FOREIGN & COMMONWEALTH OFFICE

DOCUMENTS ON BRITISH POLICY OVERSEAS

EDITED BY

S.R. ASHTON, Ph.D

AND

G. BENNETT, M.A. O.B.E, & K.A. HAMILTON, Ph.D

SERIES I

Volume VIII

WHITEHALL HISTORY PUBLISHING
in association with
FRANK CASS
LONDON • PORTLAND, OR

First published in 2002 in Great Britain by
FRANK CASS PUBLISHERS
Crown House, 47 Chase Side
London N14 5BP

and in the United States of America by
FRANK CASS PUBLISHERS
c/o ISBS, 5824 N.E. Hassalo Street
Portland, Oregon, 97213-3644

Website: www.frankcass.com

British Library Cataloguing in Publication Data

Documents on British policy overseas
    Series 1 Vol. 8: Britain and China, 1945–1950 edited by S.R.
    Ashton and G. Bennett & K.A. Hamilton. – (Whitehall
    histories)
    1. Great Britain – Foreign relations – Sources
    I. Ashton, S. R. (Stephen Richard), 1951– II. Bennett,
    Gillian, 1951– III. Hamilton, Keith, 1942– IV. Great Britain.
    Foreign and Commonwealth Office
    327.4′1

ISBN 0-7146-5164-8 (cloth)
ISSN 1471-2083

Library of Congress Catalogue Control No. 84-161776

*Published on behalf of the Whitehall History Publishing Consortium. Applications to
reproduce Crown copyright protected material in this publication should be submitted in
writing to: HMSO, Copyright Unit, St Clements House, 2–16 Colegate, Norwich NR3 1BQ.
Fax: 01603 723000. E-mail: copyright@hmso.gov.uk*

Printed in Great Britain by MPG Books Ltd, Bodmin, Cornwall

DOCUMENTS ON BRITISH POLICY OVERSEAS

Series I, Volume VIII

Britain and China, 1945-1950

PREFACE

The principal focus of this volume is not relations as such between Britain and China from the end of the Second World War to the outbreak of the Korean War in June 1950. Rather the volume is concerned with the British view of what was happening in China during these years, what this meant for the survival of British interests in the country, and how Britain perceived developments in China impacting more generally on neighbouring territories in the Far East and South-East Asia.

Britain's interest in China was largely commercial, with the one overriding political concern of Hong Kong's retention as a British colony. The future of Hong Kong was an important aspect of post-war colonial, defence and foreign policy. Here the emphasis is on foreign policy, in the sense of how decisions about Hong Kong might affect relations with a Chinese government (of whatever political complexion), and defence policy, particularly from the spring of 1949 when Hong Kong seemed to be under an imminent military threat from advancing Communist armies. The colonial dimension of policy towards Hong Kong, involving issues of the territory's economic rehabilitation and its constitutional evolution, is not covered.

In a broader regional perspective the British view of China between 1945 and 1950 was influenced by a further important consideration. Lying north of the line of the Tropic of Cancer and thus, along with Japan and Korea, identified within the American sphere of Far Eastern responsibility, China (Hong Kong apart) was not a country where British influence was expected to play a key role (No. 1). Britain's main concern in China was to recover as much as possible of its pre-war commercial position, but post-war Britain was unable to dedicate substantial financial resources to the task. In China itself therefore British influence was strictly limited. But China played a wider regional role in British policy-making by virtue of the sizeable Chinese communities living in the British colonial territories in South-East Asia. It was here, in areas lying to the south of the Tropic of Cancer, that Britain concentrated its efforts and directed what resources it had. This apparent Anglo-American division of the Far East into areas of influence, though logical for practical purposes, never became a formal arrangement with official sanction. In many ways it was artificial because developments in one area frequently impacted on those in another. The presence of Chinese communities in their own territories made the British particularly sensitive about this. They wanted to concert strategy over the Far East as a whole with the United States and the antipodean dominions. Before turning in the ANZUS (Australia, New Zealand, United States) Treaty of 1951 to America for a guarantee against a renewal of Japanese aggression, the post-war Australian government wanted a more prominent role in regional defence. Discussions were held with the UK and New Zealand and led in 1950 to ANZAM (Australia, New Zealand, Malaya), an unpublicised agreement at military staff level to establish upon the outbreak of a new war a command organisation for the countries concerned and a large area of the South-West Pacific. For Britain specifically, however, until the emergence of the Colombo Plan in 1950, success in the wider aspects of Far Eastern policy was conspicuous by its absence, and while importance had been attached in 1945 to co-operation with France, the Netherlands and Portugal, the other colonial powers in South-East Asia, ultimately this proved politically impossible. As a number of documents reproduced in this volume suggest, these regional dimensions played a significant role in both informing and influencing the British view of the unfolding events in China.

The chronological spread of documents throughout the volume is uneven. There is a separate chapter for each year between 1945 and 1949, and the volume ends with two documents in a chapter from June 1950 explaining why Britain was unable to follow up its decision to recognise the government of Communist China at the beginning of the year by establishing full diplomatic relations. The opening chapter for 1945 consists of six documents collectively establishing the main British concerns in relation to China. The number of documents rises to twelve in 1946, seventeen in 1947 and only nineteen in 1948. Much of British thinking about China over the first three and a half years of the volume was based upon speculation about how China's internal political conflict might ultimately be resolved. But there is then a sharp increase to sixty-five documents for 1949, the final year of the Chinese Revolution. Confronted now by certainty about the outcome of the conflict, policy-making was lifted from the realms of speculation to urgent consideration of what practically could be done to safeguard what remained of Britain's interests.

In order that they conform to the versions appearing in the documents, references to Chinese names and places in the editorial commentary and notes are rendered according to the spelling that pre-dates the *Pinyin* system of transliteration adopted by China in 1958 and the international community some two decades later. Occasionally, for the purpose of clarification, the *Pinyin* spelling is added in parentheses.

*   *   *   *

One of the main outcomes of the conflict in the Far East during the Second World War was the manner in which American influence superseded that of Britain in China. Prior to 1941, and before Japan's predatory incursion into Manchuria in 1931 and its swoop down the Chinese coast in 1937, Britain occupied among foreign powers in China a position of unrivalled political leadership. That position derived from the commercial pre-eminence Britain established in the nineteenth century at the principal treaty ports and a number of inland locations. It was bolstered in a military sense by the presence of naval forces on patrol in China's maritime and riverine regions. *

The extraterritorial rights and economic concessions acquired by means of the nineteenth century 'unequal treaties' had enabled the UK so to consolidate its position in China that by 1937 the total British investment was valued at £300 million. Britain's stake in China was based only in part on an import-export commodity trade that was actually (as demonstrated by the experience of cotton) in decline between the wars. More important now were direct investments in services, public utilities, real estate, banking and insurance, shipping and to a lesser extent manufacturing. British business in China was represented by a handful of companies, notably the Hong Kong and Shanghai Banking Corporation, Jardine Matheson & Company, Butterfield & Swire, the Kailan Mining Administration (a joint Sino-British venture) and the British-American Tobacco Company.

Between the wars Japan represented Britain's main rival in China. Japan's military threat was becoming increasingly apparent and commercially Japan dominated the banking and textile sectors. By contrast American influence in China was much smaller and largely confined to educational, philanthropic and missionary activity. Americans frequently elevated their interest in China to a noble cause that bordered on the messianic. American altruism was portrayed as the antidote to the rapacious greed and imperialism of other powers.

The outbreak of the Pacific War heralded a sharp role reversal for Britain and America in China. Paradoxically the interruption of trade brought about by the onset of the Sino-Japanese war in 1937 produced fresh opportunities for British business. These activities came to an abrupt

---

* The actual use of force to protect British interests in China was shown during the inter-war years to be an increasingly blunt weapon. In a climate dominated by political anarchy and rising nationalist sentiment, seasoned British observers concluded that gunboat diplomacy was only useful if kept in reserve. From the fall of the Manchu dynasty in 1912 until its capture by the Nationalists in 1928, Peking had been controlled by a succession of warlord regimes. The British welcomed the Nationalist government set up by Chiang Kai-shek at Nanking in 1928 (away from the disturbed conditions at Peking) as a modernising force, an element of stability and a guarantor of UK lives and property. That government in turn expected Britain to negotiate to remove legitimate Chinese grievances. As British interests in China moved away from trade and towards direct investment, business decisions were increasingly made locally in Shanghai and Hong Kong. Business leaders were now more inclined to seek local solutions to local problems instead of relying on force sanctioned from London. Although it was not until 1943 that the UK surrendered its extraterritorial rights in China, the experience of the inter-war years suggested that the days of extraterritoriality were numbered. How well business would fare without it became a significant issue after 1945.

halt in December 1941 when the Japanese attacked Hong Kong and invaded the International Settlement at Shanghai and the British Concession at Tientsin. In Shanghai alone about 6,000 British nationals were moved into internment camps. With Britain neutralised the initiative in China passed to the United States. This was seen first in the military sphere. From March 1942 China became part of the Pacific theatre and thus an area of American strategic responsibility. Within China itself Generalissimo Chiang Kai-shek was appointed Supreme Commander in his own theatre. The British position was that China should be recognised as an independent entity lying in neither the Pacific (American) nor Indian (British) spheres of responsibility but facing struggles for survival in Europe, the Mediterranean and the Middle East, the government in London was in no position to press its case. America's military pre-eminence was rapidly followed by American economic domination as the Nationalist Government of Chiang Kai-shek became the recipient of vast quantities of American military supplies and aid delivered under lend-lease. With the aid and equipment came innumerable American advisers, both military and technical. It was clearly to be expected that when the war was over the Americans would take the lead in China's rehabilitation.

The political consequences of these wartime developments were unwelcome from a British viewpoint. American paternalism towards China assumed a new dimension. The American aim was to arm and train Nationalist China in a manner that would enable it to become a base from which it could assist in the final destruction of Japan. Part of this preparation involved Chiang Kai-shek's elevation to a statesman of world ranking and the administration in Washington promoted the idea that once free of foreign domination, China had the potential to become a great power. At the end of the war, therefore, China would be entitled to an equal place alongside the United States, the Soviet Union and Britain in a new world organisation. Britain did not share American optimism about China's prospects. British doubts about China's capacity to become a great power derived in part from the view that China was an undeveloped country but also from the strained relationship between the Nationalist Government and the rival Communist movement ensconced at Yenan in the northern province of Shensi. As a matter of wartime expediency, Britain signed away its extra-territorial treaty rights in China in 1943. This agreement constituted recognition that conditions in China would be different once the war was over. But the UK still harboured concerns that by promoting China as a great power, America was lending encouragement to a combination of chauvinism and nationalism in China that would be resistant to attempts by British commercial interests to recover their pre-war positions in the Chinese economy.

These differences of outlook surfaced during the war in ways that gave rise at times to suspicion and recrimination. America and China believed that British policy in the Far East was still coloured by imperialism and they made no secret of their view that Britain could not, as of right, expect a return to the *status quo ante* in Hong Kong. They also suspected that Britain wanted to further its existing and future interests by keeping China weak and disunited. The counter-suspicion on the British side was that America and China were colluding in a manner designed to freeze Britain out of China at the end of the war. Anglo-Chinese wartime relations were frequently punctuated by disagreements over the terms of a British loan to China, the status of Tibet, and the Burma-China border in relation to which the British suspected that the Chinese had territorial designs on the northern boundary of the country they were fighting to recover from Japan. Recrimination on the military side could be seen in American and Chinese complaints that the British were dilatory and interested solely in the recovery of the colonial territories they had lost to the Japanese. Britain took the view that the Nationalists were wasteful and inefficient and the British criticised the manner in which Chiang Kai-shek deployed his best troops, not in combat against the Japanese but in a defensive role with a watching brief over Communist forces in the north.

However, the divisions over China were not permanently fixed. On military and other administrative matters the Americans often shared the British view about Nationalist inefficiency. Unfavourable comparisons were sometimes drawn between the Nationalists and the ideologically driven but resourceful Communists by American officials engaged in wartime efforts to bring the two sides closer together. And American solicitude towards China was never so strong that it could override the military priority of defeating Japan. In order to bring the Soviet Union into the war in the Far East as soon as possible after the defeat of Germany in Europe, the Americans and the British agreed a number of territorial concessions to Russia at China's expense in a secret protocol during the Yalta Conference in February 1945. Not until June of that year were the concessions revealed to the Chinese Government. For Prime Minister Winston Churchill the concessions represented no threat to British interests and they were to be encouraged because, if China accepted them, China would have little basis upon which to oppose Britain's recovery of Hong Kong.

Against the background of these military, commercial and diplomatic considerations, the Far Eastern Department of the FO began formulating over the first half of 1945 a new China policy to be adopted once the war was over. From this exercise a planning paper emerged in July 1945, before the Japanese surrender, that established the main principles of UK policy over the next four years (No. 1). Despite the pre-war level of investment, China was not regarded as an area of essential British priority. Senior FO officials agreed with the Treasury that financial credits should not be awarded to China for political reasons. It was beyond Britain's means to participate in China's post-war reconstruction; Britain should not compete in this respect with the US, nor involve itself in China's civil conflict (No. 6). Instead the UK should confine its efforts, first to the recovery of the British property, plant and equipment that had been lost under the Japanese occupation, and then to the negotiation of a new commercial relationship with the Nationalist Government. The weakness of Britain's position in China was said to be offset by a number of advantages, principally British experience of Chinese conditions and the natural inclination of Chinese nationalism to resist domination by any single outside power. It was expected that China would welcome good relations with the UK as a means both of protection against Soviet encroachment and avoidance of over-dependence on the US. To the extent therefore that British influence continued in China, it would be possible to overcome any potential friction that might be caused in Sino-British relations by such issues as Tibet, the Chinese overseas, the demarcation of the border with Burma, and especially the future of Hong Kong.

From this initial assessment four principal themes emerged: the internal political conflict in China, Anglo-American relations and the regional dimension, the protection of British commercial interests, and Hong Kong. Each will be examined in turn.

I

From the outset British officials accepted that the calibre of Chiang Kai-shek's Kuomintang Government left much to be desired (No. 10). Initially, however, the Generalissimo was regarded as vital to the Nationalist cause and it was not until the middle of 1947 that he was personally identified as an obstacle to peace (No. 26). Any hope of effecting an improvement in the performance of the KMT Government was regarded early on as an American responsibility. The FO and the Embassy in Chungking therefore took a detached view and approached China's conflict from what to them were the more intriguing questions of the nature of Chinese communism and its relationship (if any) with Moscow.

By virtue of a treaty with China envisaged in the Yalta protocol and concluded in August 1945, the Soviet Union had acquired substantial concessions in Manchuria. Moscow was now positioned, should it so decide, to lend direct assistance to the Chinese Communists. The British Prime Minister welcomed the prospect of Russian gains at the beginning of 1945 but shared US concern at the time of the August treaty that these should be confined within the limits of what had been agreed at the Yalta conference (No. 3). Against the background of the Soviet gains Sir Horace Seymour, HM Ambassador to China, reported in October 1945 that Chinese communism was 'at present a movement *sui generis*'. Although it had sprung from orthodox Soviet seeds it had since matured into 'a hardy Chinese product' that was unreceptive to outside influence (No. 4). The

Ambassador counselled caution about making long-term predictions and FO officials were not at one in their response to his analysis. Some argued that Communists were the same 'the world over'; others that the Chinese Communists were more in the nature of 'agrarian reformers' and as such generally more acceptable than the corrupt forces represented by the KMT.

A year later, in fresh assessments made by the FO and a new Ambassador, Sir Ralph Stevenson, the emphasis had shifted. Full-scale fighting had since broken out between the KMT and the Communists, and American mediation conducted by General George C. Marshall (No. 12) brought only temporary relief and was ultimately abandoned (No. 20). To the FO the conflict was not a dispute between two political parties 'but a civil war which has continued with intermissions since 1927' (No. 16). In the areas under their control the Communists had moderated some of their earlier hostility to the propertied classes but this was tactical and the Communists did not conceal their ultimate aim to establish a classless state. In this they 'inevitably look towards the Soviet Union for advice and support'.

The Ambassador's analysis was prompted by a review of Soviet aims in the Far East that had been drawn up by the Embassy in Moscow. In his explanation of why American mediation had failed, Sir R. Stevenson argued that neither side was interested in a negotiated settlement and that both had been encouraged in their intransigence by their great power sponsors. Dwelling at length on the reluctance of the Communists to pursue the standard Communist tactic of 'entryism' in their rejection of proposals for a coalition government, he concluded that they had more to gain by prolonging political and economic uncertainty and in preserving their own independent existence in areas bordering the Soviet Union. The Ambassador dismissed out of hand the suggestion that the Communists were simply agrarian reformers. While this might be true of the rank and file the party leaders were 'Communists first, last and all the time'. They could be trusted 'automatically to serve the best interests of the Soviet Union' (No. 17).

For the FO the Ambassador's despatch sounded an ominous note. In its own assessment the FO had assumed that UK interests in China would best be served by a negotiated settlement and thus a coalition government. If, as it appeared by the end of 1946, the Communists had 'burned their boats', the UK might have to change its hitherto neutral course and decide how much support to give to the KMT Government. Britain could not act alone. It was important to consult the United States, especially now that American mediation had been abandoned and General Marshall recalled to assume charge at the State Department (Nos. 16 and 20). In practical terms over the next twelve months the main issue for the UK was whether or not to supply weapons to the Nationalist forces. The Cabinet initially accepted the advice of the Foreign Secretary in the post-war Labour Government, Mr. Ernest Bevin, that Britain should not become involved. This position was gradually eroded, although the supply of weapons from Britain was never extensive and the details were never made public (Nos. 14-15, 24, 33, 36). Politically, the survival of the KMT Government was said to depend on the extent to which Chiang Kai-shek could cleanse his own house. The prospects were not encouraging (Nos. 21-23).

At the end of the Japanese war US logistic and military support had enabled the Nationalists to occupy significant areas in Manchuria. By July 1947 the assumption in the FO was that these gains had been squandered and that the Nationalists would not be able to hold their position in Manchuria much beyond the autumn. By then the region would have become a satellite under Soviet control. As such it would provide the base from which the Chinese Communists could penetrate China proper. With President Truman having already described Manchuria as 'the most dangerous spot in the world', Mr. Bevin wanted a 'frank' assessment of how the situation was viewed by the US (No. 25). Simultaneously the Embassy in Nanking reported that there was little evidence of house-cleansing by Chiang Kai-shek. Far from embracing reform the Generalissimo seemed determined to seek military solutions to his political problems. Amidst rumours that junior army officers might be plotting to oust him, Chiang Kai-sek's regime seemed increasingly brittle (No. 26). The American response was to send a fact-finding mission to China led by General Wedemeyer. Privately, however, a senior State Department official virtually admitted that the US 'had no China policy worth the name' (No. 28).

Against this unpromising background the head of the China Department described a communication that arrived in the FO at the end of July 1947 as 'a most significant document'. It was an account by a Canadian missionary in China of conditions in Communist-held territory in the north and it alleged in harrowing detail that the Communists were guilty of atrocities (No. 29). This first 'authentic' account was said in the FO to destroy 'once and for all the fallacy...that the Communists are not Communists at all, but a party of agrarian reformers dedicated to the ideals of true social democracy'. The document portrayed in stark reality 'what we may be up against should the Communists extend their control over all China'. While there was still no evidence that the Communists were receiving material support from the Soviet Union, the report from the missionary and the Ambassador's covering letter suggested that 'ideologically, at least, they are completely under Moscow's direction'.

But this particular episode did not end the speculation about the nature of Chinese communism. At the beginning of 1948 the FO took exception to an Embassy assessment of what China might be like under a Communist government. Sir R. Stevenson's analysis took as its starting point the New Year messages issued by Chiang Kai-shek and the Communists' leader, Mao Tse-tung. Little time was devoted to the tired and worn message of the former and the Ambassador's despatch concentrated almost exclusively on Mao Tse-tung's message, which by contrast exuded confidence in the 'imminent triumph of the Chinese Communist Party'. It was also said to represent a significant tactical shift (No. 37). By advocating conciliation towards the rich peasants and small businessmen, and a 'United Front' strategy to attract support from disillusioned liberals who had hitherto backed the KMT, the Communists were now actively 'diluting the pure milk of Communist doctrine'. The analysis highlighted important cultural differences between China and the Soviet Union and suggested that the process of turning China into an orthodox Communist state would be slow; collectivisation was unlikely to flourish in the 'land of rice fields at all levels'. The Ambassador concluded with the observations that there was no reason to believe that there would be more Communist hostility towards Britain than there would towards other powers; that US interests were likely to suffer more, even though they were smaller; and that Soviet depredations, not only in Manchuria but also in the north-western province of Sinkiang, would turn the Chinese Communists against Moscow.

With most of this analysis the FO was in diametrical disagreement. While admitting that on occasions in the past Britain had complicated relations with China by supporting for too long a tottering regime, the FO was insistent that the time had not arrived to decide what sort of relations Britain should have with the Communists if they took power. FO concern on this latter issue was twofold. First, the Ambassador's analysis led to the suspicion that the Embassy was displaying partiality towards the Communists and back-tracking on its earlier view that they had undermined American mediation in 1946 (No. 41). Secondly, within the UK, an unlikely alliance was being forged between left-wing intellectuals and business leaders with interests in China, both of whom were urging that Britain should distance itself from America's China policy and come to terms with the Communists (Nos. 39 and 40). Further exchanges took place with the Embassy. The latter refuted any suggestion of partiality (No. 42) and agreed that it would be both premature and counter-productive to recognise the Communists. But while conceding that Communism was the same the world over—'a vile and destructive ogre'—the Embassy adhered to its position that there were forces inherent in China that would render futile any attempt to impose Soviet-style orthodoxy. China's conservatism, individualism and inertia 'may emasculate even a force as virile as Communism'. Moreover, as it was still in Britain's interests to maintain trade with China, the UK should not be squeamish about 'reddening hands' and doing business with the Communists in the areas they controlled (Nos. 45 and 46). For both sides in the argument the extent of

Soviet control over the Communists remained uncertain. The FO at first assumed that the leadership was Moscow-trained but doubts were cast when an investigation was conducted into whether Mao Tse-tung had ever visited the Soviet capital (Nos. 40 and 45).

From debates about the nature of Chinese Communism and its relationship to Moscow, the argument moved from mid-1948 to one of when they would come to power. Two assessments, commissioned separately, by the Joint Intelligence Committee and the Embassy in Nanking, reached broadly the same conclusion. Although the Nationalists held the upper hand in the air and at sea, on the crucial land theatre they were no match for the Communist armies. Having always possessed the edge in leadership and morale, the Communists were now gaining numerical superiority and superiority in the quality of their equipment. But while, on a long-term basis, the Embassy found it difficult to envisage anything other than Communist domination of the whole of China, both assessments concluded this was not expected to happen immediately or even soon. A line was drawn at the Yangtse. Communist control north of the river was not in question. To the south, however, the expectation was that the Communists would be faced by problems of over-extended lines of supply and communication. They would be further handicapped by not having sufficient party members with the necessary administrative skills. A more likely outcome in the foreseeable future was either, in the south, a return to the days of provincialism and local warlords over whom a shadowy KMT government at Nanking would have no control, or, over the whole country, a coalition government dominated by the Communists but in which a rump of the KMT might still be represented. Neither assessment anticipated any threat to Hong Kong (Nos. 44 and 49). Armed with these conclusions and also, by November 1948, aware that the US was at its 'wits end' in its search for ways to improve Nationalist fortunes (No. 50), Mr. Bevin decided, for the first time, to place the China situation before Ministers.

A Cabinet memorandum of December 1948 analysed the implications for British policy and interests in South-East Asia and the Far East of a China dominated wholly by the Communists (No. 51). To protect Britain's trade and commercial interests in China itself, the memorandum suggested that the UK should keep 'a foot in the door' and have *de facto* relations with the Communists where these were unavoidable. In the Far East more generally it argued that the neighbouring countries and British colonial possessions (including Hong Kong) would be vulnerable in varying degrees to Communist encroachment and infiltration. The Federation of Malaya, Singapore, Burma, Siam and French Indo-China were said to be particularly at risk, a view already expressed in strident terms by the Chief of the Imperial General Staff (No. 47). Underlying the analysis presented to Cabinet was the assumption that the Communists would inherit a country severely weakened by years of civil war and that this would make them more receptive to continued trade, with Britain especially. It ended with recommendations that the Chiefs of Staff should examine the strategic implications if China became a Communist state, and that there should be consultation with other 'friendly' governments about protecting commercial interests and containing the threat of communism in the Far East.

The Cabinet endorsed these recommendations. Ministers suggested that in view of the uncertainty about China it would be unwise to adopt a course that would drive the Communists into the arms of the Soviet Union. They also questioned whether the time had not arrived to establish in the Far East the equivalents of the European Recovery Programme and Western Union that had been introduced in Western Europe to provide economic and military resistance to communism (No. 52). The year 1948 ended with the Ambassador asserting that 'the days of the present Chinese Government are numbered'. Agreement was reached that if Chiang Kai-shek decided to move the seat of his beleaguered government, Sir R. Stevenson should remain in Nanking (No. 54).

The final year of the Chinese Revolution proved also to be a year of reckoning for Britain's relations with China. Many of the assumptions that had guided UK policy were revealed to have been misplaced. Early indications suggested that it would not be easy to establish relations of any sort with the Communists. In the areas under their control the Communists were already using the issue of recognition in a way that was designed to make life difficult for foreign consulates (No. 58). In March 1949 Mr. Bevin went back to Cabinet over China. He explained the so far disappointing results of consultation about China with other countries, and reported the views of the Chiefs of Staff on the military implications if the Communists came to power. He also revealed that documents captured during a police raid on Communist headquarters in Hong Kong had yielded vital information about Communist plans and intentions (No. 59). The Communists were portrayed as orthodox and ruthless Marxists who would pursue a coalition arrangement only for as long as it suited them. Expediency would dictate their treatment of foreign interests.

Collective minds now turned to the question of safeguarding western interests. From the Embassy came a proposal for a Consultative Council for South-East Asia as a prelude ultimately to a Confederation for the region (No. 60). In the UK a working party of officials was set up to consider whether the Communists would be influenced by economic sanctions. Early indications suggested that sanctions would take time to work and ultimately might not be effective. It was, however, suggested that China might be vulnerable over oil, especially if the Soviet Union could not supply adequate quantities (No. 64). In March, and after considerable disagreement, the Embassy and the FO agreed a strategy for anti-Communist propaganda (No. 55).

A symbolic landmark in the unfolding events in China arrived overnight between 21 and 22 April 1949 when the first Communist troops crossed the Yangtse. But more dramatic from a British viewpoint was an incident that occurred only twenty-four hours earlier. HMS *Amethyst*, a frigate en route from Shanghai to Nanking with supplies for the British community, came under fire from Communist shore batteries, suffered heavy casualties (including the ship's commander), ran aground, and could not be rescued by other ships in the vicinity (that were also fired upon and suffered casualties). The Communists had served notice of their intention to cross the Yangtse and questions were raised as to whether it had been wise for *Amethyst* to sail so close to the expiry of the Communists' ultimatum (Nos. 65 and 66). Attempts to negotiate a safe passage for the crippled vessel at first foundered on familiar ground. Echoing their earlier stand over foreign consulates, the Communists again argued that as they had not been accorded recognition, they could not receive representations on the ship's behalf. When negotiations for *Amethyst's* release did begin, the Communists insisted that Britain was responsible because the ship had 'infringed into China's national river'. Mr. Bevin refused to comply. As this was 'the first important negotiation we are having with the Communists', concessions would 'jeopardise our whole position' and 'we may never recover from this initial step' (No. 86). After almost one hundred days in virtual captivity, the matter was resolved during the night of 30 July when, under a replacement commander and against advice from both the FO and Admiralty in London, *Amethyst* broke out and reached the open sea. The escape of the *Amethyst* was covered extensively in a rapturous British press. When the ship arrived back in the UK the commander and several crew members were decorated. To the Communists the episode represented the last gasp of a gunboat mentality.

The ending of the Yangtse incident was swiftly followed by an intriguing diversion. From Hong Kong in August it was reported that overtures had been received from no lesser figure than Chou En-lai, a member of the Politburo of the CCP who had earlier represented the Communists in the peace negotiations with the KMT. The substance of the message had in fact been known to the Americans since June. It suggested that the leadership of the CCP was split between those who believed in the inevitability of a third world war and who wanted to align China with the Soviet Union, and those (like Chou En-lai) who wanted an accommodation with the Western powers. The former faction was said to control the party's propaganda machine but the moderates controlled policy. Chou En-lai was alleged to have said in his message that the Communists should therefore be judged not by their words but by their deeds (No. 90). The message was conveyed second-hand through sources that the Embassy did not wholly trust. Mr. Bevin dismissed the message as a ploy that was 'in accordance with standard Soviet tactics'. No reply was sent.

In the FO the view was expressed that at least the message validated the policy of keeping a foot in the door. From the summer of 1949, and on the assumption that a Communist government was only a matter of time, this policy became inextricably linked with the question of whether recognition should be extended to the Communists (No. 72). British officials in South-East Asia were apprehensive at the prospect. They were especially worried that recognition would strain the loyalties of the local Chinese communities (No. 93). This concern had been expressed in a different context in 1947 (No. 31). It was reiterated in 1949 when the Joint Intelligence Committee described the Chinese in South-East Asia as 'a potentially dangerous fifth column' (No. 99).

Mr. Bevin discussed recognition in a new submission about China to the Cabinet in August 1949 (No. 94). The Foreign Secretary noted significant differences on this, and other matters, between the UK and the US. He concluded that the UK should avoid precipitate action on recognition and endeavour to keep in step with its allies in the Commonwealth and Europe as well as the US. But the balance of the argument he put before Cabinet weighed heavily in favour of eventual recognition. Practically this was seen as the only realistic way of keeping a foot in the door and thus maintaining British commercial interests in China. Politically, it was suggested that recognition would encourage China to resist Soviet encroachment. The Foreign Secretary recommended to his colleagues that as no new commitments were involved, 'we should adhere to the policy of remaining in China as long as we can'.

Discussions about China in the context of recognition were held in September with the Americans and the French (Nos. 96 and 97). On 21 September Mao Tse-tung proclaimed the People's Republic and on 1 October a Communist Government was installed in Peking. The UK responded by suggesting to the Communists that pending further study, HM consuls should be appointed for the promotion of trade. This effectively constituted *de facto* recognition. The US protested about the absence of advance notification and President Truman was especially critical (No. 100). Strategically the Joint Intelligence Committee calculated that Communist China would support the Soviet Union in its goal of world revolution. But this did not automatically mean direct Soviet control over China and it would be some years before China could be counted as a major industrial asset to the Soviet bloc (No. 99).

At the end of October Mr. Bevin recommended to Cabinet that the UK should proceed to *de jure* recognition, the timing to be decided after consultation with allies and a conference of UK representatives in the Far

East. On the vexed question of China's representation at the United Nations, the Foreign Secretary advocated that in a forthcoming UN debate on a motion put down by the representative of Nationalist China, the UK should abstain (No. 105). Subsequently the UK took the position that China's representation was a matter to be decided by a majority of UN countries. Britain's other concern was that China debates at the UN might lead to attacks on Britain's position in Hong Kong (No. 113).

Further discussions were held with the Americans and the French (No. 106) and the conference of Far Eastern representatives was held at Singapore towards the end of November. The conference, which had before it a new assessment of UK policy in the Far East, agreed that *de jure* recognition should be extended before the end of the year. But concern about the impact of recognition on the local Chinese communities was still much in evidence. The conference therefore recommended that recognition should be accompanied by tightened security measures against communism in South-East Asia, and by propaganda to the effect that there was no inconsistency in British policy (Nos. 108 and 109). Mr. Bevin reported back to Cabinet in December (No. 110) and further consultation was conducted about the date of recognition (Nos. 114 and 115). On 23 December the Prime Minister, Mr. Clement Attlee, was informed that *de jure* recognition would be extended on 6 January 1950. Whether it would serve in keeping China and the Soviet Union apart was already a matter for speculation (No. 118). The establishment of formal diplomatic relations did not follow recognition (Nos. 120 and 121). Early indications in 1950 suggested that UK commercial interests would be struggling for survival (pp. 440-441).

II

Anglo-American relations over China between 1945 and 1950 were a source of profound disappointment to British Ministers and officials. From the beginning wartime disagreements looked set to continue. In August 1945 the FO maintained that the Americans were being unduly secretive in their reluctance to share information about the draft of a new commercial treaty they were proposing to negotiate with the Chinese Government (No. 2). Mr. Bevin argued that the UK should resist where possible American attempts to dominate the China market. He believed that China would look to the UK as a way of relieving pressure from both America and the Soviet Union (No. 7). In a variation on a not dissimilar theme, a seasoned British diplomat suggested that Sino-American relations had soured and that this would be to Britain's advantage (No. 10).

On the central political question concerning China, however, it soon became apparent to the FO that American reluctance to share information stemmed, not only from reticence but also from the fact that the Americans were uncertain about their own policies. At the beginning of 1947 the FO queried whether the abandonment of American mediation in China's civil war implied a change in American policy. The State Department insisted that policy remained unchanged (No. 20), but a senior American figure had already confided that the US was in great difficulty over China (No. 15) and others were to make the same admission (Nos. 22, 28, 50).

Of equal FO concern was a perceived US reluctance to be forthcoming about their policies in a regional Far Eastern context. At the end of 1947 Mr. Bevin proposed bilateral Anglo-American talks on the Far East, an area that hitherto had occupied his attention only intermittently. Covering everywhere from Afghanistan to the Pacific, his geographical definition of the Far East was extensive (No. 35). He argued that in the west (Afghanistan to Hong Kong) UK influence was greater than that of the US and could be used as a counterpoise to US influence in the east (Korea, Japan and China). The talks that the Foreign Secretary wanted were never held, at least not in the form that he had intended. An immediate problem arose when Mr. Attlee insisted that Australia and New Zealand would have to be involved because of their shared interest on matters concerning the Far East. This introduced additional complications. The Americans were reluctant to talk to the Australians because they harboured doubts about security within the Australian Government. And the Australian Government did not want to engage in talks with the US because it disagreed with almost every aspect of American policy in the Far East (No. 43).

International support on other aspects of policy was equally problematic. India was the first country to respond when the American and selected European and Commonwealth governments were consulted about the China analysis presented by Mr. Bevin to Cabinet in December 1948 (No. 51). The Indian Government agreed that a coalition government dominated by the Communists was the most likely outcome of China's civil war. But it did not regard communism as such as a threat, either in India or in South-East Asia. If communism gained regional ground, the Indian Government argued that responsibility would rest with the colonial powers and unpopular indigenous regimes. India therefore urged the colonial powers to align themselves with the forces of progressive nationalism (No. 56). Plainly nervous that developments in China would undermine French policy in Indo-China, France was next to respond with practical suggestions about exchanging information and sharing intelligence (No. 57). The Indian and French responses were deemed unhelpful from a UK viewpoint. India's position was said to be too complacent about the threat of communism. The UK welcomed the practical suggestions made by France but equally recognised that, as in the case of the Dutch in Indonesia, wider cooperation would not be possible until the French had reached a satisfactory settlement of their colonial problems in Indo-China (No. 59).

Differences with the French over Vietnam continued to dominate Anglo-French exchanges in relation to China (Nos. 97, 106, 115).

But the main problems arose in Anglo-American relations and serious differences emerged in 1949. They were seen first when the State Department responded in March 1949 to the UK's December analysis of developments in China. US officials suggested that more emphasis should have been placed on the growing strength of nationalism in South and South-East Asia and its incompatibility in the long-run with communism. The Americans also criticised as 'repressive' the emphasis placed in the UK analysis on the need for adequate policing and intelligence. Finally, having outlined the scale of American aid that had been squandered by an incompetent leadership in China, they made clear that large-scale US regional aid could not be expected and would never be a substitute for self-help. The British Embassy in Washington described this response as 'a lament' on the failures of US policy and argued that the views expressed on policing and intelligence were difficult to reconcile with the current campaign in the US to root out communism in public life. To the FO the response was 'a mixture of defeatism and pious advice', but as there could be no co-ordinated China policy without US involvement the only way forward was to keep 'pegging away at the Americans, on the principle of the steady drip wearing away the stone' (No. 62).

The expectation, expressed more in hope than in anticipation, that the US might be persuaded to become more cooperative, never materialised. As a Communist government appeared increasingly inevitable, Britain and America moved further apart over China. On fundamentals the approach of the two governments was entirely different. The US wanted to impose more rigorous restrictions on trade with a Communist China than the UK thought necessary or desirable (No. 94). For the UK the policy of keeping one foot in the door dictated that diplomatic representation in China should be maintained until the latest possible moment. Also, and despite Mr. Attlee's concern about potential hostages (No. 72), the logic of the policy dictated that British nationals wishing to remain in China should not be discouraged. The Americans by contrast were moving inexorably towards withdrawing from China, both diplomatically and commercially (Nos. 87, 89, 94). When the American military commander in the Far East, General Douglas MacArthur, expressed his own personal views about China, the gap between the two countries appeared even wider (No. 102).

Especially worrying to the Americans were the early indications about the British stand on the question of recognition. The US argued that while resistance to communism continued in China, on the mainland or elsewhere—Chiang Kai-shek left Nanking for Canton in January 1949 and then moved his capital twice more before retreating to Formosa in December—it would be wholly inappropriate to grant recognition to the

Communists. They were also adamant, as indeed were the Australians, that if the Communists were to be recognised, they should first guarantee the territorial integrity of China's neighbours, and pledge themselves to respect China's obligations in respect of international agreements and foreign nationals and property in China. The FO noted that no such assurances had been sought from the governments of the countries that were now satellites of the Soviet Union in Eastern Europe (Nos. 105 and 110).

American concern about the drift of British policy on recognition led in July 1949 to a State Department proposal for Anglo-American talks about China. The irony of this development was not lost on the FO (No. 88) but practically nothing had changed in the American position. As the Administration published a White Paper in defence of its China policy at the beginning of August, the US was still not inclined to involve itself in economic or military help in South-East Asia (No. 91). Mr. Bevin visited Washington for talks with Mr. Dean Acheson, successor to Mr. Marshall as Secretary of State, in September. Discussions were also held at official level. On the issue of recognition Mr. Acheson acknowledged that UK interests in China were more extensive than those of the US. Upon this basis he said that the two countries were separated by 'a difference in situation rather than a difference in policy'. As long as their objectives remained the same it did not matter if they diverged over tactics (No. 96). This formula papered over cracks that re-opened when the UK announced its intentions about recognition (Nos. 100 and 114). By the end of the year US frustration at UK policy was mirrored in Britain by a sense that American policy had become inconsistent (No. 116). Anglo-American differences over China became even more pronounced during the first half of 1950 (pp. 441-442).

III

For the UK the main casualty of the Chinese Revolution was the ultimate loss of British investment and trade in (as distinct from trade with) China itself. From the outset the prospects for British commerce in China were not encouraging. Denied direct UK Government assistance (No. 1), firms and trading companies faced other major difficulties. Prominent among these was nationalist assertiveness on the part of the Chinese authorities. Expectations that properties lost during the war would be restored to their pre-war owners as soon as Japan surrendered were rapidly disappointed (No. 5). Firms could neither expect compensation if they had suffered war damage, nor subsidies if they wanted to start afresh (No. 13). Personnel shortages and a lack of China specialists in re-opening consulates compounded these problems, especially in the interior. It did not help that pre-war trade had been concentrated in the big cities and on the main lines of communication. Mr. Bevin believed that trade would bolster Britain's political influence but considerable ground had still to be made up in the opening of consulates in the interior (No. 7). However the most daunting problem in the recovery of British commerce was the condition of China itself. In the words of one seasoned UK diplomat, the country was 'in a mess—politically, militarily, financially, socially'. China's 'financial muddle' was said to be 'atomic'. Rampant inflation was the economic order of the day. The Chinese currency had depreciated to such an extent that American vegetables were cheaper than home-grown produce. Sooner or later, it was suggested, 'there is going to be an almighty crash' (No. 10).

But more optimistic voices were still to be heard. While not under-estimating the difficulties ahead, officials assumed that a new commercial treaty would be negotiated with China (No. 2). As President of the Board of Trade in the new Labour Government, Sir Stafford Cripps was an enthusiastic advocate of a proposal to send a Trade Mission to China. The aim would be to signal the interest of British industry in China's economic recovery and further development, and to counter where possible American penetration of the China market. The FO supported the Board of Trade but both departments encountered opposition from a Treasury concerned that a mission would result in requests for long-term credits. Treasury reluctance was ultimately overcome when it was made clear that the mission would not have a selling purpose; it would have an 'exploratory' function only (No. 9). Articulating what was required from the mission, a senior FO official injected a Darwinian note. In the sense that it would be exploratory the mission would also be educational. 'New methods and new men' were required in post-war China. The days when the China trade was conducted by 'rather costive firms' had gone. Firms now had to face 'the full blast of competition' and 'Oriental guile' without the 'convenient buffer of extra-territoriality & impartial justice in British courts'. A Trade Mission of industrialists and a trade union representative visited China between September and December 1946. The report it presented in 1947 was considered by some to convey an overall impression that was too optimistic about immediate prospects. The published version suggested that as a developing country China would have many attractions for British industry, but not before peace was restored, communications had been improved and a technically trained work force had emerged (No. 30).

Two British delegations visited China between 1946 and 1947. The Trade Mission was followed by an all-party delegation representing both houses of parliament that went out as a Goodwill Mission in October 1947. Led by Lord Ammon, a veteran Labour Peer, the second mission was not of high standing and the report it presented at the turn of the year was neither particularly informative nor original in its findings. In China itself the mission appears to have been noteworthy for the controversy prompted by some remarks made by Lord Ammon at a press conference about the position of British shipping in Chinese inland waters (No. 34).

Lobbying on behalf of companies and firms operating in China was the China Association in London. The originator of the proposal to send out a Trade Mission, the China Association was at first optimistic about the prospects of forging a new trade relationship with the Chinese Government. But when negotiations for a commercial treaty stalled and China's political crisis deepened, the Association changed its tactics. By March 1948 it wanted to reinsure with the Communists. Enquiries were made at the FO as to whether it would be possible to appoint an unofficial representative with the Communists while maintaining formal Embassy links with the Nationalist Government (No. 39). The Association also now shared the Ambassador's view that it would be better to have no commercial treaty at all rather than one that was unsatisfactory. As one FO official commented in April when explaining the UK position on the stalled negotiations, 'we propose like Brer Rabbit to lie fairly low and say nuffin' (No. 51).

The largest concentration of British subjects in China was at Shanghai. Attempts to negotiate compensation for the British ex-employees of the former International Settlement proved fruitless (No. 45). Concern for the safety of the British community as a whole at Shanghai led by the end of 1948 to an emergency plan for their evacuation (No. 53). They numbered about 4,000 by the spring of 1949 and while the Prime Minister especially was concerned to see their numbers reduced, it was not policy to recommend a complete withdrawal (No. 72). Having outlined in detail the extent of UK commercial interests in China in his submission to Cabinet of December 1948 (No. 51), when he next briefed Ministers in March 1949 Mr. Bevin explained that the aim was still to keep a foot in the door. Much of the UK investment in China was held in the form of immovable land and property. For the UK to pull out would involve losses to the firms concerned at much the same level as if their assets had been expropriated. It would also mean cutting Britain off from a 'potentially vast market for British goods'. Ultimately, if the Communists came to power, it was expected that they would move towards the expropriation or expulsion of foreign interests. But this would be a slow process because of the economic difficulties with which they would be confronted. The Foreign Secretary described those economic areas where he thought the Communists would be vulnerable on the one hand, and dependent on the continued functioning of British-run public utilities on the other. For as long as foreign interests remained 'reasonably unmolested', he suggested that the UK should hold the stick of sanctions against the Communists in reserve and attempt to persuade other countries to adopt a similar view (No. 59).

However, the first real threat to UK interests came not from the Communists but from the Nationalist Government. Communist armies entered Shanghai on 23 May 1949. UK Ministers were relieved that the Nationalists had decided not to defend the city (Nos. 72 and 75). But the

Nationalists responded on 20 June by blockading China's Communist-held coastline. Shanghai was effectively isolated and cut off.

The impact of the blockade was soon apparent. UK firms at Shanghai were already experiencing difficulty because of the unrealistic sterling exchange rate and because wages had been tied by the Communist authorities to the price of rice and were soaring as a consequence. By the end of July, with the added hardship of the blockade, firms were dependent for their existence on remittances from London and these were running at the rate of £350,000 a month. This was not a sum that could be sustained indefinitely; firms would soon have to cut their losses and close down. The China Association urged action to relieve the firms' plight, either by breaking the blockade (with or without US co-operation) or by exerting financial pressure on the Communists. The response from the FO was not encouraging. Mr. Attlee was informed that in lodging an appeal about the blockade with the Nationalist authorities, the Americans wanted to evacuate their nationals rather than provide them with supplies that would enable them to remain (No. 89).

When Ministers considered the blockade towards the end of June they had before them the details of an attack by Nationalist aircraft on a British merchant ship (the *Anchises*) that had occurred only twenty-four hours earlier. As a result of this incident the blockade was no longer simply an issue of providing relief for the British community at Shanghai. It was also one of providing protection for British merchant shipping in Chinese territorial and inland waters. In August, anxious to prevent supplies reaching their Communist adversaries, the Nationalist authorities insisted on stringent conditions before a British relief ship could enter Shanghai. These were deemed wholly unacceptable. Military options were under consideration when the Law Officers advised that any action to break the blockade by naval intervention would be an act of doubtful legality. There was the added complication that the UK still recognised the Nationalist authorities as the legal government of China. Shipowners were accordingly informed in September that their vessels would receive full Royal Navy protection on the open sea up to a three-mile limit of territorial waters. They would not be escorted once they entered territorial waters and HM ships would only protect them if they were attacked or bombed. If intercepted they would have to turn back or face arrest. Effectively therefore they entered territorial waters at their own risk (Nos. 94 and 98).

These limited rules of engagement brought neither protection to merchant ships nor relief to the Shanghai community. In November 1949 two of the major companies trading in China lodged a further appeal for government support in breaking the blockade. The FO and the Admiralty devised a more interventionist plan but it did not convince the First Sea Lord who was concerned that the Navy should not assume sole responsibility for any incidents that might arise. A senior FO official described his attitude as 'deplorable'. Elsewhere in the FO views were expressed that revealed little sympathy for the plight of the British merchant community at Shanghai. The basis of their complaints was 'that somebody else's war is being allowed to interfere with their business'. Parallels were drawn with the encounters between Britain and China at the end of the eighteenth and in the early nineteenth centuries. The Shanghai merchants were cast in the role of the imperial proconsuls who came away from China empty-handed. Their 'grey coolie uniform notwithstanding', the Communists shared many of the prejudices of 'the late-lamented Empress Dowager' and were in the 'classical Chinese tradition'. They concentrated on 'humiliating' the foreigner and 'making him lose face' (No. 107). A final attempt at the end of the year to get a relief ship into Shanghai had to be abandoned when the Treasury refused to indemnify the ship's owners against loss or damage (No. 111).

The blockade of Shanghai was not lifted until the outbreak of the Korean War in June 1950. By then, and despite an appeal to the Communist Government in May, conditions for the conduct of British trade and business in China had worsened considerably. Firms began reaching the conclusion for themselves that they could no longer continue. Extending into the mid-1950s, Britain's eventual financial loss in China was estimated in the region of between £200 million and £250 million. The Communists were said to have pursued a 'deliberate and consistent policy of squeezing out' British and Western interests. According to Mr. Herbert Morrison, Mr. Bevin's successor at the FO, it was 'an unhappy story as a whole' (p. 443).

IV

Of all the issues that divided Britain and China in the immediate post-war years none was more significant than the future of Hong Kong. The FO China memorandum of July 1945 touched briefly on what lay behind the differences and concluded that as the UK had lost Hong Kong to Japan in 1941, 'it is a point of national honour for us to recover it, and restore it to its normal state of order and prosperity'. The subsequent controversy over Japan's surrender in Hong Kong indicated that Sino-British relations over the territory's future would be problematic (No. 1)

Chiang Kai-shek raised Hong Kong at a farewell meeting with Sir H. Seymour in June 1946. He suggested that relations with the UK would not be 'satisfactory' or conducted with 'mutual confidence' while the question of Hong Kong remained 'without some solution'. The Generalissimo did not elaborate but hinted that the problem was 'to some extent a psychological one'. Clarification of what this meant was provided when the outgoing Chinese Ambassador in London met the Minister of State at the

FO. China wanted sovereignty over Hong Kong, leaving the UK in control on such matters as business and defence. The Ambassador was informed that the UK had more pressing matters to settle first in India, Egypt and Palestine (No. 11).

Throughout much of 1946 the FO was engaged in a major policy review about Hong Kong that involved consultation with the Colonial Office, the Embassy at Nanking and the colony's Governor (pp. 75-77). China's case for the restoration of Hong Kong was based, according to one FO official, on the analogy of a foreign power occupying the Isle of Wight. A school of thought within the FO suggested that a settlement over Hong Kong was needed in order to secure Chinese co-operation and goodwill in the recovery of Britain's position in China itself, and in South-East Asia more generally. The best defence for the British position in Malaya was said to rest in an accommodation with China over Hong Kong. A number of options were examined and a recommendation made that a settlement might involve restoring to China sovereignty over the New Territories (transferred to the UK on a ninety-nine year lease in 1898), leaving Britain in possession of Hong Kong itself. In any such arrangement safeguards would be required for Hong Kong because its airport and water supply were located in the New Territories.

Senior officials in the FO questioned many of the assumptions underlying this recommendation. They were not persuaded by the Isle of Wight analogy and particular exception was taken to the argument that policy towards Hong Kong should be designed primarily to secure Chinese goodwill. If Britain surrendered the whole or part of its position in Hong Kong it would be for one of two reasons, or possibly a combination of both. Either the UK would no longer possess the military and financial means to sustain its position, or a Government of China would sooner or later hold the UK to ransom by paralysing Hong Kong's trade and administration. The balance of the argument shifted as the debate was extended to include other interested parties. Questions were now raised as to whether there should be negotiations at all with China over Hong Kong, whether (if they were to be held) the UK should assume the initiative, and what line the UK should take. A proposal for international administration was put forward but rejected on the grounds that this would provide scope for 'Soviet mischief-making'.

All of these arguments were weighed in a joint memorandum about Hong Kong that was presented to an Official Committee by the FO and Colonial Office in November 1946. The purpose was to determine a recommendation that could be put to Ministers. A significant consideration now to be taken into account was a report by the Chiefs of Staff that Hong Kong could not be defended against a major power in occupation of mainland China. Hong Kong was therefore to be regarded as an undefended port and it was not part of UK defence policy to lock up within the territory sizeable forces that might be overrun or lost upon the outbreak of war (No. 8).

The joint memorandum argued that if a settlement had to be found the UK might offer a review of the terms of the 1898 lease. On balance, however, it concluded that the UK should not assume the initiative in starting negotiations. Instead, given the uncertainty about the colony's future that was said to exist in business circles, it suggested that it would be desirable to issue a statement to the effect that the UK intended to remain in Hong Kong. The Official Committee thought the submission too defensive in that it seemed to assume that Hong Kong would one day be lost. In suggesting amendments it recommended that the reasons for staying permanently should be stated more clearly (No. 18).

The final version of the memorandum put before the Official Committee in November 1946 was drafted by the Colonial Office, but over one issue in particular the two departments held widely differing views. As a means of restoring business confidence, the Colonial Office wanted an early announcement of Britain's intention to remain in Hong Kong. Uncertainty was said to be delaying the colony's rehabilitation and holding up investment and loan capital, especially for a new airport (Nos. 27 and 63). The FO considered the question from the wider viewpoint of China policy more generally. This in turn dictated that there should first be consultation with the US. FO officials argued that China was in no position to cause trouble over Hong Kong because it was almost on the verge of economic and financial collapse. A statement by the UK would be resented by the Chinese Government because it would be tantamount to 'kicking them when they are down' (No. 19). These differences over Hong Kong resurfaced in May 1947, and again at the end of the year. The FO continued to argue that a statement about Hong Kong would be 'out of context and gratuitous'. Politically it would also be inexpedient because no government could commit itself to a future course of action that might prove embarrassing and possibly even dangerous to the UK. There was no intention to surrender Hong Kong but equally the government could not say that the territory would never be given up. On the matter of restoring business confidence the FO took the view that investors would have to decide for themselves whether Hong Kong represented an acceptable degree of risk (No. 32). With the two main departments so divided, Hong Kong was kept off the Cabinet agenda.

Tensions surrounding Hong Kong spilled over in January 1948 when Chinese squatters were evicted from the walled city of Kowloon. This incident sparked demonstrations elsewhere in China, in one of which the British consulate at Canton was attacked and burned down (No. 38). The Chinese Government insisted that there would first have to be a settlement of its own claims over the Kowloon evictions before it could consider a British demand for compensation at Canton. These events coincided with an increasing number of student protests and anti-foreign demonstrations in China. Memories of the Boxer Rebellion at the turn of the century were revived (Nos. 29 and 34) but once the heat generated by the Kowloon and Canton incidents subsided, communism rather than nationalism was perceived as the greater threat to British interests in Hong Kong.

In October 1948 Mr. Bevin expressed concern about Hong Kong's vulnerability to Communist-inspired unrest. Its defences seemed inadequate because troops had been sent from the colony to reinforce the British position in Malaya following the declaration there of an Emergency against Communist insurgents in June (Nos. 47 and 48). The department informed the Foreign Secretary that there was in effect a stand-off in Hong Kong. On the assumption that they recognised the colony as a valuable entrepôt and as a base from which they could direct overseas propaganda (No. 59), the Communists were said to be anxious to avoid conflict with the colonial government. For its part the government viewed communism as a menace but it did not want to provoke the Communists into outright hostility. An uneasy truce existed that suited both parties. For the UK there was the further consideration that action against the Communists in Hong Kong might disrupt the military effort in Malaya (No. 48).

The Cabinet called for a review of measures to strengthen the Government of Hong Kong when it considered Mr. Bevin's assessment of China in December 1948 (Nos. 51 and 52). Mr. Arthur Creech Jones, the Secretary of State for the Colonies, presented a report in March 1949. Three localised threats to Hong Kong were identified but an organised attack by Chinese Communist forces, with or without Soviet assistance, was deemed unlikely. The level of UK forces required to meet the local threats was described and account taken of how these might impact on the Malayan operations. Other non-military ways of strengthening the government were considered. Some Ministers expressed concern that Hong Kong was becoming 'riddled with Communism' and called for pre-emptive action. However, the consensus was to avoid action that would preclude the possibility of the UK having friendly relations with a Communist government. In reaching this decision Ministers were also aware that British nationals in China represented potential hostages (No. 61).

From late April until mid-August 1949 a Hong Kong crisis descended upon the British Government. It was at its height in May and June. The rapid advance of Communist armies through southern China posed an uncertain threat to Hong Kong but one that could not be ignored. Urgent decisions were now required on the issues of what military reinforcement should be sent to Hong Kong, and the means whereby the UK might mobilise international support. In the process fundamental questions were raised about Britain's long-term prospects in the territory.

Early in May the Chiefs of Staff expressed the view that while two infantry brigades would be immediately sufficient to defend Hong Kong, should a serious Communist threat develop a division might be required. They were confident, however, that if the UK made plain its determination to hold Hong Kong an attack by a Communist army was unlikely (Nos. 67 and 68). The Cabinet approved the recommendation to reinforce the local garrison to the strength of two infantry brigade groups but then had to decide how to announce the decision. The Colonial Office and the Governor, supported by other senior officials in South-East Asia, urged that an announcement about the reinforcements should be combined with a statement that the UK had no intention of surrendering Hong Kong. In contrast to the earlier stance, official opinion in the FO had for some time been moving in the direction that a statement might after all be needed (No. 53). An option considered but rejected by the Governor was that Hong Kong might cease to be a haven for trade and commerce and become instead a fortress colony. Mindful of advice that the territory could not be defended against a major power operating from the mainland, Ministers concluded that it would be unwise to make a statement. In the words of the Cabinet Secretary, they believed that the best way of 'hanging on to Hong Kong is to keep quiet about it' (No. 71). The announcement about the reinforcements made no reference to the UK's long-term intentions and explained that the extra troops were being sent to ensure the safety of the people and to preserve trade (No. 69). In the first draft of the announcement Hong Kong was described as a 'British colony'. The final text referred only to Hong Kong.

When the Cabinet authorised these reinforcements in May 1949 it also decided against enlisting support from Commonwealth allies in Australia and New Zealand. Ministers felt that this 'might be open to the misinterpretation that we were preparing for serious consequences'. Within days the decision had been reversed. The British Defence Co-ordination Committee in the Far East had called for 'urgent' consideration of what diplomatic, economic and military action might be taken to 'form a containing ring against further Communist penetration'. Effectively this proposal reinforced the recommendations already made by Mr. Bevin in the context of China policy more generally. In Cabinet therefore Ministers now agreed that the time had arrived to consult the Commonwealth about Hong Kong on a broad basis. The view was also expressed that in the long-run it would be impossible to preserve the territory as a British colony. As an alternative it was suggested that Hong Kong might become an international port on the analogy of Trieste, but Cabinet decided that the time was not opportune to consider so radical a change of policy (No. 70).

As the Commonwealth Relations Office considered how to approach Commonwealth governments (No. 73), Mr. Bevin argued that the UK's main task in relation to Hong Kong was to avoid international isolation. He was prepared to support discussions about the colony with a Chinese government that was 'stable, unified, democratic and friendly', but at a meeting attended by the UK Commissioner-General in South-East Asia he was not in favour of a 'provocative' statement that the UK would never leave Hong Kong. He agreed that the UK should defend Hong Kong if the Communists attacked but maintained that the best means of mobilising international support would be to bring the matter before the United Nations on the basis of resisting aggression. A Cabinet Committee called for further studies of the defence problem, together with a factual appreciation of the current situation in Hong Kong (Nos. 74-76).

The upshot at the end of May was a decision to reinforce Hong Kong with another infantry brigade and a Royal Marine Commando Brigade, with supporting air and naval units. A further infantry brigade in Malaya was put on stand-by and, with regard to the movement of Communist armies in southern China, September was identified as the most dangerous time for Hong Kong. The Chiefs of Staff remained confident that with this level of reinforcement, the UK's resolve to defend the colony would not be put to the test. There was an element of risk in this policy. The Minister of Defence warned that the 'effect on Western Union of the despatch of further relatively large British forces to the Far East may be considerable'. He suggested that it would involve the call-up of over 2,000 army reservists and thus leave the UK without an effective strategic reserve for three months, a recommendation later overruled by the Cabinet's Defence Committee (No. 77 and 80). But despite the problems that would be caused in other areas of defence policy, the UK could not afford to be evicted from Hong Kong. Mr. Attlee anticipated that if this were to happen, resistance to communism in Burma, Siam and Malaya would crumble (No. 78).

Unlike the first reinforcement of Hong Kong at the beginning of May, no details were provided when the second was authorised. The new level of reinforcement might be seen as provocative and consultation with the Commonwealth had yet to take place. It would be embarrassing if the UK made a declaration about Hong Kong and Commonwealth countries then attacked it as a 'relic of colonialism'. Ministers also recognised that if the UK made it a point of prestige to remain in possession of the colony, 'it might become a matter of prestige for the Communists to force us to withdraw' (No. 80). The intention in China was still to keep a foot in the door. Expediency dictated that over Hong Kong, it would be unwise to 'rattle the sword in the scabbard too loudly' (No. 79).

The Chiefs of Staff had earlier suggested that Hong Kong should be placed under military command (No. 75). Instead a Supreme Commander of the local forces, whose views would prevail over those of the Governor in the event of disagreement or in an emergency, was appointed to the colony at the beginning of June. A directive about the new command arrangements made clear 'that the real importance of Hong Kong at present is not so much as a trading post or as a potential fortress but because of the effects of what is done there upon the Cold War. This must govern all decisions' (No. 81).

Consultation with the Commonwealth produced a varied response. All countries agreed that Britain was right to take precautions. The Government of India was more amenable than expected but apart from New Zealand, no country was prepared to offer material support. Although later offering direct support in the event of a Communist attack, the Australian Government maintained throughout that an accommodation with the Communists over Hong Kong would ultimately be necessary. Ceylon warned about the sensitivity of Asian opinion on the issue of security measures to deal with internal unrest. Canada equivocated before offering qualified support (Nos. 82 and 103).

The US was also consulted and the American reaction was largely responsible for a reassessment of British policy towards Hong Kong. Outright US support was not forthcoming. The State Department referred to the position of the New Territories and asked what action the UK proposed to take if the Communists adopted all measures short of war to force the retrocession of Hong Kong (No. 83). UK Ministers responded towards the end of June by asking Mr. Bevin and Mr. Creech Jones to consider long-term policy towards Hong Kong and to submit proposals (No. 84). At the same time a further batch of Communist documents captured during another police raid in Hong Kong arrived in the FO. They indicated that the Communists had no plans for Hong Kong in their economic strategy (No. 85).

When Mr. Bevin and Mr. Creech Jones reported back to Cabinet in the middle of August, the Communist threat to Hong Kong had receded but vigilance was still maintained. The two Ministers concluded that uncertainty over future developments in China made it neither possible nor desirable to determine long-term policy towards Hong Kong. The situation resembled that in Berlin. In both places 'the threat of Russian and Communist expansionism necessitates holding what we have and not withdrawing'. The UK was 'impelled to remain' without any clear indication of the extent or duration of the military commitment. While the UK would be willing to discuss Hong Kong with a 'friendly and democratic and stable Government of a unified China', there seemed no possibility that an exchange could take place in the near or foreseeable future (No. 92). In Cabinet Ministers advised against the inclusion of the word 'democratic' in defining the conditions under which the UK might eventually be prepared to discuss Hong Kong. The previous proposal to place Hong Kong under international control was discussed again, this time in the context of enlisting US support for the idea. It was examined afresh but rejected (No. 95).

The Cabinet's conclusions did not end the military discussions about defending Hong Kong—the garrison was in fact reduced in April 1950—(No. 101), nor the regular assessments of the extent to which it was threatened by the Communists (No. 112). It remained the UK's military position that in a wider conflict, Hong Kong could not be defended against a major power in possession of the mainland. The reinforcements were in position to deter an attack, not to fight a war. Politically it was recognised that no Chinese government would agree to the renewal of the lease of the New Territories when it expired in 1997. Without these territories Hong Kong would be untenable and before 1997 the government of the UK would have to consider the colony's status. But the Labour Government of 1949 concluded that 'some two generations in advance of the event', there was no justification in attempting to lay down the principles that might govern an arrangement with China. The 'willingness or otherwise' of the UK government of the day to reach an accommodation would depend upon how the situation developed on the mainland (No. 92).

Acknowledgements

In accordance with the Parliamentary announcement cited in the Introduction to the Series, the Editors have had the customary freedom in the selection and arrangement of documents, including full access to all classes of FCO documentation. They have followed standard practice in not reproducing specifically intelligence material. In the present volume there have been no exceptional cases, provided for in the Parliamentary announcement, where it has been necessary on security grounds to restrict the availability of particular documents selected in accordance with regular practice.

The main source of documentation in this volume has been the records of the Far Eastern Department in the Foreign Office political files classed as FO 371. Additional FO material has been consulted from the records of the Northern and Information Departments, and from FO 800, the Private Papers of Mr. E. Bevin as Secretary of State between 1945 and 1951. I am grateful to the Historical and Records Section of the Cabinet Office, and the Departmental Records Officer of the Ministry of Defence, for permission to publish and cite documents in their custody. I am also grateful to the Department of Trade and Industry for supplying information about the 1946 British Trade Mission to China (Nos. 9 and 30), and to Dr. Greg Donaghy at the Historical Section of the Canadian

Department of Foreign Affairs and International Trade for supplying copies of Canadian documents explaining the Government of Canada's position over Hong Kong in 1949 (No. 103).

The volume was researched and edited while I was on a part-time contract to the FCO from a position as General Editor of the British Documents on the End of Empire Project at the Institute of Commonwealth Studies within the University of London. I should like to thank Mrs Heather Yasamee, the head of the FCO Records and Historical Department, and her staff for their help and support. In this respect I am particularly indebted to Mrs Margaret Bryan CMG for advice and information; to Mr. Richard Bevins, Dr. Nigel Jarvis, Dr. Martin Longden, Mr. Eamonn Clifford and Dr. Christopher Baxter for their assistance with the research and their technical support; and to Mrs Diane Morrish and Miss Jackie Till for their secretarial assistance. I am especially grateful to the FCO's Chief Historian, Ms. Gill Bennett OBE, and to the Senior Editor, Dr. Keith Hamilton, for their constant guidance and support, and for their professional expertise that has enabled them to make invaluable suggestions and to iron out inconsistencies and anomalies in the typescript.

S. R. ASHTON

October 2001

CONTENTS

ABBREVIATIONS FOR PRINTED SOURCES

BFSP	*British and Foreign State Papers* (London, 1841-1977)
BoT	*Board of Trade, Report of the United Kingdom Trade Mission to China, October to December 1946* (HMSO, 1948)
Cmd.	Command Paper (London)
Cmd. 7457	*Exchange of Notes constituting an Agreement between the Government of the United Kingdom and the Government of the Republic of China for the transfer of certain British Naval Vessels to China and the Mutual Waiver of Claims in respect of the loss of other Vessels* (18 May 1948)
DBFP	*Documents on British Foreign Policy, 1919-1939*
DBPO	*Documents on British Policy Overseas*
FRUS	*Foreign Relations of the United States*
Parl. Debs., 5th ser., H. of C.	*Parliamentary Debates (Hansard), Fifth Series, House of Commons, Official Report (London)*
Parl. Debs., 5th ser., H. of L.	*Parliamentary Debates (Hansard), Fifth Series, House of Lords, Official Report (London)*
White Paper (US)	Department of State Publication 3573, *United States Relations with China, With Special Reference to the Period 1944-1949* (Washington, Government Printing Office, 1949)
Woodward	Sir Llewellyn Woodward, *British Foreign Policy in the Second World War* (London: HMSO, 1975)

ABBREVIATED DESIGNATIONS

AUS	Assistant Under-Secretary	GATT	General Agreement on Tariffs and Trade
BAT	British and American Tobacco	GOC	General Officer Commanding
BoT	Board of Trade	GRT	Gross Registered Tonnage
CATC	Central Air Transportation Corporation	HMS	His Majesty's Ship
CCP	Chinese Communist Party	JIC	Joint Intelligence Committee
CIGS	Chief of the Imperial General Staff	JMP	Jen Min Piao (Chinese dollar currency introduced by Communists)
CNAC	Chinese National Aviation Corporation	KMT	Kuomintang (Chinese Nationalist Party)
CNRRA	Chinese National Relief and Rehabilitation Administration	MFA	Minister/Ministry of Foreign Affairs
CO	Colonial Office	MVD	*Ministerstvo Vnutrennykh Del* (Soviet Ministry of Internal Affairs)
COS	Chiefs of Staff	PUS	Permanent Under-Secretary (of State)
CPLA	Chinese People's Liberation Army	RAAF	Royal Australian Air Force
CR&T	Commercial Relations and Treaty Department (Board of Trade)	SEACOS	South-East Asia Chiefs of Staff
DRV	Democratic Republic of Vietnam	SIFE	Security Intelligence Far East
ECE	Economic Commission for Europe	UN	United Nations Organisation

UNGA	United Nations General Assembly
UNRRA	United Nations Relief and Rehabilitation Administration
USN	United States Navy
WFTU	World Federation of Trade Unions

CHAPTER SUMMARIES

CHAPTER I

CHAPTER II

CHAPTER III

1947

CHAPTER IV

1948

CHAPTER V

1949

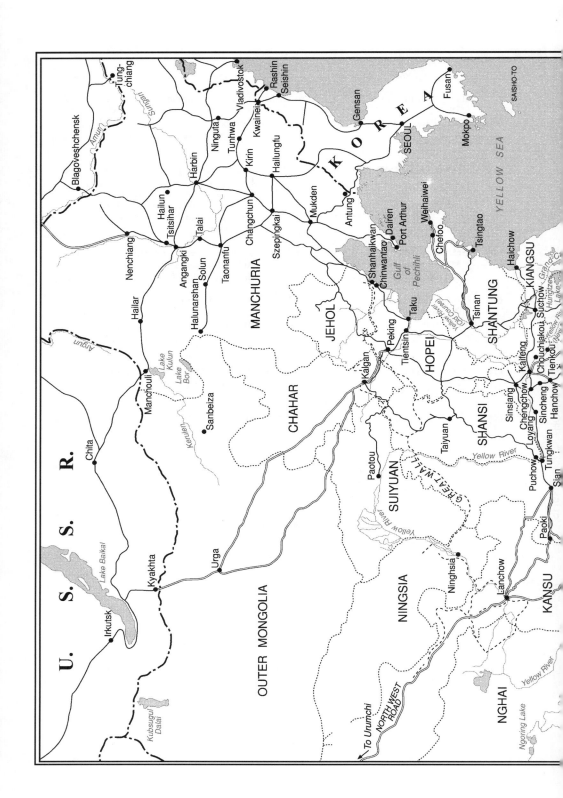

EAST CHINA

O. R. 6382

International Boundaries	–··–··–
Provincial Boundaries	··········
Railways	═══
Roads	────

MILES 100   0   100   200   300   400 MILES

SHENSI

HONAN

ANHWEI

Shanghai
Chinkiang
Nanking
Wuhu
Hangchow
Chuk
Kinhwa
Haimen
Wenchow
Ningpo

CHEKIANG

Tamsui
Tajpeh

FORMOSA

PESCADORES

PRATAS

Yangtze

Anking
Nanchang
Lake Poyang

KIANGSI

Kienow
Foochow

FUKIEN

Amoy

Chuchow
Chaochowfu
Tsungfa
Chaoyang
Waichow
Swatow
Swabue

HONGKONG
MACAO

HUPEH

PEIPING - HANKOW R.
Sinyang
Shuisien
Hankow
Hanyang
Wuchang
Shasi
Kiukiang
Yochow
Siangyin
Kaoan
Changsha
Chuchow

Hengyang

KWANGTUNG

Shukwan
Samshui
Canton
Kongmoon
Namtau

Siangyang
Ichang
Itu
Taiping
Tzeli
Changteh
Taoyuan
Sinhwa
Yuyangkwan

Lake Tungting

HUNAN

Lingling
Kweilin

Wuchow

Kongmoon

KWANGCHOWWAN

KWANGCHOWWAN
Luichow Peninsula

HAINAN

Holhow

Wanhsien
Yangtze

Chungking

KWEICHOW
Kweiyang

KWANGSI

Liuchow

Nanning

Pakhoi

Langson
Haiphong
Hanoi

SIKANG

Chengtu

SZECHWAN
Yangtze

Kunming

YUNNAN

INDO - CHINA

Talifu

Mekong

Wanting

BURMA
Kengtung

Salween
Mekong

THAILAND
M. Chieng Mai

1092/01
Foreign and Commonwealth Office Library Map Series 224(2002)
Users should note that this map has been designed for briefing purposes only and it should not be used for determining the precise location of places or features. This map should not be considered an authority on the delimitation of international boundaries nor on the spelling of place and feature names. Maps produced for the FCO Library Map Service are not to be taken as necessarily representing the views of the UK government on boundaries or political status. © Crown copyright 2002

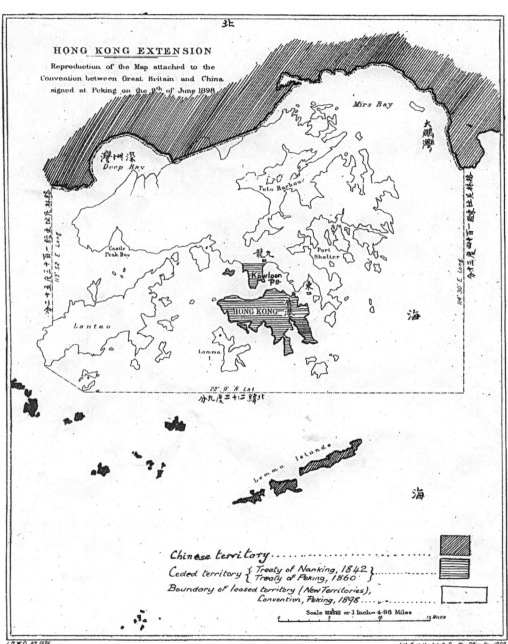

HONG KONG EXTENSION

Reproduction of the Map attached to the
Convention between Great Britain and China
signed at Peking on the 9ᵗʰ of June 1898

北

Mirs Bay

大鵬灣

澳州渓
Deep Bay

Tolo Harbour

Castle
Peak Bay

Port
Shelter

龍九
Kowloon Pᵗ

海

HONG KONG

Lantao

東

Lamma I.

22° 9' N Lat
分九度三十二緯北

Lemma Islands

海

Chinese territory ....

Ceded territory { Treaty of Nanking, 1842 }
               { Treaty of Peking, 1860 } ....

Boundary of leased territory (New Territories),
Convention, Peking, 1898 ....

Scale ≡≡≡ or 1 Inch= 4·96 Miles

15 MILES

I D W O. Nº 1376

Chapter I

1945

The memorandum reproduced below as No. 1 represented the second attempt by the Foreign Office's Far Eastern Department to define the principles of post-war policy towards China before the end of hostilities with Japan. It was a revised version of a memorandum written in March 1945. Both documents were the work of Mr. J.C. Sterndale Bennett, head of the Far Eastern Department, 1944-1946. China's importance to Britain featured more prominently in the earlier version. Here the emergence of 'a strong, stable and friendly' China was said to be as much in Britain's interests as it was in America's. 'With our world-wide imperial interest we cannot afford to be indifferent to the attitude towards us of nearly 500,000,000 Chinese, and an unstable and disunited country of that size is a standing menace to international peace and good order.'

It was equally important to allay suspicions, current in both China and the United States, that Britain did not want a strong China, either 'because we still have "imperialist" designs on China or alternatively because we fear that China may be aiming at the break-up of our colonial system in the Far East'. To allow a monopoly of American influence to emerge unchallenged in China at the end of the war might have potentially damaging consequences. In its present state of semi-development, with xenophobia still latent beneath the surface, China would not wish to place itself too much in the hands of any one foreign power and Britain would suffer as much as America from manifestations of anti-foreign sentiment. Unqualified American support of China might also bring about a collision with the Soviet Union and it would therefore be preferable if China's future could be regarded as a United Nations interest and treated as such. While recognising that Britain's ability to play a constructive role in China's post-war development would be strictly limited, the March memorandum proceeded to outline a series of measures which might be adopted. These included economic and financial aid (especially a more liberal application of the terms of the 1944 £50 million financial aid agreement—see paragraph 17 of the revised memorandum reproduced here), and military and technical assistance and training. It was suggested that this new China policy should be endorsed by Cabinet and publicised in Parliament.[1]

Two Assistant Under-Secretaries of State agreed that Britain should do what it could to help China. Both, however, cautioned that the level of such help would have to be determined by the available resources. Mr. E.L. Hall-Patch, superintending Economic Relations Department and the Economic and Industrial Planning Staff, argued that

[1] Memorandum by Mr. Sterndale Bennett of 2 March 1945 (F 1331/409/10).

Britain's external resources were now 'desperately small for our great responsibilities' and that these would have to be husbanded for use in the post-war period in areas upon which 'our whole future depends'. China was not one of these areas because financially it would not be in a position to provide immediate returns. 'To assume any fresh responsibilities in China seems to me dangerous if not impossible' and it would be 'disastrous' to appear to be competing politically and economically in China with the Americans in advance of the Stage III negotiations on the terms of an American loan to Britain. By way of counter-argument to that put up by Mr. Sterndale Bennett, Mr. Hall-Patch suggested that there might, at the end of the war, be a reaction in the United States against lavish American commitments in China, especially if these entailed increased taxation. Nor need Britain be alarmed if the American private sector became involved. American bankers and merchants would be handicapped by their own inexperience and thwarted by Chinese nationalism. Mr. Hall-Patch saw no need to make China policy an issue requiring a submission to Cabinet. Instead he recommended a policy of 'watchful passivity'. As Mr. Sterndale Bennett had suggested, Britain should seek to counter-balance any monopoly of American influence in China by involving the United Nations in China's development. The Americans might be approached for a frank exchange of views and informed of Britain's view that the task of making China 'strong, united and prosperous'—a 'vast' undertaking said to be 'so full of pitfalls'—could be tackled only on a United Nations basis.[2]

Mr. V.F.W. Cavendish-Bentinck, Chairman of the Joint Intelligence Committee since February 1944, agreed: 'After the war we shall have to cut our coat according to our cloth, and I doubt very much whether there will be sufficient cloth to do much towards clothing a strong and united China.' The immediate post-war priorities would be the restoration of internal security and the recovery of lost possessions, especially Hong Kong. These should be followed by the restoration of properties owned by British individuals and firms in China. But, Mr. Cavendish-Bentinck continued, 'I trust we shall not overrate our interest in China. China is not vital to the maintenance of our Empire and we can do without our China trade. So long as we maintain control of seaways, a direct threat from the direction of China is not serious.'[3]

Considered 'dead' by the Department in March, Mr. Sterndale Bennett's memorandum was revived in July in the version reproduced below, which was initialled by the Secretary of State for Foreign Affairs, Ernest Bevin. It was not intended as the basis for a submission to Cabinet; its purpose is explained in paragraph 31.

[2] Minute by Mr. Hall-Patch of 10 March 1945. Formerly Financial Adviser to HM Ambassadors at Peking and Tokyo, 1936, and Financial Commissioner in the Far East, 1940, Mr. Hall-Patch transferred from the Treasury to the FO in 1944.

[3] Minute by Mr. Cavendish-Bentinck of 13 March 1945.

No. 1

Memorandum on Present China Situation and on British and American Policies in China

[F 4171/186/10]

Secret   FOREIGN OFFICE, 7 July 1945

I RECENT DEVELOPMENTS in CHINA

Military Crisis of November, 1944

1. The China scene has been unusually eventful during the last six or seven months. The Japanese once more became aggressive in the summer of 1944, and by November they were rapidly overrunning the provinces of Hunan and Kwangsi, including important American airfields. Kweilin, one of the half dozen more important towns in Free China, fell on the 10th November; after that the Japanese advance, meeting with little or no resistance, continued into the province of Kweichow, and by the end of the month threatened to reach Kweiyang, an important centre where the main roads from Chungking and Kunming converge. Its occupation would have constituted a grave threat to both these cities. In early December, however, the Japanese on their own initiative suddenly pulled up, and later withdrew from Kweichow province.

2. The effect of the virtually unopposed Japanese advance was to make Chinese of all classes both despondent and humiliated. They alone of all the Allied nations were still meeting defeat. Significantly, the press abroad now only referred to the Big Three, not the Big Four as hitherto. Moreover, China had ceased to be the spoilt child of the American press, and had become instead material for 'debunking'; savage references were made to a 'moribund and reactionary régime'. Perhaps on account of the highly developed self-esteem of the Chinese people, the governing authority in China has to pay even more heed to foreign than to domestic criticism. At the end of 1944 there was plenty of both.

The Rally

(a) Ministerial changes, and return to power of T.V. Soong[1]

3. In this difficult situation the Chinese Government reacted not unsuccessfully. First, the Generalissimo,[2] anxious to retain American

---

[1] A brother-in-law of Chiang Kai-shek and China's Foreign Minister, 1941-45, Dr. T.V. Soong became Acting President of the Executive Yuan (the highest executive organ of the National Government) in December 1944. He was President of the Executive Yuan from May 1945 until March 1947. In November 1947 he was appointed to Canton as Governor of Kwantung Province.

[2] Chiang Kai-shek, leader of the Kuomintang or Nationalist Party. Elected President of the National Government of the Republic of China in September 1943, and first President of the Republic of China in April 1948.

goodwill, reorganised his administration in such a way as to make it appear that those ministers who had been chiefly stigmatized as reactionaries had been dropped. General Ho Ying-ch'in, Dr. H.H. Kung and Mr. Ch'en Li-fu were respectively relieved of the Ministries of War, Finance and Education. (In each case, however, they either retained or were given an influential post. General Ho is now Commander in Chief of all Chinese forces south of the Yangtze. Dr. Kung retained for the time being the Vice-Presidency of the Executive Yuan; and Mr. Ch'en Li-ıu was given a key Party appointment.) Far the most important development, however, was the return to power of Dr. T.V. Soong, who in December was made Acting President of the Executive Yuan, a position somewhat akin to that of Prime Minister. The Presidency of the Executive Yuan had been previously held by Generalissimo Chiang Kai-shek concurrently with his post as President of the National Government. Dr. Soong had long been in the wilderness; and only a year previously, although Foreign Minister (a post which he still retains), he had hardly been on speaking terms with the Generalissimo. Dr. Soong has outstanding ability, and probably understands the West as well as anyone else in Chinese public life.

(b) America to the rescue
4. Next, the Chinese Government committed itself to a greater degree of American tutelage in the shape of (a) the inauguration of the War Production and War Transport Boards; and (b) a Sino-American programme of reform for the Chinese army.

War Production and War Transport Boards
5. The War Production Board was set up on the 16th November to supervise productive enterprises, the importation of materials, the distribution of labour, and the financing of war production. The Board arose out of a recommendation by Mr. Donald Nelson[3] during his visit to Chungking in the summer of 1944, and American advisers are attached to it. The War Transport Board, established on the 1st January, was designed to effect in the sphere of transport, particularly road transport, the mobilisation and coordination of resources which the War Production Board set out to achieve in the economic sphere. The War Transport Board also enjoys the benefit of American advice, if not direction, having an American general as one of the deputy directors, and employing other Americans as deputy heads of the various sections.

Chinese Army Reforms
6. The Sino-American programme of reform for the Chinese army, although sponsored by the new Minister of War, General Ch'en Ch'eng, was inspired by Major-General Wedemeyer, who succeeded General Stilwell as Chief of Staff to the Generalissimo and Commanding General of

---

[3] President Roosevelt's Personal Representative in China, 1944, to advise on the setting up of a Chinese War Production Board.

the United States Army forces in the China Theatre.[4] Chief features of the programme are a reduction of superfluous units and the bringing up to full strength of other units of the Chinese Army, improved pay and rations for all Chinese troops, the attachment of a cadre of American troops to each Chinese unit, the opening of a very large training centre on American lines and run by American officers, and the placing of an American general in command of the Chinese Army Services of Supply, with a number of American officers to assist him, in order to ensure that Chinese troops get better food, clothing and equipment.

Ledo Road
7. It may also be mentioned here that the Ledo Road was opened to traffic in January. As implied by the attempt to re-name it the 'Stilwell' road, the tendency was to regard it as a purely Sino-American achievement, and to ignore both the part played by British forces in Burma, and the fact that the road runs through British territory.

Recent Ministerial Changes
8. Recently, a further strengthening and liberalization of the administration has taken place through the assumption by Dr. T. V. Soong of the substantive presidency of the Executive Yuan, and the appointment, in place of Dr. H. H. Kung as Vice-President of that Yuan, of Dr. Wong Wen-hao, Minister of Economic Affairs and Chairman of the War Production Board. Dr. Wong is a non-party man and an able and progressive administrator. Dr. Soong recently returned from the United States where he was head of the Chinese Delegation to the San Francisco Conference. The part played there by the Chinese delegation has done much to restore China's international standing and it is likely that it will also have strengthened Dr. Soong's own position at home in consequence. He proceeded to Moscow at the end of June to discuss outstanding questions between China and the Soviet Union.

Recent Military Developments
9. In April of this year the Japanese started a fresh offensive in Western Hunan with the apparent objective of capturing the American air base at Chihchiang. Chinese reinforcements, including American-trained troops with air-borne supplies, were brought up and the advance was stemmed and finally driven back with losses to the Japanese. The Chinese were jubilant over this evidence of their increasing military strength, which provided such a refreshing contrast to the humiliating *débâcle* of last autumn. In May, the Japanese began withdrawals in various parts of China. Foochow, on the coast opposite Formosa, was retaken by the Chinese in that month and in June Wenchow, further north, was

---

[4] General A.C. Wedemeyer replaced General J.W. Stilwell as Commander of the US Army Forces in China in October 1944, and continued as Chief of Staff to Generalissimo Chiang Kai-shek until May 1946.

reoccupied by Chinese troops, the Japanese withdrawing to the Hangchow Bay area in evident preparation for the defence of the Shanghai estuary against an American landing. Withdrawals also took place in Kwangsi, where the Chinese recaptured the important American air base at Liuchow at the end of June, and also reoccupied the important town of Nanning, near the Indo-China border, on the Japanese line of communication between Kwangsi and Indo-China. In effecting these withdrawals the Japanese object appears to have been to shorten their over-extended lines in China and to concentrate troops in certain strategic areas along the coast and elsewhere, in preparation for American landings.

Present Situation

(a) Inflation

10. In general, then, the situation has much improved since last December; but two obstinate problems remain, namely inflation and the Kuomintang-Communist deadlock. The cost of living continues to rise at an extravagant rate, and it is felt that the economic situation is as serious in its way as the military situation was last November. The Chungking open market retail price index in February was 94,547 compared with 100 for 1937. In the three months January to March the cost of living more than doubled itself. The increase between the 1st January and the end of May was over 150% compared with a rise of 288% for the whole of 1944. Dr. Soong is trying to combat inflation in two principal ways. The first is the absorption of idle currency by the sale to the public of gold for delivery in six months' time at an official price considerably below the open market price. To this end America is supplying China with gold to the value of United States dollars 189 million. The second is the importation of certain commodities, with a view to mopping up currency and discouraging hoarding and speculation by demonstrating that importation is again a possibility. A good start has already been made by bringing in quantities of uniforms, cotton piece goods, and yarn out of stocks amounting to 3,400 tons, belonging to the Chinese Government and purchased out of British export credits, which were lying in India. The Americans for their part also hope to make available 22,000 tons of cotton textiles this year of which 7,300 tons are already definitely earmarked from production in Mexico, Brazil and the United States of America. Dr. Soong has in addition obtained the agreement of His Majesty's Government to financing from the 1944 £50 million credit the purchase of 3,000 tons of short staple raw cotton and 200,000 rice bags from India and these are now being sent into China by air. Active consideration is also being given, both in the United Kingdom and in the United Sates of America, to Dr. Soong's further request that the Chinese Government should be enabled to purchase miscellaneous consumer goods for subsequent sale as part of the anti-inflation campaign.

(b) The Communist Deadlock

11. Negotiations between the Government and the Chinese Communists are again in suspense, and the Communists, based on Shensi province, continue to administer a large part of China independently of the Central Government. The Generalissimo, in a speech on the 1st March, rejected the Communist demand for a coalition government, which he considered could only result in friction and chaos. Instead he reaffirmed his promise that a National Assembly would be convened next November for the purpose of adopting a constitution. Democratic government would then supersede one-party rule by the Kuomintang. The Communists' answer to this is that the proposed National Assembly will be a 'mockery of democracy' and will merely produce a perpetuation of Kuomintang rule. The Government made an astute move when they included a Communist, Mr. Tung Pi-wu, in the delegation for San Francisco, thus meeting the charge that China was going to the Conference disunited. Apart from this, however, the deadlock is complete, and recently the Communists announced that they would boycott the meeting of the People's Political Council on the 7th July, which was to discuss amongst other things the forthcoming convention of the National Assembly. Perhaps even more crucial than the constitutional issue is the question of the control of the Communist armies. In his speech of the 1st March, Chiang Kai-shek let it be known that he had proposed to the Communists a compromise whereunder their armies would come under control of the National Government, but would be placed under the direct command of an American general. But the Communists declined this proposal: they were not prepared to hand their troops over to a Kuomintang-dominated government, and thus relinquish their only bargaining weapon over the constitutional issue. In this connexion it is disquieting to note that Communist troops, and not Central Government forces, have been taking over some areas of China vacated by the Japanese in their recent withdrawals, and that one or two clashes have been reported between the Communists and Chungking troops in these areas.

Future Outlook

12. While the immediate danger which threatened China at the end of 1944 has receded, the long term outlook is by no means promising. Free China is divided into two armed camps, and when once the pressure from Japan is removed, if not earlier, the danger of an outbreak of civil war will be a real one. (A particularly delicate situation is likely to arise if and when American troops land on the China coast, and are obliged to cooperate with, and perhaps arm, Communist troops in areas near the coast.) As regards inflation, it is quite possible that such remedial measures as are being taken at present will prove to be only palliatives; and if inflation continues at its present rate, no one can foretell what will be the consequences.

American attitude towards Communist and inflation problems

13. The Americans, in addition to coming to the rescue of China in her hour of need last autumn and striving to re-build her war effort, have come forward with good offices in both China's major domestic problems. Last November the new American Ambassador, Major-General Patrick Hurley,[5] went to Yenan, the Communist capital, and on his return arranged an interview between Chow En-lai [*sic*],[6] one of the Communist leaders, and the Generalissimo. However, as was perhaps to be expected, foreign mediation could achieve little in a dispute of this kind, and after his recent visit to Washington General Hurley declared American policy to be one of non-intervention in Chinese domestic affairs. In connexion with the other major problem, inflation, Mr. Leon Henderson, former administrator of the United States Office of Price Administration, visited Chungking at the special invitation of Dr. Soong, whom he later accompanied to San Francisco.

Russia

14. A summary of the situation would be incomplete without mention of the Russian factor. Of the members of the Chinese Government, only Dr. Sun Fo,[7] who is well known for his pro-Soviet sympathies, has publicly advocated Soviet participation in the war against Japan. The Government as a whole no doubt fear the possibility of Soviet demands for concessions in Manchuria or elsewhere as a price of such participation. And here it must be emphasised that there is no subject on which the Chinese as a whole feel more strongly than that of Manchuria. Its recovery is for them a *sine qua non* of the Far Eastern peace settlement. Dr. T.V. Soong's visit to Moscow reflects China's anxiety over her relations with the Soviet Union.[8]

---

[5] Special representative of President Roosevelt in China, 1944, and subsequently US Ambassador in China until November 1945. Ambassador Hurley's mission in China was primarily intended to prevent the collapse of the National Government and to keep the Chinese Army in the war. A secondary objective was to prevent the outbreak of civil war. When he resigned in 1945, he claimed that officials in the State Department had sabotaged his mission. He accused them of having aligned US policy in Asia with both Colonial and Communist imperialisms. He also declared that the Communists had been encouraged in their refusal to come to terms with Chiang Kai-shek by members of his own staff who were then, as a result of his own protests, removed to positions in the State Department where they became his supervisors. For reactions in the US to the Ambassador's charges, see *FRUS 1945*, vol. vii, pp. 722-44.

[6] Chou En-lai was the main Communist representative in the negotiations between the Nationalists and the Communists. He was in particular the Communist representative on the Kuomintang-Communist Three Man Military Committee set up in February 1946 to supervise an armistice brought about by US mediation in the civil war. The third representative and chairman was Ambassador Hurley's successor, General Marshall (see No. 12, note 2).

[7] A son of Sun Yat-sen (see No. 16, note 8) by his first wife (according to some reports an adopted son), Dr. Sun Fo made a number of lengthy visits to Russia in the 1930s and was President of the Sino-Soviet Cultural Association.

[8] On which see No. 3.

Important factors in these relations, apart from Manchuria, are the Chinese Communist question and the situation in the border territories of Outer Mongolia and Sinkiang. Up till now the Russians have shown little interest in the Chinese Communists; but should it ever come to an open clash between the Government and the Communists, it seems unlikely that the Soviet Union would then be content to remain a passive spectator. (It seems possible in fact that the Kuomintang-Communist issue may become an international issue in which Soviet Russia and the United States will be directly concerned and in which we also shall be eventually involved.) Chinese sovereignty over Outer Mongolia was recognised by the Soviet Union in 1924. In practice, however, Outer Mongolia remains independent of China and a virtual Soviet protectorate. Sinkiang was also virtually a Soviet protectorate from 1937 to 1942, in which year the Chinese Central Government, taking advantage of Russia's difficulties in the west, reasserted their authority in the province and forced a complete withdrawal of Soviet influence. Sinkiang is now in the throes of a serious economic crisis, caused mainly by the severance of trade with Russia. A Qazak revolt has also broken out in the Ili valley, near the Soviet border. Many Chinese fear that the Soviet Union may take advantage of these difficulties to reassert their influence in Sinkiang.

II THE AMERICAN AND BRITISH POSITIONS
Contrast between the two
15. A striking feature of the present situation is the ascendancy of the United States in China. The contrast between the British and American positions is brought out in the following passage from a note written by the late Sir Eric Teichman[9] in 1943:

Comparing China's foreign policy in 1943 with her attitude of ten years earlier, nothing is more striking than her dependence on America and acceptance of American leadership. Signs of this meet one at every turn, alike in the cultural, diplomatic, economic, financial and military fields. China looks primarily to America, not Britain, to defeat Japan; to furnish her with the materials and sinews of war; and to build up the great new China after the war is won. On our side, because we are not in a position to do otherwise, we have accepted this condition and have abdicated from the position of leadership which we have occupied in China for the past hundred years . . . We are not in a position to keep pace with the United States in the furnishing of financial, economic, and material assistance to the Chinese; and in the diplomatic sphere, where ten years ago we naturally took the lead, we now wait anxiously to see what the American Government may do.

[9] HM Consular Service in China, 1907-36 (retired); re-employed as Counsellor of Peking Embassy, 1942-44.

The picture drawn in the above passage is even more relevant to the situation today than it was in 1943.

American strategic responsibility

16. In view of Great Britain's vast commitment elsewhere and of her immediate danger in the West, it was inevitable and perhaps only logical that this situation should have come about. Even before Pearl Harbour, General Chennault's American Air Volunteer Group was operating in China. We on the other hand, in view of our single-handed fight with Germany and Italy and the defencelessness of our Far Eastern territories, were obliged to be particularly circumspect in the preservation of neutrality *vis à vis* Japan and even had to go to the length of temporarily prohibiting the movement of war material into China along the Burma Road. After Pearl Harbour we had to play a purely defensive rôle in the Far East and in March 1942 it was agreed by the Combined Chiefs of Staff that '... it was obvious ... that China must fall within the United States sphere of strategic influence'. The Americans have to their credit the striking achievements of the 14th United States Army Air Force based on Kunming. Between March 1941 and the end of April 1945 they had supplied war materials under Lend-Lease to the value of $458,874,000 and a further large programme believed to be of the order of $500 to $600 million is under consideration. A corollary of their ability to provide supplies on so large a scale and of the above-quoted decision of the Combined Chiefs of Staff was that the United States became responsible for presenting bids for equipment for China to the Combined Boards for munitions and raw materials in Washington and have thus come to be regarded as having the main responsibility for direct assistance to China.

The British Contribution

17. Great Britain's assistance to China in her struggle against Japan, though necessarily limited, is by no means negligible. It includes £10,000,000 advanced or guaranteed by His Majesty's Government for Chinese currency stabilisation, two export credits granted in 1939 and 1940 for nearly £8,000,000, supplies and services furnished to Chinese troops in India to a value of more than £6,000,000, supplies shipped mainly from Australia to a value of over £3,000,000, and finally the provision in 1944 of a credit of £50,000,000 for war purposes, together with a Lend-Lease Agreement for the supply of any arms, munitions, and military equipment which His Majesty's Government might be able to make available to the Chinese armies. In addition, British assistance to China during the past three years has taken the following forms:

(*a*) a small Royal Air Force training mission at the Chinese Air Staff College at Chengtu;
(*b*) a small British military unit in charge of a training school for guerrilla warfare, demolitions, etc;

(c) assistance in the sphere of technical education provided by the British Council Scientific Office in Chungking under Dr. Joseph Needham, F.R.S.;[10]

(d) assistance in the sphere of civil industrial supplies, provided by representatives of the Allied Supplies Executive attached to His Majesty's Embassy;

(e) an ambulance and transport unit sent out by the Society of Friends and subsidized by His Majesty's Government with annual grants-in-aid;

(f) the British United Aid to China fund (totalling over £1½ million);

(g) British Red Cross Assistance to the value of £1,000,000 of which £600,000 has been spent in China to date;

(h) Chinese Navy: in addition to two river gunboats and a corvette already transferred as well as the training of a small number of Chinese naval cadets, His Majesty's Government have now also agreed to transfer on Lend-Lease terms a cruiser, two submarines, 8 coastal craft and a destroyer, as well as to train the necessary crews;

(i) Chinese Air Force: His Majesty's Government have recently agreed to the transfer to India of two training schools' equipment, supplies and facilities being provided under Lend-Lease.

18. Valuable as these contributions are in themselves, they are relatively insignificant when compared with the spectacular assistance furnished by the United States, and their psychological effect is therefore small. In fact we are frequently accused both in China and the United States of lack of interest in China and of lukewarmness in China's cause.[11] It has often been alleged that we do not really want to see a strong and united China emerge from the present war. Lord Cranborne's statement in the House of Lords on the 25th January that His Majesty's Government desired to see China strong, united and prosperous has helped to dispel this impression,[12]

---

[10] Fellow of the Royal Society.

[11] As one of several illustrations of US concern, Representative M.J. Mansfield (Democrat, Montana) visited India, Burma and China in 1944 as President Roosevelt's special envoy. In his report to the President in January 1945 he commented: 'I would say that the American Military in the Far East are fed up with the dilatory tactics of the British out there. All the British are interested in is Singapore, Hong Kong, a restoration of prestige, and a weak China' (*FRUS 1945*, vol. vii, p. 16). *V. ibid.*, pp. 35-36 for the record of a conversation on 25 January 1945 between Mr. J.C. Vincent, Chief of the Division of Chinese Affairs in the State Department, and Mr. J. Keswick, Counsellor of the British Embassy in Chungking (the wartime capital of the Nationalist Government) and, in peacetime, Director of the British firm Jardine, Matheson and Company. For the FO response to the Mansfield tour and the Keswick interview, see F 682/35/10 and F 873/35/10 respectively.

[12] Lord Cranborne, Secretary of State for Dominion Affairs and Leader of the House of Lords, commented in his speech: 'There have, I believe, been unfounded suggestions in some quarters that His Majesty's Government are a little lukewarm on the question of a restoration of the unity of China. I do not know from whence these suggestions emanate, but at any rate I am very glad of this opportunity, if I can, to kill them stone dead, once and for all' (*Parl. Debs., 5th ser., H. of L.*, vol. 124, col. 749).

but the reality of our interest will always be judged not by statements but by our practical activities in relation to China.

III IMPLICATIONS OF THE AMERICAN AND BRITISH POSITIONS

Great Britain's stake in China

19. The long-term effects of the present American ascendancy obviously cannot be a matter of indifference to Great Britain in view of our great stake in China. In 1931 British investment in China was estimated at £244,200,000, i.e. 5.9% of Great Britain's total foreign investment. This sum was made up by £46,400,000 in Chinese Government obligations and £197,800,000 invested in import and export business, real estate, manufacturing, transportation, banking, public utilities, insurance etc. (see memorandum regarding foreign investments in China by C.F. Remer).[13] In 1937 the British Chamber of Commerce at Shanghai roughly estimated the total British investment in China at £300 million. A large proportion of this investment is represented by shipping, banking and other services, the maintenance and development of which after the war are of obvious importance as a contribution to our invisible exports.

America's lead in regard to post-war trade in China

20. We must clearly reckon with the probability that the ascendancy of the United States in building up China's war effort will project itself into the post-war period. American influence is increasingly predominant in many spheres of Chinese activity other than the purely military. The plans of the Foreign Economic Administration spread into the reconstruction period and even if it is not the official policy of the United States Government to use present opportunities in China with a view to post-war commercial possibilities, it is inevitable that this should be in the minds of many individual Americans, with interests in China, who are at present engaged in carrying out the policy of assistance to China. The Chinese too naturally look first to America for the heavy equipment which they will need for their post-war industrial plans. With much reason they feel that America, on account of her greater industrial resources, will be able to deliver the goods first and they probably hope that she will be prepared to do so on credit. Large numbers of Chinese students and technicians are now being sent to the United States for training primarily in connexion with war-time schemes in China. They may be expected to return to China convinced advocates of American methods and equipment. According to a recent message from Washington the Foreign Economic Administration has prepared at the request of the Chinese Government, a $1,000,000,000 post-war industrialisation plan for China calling for the construction of 953 factories and including recommendations for an internal transportation

---

[13] Not printed. Professor C.F. Remer was an American economist and author of several publications on foreign trade and investment in China.

system which would cost another $1,000,000,000. There is no indication as to how this plan is to be financed.

The outlook for British trade

21. In the face of all this, the re-establishment of the British commercial position in China after the war may be a matter of some difficulty. The Americans will have a long start and, in our post-war financial straits, we shall clearly be unable to compete with them on an equal footing. Yet the future of British trade in China may not be so unpromising as it now appears. In the first place, once the war is over there may be a reaction in Congress to lavish American commitments in China. It has been pointed out that, when deficit financing ceases, taxation will have to be on a scale to which the average American is unattuned, with the result that public expenditure in China for uncertain returns will come to be looked at with a more critical eye. Private American bankers and merchants will no doubt also enter the field; but here again it has been pointed out that after the last war they entered the China market with no experience of its pitfalls and many of their assets subsequently passed to established British enterprises. Indeed, in a recent despatch from Chungking the view was expressed that the British vested interests in the old treaty ports, especially those connected with shipping, banking, distribution and insurance, might later give us certain advantages over all the resources of the United States. The Ambassador[14] felt that there were many lines of interest to the China market in which British firms, having greater experience and commercial goodwill, could successfully compete with America. At the moment, the old-established British firms are studying how they can adapt their business to the changed conditions which will prevail in China after the war. Again, there are indications that the Chinese are disturbed over the possibility of an American monopoly of the post-war economic and commercial fields in China, with the opportunity which this would afford for the exercise of undue American political influence, and that to counteract such a possibility the Chinese are beginning to turn to British industry to supply a portion at least of their post-war needs.

Great Britain's interest in China's recovery

22. It used to be a commonplace that our sole interest in China was commercial, and this phrase was often used to disclaim all political designs on the country. But while we have an obvious interest, from the point of view of commerce alone in the recovery by China of economic and political stability, experience has taught us that we have a political and strategic interest also. A weak and unstable country anywhere is a standing temptation to aggressors and a potential menace to world peace. This is particularly true in the case of a huge agglomeration like China where all the major Powers have interests and Russia and Japan are neighbours. An unfriendly China can also be a source of much trouble in our Far Eastern

---

[14] Sir H. Seymour was HM Ambassador to China, 1942-46.

territories, like Malaya and Burma, where large Chinese populations reside. In fact our political and strategic advantage in the Far East lies in the emergence after the war of a friendly, stable and united China—apart from the fact that these are the qualities which in the wider sphere would be most helpful in a fellow member of the 'Big Five'.

Sino-British goodwill and outstanding Sino-British problems

23. The publicity accorded to America's war-time assistance overshadows the part which we have played in the evolution of modern China. But His Majesty's Government's continued support of the Kuomintang Government, from 1926 when we took the lead in meeting China's claim to Treaty revision, down to 1943, when the treaty relinquishing extraterritorial rights was signed,[15] is a fact of which the Chinese are not unmindful; and it is a useful basis of good-will on which to build future political relations. There are of course difficult problems ahead. The physical implementation of the extraterritoriality Treaty of 1943, in so far as it concerns the confirmation of British property rights and the transfer to the Chinese of the administration of the British Concessions and above all of the International Settlement at Shanghai, may give rise to many wrangles. Chinese nationalism may in the flush of victory tend once more to xenophobia, with repercussions not only on the questions just mentioned

---

[15] Under treaties concluded between the UK and China in 1842 and 1858, British subjects in China enjoyed extraterritorial rights in the sense that they were subject to British and not Chinese jurisdiction. Civil and criminal suits against British subjects were brought before HM Consular Courts and HM Supreme Court at Shanghai. Similar treaties were in force between China and other powers. Chinese legislation was not applicable to treaty power nationals, who were in practice exempt from Chinese taxation.

Certain powers (Germany, Austria and Russia) surrendered their extraterritorial rights shortly after the end of the Great War. The UK surrendered its rights in a treaty concluded in January 1943 and ratified in June 1943. The US, France and the Netherlands concluded similar treaties at about the same date.

Under the terms of the UK treaty, HMG relinquished all rights to exercise jurisdiction over British nationals and companies in China. These became subject to Chinese jurisdiction in accordance with the principles of international law. The treaty also provided for the International Settlements at Shanghai and Amoy and the British concessions at Tientsin and Canton to revert to Chinese administration. Under the nineteenth century treaties these areas had remained under Chinese sovereignty but they were administered by the UK and, in the cases of the Settlements at Shanghai and Amoy, other powers. (Britain, however, had always exercised the preponderating influence in the Settlement at Shanghai, the most important of the foreign Settlements.) The 1943 treaty included provision for the opening of negotiations to conclude a new and comprehensive treaty of friendship, commerce, navigation and consular rights. In an exchange of notes the UK relinquished rights of coastal trade and inland navigation, and the right of British naval vessels to enter Chinese waters. Most favoured nation treatment was granted to British ocean shipping entering Chinese ports open to foreign trade, and future visits by naval vessels were to be permitted only on the normal basis of international courtesy.

For the negotiation of the 1943 treaty, see Sir Llewellyn Woodward, *British Foreign Policy in the Second World War*, vol. iv (London: HMSO, 1975), pp. 510-17.

affecting the present rights and interests of foreigners and on legislation affecting foreign participation in future trade and commerce, but on the solution of outstanding political issues between ourselves and China. These issues, on which brief notes are given in the Annex to this memorandum, are Hong Kong, Tibet, the status of the Chinese communities in Malaya and Burma, and the undemarcated portion of the frontier between Burma and China.

24. There is no reason to suppose that the present Chinese Government wish to force an issue on any of these things. Indeed, in June of last year, the Generalissimo intimated informally that he was determined to ensure that relations between China and Britain should be as cordial and intimate as possible, and that the present alliance should be continued in a close friendship after the war. He let it be known that China hoped in due course to achieve a settlement of the Hong Kong and Tibetan questions satisfactory both to herself and to all concerned, and that it was his intention that there should be no Chinese interference in neighbouring British territories (Malaya and Burma).

Importance of re-established British influence

25. Given careful handling and a continuance of this goodwill towards Great Britain, there is no reason why any of the questions at issue with China should prove insurmountable. But as already indicated there is a latent xenophobia in the background and there are still doubts about our real feelings towards Chinese unity and strength. Much may depend therefore on the extent to which, from now onwards, we demonstrate our interest in, and increase our active assistance to, China. It is important that we should show where we stand and that we should increase our influence.

Limitations on scope of British assistance to China

26. Difficulties of production, transportation and finance obviously constitute severe limitations on the scope of what we can do. The demands of the war against Japan; the claims of other countries, which have built up sterling balances, upon the immediate production of such of our industry as is converted to peace-time work; and the necessity of selling our surplus products to customers who can pay for them, all limit the quantities of goods which can be made available for China. Until China's coastal ports are re-opened, transport is a bottleneck. The greater part of the capacity of the air route over the 'Hump', and of the Ledo and the Burma roads is at present taken up by the Americans for the shipment of an ever-increasing volume of military supplies for the United States forces in China and for the new Chinese army which the Americans are training and fitting out. As regards finance, the £50,000,000 credit referred to in paragraph 17 is only available under the terms of the relevant agreement, for agreed purposes arising out of war conditions, to be used during the war. Every request from the Chinese for the utilisation of this credit is rigidly scrutinised from the point of view of the 'end-use' of the goods or services concerned, and any order which cannot qualify as being for strictly war purposes or is

unlikely to be completed in time for use during the war is ruled out. As regards the post-war period, it has been laid down as a rule applicable not only to China but the whole world that, having regard to our very limited capital resources, it is unlikely that any credits will be sanctioned which cannot be justified on purely economic grounds. It will thus be exceedingly difficult to obtain credits for political purposes even when as in China they would obviously be a most valuable part of our diplomatic armoury.

Case for reconsideration of the question of credits for China

27. His Majesty's Ambassador at Chungking has suggested that any unused balance of the £50 million credit at the end of the war with Japan might be transferred to a credit for post-war purposes. The Treasury are, however, as opposed to this as they are opposed to new 'political' credits for the post-war period. Though it is useless to pursue the question further at this stage, there is a case for its ultimate reconsideration.[16] The expansion of our export trade is a matter of the utmost importance and China is a large potential market. The acceptance of orders under credits for essential services such as railways and public utilities and for enterprises designed to build up [the] Chinese economy on sound lines may be expected to contribute to the development of China as a remunerative export market for British goods and to pay long-term dividends both in goodwill and hard trade.

Possible forms of increased British activity

28. For the present, the limitations described in paragraph 26 must be frankly recognised. They are *prima facie* discouraging. But they do not rule out all assistance in the form of supplies and there are other spheres in which increased activity is worth consideration. The various immediate possibilities which suggest themselves, including some on which a start has already been made, are listed below. No doubt the march of events will quickly suggest others.

(a) *Royal Air Force collaboration in China.* His Majesty's Ambassador has said that this, if practicable, would be the best contribution from every point of view. It has clearly been impracticable up to now and may still be for some time to come, for logistic if for no other reasons. But it is a matter which might be submitted for the consideration of the Chiefs of Staff.

(b) *War-time supplies.* There is reason to suppose that Dr. T.V. Soong is sincerely appreciative of the effort we have made to respond to his call for consumer goods to combat inflation. Continued consideration will no

---

[16] The Cabinet's (Official) Overseas Reconstruction Committee considered British commercial policy in China on 24 July 1945 (ORC 2(45)2) and agreed with the Treasury that there could be no question of granting political credits to China under current circumstances (F 4712/57/10). Sir J. Grigg, Secretary of State for War, argued at the meeting that Britain's China policy was 'unrealistic' and that the reality of US competition should be accepted. 'China', he said, 'was not worth bothering about from the point of view of trade. We ran the risk of pouring great sums of money into China or loans in return for illusory commercial benefits.'

doubt be given to the provision of such goods as well as of supplies to assist China's war production within the limits of existing credits; and of war material under the Lend-Lease agreement.

(*c*) *More elastic interpretation of the £50 million credit.* A more elastic interpretation of the financial agreement which regulates the use of this credit might open the way to forms of assistance which would pay good dividends in the long run.

(*d*) *Post-war exports.* Even if the question of credits cannot be reconsidered at present, British post-war exports might be stimulated if the most sympathetic official attitude possible could be shown to those firms who have received Chinese enquiries for the purchase of equipment for post-war delivery; and if Chinese holders of frozen sterling could be given an idea of what United Kingdom export commodities are most likely to be available after the war and with what priorities.

(*e*) *Provision of technical information and increased technical training for Chinese in the United Kingdom.* It seems most desirable to encourage visits to the United Kingdom by Chinese business men and technical experts as well as by Chinese students. This in turn is likely to lead to requests for British technical assistance in China and to the adoption of British technical methods. About 170 young Chinese will be coming here this year to take up apprenticeships offered by the Federation of British Industries and British council scholarships. Certain British shipping firms who are working for the re-establishment of British influence in Chinese shipping are also giving facilities for Chinese apprentices. It may be mentioned that some 1200 Chinese technicians are being sent to the United States for training under American Lend-Lease with a view to assisting China's war effort. This offers an analogy for the use of our £50 million credit for similar purposes.

(*f*) *Assistance in the rebuilding of the Chinese Customs Service.* This is a sphere in which British influence was previously predominant and in which there seems to be a chance of re-establishing our influence. The Customs Service is not merely a preventive and revenue service but has charge of all lights and buoys on the China coast. It is therefore of great importance to shipping, in which we hope to re-establish our predominant position. The Admiralty have at present under consideration proposals for the transfer of certain vessels to the Customs Service and for the training of Chinese personnel.

(*g*) *Civil aviation.* The British and Chinese Corporation, acting in concert with the British Overseas Airways Corporation, have under discussion with the Chinese government a scheme for the development of air lines in and to China after the war. This is a scheme to which it seems desirable for us to give the maximum support.

(*h*) *Commercial Mission to China.* A project is under consideration for the despatch to China in the coming autumn of a small commercial mission to explore the possibilities of the China market both for import and export and to study Chinese legislation affecting commerce.

Anglo-American Collaboration

29. As and when conditions return to normal there will no doubt be rivalry between British and American commercial enterprises. But it is not suggested that we should attempt at this stage to enter into any competition with the Americans either in the commercial or political field in China. On the contrary our aim should be to work more closely with them. The Americans have the major strategic responsibility in China and we should not seek to force upon them a degree of collaboration which they may neither desire nor consider necessary. But American interests and our own in China have been closely identified in the past and are likely to be so in the future. There are ways in which we may be able to support them and to supplement their activities, and there may be matters in which as time goes on they may welcome our cooperation. We should not necessarily wish to be completely identified with all American activities in China in which our part would necessarily be very subordinate under present conditions. But it should be our object to convince them of our interest in China and to take advantage of opportunities as they occur to show this interest in a practical way, as indeed we have done lately in the matter of consumer goods. It may also pay us to keep them informed of such projects as the despatch to China of a commercial mission, and generally to discuss with them Chinese affairs and our attitude towards them with frankness and regularity. Our wider interests are likely to be served in this way even though we may not always meet with frankness and consideration from the Americans. Any suggestion of competition with the United States or any appearance of trying to secure advantages behind the backs of the Americans would merely give the Chinese the opportunity to play off one country against the other and do ultimate damage to our own interests.

30. Not only have we and the Americans a common interest on the political side in the establishment of a friendly, stable and united China, but there is common ground on the commercial side also. We are both interested in the conditions under which our respective nationals will be able to do business in China after the war. The recovery of property, rights and interests in occupied China, the study of Chinese commercial legislation and the conditions of future commercial treaties are all questions in which we should act, if not in concert, at least on parallel lines. We should in fact aim in all our China policy, not necessarily at collaboration with the Americans in the sense of joint action, but at much closer contact and consultation than at present.

31. The object of this memorandum is not to recommend a specific programme of action, but to urge the need for a more active policy in regard to China and for closer contact with the United States Government

in relation to China; and to provide the background against which this plea should be considered.[17]

ANNEX TO NO. 1

Outstanding Political Issues between Great Britain and China

A. *Hong Kong*

The Colony of Hong Kong comprises three areas:

(*a*) The island of Hong Kong, ceded outright to Great Britain by the Nanking treaty of 1842.

(*b*) Part of the Kowloon peninsula opposite Hong Kong, ceded outright by the Peking Convention of 1860.

(*c*) The New Territories, leased for 99 years by the Peking Convention of 1898. They include part of the mainland and a number of islands in the vicinity, of a total area of 405 square miles.

2. The reason for the lease of the New Territories, as stated in the preamble to the convention, was that an extension of Hong Kong territory

---

[17] This analysis of British relations with China remained unchanged throughout 1945 and the substance of its arguments were incorporated in a major policy paper, 'British Foreign Policy in the Far East', which the FO submitted to the Far Eastern (Official) Committee on 31 December 1945 (CAB 134/280). Here it was argued that after six years of war in Europe and four in the Pacific, the UK did not have the resources to resume 'all at once' its pre-war power, influence and responsibilities in the Far East. 'Willy nilly we have to consider where our limited resources can be applied to the greatest effect.' The Far East was divided into areas north and south of the Tropic of Cancer. The UK's limited resources were to be concentrated on Britain's dependencies to the south, including Hong Kong. To the north, in both China and Japan as well as Korea, it was assumed that the US would play the principal role in the early post-war years. Britain should aim to avoid entanglements north of the line 'as much as we can, until we have fully recuperated'.

On China itself, the paper argued that China's international status as a great power was 'unreal'. Acknowledgement of China as a great power might go far to dispel nationalist resentment at the manner in which the country had been treated in the past, but it would also create new difficulties in Britain's relations with China. It was in the UK's interests that China should become a stable and unified state. The UK should therefore deal as little as possible with *de facto* local governments, but if factionalism threatened to become permanent it would be essential to avoid the appearance of backing one faction against another. Accepting that the US was now the predominant influence in China, the UK should concentrate on the restoration of British property and such protection of Britain's rights and interests as may in future be accorded to other foreigners. China was likely to seek good relations with the UK, both as protection against Soviet encroachment and to avoid over-dependence on the US. There were possible areas of friction, most notably over Hong Kong. But if nothing emerged to replace the security for British interests formerly offered by the treaty ports and extraterritorial rights, and if China descended into chaos or split, Hong Kong would be of inestimable value, not only to the UK but also to the Chinese themselves and the Americans and any others who wished to continue a China trade.

was necessary for the proper defence and protection of the Colony. What has now become an equally important factor is that the main water supply of Hong Kong is in the New Territories.

3. In the course of the negotiations which preceded the abolition of extraterritoriality in China, the Chinese Government made a request for the rendition of the New Territories. His Majesty's Government refused to consider this question in connexion with extraterritoriality but agreed that it might be discussed with the Chinese Government after the war. Almost certainly the Chinese Government will then face us with the proposal that the Agreement of 1898 should be terminated and that the area should revert to Chinese sovereignty.

4. At no time have the Chinese Government raised the question of the status of Hong Kong as a whole, but it is generally recoginzed that their ultimate object is the 'recovery' of the whole Colony ceded to Great Britain in 1842 and 1860. The Generalissimo in his book 'China's Destiny', published in 1943, made it clear that Hong Kong is regarded as properly belonging to China and its recovery is merely being postponed.

5. In support of their claim, the Chinese can point to the fact that Hong Kong is geographically and economically a part of China and that its population is overwhelmingly Chinese. They would probably also claim that it was wrested from them under the 'unequal treaties' and that its rendition would erase the last of China's humiliations suffered under these treaties.

Against this we can set the following considerations:

(*a*) At the time of its cession in 1842 Hong Kong was a desolate island with no inhabitants except a few fishermen. British enterprise and good government have built it up to be one of the great seaports of the world, with a population of nearly a million inhabitants.

(*b*) With the removal of the protection afforded by extraterritoriality and a probability of unsettled conditions in China for some years after the war, Hong Kong is likely to acquire increasing importance and value as a base from which British merchants and industrialists can operate in China.

(*c*) Having lost Hong Kong to the enemy, it is a point of national honour for us to recover it, and restore it to its normal state of order and prosperity.[18]

---

[18] Britain's recovery of Hong Kong became a matter of considerable controversy following Japan's sudden surrender on 14 August. Under the command of Rear Admiral C. Harcourt, a task force of twenty-four vessels from the British Pacific Fleet was gathered at Subic Bay in the Philippines to sail immediately to Hong Kong. The main political difficulty arose from the fact that Hong Kong was in the operational sphere of Chiang Kai-shek whose Chief of Staff was General Wedeymer. The UK therefore faced the prospect of the colony being liberated by Chinese forces operating virtually under American direction (Volume I, No. 550). On 15 August the US Government released the text of General Order No. 1 explaining how Japan's surrender was to be conducted and received. Denying that they had any territorial designs on Hong

B. Tibet

The attitude of His Majesty's Government towards the Tibetan question
was defined in a memorandum by the Secretaries of State for Foreign
Affairs and for India dated June 23rd, 1943 (WP 43267), and the following
is an extract from that paper:

Until the Chinese Revolution of 1911, Tibet acknowledged the suzerainty
of the Manchu Emperors and a measure of control from Peking which
fluctuated from military occupation to a mere nominal link. Since 1911
Tibet has enjoyed *de facto* independence. His Majesty's Government
made repeated attempts after 1911 to bring the Chinese Republic and
the Tibetan Government together on the basis that Tibet should be
autonomous under the nominal suzerainty of China but these attempts
always broke down on the question of the boundary between China and
Tibet, and eventually in 1921 His Majesty's Government presented the
Chinese Government with a declaration to the effect that they did not
feel justified in withholding any longer their recognition of the status of
Tibet as an autonomous State under the suzerainty of China, and that
they intended dealing on that basis with Tibet in the future. The
Chinese Government have since 1921 attempted to an increasing extent
to import some substance into their suzerainty over Tibet, while the
Tibetans repudiate any measure of Chinese control. Recent references of
the Chinese Government to the subject come near to a claim that they
are entitled to treat Tibet much like any Chinese province. For example
in 1942 they proposed, contrary to the wishes of the Tibetan
Government, to post officials in Tibet to supervise the organisation of a

Kong, the Chinese argued that General Order No. 1 gave them the right to receive the
surrender because Hong Kong was within their operational sphere. They described as 'highhanded' the UK's decision to send a task force to recover Hong Kong. Mr. Bevin repudiated
China's claims at a meeting of the Far Eastern Ministerial Committee on 17 August. He insisted
that Hong Kong was a British possession and that it was not specifically mentioned in General
Order No. 1 (CO 129/591/16). The following day the Prime Minister, Mr. C.R. Attlee,
informed President Truman that the UK could not accept that Hong Kong was 'within China'
(the expression used in General Order No. 1) for surrender purposes. He requested the issue of
instructions to the effect that Japan's surrender in Hong Kong should await the arrival of the
Commander of the British naval force. President Truman raised no objection, provided that the
UK secured beforehand full military co-ordination on operational matters with Chiang Kai-shek
(*FRUS, 1945*, vol. vii, pp. 504-505; also FO 800/461, FE/45/34 and F 6113/1147/10). The
Chinese continued to insist that they should receive the surrender and UK concern about the
outcome increased when logistical difficulties delayed the departure of the task force from the
Philippines. The matter was substantially resolved when the British prisoner-of-war community
in Hong Kong seized control of the administration. The task force arrived off the colony on 29
August. The suggestion was then made that the surrender should be split, Admiral Harcourt
signing on behalf of the UK and a British military representative in China signing for the
Chinese. When Chiang Kai-shek refused to accept this the UK decided to sign on his behalf
with or without his approval. Admiral Harcourt received the Japanese surrender on 16
September.

supply route to China; and in this connexion Dr. T.V. Soong said that his Government had always regarded Tibet as part of the Republic of China. For our part we have promised the Tibetan Government to support them in maintaining their practical autonomy, which is important to the security of India and to the tranquillity of India's North-Eastern frontier. On the other hand, our alliance with China makes it difficult to give effective material support to Tibet, and we have in fact informed the Tibetans that we would be prepared to give them only diplomatic support against China. In general, two factors governing the Tibetan question are that

(a) Tibet has in practice regarded herself as autonomous and has maintained her autonomy for over 30 years;

(b) Our attitude has always been to recognise China's suzerainty, but on the understanding that Tibet is regarded as autonomous by China.[19]

C. Overseas Chinese

The Chinese communities in Malaya and Burma, numbering approximately 2,400,000 and 200,000 respectively, constitute the third outstanding political issue between ourselves and China. Under the Chinese nationality law any person of Chinese race on the father's side is a Chinese national, no matter how many generations his family may have been domiciled abroad; and thus a situation arises where about half the population of Malaya (not to mention practically the whole population of Hong Kong) possess Chinese nationality as well as British. Until recent years this has not mattered at all. The Chinese communities, although preserving their well defined national characteristics and bound by traditional ties to their home towns and villages in various parts of China, did not feel bound by any great sense of political allegiance to their mother country. During the last ten years, however, the Kuomintang has been taking an active interest in these overseas communities and propagating the Party ideas among them by means of the Party organisation, schools, chambers of commerce, and so forth. Since the Pacific War many Chinese from Malaya, Burma, Hong Kong and elsewhere have fled from the Japanese into China. These refugees have become a special subject of

[19] At the beginning of 1946 the FO considered whether the British Government should lend support to a Tibetan Mission which was intending to visit Chungking, *via* India, to discuss Tibetan autonomy with the Chinese Government. The India Office in London and the Government of India wanted to support the Mission. So too did the FO Far Eastern Department but Mr. Bevin was more cautious, commenting early in February: 'I shall need to know a good deal more of what is involved, & why we are so anxious to become involved in this business.' The matter was discussed at a meeting with the India Office on 20 February. Mr. Bevin expressed concern that a question that had remained dormant should become a live issue, involving powers such as Russia and America, 'with possible awkward decisions for ourselves'. It was therefore decided to leave the Tibetans to handle the autonomy issue with the Chinese by themselves should they so wish (F 585/71/10). Following the transfer of power on the Indian subcontinent in August 1947, the Government of India assumed all existing treaty rights and obligations of the UK with regard to Tibet.

attention for the Chinese Government, through its agency the Overseas Chinese Affairs Commission of the Executive Yuan. The idea is patently to make them into patriotic and politically minded Chinese, so that when they return to their countries of adoption they will form a politically pro-Chinese nucleus. It should, however, be mentioned that the majority of the refugees appear to have been very little influenced. Whether or not the Chinese Government will succeed in transforming the cultural allegiance to China of the overseas communities into a real political allegiance as well, is something which remains to be seen. As regards Burma, in addition to the general considerations above, the Overseas Chinese question presents an economic problem. Prior to the Japanese conquest of Burma, the Burmese legislature were showing themselves anxious to restrict further Chinese immigration. The Chinese for their part, regard Burma as a natural outlet for Chinese emigration from South-western China and there has been recent evidence of this. After the Pacific War is over, the Government of Burma will almost certainly wish to introduce legislation restricting Chinese immigration. This would involve the abrogation of certain articles in the Burma Convention of 1894 and agreement of 1897.[20]

D. *Burma: Undemarcated Frontier, etc*

Although not an immediate issue between Britain and China, the China-Burma border is liable to give rise to disputes from time to time. The northern part of the border, from about latitude 25°35' to the Tibetan frontier, remains undemarcated. The Chinese do not accept what we regard as the *de facto* boundary, represented by the Salween-Irrawaddy watershed, and never fail to challenge any of our maps which show this *de facto* boundary as a demarcated one. Their own claims to territory on the westward side of the watershed have tended to swell with the lapse of time, and in recent years Chinese official maps have appeared which show the whole of the basin of the Upper Irrawaddy, up to the Assam border, as included in the territory of China. Recently, in response to complaints about such maps, the Chinese Government has shown a conciliatory attitude. Some trouble was caused in 1942 and 1943 by undisciplined Chinese troops who penetrated westward towards the Fort Hertz and southern triangle areas. Since the end of 1944 British civil administration

---

[20] A Burma-China frontier conference was convened in London at intervals between 1892 and 1894. Acording to Dorothy Woodman, a British historian of Anglo-Burmese relations during the nineteenth century, the subsequent Convention agreed in March 1894 'reflected hard bargaining between the British and Chinese representatives and it proved to be the first round of a long-drawn-out struggle for the control of strategic areas along the border between Britain and China which was not resolved at the time when Britain transferred sovereignty to the Union of Burma in 1948' (D. Woodman, *The Making of Burma*, London, The Cresset Press, 1962, p. 294). In June 1895 China ceded part of the frontier covered by the Convention to France. Britain protested and acquired concessions from China in a revised Burma-China Frontier and Trade Convention which was concluded in February 1897 (*ibid.*, p. 324-31.)

has extended right up to the *de facto* boundary. There have been recent Chinese troop infiltrations further south, west of the demarcated boundary and in one case local Chinese military commanders have been claiming possession on behalf of China of an area leased in perpetuity to Britain under an agreement signed many years ago. When appealed to, the Chinese Government have always behaved reasonably over these border questions, and trouble has usually arisen as a result of independent action by local guerilla commanders. Unfortunately, the loyal Kachins have been the chief sufferers from these Chinese depredations.

No. 2

Letter from Mr. Lamb[1] *(Chungking) to Mr. Kitson*[2]

[F 7001/235/10]

CHUNGKING, *30 August 1945*

My dear George,

The approach of the day of the formal signature of Japan's surrender, which day would presumably be regarded as marking the effective 'cessation of the hostilities in the war against the common enemies in which they (the High Contracting Parties) are both now engaged', has set us thinking as to what would be the best time and method for implementing the requirement of Article 8 of the 1943 Extraterritoriality Treaty[3] which provides, you recall, that negotiations for the conclusion of consular, commercial, etc treaty or treaties should be entered into within six months of the end of the war.

2. This term would now be due to expire on or about the last day of February 1946, by which time one of us, the Chinese or ourselves, will have to take the initiative. The question is how soon and by whom the opening gambit is to be made. You will obviously be considering the same problem and you may therefore be interested to know as early as possible how the picture looks to us in its local perspective. I am accordingly, with the Ambassador's approval, attempting to summarise our impressions herebelow.

3. In the first place as regards the initiative, this should, we feel, be taken by us rather than by the Chinese Government, so that the onus for raising the first objections (such as may be expected with regard to our preference

[1] Mr. L.H. Lamb, Consular Service in China from 1921; Chinese Counsellor, HM Embassy, Chungking, 1945 (Nanking from May 1946); HM Minister, Nanking, 1947-1949.

[2] Mr. G.V. Kitson, Consular Service in China from 1922; Consul and Chinese Secretary at HM Embassy, Chungking, 1942-1945; Counsellor, FO, 1945; head of FO China Department from 26 April 1946 when the Far Eastern Department was divided into three separate departments for China, Japan and South-East Asia.

[3] See *BFSP*, vol. 145, pp. 129-37.

for separate commercial and consular treaties) should rest upon them instead of upon us. If that contention is accepted, the next question is whether we should lead the van or wait until someone else takes the plunge. Our own conclusion—subject to certain considerations stated further on—would be to try and chip in with drafts containing our maximum desiderata as early as possible, letting our reliable Allies such as the Dutch know in advance what we propose to ask for so that they can follow suit.

4. It would of course be admirable if the Americans would act as shock troops, particularly as one has reason to anticipate that they propose to insist with considerable toughness upon more definite guarantees for the protection of their nationals and business interests in China than are afforded by the 1943 Extraterritoriality Treaties, particularly in respect of personal security, property rights, and greater freedom of commercial enterprise. It is obviously important that we should forestall the possibility of the Chinese negotiating consular or commercial conventions on terms extremely favourable to themselves with some complacent or disinterested country and then try to impose that precedent as the basis for subsequent negotiations with us. The American draft Commercial Treaty is likely to resemble ours fairly closely, but they have adopted their usual secretive tactics in this regard and we can not therefore count upon their taking us sufficiently into their confidence in advance.[4] So it looks as though we will have to decide our tactics independently of the Americans, though, of course, in consultation with them as far as their habitual reticence and individualism permit.

5. If the above conclusions are endorsed, the remaining question for decision is when. The next few months are likely to be hectic for the Chinese administration even more than for us, first on account of the peace settlement and immediate post-war problems and secondly on account of the transfer of the capital to Nanking, which was originally optimistically slated for completion by the 'Double Tenth', but has already begun to recede into the tail end of the year, certainly a more rational hypothesis. We should perhaps try and take advantage of the chaotic state in which the Ministry of Foreign Affairs is likely to find itself to force the

[4] The State Department declined repeated requests to make available a draft of the proposed Sino-American commercial treaty. The Americans were concerned to avoid giving China grounds for suspecting that the US and the UK were colluding over the new commercial treaties. They also wanted to see a British draft which was not yet available because UK officials had produced only a statement of broad principles (F 3267/235/10). In a minute dated 14 August, Mr. Kitson responded: 'I do not believe the American profession of anxiety that there should be no appearance of collusion. There was "collusion" over the ext'rality treaty. Why not over the Commercial Treaty? The Americans sheltered for many decades before the war under our commercial leadership in China. Expecting to take over that leadership after the war they are evidently determined to strike out an independent line from the beginning. The Americans have already submitted their draft. We must hurry up & submit ours, if we are not to be left behind in the negotiations.'

pace while they may be too disorganised by the move and disturbed by the spate of similar discussions with the other foreign missions in process or in prospect, to resort so effectively to the obstructive tactics of disputing every provision clause by clause. To raise the issue too soon before we are fully briefed might leave us on a limb, especially as we are at the moment already engaged with rather delicate issues relating to Hong Kong and the atmosphere is already a bit strained; but as suggested above, we should not allow ourselves to fall too far in the rear. As a general target an appropriate time for us to broach the subject might be about one month after the hegira [transfer] to Nanking[5] if that is to take place by mid-October or some time between mid-October and mid-November if it is clear that the Ministry of Foreign Affairs and Embassies can not be moved until considerably later.

6. It could of course be argued with equal force that we should be chary of sticking our necks out as pioneers, but would rather be well-advised to sit back and watch someone else assume the onus, and then come in and claim all the same benefits on a most-favoured-nation basis. There are, however, certain risks and disabilities attached to such Ca' canny tactics, and it would therefore in our opinion be more expedient, on balance, to decide what terms we consider essential for our own interests and press for them reasonably soon, on our own initiative and without counting upon active support from the Americans, while making every effort to work in concert with them on parallel lines.

7. It is rather a pity with all this ahead that K.C. Wu[6], whose unusual command of English and comprehension of diplomatic problems and procedure would be a boon in complicated discussions of this sort, should have suddenly been translated to the Ministry of Information

8. There is, of course, a third course, namely to suggest to the Chinese that in view of the extraordinary state of affairs existing in the initial post-war phase, the six-months' period might be extended by mutual agreement, in the form, perhaps, of an exchange of letters, but this does not strike us as too commendable.

Yours ever,

Leo H. Lamb

[5] Nanking was the capital of the Chinese Republic from 1928 until 1937 when it was occupied by the Japanese. The capital then moved to Chungking until 1946 when it was transferred back to Nanking. The old imperial capital of Peking was restored as the capital when the Communists proclaimed the People's Republic in October 1949.

[6] Chinese Vice-Minister for Foreign Affairs; appointed Minister of Information in August 1945.

No. 3

Sir A. Clark Kerr[1] (Moscow) to Mr. Bevin
No. 633 [F 6893/325/10]

MOSCOW, *3 September 1945*

Sir,

In his despatch No. 511 of 24th July Mr. Roberts[2] reported on Mr. T.V. Soong's first visit to Moscow from June 30th to July 14th in order to discuss with the Soviet Government matters of common interest to China and the Soviet Union. These conversations were at the time treated as most secret in view of their bearing upon subsequent military operations in the Far East and it was left that they would be resumed after the Potsdam Conference.

2. Mr. Soong has explained to me on the 10th July that he was engaged in working out with the Soviet Government the practical implications of certain conditions of which you are aware, which were laid down by Stalin as the price of Soviet military intervention in the Far East.[3] Of these Dr.

---

[1] HM Ambassador in Moscow, 1942-46.

[2] Mr. F.K. Roberts was HM Minister in Moscow, 1945-47. His despatch of 24 July is reproduced in Volume I, No. 383. It described Dr. Soong's first visit to Moscow, 30 June—14 July, to discuss the implementation of the Yalta Agreement on the Far East (see below, note 3). Dr. Soong and Generalissimo Chiang Kai-shek only learned of the Yalta Agreement in June 1945. China's Foreign Minister revealed his concern at the manner in which, in his view, the Russians were attempting to expand the text of the Yalta Agreement to their own advantage, at a meeting with Sir A. Clark Kerr, on 10 July. *V. ibid.,* No. 180.

[3] A reference to the secret protocol attached to the agreement concluded by President Roosevelt, Marshal Stalin and Prime Minister Churchill at Yalta on 11 February 1945. Within two or three months after Germany's surrender and the end of the war in Europe, the Soviet Union agreed to enter the war against Japan on the allied side on condition:

1. That the preservation of the status quo in Outer Mongolia (the Mongolian People's Republic) should be preserved;

2. That the rights lost by Russia in the war against Japan in 1904-05 should be restored by means of

(*a*) the return to the Soviet Union of the southern part of Sakhalin and the adjacent islands,

(*b*) the internationalisation of the commercial port of Dairen, the safeguarding of the 'preeminent' interests' of the Soviet Union in the port, and the restoration of the lease of Port Arthur as a naval base of the USSR,

(*c*) the establishment of a joint Sino-Soviet company for the operation of the Chinese-Eastern Railroad and the South-Manchurian Railroad, the 'preeminent interest' of the Soviet Union being safeguarded and full Chinese sovereignty in Manchuria being retained;

3. That the Kurile Islands be handed over to the USSR.

It was understood that the agreement concerning Outer Mongolia and the ports and railroads would require the concurrence of Generalissimo Chiang Kai-shek. The USSR expressed its readiness to conclude with the National Government of China a pact of friendship and alliance in order to assist in the liberation of China from Japan. For the full text of the agreement, see *BFSP*, vol. 148, pp. 88-89.

Soong had only learned a few weeks before from President Truman in Washington. He had been in gloomy mood, full of doubts about the future. He had complained that the Russians were trying to expand these conditions to their own advantage, and he felt his responsibilities heavy upon him. He had therefore thought it necessary to return to Chungking in order to consult Chiang Kai-shek before reaching any final agreement with the Soviet Government. The main points at issue were: the recognition by China of the independence of Outer Mongolia in return for complete recognition by the Soviet Government of Chinese sovereignty over Sinkiang and for an undertaking to render no help, either material or moral, to the Chinese Communists; and the restoration to the Soviet Union of the privileged position in Manchuria which Tsarist Russia had lost in 1905, including Port Arthur and the Manchurian railways. Mr. Soong was then disposed to resist Soviet attempts to stretch these conditions, and especially to place too wide an interpretation upon the phrase 'the pre-eminent interests of the USSR' which has been used in connexion with them, provided that His Majesty's Government and the United States Government would support him.

3. During the Potsdam Conference I learned from the United States Ambassador that his government were in fact prepared to resist any Soviet attempt to push the Chinese beyond what had been contemplated.[4] But, on my return to Moscow early in August, I found the Chinese Ambassador anxious about the atmosphere in which Mr. Soong would resume his talks. It emerged however from messages exchanged between the Prime Minister and President Truman, that instructions had been sent to Mr. Harriman[5] on 5th August confirming the United States attitude as expressed to me at

---

[4] At Potsdam on 23 July, the Prime Minister Mr. W.S. Churchill sent the following minute to Mr. A. Eden, Foreign Secretary in the wartime coalition: 'Mr. Byrnes [US Secretary of State, 1945-47] told me this morning that he had cabled to T. V. Soong advising him not to give way to the Russians, but to return to Moscow and keep on negotiating pending further developments. It is quite clear that the United States do not at the present time desire Russian participation in the war against Japan' (Volume I, No. 236).

Ten months earlier, responding to an FO estimate (5 October 1944) of Soviet aims in the Far East which concluded that at the very least the Russia would want to recover the territory lost to Japan, Mr. Churchill commented: 'It will be absolutely necessary to offer Russia substantial war objectives in the Far East, and I do not see what injury we should suffer if she had—in one form or another—all effective rights at Port Arthur. Any claim by Russia for indemnity at the expense of China, would be favourable to our resolve about Hong Kong.' The Prime Minister added: 'We should not show ourselves in any way hostile to the restoration of Russia's position in the Far East, nor commit ourselves in any way to any United States wish to oppose it at this stage' (personal minute to Mr. Eden and General Ismay of 23 October 1944, F 9836/8854/61). Mr. Eden was more circumspect, advising Mr. Churchill prior to the Yalta Conference that although Russia's requirements in the Far East were as yet unknown, the issue represented 'a potential cauldron of international dispute'. To the Foreign Secretary it seemed advisable 'to go warily and to avoid anything like commitments or encouragement to Russia' (minute of 27 January 1945, F 710/185/61).

[5] US Ambassador at Moscow.

Potsdam and laying special emphasis on the traditional American 'open door' policy and upon Chinese sovereignty over Manchuria.[6] As regards the question of control over Dairen, the United States administration favoured a free port under Chinese Administration, but were in the last resort prepared to cooperate in an international administration. You will recall that you instructed me to make it clear to my United States colleague that His Majesty's Government would then also wish to share in the international administration. In the event a satisfactory Soviet-Chinese agreement was reached which made any such solution unnecessary.

4. Mr. Soong returned to Moscow from Chungking on August 8th accompanied by the newly appointed Chinese Foreign Minister, Mr. Wang Shih-chieh. His return coincided with the Soviet declaration of war upon Japan, with which I am dealing in a separate despatch. Stalin had by then returned from the Potsdam Conference, and conversations were at once resumed in the favourable atmosphere resulting from the fact that the Soviet Union was now a belligerent ally of China.

5. Mr. Soong maintained close contact with me and told me on 11th August that, although ultimately it must be largely a matter of Russian good faith, he was satisfied with the terms of Stalin's assurances about Sinkiang and with the pledges which he was ready to give about the Soviet attitude to the Chinese Communists in return for the recognition by China of the independence of the Mongolian Republic; but that Marshal Choibalsan[7] had now come forward with what Mr. Soong considered unacceptable claims for frontier rectifications. Although the proposal was repugnant to him, Mr. Soong felt that it would be necessary to recognise the independence of the Mongolian Republic in connexion with which Stalin had gone so far as to hint that Inner Mongolia might also go the way of Outer Mongolia. Agreement was in sight about the Manchurian railways; Port Arthur and Dairen; Stalin had agreed to recognise the principle of the 'open door' and Chinese sovereignty over Manchuria. I learned later that Stalin had also raised the question of war booty in Manchuria and had suggested that certain property and shares in Japanese firms should be given to the Soviet Government, but Mr. Soong had managed to persuade him that this matter should be left over for future discussion.

6. After further conversations with Stalin, Mr. Soong told me on August 14th that he had finally agreed to recognise the independence of the Mongolian Republic on instructions from Chiang Kai-shek. He had on the other hand secured the concessions that the Chinese Chairman of the new Chinese Changchung Railway (comprising the old Chinese Eastern and South Manchurian Railways) should have the casting vote on a mixed Board of Directors, that all but a few of the branch lines and the policing

[6] The texts of the messages exchanged are recorded in telegram No. 4467 to Moscow, 11 August 1945 (FO 800/461). They are reproduced in *FRUS 1945*, vol. vii, pp. 955-56.
[7] President of the Mongolian People's Republic.

of the whole railway system should be exclusively Chinese, and that no Soviet military units might travel on the railways in peace-time, though war material might pass in sealed cars. Port Arthur was to be a 'Sino-Soviet Naval Zone', the civil administration being in the hands of Soviet-dominated military commission. Dairen on the other hand was to be a free port under purely Chinese administration with certain facilities for Soviet traffic. Here again Mr. Soong said he was relying upon the good faith of the Russians about the future Chinese sovereignty of Manchuria.

7. The Soviet press which, while devoting much space to Soviet military successes in the Far East, had not mentioned Chinese affairs since Dr. Soong's arrival, announced briefly on August 15th that on August 14th a Treaty of Friendship and Alliance had been signed between the Soviet Union and China and that full agreement had also been reached on all other questions of common interest. These arrangements were to be published when ratified. The press next day published pictures of the signing of the Treaty by the Chinese Foreign Minister and Mr. Molotov[8] in the presence of Stalin. Mr. Soong left Moscow on 15th August after making a public statement expressing his extreme satisfaction that he had seen the laying of the foundations of lasting peace in the Far East. He added that the sincerity shown by Generalissimo Stalin and Mr. Molotov had convinced him of the lasting nature of Soviet-Chinese relations. Mr. Wang Shih-chieh left Moscow on the following day. The stay of the Chinese Ministers in Moscow had coincided almost exactly with the period of Soviet participation in the Far Eastern war, the Japanese capitulation having been announced in Moscow on August 14th. On August 19th messages were exchanged between Chiang Kai-shek and Stalin about the Soviet contribution to the defeat of Japan and about Sino-Soviet friendship. Many articles were published in the Soviet press at this time recording the warm welcome given to the Red Army by the Chinese population in Manchuria, but there was no comment on the Sino-Soviet Treaty until after its ratification in Moscow and Chungking towards the end of August.

8. The Soviet press on August 27th announced the ratification of the Sino-Soviet agreements and published the texts of

(*a*) the Treaty of Friendship and Alliance;
(*b*) the agreement on the Manchurian Railways amalgamated into 'The Chinese Changchung Railway';
(*c*) the agreement on Port Arthur, with a map showing the adjacent territory and islands comprised in the agreement;
(*d*) the agreement on Dairen;
(*e*) the civil affairs agreement governing the relations between the Soviet Command and the Chinese Administration after the entry of Soviet troops into the territory of the three Eastern provinces of China;

[8] Soviet Foreign Minister.

(f) the exchange of letters between Mr. Molotov and Dr. Wang Shih-chieh;

(i) on the rendering of aid by the Soviet Government exclusively to the Central Government of China,

(ii) confirming the sovereignty of China over Manchuria and Sinkiang, and

(iii) Chinese recognition of the independence of the Mongolian People's Republic, should a plebiscite of the people show that they desired it

The official Russian text of these agreements as published in the Soviet press together with English translations prepared by the Press Reading Service and the map published in the Soviet press to illustrate the agreement on Port Arthur were sent to you under cover of my despatch No. 599.[9] The Soviet press had also published messages exchanged on this occasion between

(a) M. Kalinin[10] and the President of the Chinese National Government;

(b) Generalissimo Chiang Kai-shek and Generalissimo Stalin, and

(c) Mr. Wang Shih-chieh and Mr. Molotov.

The messages exchanged between the two Generalissimos expressed confidence that the Treaty would be a firm basis for the development of friendly relations. In his message Chiang Kai-shek added that he expected the two governments to display a spirit of mutual trust and assistance.

I am sending copies of this despatch to His Majesty's Ambassadors at Chungking and Washington.

I have, etc.,

Archibald Clark Kerr

[9] Not printed.

[10] President of the Presidium of the Supreme Soviet.

No. 4

Sir H. Seymour (Chungking) to Mr. Bevin (Received 5 November)

No. 1098 [F 12049/186/10]

Confidential   CHUNGKING, 25 *October 1945*

Sir,

I have the honour to acknowledge the receipt of your despatch No. 553 of the 13th September[1] calling for information regarding certain aspects of

[1] This was a circular despatch to several posts, not one sent only to China (N 15123/10674/38).

Communist activities and organisation with special reference to their relationship with Moscow.

2. The extent to which the so-called Communist party in China is inspired by or associated with Moscow or other political headquarters in the USSR is a matter of frequent discussion. It would probably be safe to say that it is at present a movement *sui generis*, having sprung from orthodox Soviet Communist seeds, and aiming eventually at orthodox ends, but having in its present phase matured into a hardy Chinese product, unreceptive to outside, and particularly foreign, interference. Thus, while the philosophy upon which the whole Communist system of Mao Tze-tung[2] and his henchmen is based is alien, its application is native and independent. The Communists in China may therefore be classified rather in the light of an opposition or rebel element in the internal life of China than as a subordinate or associated group in a wider field under the captaincy of a nominee from Moscow.

3. How long this state of affairs will last is, of course, another question, for recent history has shown the insidious effect of Soviet influences in Turkestan and Mongolia, and there are indications that a similar policy of infiltration by propaganda is being already actively initiated in Korea and Manchuria. It is, therefore, within the realms of possibility that at some later, and maybe not so far distant, date an attempt may be made to link up the communist organisation of Yenan with the operations of the Soviet Communist machine. The assurances in the recent Sino-Soviet agreement that material assistance will only be given to the Central Government does not, of course, preclude a Soviet-Chinese Communist *entente* when this may seem desirable to the rulers of the USSR. Such a development would naturally be fostered if, as seems quite likely, serious fighting between the Central Government and the Communists should break out in North-East China.

4. Though not perhaps pertinent to the present enquiry, it is an interesting fact as illustrating how the Chinese seem to succeed in shaking off, if not actually remaining impervious to, foreign influence while retaining and modifying for their own purposes the forms and philosophies learnt from abroad, that the constitution of the Central Government with its system of Kuomintang party control in the administration is as much an outcrop of Soviet political theory as that of the Communists of Yenan.

5. Besides the actual Communists there are other Socialist or Liberal groups with political ambitions, who have recently combined with the Communists to the extent of bringing pressure to bear on the Generalissimo through the People's Political Council and by other means to agree to popular representation as opposed to the single party methods

---

[2] Chairman of the Central Executive Committee of the Chinese Communist Party.

of government, but they are not closely associated with each other and there is no apparent evidence of Moscow direction or influence.[3]

I have, etc.,

H.J. SEYMOUR

[3] Questions about the nature of the CCP, and whether it was associated in any way with Moscow, were also under consideration in London. On 10 November the JIC, then a sub-committee of the COS Committee, submitted a report on the internal situation in China which argued: 'The Chinese Communists are not a political party in the usual sense nor are they what is usually understood by the word Communists. They have their own administration and army, and control large areas of North China centering on Yenan in the Province of Shensi. Their forces were until recently also powerful around Shanghai. They are autonomous and could form an administration capable of governing China' (JIC(45)314(FINAL), F 10436/186/10). Opinion on this within the Far Eastern Department was divided. Mr. A.L. Scott (Consular Service, China, 1920-37) of the China section described as 'controversial' the statement that the Chinese Communists were not what was usually understood by the word: 'there are many people who believe that a Communist is the same all the world over, even in China, that the ultimate goal is identical everywhere, and all that is different from country to country are the methods and the rate of progress employed' (minute of 24 November). Mr Kitson disagreed, minuting on 25 November: 'I usually understand a "Communist" to mean a person adhering to and practising Marx[ist]-Leninist doctrines. The Chinese Communists are far from that; they are more in the nature of agrarian reformers.' On this latter point, Mr. Kitson continued: 'Wherever the Communists have come into contact with the peasants in recent years they have won, through their policy of agrarian reform, the peasants' enthusiastic support, which is certainly not the case with the Kuomintang and its armies, which have usually robbed and oppressed the peasants' (F 10436/186/10).

No. 5

Letter from Sir H. Seymour (Chungking) to Mr. Sterndale Bennett

[F 10179/186/10]

CHUNGKING, 1 *November 1945*

Dear Benito,

I am arranging to start for London about November 14th, but I will just send you this line as it should arrive before I do.

Last week I took advantage of General Carton de Wiart's[1] movements and went to Hong Kong from the Saturday to Monday. You will have heard all about conditions there and so I will not repeat what you already know. The place is still more or less dead commercially and must remain so until shipping gets going. I gather that according to the general plan it was assumed that no real trading could take place for six months after the re-occupation. It seems to be generally thought that this was unduly pessimistic and I hope that it may be possible to get going without such a long delay. I think the best argument we can make for Hong Kong is in

[1] Special UK military representative with Generalissimo Chiang Kai-shek, 1943-1946.

the nature of an object lesson. It looks as if Shanghai would be in a state of muddle for a long time and I believe it would be worth a real effort to get Hong Kong into a situation in which the comparison would strike everyone.

It is difficult to make out from here exactly what is happening about British properties in Shanghai. The situation seems to change from day to day and Ogden[2] is so overcome with work that it is difficult for him to produce a detailed report. I am therefore sending Lamb down tomorrow to spend two full days there and to try and get some sort of general picture of what is happening. I hope to telegraph the main points early next week.

The general picture in China is, I am afraid, rather gloomy. We hear of the troubles of British subjects in getting possession of their properties and it makes one wonder what the emissaries of Chungking are doing to their own people who have been under Japanese occupation. It seems to me they may easily get into the position where the Chinese public begins to say that the Japanese were no worse than Chungking, and if we do get this the Communist troubles will take on a much more serious aspect. This may, however be an unduly gloomy view. The rapid rise of the pound sterling in Shanghai does suggest that there is a great deal of nervousness about.

There have been no further developments on the financial and exchange front, but perhaps it is a little early to expect them. I cannot help having an uncomfortable suspicion that the Government after all their talk about realising the necessity of doing something, may after all allow matters to drift. This would entail presumably a more or less recognised black market, as the Chinese will certainly trade somehow when shipping becomes available, but it is a messy way of dealing with the problem.

We still remain dreadfully short-handed, especially as regards people with Chinese experience. We have now managed to re-open Tientsin and Canton, at least I hope we have, though we have not heard of either Whitamore's[3] or Hall's[4] arrival. I have nobody to open any other post and unfortunately cannot improvise Chinese speakers. I am afraid that this lack of personnel may lead to a lot of trouble in having to eject squatters from numerous properties. It is much easier to prevent people coming in than to get rid of them later; one can do nothing to prevent them coming in unless there is someone on the spot.

Yours ever,
H. J. SEYMOUR

[2] Mr. A.G.N. Ogden, HM Consul-General at Shanghai.

[3] Mr. C.E. Whitamore, HM Consul-General at Chungking from November 1944, at Tientsin from 5 November 1945.

[4] Mr. R.A. Hall, HM Consul-General at Canton from November 1945.

No. 6

Minute by Mr. Sterndale Bennett on the Moscow Conference[1]

[F 53/25/10]

FOREIGN OFFICE, *27 December 1945*

The Section on China in the final report of the Moscow Conference contains a passage about the participation by democratic elements in all branches of the National Government.

As this passage may be the subject of much controversy, it may be useful to record how it was arrived at.

A meeting of the Protocol Committee was called at midnight on Christmas night and the Americans had produced a rough draft with the following first paragraph under the heading of China:

'The three Foreign Secretaries exchanged views with regard to the situation in China. They were in agreement as to the need for a unified and democratic China under the National Government and for a cessation of civil strife. They re-affirmed their adherence to the policy of non-interference in the internal affairs of China.'

In the event, this text was not discussed, as M. Malik[2] made it clear that he was only able to discuss the actual texts of agreements reached, namely those on the Far Eastern Commission, the Allied Council in Tokyo and Korea, and that he was not in a position to discuss the terms of a Protocol. We were told, however, that the text on China had been shown to M. Molotov and that the latter had suggested an amendment to the above paragraph. The Americans told us that the translation of the amendment was 'for the broad participation therein of democratic elements' and that this phrase was meant to be inserted after the words 'National Government'. We understood that this did not mean that M. Molotov had agreed to the whole section on China. The American Delegation seemed to be in some doubt whether he would accept their version of what had passed between M. Molotov and Mr. Byrnes, which formed the rest of the American draft on China.

---

[1] The American, British and Soviet Foreign Ministers met in Moscow during 16-26 December 1945. Much of the discussion there on China (specifically North China and Manchuria) concentrated on the removal of those Japanese forces that remained in the country and then the timing of the withdrawal of US and Soviet troops. On these questions the UK delegation played only a marginal role. Of greater concern to Mr. Bevin was the question of what statement the Conference would make on the political situation in China. See Volume II, Chapter III.

[2] Soviet Ambassador at Tokyo.

The Drafting Committee again sat from 2 p.m. to 9.40 p.m. on December 26th. When the item on China was reached late in this session, there was disagreement between the Russians and the Americans as to the terms of the Russian amendment to the first paragraph. The Russians claimed that it should read: 'for the broad participation of democratic elements in the National Government and other organs of authority'. Sir R. Campbell[3] and I made it clear that we must entirely reserve the views of our Secretary of State on the whole amendment which seemed to us to be inconsistent with the last sentence of the paragraph, which said that the three Foreign Secretaries reaffirmed their adherence to the policy of non-interference in the internal affairs of China.

The extension of the terms of the Russian amendment clearly worried the American Delegation and Mr. Vincent opposed the addition of the extra words on the ground that their purport was not clear and that they went further than it was legitimate for the three Powers to go in extending advice to China.

At this stage I was able to consult the Secretary of State for a few minutes. He said at once that he did not feel that he could accept the Russian amendment at all. Certainly he could not accept the additional words which the Russians were now proposing to their original amendment.

Sir R. Campbell and I made Mr. Bevin's attitude quite clear in the Drafting Committee. I stated that it was not that we were opposed to the participation of democratic elements in the National Government. But we felt that it was not right for the three Powers to give joint advice in this sense, since it was in effect interference in the internal affairs of China.

A message was then brought in that Mr. Byrnes and M. Molotov had agreed to the following re-wording: 'for the broad participation of democratic elements in the National Government and its central and local branches'.

Sir R. Campbell and I said that we could not of course accept this text either.

It was agreed that the whole matter must be left to the Foreign Secretaries themselves to decide when they considered the draft text of the whole report at 11 p.m.

Mr. Cohen[4] asked whether a possible solution might not be to remove the Russian amendment from the first paragraph and work it into the rest of the document which only concerned M. Molotov and Mr. Byrnes. We said that we could only put this suggestion to the Secretary of State and could express no view on it.

[3] Acting Under-Secretary of State and deputy to Mr. Bevin on the Council of Foreign Ministers.

[4] US representative on the Protocol Committee.

When the Drafting Committee meeting was over, I discussed this point with Sir A. Cadogan[5] and the Secretary of State and the Secretary of State approved the attached brief for the meeting at 11 pm.

The meeting started as an informal meeting in one of the committee rooms, with several members of the Delegations in attendance. Shortly after the discussion on China began, Mr. Byrnes asked that everyone except the three Foreign Secretaries and their interpreters should withdraw. There is no record of what passed afterwards.[6] But M. Molotov insisted on the inclusion of the substance of his amendment and neither he nor Mr. Byrnes would accept the alternatives which the Secretary of State proposed. The only concession which they would make was to delete the words 'and its central and local branches'; and the amendment was eventually adopted in the form of: 'for the broad participation by democratic elements in all branches of the National Government'.[7]

J.C. STERNDALE BENNETT

[5] Permanent Under-Secretary of State for Foreign Affairs, (PUS) 1938-46.

[6] The record is in Volume II, No. 349, pp. 892-893.

[7] For the complete text of the Moscow Conference Declaration on China v. *ibid.*, No. 356; see also No. 361, especially note 5.

Chapter II

1946

No. 7

Memorandum by Mr. Kitson on Consular Posts in the Interior of China[1]

[*F 8999/25/10*]

FOREIGN OFFICE, *1 March 1946*

1. The following consular posts in China are open or are expected to be open in the near future:

Post	Location
Shanghai	Coast
Amoy	Coast
Canton	West River
Chefoo	Coast
Chungking	River Yangtze
Hankow	River Yangtze
Harbin	Manchuria railway
Kashgar	Interior (Sinkiang)
Macao	Coast
Mukden	Manchuria railway
Nanking	River Yangtze
Peking	Railway
Swatow	Coast
Tengyueh	Interior (Yunnan)

[1] This memorandum was prepared by Mr. Kitson on the instructions of Mr. Bevin who felt that Anglo-Chinese trade could be used to reinforce the UK's political position in China (minute of 4 March by Sir O. Sargent, PUS since 1 February 1946). Sir Ralph Stevenson, HM Ambassador at Nanking, 1946-50, discussed the subject with the Foreign Secretary in June 1946, a week before taking up his appointment. Mr. Bevin argued that the Americans were 'out to capture the China market' and that for this reason UK consular officers 'should keep their eyes open, should move about the country and should not fail to report any chances they saw for British commerce as a result of American development of the country'. The UK would not be in a position to compete in the China market for another three or four years. Mr. Bevin believed that China would welcome the UK as a 'counterweight' against Russian pressure from the north and American pressure from the Pacific (minute by Sir R. Stevenson of 13 June 1946).

Tientsin	Coast
Tsingtao	Coast
Kunming	Railway
Urumchi	Interior (Sinkiang)
Dairen	Coast

2. This gives eight posts on the China coast, four on the rivers, four on the railways, and only three which can properly be said to be in the interior—i.e. away from the coast or the main lines of communication. These three are all largely political posts. Kashgar watches British Indian interests in southern Sinkiang. Urumchi watches Sino-Russian relations in Sinkiang. Tengyueh watches the position on the Burma-Yunnan border.

3. There have been a number of British consular posts in the interior of China in the past, notably Chengtu, Tsinan and Wuchow, but all have closed down with the exception of the three mentioned in the preceding paragraph which are retained mainly for political intelligence purposes. The reason for this is not far to seek. The whole trend of commerce in China during the past 30 years has been towards the large centres of population, situated mainly on the lines of communication. These centres are not only important because they are on the lines of communication, but have all become increasingly so in recent years because of the insecurity of conditions in the interior, resulting in a drift of population towards the larger cities. Shanghai has been a notable example of the trend, and achieved a population of four millions prior to the outbreak of the Japanese war in 1937.

4. The foreign merchants have also tended increasingly to concentrate in the larger cities in China, not only because of the obvious advantages which those cities offer in the way of accommodation, convenience of access to markets and banking, warehousing and transportation facilities, but also because of the extension and gradual perfection of the native agency system. Under this system a Chinese, who is a local merchant in his own right, takes on as a part-time occupation the work of acting as agent of a foreign firm in a small interior town. He may be a selling or buying agent, according to the nature of the business. He functions in places where there is insufficient work for a full time foreign representative. The big tobacco (BAT)[2] and oil (Shell) companies have developed this agency system to perfection. It saves them enormous expenditure on foreign staff who, under this system, are merely required to undertake periodical inspection tours of agencies in the interior, and the system gives better results *vis-à-vis* the consuming public than direct sales by British subjects inexperienced in local conditions, the right kind of selling appeal, etc. Similar advantages apply in the case of buying agents. Only Chinese can satisfactorily undertake the collection, grading and despatch of articles like eggs, silk cocoons and pig's bristles, which emanate from a vast ramification of collecting points in the interior.

[2] British-American Tobacco Company.

5. That has been the system in the past, and it has worked fairly well. The Consul, whose main job is to protect and promote British trade in a foreign country, has naturally been posted where he was most needed, the large Chinese cities where British merchants have congregated. He has occasionally found himself in one of the smaller cities and has eventually had to be withdrawn because the amount of work did not justify the continued presence of a Consul. In such cases there has been nothing he personally could have done to promote or expand British trade in that particular place. The volume of trade was diminishing for reasons outside the Consul's control e.g. the silting up of a river (Chinkiang), the rendition of a British Concession (Kiukiang), or, more usually, the steady drift towards the larger centres already noted above.

6. For the future, one can only await future developments in the political, commercial and industrial field in China. Until a trend away from the big cities and back to the interior towns becomes sufficiently marked to consider re-opening Consulates in some of the interior places, the most we can probably do is (*a*) to encourage British firms in China to send their representatives on frequent visits to interior places to spy out the land and collect orders; and (*b*) to send members of the staff of Consulates in the existing posts on frequent tours of interior places to report on trade possibilities and to recommend, where necessary, the opening of a new consular post. The flag need not of course necessarily wait for trade to lead; but it has so far not been shown in China that wherever the flag is planted, or a Consul installed, trade follows, except where there are circumstances which would have caused it to flow there anyhow, Consul or no Consul.

7. In order to promote the policy suggested in the preceding paragraph, it will be necessary to re-open as many as possible of the consular posts in China which were open before the war, and at the same time to staff them adequately so that officers can have time and opportunity to make trips into the interior, away from the main centres of population, and see for themselves what are the trading possibilities. At present it has been possible to open only 12 of the 19 posts listed in paragraph 1, and these are in many cases as yet inadequately staffed. We are doing our best to remedy this, but provision of adequate career staff will be difficult until the new entrants are available in greater numbers. Meanwhile, we are taking on temporary staff, such as retired naval officers and former merchants with China experience. These have not the same experience, however, and do not carry the same weight with Chinese, as career consuls who have served in China in the past.

8. At present a considerable number of career China experts, who can speak the language and have served many years in China, are still serving in posts other than China. In many cases there are objections—e.g. health reasons—to sending them back to China; but it is suggested that China experts should wherever possible be sent to staff Chinese posts at this time, when there is a specially urgent need for them owing to the difficulties

British businessmen are experiencing in re-establishing their position under the new conditions, and when official support at the right place and time can be invaluable.

9. Manchuria is a region where the need for consular posts in the interior is most likely to present itself in the near future as China's industrialization progresses. Much will depend on the degree to which the Russians are able to establish and hold a monopoly of trade in this area, but there should eventually be room for all of us in this market. We have at present got a Consul General waiting at Tsingtao to proceed to Mukden as soon as the place is open. The Russians are however still in control and, although a Chinese mayor has arrived at Mukden, his functions are only nominal. The Chinese Government have replied to our applications to open both the Mukden and Dairen Consulates by referring to the difficulties arising from the present situation, and asking us to wait a bit. We shall in due course want also to open Harbin, the important railway centre in North Manchuria. Until these three posts are open and consuls have had an opportunity to report, it will be difficult to estimate future trading prospects, but there are obviously immense possibilities which will have to be carefully watched, and here again an adequate staff of China experts will be necessary if the ground is to be fully covered.

G.V. KITSON

No. 8

Brief for Mr. Bevin on Future Defence Policy for Hong Kong

[F 3727/113/10]

FOREIGN OFFICE, 6 March 1946

The Defence Committee is to consider on Friday, March 8th, the attached report by the Chiefs of Staff on future defence policy for Hong Kong.[1]

[1] Not printed. This report of 1 March explained that the last decision on this subject had been taken in 1938 by the Committee of Imperial Defence. Defence policy for Hong Kong had then been limited to ensuring the defence of the island itself, thus denying the use of the anchorage to an enemy. The 1946 analysis maintained: 'We do not consider that under modern conditions Hong Kong can be defended against attack by a major power in occupation of the Chinese mainland. We should not, therefore, lock up in Hong Kong against such attack forces or defences which will either not be required or else be overrun and lost.' During a war in the Pacific in which China was in friendly hands, Hong Kong might be required as an operational naval and air base. In that event mobile defences against attack from a distance by sea or air could be moved to Hong Kong at short notice. 'We therefore propose', the report continued, 'that our future defence policy for Hong Kong should be to regard it as an undefended port, so far as fixed defences are concerned.' To ensure internal security, to protect Hong Kong against piracy, and to act as a deterrent against Chinese guerrilla incursions, forces of the order of one brigade and half a flying boat squadron would be needed for some considerable time, units of

The following may serve as a brief for the Secretary of State at this meeting.

Any assessment of British military requirements in regard to Hong Kong must of necessity be qualified to some extent by the uncertainty regarding the future status of the Colony.

It is fairly certain that China will, in the near future, ask for the return of the New Territories, a portion of the Colony which was leased by China to Britain in 1898 for a period of 99 years. We refused to discuss this matter at the time of the negotiations for our 1943 Treaty relinquishing extraterritorial rights in China, and told the Chinese that in the view of His Majesty's Government it was a matter which should be left for discussion after victory was won. The question of the rendition of the Colony as a whole was not raised in connexion with the 1943 Treaty, and is unlikely to be raised in the near future.

If the New Territories were handed back to China in the near future, our military commitments would be correspondingly less, since we should no longer be required to provide military forces for the defence of the long land frontier between the New Territories and China against possible incursions of Chinese guerillas, etc. On the other hand, the rendition of the New Territories would make it even less practicable than at present to defend Hong Kong against attack by a major Power in occupation of the Chinese mainland.

It is suggested that the Secretary of State can, from the Foreign Office point of view, support the policy recommended by the Chiefs of Staff.

A paper dealing with the future of Hong Kong has recently been submitted by the Far Eastern Department.[2]

the British Pacific Fleet providing such local naval co-operation as might be required. The existing garrison of two brigades could be reduced to one brigade directly the re-establishment of the local Police Force permitted. The Defence Committee approved the report on 8 March and the Governments of Australia and New Zealand were to be informed accordingly (DO(46)30).

[2] See pp. 75-77 below. Related to the question of Hong Kong's long-term political future was the issue of how, in the short-term, the colony should be administered. Having accepted Japan's surrender, Admiral Harcourt became Commander-in-Chief of Hong Kong under a military administration. At the beginning of 1946, HM King George VI approved the return to Hong Kong as civilian Governor of Sir M. Young, who had held this position for a brief period prior to the outbreak of war with Japan. Admiral Harcourt thought the decision inadvisable, not on personal grounds but because it would be interpreted locally as 'a refusal on the part of His Majesty's Government to face the facts of 1946 and a determination to take up where we left off in 1941' (telegram to Chiefs of Staff of 6 February 1946, F 3726/113/10). Feeling that the Office should have been consulted (the King's approval had been secured by the Colonial Office), the FO agreed with Admiral Harcourt and Mr. Bevin raised the matter with Mr. Attlee (minute of 8 March). The Prime Minister responded that the Colonial Office was strongly in favour of the former Governor's return and that he would serve for a short time only to complete his term (minute of 9 March, F 3933/113/10). Civilian government under Sir M. Young was resumed on 1 May.

No. 9

Memorandum on a Trade Mission to China

[*F 8148/116/10*]

FOREIGN OFFICE, *1 June 1946*

In August 1945, shortly after taking office as President of the Board of Trade, Sir Stafford Cripps came to the conclusion that

'it would be desirable to give some tangible evidence of our interest in the industrial future of China by sending out a goodwill mission of industrialists. The purpose of the mission would be to make contacts . . . to see what they could of the country, to create an impression of the live interest of British industry in future trade with China despite present supply limitations, and generally to counteract as far as possible American penetration'.

The proposal for such a mission had already been put forward by the China Association and discussed between the Board of Trade and Foreign Office earlier in the year and it had received our support.

The President of the Board spoke to Dr. Soong, then Minister of Foreign Affairs, about the matter during the latter's visit to the United Kingdom in September,[1] and the latter suggested a postponement until the New Year when the Chinese Government hoped to be resettled in Nanking.

No further developments occurred until the last days of December 1945 when in answer to a Department of Overseas Trade enquiry, the Commercial Counsellor advised delay and suggested September 1946 as a suitable date. His Majesty's Ambassador on the other hand considered that the Mission should come as soon as possible after the Chinese Government

---

[1] Dr. Soong visited the UK from 16 to 19 September 1945. In addition to his meeting with Sir S. Cripps (no record appears to have been kept of the discussion), he also met Mr. Bevin on 16 and 17 September. Subjects raised by Dr. Soong were the future of Japan (Mr. Bevin contested Dr. Soong's view that Japan should be converted back to an agricultural economy), China's need for heavy equipment to aid its industrialisation, policy towards Korea, the Chinese communities in Indo-China and Siam, and China's communications with Burma. Mr. Bevin raised the matter of the implementation of the 1943 treaty (see No. 1, note 15), from the standpoint especially of safeguarding the position of British employees of the former settlements (letter from Mr. Bevin to Sir H. Seymour of 17 September 1945, F 7205/186/10). Contrary to UK expectation, the Chinese Prime Minister did not raise with Mr. Bevin the issues of credits or a UK loan to China. Nor were these matters raised when Dr. Soong met the Chancellor of the Exchequer, Mr. H. Dalton, on the same day, although on that occasion the Chancellor began by saying that until the UK had balanced its own imports and exports, 'we could not give much credit to anybody'. At a meeting between Dr. Soong and two Treasury officials on 18 September, the discussion was confined to China's currency problems and China's sterling balances (letter from Mr. Dalton to Mr. Bevin of 5 October 1945, F 8209/186/10).

had moved to Nanking, that is to say in April; he also suggested concentrating on the lighter industries, which would be operated by private enterprise. Similar views were expressed to the Commercial Counsellor by the head of the National Resources Commission.

The China Association in January 1946 reverted to the proposal as being now timely and offered to collaborate. The Federation of British Industries later wrote in support and asked to be consulted as to the membership of the Mission.

The Treasury (who had in July 1945 felt that since we had nothing to offer a trade mission would only raise false hopes and exacerbate rather than improve relations) expressed the view in a letter dated the 20ᵗʰ February to the Board of Trade that before a decision could be taken regarding the despatch of a trade mission to China a ministerial decision was required regarding the grant of medium or long term credits. The Board of Trade pointed out in their reply of 2nd March that what they had in mind was a purely exploratory mission, and urged an early decision. We wrote to the Treasury on 15th March strongly supporting the proposal.[2]

Eventually on 29th April the Department of Overseas Trade informed us that the Chancellor of the Exchequer had now agreed, on the understanding that it should be made, clear to the Mission that no long term credits, and only small middle term credits could possibly be granted.

[2] Mr. Hall-Patch minuted on 24 February: 'We have at the moment little to sell & there will be incredible difficulties as to price & terms of trade owing to uncertainty as to the Chinese currency situation, & the impossibility of our granting long term credits. Nevertheless I feel there is value in an *exploratory* mission: a *selling* mission might do more harm than good.

'The main value of the Mission would be to educate the people who compose it and those with whom they will be in touch on their return to this country. An entirely new situation has to be faced. The bulk of our China trade was carried on by rather costive firms with hardened arteries who have hitherto enjoyed a privileged position. That has gone and our trade has to face the full blast of competition with no chance of extended credits, with little or no possibility of enforcing contracts, with currency instability and Oriental guile with no convenient buffer of extra-territoriality & impartial justice in British courts. New methods & new men are required.

'... All Government Departments concerned should take care to indoctrinate the Mission as to the present position here and as to what it is and what is not possible (e.g. credits finance) before it leaves. The Mission should, if possible, be charged with a sense of public responsibility. They might be told that we are looking to the members . . . to provide the fresh approach and new impetus which is required in the entirely novel situation with which we are faced in China. It might be made clear that HMG cannot conduct trade (e.g. take risks which should be borne by the trader himself) . . . They can count on our support in so far as it can legitimately be given, but we cannot coddle them, we can only help when difficulties arise which only official intervention can surmount.

'If we take this line I think we are safe. It will appeal to the B/Trade & it may even bring a wan smile of assent to the face of a reluctant Treasury who are terrified at the prospect of being asked to provide credits' (F 2614/116/10). The arguments deployed by Mr. Hall-Patch were closely followed in the letter sent on 15 March from the FO to the Treasury in support of a Trade Mission (F 3374/116/10).

Telegrams were sent out accordingly to His Majesty's Ambassador and the Commercial Counsellor at Shanghai on the 7th May.

As stated in the telegram sent to His Majesty's Ambassador (No. 65)[3] it is intended that the Mission shall be a goodwill mission and not a selling mission. Part of its function would be to consider and report on the best means of securing an early reopening of trade with China. It would have no authority to enter into any commitment as regards commercial credits, or to hold out any prospects of such, without prior reference home. It would consist of five or six members including at least one representative of heavy industry. HM Ambassador was asked to approach the Chinese Government and obtain their consent and a reply (Nanking telegram No. 106 of 29th May)[4] has just been received that the 'visit is naturally welcome to the Chinese Government' and that the question of date has been referred to the authorities concerned.[5]

[3] Dated 7 May (F 8148/116/10).

[4] *Ibid.*

[5] The Mission, which was led by Sir L. Boyce, Chairman of the Gloucester Carriage and Wagon Co. (representing transport interests) visited China from September to December 1946. Other members were: Mr. F.A. Bristow, partner in the firm of Jupe and Bristow, Grain Brokers, who was nominated by the Ministry of Food (representing foodstuffs); Mr. D. Maxwell Buist, Export Director of British Electrical and Allied Manufacturers' Association (representing heavy electrical industry); Mr A.H. Carmichael, Director, Non-Ferrous Metals Federation (representing light industries); Mr R.H. Heyworth, Lever Brothers and Unilevers (representing general merchants' industries); Mr H.D. Morgan, a partner in Sir William Halcrow and Partners, consulting engineers (representing capital projects); Mr. E.K. Scott, Special Director of Dorman Long & Co. Ltd (representing the British Iron and Steel Federation); Mr. F.S. Winterbottom, a partner in Messrs Leonard Plews and Stockdale Ltd., Manchester (representing textiles); and Mr. E. Thornton, Secretary of the United Textiles Factory Workers' Association (representing trade union interests). FO briefs for the Mission are in F 12666/116/10 and the record of a briefing meeting (10 September) between the Mission and officials from government departments is in F 13276/116/10.

The Mission was instructed: 'To consider the best methods of developing trade between China and the United Kingdom during the period of transition so as to provide a firm basis for future expansion and in particular to foster Chinese interest in the United Kingdom as a source of supply for both capital and consumer goods; to convince Chinese officials and industrialists of the desire of United Kingdom industry to satisfy many of the needs of China and their ability to do so given reasonable time, and to study the possibilities for exports of Chinese goods to the United Kingdom.' The Mission also visited Hong Kong, for which purpose it was instructed to advise on the significance of the territory in relation to trade between China and the UK, and on the development of trade between the Hong Kong and the UK (Board of Trade, *Report of the United Kingdom Trade Mission to China, October to December 1946* (London: HMSO, 1948, pp. 11-12).

No. 10

Letter from Lord Killearn[1] (Singapore) to Sir O. Sargent

[*F 9715/25/10*]

Secret and Personal   SINGAPORE, *11 June 1946*

Dear Moley,

I am writing this in the air on my way back from Hong Kong to Singapore, after my short visit to Nanking and Shanghai at the invitation of T.V. Soong. I've already recorded my main impressions by telegraph: but you may care to have a letter filling in the gaps.

As you know, I went to China to talk food. There was, as you are aware, the impression in China that the reason why they were getting so little rice from South East Asia was that the British were hogging it all for British territories, and it was important for more reasons than one to scotch that yarn by getting the true facts over. Which I duly did, and I believe it has had an effect.

My activities on the food side have all been reported separately. But I could not revisit China, and meet so many old friends, Chinese and other, without forming some general impressions on the way things are going. Now, the last thing I must do is to impinge on Horace Seymour's sphere, and I trust you will not think I am doing so if I pass on these random comments.

China is in a mess—politically, militarily, financially, socially. Every schoolboy knows that, and every schoolboy knows that China has often been in a mess before. But until he visits—or, even better, revisits—China, not even quite intelligent schoolboys can realise just the sort of mess China is in now. The government consists of the Generalissimo and T.V. Soong, his brother-in-law: both able and alert as ever, but I doubt whether the foundations of government are broad enough and strong enough to carry the load. The Soong dynasty is propped up by the Kuomintang and by the Americans. The Kuomintang seems to have lost much of the driving power and popular appeal it had fifteen years ago, and the Americans are going through a typically American phase of disillusionment about China. All this naturally has a special interest for me seeing that I was the first foreign representative to present my credentials to the Kuomintang Government, now more than twelve years ago.

I am not against the Soongs. On the contrary, Chiang Kai Shek today is, to my mind, what he has always been—the only man in sight to run China. The engineer, so to speak, is first class, but I suspect the machine may be worn out, and makeshift patching and repairs which served well enough in war time are not good enough now.

---

[1] British Special Commissioner in South-East Asia. As Sir M. Lampson he had been HM Minister to China, 1926-1933.

The financial muddle is 'atomic'. Though Chinese currency has depreciated to such an extent that a coolie who used to earn twenty dollars a month now gets eighty thousand, prices have climbed even faster, and instead of falling in terms of foreign currency they are rising. American dollars are the standard currency of Shanghai, and are in common use. Even so, vegetables from America are cheaper in the Shanghai market than Chinese-grown produce! A 'Sunkist' orange costs less than a Swatow orange: even if it costs 400 dollars. Labour is so expensive that exporters of feathers from Shanghai ship away unplucked poultry—it's cheaper to pluck them in America than in China!

There is general feeling that there is going to be an almighty crash sooner or later, possibly—or indeed probably—with riots, labour troubles, and disturbances of all sorts. I must say it seems to me only too likely. The government is plainly nervous.

Meanwhile our people are in a sorry state. The Chinese enjoy flaunting their newly won power over foreign nationals, and commit all the excesses to be expected of a nation which has suddenly acquired complete control over its own affairs. Foreign firms and ships are tied hand and foot. But I am not a pessimist about the outcome, so far as British business is concerned. Admittedly, the process of adjustment will be painful, and many of the smaller foreign firms will go to the wall, and the British community in China will lessen in numbers. But the adjustment can be made, and will be made: we have something to offer—in the way of efficient management—that China needs, and the Chinese know it. In connection with our business interests, I would however say this—I do not think our representation at Shanghai, Consular or commercial, is at present impressive. And my impression was strong that we ought to do something about it at this crucial time. The stakes are high and well worth playing for.

It doesn't take long in China to learn the dominant role there which America is playing. Nothing new in that—save that during and since the war the Yanks have replaced us as the first Power in the land. But what *was* new to me was to note how irritated and impatient the Americans are growing with the Chinese, just as the Chinese are with the Americans. I suspect the honeymoon is wearing thin and that a process of mutual disillusionment has set in. Naturally China will continue to play ball as long as she continues to receive lavish supplies in cash and kind from America. But the scandals over the food etc poured in by UNRRA[2] and the notoriously corrupt practices of CNRRA[3] are having their effect—and my bet is that the American dibs will dry up fairly soon. When that happens, there will be the bust-up I have predicted earlier in this letter.

I have always believed that the Chinese had one fixed principle in their foreign policy—namely to play off the No. 2 of the moment against the

[2] United Nations Relief and Rehabilitation Administration.

[3] Chinese National Relief and Rehabilitation Administration.

No. 1. In my day it was America they were playing against us. Now the process has been reversed—which, if I am right in my analysis, should mean that we *ought* with reasonable skill to have an opportunity to regain our position and trade to some considerable extent. I am not suggesting anything so foolish or short-sighted as that we should *try* to oust the Americans: but it would be just silly and quixotic not to take our chances if and when they come to us?

As to America, I confess I am puzzled as to her aims and policy in China today. Is she playing Chiang Kai Shek, even to the extent of sending in American troops, in order to hold back Russia? If so, one can understand it, though personally I shouldn't have thought their action very wise.

That brings me to Russia. I went to China with one dominant thought in my mind—the importance of keeping her out of the Russian orbit and inside ours: even if possible her inclusion in that 'bastion of stability and peace' that I am rash enough to dream about. Well, I am now pretty clear from my talks with Chiang Kai Shek and T.V. Soong that there is little present prospect of any 'get together' with the Bear: on the contrary there is heavy dislike and suspicion. So that the nightmare of any concerted action between China and Russia in the Far East does not seem to me at all likely. This is a considerable relief, for, sitting in Singapore I have always been oppressed at the thought of what a subversive effect any such 'get together' could so easily have throughout South East Asia—in Siam, in Burma, in Malaya, in FIC and in NEI.[4]

Don't you think what T.V. Soong said to R.H. Scott[5] (see my unnumbered telegram of June 10th from Hong Kong) after the dinner in Shanghai on June 8th about the Overseas Chinese Communities was very interesting?[6] If he was sincere in what he said, his thesis is to me most

[4] French Indo-China (FIC) and NEI (Netherlands East Indies).

[5] Mr. Scott served on Lord Killearn's staff in Singapore before becoming head of the FO South-East Asia Department in April 1949.

[6] After explaining to Mr. Scott his view that the Russians would shape the course of events in Asia, Dr. Soong proceeded during this after dinner conversation to display what Lord Killearn described in his telegram as an 'unexpectedly strong antipathy towards nationalist ambitions in South East Asia'. He thought that nationalist movements in the region were 'all anti-Chinese' and that independence, especially in the Philippines and the Netherlands East Indies, would mean recrimination against the local Chinese. In both countries the Government of China would have to choose between going in to protect their nationals (this according to Dr. Soong was 'at this stage' out of the question) or withdrawing them to China. He was less concerned about Malaya because with almost half of the population, the local Chinese were numerous enough to look after themselves. The Siamese were 'too cowardly and too frightened of China to do much'. In Indo-China there was doubt as to whether it was in China's interests that French control should go. It was much the same story in Burma. 'All these peoples', said Dr. Soong, 'dislike us because we are cleverer and more hard working and successful than they are. They are jealous, [and] in many ways it suits us better to have Western powers controlling them than to have a group of unstable and inefficient independent little states in Asia' (F 8667/87/61).

surprising. I only hope it is true—and that instead of turning the heat on in these areas he is going to do just the reverse. But can it in fact be true? I confess I am sceptical.

Yours ever,
KILLEARN

No. 11

Sir H. Seymour (Nanking) to Mr. Bevin (Received 16 July)

No. 679 [F 10316/25/10]

Secret   NANKING, *20 June 1946*

His Majesty's Ambassador at Nanking presents his compliments to His Majesty's Principal Secretary of State for Foreign Affairs, and has the honour to transmit to him a memorandum on Hong Kong.

ENCLOSURE IN NO. 11

The Generalissimo and Mme. Chiang entertained my wife and myself at a farewell luncheon today. After luncheon I had a talk with his Excellency, at which the Minister for Foreign Affairs and Dr. Wellington Koo[1] were present.

After I had raised the question of visits by His Majesty's ships to Chinese ports (recorded separately)[2] the Generalissimo spoke of Sino-British relations in general, saying that they had much improved in the last few years. He agreed that, in the main political questions now before the world's statesmen, Chinese and British interests were very similar. But he thought that China's relations with Britain would not be so satisfactory, or conducted with such mutual confidence as her relations with the United States, so long as the question of Hong Kong remained without some solution. It would, he said, not be difficult to find a solution under which the material interests of all concerned would be safeguarded. The question was to some extent a psychological one, and public confidence in British policy would not be fully established unless a solution could be found. As an illustration His Excellency mentioned the recent repeal of the American exclusion acts affecting Chinese immigration to the United States: the practical effect was very small indeed: the moral effect had been very satisfactory.[3]

[1] Chinese Ambassador to the UK, 1941-46.

[2] Not printed.

[3] In an attempt to curb the influx of cheap Chinese labour, a number of exclusion acts were introduced in the US at the end of the nineteenth century, and again in 1924. They were repealed in 1943 when a law was introduced setting an annual immigration quota and extending citizenship privileges to Chinese.

3. The Generalissimo mentioned incidentally that in the discussions with the Soviet Government over Port Arthur and Dairen the Russians had argued that as the Chinese allowed the British to stay in Hong Kong they could hardly object to the presence of the Russians further north. His Excellency added that this argument was in fact not of any particular importance, but he mentioned it because it had been put forward on the Russian side.

4. In conclusion the Generalissimo asked me to let His Majesty's Government know, on my return to England, of his views on this matter, and of the importance which he attached to it as a means of promoting those cordial relations between China and the United Kingdom which it was his wish to see.

5. As I know from recent correspondence that His Majesty's Government have not yet decided upon their future policy in regard to Hong Kong I did not enquire further into the Generalissimo's views (which are probably not very definite as yet) beyond confirming that I had correctly understood that he contemplated some arrangement under which our material interests would be safeguarded. I promised of course, to convey to the Secretary of State for Foreign Affairs what he had said to me.

6. In view of the circumstances in which this conversation took place, on the eve of my departure, it could be taken, if that should suit His Majesty's Government, as an opening of the question by the Chinese Government. On the other hand, it could equally be taken as a more or less informal message to the effect that the Chinese Government want the question raised. As was to be expected the Generalissimo made no distinction between the colony and the leased territory, speaking throughout of Hong Kong. His emphasis on the psychological aspect of the matter seems to suggest that the question of sovereignty will be of first-rate importance from the Chinese point of view.[4]

H. J. Seymour

[4] In June, shortly before leaving London to take up his new post as China's Ambassador to the US, Dr. Wellington Koo discussed Hong Kong with the Minister of State at the FO, Mr. P. Noel-Baker. Referring to the conversation between Chiang Kai-shek and Sir H. Seymour, the Ambassador asked if discussions between China and the UK over Hong Kong were likely in the near future. Mr. Noel-Baker replied that for the UK, the more pressing matters of India, Egypt and Palestine would have to be settled first. The Ambassador accepted this but he also outlined a possible settlement over Hong Kong that would, he said, be acceptable to his government. While the Hong Kong question was of great 'sentimental' appeal in China, there was also, on such issues as business and defence, a 'practical side' of the matter. Nominal sovereignty over Hong Kong might therefore pass to China, while in practice for many purposes the UK would retain control. Reporting the discussion to Mr. G.A. Wallinger, the British Minister at Nanking, the FO commented that 'the Ambassador appeared to understand that he and his Government would do well not to raise the question again at present' (letter of 27 June, F 10070/25/10).

No. 12

Sir R. Stevenson[1] (Nanking) to Mr. Bevin
(Received 9 August, 1.50 p.m.)

No. 376 Telegraphic [F 11588/25/10]

Important   NANKING, *8 August 1946, 6.10 p.m.*

I presented my letters to Chiang Kai-shek at Kuling on August 7th.

2. Our conversation at the time of presentation was confined to polite generalities but he entertained me at dinner the same evening and we had a talk lasting about an hour and a quarter in the course of which I elicited from him his views on the very serious situation in China.[2] He told me that he was convinced that Communists had no real intention to reach a satisfactory compromise with the Central Government. On the contrary they sought to dominate it. He had therefore come to the conclusion that the only course was to defeat them militarily. When I suggested that this might be a long and arduous task which would leave China in complete economic chaos he replied that defeat of main Communist forces should not take long and that once this had been achieved he hoped Communist leaders would be in a more accommodating frame of mind and that some compromise with them might be possible.

3. Incidentally, this expression of Chiang Kai-shek's views confirmed what I had heard from General Marshall whom I had seen earlier in the evening. He told me that Central Government are staging a large scale operation in Shantung against Communists which they intend to follow up with a view to further operations in Jehol and subsequently in Manchuria.

---

[1] See No. 7, note 1.

[2] The clashes between the Nationalist Government and the Communists, to which reference had been made in July 1945 (see No. 1, para. 11), had escalated by the end of the year almost to the point of full-scale civil war in northern China. Under the auspices of General G.C. Marshall, who succeeded Major Hurley as President Truman's Special Representative in China with the personal rank of Ambassador in December 1945, an armistice was signed in Chungking on 10 January 1946. Military issues between the two sides were to be examined by a three-man committee (see No. 1, note 6). Political issues—the convening of a National Assembly and the revision of the 1936 constitution (never implemented because of the onset of the Japanese war the following year) to broaden the basis of the government—were to be examined by a Political Consultative Council. Differences between the two sides over percentages of representation and the allotment of portfolios led the Communists to boycott the National Assembly. Convocation had been planned for 5 May 1946 but the Assembly was postponed indefinitely at the end of April. Meanwhile the military armistice had broken down. The Communists refused to admit central government control over Manchuria (for more on which see No. 17) or the application there of the terms of the armistice. Fighting broke out north of Mukden and then spread to China proper. General Marshall again stepped in and while his mediation had some success in stopping the fighting in China, there was little prospect of a settlement in Manchuria ('China: Some Current Trends and Recent Developments', memorandum by Mr. Kitson of 23 May 1946, F 7701/25/10).

He considers that military leaders on both sides have the bit between their teeth and will not listen to protests of moderate elements. In his view Central Government could keep up military operations on a large scale for perhaps two months and thereafter the country would sink into economic chaos and provide most favourable conditions imaginable for the spread of Communism.

4. In his conversation with me Chiang Kai-shek did not (repeat not) refer to Hong Kong. So far as concerns Anglo-Chinese relations we spoke merely of the desirability of increasing trade between our two countries.

No. 13

Letter from Mr. Kitson to Mr. Lamb (Nanking)

[*F 10812/33/10*]

FOREIGN OFFICE, *16 August 1946*

My dear Leo,

I am sorry not to have replied earlier to your two letters 467 (32/163/46) of 12th April and 579 (54/163/46) of 20th May about financial aid to firms in China by His Majesty's Government.[1] The delay has been due to the need for consultation with the Treasury.

2. If His Majesty's Government were going to finance British firms hit by war damage in foreign parts, they manifestly could not stop at China: and we can see no hope of our being able to face a world-wide programme. We must therefore make it entirely clear that any possibility of finance by His Majesty's Government is ruled out. If there are good prospects of British companies doing profitable business in the future, they should have no difficulty in raising fresh money by private enterprise; and their applications for such investment could be considered. If the existing shareholders of some companies have lost their money, they may decide to close down and clear out; if they do it will be because the future prospects do not seem to them attractive enough to encourage them to put in fresh money. In any case there could be no question of giving subsidies to rebuild these unprofitable connexions.

[1] Both letters dealt with the question of financial aid to firms suffering from war damage. In the first, No. 467 of 12 April (F 32/163/46), Mr. Lamb enclosed a letter, dated 18 March, from the owner of the Hankow Ice Works (established 1901) to the Consulate at Shanghai, appealing for UK Government cash support to replace the equipment which had been looted by the Japanese. Mr. Lamb held out little prospect for the owner in question. Another constant concern at this time was the slow rate at which many properties were being restored to their former UK owners (F 6952/47/10).

3. For your *confidential* information I would add that the whole question of British investment in China (and overseas generally) is at present under exploratory consideration by the Treasury and Board of Trade. When it is known what would be required for the salvage of efficient British undertakings in China and an idea has been formed as to the relative priority of new investment in railway, steelworks and other possible schemes, it will then be for consideration whether priority could not and should not be given in the case of applications to invest in China to those which are for the purpose of rehabilitating established undertakings there which have suffered from the Japanese occupation. But that is really a separate matter from the question of financial aid to firms in China by His Majesty's Government.

4. There remains the possibility that British firms in China might eventually receive some sort of financial compensation for their war damage claims. It is necessary here to sound the warning, however, that His Majesty's Government have entered into no commitment as regards payment of claims of British subjects in China, and that any payments that it might be possible to make eventually from the still quite unknown and problematical amount that might accrue to His Majesty's Government from Japanese reparations could probably only be for the comparatively distant future. There could obviously under this heading, be no question of any 'immediate cash advance', such as the smaller enterprises to which you refer stand in need of.

5. I am copying this letter to Hutchison[2] at Shanghai.

Yours ever,

G.V. KITSON

[2] Mr. J.C. Hutchison, Commercial Counsellor at Shanghai.

No. 14

Sir R. Stevenson (Nanking) to Mr. Bevin
(Received 18 September, 2.35 p.m.)

No. 528 Telegraphic [F 13859/119/10]

Secret. Guard   NANKING, *18 September 1946, 12.35 p.m.*
Repeated to Washington, Moscow.

General Kwei Yung-Ching[1] formerly Head of Chinese Military Mission in Berlin has approached General Sir A. Carton de Wiart[2] on the instructions of Chiang Kai-shek with a request for the assistance of His Majesty's Government in obtaining certain war material. General Carton de Wiart brought him to see me this morning.

[1] Chinese delegate to the Allied Control Commission in Berlin, 1945-46. Deputy Commander-in-Chief of Chinese Navy, 1946, and Commander-in-Chief from 1948.

[2] See No. 5, note 1.

2. General Kwei, after expatiating on the political situation of the World and the inevitability of an eventual clash between the Soviet Union and the democratic powers, emphasised the vital necessity of attaining Chinese unity and consequently of the Central Government defeating the Communist troops in China in the shortest possible space of time. He confirmed that in these circumstances Chiang Kai-shek had charged him personally to approach us in the greatest secrecy and ask for our help.

3. The position was, he said, that with economy, the Central Government's forces had enough munitions to last them for a year and a half. But if they required to make an all-out effort, such as now was necessary, they must acquire further stocks. They had approached the United States authorities for supplies of ammunition for 150,000 American rifles in use in Chinese army but had met with continual delays and postponements on various pretexts. In answer to a question put to him at this juncture he affirmed that the Central Government had evidence of direct supply to the Communists by the Soviet Union of Russian and German war material.

4. At this point General Kwei made a digression on the theme of the superior knowledge and juster appreciation of the world situation on the part of Great Britain as compared with the United States of America and the greater ability of the former to maintain the necessary secrecy in important and delicate matters.

5. He went on to ask whether it would be possible for His Majesty's Government to supply munitions from ex-German stocks in British zone of occupation in Germany. The main need was small arm ammunition (7.9) of which they required at least 6,000 million rounds. They would also like certain quantities of rifles and machines guns particularly if they were forced through lack of ammunition to store their United States rifles. In such a case they would require more 7.9 ammunition than the quantity mentioned above. He explained that it would serve no useful purpose to be more explicit about the exact needs of the Chinese Government until they know whether His Majesty's Government were in a position to ...[3] them as suggested when all necessary information would of course be forthcoming.

6. I undertook to pass Chiang Kai-shek's request on to you and to emphasise its secrecy. I told General Kwei that he naturally could not expect me to comment on it as it obviously raised wide political issues which could only be weighed up in London.

7. From a local point of view this approach is interesting on two counts. It shows

(a) That the Central Government have completely abandoned any idea of reaching a compromise with the Communists and are only paying lip service to American efforts to halt civil war; and

[3] The text was here uncertain.

(*b*) That the United States authorities are in fact cutting down supplies of war material in an attempt to ensure that the Central Government will be more amenable.[4]

[4] Mr. Bevin commented on this telegram: 'I am against this. We ought not to show any desire to the US that we want to supply. I would speak to Mr. Byrnes next week.' The Secretary of State discussed China with his American counterpart in Paris on 13 October: see No. 15 below.

No. 15

Sir A. Duff Cooper[1] *(Paris) to Foreign Office*[2]
(Received 14 October, 3.29 p.m.)

No. 930 Telegraphic [FO 800/461]

Immediate. Top Secret   PARIS, *14 October 1946, 4.10 p.m.*

For Prime Minister from Foreign Secretary.

I went to see Mr. Byrnes on October 13th.

2. The first subject I discussed with him was the question of supplying arms to China (see Nanking telegram No. 528).[3] I said that I had understood from Nanking that Chiang Kai-shek had asked our assistance in obtaining war material. It was difficult to understand why the Chinese should approach us, having regard to the close association of the United States with China and the fact that Chiang Kai-shek was actually negotiating in the United States. My reaction, I said, was that we should not touch this business at all.

3. Mr. Byrnes expressed gratitude explaining that the United States were in very great difficulties in China. There had been an understanding between General Marshall and Chiang Kai-shek and Soong that the Government forces would attack Kowloon [*sic*][4] and on this footing the negotiations with the Communists were being conducted. But Soong and Chiang Kai-shek had seen Marshall and had put up an ingenious suggestion that negotiations should be suspended for so many weeks in order that they might take Kowloon, after which they would accept the

[1] HM Ambassador at Paris.

[2] Mr. Bevin was in Paris for the conclusion of the 21-nation Peace Conference that opened in July and ended on 15 October.

[3] No. 14.

[4] The reference was presumably to Kalgan (today Zhangjiakou) which at the time was the capital of Chahar to the north-west of Peking, and the most important Communist centre next to Yenan. The sentence in question should also presumably read ' . . . the Government forces would *not* attack Kalgan . . .' (editor's italics). The Kalgan crisis is covered extensively in *FRUS 1946*, vol. ix, pp. 258-362. Government forces captured Kalgan on 11 October. See also No. 16, Annex, para. 8, and the Embassy's annual report on China for 1946, sent with Sir R. Stevenson's despatch to Mr. Bevin of 14 March 1947 (F 4491/4491/10, paras. 9-10).

settlement which Marshall had put forward. Marshall had informed them that this was going back on their word. It was a trick to which he could not be a party. He had cabled the President to ask his permission to return home and leave the whole business. Marshall had expressed the view that the Communist armies were acting quite genuinely in endeavouring to come to a conclusion but the Government was not in this matter, in his view, acting straight. Mr. Byrnes read to me certain references from Marshall's report. He said that the President had decided that Marshall could return whenever he felt he ought and at the present moment owing to Chiang Kai-shek's and Soong's attitude, the United States were considering withdrawing all their marines from Northern China and leaving it.

4. I made no comment but Mr. Byrnes emphasised that he felt that the Chinese Government was exploiting them and if it were not for the Russian attack about their troops being in China he thought withdrawal would have taken place already. Mr. Byrnes seemed very perturbed about the whole position. I thereupon said that in view of what I had now learnt I would advise my Government not to touch it at all and to keep completely clear of the whole business. In fact, that had been my first reaction because Great Britain has so much on her hands that she does not want to be involved in any internecine difficulties in these countries.

5. I would recommend that based on his information steps should be taken at once to say that His Majesty's Government cannot agree to this request.[5]

---

[5] Copies of this telegram were sent to the Prime Minister. The Cabinet discussed Chiang Kai-shek's request for arms on 15 October and endorsed Mr. Bevin's recommendation that it should be rejected. Conveying the decision to Sir R. Stevenson, Mr. Bevin also explained that at the beginning of September 1946, the US had decided not to permit the export of any further supplies of arms and munitions to China (telegram No. 910 to Nanking of 16 October 1946, F 13859/119/10).

No. 16

Minute from Mr. Dening[1] to Mr. Bevin

[F 15359/384/10]

FOREIGN OFFICE, *18 October 1946*

Some weeks ago you agreed that we should ask the United States about their policy in China, and you suggested that, in the light of their reply, we should consider what our own policy towards China should be.

[1] Mr. M.E. Dening, Chief Political Adviser to Supreme Allied Commander, South-East Asia, 1943-1946; Assistant Under-Secretary of State (AUS), 1946-50.

We asked the State Department and received their reply (though from your conversation with Mr. Byrnes in Paris it would appear that United States policy in China is somewhat uncertain).[2] At the same time they said they would be grateful to learn in due course what our own policy towards China was. This has been considered by the department and their recommendations in brief are as follows:

(i) that HM Government should keep in step with US policy in China in so far as it is affording moral support to the National Government of China and encouraging, to the greatest possible extent, the development of a strong and stable government on a broad democratic basis;
(ii) resist ultra-nationalistic attempts to discriminate against British commercial interests in China and encourage HM Ambassador to uphold our interests vigorously where there are threatened;
(iii) widen our cultural relations with China as far as circumstances permit.

A suggestion has been made to the Parliamentary Under-Secretary by Mr. Rees-Williams[3] that he might raise the question of China on the adjournment. The question of Allied troops in non-enemy countries has also been put on the agenda of the United Nations Assembly. It would therefore seem necessary to make up our minds what our attitude is to be.

The situation is always embarrassing when a friendly Power is engaged in civil war. It is even more embarrassing when, as in this case, the United States Government stands behind the National Government of China (even if a little uncertainly) while the USSR stands behind the Communists. We are fortunately not involved beyond a possible battle of words. But I submit we should do nothing which would appear:

(*a*) to weaken the position of the National Government of China with which we are in friendly relations;
(*b*) to criticize the policy of the United States who are after all trying to do in China what we have been trying to do in Indonesia, namely to bring the conflicting parties together.[4]

If our policy towards China as recommended is approved, it is suggested that, apart from any statements which may have to be made in Parliament or in the United Nations Organisation, its implementation should be conducted through diplomatic channels. Occasions may arise when a word to the Chinese Ambassador here or through our Ambassador in Nanking

[2] See No. 15; for the State Department response, see note 13 below.

[3] Labour MP for Croydon South who chaired the Burma Frontier Areas Committee of Enquiry, 1947, and who was Parliamentary Under-Secretary of State at the Colonial Office, 1947-1950 (Lord Ogmore cr. 1950).

[4] A reference to British efforts to mediate in the Indonesian war of independence (1945-1949) between the republican nationalists and the Dutch colonial authority.

may help to achieve the desired object. We should also let the State Department know our views.[5]

ANNEX TO NO. 16

British Policy towards China

This paper recommends that HMG should:

(i) keep in step with US policy in China in so far as it is affording moral support to the National Government of China and encouraging to the greatest possible extent the development of a strong and stable government on a broad democratic basis;

(ii) resist ultra-nationalistic attempts to discriminate against British commercial interests in China and encourage HM Ambassador to uphold our interests vigorously where these are threatened;

(iii) widen our cultural relations with China as far as circumstances permit.

2. On 29th August, in a telegram to Washington (No. 8501), HMG sought a clarification of US policy in China.[6] On 4th September the State Department gave their views (Washington telegram No. 5482)[7] and indicated broadly that the United States were pursuing a waiting policy in China while endeavouring to convince Chiang Kai-shek that statesman-like agrarian concessions and reform throughout the country would bring the Communists within reach of a settlement. The State Department had hinted that they would be grateful to have an indication in due course of the policy which HMG proposed to develop in China. We have therefore an obligation to reply to the US Government.

3. Conditions in China today are subject to constant change and are mainly influenced by:

(a) the internal political situation
(b) the policy of the United States
(c) the policy of the Soviet Union.

4. As regards (a) the essential fact about the Kuomintang-Communists situation is that it is not a mere dispute between two political parties but a civil war which has continued with intermissions since 1927. The Communists at the outset enforced pure communist theories, liquidating the propertied classes and distributing the land to the peasantry, but on their removal to North West China have pursued a far milder policy of agrarian reform and of associating the populace, at least nominally, in the machinery of the Government. This policy has worked in a purely agricultural region such as North Shensi but it may be doubted as to how far it could be applied to large cities and industrial areas generally, where

---

[5] Both Sir O. Sargent and Mr. Bevin wrote 'I agree' at the end of this minute.

[6] F 11597/25/10.

[7] F 12949/515/10.

the problems involved would be different and more complicated. In any event the Chinese Communists have themselves made it clear that they regard the present policy as a short-term one to be pursued until such time as China is ripe for the adoption of unmodified Communism. Moreover, the 'three three's' system in force in the Communist area, by which the Communists restrict themselves to one third of the members elected to local bodies, is not as liberal as would appear at first sight since the local population is largely illiterate and unversed in administration, and the Communists inevitably remain the dominating influence. Finally the Communist policy in China as in other countries is to retain direction and control until the achievement of the classless state and they therefore inevitably look towards Soviet Russia for advice and support. The Kuomintang programme on the other hand is more gradual and envisages the enforcement of full constitutional Government in accordance with the Third Stage of Dr Sun Yat-sen's[8] plans for national reconstruction, after the people have been educated in the task of local self-Government. The Kuomintang for its part looks not towards Soviet Russia but towards the United States of America in particular and the United Kingdom and France in the second place. A constitution was drafted by the Chinese Government in 1936 and was to have been submitted to a National Assembly in the following year. The war against Japan followed but eventually it was arranged to convoke the Assembly on the 12th November, 1945. Differences with the Communists led to a postponement, first to the 5th May, 1946 and then indefinitely, but the Chinese Government, disregarding protests by the Communists, have now officially fixed the 12th November, 1946 as the date of meeting. The task of the National Assembly will be to adopt a constitution and so inaugurate the era of Constitutional Government in China. The fact however is that the Chinese people are in the mass hopelessly ill-equipped for self-Government, and herein lies the reason for the insistence of the Communists on the formation of a coalition Government as an essential preliminary step, and for the reluctance of the Kuomintang to surrender its present exclusive control over the Government.

5. In industrial and commercial matters the Kuomintang programme is based on Dr. Sun Yat-sen's 'International development of China' and stipulates that the industrial reconstruction of China shall be carried out by the State. It specifically provides for all enterprises of a monopolistic or national character such as steel industries, principal railroads, air transportation, large-scale hydraulic projects, etc., to be operated by the State, and for all other economic enterprises to be undertaken by private individuals, except that those requiring large capital may either be aided by

[8] Father of the Chinese Republic, leader of the Nationalist Kuomintang (formed as a political party in 1912 after the Chinese Revolution of 1911), and President of the Nationalist Government at Canton in 1923 when he allied with the Communists. Sun died in 1925, two years before the break between the Nationalists and the Communists.

the Government or jointly operated by the State and private interests. In particular the exploitation of petroleum in China is reserved to the State, and the Chinese Government is also interested in textile manufacture and merchant shipping and is extending its activities over an increasing range of industry. The interim programme of the Chinese Communist Party also allows for development of private capitalism *pari passu* with the operation of key industries by the State, but there seems little doubt that the eventual goal is on the usual Communist lines.

6. In regard to land, the Land Law recently promulgated by the Chinese Government subjects land holdings to severe limitations for residential, agricultural and industrial purposes and provides for surplus land over the amount laid down to be sold to private interests or expropriated to public purposes. Special provision is made for purchase of land by persons actually cultivating it.

7. Perhaps the most disquieting feature of the present situation in China is the heavy and increasing inflation—the Chinese dollar is now officially quoted at 3,320/3,370 to 1 US dollar—and it is now cheaper to produce goods in the USA and ship them to China rather than manufacture them locally. This arises mainly from the necessity of financing large unproductive military expenditure, which in present circumstances can be done only by issuing further bank notes.

8. Recently the Chinese Government forces have re-captured Kalgan to the north-west of Peking, and this is the culmination of a number of successes scored by them in occupying territory previously held by the Communists. The Communists however still retain portions of the Peking-Hankow railway north of the Yellow River, part of the Tientsin-Pukow railway, about two thirds of Shantung, and large parts of other provinces in North China together with North Manchuria. The likelihood is that the Communists will again take to guerrilla fighting and attempts to bring about their final defeat would be like chasing a ball of mercury.

US Policy

9. As regards (*b*) the US towards the end of 1944, engaged in stepping up its offensive against Japan, determined to mobilise the Chinese war potential to more effective participation in the common effort. Reforms in the Chinese military and economic spheres, introduced on American insistence, were accompanied by attempts to bring the Communists and Kuomintang together. Efforts by General Hurley, then US Ambassador, ended in failure,[9] and he was replaced in December 1945 by General Marshall. Reference should here be made to the Declaration of the three Foreign Secretaries at the Moscow Conference in December 1945 that 'the three Foreign Secretaries were in agreement as to the need for a unified and democratic China under the National Government, for broad participation by democratic elements in all branches of the National

[9] See No. 1, note 5.

Government, and for a cessation of civil strife'.[10] Fortified by this
declaration General Marshall was able to bring the two sides together and
on 10th January, 1946 an armistice agreement was signed in Chungking.
Fighting however broke out over Manchuria, where the Chinese forces
gained notable successes in May and June, and this spread later, after truce
talks in June had finally broken down, to the rest of China. Finally, on the
10th August, General Marshall and Dr. Stuart[11] issued a statement virtually
admitting the failure of General Marshall's efforts to achieve a settlement
and placing the responsibility for the failure squarely on the shoulders of
the two parties concerned.[12] In fact, the American efforts have been
directed towards persuading Chiang Kai-shek to accept a compromise with
the Communists and to admit them and other small democratic groups to
participation in the administration, but the irreconcilable nature of the
dispute between the two parties virtually foredooms these efforts to failure.
The US Government, feeling that further pressure was necessary, decided
about the beginning of September to allow no further exports of arms and
munitions of war to China, but they nevertheless agreed to transfer to
China some US $800 million worth of non-warlike materials from stocks in
the Pacific islands. In addition, they are now considering withdrawing their
marines from North China, where their presence, while largely contributing
to the success of the Government in gaining control of that area, has
undoubtedly prevented complete chaos. The presence of the US fleet in
Tsingtao has also stood in the way of Communist control of the whole of
the key province of Shantung and restricted them largely to the interior,
except for the minor port of Chefoo.

Soviet Policy
10. Russia has up to the present been content to play a waiting game in
the Far East. She already has a defensive zone in Sinkiang, Outer
Mongolia and Manchuria, and China proper would only be a secondary
line of defence. The Chinese Government have perforce recognised the
independence of Outer Mongolia and in Sinkiang they have been
compelled to concede the demands of the tribal peoples in circumstances
which give rise to strong suspicions of Russian support behind the scenes.
In Manchuria the Soviet armies withdrew by the end of April 1946 after
stripping the country of key machinery on the grounds that this was 'war
booty' but they continue to maintain forces not only at Port Arthur but
also at Dairen. Their withdrawal from Manchuria was followed by
occupation by the Chinese Communists but Chinese Government forces
ferried to Manchuria in US vessels have succeeded in occupying the main
cities and lines of communication in southern Manchuria except on the

[10] See No. 6.

[11] Dr. J. Leighton Stuart, US President of Yenching University, Peiping (Peking). Assisted
General Marshall in mediation between Nationalists and Communists in June-July 1946. He was
appointed US Ambassador to China during July 1946.

[12] *FRUS 1946*, vol. x, p. 1.

Korean border, only north Manchuria with Harbin continuing in Communist hands. While however the Soviet Government have taken no overt line in the Chinese political situation, the presence of US troops in China has in recent weeks been persistently attacked, and there is at least a strong presumption that with the withdrawal of US forces the Soviet Union would feel free to exert pressure upon China in the same way as she has done in the case of Persia.

11. Up to the outbreak of the war in Europe in 1939 Great Britain may be said to have occupied the dominant position in China. Since then a great change has taken place and our place is now occupied by the United States, to whom China looks primarily alike in the cultural, diplomatic, economic, financial and military fields. We ourselves abandoned our privileged position in China with the signature of the Treaty of 11th January, 1943 renouncing extra-territorial rights and ancillary privileges, and our interests in China today are purely commercial and cultural. As a result of the war therefore US have replaced United Kingdom as the Western Power capable of exercising principal influence and pressure in China. We are interested in the political situation in China only insofar as unstable conditions hamper the development of our trade and cultural relations, and also to the extent that, if China were to come under the domination of the Soviet Union, this would be liable to threaten our position in South East Asia where there are large Chinese communities and also in Burma and India. There is at present no reason to suppose that Soviet policy in the Far East is motivated by aggressive as opposed to defensive designs. But her actions must be carefully watched. Russia's active entry into the China area, e.g. by lending material support to the Chinese Communists, would call for a reconsideration of our policy in consultation with the US Government.

12. While unable to compete with the USA in China at the present time, we have a number of assets in that country not enjoyed by the Americans, such as long experience in shipping, banking, insurance, distribution and other services, which should stand us in good stead and enable us to reassert ourselves as soon as we are in a position to participate more fully in world trade. Meanwhile, we must reestablish and retain our commercial position in China as far as possible, so as to be able to take advantage of the opportunities when they come. Strong nationalist influences which have emerged in China after the war have a general anti-foreign complexion and tend to discriminate against British interests and to prevent the restoration of British property. Chinese military forces in Government organisations continue to occupy British properties in all the main centres and persistent representations by HM Embassy and Consular Officers have brought steady albeit slow progress. The position is particularly difficult as regards shore and floating premises of British shipping firms. For example, Messrs. Butterfield and Swire still await restoration of part or all of their premises at Canton, Hankow, Nanking and Shanghai. The China Navigation Company Ltd still report a total of over 30 launches, lighters,

tugs, etc., in the hands of the Chinese authorities. In the case of the Zoong Sing Mill the legal rights of the British owners are usurped by certain Chinese ex-collaborators who are now running the mill, and representations so far made have been unsuccessful. The chauvinistic tendencies in question must be resisted if British firms are to be able trade successfully in China and HM Ambassador and Consuls should be encouraged to display firmness in calling for the restoration of British properties and securing fair treatment of British interests. Support might be given where necessary by suitable statements in Parliament.

13. Reports have been received from China that the Communists might be encouraged to put the whole matter on an international plane. It is not clear what the Communists have in mind for this purpose or whether they are being prompted by Moscow, but the possibility remains that the question of China might be brought up in the United Nations either by the Soviet Union or one of her satellites.[13] There are also indications that the

[13] Sir R. Stevenson reported on the *impasse* in negotiations between the National Government and the Communists in August. In conversation with Mr. Wallinger, Dr. Wang Ruofei, a CCP negotiator, explained that while the Communists would continue to negotiate, their real hope was that the Americans would end their mediation, withdraw General Marshall and 'put the whole matter on [an] international plane'. Dr. Wang declined to be drawn on what this meant, but it was assumed that he had in mind an appeal by the Communists to the Soviet Union and the UK on the basis of the declaration on China at the 1945 Moscow Conference, and that the Communists did not rule out reference to the United Nations on the grounds that the situation in China constituted a threat to peace (Nanking telegram No. 380 of 10 August, F 11597/25/10). Mr. Bevin commented on this telegram: 'We must keep clear of being involved in negotiation. This must be left to USA.'

Reviewing the China situation at the beginning of September 1946, the FO envisaged three possible outcomes: first, a negotiated and durable settlement; secondly, the failure of negotiations and full-scale civil war (the effect of this in the short-term on the UK position in China and the Far East generally 'could not fail to be serious'); thirdly, 'the emergence from the civil war of a Communist Government under the leadership of someone like Mao Tse-tung, loyal less to Marx-Leninist ideology than to the native precepts of agrarian reform and social democracy practised by the Yenan régime, and bringing to China a relatively honest and efficient administration'. It was anticipated that such a government would clash with the Moscow-sponsored Communists in the CCP and that the party might split. The chances of the agrarian reformers surviving such a split and emerging from it strong enough to rule China were too slender to be relied upon. UK interests in China would therefore be served best by a negotiated settlement, in accordance with the Moscow Declaration. The role of leadership in China had now been assumed by the US and it was important that the UK should keep in step with the US (especially on any question of reference to the United Nations) and be kept informed on the general direction of US policy (memorandum on China of 1 September 1946, F 13295/384/10).

When consulted by HM Embassy in Washington, Mr. Vincent of the State Department was not overly concerned at the prospect of China being referred to the UN. The Russians might use the occasion to embarrass the US but they would have difficulty protesting about the presence of 20,000 US marines in China when they had a force of their own of about 60,000 in Dairen and a huge army in Korea. The US would find it more difficult to explain the presence in the Philippines of 60,000 US troops. According to Mr. Vincent, the US was not about to change its policy in China. All-out support for Chiang Kai-shek, for which purpose a large US

question of China may be debated in Parliament. It is submitted that the policy outlined in the first paragraph of the memorandum should form the basis of replies if China is debated in public. On the question of US troops in China it is submitted that we should vigorously oppose any resolution placed on the agenda of the United Nations on the grounds that no threat of international peace exists and that there have been no prior negotiations with the powers immediately concerned. We are interested in the failure of any Soviet motion in regard to the maintenance of troops in non-enemy territories elsewhere and we should therefore want to give the US any support we properly can in the matter of US troops in China. The Chinese Government have already said that the US troops are there with their approval and we should make it clear that we consider the matter one between the US and Chinese Governments exclusively.

14. The situation in China is constantly changing and HMG are for the present unable to undertake any further commitments in the Far East. In these circumstances it is necessary that our policy should both be broad and flexible. It follows that the recommendations in paragraph 1 of this memorandum represent the limit to which we can go for the present and we should reply to the US Government enquiry in this sense.

army would be required, was out of the question, as was a complete American withdrawal. There remained therefore the present plan of 'holding the ring' and persuading the combatants by all the means at General Marshall's disposal that continued fighting was merely draining the strength of both sides. If the Russians entered the arena the picture would change and the US would be forced to reconsider its policy. In the meantime Mr. Vincent requested an indication of what policy the UK proposed to develop for China (Washington telegram No. 5482, 4 September, F 12949/515/10).

No. 17

Sir R. Stevenson (Nanking) to Mr. Attlee[1] (Received 10 December)

No. 1494 [F 17620/25/10]

Secret. Guard. Light [2]   NANKING, *23 November 1946*

Sir,

I have read with great interest Mr. Roberts' despatch No. 659 of 30th August giving a comprehensive review of Soviet policy in the Far East.[3] In the last paragraph of that despatch my comments are invited.

[1] Mr. Bevin was in New York for a Council of Foreign Ministers meeting on the European peace treaties.

[2] The code 'Light' was introduced in August 1946, specifically to ensure that higher authority in the FO saw certain telegrams. The system proved less than satisfactory and was discontinued in January 1950.

[3] In this despatch (F 12910/12635/233) Mr. Roberts argued that a review of the main trends of Soviet policy in the Far East, as seen from the Embassy in Moscow, was overdue. He had

2. So far as it is possible to judge the situation form here I am in agreement with the conclusions drawn by Mr. Roberts on the aims and scope of Soviet policy. I think, however, that a general survey of the scene as it appears from Nanking would provide you with a more useful commentary than a detailed consideration of Mr. Roberts' despatch.

3. In the course of this survey, in the compilation of which I am much indebted to the assistance of Mr. G.A. Wallinger, His Majesty's Minister at this Embassy, an attempt will be made to estimate the policy and intentions of the Chinese Communist Party, which I am convinced accurately reflects the desires of Moscow, the policy of the Chinese Government towards the Soviet Union, the policy of the United States in the Far East and the policy of the Chinese Government towards the United States, all of which are inter-related and inter-dependent. Great Britain comes less directly into the picture but broadly speaking our interests are regarded as similar to those of the United States, so far as the Soviet Union is concerned; and therefore the Chinese Government's hope for support against future Soviet pressure includes the hope for such help from us also though—for practical reasons—not necessarily in the Far East. It is thus the attitude of the United States towards present and future Russian encroachments in the Pacific area on which their main interest is naturally focussed.

already suggested, in an earlier despatch (No. 189 of 17 March 1946), that while Soviet tactics and timing were opportunist, fundamental Soviet policy and methods tended to be very similar throughout the world (see Volume VI, No. 82). In his despatch on the Far East he therefore argued that it would be a mistake to view Soviet policy in isolation. His comments were to be studied in the context of the general world outlook summarised in his March despatch, and also in the light of a still earlier study he had made of Soviet policy in the Middle East (despatch No. 30 of 16 January 1946), a region in which Soviet policy came more directly into conflict with British interests (see Volume VII, No. 8.iii).

He reached the following conclusions in his Far Eastern despatch. (*a*) A combination of factors (historic, geographic, economic, strategic and ideological) would encourage further Soviet expansion. Available indications suggested that this would be achieved through zones of influence rather than direct annexation. (*b*) Such expansion would increasingly bring Soviet interests into conflict with those of the US. (*c*) The Soviet authorities were not as yet disposed to precipitate a clash with the US, in part because they feared American strength and partly because they had not had the time to prepare the ground in China and elsewhere. (*d*) The Russians were fully absorbed with problems in Europe and the Middle East. In the Far East they could do little more than play a waiting game, leaving the Americans to make mistakes and 'putting spokes' where possible in the American wheel. (*e*) The Soviet Union would never willingly abandon its aspirations in the Far East. The degree of Soviet commitment in the region would depend at any one time on the strength and continuity of the American interest, internal developments in China and Japan, and the Soviet capacity to pursue an active policy simultaneously on three fronts. (*f*) There was no direct Soviet threat to the main area of UK interest which lay in South-East Asia. Soviet propaganda about oppressed colonial peoples could be counteracted by progressive political, economic and social policies in the region.

Background

4. In paragraphs 5 to 9 of his despatch Mr. Roberts gave an ample picture of the historical background of Sino-Soviet relations and I think therefore that for the purposes of this survey there is no need to go further back than the Sino-Soviet Treaty of 1945. From the standpoint of the Kuomintang, that treaty had one sterling advantage: it gave positive Soviet recognition to the Chungking régime as the sole recognised Government in the China to be. Though officially heralded by a controlled press as the first step in a new era of Sino-Russian co-operation, the treaty was not considered to be a happy document by most Chinese. Apart from the abandonment of Outer Mongolia, the potentialities of the Dairen, Port Arthur and railway clauses were by no means ignored: and in the subsequent Manchurian occupation period, the activities of Malinovski's[4] troops provoked ever more open expressions of public (but not official) criticism. The publication of the secret clauses of the Yalta Agreement[5] gave an opportunity for popular demonstrations, which were certainly not impeded by the Government. In these demonstrations, demands were made for the early evacuation of Manchuria and the latent xenophobia of the hot-heads and students was allowed to have expression. So far as official circles were concerned, the revelation of the secret clauses caused an attack of cold feet. Recently Dr. Chiang Mon-lin, the Secretary-General of the Executive Yuan, talking to a member of my staff about the eventual return of the capital to Peking, said sadly, that there had been a time when the Government had almost decided to move there from Chungking but then 'the news that Port Arthur had been sold over our heads to the Soviet Union shook the Government and we came to Nanking instead'. I give the story not so much because I believe it to be strictly truthful but because it seems to me to illustrate the general feeling both of fear of Russia and of uncertainty about the reliability of the western democracies. Subsequent demonstrations of American and British firmness in their dealings with the Russians may have gone some way to allay the uncertainty; and as it became known that, in what Mr. Roberts calls 'an elemental act of kleptomania,' Soviet troops had stripped the industries of Manchuria, official opinion seemed to harden; and, though criticism of the Soviet Union was not actually encouraged in the Kuomintang press, independent newspapers such as the *Ta Kung Pao* became more forthright and there was a general tendency to permit freer discussion of Sino-Russian problems. We in this embassy have found a disposition in the Wai Chiao Pu[6] and among officials generally to accept us as being, broadly speaking, on what they consider to be the right side of the fence; and this careful move towards co-operation culminated in the communication to me, at Dr.

[4] Marshal R.Y. Malinovski was Commander of the Soviet forces in Manchuria.

[5] See No. 3, note 3.

[6] Chinese Ministry of Foreign Affairs.

Wang Shih-chieh's[7] behest, of the very secret report on the extent of Soviet's depredations in Manchuria, sent to Mr. Dening under cover of Mr. Wallinger's letter No. 1349 of 1st November, immediately after the Japanese collapse.[8]

American policy in China

5. I have mentioned the uncertainty felt by the Chinese about the policy of the western democracies. In fact, of course, Nanking's policy *vis-à-vis* Moscow requires to be set against the general background of Soviet relations with the rest of the world (on which we here do not need to comment) and, specifically, of American post-war policy in China, Korea and Japan. That policy grew out of a war situation in which Kuomintang China was being armed and trained to assist in, and to provide a base for, the final destruction of Japan. This military policy continued after the sudden collapse of Japan, partly because of its own momentum and the existence of continuing commitments, and partly because, so long as Soviet troops were in Manchuria, the Americans could clearly not risk a military evacuation of China. This did not, however, mean that the shortcomings of the Kuomintang's authoritarian régime were ignored by Washington and the distressing Hurley episode late in 1945[9] did at least have the merit of causing some crystallisation of United States thinking about China. President Truman's statement of China policy in December 1945[10] was reinforced by the declaration on China of the three Foreign Ministers at Moscow:[11] and at the turn of the year General Marshall came to China on

[7] See No. 3, para. 4.

[8] F 16903/757/10. The report, dated May 1946, contained summary lists of the industrial equipment and material removed by Soviet troops from North-East China. Also forwarded, on film, were maps from the report showing the area and locations from which the equipment had been removed. The film, however, could not be developed because it was under-exposed and it was destroyed. In April 1946 Mr. Roberts reported a conversation with the Chinese Ambassador in Moscow in which the Ambassador explained that Chiang Kai-shek's son (Chiang Ching Kuo) had visited the Russian capital in December 1945 in an attempt to reach agreement with the Russians about economic assets in Manchuria. The Russians proposed that the war booty to which they believed themselves entitled should be put into a pool and run by Sino-Soviet industrial concerns in which the USSR would predominate. Covering the greater part of Manchuria's industrial assets, the booty was valued at $36 billion. The Russians insisted that they would not withdraw their troops from Manchuria until China agreed to this proposal; the Chinese for their part insisted that they would not even discuss such a proposal until Soviet troops had been withdrawn (letter No. 299/38/46 from Mr. Roberts to Mr. Sterndale-Bennett of 25 April 1946, F 6593/109/10). Soviet troops were withdrawn from Manchuria at the end of April 1946 (see No. 16, Annex, para. 10).

[9] See No. 1, note 5.

[10] The statement (dated 16 December) was in effect a brief for General Marshall on his mission to China. It reaffirmed the US commitment to 'a strong, united and democratic China', pledged US support in arranging a ceasefire between the National Government and the Communists, and called for the summoning of a representative national conference to resolve the political deadlock (*FRUS 1945*, vol. vii, pp. 770–73).

[11] See No. 6.

a mission of mediation, to create internal peace and a situation under which a 'unified and democratic China' might become a practical proposition. He had, and continued to have, wide powers and more than ordinary latitude in carrying out his task though he has recently expressed to my United States colleagues some uncertainty about the effect on his position and influence in the United States of the Republican victory at the polls.[12] However that may be, it is questionable whether the carry-over of the military policy mentioned above has helped him but he has evidently not considered its complete reversal to be justified. At this stage then there were: (*a*) United States armed forces in China [in] considerable (but diminishing) strength, giving direct assistance to the Kuomintang by carrying troops, supplying equipment and even (in Peking and Tientsin) making certain by physical occupation that territory would not fall under less desirable control; (*b*) a small but important United States Military Mission, which developed into the 'Military Advisory Group in China' (MAGIC), occupied in the reorganisation of the Ministry of National Defence; and (*c*) preparations in the form of engineering, agricultural and mineralogical surveys (confined, so far as I know, to non-Communist territories) to give extended economic assistance to China. On the other hand General Marshall was trying to exert pressure on the Kuomintang to offer such terms to the Communists as would enable the latter to allow the incorporation of their troops into a national army and their participation as a political party in the legislative and administrative processes of Government. The incompatibilities in the administration of these two policies were soon to become obvious but in January and February of this year, when, in the first flood of gratification over General Marshall's presence, a large measure of agreement was reached both on political and military problems, there were hopes of an effective compromise. If civil war could be avoided, there would be no political grounds for criticising American aid and the foundations would have been laid for the inauguration of a régime sufficiently democratic, in the western sense, to pacify American critics of the Chinese political set-up.

The start of the Civil War and the concurrent negotiations

6. Unfortunately, however, the two main parties in China showed greater interest in continuing the process, which had marked the period immediately following the Japanese collapse, of acquiring control of liberated territory by military occupation. It would, I think, be stretching the available evidence too far to state definitely that it was Yenan who took the first step to torpedo the Political Consultative Conference agreements of January 1946. It is, however, the case that the move of the Communists, baulked further south, to occupy large areas in Manchuria was particularly significant: and that their task was facilitated by the timing and manner of

[12] The Republicans gained control of both the House of Representatives and the Senate as a result of mid-term elections in the US in November 1946.

Soviet military withdrawals in the early part of the year. It has also been more or less conclusively established that Malinovski left in those areas very considerable stocks of Japanese arms and military equipment, which now form the main reserves of the Chinese Communist troops.

7. As to the forces of the Central Government, their reoccupation tasks in Kwangtung, Kuangsi, the coastal provinces and the Yangtse valley had been heavy and it was not until about February that serious attention could be devoted to Manchuria. As, however, Communist forces were in occupation of a broad belt of 'liberated areas' in Shantung, Kiangsu, Arhsci and Honan, it was only by ship and by air that Kuomintang troops could be moved northwards. It must therefore be emphasised that it was only possible for Chiang Kai-shek to tackle the Manchuria problem, first because American marines had taken over the Tientsin, Peking, Chinwangtao triangle for him and secondly because American transportation was made available to his troops and equipment. During all this period of land-grabbing there had been few important engagements between Communist and Kuomintang forces, and Manchuria once again provided the scene for the first serious clashes in 'China's undeclared civil war'. At this point—which may be put as mid-April last—China entered upon the strange phase of fighting and negotiation which has continued ever since. Though General Marshall, with his complex organisation of a tripartite executive head-quarters in Peking and tripartite field teams investigating and endeavouring to find local settlements for 'incidents' between Kuomintang and Communist forces, continued indeed to provide the machinery for mediation, neither party was prepared either to use it honestly or to reject it. On the Kuomintang side, the existence of confidence in the capacity of troops trained and equipped by America makes it comprehensible that the temptation to military adventure proved attractive; but the purposes of Yenan began to be suspect. It seemed in January last that the Chinese Communist Party then had everything to gain from whole-hearted co-operation with General Marshall; while a compromise would indeed entail the abandonment of the precarious independence enjoyed by Yenan (and the difficulty about the incorporation of Communist troops was obviously the most serious obstacle), they would be able to profit by the considerable guarantee of Kuomintang good behaviour provided by the General's presence (with the cutting off of vital American economic aid as his sanction) to get into the administration and into the national army and then to work from within.

8. However, neither party really 'played ball' with General Marshall. The Communists, as stated above, took steps to extend their control over Manchuria and the Generalissimo launched the offensives which eventually took his troops into Kalgan and Antung and virtually cleared the Communist pockets in northern Kiangsu, Hupeh and Honan. The launching of his troops gave the impetus for Soviet propaganda, followed in due time by that of Yenan, to begin to busy itself with American 'imperialistic intervention' in China.

9. In the United States, the stage had probably already been set by the withdrawal of the Soviet forces from most of Manchuria for a modification of the policy of military aid; and political pressure from the Left led to the decision in September to withhold further military supplies. The position was anomalous: it was well understood here in China that had it not been for the presence of General Marshall, Chiang Kai-shek would have launched his full-scale attack on the Communists earlier than he did. Now the sands were running out and Chiang Kai-shek was likely to be cheated out of such advantage as he might have gained from a military triumph while Yenan was enabled to indulge in delaying tactics at the conference table. Once the Generalissimo had decided on an active policy, the possibility of the failure of General Marshall's mission had to be contemplated; and the tactics of the two protagonists became directed principally towards jockeying themselves into such a position that, if and when he left, the main share of the blame for his failure would lie, in the eyes of the world, with the other party. The fact that the Generalissimo deemed it necessary to read the Communist troops a salutary lesson entailed his taking a considerable risk of General Marshall saddling the Kuomintang with the blame; and the period from April to September saw him, on the one hand pushing the Communists out of a series of their strongholds and on the other conducting a long drawn-out negotiation of offer and counter-offer in Nanking. Again it seemed that had the Communists at that stage taken a chance and accepted one of the offers, the party would have stood to gain, but they did not take that chance and the Generalissimo's gamble paid.

10. Two other factors must be mentioned to complete the picture: the whole atmosphere throughout this period was being poisoned by the violent propaganda being issued by both sides, which only served to embitter the existing feelings of mutual distrust; and the tasks of rehabilitation and reconstruction in the finance, trade, industry and communications of this war-ravaged country suffered as a result of the Government's decision to attempt the imposition of a military settlement of their dispute with Yenan.

11. From the point of view of the Kuomintang, the Generalissimo seems to have played his hand with great skill. His *villegiature* in Kuling from mid-July till 26th September made it necessary for the mediators to come to him out of the heat of Nanking and, while the issue of a sharply-worded joint statement by Dr. Stuart and General Marshall in mid-August undoubtedly shook him,[13] he held on to his policy and so timed a not unreasonable offer of terms to the Communists (made just before the fall of Kalgan on 11th October) that General Marshall, who was seriously considering throwing his hand in in such a way as would have placed a major share of the blame for his failure on the Kuomintang, was prevented from taking this step. The Communists refused to negotiate on this offer

[13] See the Annex to No. 16, para. 9.

and maintained their refusals in the face of a series of later offers in which more and more Communist desiderata were met. Meanwhile, of course, the armies of the Kuomintang absorbed more and more territory. The cease-fire of 9th November and the subsequent convening of the National Assembly were the culminating points of this skilful combined military and political operation by which the Generalissimo has made it unlikely that, if General Marshall still decides to go, he could ignore the fact that Chou En-lai has turned down very reasonable offers.

The Policy of the Chinese Communist Party

12. This rather long analysis of recent events seems required for the present position of the Chinese Communist Party. The main deduction to be drawn from it is that the party are not in fact interested in a compromise agreement with the Kuomintang *at present*. Personally, I have always thought that arguments along the line that the Chinese Communists are more Chinese than Communist and more agrarian reformers than Communist are misleading. I would be prepared to accept them as possibly a fair enough description of the rank and file of the party's supporters in China; but I am convinced that, here as elsewhere, the leaders of the party are Communists first, last and all the time. They can thus be trusted not only to follow the 'Party Line' in all circumstances, but automatically to serve the best interests of the Soviet Union. At first sight it seems puzzling that Yenan should have passed up opportunities for that 'penetration of the Government by means of a "democratic" coalition' which, in paragraph 17 of his despatch, Mr. Roberts rightly describes as a 'standard example' of Communist tactics. Can the decision to do so be reconciled with purely Chinese interests? In my view it cannot; and I think that the reason for it must be sought in what the Communist leaders consider to be the best interests of their creed, which coincide so conveniently, here as elsewhere, with the interests of the Soviet Union. It is true that in any coalition now offered the Communists and their sympathisers of the Democratic League[14] would be in a minority, and that, as a rule, Communist Party leaders prefer to have at least a fairly dominating position in any coalition entered; it is also true that the Kuomintang would certainly try to double-cross their Communist colleagues, and that, in the present atmosphere of bitterness and hatred, the coalition would be an uncomfortable and gimcrack affair. But from the point of view of China and the Chinese people these are certainly not sufficient grounds to justify a policy which will indefinitely prolong civil strife and discord and proportionately delay reconstruction and rehabilitation. The arguments used by Chou En-lai have been, for the most part, legalistic and 'procedural' and have had the appearance of being put forward on tactical grounds. It seems to me, therefore, that the true explanation is that the advantages of 'penetration' in China are considered

---

[14] The Democratic League was founded as a political party during the war. Considered liberal at the outset, it was outlawed in October 1947 on the grounds that it had been infiltrated by Communists (F 8197/154/10).

by the party both in Yenan and in Moscow to be outweighed, at present, by those to be won by the continuance of the present state of political and economic chaos and by the continued maintenance by the Communist Party of an independent armed force, based on the border regions which lie so conveniently on a large sector of the Sino-Soviet frontier. It is, moreover, more than likely, in my view, that the negative policy of Yenan has also been dictated by the following considerations: (*a*) Coalition in China now would have been obtained under American auspices. (*b*) Such a coalition could probably only be maintained so long as the need for American economic aid could be used by General Marshall (and/or his successors) to enforce 'democratic' practices upon the fundamentally authoritarian Kuomintang. (*c*) The creation of such a coalition would have the effect of consolidating American influence in an area where such influence could hardly be appreciated in Moscow. I believe these to be the real reasons for the Communists' attitude and that there are no valid 'Chinese' reasons for it.

American Policy in the Far East excluding China

13. I mentioned above that Nanking's policy *vis-à-vis* the Soviet Union must be considered in the light of American policy not only in China but also in Korea and Japan. We here are in no position to comment upon the situation in Korea, though we would not, I think, challenge the views expressed in paragraph 12 of Mr. Roberts' despatch, and there is, I believe, some disquiet in Nanking at the possibility that Korea may not be able to 'avoid sliding into Soviet control'.[15] I have little doubt that here it is appreciated that Soviet policy in Korea may be an earnest of the dynamism to come in Soviet policy elsewhere in the Far East.

14. As to Japan, the development of General MacArthur's[16] policy is causing very definite qualms in Chinese minds, the effect of which is again appreciably to lessen confidence in the continuity of United States policy. This trend has been signalised in a number of articles in such newspapers as the *Ta Kung Pao*, which see in the policy of the Supreme Commander Allied Powers an attempt to build up Japan as the main focus of American resistance to the Sovietisation of the Far East. If Japan is again to develop as a strong economic unit, what will [the] Chinese economy have gained from the long war? The Japanese threat will still hang over a China which, owing to its own internal troubles, has not yet been able to set its foot on

[15] In para. 12 of his Far Eastern despatch (see note 2 above), Mr. Roberts commented: 'And it is hard to see how all Korea can avoid sliding into Soviet control unless America is prepared to keep the country partitioned indefinitely and run the southern zone by herself; and this she has until recently appeared unlikely to be prepared to do over a long period. Apart from its natural wealth, Korea is probably regarded by the Soviet Union as strategically important, largely because it provides a shield for Vladivostok and the Soviet land frontier, but also because it reaches out towards the Japanese islands.'

[16] General Douglas MacArthur, Commander-in-Chief, US Forces in the Far East, and Supreme Commander, Allied Powers in Japan.

even that relatively narrow road to recovery which SCAP[17] has constructed for Japan. The fact that such arguments are being heard (and are illustrated in the deliberations of the Allied Council in Japan where the Chinese member often finds himself voting with his Soviet (and British Commonwealth) colleague against Mr. Atcheson)[18] is bound to affect Chinese policy *vis-à-vis* the Soviet Union.

The Policy of the Chinese Government towards the Soviet Union

15. Mr. Roberts considers that Soviet policy towards China at the moment is 'to sit back, make her policy appear respectable and wait on events.' I think that Nanking's appreciation of the position would be basically similar, and that the Chinese Government's policy to Moscow might be described in exactly the same terms, possibly substituting the word 'friendly' for the word 'respectable.' Mr. Roberts considers that an American failure to play the China hand successfully might give Soviet policy its opportunity. That, too, is just what Nanking fears; and it provides, to my mind, one explanation why the Generalissimo, in his latest offers for a compromise, went so far to meet Communist demands. The Chinese Government ardently desire an American success in China—or at least they hope for that unqualified American support against the 'rebels' of Yenan which can only be forthcoming if Yenan is publicly shown to American opinion to be in the wrong. Meanwhile, the lack of definition in Soviet policy permits an equally indefinite line in Nanking, and circumstances have not, except in Sinkiang (and to some degree in Manchuria, particularly at the time when there were negotiations over Soviet withdrawals from the province), made it essential for the Government to get to grips with the unhappy problems which Soviet neighbourliness normally creates.

16. In Sinkiang the Generalissimo has appointed, in General Chang Chih-chung,[19] one of his strongest men to try to clean up a situation in which Soviet intrigues were almost certainly an active irritant to more or less permanently dissatisfied tribal elements. That Chang's intervention has had the measure of success in tackling the problems of that unruly area, which recent reports from His Majesty's Consul in Tihwa indicate, seems to me to show that it is Chiang Kai-shek's intention to go as far as his limited resources of capable administrators permit to put his house in order against the day when the Soviet policy may cease to be one of sitting back. At the moment at least that policy is not aggressive, even in Sinkiang; but one may perhaps expect that there will be sufficient intervention to baulk the establishment by the Central Government of too great an influence over the newly constituted authorities in that province.

[17] Supreme Command(er) Allied Powers.

[18] Political Adviser to General MacArthur.

[19] Member of the Standing Committee of the KMT Central Executive Committee, appointed Chairman of Sinkiang, March 1946.

17. For the rest the policy of China is nervously watchful. By comparison with her northern neighbour she is so weak that no more positive policy is perhaps possible and the tempo of Sino-Soviet relations is that imposed by Moscow. The necessity to walk warily is such that even the hotheads of the Kuomintang, who are permitted from time to time to twist the lion's tail in Hong Kong, are not allowed to ask embarrassing questions about Port Arthur and Dairen. The Government are no doubt happy that, for the moment, the shape of their future relations with the Soviet Union is not being worked out on their long mutual frontier, but rather at the meetings of UNO and of the Foreign Ministers. Those meetings deal at present with matters outside the Far East, and China's practised diplomatists can air judicious views and stress their concern for 'dependent peoples' without unduly committing themselves; but they realise that their trials are to come, with the Japanese Peace Treaty and such prickly subjects as the definition of 'war booty', with particular reference to Manchurian machinery, lying ahead. For the moment, therefore, it seems wisest in Nanking to see how things develop elsewhere and to decide on a policy after experience has shown how far America and Britain are likely to go in withstanding Soviet pressure.

18. It seems to me that the position can fairly be summed up as follows:

(a) The Chinese Communist Party—and the Soviet Government—consider that a fluid situation in China, with independent Communist armed forces based on the border regions, is more advantageous than a China united under United States influence.

(b) The Chinese Government's policy towards the Soviet Union consists in waiting on events. It is based on fear tempered by the hope that the United States and less directly Great Britain will be compelled in their own interests to support China against Soviet pressure.

(c) The Chinese Government are mistrustful of United States policy in the Far East as a whole, but they are ardently desirous of securing the unqualified United States support, which they hope would accrue to them if the Chinese Communists could be shown clearly to the American public to have been responsible for the failure of General Marshall to establish a 'strong united and democratic China'.

(d) United States policy towards China itself has not yet definitely crystallised. It has suffered from a duality which was perhaps unavoidable; but it is based on a genuine anxiety to see that the people of China have a reasonable deal and on the desirability in the interests of the United States of having a China sufficiently strong and united to resist Soviet encroachments.

I have, etc.,

RALPH SKRINE STEVENSON[20]

[20] On 13 December Mr. Kitson minuted on this despatch: 'The suggestion that the Communists are reluctant to enter a coalition functioning under American sponsorship is, I think, the right

explanation of their attitude, and reinforces the conclusion that they are acting under Moscow's guidance.

'If it is the case that the Communists have in fact burned their boats and abandoned plans for entering a coalition government, we shall have to reconsider our policy which contemplated working for such a government, and decide, in consultation with the Americans, on the extent of the support we should give to the present Kuomintang-dominated government, or whether we should leave that government to fight its battles unaided.'

Four drafts of the memorandum reproduced below were drawn up before this version was agreed and submitted to the Cabinet Far Eastern (Official) Committee in November 1946 as FE(O)(46)122. The aim throughout had been to define the principles of policy, first for the benefit of UK traders who needed confirmation of whether or not the UK intended to remain in Hong Kong, and secondly in anticipation of a Chinese campaign for Hong Kong's return. An agitation for this purpose had already started and although not as yet serious, the expectation was that it would continue and make relations with China difficult (F 3604/113/10).

The first draft emerged in February 1946. It was the work of Mr. Kitson, an exponent of a school of thought in the FO that an accommodation of some sort over Hong Kong should be reached with China. The draft began with the observation that China's case for the colony's return was a matter of 'prestige and national self-respect'. An analogy was drawn with a foreign power having been in possession of the Isle of Wight off the south coast of England for a comparable period. The arguments for the retention of Hong Kong were that it was largely a British creation and that the Chinese population lived voluntarily under British administration. With the abolition of extra-territoriality, the value of Hong Kong as a base for the China trade had increased. Cession might have a knock-on effect and would be seen as a sign of weakness. China would be encouraged in its claims and ambitions in South-east Asia, especially in Malaya. Strategically, Hong Kong formed part of a forward defensive system covering the main areas of British interest in the Far East. It was also possible that new methods of warfare would increase Hong Kong's strategic importance. (These comments were made before the COS reported that Hong Kong should be regarded as an undefended port, see No. 8.) Having accepted concessions to the Soviet Union in Manchuria, China would not be in a position to claim that the status of Hong Kong was unique. It was not expected that the Chinese authorities would force the issue in the near future but when they did their position would be much stronger than that of the UK. On the basis, therefore, that Chinese goodwill and co-operation were needed for the re-establishment of the British position in China specifically and in the Far East more generally, the best defence of the UK position in Malaya was said to lie in an accommodation over Hong Kong. In the words of the draft, the 'Chinese tide' had to be met somewhere and it was futile to attempt to stop it at the shores of Hong Kong.

The draft examined four possible solutions. The first, a straightforward return of the whole colony, was ruled out. The second envisaged the return of the New Territories (the leased portions), while retaining sovereignty in Hong Kong itself (including the ceded part of Kowloon). Safeguards would be required for Hong Kong because its airfield and water supply system were both in the New Territories. The third involved the reversion of the whole of Hong Kong to Chinese sovereignty, with China then, of its own accord, leasing Hong Kong and Kowloon to the UK for a period of say thirty years. No change in Hong Kong's status was envisaged in the fourth solution. Instead effort should be concentrated on modernising its administration 'in line with the current trend of colonial emancipation'. In place of the 'Crown Colony of Hong Kong', the territory might be renamed the 'Free Port and Municipality of Hong Kong'. The draft recommended the second solution, upon the basis of the agreement reached when the 1943 treaty was concluded (see para. 3 of the memorandum reproduced below).

Senior FO officials contested some of the draft's assumptions and also its recommendation. Mr. Sterndale-Bennett was not convinced by the Isle of Wight analogy. '[A]re we prepared to carry it to its logical conclusion, and, say, cede Gibraltar to Spain?' (2 March 1946). Moreover, Mr. Sterndale Bennett argued, as did Sir O. Sargent, that any Hong Kong policy designed primarily to secure Chinese goodwill was an illusion. As the PUS put it (19 March), if the UK surrendered the whole or part of the territory 'it will either be because we have no longer the physical means (military and financial) to maintain our position or because we anticipate that sooner or later the Chinese Government will be able to hold us up to ransom by paralysing our trade and administration in Hong Kong.' This was to be made clear in a new draft (F 3237/113/10). Mr. Bevin commented at this point: 'I agree with Sargent but before circulating I would like PM to see & comment; he is deeply involved.' [1]

The second and third drafts of the memorandum are in F 5107 and F 5830/113/10 respectively. Mr. Hall-Patch commented (23 April) on the third draft that endless problems would ensue if Hong Kong and the New Territories were placed under different administrations. The distinction between the two was known only in official circles. The Chinese people and opinion in the US ignored it. Both thought only in terms of Hong

---

[1] Although Mr. Bevin was not involved in the subsequent redrafting of the memorandum, he continued to take an interest in Hong Kong. In October 1946 he received a letter from Sir S. Cripps enclosing a copy of a letter sent to the President of the Board of Trade by Dr. D.J. Sloss, retiring Vice Chancellor of Hong Kong University and a member of the Governor's Executive Council, 1940-1941. Dr. Sloss was critical of British policy in Hong Kong: 'It must be recognised that in a hundred years, we have done almost nothing by education, social services or political education to foster a "Hong Kong" patriotism among the Chinese.' With the exception of a proposal to establish a Municipal Council in the territory (see below, note 2), there were no new ideas and even less evidence of British interest in China as a whole. The prevailing mood in Hong Kong was said to be one of 'disillusion' and the situation was being exploited by anti-British elements among the local Kuomintang. Mr. Bevin commented on the correspondence that he too was concerned about affairs in Hong Kong and he directed that the matter should be raised with the Colonial Office (F 15424/113/10). In its response (21 November) the Colonial Office denied the charges and claimed that Dr. Sloss was out of touch. The Foreign Office did not press the matter but officials used it as an opportunity to update Mr. Bevin on the redrafting of the memorandum about long-term policy towards Hong Kong (F 16901/113/10).

Kong as a whole. Mr. Hall-Patch argued that nothing was to be gained by the alternative of the UK standing firm on the status quo. He urged a bold initiative based on a system of international control for Hong Kong. The UK and China should each have a twenty-five per cent controlling interest, with the remaining fifty per cent being divided among the maritime powers in proportion to their respective shares in the registered ocean-going tonnage of world trade. Favoured by the outgoing Ambassador, Sir H. Seymour, international control was ruled out on the grounds that it would afford too many opportunities for Soviet mischief-making (F 8364, 10372 / 113/ 10, letter to Sir O. Sargent, 11 June, minute by Mr. Dening, 13 July).

The fourth draft of the memorandum incorporated details of the exchanges over Hong Kong between Chiang Kai-shek and Sir H. Seymour and Mr. Noel-Baker and Dr. Wellington Koo (see No. 11). It now took account of the views of Sir M. Young, the Governor, who opposed any concessions on the grounds that they were not wanted by the people of Hong Kong, and who was beginning a process of introducing modest constitutional reform in the colony.[2] The Colonial Office, anxious above all to restore business confidence in Hong Kong and in the middle of attempting to raise a rehabilitation loan, argued that the memorandum should state why it would not be acceptable for the UK, either to take the initiative in opening negotiations with China or to make concessions. The version reproduced here was finalised in the Colonial Office and includes textual amendments suggested by the Far Eastern (Official) Committee; F 1167, 5641, 10572, 12400/113/10.

[2] In March 1946, in preparation for Sir M. Young's reinstatement (see No. 8, note 2), the FO received from the Colonial Office the text of a statement the former Governor intended to make upon his return to Hong Kong (F 3865/113/10). It proposed the establishment of a Municipal Council and throughout referred to Hong Kong as the 'colony'. Mr. Kitson disliked the text. He thought it would irritate the Chinese 'because of its reference to Hong Kong as part of the British Colonial Empire'. Moreover, self-government in Hong Kong, 'even if it were exercised entirely by Chinese, would not in the least interest or attract China so long as the Colony remains, and shows every sign of remaining, under the British Raj' (minute, 15 March). Sir O. Sargent thought Mr. Kitson's criticism 'a bit captious' and explained (20 March): 'Surely it would be wrong to deny the Colony self-government because we wished to make its grant part of some eventual bargain with the Chinese Government over Hong Kong.' Mr. Bevin agreed with Sir O. Sargent. The Colonial Office subsequently accepted the FO's suggestion that it would be more appropriate to substitute the word 'territory' for 'colony' in the statement which Sir M. Young made when he returned to Hong Kong in May (F 5707/113/10, F 5856/113/10). In June Sir H. Seymour reported adverse comment about the statement in the Shanghai press. Mr. Kitson was not surprised and referred to his earlier criticism. Mr. Dening minuted (14 June): 'The statement was bound, to my mind, to give rise to the suspicion that it means that we are determined to remain in indefinite possession of Hong Kong' (F 8370/113/10).

No. 18

Joint Memorandum by the Foreign Office and the Colonial Office on the Future of Hong Kong

[*F 16900/113/10*]

Top Secret   *29 November 1946*

1. The Colony of Hong Kong consists of three areas, two of which were ceded outright to Great Britain. The remaining area is leased. The areas are:

(*a*) The island of Hong Kong, ceded outright to Great Britain by the Nanking Treaty of 1842, with an area of about 32 square miles.

(*b*) Part of the Kowloon Peninsula opposite Hong Kong, ceded outright by the Peking Convention of 1860, with an area of about 3 square miles.

(*c*) The New Territories (sometimes referred to as 'the leased territory of Kowloon'), leased for 99 years by the Peking Convention of 1898. They include part of the mainland and a number of islands in the vicinity of a total area of 359 square miles.

2. The reason for the lease of the New Territories, as stated in the Preamble to the Convention, was that an extension of Hong Kong territory was necessary for the proper defence and protection of the colony. What has now become an equally important factor is the much closer economic intercommunication between certain parts of the new territories and the colony itself, e.g. the fact that with one exception the only existing airport, and all alternative sites for an airport, are in the new territories, the construction in recent years of large waterworks in the new territories for supply of water to Kowloon and Hong Kong Island, and the extension into the new territories of docks, industrial and commercial buildings and residential extensions of the urban area of Kowloon.

3. In the course of the negotiations which preceded the conclusion, in 1943, of a treaty providing for the abolition of extraterritoriality in China, the Chinese Government made a request for the rendition of the New Territories. His Majesty's Government refused to consider this question in connexion with extraterritoriality, but intimated that, if the Chinese Government desired that the question of the lease of these territories should be reconsidered, that was a matter which, in the opinion of His Majesty's Government, should be discussed when victory was won. The Chinese Government thereupon reserved their right to raise the question later.

4. In June and July of this year Generalissimo Chiang Kai Shek and Dr. Wellington Koo referred to the 'Hong Kong problem' and the desirability of finding an early solution, in the course of conversations with Sir Horace

Seymour and the Minister of State respectively.[1] Copies of the two documents reporting these conversations are attached (Annex III).[2] More recently, there has been some Press agitation in China and Hong Kong, which is now, however, dying down, on the particular question of the resumption of Chinese jurisdiction within the Walled City of Kowloon.

5. These events, linked with other indications of the resurgence of Chinese national feeling regarding Hong Kong, and the possibility that the informal approaches referred to above will be followed by a formal request for the opening of negotiations, make it desirable to examine (1) the question whether we should take the initiative in opening negotiations with the Chinese, (2) the line that we should take in the event of negotiations undertaken on our initiative, and (3) the modification to (2) that might be necessary if it were left to the Chinese to open negotiations.

6. The main arguments for and against our taking the initiative are briefly:

Arguments for

(*a*) The Chinese would undoubtedly welcome an initiative from us. The conversations referred to in the fourth paragraph have made this clear, and with the example of India, Egypt and Trans-Jordan before them, the Chinese Government probably look for a generous gesture in regard to Hong Kong.

(*b*) It would meet with whole-hearted approval in China and the United States (except, perhaps in business circles in the latter country) and thus strengthen our relations with those countries. It should create a favourable atmosphere for our long-term objective of freedom of commercial opportunity in China and the Far East generally.

(*c*) The Chinese, having already raised the matter informally, might be expecting us to make the next move, and any failure on our part to do so may be attributed to lack of sympathy with their cause.

(*d*) The danger of the Chinese Government, in ignorance of our attitude, committing itself publicly in the near future to demands for the return of Hong Kong.

(*e*) The danger, in the absence of any move from us, of our position in Hong Kong being progressively undermined by Chinese propaganda and political activities in the Colony.

(*f*) The possibility, if we left the initiative to the Chinese, of our being forced, as a result of the tactics envisaged in (*e*), to concede more than if we took the initiative ourselves.

(*g*) The lack of adequate security of tenure in the leased territory in present circumstances for the construction of any new projects, e.g. new airfield, involving substantial expenditure.

---

[1] See No. 11.

[2] Of the four annexes attached to this memorandum (the fourth being the map of Hong Kong reproduced on p. LII), only Annex II is reproduced below.

Arguments against

(i) Unless we are going to offer substantial concessions, an approach on our part may do more harm than good to our relations with China and the United States.

(ii) We should put ourselves in a false position by initiating negotiations, since it is the Chinese themselves and not we who are not satisfied with the present position (subject to (g) above).

(iii) A formal approach from us would be inconsistent with what the Minister of State told Dr. Wellington Koo in the course of the conversations referred to in the fourth paragraph of this memorandum, namely that he (the Minister of State) thought it unlikely that the Secretary of State would desire to open any new subject of conversation in the early future, that is, until India, Egypt, Palestine and other questions were settled and out of the way. The more immediate preoccupations of the Secretary of State for Foreign Affairs are presumably no less now than they were in June when this conversation took place.

(iv) Generally speaking, the existing uncertain political situation in China seems to make it undesirable to negotiate with the present Government any important matters which can be deferred.

7. The following appear to be the factors to be taken into consideration in formulating the line to be taken in the event of negotiations with the Chinese whether on our own initiative or on that of the Chinese.

(a) Chinese goodwill and co-operation are necessary for the re-establishment of our position in China, in the Far East generally, and in Malaya in particular, whereas China has no essential need in which she is dependent on us.

(b) China is in a position at short notice to paralyse the entrepot trade of Hong Kong, on which the Colony depends.

(c) There is no distinction in the Chinese mind between the ceded portion of the colony and the leased area (the New Territories). China wants the return of the whole Colony.

(d) China would not expect an immediate transfer of Hong Kong to Chinese control and would probably be content with sovereignty, leaving administration and control in our hands very much as it is at present.

(e) The insecurity of our present tenure of the leased territory for new projects involving substantial expenditure (e.g. the airfield project estimated to cost £4,000,000). *Note.* There is however a proposal to site the new airfield in the ceded area of the Colony. This is under consideration. The estimated cost is £10,000,000.

(f) The present agreed policy with regard to the defence of Hong Kong is briefly that, since the Colony cannot be defended against attack by a major power in occupation of the Chinese mainland, Hong Kong should be regarded as an undefended port so far as fixed defences are concerned, but that plans and preparations should be made to enable the necessary mobile defences to be introduced at short notice should we require to use Hong Kong as an operational Naval and Air base in the event of a war in the Pacific, during which China was in friendly hands. The present and future garrison of Hong Kong, augmented by reinforcements from South East Asia, is considered strong enough to repel small scale aggression by a hostile Chinese war lord.

(g) The great value to British, Chinese and other trade interests in China and throughout the Far East, of ensuring that Hong Kong will continue as a base providing conditions in which business can be transacted with reasonable security, and the difficulty in which British trade interests would be placed if there was no such base.

(h) The effect of our position in other Colonial territories of the relinquishment of sovereignty over Hong Kong to the Chinese. For example, Gibraltar, Cyprus, British Honduras, Falkland Islands are or have been the subject of claims by foreign countries. The return of Hong Kong to China might give rise to claims by foreign countries in respect of other Colonial territories.

(i) The effect on the territory and its inhabitants of the relinquishment of sovereignty over Hong Kong to the Chinese. Judging by what has happened in Shanghai,[3] the immediate effect of an early return would undoubtedly be detrimental.

(j) If, in return for sovereignty, the territory were leased to His Majesty's Government, the conditions would have to provide the same security for defence and capital investment and for other measures for the rehabilitation and development of the territory as there would be if the territory had remained a British Colony. For this purpose the period of the lease would have to be such as to attract capital for the rehabilitation and development of the Colony and it would probably have to secure, for the administration, jurisdiction and control substantially on the existing basis. It is likely, therefore, that the conditions of the lease would have to be such that the Chinese would acquire sovereignty in name only. This might satisfy China for the time being, but the arrangement might give rise to criticism in America and elsewhere.

(k) There is reason to believe that the people of Hong Kong do not wish to be ruled by a Chinese administration, although it is recognised that were it practicable for a plebiscite to be held on the matter there would probably be an overwhelming majority vote in favour of transfer, since this is not a matter on which it can be hoped that the real feelings of the Hong Kong Chinese would be revealed.

(l) Sir Horace Seymour's view that the usual Chinese technique is to take what they can get as a first instalment towards the attainment of their full objective. Any concession that may be offered now may, therefore,

---

[3] A reference presumably to the deteriorating economic position of Shanghai.

prove to be the beginning of the end of Hong Kong, so far as we are concerned, unless we have a clear understanding with the Chinese that whatever is agreed is to be a final settlement. Whether this is possible, in view of their usual technique, seems to be open to question.

(*m*) The assurances respecting Hong Kong which have been given by Ministers in the past (Annex I)[4] and on the strength of which British firms have invested further large sums of money in Hong Kong since its liberation.

(*n*) The desirability of a clear understanding with China at the outset of any discussions as to their scope, particularly if it is decided that there can be no question of the return of Hong Kong to China or the transfer of sovereignty under the above conditions. [A public announcement would also be desirable in view of the effect of any uncertainty as to the future of the Colony on the necessary measures for its rehabilitation].[5]

(*o*) If it is decided that Hong Kong should not be returned to China and that there should be no transfer of sovereignty on any conditions, the question resolves itself into one of reviewing the terms of the 99 years' lease which we have of the New Territories and which has some 50 years to run.

(*p*) From our point of view, the most satisfactory basis on which to negotiate in respect of the New Territories would be to undertake with the Chinese a joint review of the lease in the light of the changes which have occurred since it was first made and present-day circumstances and conditions. Any approach on these lines could be linked with the 1943 discussions. On this basis we should be able, in the course of negotiations and if necessary, to offer them to surrender the lease on certain conditions, which it is suggested should be those set out in Annex II.

[4] This Annex consisted of extracts from parliamentary statements made by Ministers about Hong Kong, dating back to October 1942. They included two statements by Mr. Attlee, the first of which (8 November 1944) was made when he was Lord President of the Council. Asked if encouragement would be given to British firms to prepare plans for re-establishing themselves in Hong Kong, Mr. Attlee replied: 'That is obviously so.' More recently (23 August 1945), the Opposition leader, Mr. Churchill, had asked Mr. Attlee whether the Government was taking action to restore British administration in Hong Kong as soon as the Japanese surrender had been received. Now Prime Minister, Mr. Attlee replied: 'Plans for re-establishing British administration in the Colony are fully prepared.' Mr. Churchill then asked if the Prime Minister recalled the numerous occasions, and especially at the Cairo Conference in 1943, when the Government had made it plain that no modification in the sovereignty of UK territories in the Far East was contemplated. Mr. Attlee responded: 'I have a very full recollection of those statements and I will bear them in mind.' It may be noted, however, that none of the statements included in Annex II amounted, in terms, to a declaration of intent to remain in Hong Kong.

[5] Parenthesis in original.

Possible Courses

8. The factors set out in the preceding paragraph seem to point to two possible alternatives in the event of our becoming involved in negotiations. The first to transfer the sovereignty of Hong Kong to China in return for a lease, the conditions of which would offer substantially the same security and encouragement for investment and the carrying out of other measures for the rehabilitation and development and defence of the Colony as exist at present; and the second to confine the negotiations to a review of the lease of the New Territories

9. It is difficult to see what grounds other than political expediency could be advanced in favour of the first alternative, and it would clearly be impossible to attempt to differentiate, on those grounds, between China's claim to the return of Hong Kong and the claims of other foreign governments to the return of British territory which once belonged to them. The recognition of China's claim in this manner would undoubtedly stimulate pressure from those other governments who would see in it a readiness on the part of His Majesty's Government to entertain similar claims. Other important factors to be considered in connexion with this alternative are (*a*) the Ministerial assurances respecting the future of Hong Kong which have been given in the past, and (*b*) the likelihood that once we indicated that we were prepared, in principle, to give up sovereignty we should not, in fact, be able to secure the conditions we considered to be necessary. In other words, it would be difficult to make any acceptance of the Chinese claim to sovereignty the subject of conditions. If however, we succeeded, there is the possibility that the transfer of sovereignty on those conditions would give rise to criticism in American and elsewhere.

10. On the other hand, an offer to review the lease of the New Territories on the lines suggested in paragraph 7(*p*), in accordance with the second alternative, would minimise the danger of (1) giving excuse for claims for the return of other British Colonial territories and (2) giving the Chinese grounds for demanding further concessions in the future in accordance with their usual technique.

11. This offer represents the line we would propose to adopt in the event of negotiations being undertaken on our own initiative. It would probably be desirable to seek a clear understanding with the Chinese before the discussions opened (*a*) that the status of Hong Kong excluding the New Territories would be excluded from the discussions (*b*) that the agreement reached as the result of the discussions should be regarded as the final settlement of the so-called Hong Kong question.

12. If it were decided to leave the Chinese to take the initiative in raising the matter, the nature of our response would depend on the timing of the Chinese action. Were the Chinese Government to raise the matter in the near future, it would seem preferable to reply that, in view of the existing instability of political conditions in China, any discussion of the Hong Kong question appears to His Majesty's Government to be inopportune at the present time. If, however, the Chinese Government delayed their

initiative until conditions in China became more settled, we should then hope to maintain a line similar to that indicated in paragraph 10, though it is realised that such an offer would probably fall far short of the Chinese demands. Were the Chinese, however, to press for a wider settlement and at the same time to make a positive attempt to undermine our position in the Colony either by subversive action or by open boycott, we should then be faced with the necessity of deciding whether to maintain our attitude, regardless of the consequences, or to recede from our position and to make, as a matter of political expediency, an offer to transfer sovereignty in return for a lease on suitable terms.

Conclusion

13. Our conclusion is that although the arguments for and against our taking the initiative are finely balanced and there may be tempting advantages to be gained from adopting the first course, it would be wiser on the whole to refrain from taking the initiative and offering to open with the Chinese Government the discussions on the leased territories contemplated in 1943. We feel however that, in order to lessen the uncertainty regarding the future of Hong Kong which we understand exists in business circles, it would be very desirable for some reassurance to be given in a public statement that we intend to retain Hong Kong.[6]

[6] The Far Eastern (Official Committee) considered this memorandum on 11 December 1946 (FE 14(O)(46)2). In the event of the UK deciding not to take the initiative in opening negotiations with China, the Committee recognised as an important point the question whether a public statement should be made to the effect that the UK intended to retain Hong Kong. Mr. MacDougall, Colonial Secretary in the Hong Kong government, argued that some measure of reassurance was required for the local population and the business community and to enable important capital projects to proceed. Mr. Lamb from the Embassy in Nanking suggested that the great mass of the Chinese people were not interested in Hong Kong and that the 'politically minded few' were responsible for the agitation over rendition. He was against a public statement on the grounds that this would serve only to bring Hong Kong questions to 'the forefront of public feeling'. Mr. Young of the Treasury argued that no decision, about initiating negotiations or making a public statement, could be taken until permanent policy towards Hong Kong had been settled. The memorandum gave the impression that the UK was fighting a delaying action in Hong Kong that ultimately would be lost. He was not convinced that this was the correct representation. In more general discussion there was support for the view that the memorandum should be expanded so as to bring out more clearly the reasons why Hong Kong should be permanently retained. This could be achieved without altering the structure of the memorandum. However, the way in which the conclusions were set out might have to be altered 'e.g., on the points whether anything should be said as to the possibility of negotiations with China being initiated from the British side, and as to the desirability of making a public statement that we intended to retain Hong Kong' (F 1807/113/10).

ANNEX II TO No. 18

Conditions which it is suggested should be attached to the surrender of the lease of the New Territories

1. The re-drawing of the frontier between the ceded territories and the leased territories so as to include within the ceded territory the whole of the built-up area of Kowloon and certain islands which at present fall within the leased territory. In other words, the Colony of Hong Kong would then consist of the Island of Hong Kong plus Kowloon and the area described in Section 39(*b*) of the Hong Kong Interpretation Ordinance as 'New Kowloon', together with certain of the New Territories islands.

2. Joint management of that part of the water supply system which would run beyond the Colony's new boundary.

[It may also be desirable (*a*) in connexion with 2 above, to stipulate that there should be a joint control as well as joint management and there should also be an understanding about the grant of facilities to the Hong Kong Government for constructing any further installations in the New Territories (e.g. a new airfield) which might be regarded as necessary or desirable in the interests of the Colony: (*b*) to add the further condition that the Chinese Government will recognise the existing rights of the individuals who have settled in the New Territories, unless, of course, this would be a normal condition and need not be specifically stated.][7]

[7] Parenthesis in original.

Chapter III

1947

No. 19

Letter from Mr. Bevin to Mr. A. Creech Jones[1]

[*F 527/376/10*]

FOREIGN OFFICE, *28 January 1947*

I[2] understand it to be your wish that the Far Eastern (Official) Committee should proceed with their paper on Hong Kong which has been in preparation for some time, and that you are in particular anxious that there should be some statement in public which would reassure both people here and in Hong Kong about the future status of the Colony.[3]

The question of Hong Kong is closely bound up with our relations with China, and these in their turn must be considered in relation to the American attitude towards China. The appointment of General Marshall as Secretary of State[4] after his experience in China may affect the official United States outlook, and until I have met General Marshall and have ascertained his views about China I would much prefer that we should not become involved in consideration of the Hong Kong problem. If we were to engage in discussions about Hong Kong with the Chinese Government at a time when the United States might be contemplating a change in their policy towards China, this would be likely to operate to our disadvantage.

On the question of a public statement, though such a statement would no doubt do much to reassure the public, there is on the other hand the distinct possibility that the Chinese might feel impelled to increase their pressure in order to show that they do not accept our view about Hong

---

[1] Secretary of State for the Colonies.

[2] Opening and concluding salutations were omitted from the filed copy of this letter.

[3] A shorter version of the Hong Kong memorandum (see No. 18), incorporating the comments made by the Far Eastern (Official) Committee, was produced by the Colonial Office and sent to the FO on 14 January 1947. The Colonial Office was still anxious for ministerial decisions (*a*) on whether a statement of intent to remain in Hong Kong should be made, and (*b*) what line the UK should adopt if China asked for discussions about the leased territories.

[4] In January 1947.

Kong. In spite therefore of the advantages which may derive from a public statement, I think on balance it would be better to remain silent.

In these circumstances I hope you will feel disposed to agree that consideration of the Hong Kong problem should be deferred, at any rate until I have seen General Marshall and have been able to find out what his general attitude towards China is.[5]

[5] The Colonial Office replied to this letter on 4 February, arguing that while it was important to know what line General Marshall proposed to take, there was nothing to stop the UK deciding its own position. A statement about Hong Kong was needed because the uncertainty was impeding rehabilitation and development. While the Governor and local businessmen were worried about investment prospects, the local Chinese population were looking over their shoulders at China and the KMT and were reluctant to participate in the new constitutional reforms which had been proposed for the colony (F 1544/376/10).

On 8 February the Colonial Office raised the cost of the new airport. The Governor was convinced that an airport of international standing was essential to the colony's recovery. There was only one possible site in the ceded area and it was estimated that it would cost £10,000,000 and take four years to construct. The alternative site in the New Territories was estimated to cost only £4,000,000 and could be built within eighteen months (F 2493/376/10). The FO remained unimpressed. The Colonial Office wanted to include the point about the airport in a new memorandum for the Far Eastern (Official) Committee, but Sir Norman Brook, the Cabinet Secretary, ruled that the Committee could not consider a new paper until the main policy issue had been resolved. If the FO and CO could not resolve their differences, they would have to make separate representations to the Cabinet.

Mr. Dening suggested that it was for the CO to act first and added that China was unlikely to take any steps in the near future for the recovery of Hong Kong because the country was 'on the verge of economic and financial collapse'. A statement to the effect that the UK intended to remain in Hong Kong would give 'deep offence' to the Chinese Government and would be tantamount to 'kicking them when they are down'. This was a new and 'cogent reason' why no statement should be made. In the meantime there was no reason why the Colonial Office should not proceed with their Hong Kong projects, and why HMG should not give its blessing to the floating of a proposed loan in the City (F 1544/376/10, minute by Mr. Dening, 13 February 1947). These arguments were repeated in a letter from Mr. Bevin to Mr. Creech Jones on 25 February.

No. 20

Lord Inverchapel (Washington) to Mr. Bevin
(Received 16 February, 12.56 a.m.)

No. 1016 Telegraphic [F 2089/76/10]

Important WASHINGTON, *15 February 1947, 7.36 p.m.*

Repeated to Nanking and Moscow.
Your telegram No. 1104.[1]

[1] On 18 December 1946 President Truman had issued a statement reviewing the history of General Marshall's visit to China. This statement revealed that the numbers of US troops in China had been reduced from the 1946 peak of 113,000 to 16,000 marines who remained in

Abandonment of United States mediation in China.

Vincent, the Principal State Department Adviser on Chinese affairs, having returned after brief absence from Washington, member of my staff yesterday spoke to him on the lines of your paragraph 2.

2. Vincent said that he would add nothing to the authoritative statement that had already been made: mediation had been abandoned because there was no point in continuing a fruitless negotiation. Up to March 1946 Marshall had had some success—considerable success in fact—but since then neither side had been willing to cooperate to the extent necessary to bring about peace and unity.

3. Abandonment of mediation did not, however, denote a change in United States policy towards China. This policy remains as described in the President's statement of December last—'When conditions in China improve, we are prepared to consider aiding in the carrying out of other projects, unrelated to civil strife, which would encourage economic reconstruction and reform in China and which, in so doing, would promote a general revival of commercial relations between American and Chinese business men.' Vincent said that this was not a sterile policy. Stuart would look round for specific projects and if he saw an opportunity of bringing nationalists and communists together on an economic project—e.g. a Yellow River development[2]—he would do his best to make it successful. There was in fact a very large sum of money still earmarked by Export-Import Bank for such purchases. Certainly there was no

---

North China to supply Executive HQ and to guard its lines of communication to the sea. The statement also explained that the US continued to recognise the Nationalist Government and regarded China as a sovereign state. According to the President China's political problem had to be solved internally; the US would not involve itself in China's civil strife, 'but we will stay with the problem of furthering peace, unity and economic recovery . . . We do not intend "to wash our hands" of the problem' (*FRUS 1946,* vol. x, pp. 610-17). On 28 December General Marshall asked to be recalled from China (*ibid.,* pp. 661-65) and in a statement published on 8 January 1947 the new Secretary of State declared that the extremists in the two contending parties—the 'dominant reactionary group in the Government and the irreconcilable Communists'—were the main obstacles to peace.

In telegram No. 1104 to Washington of 5 February, the FO sought clarification of the significance of these developments: 'Any drastic modification of United States policy would of course have potentially serious repercussions on our interests there, and for this reason it would be helpful to have fore-warning of any such change.' The Embassy was therefore asked (in paragrah 2 of telegram No. 1104) to secure as soon as possible 'an authoritative indication of the real significance of the abandonment of United States mediation' and whether it was likely to lead to any fundamental change in US policy towards China (F 1209/76/10).

[2] i.e. a scheme to divert the Yellow River to its original course, involving the resettlement of 250,000 people, and the creation of new irrigation channels which were expected to benefit millions. $5 million had been invested but the project was plagued by the political deadlock in China, each side appearing to be more interested in the military advantage to be gained from the scheme. Mr. Wallinger described as 'a typically disgusting piece of Chinoiserie' the fact that the project should become the subject 'of a politico-strategic bargain between the contending parties' (letter to Mr. Kitson of 25 January 1947, F 2646/2646/10).

intention of adopting an attitude of 'letting them stew in their own juice'. On the other hand General Marshall was unlikely to veer towards a policy of all out assistance for Chiang Kai-shek.

4. When asked whether the State Department had any indications of increased Soviet activity, Vincent replied that he thought the Russians were well satisfied with the present conditions in China: a state of turmoil was what they wanted. They would be unlikely, in his opinion, to repeat their active role of the 1920s and would prefer instead to concentrate on linking agricultural system of Northern Manchuria to the industrial belts of Eastern Siberia. Now that the Japanese menace had been eliminated he judged that the Russians would consider it unnecessary to do more than encourage persistence of a communist clique in Northern Manchuria and Northern China.

5. In conclusion Vincent said that there were of course influential proponents: theoretically that now was that time to encourage economic reconstruction and reform in China by immediate use of fund earmarked by Export-Import Ban[k]. There was nevertheless strong opposition in New York to such action and he thought the United States Government had no other alternative at the moment than to watch, and to proceed, whenever the opportunity occurred, on the principle of assistance by successive projects.

No. 21

Letter from Sir R. Stevenson (Nanking) to Mr. Dening

[*F 4120/76/10*]

Secret. Guard   NANKING, *7 March 1947*

My dear Dening,

We have been thinking a good deal here about Vincent's views on the situation in China as set forth in Washington telegram No. 1160 to the Foreign Office.[1]

[1] This telegram of 23 February reported a conversation with Mr. Vincent on China's economic situation. He explained that no decision had been made to provide aid to China in the current crisis (cf. No. 20). Personally he could see no way in which the US Government could help, and there was no prospect of balancing the budget when 60-80% of expenditure was on the armed forces. Asked if a financial collapse would mean the downfall of Chiang Kai-shek's regime, Mr. Vincent responded that a plank already laying on the ground could not be knocked down but it might rot. China was unlikely to find itself without a government but the present regime might disintegrate. Centrifugal tendencies were always at work in China and government weakness might lead to a loss of control in outlying districts. With the exception of areas that they had already lost, Mr. Vincent did not feel that this would open up any new territory to the Communists. It was more likely that provincial warlords would take over and put up stiff resistance to the central government. At the end of the conversation Mr. Vincent suggested that the present crisis scarcely affect the 'vast majority' of the Chinese people; he

There are one or two points on which we join issue with him. Of these the main one is his view that the present crisis scarcely affects the majority of the Chinese people. This simply is not true. The self-sufficiency of the Chinese peasant (85% of the population) is a thing of the past. Scarcity of essential commodities, disruption of communications, currency inflation with sky-rocketting [*sic*] prices and military exactions by both sides make his life almost unendurably hard. Moreover a new element has appeared on the scene in the shape of the agrarian policy of the Chinese communist Party which has undoubtedly appealed to the cupidity of many millions of peasants. Thus not only economic but political factors have an increasingly direct influence on him. Therefore Vincent's view mentioned above strikes us as too easy an alibi for laisser-faire and for salving the conscience.

Another point on which we don't see eye to eye with him is his forecast that 'the weakness of the Government might lead to loss of control of outlying districts'. We think that this is greatly under-stating the probabilities. In our view separatism would start much closer [to] the centre, very probably with the Canton bloc (Kwangtung, Kwangsi and Kweichow). In this connexion it is noteworthy that early in the recent financial and economic crisis not only Canton but Peking, Kunming, Chungking and other provincial cities also came out with restrictive measures dealing with foreign exchange, gold bar speculation etc. in advance and quite independently of the Central Government. That there is serious discontent with the Central Government's administration has been clearly demonstrated in Formosa where, though we have no direct information yet from our Consul, it is obvious that the recent disturbances were of a pretty serious nature.[2] In normal circumstances a return to semi-autonomous administrative areas might not greatly disturb British and other foreign interests. But, what with the general economic and financial debacle and the ideological struggle, regional governments would themselves be in as bad a position as the Central Government and it is clear that such a disintegration would be to the advantage of no country in the world with the exception of Soviet Russia.

While it might well be beyond the powers of the Communists to take complete and immediate advantage of a state of chaos in China, they would obviously set about extending their power wherever they could and in time might be as successful as was the Kuomintang when faced with a more or less similar situation in the early years of the Chinese Republic. This would doubtless take a considerable period of time and, meanwhile, the sufferings of the Chinese people would be indefinitely and hideously prolonged and at the end of it such foreign interests as survived would be faced with the unpleasant prospect of dealing with a Communist Government on the Soviet satellite model and the whole situation in the

thought that China would emerge from it 'as she had emerged from many other[s]' (F 2459/37/10).

[2] See No. 23 below.

Pacific would be radically altered to the grave disadvantage of Britain and America. On the other hand of course it would not be to our advantage that the Kuomintang should hold undisputed sway over China. Fundamentally they are just as hostile to foreign interests as the Communists are to Western democracy. It is perhaps therefore as well that the likelihood of a complete triumph of the Kuomintang is exceedingly remote.[3]

In all the circumstances it seems to us that the best that we can hope for, both from the point of view of the Chinese people and of our own interests, is to secure in China the same kind of balance between Communists and non-Communists that we hope to maintain in the rest of the world i.e. an armed peace—if nothing better can be achieved—with neither side in the ascendant.

The first step towards attaining this aim is obviously to stop the civil war. The only country which is physically capable of bringing pressure to bear on both sides in China, and thus to tip the scales as required to secure some kind of an equilibrium, is the United States of America. So far as the Kuomintang is concerned this pressure would be in the economic field and so far as the Communists are concerned it would consist of the threat to give material support to the Kuomintang. Such pressure obviously could not be used openly as it would then defeat its own object. More particularly would this be so in the case of the Communists. Indeed, last summer General Marshall went so far as to say in conversation with the Communist leaders that their continued intransigence would drive the United States of America into all-out support of the Central Government. The Communists' immediate reaction to this was to say that in such a case nothing would remain for them but to fight on to the end. If however the Communists saw of their own accord that the United States Government were prepared in certain circumstances to give active support to the Central Government they might think better of their refusal to negotiate.

On the other hand it would not be possible for the United States Government to support the Central Government unless they were satisfied that the latter had done everything in their power to put their house in order both politically and administratively. Admittedly Chiang Kai-shek would have to be very thorough in his house-cleaning before he would be able to satisfy the United States Government and American public opinion of his good faith. Dr. Leighton Stuart, however, who knows him well has never during recent months wavered in his opinion that Chiang Kai-shek would be ready to do anything in this direction which the US[4] Government asked him to do.

[3] Mr. A.L. Scott commented on this paragraph (27 March): ' . . . even if one were to concede that the KMT and Communists are equally hostile to foreign interests, it w'd. still be better for us to have a govt. in China whose concept of the word "democracy" resembles in some measures at least our own, and which is not under the sole influence of Soviet Russia.'

[4] 'US' was inserted in manuscript on the filed copy.

Supposing, for the sake of argument, that Chiang Kai-shek did go far enough in his house-cleaning to enable the United States Government to express their approval this might be done in a public statement which could be accompanied by an appeal to both sides (*a*) to stop fighting (*b*) to cooperate in restoring rail communications, possibly under American supervision and guarantee that they would not be used for transporting troops, and (*c*) to withdraw all conditions on both sides and resume negotiation on the basis of the Political Consultative Conference resolutions of January 1946. If the Communists knew that a refusal by them to accede to this appeal would probably entail United States help to the Central Government to restore rail communications through, for example, the resumption of the supply of munitions to the thirty-nine divisions equipped with American arms, they might well consider it more advantageous to negotiate.

Of course all this might fail in its desired effect of stopping the war—and I fear that the Party line from Moscow might ensure that it did. But even so something would have been gained, the air would have been cleared, the real aims of the Communists would have been publicly established, and even a partial house-cleaning by Chiang Kai-shek would be to the good..

I know that Dr. Stuart is thinking generally along these lines for I have had many long conversations with him in which we have discussed all these ideas and possibilities though I doubt whether he has made any concrete suggestions to Washington. Incidentally in connexion with the supply of munitions to the American equipped Chinese divisions, he told me the other day that General Marshall was fully conscious that the cessation of supply was in fact, since it was virtually demilitarising these formations, a direct aid to the Communists and that it worried him a good deal. I also know that Walton Butterworth, the United States Minister here is inclined to think that the United States Government might in certain circumstances be ready to make an encouraging statement.

I apologise for having burdened you with this over-long letter but Vincent's attitude seemed to us here to be shortsighted and unconstructive. If, of course, in saying that he did not see how the United States of America could help, he was talking about the task of bolstering up China's tottering economy in present circumstances he was dead right. There is no possible hope of improvement until military expenditure can be reduced, i.e. so long as the civil war goes on. In present circumstances therefore it would be absurd for the United States Government to throw good money after bad. The only hope of alleviation for China's sufferings is to stop the civil war and the United States of America is the only country that might conceivably be able to help in doing that. Anything that we can do to encourage them not to abandon hope would I think we worth doing.

I am sending a copy of this letter to Sansom at Washington.[5]

Yours ever,

RALPH SKRINE STEVENSON

[5] Sir George Sansom was adviser to HM Ambassador at Washington.

No. 22

Sir M. Peterson (Moscow)[1] *to Foreign Office*

(Received 15 March, 10 p.m.)

No. 114 Telegraphic [*F 3569/76/10*]

Immediate. Top Secret   MOSCOW, *16 March 1947, 12.56 a.m.*

Repeated to Nanking and Washington.
My immediately preceding telegram.[2]
Following from Secretary of State.

China

In the course of the conversation reported in my telegram under reference Mr. Marshall last night gave the following picture of the Chinese situation as he saw it.

2. He thought it could hardly be worse and offered every opportunity to the Chinese Communists and to the Russians. It was no satisfaction to know that everything was now happening against which he had warned the Chinese Government months ago. He had then told them that unless they modified their policy they were faced with military or economic chaos, or both. Instead of restricting their military operations to essential objectives within their reach the Government were rapidly expending their best American trained divisions and running through their ammunition and equipment in operations which either resulted in costly failure or in purely transitory occupation of territory. Whenever the Government forces attempted to extend their occupation beyond large centres and railway

[1] HM Ambassador in Moscow.

[2] This telegram of 15 March reported a conversation between Mr. Bevin, then in Moscow for a meeting of the Council of Foreign Ministers, and Mr. Marshall about a request from M. Molotov for an informal exchange of information about China (F 3553/76/10). M. Molotov had raised the matter in the second plenary meeting, suggesting that the foreign ministers might exchange information about the implementation of the 1945 Moscow Agreement on China (see No. 6). Mr. Bevin took the line that the 1945 meeting had been an informal discussion and that it would be improper to discuss Chinese affairs at a full Council meeting in the absence of a representative from China. He was supported by M. Bidault, the French Foreign Minister, and by Mr. Marshall (Moscow telegram No. 27 of 11 March, F 3292/76/10.) M. Molotov dropped the proposal but declared that 'public opinion' would be disappointed.

lines they failed to secure the cooperation of the local inhabitants, who were terrified of the results to them personally when the Communists infiltrated back in areas from which the Government troops had moved on. The only efficient General on the Government side had agreed with Mr. Marshall, but he had been overruled by the Kuomintang reactionaries, who were digging their own graves as well as ruining China. The economic chaos which Mr. Marshall had predicted had already come to pass, and it would not be long before it was followed by military chaos. In fact on present showing it was only a matter of time before the Communists were in a position to take over the whole of China north of the Yangtse Valley and possibly even to extend their hold south of it especially in the big towns whose economy could only be kept going by coal from the north.

3. Mr. Marshall said that he had never been able to get any reliable intelligence regarding the strength in men and armaments of the Chinese Communists nor to discover whether they were receiving any direct assistance from the Soviet Union in addition to the Japanese armaments which they had taken over in Manchuria and Northern China. The Chinese Communists had always claimed to have got their arms by direct capture from the Japanese and from defeated Chinese Government troops.

4. Mr. Marshall and General Bedell Smith[3] who was present both clearly felt that the present situation in China was extremely favourable to the Russians and this seemed to have strengthened the American determination not to be drawn into anything more than a restricted exchange of information.

[3] US Ambassador in Moscow.

No. 23

Note by Mr. Scott on Formosa[1]

[*F 6408/2443/10*]

FOREIGN OFFICE, *7 May 1947*

We have a Consul, Mr. G.R. Tingle, in Formosa. He is stationed at Tamsui. The latest report from him is dated 15th March and describes the disorders which began in Formosa on 27th February. A number of

[1] This note by Mr. Scott was written in response to a query from Mr. H. McNeil (Mr. Noel-Baker's successor as Minister of State at the FO), who had heard from an MP of 'some dreadful incident' in Formosa involving a massacre of 'some hundreds' of local people. Unable to discover the full details, Mr. McNeil asked what representation the UK had in Formosa and whether information were available about the behaviour of Chinese troops (minute by Mr. McNeil of 5 May).

Following the Sino-Japanese war of 1894-95, Formosa (Taiwan) was ceded to Japan by the

telegrams have since been received from HM Embassy at Nanking. There are about 25 British subjects in north Formosa.

There has for some time been widespread and deepseated discontent in Formosa against the Chinese officials from the mainland, who appear to have been exploiting the island in a highhanded way and to have excluded native Formosans from all higher branches of the administration.

An incident at Taipei on 27th February, when a woman hawker was manhandled by police for selling blackmarket cigarettes, proved the spark to the explosion, and on the following day processions were formed one of which was fired on from the Governor General's offices, and this in turn led to widespread attacks on mainland Chinese, many being beaten to death with the utmost ferocity, and on their property. The disorders later spread to other places on the island. Faced with a threatening situation, the Gov. Gen. (Chen Yi) temporized and promised to consider a long series of demands put forward by the Formosan representatives. These however included obviously unacceptable demands for the abolition of Garrison HQs, the laying down of arms by the national forces on the island and the organisation of sea, land and air forces in Formosa by the Formosans. Chinese Govt. reinforcements were promptly sent to the island, and on their arrival measures, accompanied it would appear with considerable brutality, were taken to quell the revolt; some 800 Formosans it is estimated were killed. At the same time the Central Government Minister of Defence was sent to the island on a special mission of investigation, and on his return he made a press statement promising the removal of the main abuses, greater participation by the Formosans in their own affairs and leniency towards all except 'leading rioters and Communists'. The US Ambassador informed HM Ambassador in mid-April that he had urged C[hiang] K[ai-]s[hek] to appoint as Governor some really able man and attach to him foreign advisers not exclusively American. C.K.S. appeared receptive and there are some hopes therefore that the Ch[inese] Government will now pursue a sound and conciliatory policy in Formosa.[2]

A.L. Scott

Treaty of Shimonoseki. Under the Cairo Declaration of 1943 and the Potsdam Agreement of 1945, Formosa was to be returned to China once Japan had been defeated. Chinese administration was restored in 1945 but it was not until the Japanese Peace Treaty of 1951 that Japan formally renounced sovereignty. Thereafter the legal status of the island was in dispute, with the Communist government of mainland China and Chiang Kai-shek's exiled government

[2] Mr. Kitson noted on 7 May that the Governor General, Chen Yi, had been replaced by Mr. Wei Tao-ming, a former Ambassador to Washington.

No. 24

Minute from Mr. Dening to Sir O. Sargent

[*F 7569/13/10*]

FOREIGN OFFICE, 26 June 1947

Embargo on supply of arms to China

Sir R. Stevenson has asked us in his telegram No. 552 of 29th May[1] whether it is now proposed to abandon our policy not to supply war material to the Chinese Government. This enquiry arose from a report from Washington (telegram No. 3098 of 27th May)[2] that Mr. Marshall has decided that licences for the export of arms to China should no longer be refused.

You will recall that the decision not to supply war material to China arose from a conversation which the Secretary of State had with Mr. Byrnes in Paris last October, and that it had the approval of the Prime Minister.[3] That decision has remained in force ever since, and it is now for consideration whether our policy should be changed or whether we should stick to the decision. The United States have never publicly declared the existence of an embargo on the supply of war material to China. For our part, however, the Lord Chancellor[4] declared in the House of Lords on 23rd January that:

> So far as the supply of arms to China is concerned, it is certainly the fact that we are sending nothing . . . We are pledged under the Moscow Declaration[5] not to interfere in Chinese internal affairs and we shall continue to adhere to that pledge.

We are now told in Washington telegram No. 3205 of 3rd June that, according to the State Department, the removal of the embargo is not a change in policy and that they have taken pains to prevent it from appearing to be one. According to this telegram, and also according to a member of the American Embassy with whom I have spoken on the matter informally, export licences have so far only been granted for a particular order.[6]

It is, as so often happens, not very clear what the United States policy is, and I doubt whether we shall get anything much more explicit if we ask

---

[1] F 7375/13/10.   [2] F 7185/13/10.   [3] See No. 15.

[4] Lord Jowitt. *Parl. Debs., 5th ser., H. of L.*, vol. CXLV, col. 156.

[5] See No. 6.   [6] F 7569/13/10. The order in question was for a quantity of rifles.

Lord Inverchapel to approach Mr. Marshall. It looks as if the United States wish to get the best of both worlds and to supply China with war material as and when they think fit without disclosing to the world at large that they are doing so or that they have reversed the policy introduced last year.

This does not help us at all, and I submit that we must make up our own minds what it is we should do. Sir R. Stevenson's request relates on the one hand to specific requests for arms and ammunition and on the other to wireless sets and early warning radar.

Three possible courses suggest themselves:

(*a*) To reverse our policy and to supply all the materials requested. We should have to be prepared to face questions in Parliament if we do so, and since the United States gave no publicity either to their original policy or to their reversal of it now, we should be unable to quote the United States in support of our own decision;

(*b*) To adhere to our original policy, and to refuse all the Chinese requests. This might, as Sir R. Stevenson points out in paragraph 2 of his telegram, antagonise the Chinese, who know that we were keeping in step with the United States in refusing material, and that the United States are now supplying material;

(*c*) To grant requests for wireless sets and radar equipment, in view of the fact that these are not offensive weapons, and can justifiably be supplied to the Central Government for national defence. It is also for consideration whether we should not supply ammunition for HM ships on loan to the Chinese Government where the nature of the armament is such that United States ammunition cannot fit. These warships are not likely to be so directly involved in the Kuomintang-Communist conflict as the land forces. A note of the position as regards these warships is attached at Annex A.[7]

None of these courses is without its disadvantages, but of the three the last is the least objectionable, and I would recommend that we should reply to Sir R. Stevenson in that sense. But in the case of ammunition for the warships, we can wait for the Chinese to make application and there is no need to offer it in advance.[8]

M.E. DENING

[7] Not printed; cf. No. 36, note 3.

[8] Sir O. Sargent noted on 27 June: '(*c*) is I think the right course. So proceed.'

No. 25

Minute by Mr. Kitson on the situation in Manchuria

[*F 9619/86/10*]

FOREIGN OFFICE, *9 July 1947*

1. The Chinese Communists opened an offensive in Manchuria in May, and on June 19th Chiang Kai-shek admitted to the American Ambassador at Nanking that the military position of the Central Government in Manchuria was 'hopeless'. Since then, the Central Government forces have staged a counter-offensive with some success, but expert opinion considers that, failing substantial help from America, the Chinese Central Government will not be able to hold Manchuria much beyond the autumn.

2. If the Central Government loses Manchuria it is generally believed that this area will sooner or later become a Chinese Communist satellite state under the domination of the Soviet Union, who will then use it as a base for political penetration into China proper. China is unlikely to acquiesce in this development any more than she did in the creation of 'Manchukuo'[1] by Japan but, in the absence of American assistance on a scale sufficient to enable the Central Government to defeat the Communists decisively in the field (which the US Govt. shows no signs of providing), it is difficult to see what the Central Government can do about it.

3. In making his statement that Manchuria was the most dangerous spot in the world today,[2] President Truman perhaps had in mind the extension of Soviet influence through the creation of another satellite state in Manchuria; but this is surely happening, or promising to happen, in other Soviet border territories? It is otherwise difficult to justify the President's statement, and it is possible he may have been merely voicing, unbriefed, his personal reactions to an official statement by the Chinese Government, which must have appeared in the Canadian press about that time, accusing the Soviet Government of helping the Communists in Manchuria and obstructing the resumption of Chinese Government administration over Dairen and Port Arthur in contravention of the Soviet undertakings in the 1945 Agreement. HM Ambassador, in reporting this statement, considered

---

[1] i.e. the puppet state established by Japan in Manchuria in 1932: see *DBFP*, Second Series, Volume IX, Chapter V.

[2] In telegram No. 573 of 3 July to the Dominions Office, the UK High Commissioner in Canada reported that Mr. Mackenzie King, the Canadian Prime Minister, had been told during a private talk with President Truman that Manchuria was the most dangerous spot in the world and that it would need watching. Mr. Mackenzie King expressed surprise and asked if the UK had further information.

it obvious that this sudden show of defiance of the Soviet Union was playing to the gallery of an anti-communist public in the United States.[3]

G.V. KITSON

[3] Mr. Bevin noted in the margin against this minute: 'I feel we ought to ask USA frankly as to their policy in this field. EB.'

No. 26

Minutes by Mr. Kitson and Mr. Dening on China's political situation

[F 9179/76/10]

FOREIGN OFFICE, *10 July 1947*

This paints a gloomy outlook.[1]

I think it is now, unfortunately, time to say that Chiang Kai-shek is himself the main obstacle to peace in China. Nevertheless, his prestige is still high, and it would be a bold man, or group of men, who could stage a revolt aimed at his removal. The loyalty of the army would be the decisive factor in any such attempt, and recent stories of collapse of morale among the US trained divisions do not encourage hope that in a show-down sufficient troops could be rallied to Chiang Kai-shek's support to quell the revolt.

It remains to be seen what instructions Mr. Butterworth will carry back from Washington, but I think Chiang Kai-shek has gone too far to carry out any house-cleaning, i.e. by getting rid of his reactionaries & calling off the all-out offensive against the Communists as a preliminary to a resumption of negotiations & a reorganisation of the Government with Communist participation.

G.V. KITSON

[1] Mr. Kitson was commenting on Nanking telegram No. 663 of 7 July, in which Sir R. Stevenson reported that US hopes for 'house-cleaning' action by Chiang Kai-shek had been disappointed. The resolution passed by the State Council on 4 July to mobilise national resources for an all-out offensive against the Communists, suggested that Chiang Kai-shek was once again relying on 'traditional methods' to save the situation. The Ambassador had been informed by his American counterpart of the existence of a plot to oust Chiang Kai-shek by a group of military leaders, 'not of first but of second rank'. The objective of those involved was to come to terms with the Communists and it was possible that they had already 'started haggling' with Communist leaders. Chiang Kai-shek knew something of what was going on but no more, and whether he intended to take action against the plotters depended on the success of his all-out effort against the Communists. In the meantime Mr. Butterworth, the US Minister at Nanking, had been recalled for consultation. Dr. Stuart, the US Ambassador, hoped that as a result of this consultation Mr. Marshall would give Chiang Kai-shek one more chance to put his house in order. Sir R. Stevenson agreed with Dr. Stuart's assessment that Chiang Kai-shek was the only leader capable of giving China a new start and that the proper course for the US Government was 'to try and convince him of the necessity for such action'.

On another paper the S[ecretary] of S[tate] has intimated that he wishes us to ask the Americans about Manchuria.[2] I think the time has come for us to ask the Embassy to find out how the State Department view the China situation in general. We do not as a rule get much out of them, but it will do no harm to indicate our continuing interest and anxiety. I imagine the Americans may be feeling a little sensitive about the subject; for such as it has been their China policy has so far failed to pay dividends.

M.E.D.

[2] See No. 25, note 3.

No. 27

Minute by Mr. Kitson on Hong Kong airport

[*F 9693/376/10*]

Secret   FOREIGN OFFICE, *16 July 1947*

I had an interview in the Colonial Office this morning with Sir Alexander Grantham,[1] the Governor-designate of Hong Kong, who is leaving this country for Hong Kong on July 19th.

2. We discussed various problems concerning Hong Kong in which the Foreign Office were interested. Among these was the question of the construction of an airfield. There are two schemes, one to construct in the ceded territory of Hong Kong at an estimated cost of £23 millions, and the other to construct in the New Territories at a cost of £4 millions. I gather that the choice between the two schemes, or whether there is going to be an airfield at all, has not yet come up for decision. When it does, Treasury will obviously be inclined towards the cheaper scheme, though it may be that even four millions will be too much to spend in these days. The disadvantage of building in the New Territories, of course, is that they are leased and not ceded, and there can thus be no permanent security of tenure. Apart from that, the Chinese may well demand a curtailment of the lease (which has another 50 years to run), and there could be no assurance that we could effectively resist such a demand or that, in any compromise reached with the Chinese on the subject, we could retain even partial control of the airfield. We have already said all this semi-officially to the Colonial Office, and I repeated the above arguments to Sir Alexander Grantham, who sounded me on the proposal to build in the New Territories, which he himself evidently favours.

3. I also pointed out that on the last occasion an attempt was made to construct an airfield in the New Territories, soon after the end of the war, there was violent Chinese opposition, one argument advanced being that the Chinese Government should have been consulted before we embarked

[1] Governor of Hong Kong, 1947-57.

on any long-term constructional project in the New Territories. The project had eventually to be dropped for technical reasons—though no doubt the Chinese interpreted its abandonment as a concession to their opposition. I said that if a further attempt were made to construct in the New Territories, the same kind of opposition might be anticipated. Much would depend, however, on political conditions inside China when the project was undertaken. If the Central Government's authority disintegrated, I thought one could proceed with such a scheme, and even press it against local opposition, with much greater impunity than if a strong Central Government remained in power, capable of damaging British interests in China as well as in Hong Kong and possibly even Malaya.

4. I thought that any opposition was likely to be engineered as much by the extreme nationalists, who seek every pretext to agitate for the rendition of Hong Kong, as by the vested interests who want to see Canton, rather than Hong Kong, as the main centre of air travel in South China. The latter's opposition might well be strengthened in the event of the establishment of a separate régime in South China.

G.V. KITSON

No. 28

Sir J. Balfour[1] (Washington) to Mr. Bevin

(Received 17 July, 6.40 a.m.)

No. 3973 Telegraphic [F 9956/76/10]

Secret   WASHINGTON, *16 July 1947, 11.42 p.m.*

Repeated to Nanking and Moscow.
Your telegram No. 7045: China political situation.[2]

[1] HM Minister at Washington.

[2] This telegram of 14 July was sent in response to Mr. Bevin's suggestion that the US Government should be asked how it viewed the situation in Manchuria (see Nos. 25, note 3 and 26). It argued that if the Chinese Government lost control of Manchuria the region would sooner or later become a 'Chinese Communist satellite state under aegis of the Soviet Union', which would then use it to penetrate China proper. Such a development was the more likely because the internal situation in China was one of 'uneasy suspense' and there were already signs that the Shanghai money market was on the verge of another crisis. The telegram repeated the arguments that developments in China would have potential repercussions in South-East Asia, and that any weakening of the central government's authority would have an effect on UK trading interests in China. In the light, therefore, of the US Government's decisions, firstly to allow the $500 million credit in the Export-Import Bank to lapse, but secondly to lift the ban on licenses for the export of arms, the US Government was now asked for its views on the situation in China generally and in Manchuria in particular. Information was also requested about how the US viewed the situation in Korea (F 9620/86/10).

The announcement of the departure of the Wedemeyer Mission[3] gave a good opportunity for a member of my staff to raise with Vincent the subjects referred to in your telegram under reference. Vincent began by saying that reports of Stuart and Butterworth had been admirable in every way but it could not be expected that either would be able to assess the military position well enough to enable Marshall to form a judgment on the situation which had now developed.

2. Vincent recalled that United States policy had derived from the broad principles enunciated at Moscow in December, 1945—'the need for a unified and democratic China under the National Government for broad participation by democratic elements in all branches of the National Government, and for a cessation of civil strife'.[4] The President had endorsed that policy in his statement of 18th December, 1946,[5] and had said that 'as China moved towards peace and unity along the line mentioned, we were prepared to assist the Chinese economically and in other ways'.

3. Unfortunately, there had been no progress towards a unified and democratic China, nor had there been a cessation of strife. The requisite conditions for the implementation of United States policy as announced in 1945 and 1946 were simply not there and the Secretary of State had therefore come to the conclusion that it was high time to re-assess the military and economic positions.

4. There had been numerous reports that the Soviet authorities were giving material aid to the Communists. United States foreign service officers had found no evidence that this was so and Marshall thought that an experienced General should ascertain the facts. Vincent went on to say that Marshall and Wedemeyer had discussed the peculiar logistic problem confronting the Nationalist forces, which was that about 50 per cent of the material sent to the forward zones was immediately lost to the Communists. Vincent was not, however, to be drawn on whether this indicated that one of Wedemeyer's duties was to estimate the quantity of material which would be necessary to ensure the crushing of the Communist armies.

5. The conversation then touched on the economic aid which the United States were still prepared to give China. This was of course on the limited project basis. But the Chinese did not like this since it showed to the world that the Nationalist Government was receiving only limited support from United States. As Vincent put it the Chinese infant had been suckled at the ample lend-lease bosom of the United States and was finicky about condensed milk.

[3] General Wedemeyer (see No. 1, note 4) was sent on a fact-finding mission to China in July and August 1947. See notes 6 and 8 below.

[4] See No. 6.

[5] See No. 20, note 1.

6. As regards Manchuria in particular Vincent was of the opinion that the position had really been lost when the agreement was made to allow the Soviet Government to have rights on the railway and in the Kwantung Peninsula.[6] But Chiang could have re-established Nationalist authority through a semi-autonomous administration in Manchuria: instead of doing this he had sent carpet-baggers to the area and very quickly alienated the sympathy of the Manchurians. Vincent thought it probable that Soviet influence would grow and that the Russians would be astute enough to limit their operations to leavening the movement.

7. Vincent almost admitted that the United States had no Chinese policy worth the name. He said that the situation had changed so much—deteriorated in fact—since their broad intentions had been stated at the end of 1945 and endorsed in December, 1946, that it was now necessary to take stock of the position. That was why Wedemeyer was being sent to China and it would not be possible to decide on a course of action until after his report had been studied. It is therefore still too early to say whether there will be a change of policy.

8. It was obvious, Vincent finally said, that the mood of Congress would have to be taken seriously into account in the formulation of any proposal for China. It was more and more difficult to secure approval for allocations for aid to foreign countries. Even if . . .[7] important political clash of interests in the Far East became apparent it did not follow that Congress would agree to stand behind an expensive programme.

9. Korea will be dealt with in a separate telegram.[8]

[6] A reference to the Sino-Soviet agreement of August 1945 (see No. 3). Mr. Kitson minuted on 28 July that 'the pass had already been sold in this respect by the Yalta Agreement' (see Volume I, No. 180). As a result of these two agreements, Mr. Kitson argued: 'The only thing which could stop the extension of Soviet control over Manchuria would be an all-out Nationalist military offensive, with American backing in guns, equipment and training, to inflict a decisive defeat on the Communists in Manchuria.' Such action would bring the US into conflict with the Soviet Union and probably explained President Truman's reference to Manchuria as the 'most dangerous spot in the world' (see No. 25). Also, Chiang Kai-shek's armies were 'a doubtful horse to back' and the US would therefore 'shrink from trying to underwrite China's recovery of Manchuria' and would attempt to stop Soviet infiltration at the Great Wall, south of Manchuria. Mr. Kitson observed that the China problem had ceased to be political and was now military. To save the 'tottering Nanking administration', Chiang Kai-shek's 'demoralised armies' would have to be reorganised and re-equipped, and urgent financial and economic assistance would be needed. It was assumed that General Wedemeyer was being sent to China 'to assess the cost and, doubtless, the likelihood of success'.

Commenting that Mr. Vincent had been 'unusually frank', Mr. Dening doubted that Congress would sanction the allocation of 'further vast sums' to bolster the Chinese Government, unless 'concrete evidence' became available that the Russians were aiding the Communists. The US administration was therefore in an 'unenviable position' (minute of 28 July). Sir O. Sargent noted 'A gloomy outlook', and Mr. Bevin added 'Very bad'.

[7] The text was here uncertain. Both 'an' and 'no' were suggested on the original.

[8] At the end of his visit to China, General Wedemeyer issued a statement which, in the words of Sir R. Stevenson, recapitulated 'with almost brutal frankness' the 'deficiencies and failings of China today'. The statement called for immediate and far-reaching political and

economic reforms by the central government to regain and maintain public confidence. 'Promises', it said, 'will no longer suffice. Performance is absolutely necessary. It should be accepted that military force in itself will not eliminate communism' (F 12620/76/20, Nanking despatch No. 476 of 29 August). According to the US Ambassador, General Wedemeyer was even more forthright in private talks with members of the State Council of the. Chinese Government and with Chiang Kai-shek. Those concerned were said to be 'badly shaken' (Nanking telegram No. 821 of 27 August, F 11861/76/10). On the Wedemeyer Mission, see *FRUS 1947*, vol. vii, pp. 635-784.

No. 29

Minute by Mr. Kitson on alleged Communist atrocities in China

[*F 9849/76/10*]

FOREIGN OFFICE, *30 July 1947*

The enclosure in Sir Ralph Stevenson's letter headed 'Conditions in North Honan', and particularly the appendix to that enclosure, is to my mind a most significant document.[1] It is the first really authentic and circumstantial account we have had of conditions under the rule of the Chinese Communists in north China since the end of the war. It destroys once and for all the fallacy, sedulously cultivated from the time of the stage-managed wartime visits of foreign newspaper correspondents to Yenan, that the Chinese Communists are not Communists at all, but a party of agrarian reformers dedicated to the ideals of true social democracy. The evidence gathered by Canadian missionaries shows how far those foreign correspondents (many of whom have written books on the subject) were led up the garden path.

2. The fact that the conditions described in these documents are not a purely local manifestation, confined to one area of North China, but represent part of a systematic ideological plan being enforced by the Communists in all areas of China under their control, is shown by a report from our Consulate-General in Tientsin based on investigations carried out

[1] The reference was to a report by the head of the United Church of Canada Missions in China about conditions in the Communist areas of North Honan province (now Henan). The report was sent to Mr. T.C. Davis, Canadian Ambassador at Nanking, for onward transmission to the United Church. The missionary author wanted no copies to be left in China and had not even retained a copy for his own files. Mr. Davis was so impressed with the report that he requested permission from the author to deliver copies to the British and US Ambassadors. This was granted, again on condition that no copies were left in China and that the source of the information was never disclosed publicly. The Canadian Ambassador sent a copy on 25 June to Sir R. Stevenson, who sent it to Mr. Dening on 2 July. In his covering letter he commented: 'In general it has been sufficiently established that the Communists have a particular hate against the missionaries who are singled out for special victimisation wherever the Communist armies take over, usually on the grounds either that they own too much property and exploit the labour of the farm labourer, or that they have helped the Japanese during the war.'

by a British missionary who visited Lingyuan, in Jehol province, north of
the Great Wall, some 400 miles from the area covered by the enclosure in
Sir R. Stevenson's letter—see F 9547/2753/10.[2]

3. The same 'levelling process' and complete disregard of all normal
conceptions of the value of human life are apparent in both areas. A salient
feature of Communist methods is the suppression of all activities that do
not minister directly to the upbuilding of Communist tenets and
organization. 'People are thus bereft of freedom of thought, speech and
action.' The brutal means used to bring about this result are described in
Appendix A to the enclosure, which should if possible be read in its
entirety if we are to understand what we may be up against should the
Communists extend their control over all China. The portions marked on
pages 1, 3, 5 and 6 merit particular attention.[3]

4. We have still no evidence whether the Chinese Communists are
receiving material support from Moscow, but these papers suggest that
ideologically, at least, they are completely under Moscow's direction, and
that politically, and in the sphere of foreign relations, they will place the
interests of the Soviet Union before those of the Chinese people, whom

---

[2] In a letter of 27 June Sir R. Stevenson forwarded a letter of 3 June from the Consulate-
General at Tientsin based on an account by R.N. Tharp, a young missionary of the 'Christian
Missions to Many Lands, Jehol'. Communist troops engaged in the capture of Lingyuan were
said to have been well-armed, disciplined and restrained. They removed all forms of transport
from the town, but looked after the wounded from both sides in the fighting. Persecution and
'systematic liquidation' were said to have been in evidence during the second phase of the
town's capture, but this was undertaken by 'a completely disorganised rabble' nominally under
the control of a political commissar. In his forwarding letter, the Ambassador commented: 'We
are not at the same time prepared to assume that Communist troops always behave in this
punctilious manner wherever they go or that the inhabitants generally welcome them. Even in
this case, as you will observe, they took away most of the local vehicles. In this respect,
however, they are at least no worse than the Central Government forces'.

[3] The marked portion on p. 1 explained the methods of 'Tou Cheng', the spirit of revenge
and retaliation, used by the Communists against wealthy families or landowners in a
community. Villagers were encouraged to volunteer their opinions in order to achieve a
prosecution. The reference on p. 3 described a 'mob trial' of a wealthy villager whose son was
an officer in the Nationalist Army. The victim was forced to reply to accusations against him
made by everyone in the village. When asked if they were satisfied, the villagers demanded that
he be 'dragged', i.e. hauled over a rocky road and subjected to repeated questioning. His
suffering was ended when his grandson broke his skull with a large stone: his body 'did not
resemble a human being'.

The reference on p. 5 again dealt with a case of Tou Cheng, this time against a pregnant
woman whose crime, it was alleged, was that her husband had been in the Nationalist Army.
She was sentenced to death and killed, and 'the child was taken from her womb and held by
the heel, for all to see'. Asked what should be done with 'the offspring of a traitor', the crowd
replied 'kill it'. The child was 'dashed to pieces on the hard ground'. The reference on p. 6
described how a Nationalist soldier captured by the Communists was bound by his four wives
and suspended by the feet above a cauldron of water, under which a fire was lit. The eldest
wife refused, but threatened with the same fate joined the three others in lighting the fire. When
the water was hot, the body was lowered and the victim drowned and boiled. This was called
'The White Boil'.

they will attempt to regiment and coerce in the same way as Communist minorities have done in other countries within the Soviet sphere of influence (note Sir R. Stevenson's analogy with Yugoslavia).[4]

5. The Americans, who have copies of these documents, must be aware of all this. They alone, of course, are in a position to help Chiang Kai-shek's Government to stem the advancing tide of Communism in China. On another paper I have minuted as to the possible significance of the Wedemeyer Mission in this connexion.[5]

Query. Bring this paper to the attention of the Russia Committee.[6]

[4] Mr. Hankey (FO Northern Department) noted against this paragraph: 'I agree.' In his covering letter Sir R. Stevenson commented: 'The proceedings of public trial, of which we have heard a good deal of late, though without this wealth of first hand detail, give one a shock in this 20th century and unpleasantly recall the days of the Boxers. They are a faithful reflection of analogous "People's Courts" instituted by the Communists in Yugoslavia but seem to be even more brutal in their methods.' (The Boxers were a secret nationalist organisation (I Ho Ch'uan) and the leaders of an uprising in Peking in 1900 against foreigners and foreign influences.)

[5] See No. 28, note 6.

[6] Established in April 1946 as an interdepartmental committee of officials, the Russia Committee was briefed to conduct a regular review of Soviet activities, policy and propaganda throughout the world. For its precise terms of reference, see Series I, Volume VI, p. 328. No record of a discussion about alleged Communist atrocities has been found in the Committee's papers.

No. 30

Letter from Mr. H.O. Hooper[1] (Board of Trade) to Mr. A.S. Gilbert[2]

[F 12378/37/10]

BOARD OF TRADE, *8 September 1947*

I[3] gather that the trade mission which went to China[4] are excusably anxious that their report should be published and I imagine that you will be dealing with the question of publication.[5]

[1] Assistant Secretary in the Commercial Relations and Treaties (CR&T) Department of the Board of Trade.

[2] Assistant Secretary in the Overseas Division of the Board of Trade.

[3] Opening and concluding salutations were omitted from the filed copy of this letter.

[4] See No. 9.

[5] A draft of the report had been submitted in March but was not presented to the President of the Board of Trade until August 1947. A 226 page typescript is at F 11888/37/10. The report was positive in its estimate of the long-term opportunities for trade, but also emphasised the immediate handicaps and drawbacks, including inflation, a weak currency, poor communications and political uncertainty because of the civil war. The caveat desired by the Board of Trade did not appear in the form recommended by the Board when the report was published in 1948. However, in the conclusions, following immediately after the argument that in the course of time and at an increasing pace China would tend to become industrialised, the report stressed that 'it would be wrong to assume that such a development will be speedy or

From the CR&T point of view, I think it most undesirable that this long and in itself admirable report should be published without a clear indication that it is a forecast of opportunities that may be enjoyed in the future rather than a statement of opportunities which can be exploited now. Without this it is obvious that exporters will get the general impression that HMG is anxious to stimulate an energetic export trade with China, and, though there are some passing references in the report to the difficulties impeding current trading, the actual recommendations are so numerous, so practical and so detailed that their accumulative effect is bound to swamp any general caveat embodied in the text.

We cannot afford to encourage exports to China until our hard currency position is better and we may have actively to discourage them. Exporters are already doing rather too well. In these circumstances, I am sure that if the report is published (and I suppose it must be) it should be given some kind of foreword containing our reservations.

I am copying this letter to Scott at the Foreign Office.

that China can within foreseeable time become an industrial nation to a degree usually implied by that term. It will take many years, perhaps even generations, to build up a technically trained force sufficient for China's industries even on a modest scale' (Board of Trade: *Report of the United Kingdom Trade Mission to China, October to December 1946* (London, HMSO, 1948) pp. 171-72; see also Aron Shai, *Britain and China, 1941-47: imperial momentum* (London, Macmillan, 1984).

No. 31

Note by China Department on Chinese National Assembly Elections

[F 12881/36/10]

FOREIGN OFFICE, *15 September 1947*

Elections are to be held shortly for the Chinese National Assembly & Legislative Yuan, and the Chinese Govt. are making preparations for the Chinese communities in Malaya, Borneo, Hong Kong and other countries to elect members thereto.

The Colonial Office regard this as objectionable as tending to make these Chinese communities look towards China rather than to their local Governments, though participation in such elections is probably not an offence under the laws of the British territories concerned. To ban the elections would in any case be somewhat delicate, as the Chinese Govt. may choose to make an issue of the matter and foment agitation, particularly in respect of Hong Kong.

The Siamese Govt. have informed the Chinese Govt. that the elections cannot be permitted in Siam. HM Ambassador in Nanking believes that such elections should not be tolerated in Hong Kong.

It is proposed to instruct HM Ambassador to inform the Chinese Govt. that the extraterritorial application of the Chinese electoral law involves unwarrantable interference with the sovereignty of local Governments and to seek an assurance that no further attempt will be made to apply China's electoral law in British territories. A similar communication made in 1938 remained unanswered.

There seem no good legal grounds for objecting to such elections if conducted by post.[1]

CHINA DEPARTMENT

[1] Mr. F.T.A. Ashton-Gwatkin, Senior Inspector of HM Missions, minuted on 15 September: 'It would never have occurred to us to rope in our communities in say the US or Argentina to vote in a UK general election, but I think Nazi Germany used to rope in the *Auslandsdeutsche* [Germans abroad] to vote for Hitler—recording their vote, if I remember rightly, on board a German steamer. But that is not a precedent which we would think the Chinese would invoke to justify what looks like most unwarrantable trespassing in other peoples' territory. Although these nationalistic questions are very delicate ground yet I think that HM Ambassador should be instructed at once to tell the Chinese that they cannot do that kind of thing. It would incidentally be a kind of revival of extra-territoriality which the Chinese so much objected to in China and which has now been abolished there.'

In Nanking telegram No. 158 to Singapore of 25 November, repeated to the FO, Mr. Lamb reported that the Chinese Government had decided not to proceed with elections in British territories (F 15617/36/10).

No. 32

Minutes by Mr. Scott and Mr. Dening on future policy regarding Hong Kong

[*F 15520/376/10*]

FOREIGN OFFICE, *28 November and 1 December 1947*

The last word by our Secretary of State on the subject of a statement about Hong Kong is contained in F 6588/376/Green.[1] He then told the Secretary of State for the Colonies that he was not in favour of such a statement.

[1] When the Colonial Office returned in May 1947 to the issue of a statement about Hong Kong (see No. 19) Mr. Bevin again told Mr. Creech Jones that he was not in favour (F 6588/376/10). Another attempt to raise the issue was made by the Colonial Office in November 1947. Portugal had by then stated publicly that it did not intend to hand over its own territory of Macao and this, according to the Colonial Office, had led to 'unfavourable comparison' with the UK's attitude towards Hong Kong. The uncertainty was continuing to affect Hong Kong's ability to raise money for rehabilitation and reconstruction. Moreover, the Colonial Office did not accept the FO view that China was in no position to take action against Hong Kong, and cited as evidence the recent attempt (see No. 31) by the Chinese Government to organise elections among the local Chinese in both Hong Kong and Malaya (letter from Mr. N.L. Mayle to Mr. Scott, 20 November). Mr. Scott's reply of 4 December followed closely the arguments put forward in the minutes reproduced here. For the Portuguese position over Macao, and the refusal of HMG to associate itself with Portuguese policy, see F 9158/376/10.

I cannot myself see that any useful purpose would be achieved by HMG now making a declaration that it intended to retain Hong Kong in perpetuity.

The hesitations of firms about putting money into Hong Kong arise primarily from the uncertainties of the situation in the Far East, more particularly in China, and it is the Chinese attitude which is really the governing factor.

We know that the aim of the Chinese Government is the eventual recovery of Hong Kong, but in present circumstances they are prepared to let their ambitions remain dormant, although every now and then they try to argue that the New (Leased) Territories are in some way different from Hong Kong proper.

If, however, we issued any statement I fear that the only result would be that the Kuomintang hotheads would be given a loose rein and, as Hong Kong's prosperity depends on Chinese goodwill, the last state would be worse than the first.

A further consideration is that we should almost certainly receive no support from the Americans if we made a statement about Hong Kong, and, if the Chinese appealed to the United Nations they would, as indicated in the press extract enclosed in Mr. Mayle's letter,[2] doubtless receive considerable support.

My general conclusion therefore is that there is still no case for the issue of any statement about Hong Kong, and that, while such a statement might at first reassure possible investors, Chinese reactions would soon turn such reassurance into greater uncertainty than at present is said to exist.

I would propose to reply to Mr. Mayle on the above the lines.

A.L. SCOTT

I do not think it desirable to bother the Secretary of State with this question again at this juncture. Since the approach from the Colonial Office is only on the departmental level, I think we should reply in the light of this and the preceding minute.

---

[2] The enclosure was a cutting from the Paris edition of the *New York Herald Tribune*, 18 October 1947, which included extracts from a book by the former US Secretary of State, Mr. Byrnes, *Speaking Frankly*. Hong Kong was mentioned as a subject that had been discussed at Yalta in the context of voting rights in the Security Council of the proposed United Nations Organisation. The US had proposed that unanimity should be required for all categories of decisions in the Security Council except one. In decisions involving the peaceful settlement of disputes, a permanent member of the Council would not cast a vote if it were party to the dispute in question. Supporting the proposal, Mr. Churchill argued that it would give both the UK and China the right to state their positions on Hong Kong, but the UK would not be required to return Hong Kong to China 'if we did not feel that was the right thing to do'. Marshal Stalin challenged this interpretation, and argued that China would not be satisfied with the right only to state an opinion. China would demand a decision on the matter and would in all probability 'have some friends' for its position in the General Assembly (James F. Byrnes, *Speaking Frankly*, London, 1947, pp. 34-37).

We still think it undesirable to make any statement about Hong Kong. To do so would appear to the Chinese to be out of context and gratuitous, and this might provoke an outburst which would be bound to affect adversely our relations with China at a time when we are anxious to exert our influence upon her not to throw in her lot with the Soviet Union and to agree to American proposals for a Japanese peace settlement.

I should have thought that no government of this country, of whatever political complexion, ought to commit its successors (again of whatever complexion) to a course of action in international affairs which might be actually embarrassing if not dangerous to the United Kingdom at some unforeseen time in the future.[3] We may once have said, for all I know, that we had no intention of giving up Burma, but we are doing so on the 4th January, 1948, and the Opposition did not oppose the third reading of the Burma Independence Bill. If the Government were to declare to-day that we have no intention ever of giving up Hong Kong, then they may embarrass some government of the future which might, in a different set of circumstances, feel obliged to give up Hong Kong. Nor would the investor bless the government of today for giving him an assurance by which in the future they may not be able to abide.

As to the investor, either Hong Kong must seem to him an acceptable risk or not. If it is not acceptable, then I think HMG would be very unwise to try to make it so by offering perpetual guarantees which we are not in a position to do.

Obviously we do not want to give up Hong Kong now, and I should say that we would be most reluctant to give it up at any time if we could avoid doing so. But whether we can always avoid doing so is something which no Minister today could possible answer.

M.E.D.

[3] This sentence and the last paragraph in Mr. Dening's minute were repeated in Mr. Scott's reply of 4 December to Mr. Mayle (see note 1 above).

No. 33

Minute by Mr. P.W. Scarlett[1]

[F 16276/13/10]

FOREIGN OFFICE, *12 December 1947*

When HM Ambassador visited Canton last week Dr. T.V. Soong, Governor of the Provinces of Kwantung and Kwangsi, expressed grave

[1] Head of China Department from December 1947 and of the Far Eastern Department from November 1948 until February 1950. The re-formed Far Eastern Department had responsibility for China, Japan, Korea, the Philippines and general Pacific questions. A separate department continued to deal with South-East Asia.

concern over banditry in these Provinces. The military resources at his disposal were inadequate to meet the problem and Dr. Soong proposed to raise a special Peace Preservation Corps (gendarmerie) armed with captured Japanese rifles for which, however, ammunition was very short. He emphasised the serious effects on the position of Hong Kong should public order in Kwantung deteriorate and enquired informally whether His Majesty's Government had at their disposal any stocks of suitable Japanese ammunition and, if so, whether they would sell it to China. If HMG were willing to consider the matter, Dr. Soong would ask the Central Government to make a formal approach.

After discussion with the Governor of Hong Kong, Sir R. Stevenson asks[2] that this approach be sympathetically considered. China Department support this recommendation for the following reasons:

(1) the supply of this ammunition to preserve internal security in Kwantung would not contravene the principle of non-interference in the internal affairs of China neither would it represent participation in the present conflict between the Kuomintang and the Chinese Communists;

(2) Kwantung is remote from the present area of that conflict;

(3) any deterioration in law and order in Kwantung is of direct interest to Hong Kong;

(4) there are at present various points of tension between Hong Kong and the Chinese authorities—squatters at Kowloon, smuggling, the presence of dissident elements etc. The proposed concession would therefore be correspondingly valuable in the interests of Anglo-Chinese good relations;

(3) in June last the United States Government withdrew their embargo on the supply of arms to China and have recently agreed to make munitions available to China on payment. If we refuse the present request the Chinese will almost certainly turn to the Americans. On the other hand, there could be no grounds for objection from the American side if we meet it.[3]

[2] Nanking telegram No. 1134 of 9 December. Dr. Soong's specific request was for 6.5mm. ammunition for the 30,000 to 40,000 captured Japanese rifles he had at his disposal. His approach to Sir R. Stevenson was made informally because he did not want to advise the central government to make a formal approach if the answer would be negative. In agreeing to raise the matter in London, the Ambassador told Dr. Soong that he was not optmistic about the outcome.

[3] The FO had, in October, rejected further appeals made by the Chinese Ambassador and Air Attaché in London for arms for use in the civil war (F 13972/13/10). On 12 December Mr. Dening recommended that this new approach from Dr. Soong should be approved: it could be defended in Parliament and it was unlikely that the US would object. It emerged, however, that the UK had destroyed its stocks of Japanese small arms ammunition on security grounds. The War Office believed that some had been kept by the Australians (minute by Mr. Scarlett, 20 December). A more substantial request for armaments was considerd at the beginning of 1948 (see No. 36).

No. 34

Report of the British Parliamentary Goodwill Mission to China, 1947[1]

[*F 1517/361/10*]

15 December 1947

In a letter from the Foreign Office dated 22nd August last,[2] the delegation was asked to furnish a report on its return, chiefly on the headings set out in that letter. We propose to deal with these in the order in which they appeared.

As a preliminary we would mention that on the journey out the mission called, among other places, at Karachi and had (at his own request) an interview with Mr. Jinnah, the head of the Pakistan Government, who discussed certain matters concerning the difficulties that confront his administration, particularly with regard to the Punjab.

Our Chairman spent the night at Government House, Calcutta, by invitation of Mr. Rajagopalachari, Governor of Western Bengal. Among other foreign states visited were Burma (Rangoon) and Siam (Bangkok).

In all places the utmost courtesy and hospitality were extended to us, the only exception being at Bangkok, where no connexion was made with the British Ambassador—probably due to the fact that the 'plane arrived a day late; the Chinese Ambassador extended to us courteous and generous hospitality.

Turning to the visit to China, we were asked in the letter referred to above to comment on the following subjects:

(a) *The position of Chiang Kai-shek*

This is not very easy to answer. His own personal character we have every reason to believe is appreciated and stands in high regard; but he is certainly suffering from some sort of reaction against many of the people in his immediate entourage.

There can be no doubt there is very little enthusiasm on the part of the Chinese people in connexion with the civil war and there is certainly nothing of what we know as patriotic fervour. We had the advantage of dining with the President (which term is preferred—rather than Generalissimo) and Madame Chiang Kai-shek at Nanking. During the

[1] A British Parliamentary Goodwill Mission had visited China in October 1947. It was led by Lord Ammon (aged 72), a Labour Peer and Government Whip who had led a Parliamentary Mission to Newfoundland in 1943. Other members were: Lord Amulree, a Liberal Peer and doctor; Mr. F. McLeavy, a trades unionist and Labour MP for Bradford East; Mr. J. Harrison, trades unionist and Labour MP for Nottingham East; Mr. W. Roberts, Liberal MP for Cumberland, and Mr. M.A. Lindsay, described in one notification of the Mission as 'a well-known author and explorer', Conservative MP for Solihull (F 13157/28/10). This Report was communicated to Mr. Mayhew by Lord Ammon on 23 January 1948.

[2] F 10836/28/10.

course of a long conversation afterwards, in reply to a question as to when he thought there was a possibility of a termination of hostilities, the President said that within six months, or at the most twelve months, they expected to clear the whole of the rebel element from within the 'Great Wall'.

The civil war overshadows all other problems in China and is most noticeable in the North. It was at no time suggested to us that Great Britain should attempt to assist the Government in the civil war. Nevertheless from various quarters there were suggestions that the pressure of the Communists from without and the inflation within would inevitably result in the disintegration of the Government, unless substantial help from outside was soon forthcoming.

The Kuomintang seem to be losing ground. This arises as much, we think, on account of the economic conditions as from the continuance of the civil war itself.

Later, it was conveyed that the President would like to talk over the matter again with the delegation, but unfortunately this conversation did not ensue, as during the time between the despatch of the President's cable and our reply, fresh trouble broke out in the North which called for his personal attention.

(b) *The morale of the Chinese Army*

Of the Chinese army at the front we are unable to speak. Those we saw within the non-combatant army looked fairly well dressed and otherwise well set up; but from conversation with some of them we gathered there was a good deal of discontent owing to the fact that their pay is often in arrears, and generally no great enthusiasm was evinced. But it must be repeated that as far as those in the active fighting line are concerned, we have no knowledge. The question was put to a number of Generals and other high officers in the Government army as to how things were going, but nothing definite could be extracted.

Se far as we could see, it appeared that unless some intervention can come from outside, either the war can go on interminably or there will have to be an agreement as to partition.

(c) *The value of British United Aid to China*

We are not quite clear as to what this question means. If it refers (as it probably does) to Lady Cripps' Fund,[3] then there was ample evidence, in work done on behalf of the 'derelict' children and others in need, that it had been of very substantial help. It is true that here and there among the British community one did hear comments to the effect that they thought such aid was not necessary having regard to the stringent conditions obtaining at home. But so far as we could gather from the Chinese and

[3] Lady Cripps was the wife of Sir Stafford Cripps, Chancellor of the Exchequer, 1947-50. The report was correct in its assumption that 'Lady Cripps' Fund' was a charitable foundation known as 'British United Aid to China'.

those concerned with the administration of the Fund and the care of distressed persons, it has been of undoubted benefit.

British stock stands very high; in fact it is much higher than that of the United States. The Chinese appear to have a hope that in some way we might intervene in order that this draining of the blood and treasure of China might cease. Over eighty per cent of their revenue is expended in war potential.

(d) The Chinese Communists

The Mission was invited to visit Communist areas, but as we were the guests of the Chinese Government, who quite evidently did not approve of our so accepting, it was thought inadvisable to pursue the matter.

It is difficult to say what is their strength and influence, although there is proof that many who are in the Communist ranks are not there willingly. For example, a memorandum was handed to us in Nanking from the people of Inner Mongolia, in which they pointed out that they were quite unwillingly supporters of the Communists, with whose ideologies they had no sympathy, but by the nature of their geographical position they were fairly helpless.

A good deal of what is called Communism is just plain banditism. It is estimated there are not less than 40,000 organised bandits in the province of Kwantung alone; and when we visited Fatshan, which is a little off the regular road, we had to have almost an army to protect us, although no occasion for such was apparent.

We gathered from numbers of the refugees who are flowing into Southern China that the farmers feel bitter against the Communists, who destroy their crops, loot their possessions and force their young men into the army. What percentage of the Communist army these enforced conscripts constitute it is impossible to say; but they cannot be too willing participants and presumably it is only the necessity of having to live on the land which forces them to act with the Communists.[4]

(e) The attitude of the Chinese Government and people towards this country

The attitude of the Chinese Government and people towards this country is undoubtedly friendly. Wherever we went we were received with the most cordial welcome from all sorts and condition of people—not only from members of the Government but from the universities, schools and welfare associations, which brought us into touch very largely with what

---

[4] Lord Ammon was asked by Mr. Scott to report separately on the issue of whether there was evidence to suggest that the Russians were assisting the Communists. In his reply of 4 December Lord Ammon reported a conversation with the Commissioner of Police at Tientsin who advanced what seemed to be 'conclusive evidence' that the Russians had handed over captured Japanese weapons. When questioned, Chiang Kai-shek had taken the opposite view that there was no evidence of Russian assistance. Lord Ammon concluded: 'I cannot advance any further evidence, beyond just a comment that it is difficult to imagine how the rebels can get sufficient supplies of munitions except through some outside source, and certainly they seem to be better armed than the Government troops' (letter to Mr. Bevin of 4 December, F 16079/28/10).

one would call popular opinion—keeping in mind, however, that 'popular opinion' apparently does not include the tremendous mass of poverty-stricken people in China who have all they can do to rake up a living or a mere existence.

We did sense something of a tense atmosphere in the universities. Since the big demonstrations in the summer there have been sporadic outbreaks of conflict between students, sometimes supported by members of the faculty and the Government in many parts of China. We had the most cordial reception from the students, who were evidently very friendly towards this country, and so far as it was possible we took every opportunity of strengthening that feeling.

We were assured by the British community that there was very little anti-British feeling in China.[5] There is some feeling against all foreigners, but it is the Americans, and not the British towards whom hostility is primarily expressed. Some Chinese blame the Americans for prolonging the war by intervention and those who sympathise with the Communists are angered by the American policy.

In addition we were favourably impressed by the attitude of the British business community. Many of them, in spite of the difficulties under which they attempt to do business at the present time, seem to have a real understanding and sympathy with the Chinese. We soon became aware of the fact that very many of this community had spent a large part of the war in Japanese concentration camps, and out of this experience there may have been born a philosophic attitude towards present difficulties.

(f) Long-term British prospects—effects of American competition and Chinese nationalism

Just now the Chinese are very much on top of themselves with their newly-found nationalism and are what one might call a little 'heady'; but we have every reason to believe that the prospects of trading in the long run are good. British business men in China feel that a country of 400,000,000 people cannot live forever without world trade; but they see little or no prospect of doing much business until the civil war is over and economic stability is restored throughout the country.

We were particularly involved in a controversy in press conferences about British shipping in Chinese waters.[6] From the start a confusion arose

[5] Mr. A.L. Scott minuted on 30 January 1948 that this 'read strangely in the light of recent events in Kowloon and Canton' (cf. No. 38 below). He continued: 'The fact is that there is a great deal of latent anti-foreign feeling in the mass, and a great feeling of friendliness to individuals: anti-British feeling can easily be aroused especially in South China over Hong Kong. The intelligentsia in particular are nearly all xenophobes. The most violent of the demonstrators at Canton appear to have been students from Chung Shan University.'

[6] The *Peiping Chronicle* of 15 October reported Lord Ammon as saying at a press conference that any ship flying any flag was allowed to sail unimpeded up the River Thames and the Manchester Ship Canal (16584/28/10). When asked at a press conference what might be done to improve trade between the UK and China, Lord Ammon, according to his own account, replied that China's inland waterways should be opened to British shipping. His remarks

as to whether the Mission, through its leader, had asked for rights of port-to-port trading or whether what was intended to suggest that Nanking and Hankow should again become ports for ocean-going shipping. The Mission received a mixed press on this issue towards the middle of our stay; but before we left China there were more favourable comments, both in the press and in conversation. We quote two instances from the *China Press*:

One, dated from Shanghai on November 6th, was headed:

AMMON ARGUMENT SUPPORTED

and in the course of a leading article it was said

'The gain to British shipping firms, for a long time the chief carriers of freight along the Yangtse, should be obvious; but the gain to China's national economy as a whole should be even more obvious. We believe in this case the point has nothing to do with national sovereignty.'

From another paper we quote the following:

'For the time being at least permission for foreign ships to navigate Chinese rivers means only quicker rehabilitation and acceleration of mobilisation measures. We do not see what harm China suffers in consequence.'

The difficulties confronting the resumption of trade are obviously very great. The Chinese wish to buy from Britain and believe there is much that we have to offer. The increasing economic difficulties, of which the steadily falling dollar is an index, result in new restrictions being constantly imposed. However, the total prohibition of any particular import is not in fact in China an insuperable barrier. To give an example: while we were in China shark fins were banned as a course at meals as being an expensive imported luxury. Within a fortnight it was announced that existing stocks might still be consumed, and we were probably not wrong in drawing the conclusion that further imports would continue to arrive.

China today desperately needs to export, but it appears that the business interests dominating the Government are those of importers and not exporters. This is probably one amongst many of the factors which may undermine the economic position of the National Government.

The position of British traders in China today is vastly different from what it was when extraterritoriality protected them and the concessions provided a secure base for operations.

In spite of this, and particularly in the light of the quotations from the *China Press* concerning resumption of trade on the waterways, the outlook is not too gloomy and trade seems capable of revival.

In conclusion we would like to express our personal thanks to our generous Chinese hosts and to all who did so much to make our journey

resulted in adverse comment in sections of the Chinese press about a return to the unequal treaties (letter to Mr. Bevin, 25 November, F 15815/28/10).

interesting and profitable—not least to the Consular and allied services whom we met and members of the several British communities.

AMMON
FRANK MCLEAVY
MARTIN LINDSAY
AMULREE[7]

[7] One member of the Mission, Mr. Roberts, did not sign the report. Mr. Scott attributed his reluctance to the fact that he sympathised with the 'anti-Kuomintang view of the students with whom he came into contact'.

No. 35

Minute from Mr. Bevin to Mr. Attlee

[FO 800/462]

Top Secret   FOREIGN OFFICE, *22 December 1947*

Prime Minister,

I have been considering what steps should now be taken to implement the proposal to have talks with the Americans on an official level about the Far East.[1]

2. Although Mr. Marshall agreed to the inclusion of Canada and Australia in the scope of these talks, I am on reflection very doubtful whether, on security grounds, it would be wise to have so large a gathering in the first instance. Our Middle East talks[2] have shown that it is possible for UK and American officials to get round a table without attracting attention, but the risk of leakage will increase if we add to their numbers. Much as I appreciate, therefore, the concern of the Secretary of State for Commonwealth Relations to include at any rate Canada and Australia, I feel we should aim in the first instance at bilateral conversations. We should of course keep the Dominions informed and try to bring them in at an appropriate stage before reaching any final conclusions.

3. I consider that the talks should cover the political, economic and strategic field for the whole region from Afghanistan to the Pacific and that we should recommend this to the United States. My reason is that from Afghanistan to Malaya inclusive, and beyond to Borneo and Hong Kong, British influence at present exceeds that of the United States. In China,

[1] During discussions with Mr. Bevin in London on 17-18 December, Mr. Marshall had agreed to official Anglo-American talks on the Far East.

[2] Secret Anglo-American talks on the Middle East, involving the FO, the State Department, and the British and American Chiefs of Staff, were held in the Pentagon between 16 October and 7 November 1947. The main concern of both countries was to prevent the Soviet Union gaining influence in the region. The UK record of the talks is in FO 800/476, ME/47/21. For the US record, see *FRUS 1947*, vol. v, pp. 488-626.

Japan and Korea on the other hand, though our prestige remains high, our economic and financial position does not enable us to enter into any material commitments. Our influence in the western part of the area I have designated might therefore be used as a counterpoise to American influence in the eastern part. Up to now the Americans have shown an apparent reluctance to be frank about their policy towards China, Japan and Korea, and I feel that these talks might pave the way to a better understanding in the future.

4. I realise, of course, that to cover this area means to bring in India and Pakistan, but I think the scope of the discussions should be confined to UK policy in these Dominions.

5. I should like to consult with the Minister of Defence and Secretary of State for Commonwealth Relations (to whom I am sending a copy of this minute) in order to put concrete proposals before you.[3]

[3] Mr. Bevin discussed this proposal with the Prime Minister on 23 December and it was agreed that the Dominions would have to be involved from the outset. It then emerged that the US would fight shy of any Dominion participation because of doubts over security within the Australian Government. The proposed talks with the Americans were therefore put on hold. In the meantime the Minister of Defence, Mr. A.V. Alexander, reported in a letter of 19 January 1948 to Mr. Bevin that the Chiefs of Staff felt that discussions on Western Europe were more important than talks on the Far East. They did not, however, wish to press their view to the point of giving the Americans the impression 'that we do not want to play on Far East questions' (AN 517/45/45). The talks with the US never materialised for reasons that are explained in No. 43.

Chapter IV

1948

No. 36

Minute from Sir O. Sargent to Mr. Attlee
PM/48/OS/1 [FO 800/462]

FOREIGN OFFICE, *1 January 1948*

Prime Minister

The Chinese Government, through their agent in Canada, have asked us to supply 1000 Hispano-Suiza guns as armament for Mosquito aircraft which are being sold to them by the Canadian Government. The guns are available and the value of the order would be about £30,000.

2. The policy of His Majesty's Government which is based on the Moscow Declaration of 1945,[1] has been not to supply arms to the Chinese Government as long as the present civil war continues. A request from the Chinese Government for war materials addressed to us in October 1946 caused the Foreign Secretary, who was then in Paris, to discuss the problem with Mr. Byrnes. In agreement with the United States Government the embargo was maintained.[2]

3. I think the time has come to reconsider this policy of complete embargo in the light of:

   1. the situation in China,
   2. the present attitude of the US Government and Canadian,
   3. in view of the developments set out below, I would recommend that this particular request of the Chinese Government for the supply of Hispano-Suiza guns be met, and that future requests by the Chinese for war materials be considered on their merits as they reach us.

4. The military and economic situation is widely admitted to be critical, even in official Chinese circles. The Communist forces, hitherto largely confined to North China, have recently broken into the Yangtse basin, while in Manchuria they have successfully renewed their offensive and

[1] See No. 6.
[2] See Nos. 14 and 15.

Mukden is now virtually invested. Inflation continues to gather pace and Sir R. Stevenson reports that the Central Government's prestige has fallen in recent weeks. It would seem to be in the interests of HMG that the Central Government of Chiang Kai-shek should not collapse since the only viable alternative is a Communist and ultimately a Russian-dominated Government.

4. [*sic*] Though we are committed under the Moscow Declaration to non-interference in the internal affairs of China, the only Government which we recognise is that of Chiang Kai-shek. It is, I submit, in this context that the question of the supply of arms must be considered. In June 1947 the United States Government appear to have reversed their policy of prohibiting supplies by deciding to grant licences for the export to China of such war materials as China could buy. The Canadian Government, who had assured us as recently as May 1947 that their policy was to 'maintain a complete embargo on all export of arms to China', have lost no time in following the United States lead by arranging to sell to the Chinese Mosquito aircraft in substantial quantities (the number varies from 150 to 300 machines). It is for these reasons that the guns are required.

5. In the present instance Messrs. Rolls Royce might have sold £1 million worth of engines from surplus reconditioned stock had not the embargo intervened. The aircraft (which are a British type) are none the less fitted with Rolls Royce engines, manufactured under licence in America during the war and surplus to requirements. Clearly, then, our policy no longer even prevents China from receiving British equipment. It merely debars British firms from selling.[3]

O.G. SARGENT

[3] Sir O. Sargent and Mr. Dening discussed this minute with Mr. Attlee on 2 January. The Prime Minister approved the release of 1000 Hispano-Suiza guns as armament for Mosquito aircraft, subject to the US Government's being notified in advance and to the Canadian Government's being informed. He also directed that no publicity should be given to the decision (minute by Mr. Dening of 19 January, F 22/34/10).

On a more public basis and in order to assist in the post-war reconstruction of the Chinese Navy, the UK transferred to China in May a cruiser, eight harbour defence motor launches (already on loan to China) and, for a period of five years, a destroyer (Cmd. 7457, 1948).

No. 37

Sir R. Stevenson (Nanking) to Mr. Bevin

No. 83 [*F 2535/33/10*]

Confidential   NANKING, *2 February 1948*

Sir,

I have the honour to enclose herewith copies of the President's New Year message and of Mao Tze-tung's report to the Central Committee of the Chinese Communist Party, which was made on Christmas Day.[1]

2. The President's remarks contain little that is new and do not seem to be inspired by any large measure of self-confidence. He speaks of the two great strategical objects which have been achieved by the nationalist forces, but one of these (the capture of Yenan) has been singularly barren of results and the second (the Government offensive in Shantung) brought, for the most part, but temporary gains. The price paid is admitted to have been a heavy one. It is of interest to note that the President takes to task the inhabitants of big cities, who have so often impressed foreigners by their lack of patriotism and general insouciance, on the ground that they have made the economic situation worse than it need have been.

3. On the other hand Mao Tze-tung's report breathes a spirit of complete and unshaken confidence in the imminent triumph of the Chinese Communist Party. A very brief review of it is given later in this despatch (see paragraphs 5 and 6 below) but in connexion with its advocacy of a united front, it is convenient to digress for a moment and touch on the statement of policy recently issued in Hong Kong by the Kuomintang Revolutionary Committee (please see Chancery letter No. S/O 51 of January 27th)[2] together with the historical background of that policy. This Committee of left-wing Kuomintang members, with a leavening of Democratic League[3] and others, favours a return to the principles enunciated by the First National Party Congress of the Kuomintang, which was held in Canton in January 1924. That Congress endorsed the policy of co-operation with Russia and the admission of Communists to the Party. (Dr. Sung Yat-sen had had a full discussion with the Soviet envoy Joffe[4]

[1] Not printed.

[2] Issued on 1 January 1949, this statement called for the overthrow of 'the re-actionary dictatorial rule of Chiang Kai-shek' and a return to the three main policies of the Chinese Revolution that had been agreed by the Kuomintang in 1924. These were association with Russia, admission of CCP members, and assistance to the workers and peasants (F 12258/154/10).

[3] See No. 17, note 14.

[4] Adolf Joffe or Yoffe was chief delegate on the Soviet side (until January 1918, when he was replaced by Leon Trotsky) in the negotiations preceding the Treaty of Brest-Litovsk between Bolshevik Russia and Germany. He made a declaration with Dr. Sun Yat-sen in January 1923

and had been greatly impressed with the merits of Communism; it must, however, be added that, while an interesting comparison can be made between Sun and Lenin, they differed in that the former was at the same time a warm admirer of many western political ideas, as his hotch-potch constitution bears witness.) In fact, if Dr. Sun threw himself into the arms of the Russians, it was not entirely by design. Approaches to the British, American and German Governments for assistance in training the Cantonese forces had been unsuccessful. With Russia it was different. Borodin's[5] services were made available and he undertook to obtain from Russia not only arms and ammunition, but civil and military experts.

4. The Russian part in the reorganisation of the Kuomintang was important; equally so was their work in ensuring, by efficient preliminary propaganda, the success of the Northern expedition of 1926.[6] So thoroughly was this work done that it is almost certain that Communist cells in Hunan (and probably also in Kiangsi) have survived up to the present time. The sequel to the Soviet-Kuomintang alliance is well known. Chiang Kai-shek and others became violently anti-Communist, and lack of tact on the part of the Russian advisers no doubt added fuel to the flame. The Chinese communists, after years of effort, were at last prised out of Kiangsi by Chiang and made their historic trek to North-west China.[7]

5. It is to the period of the Communists' sojourn in Kiangsi (1931-1934) that some of Mao Tze-tung's most interesting passages refer. He stigmatises the 'ultra-left and erroneous policy' carried out during this period in dealing with agrarian reform and with the 'petty bourgeoisie and middle bourgeoisie economic elements'. As far as is known, this is the first occasion on which an explicit recantation of former errors has been made by the Leader of the Chinese Communist Party. Nowadays the harsh policy of victimising the richer peasants and landlords is no longer regarded as correct. Instead, they are to be treated in the same way as the mass of the peasants. The views of the middle class of peasants should be considered and concessions should be made to them if necessary as (presumably on account of the fact that they are very numerous) it is of great importance to attach them to the Communist Party. Again, the small business man was formerly harshly treated, whereas it is now clear that 'the economy of independent small industrial and commercial business men, and the economy of small and private capital' have an important part to play in the future China as contemplated by Mao. (This dilution of the pure milk

as a result of which Chinese Communists were admitted to the Kuomintang and Soviet aid to China in arms and advisers was increased.

[5] Michael Borodin was the main Soviet emissary in China in the 1920s and a key influence in steering Kuomintang policy in an 'anti-imperialist' direction.

[6] A reference to Chiang Kai-shek's Northern expedition which expanded the area of China controlled by the Kuomintang. Its success was in part the result of Communist help in organising pro-KMT risings among the peasants and workers.

[7] See *DBFP*, Second Series, Volume XX, Nos. 211, 268 and 313.

of Communist doctrine is reminiscent of the tactical concessions and withdrawals made by Communist parties in South-eastern Europe—particularly Yugoslavia—before they had established themselves firmly in control.) From Section E of the report it will be seen that the Party claims a membership of no less than 2,700,000, making it the largest Communist party outside Russia, but that not all members are considered worthy and the possibility of a purge is indicated.

6. He stresses the necessity for the 'broadest United Front' to carry through the 'Chinese New Democratic Revolution'. Inevitably, any 'United Front' (even that which the Kuomintang Revolutionary Committee appear to have in mind) must (in Mao's words) be under the 'firm leadership of the Chinese Communist Party'. Finally after drawing attention to the establishment of 'Cominform' in Europe[8] he says 'all anti-Imperialist forces of the various eastern countries should also unite to oppose oppression of imperialism and reactionaries'. Some may think this an allusion to the rumoured establishment of a Far Eastern Cominform at Harbin. This supposition appears to me to be premature. There is little doubt that Mao Tze-tung as leader of the largest Communist Party in the Far East is in a position at any moment to create a Far Eastern Cominform, should this appear desirable in Moscow, but there is as yet no confirmation that such a step has been taken.

7. In estimating the degree of support for or acquiescence in, a United Front, it must be remembered that the Kuomintang Revolutionary Committee by no means comprises all those in favour of an understanding with the Communists. There is, first of all, a mass of more or less inarticulate liberal opinion which sees no military solution of the Kuomintang-Communist dispute. Secondly, there are important elements in North China who are so heartily sick of the civil war and the inefficiency and rapacity of the present Chinese Government that they would be likely in the event, say, of the loss of Manchuria to seek agreement locally with the Communists. There are also the followers of the proscribed Democratic League whose main objective remains the termination of the civil war by negotiation. Finally, there are numbers of influential people like Shao Li-tzu, Secretary General of the People's Political Council, who would be in favour of the elimination of the Generalissimo, by means, for instance, of an extended trip abroad during which negotiations could be initiated by the Vice President of the Republic to which post they would like to see Li Tsung-jen,[9] at present in charge of the Generalissimo's Northern Headquarters, elected.

8. Many competent observers are convinced that despite American help to the present Chinese Government the establishment of some degree of

[8] The Communist Information Bureau was established at a conference of East European communist parties at Warsaw in September 1947.

[9] Appointed in September 1945 director of Chiang Kai-shek's provisional headquarters in Peking.

Communist control over part, if not over the whole of China, is only a question of time. Whether this is certain or not, it is tempting to speculate on the form which Communism would assume in China and the effect it would have on foreign interests. Optimists will cling to the hope that the many differences between Chinese and Russian society will force it to adopt modifications which will render it less objectionable to Western susceptibilities. The Kuomintang Revolutionary Committee has condemned the Bureau of Statistics, which is the Kuomintang version of the MVD.[10] It would indeed be unfortunate for the Chinese people if the Bureau, which is universally detested by all progressive elements, were to be sovietised. The MVD has a far longer pedigree and a far greater measure of acceptance—or so at least it would seem—than has the Bureau; but it is difficult, if not impossible, to imagine a regime under Communist leadership without a political police department and it can be taken for granted that some organisation of the kind will exist if only to deal with 'counter-revolution'.

9. There are great differences in the cultural sphere between China and Russia. It does not seem that any class in the latter country ever corresponded to the scholar gentry, which has played such a large part in making China the country she is. The Academia Sinica bears at present no resemblance whatever to its Russian counterpart; in general the attitude to culture in China is very much less self-conscious. Here the students have traditionally been leaders of public opinion. At the present time, when there is no 'middle way' and they are forced to choose between the Kuomintang and the Communists, many of the best students choose the latter. There is a continual trickle, amounting in some months to a few dozen and in others to a hundred or more, of students from Peking to the Communist areas. Nevertheless, the 'middle way' remains that which the student would prefer to see adopted, and it is possible that this general attitude would make itself felt in a Communist China.

10. Two most obvious points remain to be made. First, China cannot exclude foreigners by means of an iron curtain, for she has far too many of her own nationals abroad. She depends on remittances from the latter and will continue to absorb their ideas. The process of turning China into an orthodox Communist state would therefore be extremely slow, if, indeed, it ever proved possible. Secondly, South China (like North China) must change her form of agriculture; but even the purest Soviet doctrinaire will agree that collectivisation is impossible in that land of rice fields at all levels. Apart therefore from re-distribution of land, co-operation, fertilisers (at present used on a large scale only in Taiwan) and an attack on the problem of debt would appear to be the lines on which a Communist-dominated regime would concentrate.

11. So far as British interests are concerned it is impossible to guess what effect such a regime would have. There is no reason to suppose that there

---

[10] *Ministerstvo Vnutrennykh Del* (Soviet Ministry of Internal Affairs).

is any more hostility towards Britain among the Chinese Communists than towards any other foreign country, leaving aside the United States of America. Nor is there any particular reason to suppose that Mao's report which only attacks America was edited in order to make it acceptable in Hong Kong (though this is, of course, not impossible) as Communist publications there have not troubled to be markedly tender towards us. All that can be said with certainty is that the question of the treatment to be meted out to British interests would be decided on grounds of pure expediency. Indications have it is true been given from time to time by the Communists that foreign traders would be encouraged to continue their activities, but no doubt everything would depend on how the situation developed. The Kailan Mining Administration would very probably be nationalised as would the other mines in which we are interested. British shipping interests in China have not so much to lose, now that they no longer enjoy cabotage rights and it does not seem likely that they would be any worse treated than they are at present.

12. As regards Soviet Russia, it seems possible that, while so much else is in her favour, she would find that her policy in Sinkiang, which appears to be aimed at the absorption of part of that province, and at Dairen would cause her the same kind of embarrassment as did her Mongolian policy in 1924.[11]

13. Of all foreign commercial interests those of the United States are the most likely to be adversely affected. They are not so deeply rooted as are ours, nor are they of course so extensive. It seems unlikely that they would persist in trying to weather the storm. But the major effect of a change to Communist leadership would naturally be on the political and strategic interests of the United States of America and would presumably lead the United States Government to concentrate on a wide defensive ring based on Japan.

14. Finally, there is little doubt that the work of all foreign missionaries would be rigorously curtailed except where it is of immediate practical benefit to the local inhabitants, as in the case of hospitals and dispensaries. Religious activities would certainly be stopped and educational establishments taken over by the authorities.

15. I am sending a copy of this despatch with enclosures to His Majesty's Ambassadors in Moscow and Washington.

I have, etc.,

RALPH SKRINE STEVENSON

[11] A treaty of May 1924 between the Chinese Republic and Soviet Russia acknowledged Chinese sovereignty over Mongolia but in effect recognised the territory as a Soviet protectorate.

No. 38

Minute by China Department on Kowloon Walled City

[*F 2022/154/10*]

FOREIGN OFFICE, *4 February 1948*

Before it is possible to reach a settlement with the Chinese Government on the question of the Kowloon walled city, it is necessary to decide whether His Majesty's Government wish to admit the principle of Chinese jurisdiction over the 6½ acres of waste land known as the 'Walled City', or not.

This paper summarises the history of the fifty-year-old controversy, recent developments, the various suggestions which have been made for a negotiated settlement with the Chinese, and recommends a course of action.

1. *Historical Background*

Under the Anglo-Chinese Convention for the extension of Hong Kong territory dated 9th June, 1898, it was agreed that 'within the city of Kowloon the Chinese officials now stationed there shall continue to exercise jurisdiction except in so far as may be inconsistent with the military requirements for the defence of Hong Kong. Within the remainder of the newly leased territory Great Britain shall have sole jurisdiction.' An Order in Council issued 20th October, 1898 providing for the Government of the leased territories at Hong Kong laid down (Article IV) that 'the Chinese officials now stationed within the city of Kowloon shall continue to exercise jurisdiction therein except in so far as may be inconsistent with the military requirements for the defence of Hong Kong'.

Disturbances occurred after the signing of the 1898 Convention and repeated attacks were made on the British forces by Chinese troops in uniform and local mobs. Representations made to the Chinese authorities having led to no result, the Governor of Hong Kong was authorised to deal with the matter locally, and, with the approval of Her Majesty's Government, the city of Kowloon was occupied on the 16th May, 1899 by British forces. In reply to complaints addressed to Her Majesty's Government through the Chinese Minister in London at the expulsion of Chinese troops and officials from the city of Kowloon, the Secretary of State in a note of the 30th May, 1899, stated as follows:

In view of the fact that the Chinese Government do not hold themselves responsible for attacks by local mobs on British troops, the obligation falls on Her Majesty's Government of performing the duty which is usually performed by the Sovereign of the country, but which the Chinese Government declined. After the recent experience which they have had not only of the worthlessness of the protection extended by the Chinese garrison of Kowloon, but of the additional danger involved in its presence, it is impossible for Her Majesty's Government to allow the resumption of Chinese authority within that city.

The Chinese Government made further strong representations but Her Majesty's Government refused to yield, and a second Order in Council was issued on the 27th December, 1899, revoking Article IV of the Order in Council of the 20th October, 1898, and applying the provisions of that Order in Council to the city of Kowloon 'as if the said city had by the said Order in Council been declared to be part and parcel of Her Majesty's Colony of Hong Kong'.

No question appears to have been raised as to our position until 1933 when the Hong Kong Government proposed to expropriate certain Chinese owners of property in the city of Kowloon. Chinese protests at this proposal claimed that 'the city of Kowloon remains under the jurisdiction of China', and our legal position was then examined with the conclusion that from the point of view of jurisdiction we were not on very strong ground but that a prescriptive right had been established for the exercise of British jurisdiction in the city of Kowloon in as much as the Chinese Government having tacitly acquiesced for over thirty years could not now say that we were not rightly there, or, alternatively, that the exercise of Chinese jurisdiction was still inconsistent with the military requirements for the defence of Hong Kong as laid down in the Convention of 1898.[1]

The matter continued to be the subject of dispute throughout 1935, 1936 and the first half of 1937, the Chinese maintaining their attitude on the jurisdictional issue while we argued for the most part that the clearance of the area in question was necessary on the grounds of public health and civic amenities. On the outbreak of hostilities between China and Japan in July 1937, the matter went into abeyance where it remained until the present time.

2. *Recent developments*

In recent weeks agitation has been artificially stimulated by Chinese elements with the obvious purpose of reviving the question of jurisdiction over the walled city. Though the reason for reviving this question at this particular juncture is as yet obscure, the agitation gave rise to incidents over the eviction of squatters from the site of the walled city by the Hong Kong administration as a normal precaution against fire and disease.[1]

Initially on the 6th January, 1948 the Chinese Government made a formal protest to His Majesty's Embassy against the evictions in the course

---

[1] The sequence of events which led to the eviction of Chinese squatters from the Walled City of Kowloon, an area no larger than Berkeley Square in London, began in November 1947 when the Hong Kong Government issued eviction notices. These were ignored and on 16 December the local magistrate ordered all illegal persons to be evicted and all unauthorised structures dismantled. A week later details of alternative accommodation sites for the squatters were published. On 5 January 1948, the evictions were carried out, with police backing, and two arrests were made for incitement to resist. On 12 January some of the squatters returned. Police action to remove them led to four injuries and one fatality (F 860/154/10).

of which the question of jurisdiction was not raised. By January 8th their attitude had hardened and His Majesty's Ambassador received a memorandum which painted an exaggerated picture of protests disregarded and of Chinese evicted from humble dwellings by large detachments of police, and requested His Majesty's Government to prevent the Hong Kong Government from continuing their eviction measures and immediately to order the release of those arrested, the cessation of further arrests and the provision of proper accommodation for those dispossessed. The memorandum sought to justify this attitude on the grounds that the Chinese Government have never relinquished their jurisdiction over Kowloon walled city, and concluded with the following paragraph:

> The Ministry of Foreign Affairs now formally declare to the British Embassy that, in accordance with the provisions of the said Convention, the Chinese Government enjoys jurisdiction over the City of Kowloon and that they have no intention whatsoever of renouncing this jurisdiction. The Chinese Government are quite unable to consider as legitimate any measures in breach of the Convention of 1898 respecting an extension of Hong Kong territory adopted by the British Government, either in the past or in the future. Should the British Government have a different interpret[at]ion of the said Convention, they should seek an equitable and legitimate settlement through the usual diplomatic channels.

The Chinese Press simultaneously took up the same line of argument and began assiduously to fan the spark of anti-British feeling with every propaganda device. From informal conversations at the Chinese Ministry of Foreign Affairs it soon became clear that as a result of all the agitation the matter had by January 15th become one of 'face'. Support for this view is lent by a further note from the Chinese Minister for Foreign Affairs formally demanding:

> (1) the withdrawal of the Hong Kong police stationed in Kowloon City;

> (2) the payment by His Majesty's Government of appropriate compensation for the physical injuries and property losses suffered by the inhabitants in Kowloon City;

> (3) an enquiry to establish who fired and who issued the order to fire in Kowloon City on January 12th and their punishment.

The only written communication which has so far been made to the Chinese on the British side is contained in a note addressed to the Chinese Ministry of 24th January. In this we specifically decline to go into the jurisdictional issue but, after a full statement of the facts of the case, make it clear that the Hong Kong Government was fully justified in deciding to clear the area and showed every consideration for the squatters in the measures taken to evict them consistent with good administration and the maintenance of law and order. Further, that in His Majesty's Government's opinion it would be quite wrong for the Hong Kong Government, on account of the jurisdiction issue, to refrain from taking such administrative measures in respect of Kowloon City as are necessary in the interests of the community as a whole. The note goes on to express regret at the standpoint adopted by the Po On Magistrate[2] and at the local Press, and concludes with the request that steps be taken to bring the facts of the case before the Chinese public.

In conversations both in London and Nanking it has been represented to the Chinese from the first that they were deliberately confusing the issue by raising the question of jurisdiction in connexion with a purely administrative matter. We were not prepared to pander to Chinese agitation but all proper steps would be taken to see that no-one with a right to live in Kowloon City was expelled.

3. *Proposals for a settlement*

(a) The Chinese Minister has made the tentative and personal suggestion that since a Customs Agreement has been concluded recently between China and the Government of Hong Kong[3] a possible solution of the Walled City controversy might be reached by allowing the Chinese Maritime Customs to use the site for their offices and customs sheds. This suggestion was put to the Governor who rejected it both on its merits, since the site is judged unsuitable and also because it would be regarded locally as complete surrender to the Chinese claim.

(b) The Chinese Minister for Foreign Affairs has proposed that the site be turned into an unfenced garden in which should be erected one building for the office of the Commissioner for Foreign Affairs of the Provinces of Kwantung and Kwangsi, any necessary police, guards or park-keepers being provided by the Hong Kong Government. The Governor considers this proposal open to even graver objection than that in (a) above.

(c) The Government of Hong Kong have already announced their intention of tidying up the area and making it into a public park for the benefit of the community. Sir A. Grantham is willing for this proposal now to be put forward to the Chinese Government, adding that the park would be called the Sun-Yat-Sen Memorial Park and that it would be policed and maintained by the Hong Kong Government.

(d) His Majesty's Consul General, Canton, has offered the suggestion that the area be allotted to the Chinese Government as the site of their future

[2] Po On is the Cantonese reading of Bao-an, the name of a town to the north-west of Hong Kong, on the Pearl River delta.

[3] This agreement, signed at Nanking on 12 January 1948, provided for the limited operation in Hong Kong of the Chinese Maritime Customs in order more effectively to control smuggling between Hong Kong and China. For the UK therefore it represented a partial surrender of sovereign rights, which made it all the more important that the agreement was signed on behalf of the UK by the Ambassador, not by the Hong Kong Government (F 2153, 11013/179/10; F 10180/154/10).

Consulate-General. On this the Governor has commented that it affects the Sovereignty issue more than does the park proposal but that it does not settle it. Moreover, it would, in His Excellency's view, be claimed as a victory by the Chinese.

(*e*) Finally the Chinese Embassy in London have echoed proposal (*b*), adding the rider that police, water, electricity and other public utility requirements would be provided by the municipal authorities of Kowloon leased territory.[4]

Proposals (*a*) and (*b*) are clearly unacceptable. Proposal (*c*) as it stands offers no solution to the jurisdictional issue. Proposal (*d*) has certain merits in as much as there is an aura of extraterritoriality about Consular premises which should commend it to the Chinese, though this claim has little or no foundation in international law. Moreover, it is one of the Governor of Hong Kong's express wishes to see Chinese representation regularised by the appointment of a Consul-General. To propose this solution is, however, open to a risk inherent in the fact that the Chinese Government have shown no sign of wishing to make any such appointment. We might thus be faced in the end with a Chinese Government building, housing the Provincial Commissioner for Foreign Affairs.

4. Though the Chinese attitude on the Walled City issue has all the appearance of blackmail there is no doubt of the existence of a genuine feeling on the part of many Chinese for the return of Hong Kong to China, and it is evidently the policy of the Kuomintang to keep agitation alive on this subject until they regard the time as ripe for making a formal approach. To shelve the issue of jurisdiction over the Walled City once more would merely be to provide the Chinese Government with the means of sustaining agitation, and it would therefore seem to be in our interests to achieve a settlement if we can do so without seriously weakening our own position in Hong Kong.

5. *Recommendation*

In these circumstances it is recommended that a solution be sought whereby we accept the principle of Chinese jurisdiction over Kowloon Walled City but the Chinese agree not to attempt to exercise that jurisdiction in practice.

A public garden controlled by the municipal authorities of Kowloon Leased territory offers such a solution and so would a Chinese consular compound, if the Chinese could first be induced to agree in principle to the appointment of a Consul General.[5]

---

[4] The UK also proposed that the area should become a Garden of Remembrance for the war dead. The Chinese Government was prepared to consider this but insisted on appointing five of the seven members on a proposed Board of Management. As with the other proposals, the Chinese also wanted jurisdiction (F 3133/154/10).

[5] The dispute over the Kowloon evictions was never resolved. On 16 January, in retaliation, Chinese demonstrators sacked and burned down the office of the UK Consulate General at

Canton and adjoining British property. A report by Mr. Hall, the Consul-General at Canton, was forwarded by Sir R. Stevenson on 7 February 1948 (F 2019/361/10). The Chinese government refused to consider a UK claim for compensation (estimated at first at £300,000 but later reduced to £225,000) unless their own claim to Kowloon were settled first. Mr. Dening minuted on 18 October: 'Though we refuse to allow Canton and Kowloon to be linked, the fact is that there is *no* prospect that the Chinese Govt. will give us satisfaction over Canton unless the Kowloon incident is first settled' (F 2019/15305/362/10).

No. 39

Minute by Mr. Dening

[F 4392/33/10]

FOREIGN OFFICE, *19 March 1948*

The China Association invited the Minister of State[1] and me to lunch at the Savoy on 12th March to discuss the China situation informally. Mr. W.J. Keswick[2] was in the chair, and in addition to Mr. Mitchell,[3] there were representatives of Shell, ICI,[4] Unilever and the BAT.

Mr. Keswick spoke on behalf of the Association and said they were very concerned about the situation in China. The Communists appeared to be achieving a considerable measure of success, and British mercantile interests, whose investments in China amounted to £300 million (as compared to £87 million of the United States), had to consider what the prospects were and what HMG might be prepared to do. Mr. Keswick wondered whether, in view of the possibility of Communist success, it would not be possible to appoint some unofficial representative with them while maintaining our Embassy with the National Government of China.

This led Mr. Keswick to the question of representation. In view of their anxieties, the China Association wished to be assured that HMG were fully conscious of the necessity of adequate representation in China. The Minister of State, in dealing with these points, said that HMG were fully aware of the situation in China and were watching it very closely. As to representation, both Shanghai and Canton had been mentioned, and the Minister of State explained that Mr. Ogden[5] was leaving; that we were fully conscious of the necessity of appointing a good successor but that we should probably have to go outside the former China Service in order to find him. Mr. Keswick, speaking for himself, but apparently with the agreement of the others present, said that he was inclined to think that

[1] Mr. H. McNeil. [2] See No. 1, note 11. [3] Secretary of the China Association.
[4] Imperial Chemical Industries [5] See No. 5, note 2.

selection from outside China might be a good thing. He also stressed the necessity of a good man at Canton. The Minister of State said that several moves were in contemplation in the near future which, we hoped, would tend to strengthen our representation in China.

On the question of representation with the Communists, the Minister of State made it clear that in present circumstances we could not contemplate such a step. If the Communist successes were such as to raise the question of whether British merchant interests should trade with them, that was for them to decide, and were they to find it possible to trade with the Communists, we should raise no objection. But for HMG to have contacts with the Communists would be quite another matter.

Our hosts raised the question of what would happen if Communist successes enabled them to gain possession of the larger cities, in particular Shanghai, where most of the British capital was invested. Would we be prepared, as was done when the Japanese were in Shanghai, to maintain an Embassy office there while possibly evacuating the main Embassy to Canton or somewhere in the south? The Minister of State indicated that we should have to consider the situation when it arose, but he was not prepared to state in advance that we would necessarily leave an Embassy office in Shanghai.

Allusion was made to the fact that we had not yet secured compensation for the destruction of our Consulate-General and adjacent buildings at Canton.[6] We had given the Chinese virtual extraterritorial rights in Hong Kong by virtue of the Customs Agreement[7] and appeared to have secured no *quid pro quo*. Mr. Keswick expressed the view that it was always a mistake to give the Chinese anything without securing something in return. When pressed as to what he would propose in relation to Canton, he suggested that Chinese claims for railway material commandeered by the army, as to which he was representing the Chinese Government, might be offset against our claims for Canton, which he assumed to amount to something in the nature of £100,000 (he did not disclose how he arrived at this figure). There were two Chinese claims, one of which he considered to be a good one, and the other possibly a bad one. The first was for material commandeered by the British military authorities before the Japanese attack on Hong Kong, and this he thought ought to be met. The other was for material which was presumably seized by the Japanese when they took Hong Kong, and the claim was therefore more doubtful.

At the close of the proceedings, the Minister of State suggested that if the China Association wished to be able to give its members some assurances about HMG's continuing interests in Chinese matters and about representation in China, they might address a letter to the Secretary of

[6] See No. 38, note 5.

[7] *V. ibid.*, note 3.

State on the subject. In that event Mr. McNeil felt sure that the Secretary of State would be willing to reply on the lines he had indicated.

M.E. DENING

No. 40

Memorandum by China Department on the Chinese Communists[1]

[*F 10028/33/10*]

Confidential   FOREIGN OFFICE, *1 April 1948*

It is now being argued that with the increasing success of the Chinese Communists His Majesty's Government should accord them recognition and open up trade with the territory controlled by them, namely, the so-called 'liberated areas', on the ground that the present Kuomintang Government at Nanking is down and out and in any case is inefficient and corrupt, and therefore unworthy of our continued support.

The present is therefore a suitable time at which to review the position of the Chinese Communists.

Communism has a history of about thirty years in China. Sun Yat-sen concluded an agreement with the Bolshevik M. Joffe at Shanghai in 1922.[2] In 1924 Chinese Communists were officially admitted members of the Kuomintang, and with Russian inspiration and guidance the Kuomintang armies penetrated into Central China. The split came in 1927. In that year M. Borodin and other Russian advisers were dismissed and a Chinese Communist Soviet was set up in the province of Kiangsi. After several campaigns the Communists made their celebrated 'Long March' and re-established themselves in the comparatively poor agricultural province of Shensi in 1935-36 with their headquarters at Yenan. There they developed a policy of agrarian reform, and largely abandoned the more ruthless and savage features of their régime in Kiangsi. With the outbreak of hostilities against Japan in July 1937 a working arrangement was reached with the Kuomintang, which, however, did not survive more than a few years, and

---

[1] This paper was prepared on Mr. Dening's instructions for consideration by the Russia Committee. In recent Parliamentary debates (cf. No. 41, note 9 below) there had been criticism of the Chinese Government and of US support for it, arguing that the Communists were more Chinese than Communist, Chiang Kai-shek's Government was rotten and its days were numbered, and that the UK should 're-insure' with the Communists as they were bound to win. The criticism was not confined to 'intellectual Left-Wingers'; some UK China merchants were also wondering whether to make contact with the Communists (see No. 39). The object of the memorandum according to Mr. Dening, was to 'put matters into their proper perspective'.

The Russia Committee recommended the memorandum should be recast as a Cabinet paper, and the version printed here was intended for submission to the Cabinet. However, Sir O. Sargent ruled that as the memorandum did not propose any action it should be printed and circulated to the King, Cabinet and Dominions instead (F 4391/33/10, F 2915, 8166/765/38).

[2] The date of the agreement was January 1923: see No. 37, note 4.

for the latter part of the war the Yenan area was closely blockaded by crack Kuomintang troops. After Japan's offer to surrender in August 1945, the Communist armies moved north-eastwards into North China, but were baulked of gaining control of the Peking-Tientsin area by the presence of American marines and by the action of the United States High Command in flying in Chinese troops to these areas. The Soviet armies in these circumstances delayed their evacuation of Manchuria until the Communist forces could be ferried across from Shantung and eventually withdrew in April 1946, leaving Japanese arms and ammunition to be picked up by the Communists.

In the meantime the three Foreign Secretaries of the USSR, United Kingdom and United States had decided at the Moscow Conference in December 1945 'as to the need for a unified and democratic China under the National Government, for broad participation by democratic elements in all branches of the National Government, and for a cessation of civil strife'.[3] In pursuance of this declaration, General Marshall, who on the resignation of General Hurley had gone to China as President Truman's Special Envoy, was able in January 1946 to bring the Kuomintang and the Communists together and an armistice agreement was signed. Differences soon developed, however, as to the integration of the Communist armies in the Nationalist forces and regarding the extension of the agreement to Manchuria. By June large-scale fighting had broken out in Manchuria which soon spread to the rest of China. Further attempts at compromise were pursued under General Marshall, but it became evident towards the close of 1946 that the Chinese Communists no longer desired entry to a coalition Government and a reorganised national army, and were pursuing a policy at variance with their interests as a purely Chinese political group. It is scarcely a coincidence that the breakdown of efforts at compromise coincided with a marked deterioration in relations between the United States and Russian Governments. The delay occasioned by these unprofitable negotiations worked in favour of the Communists, who at the end of 1946 were relatively stronger to the Kuomintang than they were at the beginning of the year. In January 1947 General Marshall threw in his hand and returned to the United States to become Secretary of State.[4] During 1947 the Communists persistently refused to enter into negotiations except on obviously unacceptable terms. General Chiang Kai-shek in July 1947 finally broke off negotiations by the issue of a general mobilisation order against the Communists,[5] whom he described as outlaws and rebels.

The Communist policy of systematically wrecking communications and any plant essential to the economic life of the country has met with growing success and, besides gaining control of nearly all Manchuria except for the towns of Mukden, Kirin and Changchun, where the position of the

[3] See No. 6.   [4] See No. 20, note 1.   [5] See No. 26, note 1.

Government forces is now critical, they have established themselves in force in Central China and have even penetrated the rice-growing province of Hunan, across the River Yangtze. With inflation gathering force by leaps and bounds the financial situation of the Chinese Government has grown from bad to worse. There has been a marked deterioration in morale in the Nationalist armies and among Government officials generally, particularly since General Wedemeyer's public strictures in August 1947,[6] and there is the feeling that the programme of American aid amounting to United States $540 million now under consideration by the United States Congress will have come too late to be effective.[7] Nevertheless, the Chinese Government have not abandoned hope that the United States Government, despite its dissatisfaction with the corrupt and reactionary elements in the Kuomintang, will take adequate steps to ensure that China does not fall under the control of the Chinese Communists and hence become subject to exclusive Russian influence.

Those sympathetic to the Chinese Communists have long argued that they are merely agrarian reformers and are 'more Chinese than Communist' and that their coming into power in China will not necessarily mean that China will become a dependency of Soviet Russia. As to these contentions, His Majesty's Ambassador at Nanking stated in November 1946 that he was convinced that whatever the rank and file might be 'the leaders of the party are Communists first, last, and all the time. They can thus be trusted not only to follow the "Party Line" in all circumstances, but automatically to serve the best interests of the Soviet Union.' He went on to express surprise that the Chinese Communists should have let fall opportunities for penetration of the Government by means of a 'democratic' coalition, and this he points out cannot be reconciled with purely Chinese interests. He concludes 'that the reason . . . must be sought in what the Communist leaders consider to be the best interests of their creed, which coincides so conveniently here and elsewhere with the interests of the Soviet Union'.[8]

It is natural that, established in purely agricultural areas, the Chinese Communists should have concentrated primarily on satisfying the land-hunger of the peasantry.

[6] See No. 28, note 8.

[7] The amount and nature of US aid to China were under protracted discussion by Congress, with two rival bills under consideration. The House of Representatives Bill, backed by the Republican Opposition and influential military figures such as Generals MacArthur and Wedemeyer, emphasised the importance of military aid to China and placed it in the same category as the military aid being provided to Greece and Turkey. The Senate Bill concentrated on economic aid and had the support of General Marshall and the State Department. The matter was finally resolved on 3 April by Presidential approval of the Economic Cooperation Act which included the provision to China of $463m over 12 months made up of $125m of military-type aid and $338m of economic aid: see *FRUS 1948*, vol. viii.

[8] See No. 17, para. 12.

It is, however, also evident that the Chinese Communists are growing more ruthless with increasing success, and there seems every logical reason to expect that, since the Communist leaders are confirmed Marxists, the land will not be allowed to remain indefinitely in private ownership but will be collectivised, and that all classes except the proletariat will be liquidated. It is true that the Slav mentality, with its emphasis on the abnegation of the individual, is in strong contrast with the individualism of the Chinese character. It is equally true that in 1927 the Kuomintang threw off Russian tutelage and expelled the Communists. On the other hand, Chinese communism is a far stronger force today than it was in 1927. Indeed, it is already, in those areas where it has gained control, in a fair way to transforming Chinese life and character in a way which, unless soon altered, seems likely to become permanent. The principal Chinese Communist leaders, such as Li Li-san in Harbin and Mao Tze-tung in North China are Moscow-trained[9] and maintain constant radio communication with Moscow. No doubt a certain latitude will be permitted at first to private enterprise, but Mao Tze-tung has made it clear that Chinese Communism is a part of the world revolution and that the ultimate aim of the Chinese Communists is the realisation in China of the full Marxist-Communist programme. In this connexion it is interesting to note that Mao Tze-tung, in a report to the Central Committee of the Chinese Communist Party on 25th December 1947,[10] made it clear that the party relied on 'the strength of the Socialist Soviet Union' and on the 'science of Marxism-Leninism'; and in the report occur passages like the following: 'American imperialism and its running dogs in various countries have . . . organised a reactionary camp against the Soviet Union and the new democratic countries of Europe, against the workers' movement in the capitalist countries, against the national movement in the colonies, and against the liberation of the Chinese people . . . All anti-imperialist forces of the various Eastern countries should unite to oppose the oppression of imperialism and the reactionaries within each country.'

The probabilities, therefore, are that the Chinese Communists, if they succeed to power, will follow those policies which are agreeable to the Soviet Government. There is certainly no evidence to suggest that Chinese communism is *sui generis*, and that the pattern of events elsewhere will not apply in China also, with the usual variations to meet special local circumstances.

[9] On this see No. 45, para 9.   [10] Cf. No. 37.

No. 41

Letter from Mr. Dening to Sir R. Stevenson (Nanking)

[*F 2535/33/10*]

Confidential   FOREIGN OFFICE, *8 April 1948*

Dear Stevenson,

You will like to know that the Secretary of State has read with interest your despatch No. 83 (1/1020/48) of the 2nd February,[1] with which you forwarded copies of the President's New Year Message and of Mao Tse-Tung's report to the Central Committee of the Chinese Communist Party. He discussed it with me afterwards when his chief comment was that the despatch did not give him much help in formulating policy, though he readily agreed that this was perhaps expecting the impossible until we had some far clearer idea of what the American line was likely to be.

2. At the same time your despatch has raised a number of questions in our minds on which I should welcome your comments.

3. In the first place there is marked contrast between the views expressed in this despatch on the Chinese Communists and those contained in earlier reports, notably in your despatches Nos. 1494 of 23rd November, 1946,[2] and No. 145 of the 14th March 1947,[3] also on those about the Communist treatment of foreign interests in paragraph 6 of Lamb's letter to Scott, No. 691 of the 10th September 1947.[4] Is this deliberate? We rather fancy not, since all the information received from the Embassy recently is to the effect that Chinese Communists are pursuing a policy more cruel and more Marxist, but more successful, than a year ago.

4. We also note that only one short paragraph is given to Chiang Kai-shek's speech, while Mao Tze-tung's report gets twelve. We feel that the state of affairs in regard to the policy of the Chinese Communists is

---

[1] No. 37.

[2] No. 17.

[3] This, the Ambassador's annual report for 1946, commented (para. 9) on a 15-day ceasefire in the civil war arranged in June of that year: 'While both sides were undoubtedly prevaricating, it began to be clear to unbiased observers that the Communist attitude was now stiffening to such an extent as to cast doubts upon their desire for any compromise. Yenan's propaganda had begun at this stage to take a strongly anti-American line and General Chou-En-lai in Nanking took refuge, in his public statements, in cloudy generalisations and procedural arguments' (F 4491/4491/10).

[4] Commenting in this letter on the situation in Manchuria, Mr. Lamb concluded with his own belief that in their treatment of foreign interests, in Manchuria or elsewhere, the Communists would be no better than their Kuomintang adversaries. British business, missions and residents could expect to be 'bled white, exploited, reviled, and/or squeezed out under a Communist regime just as much as under any other Chinese system of government without the protection of extraterritoriality and the "gun-boat policy".' There was little to choose in this respect between the Communists and the Kuomintang 'whose slogans equally echo chauvinism and xenophobia and whose spirit is one of repression' (F 13215/76/10).

(according to your reports over the last few months) correctly represented by the 9th paragraph of Chiang's speech[5] and not by Mao's statements quoted in paragraph 5 of your despatch. Your reports have in fact indicated that the Communists are levelling everybody down to the lowest point. Consequently the Communist line does not appear to be to 'solidly unite with middle peasants', or if it is their line, it is certainly not their practice.

5. We see too that you continue to think good of the Democratic League. But, whatever the leaders may be, there seems little doubt that many of the rank and file are communists or fellow-travellers. Perhaps your views will have been modified now that you have received the recent Hong Kong despatch on the January 1948 session of the League's Executive Committee,[6] reporting a strong movement in favour of purging from the League those who do not support the Communist ticket.

6. Then as to your speculations (paragraphs 10-14) 'on the form which Communism would assume in China and the effect it would have on foreign interests'. Is it true that the 'process of turning China into an orthodox Communist state would therefore be extremely slow, if, indeed, it ever proved possible'? Certainly we doubt if the reasons given for this view are valid. We particularly do not agree that, because there are large numbers of Chinese residents abroad, China herself cannot or will not exclude foreigners. Moreover, remittances from overseas Chinese in pre-war days certainly helped China's balance of payments considerably, and it was overseas Chinese who financed Sun Yat-sen and have financed the Kuomintang (though recently subscriptions are said to have fallen off owing to dissatisfaction with Kuomintang policies and practice). Perhaps collectivisation *may* not be possible in South China. North China on the other hand would appear to be an ideal field for collective farming on a large scale and some collective system may even be devised for the special conditions of South China, which incidentally contains a much higher proportion of lease-holders than North China.

7. As to the effect on British interests, you are no doubt correct in saying that the attitude of the Chinese Communists will be dictated by expediency. But do you really think that in practice 'there is no reason to suppose that there is any more hostility towards Britain among the Chinese Communists than towards any other foreign country, leaving aside the USA'? I should have thought it more probable that once they are in the

---

[5] This para read: 'Wherever the Communists go, they give lip service to "land revolution". Actually all they do is to instigate the loafers and ruffians to dominate the villages and to bring pressure to bear on the law-abiding farmers. They appeal to the people's mob psychology and create a reign of terror. They encourage killings among family members and break up homes. In areas under their control, the Communists have forced women to form "comfort corps", so as to satisfy the lust of those in the Communist armed forces. They have formed "juvenile corps" of youngsters and taught them how to plot against their own parents and elder brothers.'

[6] Cf. No. 37, para. 3.

saddle the Chinese Communist Party may be expected to treat capitalist countries alike, and that in these matters they may well follow the Russian attitude. Mao's report seems evidence enough to justify such an expectation. No doubt British interests are so hampered and restricted at present that they feel that the Chinese Communists will be no worse than the present Chinese government, but I think they will be very unwise to count on the honeymoon period being more than temporary, and that the last state under Communist rule will ultimately be worse, and more irremediable, than the first state under the Kuomintang. Deductions from what has happened elsewhere must surely bear out this view.

8. This leads me to the suggestion in paragraph 12 that 'Soviet Russia. . . would find that her policy in Sinkiang and at Dairen would cause her the same kind of embarrassment as did her Mongolian policy in 1924'. It is of course conceivable that the Russians may overplay their hand, and that their acquisitiveness in Sinkiang and Manchuria will turn the Chinese Communists against them. But there is surely no evidence of this at present, and it would be unwise to make the assumption. If the Soviet Union gains complete control in Sinkiang and Manchuria—a process which would presumably be achieved by setting up administrations similar to that of Outer Mongolia—it will be in a strong position to put the screw on China proper and to eliminate American influence. By then it may not matter whether Communist China likes the prospect or not; it may be compelled to follow the Moscow line.

9. There are, I think, two aspects of the situation which we have to consider here. In the first place we have to consider objectively the respective merits and demerits of the Kuomintang and the Communists. This subject is dealt with in a paper recently prepared in China Department, of which I enclose a copy, and on which we should be grateful for your comments.[7]

10. Secondly we have to consider what our attitude should be towards the Kuomintang and the Communists. On previous occasions in China we have sometimes lingered too long in our support of a tottering régime and this has complicated our relations with the new one when it came into power. This was notably the case when Chiang Kai-shek himself came into power. But I think this second question should be considered quite separately. The question of our relations with the Communists, if they should succeed in seizing power, is one with which we need not, I think, deal at present. It may well be that if this should occur we should wish to maintain our contacts with China through our Embassy and Consulates as long as we can, and that if British merchants can contrive to trade with Communist China we should at any rate not discourage them from doing so. But it would be quite a different thing to try to reinsure now. I am sure it would be wrong, and it would only complicate our relations not only with the National Government but with the United States.

[7] See No. 40.

11. I have thought it better to comment upon your despatch in a semi-official letter. But apart from any reply you may wish to send on the same basis, it would be very valuable to have from you a further despatch dealing with the two aspects of the situation which I have mentioned. There is a good deal of interest on the subject here at present. The China Association recently invited the Minister of State and me to a private luncheon at which they voiced their doubts and fears.[8] In another sphere Lord Lindsay of Birker has been quite active, and apart from his recent speech to the House of Lords[9] he called on the Minister of State to advocate at any rate an official investigation into the merits of the Chinese Communists. You will doubtless also have seen an interchange of correspondence in the *Times* between Mr. Harrison MP (of the China Parliamentary Delegation) and Michael Lindsay.[10] As you may imagine the Lindsay family thesis is that we do not know what is going on in the 'liberated' areas or in the minds of the Communists, that the latter can probably still be won over to our side, and that we should at any rate trade with them.

Yours ever,

M.E. DENING

[8] See No. 39.

[9] Speaking in the House of Lords on 3 January 1947, Lord Lindsay described the Nationalist Government of China as 'totalitarian'. He had heard that Moscow did not control the Communists in the north. To establish whether this was correct he suggested that the British Government should send an envoy to talk to the Communists (*Parl. Debs.*, 5th ser., H. of L., vol. 145, cols. 110-23). Lord Lindsay had never visited China, and the FO believed he was influenced in his views by his son, Michael Lindsay, who had a Chinese wife and had spent four years with the Communists in north China from December 1941. During this time he had organised the Yenan radio broadcasts in English to the outside world. In 1946 he had been invited to give a lecture to the Joint Intelligence Staff on his experiences in Yenan (minutes of a meeting of the Russia Committee on 7 May 1946, N 6092/5169/38). Notes dated 2 February 1948 prepared for a meeting between the Prime Minister and Lord Lindsay indicated that Michael Lindsay was suspected of continuing to advise the Chinese Communists on propaganda methods (F 16430/33/10).

[10] In a letter to *The Times* of 18 March Mr. Harrison, a member of the 1947 parliamentary delegation to China (see No. 34, note 1), observed: 'The Communist appeal contains a strong element of nationalism, but that particular feature does not make the Communists any less Communistic . . . My whole experience leads me to think that the Communists of China will develop according to type.' He maintained that the 'fanatical leaders of the Communist guerrillas' had been trained in Moscow. Responding in a letter printed on 5 April, Michael Lindsay argued that there were clear differences between Russian and Chinese Communism: 'Communist principles applied with an objective respect for the common people and for the realities of the Chinese situation have enabled the Chinese Communist Party to govern without resort to the secret police methods of Russian Communism.' He denied that the CCP leaders were Moscow-trained and argued that the majority, including Mao Tse-tung, had never visited Russia (cf. No. 45, note 11 below). If the CCP had become more extreme and pro-Russian over the past two years, it was because the US had failed to protest against Chiang Kai-shek's repudiation of the US-sponsored mediation agreements.

No. 42

Letter from Sir R. Stevenson (Nanking) to Mr. Scarlett

[*F 6505/33/10*]

NANKING, *20 April 1948*

Dear Peter,

I have seen your confidential letter (F 3692/361/10) of the 24th March to Leo Lamb.[1]

We fully appreciate the delicate hint that we should not let irritation, however justified, with the Kuomintang run away with us. We hasten therefore to assure you that we completely share your preference for non-Communist organisations. You need have no qualms whatever on that score. We have no illusions about the intentions of the Communists. Our doubts, if any, are confined to the degree of success which they might have in carrying out their intentions in this immense and intractable country.

If we report more fully on the shortcomings of the Kuomintang than on those of the Communists, the reason is simple—we have much more information about the areas under the control of the Central Government in which not only this Embassy but all our Consulates are situated. We propose therefore to continue to report without prejudice the facts of the situation and of prevailing conditions in China so far as we are in a position to observe them. I am sure you will agree that this is right.[2]

Yours ever,

RALPH SKRINE STEVENSON

[1] This letter was a reply to Mr. Lamb's letter of 21 February enclosing a copy of a press statement by Wu Te-chen, Secretary-General of the Kuomintang, refuting a *Times* editorial of 14 February which argued that there was little to choose between the KMT and the CCP because both aimed at a one-party dictatorship. The statement was viewed by the FO and the Embassy as evidence that the Kuomintang took seriously adverse comment in the foreign press. Mr. Lamb suggested this might be exploited and that the UK press should expose 'the more flagrant sins' of the Chinese Government, especially with regard to what was seen as its failure to implement many provisions of the 1943 treaty abolishing extraterritoriality. In his letter of 24 March Mr. Scarlett had replied: 'We are of course not unaware of the many faults of commission and omission of the Kuomintang, and the gap between promise and performance is I gather notorious. Nevertheless we confess to a preference in present circumstances for a Party that runs under a non-Communist label. It is at least a sign of grace that the Kuomintang should be sensitive to Western criticism, to which the Chinese or any other Communists would be impervious.'

[2] Mr. Scarlett noted on 6 May on this letter: 'Touché!'

No. 43

Letter from Mr. Dening (Canberra)[1] to Sir E. Machtig[2]

[F 7706/6139/23]

Top Secret and Personal   CANBERRA, 7 *May 1948*

Dear Machtig,

As the only non-Australian stenographer is away with the High Commissioner, I have perforce to write this in manuscript. I wonder whether you would be good enough to have copies made for Sargent and also for the High Commissioner here.[3]

You will have had the various telegrams about my visit, but before I go off to-night I feel I should fill in the picture, which on the whole I find a discouraging one.

I dined alone with the High Commissioner on my first evening here and we had a long talk, in the course of which I asked his advice as to how I should make my approach to the Prime Minister[4] and Dr. Evatt[5] on the morrow. He gave it as his view that Evatt has latterly been feeling somewhat isolated, both politically and internationally, and that for that reason he has tended to become somewhat more amenable. He was however a very different man when in the presence of the Prime Minister than when he was on his own.

This I found to be the case. Our first interview passed off very well. The Prime Minister did most of the talking, while Evatt was subdued and said little. Chifley I thought showed a very clear insight into and understanding of the European situation and of the general international situation. For his part he seemed to have no illusions about Soviet aims. And after his preliminary reactions against secret talks he seemed to respond readily to the idea, and even Evatt raised no serious objections at that stage, though he clung rather (and still clings) to the idea that representations should be

---

[1] Between April and early June 1948 Mr. Dening visited Australia, New Zealand and Canada in furtherance of the proposal that Anglo-American talks on the Far East should be convened (see No. 35), ending his trip in the US. The reason given publicly for his tour was to discuss the Japanese peace settlement, and to make this more credible he also visited Pakistan and India, although those governments were not informed of the real purpose of his trip (F 6139/6139/23). He carried with him a letter from Mr. Attlee to the Dominion Prime Ministers explaining that the UK had for some time intended to raise the issue of Far Eastern policy but that for security reasons correspondence should be avoided (FO 800/462, FE/48/5).

[2] Permanent Under Secretary of State for Commonwealth Relations.

[3] Mr. G. Kimber was UK High Commissioner in Australia, 1946-48. Mr. Bevin wrote on the filed copy of this letter: 'Has the PM seen this?' Sir E. Machtig's private secretary was asked to ensure that it was sent to the Prime Minister.

[4] Mr. J.B. Chifley, Prime Minister of Australia, 1945-49.

[5] Australian Minister for External Affairs.

Ministerial and he the man. I hope I made it clear, however, that Ministerial representation would make secrecy impossible.

When we left the Prime Minister Evatt said he wanted to talk to us, but he went away and did not return. The High Commissioner and I came away feeling we had had quite a satisfactory interview, and he left immediately afterwards on his tour.

The next day I was invited to see Dr. Evatt, and he had Burton[6] with him. The House was sitting and Evatt was summoned away several times in the course of the conversation to which he contributed little. But though he was quite friendly, he raised once more all the difficulties which had been raised (and I thought overcome) the day before. Burton showed no enthusiasm for our proposals at all. He immediately launched into an attack on American policy the world over, and said that there were a number of subjects on which Australia and the US could never agree. I said it was a sorry outlook if we were to accept our disagreements as final. Burton then went on to indicate that the Soviet Union were not as bad as they were painted. It was the US attitude towards Russia which was vitiating the whole world atmosphere and preventing the settlement of any problems, including the Japanese problem.

Evatt returned at this stage, and as it was nearly lunch time, the party broke up, Evatt saying that while he thought the talks might do good and could do no harm, he would have to consider further the questions of representation and the scope of the talks. He suggested I should have further talks with the Department.

That afternoon I went to External Affairs, where I was confronted by Burton and three others: MacIntyre[7] (who looks after the Far East Section) Plimsoll[8] (who was on the Far Eastern Commission) and one young man whose name I did not catch.

The meeting was quite informal, and we had drinks as it progressed. But I found the departmental attitude depressing to a degree. Appeasement of the Soviet Union appeared to be their main aim. As regards the Japanese peace settlement, I was asked whether I did not think an approach to Moscow, cap in hand, to enquire whether the Russians would attend a conference without commitment, if it were summoned, should not be the first step. If this was successful, we could then put America on the spot. I said drily that I thought such a proposal would hardly commend itself to my Secretary of State, and that the only result would be so to alienate the Americans that they would be unwilling to discuss anything with us.

At this stage Burton repeated his performance over the Soviet Union and the US. I disposed of his arguments but obviously left him unconvinced. The others did not enter into this part of the discussion and

---

[6] J. Burton, Secretary, Australian Ministry of External Affairs.

[7] Mr. L.R. McIntyre, Officer in Charge of the Pacific Division, Australian Department for External Affairs, since September 1947.

[8] Mr. J. Plimsoll, First Secretary, Australian Permanent Mission to the UN.

Plimsoll (who is really a very good man) uttered not a word throughout the proceedings.

But MacIntyre thought there would be difficulty in holding conversations at the official level, and he did not believe they would remain secret. The Soviet Union would get to know, and then all chance of Soviet participation in a Japanese peace settlement would have been lost. To this I said that it was possible to keep talks secret, and we had done so. As to the Soviet Union, our experience was that they did what they wanted to do, and I thought we could safely assume that their course of action would be one which suited their own interests—it was as simple as that.

Then MacIntyre said that if the scope of the talks was to be as wide as I had suggested, Australia would have to send a number of men. This was obviously advanced as an additional argument against official representation.

Finally I said that if the views expressed were those of the Australian Government, there did not seem to be anything more I could say, and no doubt they would in due course be communicated to the United Kingdom.

I am given to understand that everyone in the Department of External Affairs speaks with the voice of Dr. Burton who, in turn, speaks with the voice of Dr. Evatt. If the departmental view remains as it was put to me, then not only do I think the talks will fail, but I gravely doubt whether it would be wise to hold them at all.

We had some desultory conversation about the Japanese peace settlement, and on this subject I do not think there is any wide divergence of view between us. But while we hope to steer American policy in the right direction by diplomacy, the present Evatt-Burton inclination would seem to be to accomplish it by an openly provocative attitude. They may modify this view, but until they do, the outlook is gloomy. Their attitude towards world events is almost unbelievably unrealistic.

To-day I went with Kimber to see the Prime Minister. But Kimber was excluded, and when I saw Chifley he explained why. He said he wanted to speak to me alone because he thought I might have some special message to convey to him from Mr. Attlee or Mr. Bevin. He was aware that there were occasional passages between Dr. Evatt and Mr. Bevin, and perhaps we had not liked some of the telegrams which the former had sent. The Prime Minister then launched into a lengthy discourse in which he surveyed the international situation and expressed his sympathy and understanding for Mr. Attlee and Mr. Bevin in their difficult task. Though he raised the perennial question of consultation, he said he quite realised that it was not always possible to consult Australia in advance.

I gained the impression that the whole interview, which might have been conducted by General MacArthur, was designed to show that the Prime Minister has much more tolerance and understanding than Dr. Evatt (which I do not doubt for a moment is the case).

When I was given an opportunity to speak I touched on the security point[9] and told him of Mr. Bevin's anxiety to keep Dr. Evatt fully informed and of the difficult position in which he had been placed. Mr. Chifley said 'I quite understand' and then delivered his views at length on security. For himself, top secret messages delivered to him were locked up and then burned. He seemed to think that adequate measures were being taken to tighten up security, but I thought he treated the whole question a little light-heartedly.

I told Mr. Chifley that Mr. Bevin had expressed the hope that he might find the time to visit London. The Prime Minister said he would like to. His difficulty was that a referendum was about to take place and then there would be a further session of Parliament. Then the United Nations Assembly would be held and Dr. Evatt would have to go to that. He and Dr. Evatt could not be away at the same time. On the other hand he did not entirely exclude the possibility of a visit.

All this time we had not touched on the purpose of my visit, and I came away with the impression that Mr. Chifley was not unaware of what had been going on, and while not prepared to discuss the matter in detail, was anxious to smooth things over. His manner was throughout very genial, but though the interview lasted for the best part of an hour and he did virtually all the talking we did not get down to anything tangible.

The only thing was that he accepted the Far Eastern talks in principle, and said it was vital for Australia to know which way things were going in the Pacific.

So there we are. If the Prime Minister were really at the head of foreign affairs, I should expect no difficulty, but since the actual conduct of affairs will be in the hands of Evatt and Burton, I am very dubious about the outcome of our proposals. And as the Americans can hardly be unaware of the Evatt-Burton attitude, since it is common talk in the diplomatic corps in Canberra, I confess I shall be rather surprised if they agree to five power talks. Nor am I satisfied that, in the existing frame of mind here, we can be sure that the talks will be kept secret if they are held.

I confess that I find this rather discouraging, though not surprising. No useful purpose can be served by my staying on at present, so I am off tonight.

[9] See No. 35, note 3.

Excuse the length of this screed![10]

Yours sincerely,

M.E. DENING

[10] Mr. Dening arrived in Washington at the end of May. He told the State Department that the Dominion Prime Ministers had agreed 'in principle' to participate in secret Far Eastern talks, but Mr. R. Lovett, Under Secretary of State, did not think the time was right. He expressed particular doubts about Australia (and was especially critical of Dr. Evatt's public statements), and asked Mr. Dening 'point blank' if Australian security could be depended upon. Mr. Dening 'could only reply that he hoped so'. Mr. Lovett also argued that in a presidential election year no one could predict what policies a new Administration would follow; if the US went into recession there might be strong pressure for cuts in foreign commitments. He anticipated 'immediate adverse reactions' if Congress received any inkling that the State Department was about to hold talks on the Far East (Washington telegram No. 2541 of 29 May, F 7716/6139/23).

Mr. Dening subsequently had discussions with US officials about Japan and found them in no hurry to conclude a peace treaty. Reporting on his talks he commented: 'I wonder whether the fact that Congress passed ERP in an election year has not led us to believe that more is possible in this election year than is in fact the case' (letter to Mr. Wright, 1 June, F 8014/6139/23). On 2 June he discussed China with Mr. Butterworth (now Director of the Office of Far Eastern Affairs) and other officials. The conversation covered military supplies, economic aid (in the context of which Mr. Butterworth 'compared the "tea cup" of Greece to the "ocean" of China'), the rising Communist threat and the need for close Anglo-American consultation, bringing in France also. For the record of these talks, see *FRUS 1948*, vol. viii, pp. 77-79.

No. 44

Report by the Joint Intelligence Committee on the Military Situation in China

JIC (48)30(0) Final (Annex)[1] *[F 5777/33/10]*

Top Secret   MINISTRY OF DEFENCE, *13 May 1948*

Present military situation

Although, by virtue of training and advisory assistance by the American Military Aid group the Central Government have increased command of air and sea, the present course of the Civil War is definitely going in favour of the Communists. This is particularly the case in Manchuria where recent Communist successes have effectively isolated Mukden and Changchun. The Communist capture of the important port of Yingkow has left the Central Government only the ports of Chinwangtao and Hulutao through which to send up reinforcements. The value of these is

[1] The covering Report stated that the JIC had prepared their appreciation of 'the military situation in China and of likely developments including repercussions on the defence of Hong Kong' in response to a letter from the Colonial Office. They had consulted HM Ambassador at Nanking and the JIC (Far East).

dependent upon the ability of the Central Government to restore and maintain land communication with Mukden.

2. Government forces in North China are also effectively isolated by land from the south by a wide belt of Communist held territory stretching from the Shensi border to the sea. They are therefore dependent for most supplies on the port of Tientsin. The Communists are at the same time regaining ground in Shantung and maintaining considerable pressure in the area between the Lunghai railway and the Yangtse River (from the vicinity of Shasi to the vicinity of Anking) though they do not at the moment hold any part of the north bank of the river. South of the Yangtse, Communist cells are in being but temporarily quiescent except for an active force (about 35,000) in the Luichow Peninsular area.

3. The present strengths and locations of the Communist and Nationalist forces are given at Appendix A[2] and on the map attached.[2]

4. A serious shortage of ammunition is reported by the Nationalists while the Communists continue to increase their supplies by the capture of Government stocks.

5. The effective use of captured weapons by the Communists has been noticeable particularly in the artillery arm in Manchuria, where the value of their training schools is beginning to be felt.

6. The Air Force is the principal Central Government asset. Isolated cities and garrisons have been supplied, and troops lifted. The Communists as yet have only an Air Force in embryo, though some training of pilots has taken place. No air opposition has yet been met by the Nationalist Forces.

7. Nationalist forces, though numerically superior to the Communists, suffer several disadvantages besides that of having to occupy a very large area.

(*a*) The officers are inefficient and, especially in the higher grades, are frequently appointed for personal or political reasons apart from any military qualifications.

(*b*) Graft and corruption permeate much of the Nationalist forces.

8. The nucleus of the Communist forces, at least for the present, have relatively high morale, good discipline and efficient officers. The Communist forces have so far not committed themselves to the strain of administering any large commercial or industrial area. Since they live off the countryside they are able to harass the Government lines of communication, particularly the railroads, and make frequent raids on the municipal areas for supplies without detriment to their future needs.

[2] Not printed.

Likely developments

9. We consider it probable that the military situation of the Nationalist forces will continue to deteriorate with corresponding deterioration in the authority of Central Government. Nevertheless it is unlikely that such adverse developments would immediately lead to a political collapse of the Central Government, although they would obviously undermine not only its prestige but also its effective authority, which is already declining throughout the greater part of China.

10. It is probable that the Nationalist forces will fail to hold Mukden in which case the whole of Manchuria, except the Port Arthur Naval Base Area which is occupied by Soviet forces, will fall into Communist hands. When the Communists have consolidated their gains North of the Great Wall they are likely to take over the Peking-Tientsin area as far South as the present course of the Yellow River.

11. Other developments likely to take place are:

(*a*) An increase in the size and number of Communist-dominated areas and some consolidation as far South as the Yangtze River.

(*b*) south of the Yangtze River existing Communist pockets will be militarily reinforced.

12. In the South there is no political opposition party capable of taking over the administration of the country. In these circumstances continued control by the Kuomintang from Nanking, however nominal, is likely, although the possibility of disintegration and collapse cannot be excluded. In this latter event, separate regional governments would most probably be set up by Kuomintang elements opposed to the present Nanking Government and prepared to compromise with the Communists.

13. It is possible that a Communist Air Force may shortly emerge. This would have the effect of largely neutralising the Nationalist tactical air force and might gravely interfere with the supplies of the Nationalist forces in North East China, particularly those just south of the Great Wall.

14. The USA has granted China 338 million US dollars for relief and reconstruction, and another 125 million dollars for other purposes to be agreed with the Chinese Government, including military aid.[3] We consider, however, that this aid will not prove effective in time to prevent the developments outlined in paras 9-11 above but may result in stabilisation thereafter.

Military threat to Hong Kong

15. We consider that it is unlikely that the Communists will be able to overrun South China, including Canton, owing to the hardening of resistance by the provincial Chinese troops of the Central Government and to increasing American support. However, should the present control of the Central Government in South China be seriously weakened it is probable

[3] See No. 40, note 7.

either, that disaffected elements of the Kuomintang will set up separate regional governments, or, that there will be a revival of local war lords and provincial antagonisms.

16. The military threat to Hong Kong may take the form of attack by irregular bands, owing nominal allegiance to the Kuomintang or to the Communist Party. The threat would be particularly real during any period of transition. Such an attack would be likely to be disowned officially. We consider that there will be no direct military attack on Hong Kong by the regular forces of the Chinese Government or of the Chinese Communist Party whichever controls South China.

17. Anti-British propaganda for the return of Hong Kong is likely to continue in any circumstances, and if there is a serious deterioration in relations between the Government of Hong Kong and the Chinese authority in control of South China, strong economic pressure may be brought to bear by boycotting the colony, by interfering with the passage of its supplies from South China, and by fomenting strikes within the colony.

18. In the unlikely event that Canton or the hinterland of Hong Kong should fall to the Communists, we consider that the chances of attack by irregular bands are probably greater than if the district remains as at present under Central Government. In any event the Communists could be expected to exploit the opportunity of directing and assisting vigorously the subversive activities of Chinese Communist groups in Hong Kong and the influence of the Kuomintang in Hong Kong could be expected to weaken. In this case some of the more responsible Chinese in Hong Kong might show increased loyalty to the British.

19. Should Communist pressure on the Central Government of China result in the establishment of a non-Communist warlord in control of Canton we consider the chances of such a warlord attacking Hong Kong would be remote. The danger of attack from irregular bands would depend on the degree of authority such a warlord had established over the immediate hinterland of Hong Kong.

No. 45

Letter from Sir R. Stevenson (Nanking) to Mr. Dening

[F 8032/33/10]

Confidential   NANKING, *25 May 1948*

My dear Dening,

I hope we were wrong in deriving from your letter (particularly paragraphs 3 and 4) of 8th April (F 2535/33/10)[1] a faint suggestion of lack

[1] No. 41.

of consistency or objectivity in our reports about the Chinese Communists. If so you may be assured that none of us are conscious of any such intention.

2. Any apparent contrasts or even contradictions in our reports relating to this vital topic are a natural reflection of notable developments or changes in the general picture which have altered the perspective of modified our reading of the portents. For example what we tried to emphasize in our despatch No. 83[2] was the introduction of a new factor in the policy of the Chinese Communists in Mao Tze-tung's Christmas Day message, since repeated and elaborated in various statements by prominent communists, namely the extension of the promises of the benefits of life under a communist regime to the 'middle-farmer' class and small capitalist. This appeal for the support of the bourgeois and urban elements in addition to the landless peasant—though admittedly merely a variant of the usual Communist procedure—is undoubtedly an interesting step, which is being taken seriously by the Central Government judging by their subsequent spate of counter-promises to implement the 'land for the tiller' programme. Chiang Kai-shek's New Year's speech on the other hand was a replica of so many others delivered during the last several years which merely inveigh against the communists as the cause of all China's current evils, including official corruption and inflation. It did not therefore seem to call for the same attention as Mao's disclosure of a new platform, to the significance of which we devoted greater space.

3. I hope that it will be clear from our reports that we take the declarations of the Communists no less than those of Chiang Kai-shek and the Kuomintang equally at their face value. In neither case have we any inducement to proclaim their sincerity. There must inevitably, however, be a difference in our analysis of them as living continuously in territory under Central Government administration over a number of years our reports and criticisms of Kuomintang activities are based on what we see and know first hand, which does not happen to be conducive of better things to come. On the contrary events such as the practical repudiation of the 1943 Treaty obligations,[3] the recent Canton incident,[4] and various discriminatory

---

[2] No. 37.

[3] In taking over the administration and control of the former International Settlements and British concessions in China, the Chinese Government, under article 4 of the 1943 treaty (see No. 1, note 15) undertook to make provision for the assumption and discharge of the official liabilities and obligations of the areas in question. These related especially to the British ex-employees of the former International Settlement in Shanghai, more than 500 in number, most of whom had spent the greater part of their working lives in China. The Chinese Government appointed a Liquidation Commission, to which foreign advisers were attached. The latter recommended for the ex-employees the payment of substantial sums for pension, superannuation and other allowances on the basis of continuous service up to 30 September 1945, when the Chinese assumed complete control of the Shanghai Settlement. Since then negotiations had stalled because of a serious difference between the two sides as to the appropriate date for calculating benefits owing to the ex-employees. The UK argued that it

or damaging restrictions or activities against British interests, clearly constitute a continued deterioration in conditions from our point of view. In the case of the Communists on the other hand we have obviously much less factual material to work on and our views are necessarily speculative, and for that very reason perhaps subject to greater variation. In exploring the prospects of Communist extension over China from the point of view of the effect locally and further afield, we are largely dependent upon second hand information and have to weigh such evidence as reaches us against the political or sentimental bias of the narrator. There is no doubt, however, that acts of cruelty and atrocities have been committed by the Communists (and for that matter also by the Central Government in this war of bitter retaliation), particularly through the people's courts. Both sides are generally regarded with disfavour and fear by the common people, hence the need for the active propaganda now being directed by each contestant to the respective classes more naturally inclined towards the other camp. The public have by now become sceptical of Kuomintang promises of reform particularly when they serve up as new such old and frequently discarded chestnuts as the 'land for the tiller' policy. With the Communists, on the other hand, there is always the possibility of their being sufficiently shrewd and practical to implement some of their declarations of decent treatment and improved conditions. It is after all in the Communists' own interest to suborn the natural allegiance to the Kuomintang of the middle level of the people who represent the solid yeoman class. Reports on Communist political activities are therefore more apt to reflect a wistful, if not wishful, hope, which is at any rate manifest in North China, that things cannot be as bad under any regime as under that of the Kuomintang today.

4. This of course brings us to the vital and vexed question of the extent to which the Chinese Communist leopard can divest himself of or avoid developing Soviet spots. Or, to put the proposition in a different and more specific form, how far, if at all, will ingrained Chinese customs and characteristics resist the impulses of communism as applied in the USSR. This is perhaps not the same thing as whether Chinese Communism will be *sui generis*—it depends, of course, upon exactly what interpretation one happens to give to this general term. In any event our conclusion, subject to some variations in opinion in certain respects, is that while Communism cannot be otherwise than Communism, a vile and destructive ogre,

should be 30 September 1945 but the Chinese recognised no service for compensation purposes after 8 December 1941 and the outbreak of the Pacific War. The issue engaged Mr. Bevin's personal interest and he called for periodic progress reports. However, faced by continuing deadlock the FO appealed to the Treasury in May 1948 for funds to enable the ex-employees to receive their full entitlement. In the case of Shanghai this involved a total lump sum payment of £1,250,000, plus pensions of about £30,000 p.a. Much smaller sums were involved for the ex-employees of the settlements at Canton, Tientsin and Amoy (F 6268, 10336/38/10).

[4] See No. 38, note 5.

wherever it is planted and made to flourish whether in fertile or reluctant fields, nonetheless it may not be able to overcome or supplant certain forces, inherent in the people or the soil of China, in which case being exploiters of expediency the master minds in Moscow will of course amend their directives accordingly in deference to such potential stone walls. We do not believe, for example, that collectivist theories will in the long run be able to stand up against the age-old yearning of the Chinese peasant to own his land for the security of his family no less than of himself. The recognition of this fundamental characteristic (as well as more recently of the parallel instinct of the Chinese for individual business enterprises) is to us clearly indicated in the Mao Tze-tung and other Chinese Communist pronouncements of intent. In this connection supporting testimony to this thesis is provided in the article on the history of agrarian reform in China by a Chinese expert quoted in paragraph 3 of Lamb's semi-official to Dening No. 256 (24/840/48) of 3rd May.[5] We are thus of the opinion that it will at least be a very slow process to convert China to Communist orthodoxy. Few would be so rash, however, as to hazard the assertion that Chinese conservatism would absorb and stifle communism, though it would be equally foolhardy to ignore the historical fact of China's genius for implanting or super-imposing the native culture and way of life upon the foreign invader, who thereby in the passing of time lost his initiative and virility. The inertia and corruption of China are potent—and inertia, unlike corruption, may emasculate even a force as virile as Communism.

5. In any case we must consider the effect upon British interests of the progressive impact of Communism, whether of the orthodox Soviet pattern or in a modified Chinese form, and equally what policy could be adopted to cope with or forestall the resultant effects. This aspect of the situation is being dealt with more extensively in a despatch drafted in accordance with the suggestion in paragraph 11 of your letter.[6] Generally speaking however despite recent indications of a less actively hostile attitude towards foreigners, including missionaries, in areas under Communist occupation, we do not expect any great consideration for British or other foreign interest. As you say in paragraph 7 of your letter any improvement in the initial stages is unlikely to be lasting, and we have never felt that the honeymoon period, if any, would be more than a fleeting one. Such a honeymoon, it may be confidently assumed, would be one of convenience and not of love. In fact it could not be otherwise in a country like China where xenophobia is already endemic without infection from Moscow. After all anti-foreignism is a fundamental element in Kuomintang political

[5] Not printed. The article in question was by Chen Han-seng and it appeared in *The China Weekly* of 17 April 1948. Arguing that whereas the Soviets nationalised land and redistributed only its use, the Chinese Communists redistributed both the ownership and use of the land, the author concluded that the Communists' land reform programme in China represented 'an indigenous solution of the country's gravest problem' (F 7080/355/10).

[6] No. 46 below.

philosophy as 'China's Destiny'[7] so clearly indicates. Therefore the moral would seem to be that even if the short term view shows some possibility of improvement in the treatment of British interests under a Chinese Communist regime, in the long run if Communism comes to stay the ideological reaction against non-communist states will inevitably set in to our detriment.

6. There is therefore no doubt in our minds that our bread is not buttered on the side of the Communists, so that sour and rancid as it undoubtedly is, we must adhere to the Kuomintang. We certainly would not think of advocating any olive branch to the Communists. Such a move would in fact have the additional demerit of antagonising American opinion—and Anglo-American solidarity is as important in China as anywhere else. Any action on our part capable of interpretation as trying to 'cash in' on present American unpopularity in Chinese Communist circles owing to their active aid by emphasising that we at least are not so actively bolstering up the 'reactionary' forces of Chiang Kai-shek, would be a crass political blunder. At the same time while doing our best to combat Communism as a creed (see our despatch No. 383 (10/1026/48) of 12th May, 1948)[8] we think it would be prudent not to provoke gratuitously the enmity or resentment of the Chinese Communists at the risk of exposing our nationals in Communist areas to retaliation. It is also to our interest to avoid making it too difficult for any of our Consuls to stay on at his post in the event of Communist occupation (e.g. Mukden).

7. While there is no question of making overtures to the Communists, we must nonetheless recognise the practical necessity of dealing with them *de facto* in areas under their control whether now or later. However impotent we may be to stem the progress of the Communist hordes in China (and who knows whether even the Army Advisory Group and other United States aid to China can provide the requisite blocking power), we can not afford to abandon our struggle to protect British interests. And if there should happen to be a chance to promote British trade, etc., we should surely not fail to take it up through over squeamishness about reddening hands. It might in fact be a contribution to the anti-communist cause if one

[7] Chiang Kai-shek, *China's Destiny,* originally published in 1943, first English edition (New York, Macmillan), 1947.

[8] This despatch was a response to an FO circular of 28 January on how to disseminate anti-Communist publicity. In the Chinese context, the despatch argued that overt action should be avoided as this would lead to a charge of interference in China's internal affairs. It suggested that the aim of publicity in China should be to assail Communism generally rather than the Chinese Communists: 'The objective of this would be to counteract as far as possible a tendency, already discernible in North China, to regard a Communist regime as being at least likely to be less burdensome than that of the Kuomintang. It is suggested that this might be accomplished by giving as much publicity as possible to events and statements by prominent personalities in Western Europe and adjacent areas, exposing the totalitarian nature of Communist rule and the injustices and hardships of existence in a Communist state' (PR 373/11913).

could, by participation through non-official British channels in the fostering of trade with Communist areas, underline the real need for Sino-foreign trade on a liberal basis (a principle which the present Kuomintang government has consistently ignored) in the hope that this appeal to the commercial instinct of the Chinese may weaken his faith in the more sterile tenets of Sovietism. But there is no question of recognition of the Chinese Communists—nor were we aware that the question of doing so had been seriously mooted as stated in the introductory sentence in the China Department's memorandum of April 1st enclosed in your letter.[9]

8. Otherwise we find ourselves in general agreement with this presentation of the situation though, doubtless owing to its essential quality of brevity, as well as to the fact that it sets out with a definite theme as declared in the preamble, it tends to concentrate upon the shortcomings of the Communists as for example with regard to the abortive Marshall peace negotiations, which in fact were equally sabotaged by the Kuomintang (Chiang Kai-shek's 'ante' being raised, no less than Chou En-lai's, according to whose fortunes of civil war seemed to be at the moment in the ascendant).[10] The verdict of history in this regard must surely be that neither side sincerely aimed at a peaceful solution—Chiang Kai-shek can never really have wavered from his intention, born in 1927 (when the Kuomintang, itself the child of Soviet Communism—of which it retains many features—broke away from Soviet tutorship and started to hunt its former associates) and maintained during the Pacific war, to eliminate the Chinese Communists. It is in fact inevitably and essentially a life and death struggle between two ruthless foes, each of whom seeks to be lord of the jungle. In the circumstances there is no genuine prospect of the minor parties playing anything but a subordinate role. We had at one time, however, entertained a faint hope that the Democratic League, who had produced one or two good performances in the People's Political Council and in the way of political pamphlets, might prove to be the bridge between the two conflicting elements. In the event it is evident that it never had a chance and its members eventually found themselves faced with the choice of more active alignment with the Reds or taking a very back seat. The proscription of the Democratic League by the Central Government drove all except the more moderate into the enemy's camp and was therefore in our opinion a major political error. The League having been reduced to the role of a Communist stooge or an émigré manifesto-

[9] See No. 40.

[10] A reply to this letter, drafted in June for Mr. Dening's signature but never sent, argued in its final paragraph: 'As regards the breakdown of the Marshall peace negotiations, I am afraid we are quite unrepentant in attributing the chief blame to the Communists. As the Ambassador himself observed in his telegram No. 741 of the 16th November 1946, "I find it difficult to reconcile Chou's rejection with the interests of the [Communist] party as a Chinese (repeat Chinese) political group". So it seems to us now.' Sir R. Stevenson's telegram under reference is at F 16592/25/10.

producer can now be discounted as an independent political entity, which is perhaps unfortunate for China as its ranks seemed at one time to contain a number of potential 'liberal' leaders.

9. As a matter of detail we noticed that in the eighth paragraph of the China Department memorandum Mao Tze-tung is referred to as 'Moscow-trained.' If this is intended to mean that he was actually educated or indoctrinated in Moscow, we should be interested to learn the authority for this statement of which we appear to have no confirmation.[11] In any case I must confess on our part to an error in paragraph 10 of my despatch No. 83, which was clearly responsible for the misinterpretation of my meaning contained in paragraph 6 of your letter. As drafted the relevant sentence was 'China cannot altogether exclude foreign influences' which (though I unfortunately failed to notice it) was typed in the despatch itself as 'China cannot exclude foreigners', an obvious *non sequitur*. While the existence of large overseas Chinese communities need not necessarily prevent China from closing her frontier, it would at the same time make it difficult to set up an 'iron curtain' impervious to the infiltration of foreign influences and ideas through the extensive contacts of these overseas Chinese with their families and friends in China.[12]

[11] Investigations in July 1948 by the Far East Section of the FO Research Department uncovered Moscow despatch No. 659 of 30 August 1946, which stated: 'At the last Congress of the Third International in Moscow in 1935 China was represented by three leading members of the Yenan group, Mao Tse-tung himself . . .' The despatch also stated that Mao was elected a member of the Communist International and remained on the Executive Committee of the Comintern until its dissolution in 1943 (F 4391/33/10). In July 1949 the Embassy in Nanking returned to the issue of Mao's participation in the 1935 Congress, which ended in Moscow on 20 August 1935, while the Long March of the Communists in China did not end until 22 October 1935. Mr. G. Burgess of Far Eastern Department sought further clarification in July from the Embassy (F 8072/1015/10), which admitted that no evidence could be found to substantiate the assertion that Mao had been in Moscow (F 11132/1015/10). Further investigation led Mr. Burgess to conclude (15 August 1949) that while Mao had been elected to the Executive Committee of the Comintern, it was still not certain he had ever visited Moscow: 'it looks very much as if he did not. On the other hand the friendly recollection is that the organisation of his journey, whether implemented or not, was carried out very conspiratorially and by the Russians. It remains possible therefore that his visit was also conspiratorial (e.g. that he did not speak, or appear at plenaries or in the Press). A reason for this cld. presumably have been that the long marchers shld. assume that some of their leaders were sharing all their discomforts. But this is mere speculation.' According to a recent biographer, Mao's first visit abroad was to Moscow from December 1949 to February 1950 (Philip Short, *Mao: A Life* (London, 1999) p. 420). Of the thirteen members of the CCP Politburo elected by the Central Committee in 1945, Mao was one of six members who had not studied in the Soviet Union (James Tuck-Hong Tang, *Britain's Encounter with Revolutionary China, 1949-54* (London, 1992) p. 21).

[12] This despatch was signed by Mr. Lamb in the absence of the Ambassador.

No. 46

Sir R. Stevenson (Nanking) to Mr. Bevin

No. 415 [F 8050/33/10]

Confidential   NANKING, *25 May 1948*

Sir,

In my despatch No. 83 (1/1020/48) of 2nd February last[1] I commented upon a report made to the Central Committee of the Chinese Communist Party by Mao Tze-tung which contained several interesting items regarding the policy and objectives of the Chinese Communists. In particular Mao Tze-tung's review of the programme of his party indicated a significant modification of the purely agrarian policy designed for the landless peasant, inasmuch as he admitted the need to make concessions to the middle classes and the important part which the small business man was capable of playing in the China of the future under a Communist regime.

2. This attempt to appeal to a wider range of the population has manifested itself with even greater clarity in various subsequent statements by prominent Chinese Communist personalities, such as those which formed the subject of my despatches Nos. S/O 281 (112/1020/48 and S/O 293 (117/1020/48) of 11th May and 19th May respectively.)[2] There can be little doubt that such promises of recognition and favourable treatment would be attractive to a considerable section of the rural and urban communities, particularly in Northern China where public morale is likely to be at a lower ebb, and where the local population have had little cause for contentment with the conditions of life under the Central Government since the time of the Japanese surrender. It is at least evident from the subsequent declarations by spokesmen of the Central Government promising land reforms in favour of the tiller of the soil that the directors of Kuomintang propaganda are fully alive to the potential effectiveness of this new departure on the part of their adversaries.

3. The progressive deterioration of the economic situation in China unfortunately affords particularly favourable soil for the planting of the Communist seed. Intelligent foreign observers have in fact reported that

[1] No. 37.

[2] Despatch No. 281 commented: 'the Communists are raising their sights to take in the "Kulaks", whereas the Kuomintang are countering by gestures to the landless peasant. The same trends of policy are also noticeable in respect of the small capitalists and industrial labourers' (F 7781/366/10). No. 293 referred to statements on labour and taxation by Chen Po-ta, a member of the Central Committee of the CCP. On labour he suggested that it would be a mistake to fix wages at a uniformly low level and to afford no incentive for 'special exertion'. On taxation he argued that a distinction should be made between taxes on manufactured capital goods and the necessities of people's lives (F 8033/33/10).

there is a tendency on the part of the man in the street, especially in the North, to regard the prospects of life under a communist administration as a possible improvement. It is at the best a choice of two evils to the victims of the upheavals and depredations of civil war and the detrimental effects of incompetent and corrupt officialdom. It is probable, moreover, that certain of the known attributes of Communist government in other countries may not be as repugnant to the average Chinese as they would be to the inhabitants of countries where the principle of personal liberty has been established. Arbitrary exactions and impositions, disregard of *habeas corpus*, and the operations of secret police, for instance, are no novelty in this country where such totalitarian practices have survived despite the replacement of the supreme Emperor by a republican government.

4. This does not, of course, mean that the Communist philosophy is inherently attractive to the average Chinese mind. On the contrary, despite a good deal of sympathy among liberal and intellectual circles (notably, of course, in North China universities), some aspects of the orthodox Communist creed, such as collectivism of land cultivation, are in conflict with the peasant's deep-rooted desire to own the soil he cultivates as the best security for the likelihood of his family no less than himself. The recognition by the Communists of this important factor is demonstrated by the insistence in their agrarian reform platform upon the distribution of land to the individual peasant, thereby proving by their readiness to adjust their policy according to expediency, greater adaptability and skill than the Kuomintang in the exploitation of psychological opportunities. Thus, though the ferocity of some of the Communists' methods, such as the persecution of unfortunate victims through the people's courts, has been the cause of a considerable flow of refugees bringing tales of horror into other parts of China, the failure of the Kuomintang to improve the lot of the masses cannot but render the common people more susceptible to Communist propaganda. The menace of Communist infiltration tactics is therefore a real one from the point of view of the Chinese people, in whatever modified form it may be presented. For although they might have reason to hope for some improvement in the conditions of existence for the lower classes of society in the initial period of Communist domination, they would not of course be justified in looking forward to any such betterment being long-lived.

5. The same conclusion is, of course, equally inescapable with regard to British and other foreign interests. No one can deny that the anti-foreign basis of present Kuomintang policy, as interpreted, for example, in *China's Destiny',*[3] and practised in such ways as discriminatory restrictions upon foreign enterprises, the practical repudiation of the obligations of the Chinese Government under the 1943 and other treaties for the relinquishment of extraterritorial rights, and organised and often violent

[3] See No. 45, note 7.

agitations as occurred in Shameen[4] and Kowloon City. Nonetheless there may be some hope of improvement in the attitude towards the foreigner of the Kuomintang leaders with greater political maturity, whereas experience in other countries has amply demonstrated that Communism only produces deterioration. The balance between the potential benefits or disadvantages of the existing government and a Communist government is however more difficult to appraise in China than in other countries where the issue is a clearcut one between the Communists, whose hostility to us is patent, and their opponents whose friendship has been proved. In China, on the other hand, xenophobia is a national characteristic and has therefore to be reckoned with irrespective of the political complexion of the party in power. In this respect there are interesting indications that the Chinese Communists are becoming conscious of the need to bid for foreign sympathy by dissipating, or at least lessening, the unfavourable impression created abroad by their previous rough treatment of foreigners, especially missionaries. Whereas all accounts from eyewitnesses used to stress the brutal treatment accorded to foreigners, of whom Catholic missionaries were the worst sufferers, there have recently been indications of a studied policy of at least moderate respect for foreign persons and property in Communist areas. Certain members of foreign missions in Hsienhsien in Hopeh, for example, are being left comparatively unmolested and have even been permitted by the Communists to make trips to Tientsin on several occasions. There is also reason to believe that the Roman Catholic Bishop and his personnel at Ssupingkai in Manchuria, since its capture by the Communists, are being reasonably treated and may be permitted to evacuate. Though the news of two British employees of the Yee Tsoong Tobacco Distributors Limited (formerly the British American Tobacco Company) who were in Yingchow (Newchwang) when that port was recently occupied by the Communists, is perhaps not quite so encouraging, less anxiety is felt with regard to their safety than would certainly have been the case a few months ago. There have also been hints that the Chinese Communist leaders would be disposed to enter into business relations with foreign interests presumably in anticipation of the time when they may control trade centres such as Tientsin.

6. It would however be unduly rash to place much faith in these tokens of diminished hostility towards us. Whatever may be the modified appearance of Communism as applied in China in order to adapt itself to native characteristics, Communism is fundamentally hostile to the non-communist state and this hostility would sooner or later manifest itself in China even independently of Soviet direction. That Moscow will strive to exert its direct authority to the utmost over the Chinese Communists is equally a foregone conclusion. In doing so the orthodox Soviet communism may encounter obstructions and even set-backs in the face of Chinese obstinacy and inertia, but its baleful influence must inevitably prevail.

[4] A reference to the disturbances at Canton following the evictions at Kowloon: see No. 38.

Visitors to Communist areas have been impressed in this general connection with the much greater enthusiasm for Stalin and Soviet doctrines of the younger elements as contrasted with the older members of the community.

7. It is therefore evident that, despite the indisputable short-comings of the present government in China, no encouragement should be extended by us to the Communists regardless of any blandishments. At the same time it would obviously be imprudent to make gratuitous gestures of hostility in view of the British interests which are or may become hostages in their hands. It is nonetheless clearly expedient for us to render such assistance as we properly can to the Central Government and to align ourselves as far as possible with United States policy in this respect. The difficulty in doing so, however, is that United States policy is itself still somewhat indefinite and occasionally inconsistent. This is largely due to the fact that the utility of any active help to the Central Government depends upon the extent to which they are prepared and competent to take definite steps to use their own resources and those derived from abroad (e.g. United States aid) to the fullest advantage. The pouring of further money and materials into the country is inadequate by itself, and without genuine co-operation by the Chinese themselves the result would be no less abortive and futile than the operations of UNRRA. The American authorities, both at Nanking and at Washington, have been long striving to instil into the Generalissimo a sense of urgency and the necessity for more vigorous self-help but success has been hampered by the sort of political considerations illustrated in my telegram No. 443 of May 20th.[5] It is difficult therefore to avoid the conclusion that the only chance of effectively countering the threat of further expansion of the Chinese Communists into China is by actual foreign military assistance, though not necessarily by armed intervention. Such a step neither the United States of America nor any other democratic power can, however, take light-heartedly. Nonetheless only a military resolution of the situation seems to offer any hope of permanency. A peaceful solution by parliamentary process is no longer possible, if indeed it ever was, even at the time of the Marshall mediatory mission. And in view of the bitterness of the struggle, which is in effect a straight issue of Communist or Kuomintang domination over the whole of China, a compromise peace by a territorial division of administration seems almost as unattainable, though this, I believe, is the solution contemplated by the United States authorities in China. As things are at present the civil war, with its concomitant economic chaos, threatens to continue inconclusively and indefinitely, and, so far as can be estimated at present,

[5] This telegram referred to differences within the Chinese Government over senior appointments and to views expressed in *Life* magazine by William Bullitt, a former US Ambassador, to the effect that Mr. Marshall had been wrong to neglect China, that President Truman would be defeated at the presidential election, and that with the replacement of Mr. Marshall, the US would provide substantial military assistance to China (F 7408/33/10).

neither side is likely to listen to reason or to abandon the struggle through sheer exhaustion.[6]

I have, etc.,

(In the absence of HM Ambassador)

L.H. LAMB

[6] Sir R. Stevenson offered a further assessment of prospects in China when he visited the UK in the autumn and attended a meeting of the Russia Committee on 30 September. Arguing that the continuation in power of the Chinese Government would depend upon its holding of the financial position, the Ambassador anticipated that the 'gold yuan', a new currency introduced in June, was likely to collapse as soon as Chinese traders discovered means of evading the currency regulations. When that happened the Government's authority in the provinces would diminish and Communist influence would increase. Nevertheless, it was doubtful whether an effective Communist central government could govern 'in accordance with the doctrines of Lenin and Stalin except as a very long-term measure'. But even the existence of 'shadowy' Communist government would have repercussions in Malaya, Siam and South-East Asia generally, and such a government would vote with the Soviet bloc at UN meetings (N 10730/765/38).

No. 47

Extract from a Memorandum by the Chief of the Imperial General Staff on the General World Situation[1]

CIGS/BM/31/2562 [*FO 800/453*]

Private and Top Secret   WAR OFFICE, *18 August 1948*

1. It is becomingly increasingly clear to me that the general world situation is getting very grave. The religion of Communism, operated from Moscow, is slowly drawing the world towards great dangers; the full significance of these dangers is difficult to comprehend.

The Defence Committee has decided to submit a paper to the Cabinet, setting out the measures recommended as necessary to be taken immediately to place the Armed Forces in a better state of preparedness.[2]

[1] Field-Marshal Lord Montgomery of Alamein sent this memorandum to Mr. Bevin on 19 August with a covering letter which read: 'From time to time I write a memorandum for the Military members of the Army Council, and certain other very senior members of the War Office Staff, giving them my views on the situation. Such Memoranda are intended to influence War Office thought and policy, and to ensure that in our work in the War Office we face up to practical realities and do not bury our hands in the sand like an ostrich.'

[2] The consideration by the Chiefs of Staff, the Defence Committee and the Cabinet of Britain's state of preparedness for war was prompted by the Berlin airlift crisis, and will be documented in a forthcoming volume of *DBPO* covering Berlin during the Cold War. In a memorandum of 3 July 1948, 'Western Union Defence Organisation' (COS(48)147(0), Annex II, DEFE 5/11), the Chiefs of Staff had expressed the view that a general war was unlikely until the USSR had completed its second post-war five-year plan, and that in such circumstances the main defence burden in the Far East and Pacific would rest with the US based on Japan and

Meanwhile in the War Office we must be clear as to the impact of the growing dangers on our own affairs; we must be certain that we are not trying to do things which are not really capable of being done with the resources at our disposal. After all, we must be clear as to the essentials for success in those areas in which we cannot afford to fail.

2. The following notes give my views on the three *main* centres where trouble is likely to break out and where the consequences would be disastrous if we suffer defeat:

Western Europe
Middle East
Far East. ...[3]

The Far East

13. A surge of Communism is raging in the Far East. It has its origins in China.

14. In Burma, about one third of the Army has gone over to the Communists.[4] It is my view that the situation in Burma is very grave; the whole country will go Communist very shortly.

15. Malaya is seething with disorder.[5] The trouble is being handled by Chinese Communists, who are being reinforced through Siam. The

the Rykus. 'The task of the Commonwealth and other allied forces in the Far East is likely to be confined to maintaining internal security in the areas in which they are allocated.'

[3] Only the section relating to the Far East, and the Conclusion to the memorandum, are reproduced here. On Western Europe Lord Montgomery described as the 'supreme requirement' a determination on the part of the countries concerned 'to defend their homelands to the death'. A second essential was an organisation, under the control of a supreme commander, that would produce the necessary forces. Both were lacking in a state of affairs described by the CIGS as 'appalling'. Militarily France would have to be the 'hard core' of Western Europe and the UK and US 'should at once concert measures to effect the military rebirth of France'. On Berlin Lord Montgomery doubted that the airlift would be able to keep the city supplied during the winter months. The allies could not remain indefinitely in Berlin in defiance of the Russians. They should work towards a conference on Berlin, set up 'under proper conditions and not under pressure'. On the Middle East the CIGS argued that the policy of retrenchment was 'out-of-step with the trend of events' in its assumption that there would be an early return to settled peace-time conditions. He urged especially the retention in Egypt of a nucleus military base capable of rapid expansion to meet the needs of war.

[4] Burma became independent from British rule on 4 January 1948. Almost immediately the new government faced a revolt by Communists and the People's Volunteer Organisation, the para-military wing of the Anti-Fascist People's Freedom League which led the movement for independence. There were also disturbances among Burma's ethnic minorities which escalated in the case of the Karens, the largest minority, into an open rebellion at the beginning of 1949.

[5] A State of Emergency was declared in the Federation of Malaya in June 1948 following the murders of three European planters. In July the Malayan Communist Party was proscribed. The British Government did not, however, claim that the Malayan Communists were linked with Communists elsewhere as this would complicate attempts to reach an understanding with the CCP over UK interests in China. In October 1948 the Chinese Ambassador in London lodged a protest with the FO about the severity of some of the measures adopted under the Emergency. A Chinese Consul at Ipoh in the state of Perak in Malaya had reported the

reinforcements of troops we are sending out will not be sufficient to put things right, though they will help to restore confidence and to hold the situation until the Civil Administration can recover its breath.

If the Army is to defeat the troubles in Malaya we would require a force of from three to four Divisions: which we have not got.

What is really required in Malaya is very firm Government by the local administration, good District Officers, a first class police force, a highly efficient CID and police intelligence organisation, a sort of Home Guard organisation on the part of the inhabitants, and so on.

Unless very firm and strong action is taken in Malaya in these respects we may well lose that territory.[6]

Conclusion

16. And so the general picture is sombre, if not black. And we are unable to do very much about it because of the parlous state into which our Defence Services have been allowed to get.

17. The first shock of all the troubles will fall on the Army. The troubles in Malaya require soldiers.

If the Middle East is set alight, not by war but by Communism and racial antagonism, soldiers will be required in Egypt, in Libya, in the Horn of Africa; the first demand of everyone will be for more troops.

18. When troubles break out they can usually be handled *provided there are adequate troops on the spot in the first instance,* so that initial outbreaks can be dealt with promptly and firmly. Unless this can be done, the quelling of disturbances takes a very long time and, in the end, costs a great deal in human life and in money.

19. If we are to win through the next six to twelve months, we must take immediate steps to see that the troops we have on the spot in the Middle East are adequate to deal promptly and firmly with disturbances when that vast area is set alight. Similarly for the Far East; but here Australia should be asked to lend a hand.

20. In the West, we cannot do a very great deal ourselves at present. But we must see that the continental nations of the Western Union do

burning of 300 Chinese homes. The occupants had been rendered homeless and they had not been given time to remove their belongings (F 14871/1437/10).

[6] Commenting on 23 August on paragraphs 13-15 of this memorandum, Sir O. Sargent agreed that while troops in large numbers would be required to restore the situation in Malaya, the security of British and other 'friendly' territories in the Far East could be achieved 'only by the provision of adequate police forces and intelligence services'. Without apportioning blame to the colonial government which was having to build up security forces afresh after the Japanese occupation, he described the police forces in Malaya as 'inadequate'. 'There is no doubt', he commented, 'that we lack information about communist and other subversive activities in the Far East, and their connexion with Moscow'. If adequate police and intelligence services could be established, there was a reasonable prospect of 'nipping subversive movements in the bud' before the situation developed as it had in Malaya. The problem should not be seen in isolation, and the UK should pool information and co-ordinate resources with Burma, Siam, French Indo-China and the Dutch East Indies (FO 800/453).

something about it, and we must build up a high morale on the continent. We must always remember that, fundamentally, the West is the vital theatre in the long run.

21. In the end, it comes down to a question of manpower and equipment.

As regards manpower. So long as the world is in its present state, I do not believe we can handle our problem with National Service for only 12 months.[7] I think it may well have to be longer. The whole system of the manner in which the Fighting Services get their manpower was drawn up on the assumption that the world was to be a peaceful world.

The world is not peaceful. Therefore the whole subject needs urgent examination.

As regards equipment. This matter is already being taken up by the appropriate Departments. The immediate need is for technicians to repair and make serviceable much of our reserve stocks.[8]

M. OF A.

[7] The Cabinet decided in August 1948 to suspend releases from the armed services and to retain conscription for six months from 1 October (CM 57(48)2, 26 August, CAB 128/13).

[8] Mr. Bevin did not discuss this memorandum with Lord Montgomery as the question was being 'thrashed out' in the Defence Committee, but he instructed that consideration be given by the Foreign Office to consider how best to pool information and co-ordinate resources with other governments as suggested by Sir O. Sargent (see note 6 above).

No. 48

Minute by China Department on the Communist threat to Hong Kong[1]

[F 15770/154/10]

FOREIGN OFFICE, *19 October 1948*

The Chinese Communist Party in Hong Kong on the 18th June issued a statement to the effect that it had neither connexion with, interest in, nor connivance of, the activities of the Malayan Communist Party. It is believed that in matters of high policy Chinese Communists in Hong Kong receive their orders from the Central Committee of the Chinese Communist Party. In so far as Hong Kong is concerned, their line is to avoid incurring the displeasure of the authorities and this has been in fact the basis of the Communist Party's activities in Hong Kong over the past

[1] The background to this minute was an expression of concern by Mr. Bevin that should there be Communist trouble in Hong Kong, the British Government would be criticised for having sent troops to South-East Asia (Malaya primarily) from the colony. Mr. Scarlett minuted on 16 September: 'On the basis of recent reports I think we can reassure him [Mr. Bevin] that the Communists fully realise the usefulness of Hong Kong as their one remaining "entrepôt" in the South & in consequence have never been more careful.'

year. Hong Kong as a base from which to direct activities abroad is too valuable to be frittered away in local activities which might result in the banning or even expulsion of the Party with its leaders. There is said to be no separate Hong Kong Communist Party.

The attitude of the Chinese Communist Party is of course dictated by the problems of the conflict in China between the Chinese Communists and the Kuomintang, who are still in effect the Chinese Government. The Kuomintang, in Hong Kong as elsewhere, pursue a policy of trying to assert control over 'overseas Chinese' residents in Hong Kong, and their programme includes the eventual recovery of Hong Kong. But as long as the present civil strife in China continues the energies of the Kuomintang are more likely to be concentrated on counteracting Communist propaganda and boosting the Nanking Government than on embarrassing the Hong Kong authorities.

It is obvious in the circumstances indicated that action against one Party or the other would destroy the existing balance and enable the Party not affected to create difficulties for the Hong Kong Government. The latter were therefore recently authorized to maintain their existing policy of non-interference with political refugees etc. provided their activities are not detrimental to law and order. Warnings have been given to political dissidents such as ex-General Li Chi-shen[2] and the China Democratic League, but no such warnings have been needed in the case of the Communists. The Hong Kong Government recognize Communism in the colony as a potential menace, and extreme vigilance is exercised in order that no subversive movements may be hatched underground.

Should of course the civil war in China take a decisive turn the situation will be radically altered. In this connexion it should be borne in mind that hostility to British retention of Hong Kong will be inherited by *any* future government of China, or of the south of China, whatever its political complexion. In the meantime the Chinese Communists who use Hong Kong as a liaison and propaganda centre appear to be determined to refrain from any overt activity which would afford the Hong Kong Government reason for taking action against them. There is the further consideration to be borne in mind that, if action were taken now against the Communists in Hong Kong, the consequences might well be such as to require military action which His Majesty's Government would be unable to provide without prejudicing the progress of operations in Malaya.

---

[2] Li Chi-shen was the focal point in Hong Kong for rallying opposition to the Nanking government. Formerly a military governor of Kwantung province, he was expelled from the Kuomintang in August 1947.

No. 49

Mr. Lamb (Nanking) to Mr. Bevin

(Received 18 November, 3.47 p.m.)

No. 1010 Telegraphic [F 16258/33/10]

Important. Secret   NANKING, *18 November 1948, 3.11 p.m.*

Your telegram 853.[1]

Since the beginning of the Communist offensive in October the Government have lost approximately 500,000 men with all their equipment plus most of the equipment of approximately 10 divisions recently evacuated from Hulutao. The Communists are therefore expected, either on local basis if various battle areas are considered separately, or on overall basis, to concentrate superior force against remaining Government forces. The latter do not possess the fighting spirit which alone might enable them to overcome this handicap. The Government's only material advantages relative to the Communists are their air force and navy. The former is badly handled and comparitively [*sic*] ineffective while the latter is obviously incapable of having much effect in this type of war-fare.

2. The present position and future prospects by areas are as follows:

(*a*) North China

The Communists are now moving troops in preparation for delivery of final blow to Fu Tso I[2] who according to recent positive indications does not intend to await this but will withdraw to his own territory. The Communists should therefore be in control of the Peking Tientsin area well before the end of the year. The main military advantage gained from this is the control of two main railways which will enable them to produce any amount of force south of the Yellow River. The Government's position at Taiyuan cannot long survive fall of North China even if it does not precede it. This would give the Communists full control of another railway which will be useful for holding in check the independent North Western leaders who are however unlikely to be concerned with anything beyond trying to consolidate their own territories for bargaining purposes.

(*b*) Central China including Nanking and Shanghai area.

It is evident that the Communist objective is the destruction of the Government force in Hsuchow area followed by advance towards Nanking. Slight delay may be imposed on this programme by the failure to take

[1] This telegram of 16 November requested an appreciation of the overall military situation in China, with particular reference to the growing threat to Hong Kong (F 15798/33/10).

[2] General Fu Tso-yi, appointed Commander-in-Chief, North China Rebel Suppression Headquarters, December 1947, and Deputy Director of Chiang Kai-shek's Headquarters in North China, February 1948.

Hsuchow by the first direct assault, but the Communists have enough force available and not committed in the Hsuchow battle to prevent eventual escape southwards of any Government troops. The subsequent fall of Nanking is merely a question of time and Shanghai follows automatically. This pessimistic forecast is largely inspired by my impression of the complete absence of morale and therefore of fighting value among the Government troops.

(c) South of Yangtse

If events move as in (b) there will be virtually no regular Government troops left in this area except such as can be moved south from Hankow and four weak brigades in the Canton area. There will be no equipment available for the new forces. Communist domination of this territory therefore seems to depend on how fast they choose to move but they are likely by this time to be faced with considerable problems of administration and rehabilitation in territory already gained and may therefore be content to devote a fairly lengthy period to military and political infiltration of the South. Any indication of an intention on the part of America to try to consolidate an anti-Communist bloc in the South would inevitably tend to make them speed up the process of military conquest.

(d) Formosa

I assume that the Americans intend to hold this at all costs.

(e) West and South West China

So far as one can judge there is some Communist penetration of Yunan but not much in Ssuchuan. The latter province may therefore link itself for a time with the independent North West but cannot indefinitely survive the difficulty of the stranglehold imposed by Communist control of the Yangtse valley. The size and geographical position of Yunan may well cause it to be the last province to be over-run. On the other hand it is liable to be subjected to pressure from all sides including the South.

(f) In the circumstances stated in (c) above Hong Kong . . .[3] not be subject to direct military pressure for some time (exactly how long it is impossible to guess at this early stage) unless the Communists are forced by threat of outside intervention in South China to take urgent military action. Even then it does not follow that Hong Kong itself would be attacked. Economic and political factors on account of which they might prefer Hong Kong to remain free port under British administration are too well known to need repetition. But there would inevitably be the tendency among the local population including those who now support the Kuomintang to transfer their homage to new ruling party or group in China. This would impede Communist efforts to secure virtual control of the life of the port by ostensibly legal political means.

3. All forecasts in the preceding paragraph are based on the assumption that the Communists are compelled to continue the war of conquest. I am however inclined to the opinion that an early settlement with formation of

---

[3] The text was here uncertain.

a coalition Government is more likely.[4] Although main military considerations would not be greatly affected by such an outcome, it might result in reducing expansionist momentum of the Communists and in fomenting a desire to win foreign recognition by outward signs of good behaviour. In such circumstances direct military threat to Hong Kong would be less probable and there might even be a tendency to keep any disruptive propaganda campaign within the bounds.

4. The inescapable conclusion is that eventual Communist domination of the whole of China cannot be prevented. This might not result in direct military threat to Hong Kong but would increase internal political difficulties of the Colony. Though the danger, and eventual fate, of any coalition Government which includes Communists are apparent this is the most probable eventuality in the near future. In such an event it might be politic to accept this situation however unpalatable in hope of being able later on to exploit internal strains which are sure to develop rather than to try to bolster up the remnants of the present hopelessly decayed régime or to attempt to establish a new one by force of arms in the south; in this connexion I understand that the United States Ambassador has been informed that the President does not intend to take any action towards increased aid to China until the new Congress meets in March.[5]

[4] During the first Conference of HM representatives and colonial governors in the Far East and South-East held at Bukit Serene in Singapore on 18 and 19 November 1948, Sir R. Stevenson argued that if the Communists penetrated further than the Yangtse and were in virtual control of the whole of China, they would would still only be part of a Communist coalition. The actual degree of authority they would wield in such a coalition was doubtful. 'China was so enormous and the country so difficult that it would be a considerable time before the Communists would be in a position to give any material help to peoples in the South and West of China' (F 5158/10110/61).

[5] Mr. Dening commented on this telegram on 23 November: 'I do not think any useful purpose will be served by bolstering up Chiang Kai-shek's régime, because it has grown too rotten. Nor do I believe the Americans could have the technique even if such a course were feasible.

'In general I agree with Mr. Lamb's analysis. I do not know that *we* shall be able to exploit internal strains in a communist-dominated China, but the strains may, so to speak, exploit themselves. The 100% communists will be rather thin on the ground by the time they are spread all over China, and the natural resistance of the Chinese to regimentation will not be as easy to overcome as it was in Poland and Jugoslavia. I do not suggest that the stranglehold will not eventually be complete; merely that it is likely to take time.'

No. 50

UK Delegation to UN General Assembly (Paris) to Mr. Bevin

(Received 20 November)

No. 109 Saving: Telegraphic [F 16331/190/10]

Secret   PARIS, 19 November 1948

Repeated to New York Saving.

China.

I[1] saw Marshall this evening. He said that he was very glad to talk about United States' policy towards China. He went on to do at considerable length, involving a great deal of local history which I cannot attempt to report.

2. He said that the Chinese Government had now made some impossible applications to the United States Government which they did not mean to meet at all. The Chinese had asked that military supplies should be increased, that a pre-eminent American military figure should be immediately appointed as a Supreme Adviser, although in fact he would be a Supreme Commander, of the Chinese forces, and that the personnel of the existing military mission should be spread over Chinese divisions and attached again as advisers, but actually as Divisional Commanders. On the political side he said they were being asked to use their influence to build up among the small Chinese parties political support for Chiang Kai-shek.[2]

3. He said that the American Government were resisting all these demands. First of all on the supply side he said that he doubted if he had any real estimate of how much equipment they had made available to the Chinese. Although the appropriation was only $X million in actual figures he said that the price of supplies was so written down that the actual movement of supplies had become a major operation. Even if they had been willing to meet the Chinese request they had not at present the availabilities [*sic*].

4. They were refusing to attach a pre-eminent military figure because they did not think even if they had been willing to do so that a military

---

[1] Mr. Hector McNeil, Minister of State, FO, 1946-50. At the second session of the UN General Assembly in New York in November 1947, a Franco-Swedish proposal that the third session should be held in Europe was carried by 32 votes to 17, with 8 abstentions. Paris was announced as the venue in February 1948.

[2] Asked to obtain clarification of how the US might enlist support for Chiang Kai-shek among the small Chinese parties, Sir O. Franks (UK Ambassador at Washington, 1948-1952) replied that the head of the Chinese Affairs Division within the State Department had no knowledge that such support had been requested. 'He remarked that such a request would be even more fantastic than those to which State Department were by now accustomed to receive from Chinese' (Washington telegram No. 5417 of 29 November 1948, F 16969/190/10).

figure could catch up with the details of the military situation sufficiently to become an effective commander of the Chinese forces in trying to cope with the crisis which they judged would show itself over the next few months. (He said that their intelligence and his judgement was that the Communists would continue to push south.)

5. Similarly they did not dispense their military mission as Divisional Commanders because, he said, this, like the political pleas, was only an attempt by the Chiang Kai-shek Government to entangle America hopelessly in China and would only have resulted in America doing what the Soviet[s] most wanted them to do.

6. However, he went on to say that the policy of the United States was to continue to support Chiang Kai-shek for as long as he was supportable and that they would continue to make available the military supplies which they had contracted to make available. He stressed that he did not want to imply by anything that he had said that they were weakening in their support of Chiang Kai-shek.

7. Nevertheless, he went on at great length to show me that they were at their wits end for any palliative even for the present situation. He reaffirmed his admiration personally for Chiang Kai-shek but said that the whole administration was corrupt and that the graft was becoming worse rather than better. He said that they were exceedingly distressed about the state of the Chinese forces and even more distressed about the leadership in the Chinese forces. There were only three commanders in the field that he thought anything of. The military situation was so bad that something between six and seven divisions had recently surrendered in three operations with their total equipment. This meant, he said, that the Chinese forces were giving more arms and equipment to the Communists in a week than they, the United States, could produce for China in twelve months.

8. Moreover, he said that to dissipate their men or their material further in China could only be done at the expense of Western Union or the Atlantic Pact. This would be completely what Russia wanted them to do. Their effort would be dispersed and they would be making a maximum effort in the field, i.e. China, furthest from their base and with the least reliable of allies.

9. Despite this gloomy interview which went on for rather more than an hour, he kept saying again and again that he had great faith in the Chinese people and that they had a habit of extricating themselves from just such situations as these. The only time he descended to any precise discussion of an alternative leader to Chiang Kai-shek was when he mentioned T.P. [*sic*] Soong, whom he said seemed to have been establishing the elements of an alternative administration in, I think, Canton (he said that T.P. Soong was governing three provinces in the South).[3]

[3] Presumably this is a reference to Dr. T. V. Soong. Cf. Nos. 1, note 1, and 33.

10. He also spent some time saying that although the Chinese Communist was a Marxist and a Leninist he was different from other Communists. I intervened here because I must say that I thought some of his generalisations upon this subject rather ingenuous.

11. He was, as you can see, very forthcoming and not in the least panicky about the situation despite its gravity. I took the opportunity of mentioning our difficulties in extracting much information from Washington. He assured me that there was no reason for this and said that he would take steps to see that this position was repaired.

No. 51

Memorandum by Mr. Bevin on recent developments in the civil war in China[1]

CP(48)299 [*CAB 129/31*]

Secret   FOREIGN OFFICE, *9 December 1948*

I circulate to my colleagues herewith a paper regarding developments in the Chinese civil war.

This paper is designed to show the implications on British policy and interests in the Far East of a Communist domination of China. The present position in China is that the Communists already virtually control north China and it is merely a matter of time before this control is extended. The result may either be the disappearance of Chiang Kai-shek and the creation of a coalition dominated by the Communists, or an attempt by Chiang Kai-shek to keep his government in being in some part of China, which would result in a continuance of civil war. It is assumed that in either event Communist domination of China will only be a matter of time. It is also assumed that the Chinese Communists, if ever they succeed in surmounting their economic difficulties, will adopt the policies of orthodox Communism.

The only Power which could contribute financial, material and military resources for counter action against the Chinese Communists in China is the United States, but it seems unlikely that such counter action will be taken or, if taken, will be effective.

The political effects of this state of affairs on neighbouring countries are separately considered. The general conclusion is that Communist activities in all these countries will be increased and that contacts between Communists in these countries will be facilitated. The economic effects in

---

[1] Mr. Bevin had commissioned this paper on the political, economic and strategic consequences to the UK of Communist domination of China at an Office meeting on 6 November, with a view to consultation with Dominion Governments. It was drafted in the Far Eastern Department under the direction of Mr. Dening.

these areas are likely to be an increase in labour troubles and disturbances in the production of vital commodities.

In China it can be assumed:

(i) that there will be an immediate period of dislocation when foreign commerce generally will be at a low ebb;

(ii) that there will follow a period in which the economic difficulties of the Communists may dispose them to be tolerant towards foreign trading interests;

(iii) that the present nationalist tendency towards foreign investments and capital installations will thereafter be enhanced and that the intention to work rapidly towards the exclusion of the foreigner will be strengthened;

(iv) that there would be a tendency to subject foreign trade, both import and export, to close governmental control, which would not altogether suit the types of trade United Kingdom merchants aim at doing in and with China.

But British interests in China might be able to carry on at least for a time and we should encourage this.

It is recommended:

(i) that we should consult Commonwealth countries, the United States, France, Netherlands, Burma and Siam as to the best means of containing the Communist threat to all our interests;

(ii) that all necessary steps should be taken to strengthen our own position in Colonial territories in the area; and

(iii) that we should consider in consultation with friendly Powers whether the economic weakness of Communist-dominated China might not offer an opportunity to secure reasonable treatment for our interests.

E.B.

Annex to No. 51

I Political Appreciation

The Government of the Republic of China under President Chiang Kai-shek has virtually lost control of the whole area north of the River Yangtze as the direct result of military failures in Manchuria. Moreover, it seems highly unlikely that the Government forces, whose fighting value is at best problematical, will be able to hold their ground on the south bank of the river in the face of determined pressure from the Communists. The northern Communist armies now hold the initiative and are making an all-out drive on Nanking with intent to dislodge the Central Government from its capital. The consensus of expert opinion is that success is merely a matter of time.

2. Following on the Communist occupation of the whole area north of the Yangtze the political situation is likely to take one of two courses:

(*a*) The disappearance from the scene of Chiang Kai-shek, when the Government, headed by Vice-President Li Tsung-jen and with the support of certain military leaders, may try for a military truce and a subsequent political arrangement by negotiation with the Communists. As the latter hold the whip hand it is likely to rest with them whether such proposals are accepted or not.

(*b*) The withdrawal of Chiang Kai-shek and a small number of his henchmen to Canton or elsewhere in China proper in a die-hard attempt to continue the war. Although this is compatible with Chiang Kai-shek's present mood and would suit those members of the Kuomintang whose fate is linked with his, it is doubtful whether the essential quota of Government servants would be able or willing to follow. In any event he and his associates are now so completely discredited in the eyes of the people that their continued existence as a shadow government would be entirely dependent on American support, which would have to be much more extensive than anything so far undertaken. A withdrawal by Chiang Kai-shek to Formosa would hardly affect the course of events on the mainland.

3. Of the above alternatives the first is likely to be the more welcome to the Communists, since it would give them control over Nanking and Shanghai without driving away the administration and financial elements, which they would find it difficult to replace from their own resources. Further, if they attach importance to the international position they would thus step overnight into the controlling position in a recognised government. To the extent that they are guided by Moscow they may be encouraged to pursue this policy with a view to strengthening the opposition to the Western Democracies in the United Nations.

4. Much has been written which suggests that the Chinese Communists are Communists only in name. Justification for this view lies in the fact that up to the present there has been no need for Moscow to take any overt hand in the civil war or for the Chinese Communists to make any appeal to their compatriots save that of relative honesty, relative efficiency, an ostensibly fair deal in the matter of land reform and above all peace. On the other hand, a careful study of their official pronouncements shows that their leader, General Mao Tse-tung, pays at any rate whole-hearted lip service to the Marxist-Leninist philosophy, while the Moscow press has avoided comment on his successes with such scruple over so long a period as to suggest that it is in the interests of Soviet policy not to trouble the pipe dreams of the complacent. Inasmuch as the Communist administration appears to be better disciplined and less corrupt than that of

the Central Government, it may well be that if it is their policy to develop and exploit Chinese resources their initial attitude to foreign technical ability and trading interests may be encouraging. It would, however, be highly dangerous to assume that this initial honeymoon period would be likely to ripen into any enduring bond.

5. It is nevertheless clear that, by whichever means the Communists acquire control of the area south of the Yangtze, they must inherit the economic ills of the land. If they do so by entering a coalition Government the drain on the exchequer from civil war would cease, but it may be assumed that the Central Government has already reached such a degree of insolvency that the advantage of this is likely to be more apparent than real. In our present ignorance of Communist internal policies it is impossible to measure the degree of handicap which this state of affairs will represent, but its existence can hardly fail to induce the Kuomintang's successors to seek to maintain the country's export trade in order to pay for her essential imports, and in this connexion some initial benefit to British traders may accrue. Moreover, it is also fair to assume that General Mao Tse-tung will be hard put to it to provide the necessary administration, the more so as the number of his efficient followers is probably limited and will become somewhat thin on the ground when the whole of China falls to be administered. This factor, too, may well tend to shelter British interests for some time from the full force and fury of Communist theory and practice. But of the ultimate intentions of Mao Tse-tung, if he succeeds in surmounting local difficulties, there is little doubt.

6. In either event the Communists would almost certainly require a fairly lengthy period of preparation and infiltration before moving very far south of the Yangtze. Even in the absence of any coherent opposition, therefore, the eventual Communist domination of the whole of China is likely to take some little time. Whether advantage can be taken of the breathing space to create an anti-Communist *bloc* (for which American aid would be essential) remains to be seen, but as already indicated, the prospects are very doubtful.

II AMERICAN POLICY TOWARDS CHINA

7. The United States Government have been under considerable pressure from the Chinese to increase their military aid to the Nationalist forces and to issue some firm statement in support of the Central Government's cause. President Chiang Kai-shek has appealed to Mr. Truman not only for supplies but for the appointment of a pre-eminent American figure as Supreme Adviser to the Chinese forces who would in fact be a Supreme Commander, and that the personnel of the existing Military Mission should be spread over Chinese divisions, again as Advisers but in fact as Divisional Commanders. On the political side they have been asked to canvass support for Chiang Kai-shek among small political parties in China. Mr. Marshall has explained that it is his Government's intention

to refuse these hysterical requests but at the same time to continue to support Chiang Kai-shek so long as he is supportable by hastening deliveries of such supplies as the Americans have contracted to make available under the grant for aid to China already voted by Congress. Madame Chiang's visit to the United States to canvass her husband's cause thus represents no mean embarrassment to United States authorities.[2]

8. It is noteworthy that the United States Ambassador to China, who has long been a staunch advocate to giving the fullest aid to the Central Government, has now reached the conclusion that it is too late for such a policy to be effective. We may thus assume that Washington will stand by their present policy of limited commitments on Chiang Kai-shek's behalf. The State Department are, however, in a dilemma, since if they were to issue some statement calculated to assist Chiang Kai-shek, they would be concealing the true facts from the American public and being dishonest with Congress. If, on the other hand, the State Department revealed the true facts to the American public, they would, in Mr. Lovett's words, 'pull the rug out from under Chiang Kai-shek's feet'. To a lesser extent this same dilemma must condition any references to the Chinese situation which His Majesty's Government may feel obliged to make in Parliament.

III POLITICAL EFFECTS ON ADJACENT AREAS

(a) Japan

9. The spread of Communism in China will enhance the political and strategic importance of Japan as the most important non-Communist area in East Asia, and seems certain to strengthen the determination of the United States Government that Japan shall not fall under Communist domination. United States policy towards Japan is largely determined by strategic considerations arising out of the tension in Soviet-American relations. The Americans no longer appear to regard Japan as a potential threat to security, but as potential help in the case of war with the Soviet Union. This trend in American policy is being scrutinised very carefully by certain Commonwealth countries, notably Australia and New Zealand, who would consider that their security was threatened by the restoration of Japan, unless it were kept under strict Allied control. For this reason, besides its more direct effects on the United Kingdom's own interests, the United Kingdom must also watch it carefully. It is, moreover, a trend which seems certain to be strengthened if China becomes lost, wholly or in part, to the democratic world. The Americans are likely to become more determined than ever to ensure that the Japanese standard of living is maintained at a level high enough to give the Japanese worker no incentive to turn to extreme political courses; and their conviction that it would be unwise to conclude a Treaty of Peace in present circumstances and that the

[2] Madame Chiang Kai-shek visited Washington in December 1948: see *FRUS 1948*, vol. vii, pp. 608-10, 626, 653.

military occupation of Japan must be continued for an indefinite period will be strengthened.

(b) Hong Kong

10. Communist domination of China down to the Yangtze is not in the first instance likely to affect Hong Kong very seriously. The colony's major problem is likely to be a steady stream of refugees. If, as may be expected, the Communists continue southwards, they may well try to 'soften up' Hong Kong by instigating strikes to coincide with their advance. Since labour in public utilities and on the waterfront in Hong Kong is mainly Communist in sympathy, such strikes might temporarily paralyse the colony. Serious clashes between Communist and Kuomintang supporters might also occur.

11. If all China were dominated by the Communists, the retention of Hong Kong as a British colony, in the absence of strong British naval and military forces, might depend on whether the Communists found the existence of a well-organised, well-run British port convenient for their trade with the outside world. In that event, while Hong Kong might be faced with a vast refugee problem, the colony could continue its life, but would be living on the edge of a volcano. Meanwhile the Communists would no doubt continue their infiltration tactics. If, on the other hand, the Communists were to demand the rendition of Hong Kong to China, they would use every method short of war to undermine it.

(c) The Federation of Malaya and Singapore

12. Communist control of China down to the Yangtze would not have such serious effects on Malaya as Communist domination of the whole of China, because most of the Malayan Chinese come from South China and because the Communist-controlled areas would not be contiguous to the frontier of French Indo-China. The following reactions among Malayan Chinese during such a period could, however, be expected, while some of the effects forecast in paragraph 13 below would also be felt:

(i) an intensification of Kuomintang activity. An increase in Kuomintang activity has already been reported in recent weeks (including paper plans for an underground cell system);

(ii) strong support for the China Democratic League and the Kuomintang Revolutionary Committee, which would increase if a coalition Government were formed in China;

(iii) increased political activity by the Chinese community, with agitation for increased representation of the Chinese in the Federal or State Councils, to which the Malays would react strongly.

13. Communist control of the whole of China would be a grave danger to Malaya and would mean that:

(i) Militant communism would be very close to Malaya's northern frontier, with Siam and French Indo-China as poor buffers;

(ii) the morale of the Malayan Communists would be bound to improve;

(iii) there might very well be increased activity by China Communist Party agents infiltrating into Malaya. A number of China Communist Party agents are already reported to have reached Singapore;

(iv) a comparatively small increase in the successes of the Malayan Communists might have wide repercussions among the passive Chinese community, since Chinese morale as a whole in Malaya has never been good, and is very sensitive to bandit successes, intimidation, and propaganda;

(v) the Chinese population in general might well be even less ready to co-operate actively with the Malayan Government than at present. They will continue to sit firmly on the fence and hope that a Communist administration in China will turn out to be peaceful and reformist;

(vi) subversive activities by Kuomintang diehards might well continue, though admittedly without the backing of the Chinese Government, which it has hitherto enjoyed to the detriment of good government in Malaya;

(vii) there would be some increase in illegal immigration into Malaya and there might also be a demand for asylum for political refugees;

(viii) there would be repercussions among the Malays to any increase in Chinese political activity and also if militant communism were to spread in Indonesia.

(d) Sarawak and North Borneo

14. In Sarawak and North Borneo it is expected that Communist successes in North China will probably lead to an increase in Communist sympathies among the local Chinese population and reinforcement of present Communist attempts to persuade Chinese *intelligentsia* that national aspirations can now best be achieved through communism. At the same time a parallel increase in Kuomintang activity may be expected in the form of tightening control over registered societies, and increasing pressure on the Communists.

(e) Foreign Territories in South-East Asia

15. In general, it may be expected that Communist successes in China will stimulate Communist movements throughout the area. If the Chinese Communists succeed in overrunning the whole of China, the possibilities of contacts with the Communists in Indo-China, Siam and Burma will be greatly facilitated, and it may be expected that Communist agitation in various forms will be accelerated to a marked degree.

16. *Burma.* The frontier between Burma and China is in part undefined, and in view of the fact that the present Burmese Government lacks effective control, it would be difficult to prevent the infiltration of Chinese Communists and a link-up between them and Burmese Communists against the Government were the whole of South-West China to come

under Chinese Communist control. The general disorder in Burma might render it very difficult to cope with any considerable increase in Communist strength. There might also be the two further dangers of communism seeping over the border into India and Pakistan (East Bengal), and of the Chinese Communists pressing China's extensive frontier claims against Burma.

17. *Indo-China.* Direct contact between Communist-controlled China and Northern Indo-China will greatly increase the difficulties of the situation in the latter territory, where the failure of the French Government to take effective measures to seek a solution has resulted in an alliance between the Nationalist and Communist elements. The French forces in Indo-China are already stretched, and if the Viet Minh[3] were to be strongly reinforced as a result of a Communist-controlled China, the situation might well become untenable for the French, at any rate in the north. There would be an increased threat to South-East Asia in general through the strengthening of the Communist position in Indo-China.

18. *Indonesia.* Apart from the psychological effect of a total Communist victory in China upon Communists in Indonesia, it is doubtful whether any very early reactions would manifest themselves in view of the defeat administered to the Communists in their recent attempt to wrest power from the Republic. But if the Dutch were to fail to reach a settlement in the near future and were to take military action against the Republic, this might lead to an alliance between the Nationalists and the Communists which might result in a long period of disorder with serious consequences not only to Indonesia but to South-East Asia as a whole.

19. *Siam.* There is quite a strong Chinese Communist element in Siam which so far has not caused serious trouble, but encouraged by the situation in China it might well get out of hand, and it is by no means certain that the comparatively inefficient administration in Siam would be able to deal with it effectively. There is a considerable danger that if the Communists got out of control in southern Siam, they might combine with Communist elements in Malaya, thus rendering the suppression of the latter immeasurably more difficult.

20. *Sinkiang and Tibet.* Chinese Communist control in Sinkiang would facilitate increased Russian pressure, which is already apparent in that region. It is just conceivable, however, that if the Russians sought complete domination in Sinkiang, this might cause a rift with the Chinese Communists, whose nationalism would not take kindly to Russian acquisitiveness. In Tibet, it is not likely that the Tibetans would welcome Chinese Communists any more than they welcome attempts at domination by the National Government of China. But obviously the potential danger

---

[3] Abbreviated and popular name for Viet Nam Doc Lap Dong Minh that constituted, under the leadership of Ho Chi Minh, a coalition of Communist and Nationalist groups fighting for Vietnamese independence from French colonial rule.

is greater as the area to the north and east of Tibet comes under communist domination.

(f) India and Pakistan

21. The political consequences to India and Pakistan of Communist domination of China would be indirect but none the less formidable. They would be moderated or delayed to the extent that Communist domination did not spread over the whole of China. They would consist in the first instance of the great moral effect of China becoming a Communist State. India, and to a lesser extent Pakistan, are the field where Western and Asian civilisations meet, and there is always a tension between them. Hitherto, Russia has been a third factor; but the adoption of communism by a major Asiatic country would be likely to cause it to be regarded in India and Pakistan more favourably than when it was predominantly a northern and western development. Although China has no common frontier with India, a Communist-dominated China would certainly result in a strengthening of communism in Burma, and the countries to the north of India—Tibet, Nepal and Bhutan—would gradually be penetrated by Communist influence. Thus there would at once be a threat of political and strategic encirclement of India and Pakistan's land frontiers by Communist states, which might in a relatively short time become a reality.

22. The political consequences of this situation may be summarised as follows:

(i) The Indian Communists would derive enhanced prestige and greater influence. At present they are a small but vigorous minority. They would be fortified by the infiltration of Communist agents and Communist finance through Burma, Eastern Pakistan, and through North-West Pakistan.

(ii) The Indian Communists would redouble their efforts to acquire influence over organised labour. They already have an influential trade union organisation under their effective domination. The agricultural population is illiterate and politically inert and therefore the urban population of India, which is small, has an influence out of all proportion to its size.

(iii) Any economic disaster, such as a famine, would give communism an opportunity to spread to rural areas.

(iv) The present attitude of neutrality on the part of India in foreign policy as between the Communist States and the Western democracies might harden as Communists rises [*sic*] to power in Asia. On the other hand, Hinduism is strongly opposed to communism in outlook and initially at any rate the Nehru Government[4] would be likely to make a determined stand against communism, their ability to maintain it

---

[4] Pandit Jawaharlal Nehru, Prime Minister of India, 1947-64.

depending on their ability to provide progressive improvement of the economic condition of the masses.

(v) Burmese rice might be diverted away from India if Burma went Communist and joined in any attempt to overthrow the existing regime in India. This would be a powerful factor militating against an improvement in India's economic condition.

(vi) The Government of Pakistan would be likely to be strongly anti-Communist if their disputes with India, particularly over Kashmir, were disposed of. Until that happens, however, there is a possibility that Pakistan might prefer Russian support against India, even with some knowledge of Russia's price, to absorption or conquest by India, which she still regards as India's primary objective. A solution of the Kashmir dispute would therefore become even more essential from our point of view if the Chinese Communists succeed in controlling China.

IV Economic Effects

23. The main economic effects of a Chinese Communist advance depend again on whether the advance is stopped at the Yangtze or continues over South China. The main fields in which our economic interests might be affected (depending on the extent of the advance) would be:

(*a*) British commercial property and investments in China;

(*b*) China-United Kingdom trade;

(*c*) Shipping;

(*d*) The economy of Hong Kong;

(*e*) The economy of South-East Asia;

(*f*) Overseas Chinese remittances.

24. In general it might be assumed that, wherever the Communists might get to, there would be an initial period before any stable administration could get going there, when foreign commerce and business generally would be at a low ebb. This could not, however, be a very much worse state of affairs than that existing in China at present, with the lack of easy and safe internal communications, extremely inflated prices, the restrictive attitude of the present National Government towards foreign trade, shipping and business, and the prevalent corruption. During this period the economies of Hong Kong and the South-East Asian countries generally would probably be affected mainly (and in the case of Hong Kong, seriously) by labour disturbances and refugees, but only to any great extent if the advance continued beyond the Yangtze. There is, too, a possibility that the Communists might decide to by-pass Shanghai, isolating it from its hinterland. In this event the city would be faced with starvation, and not only would the danger to British life and property be increased,

but we and the Americans would be under considerable pressure to supply it by sea.

25. In the longer term much depends on the attitude the Communists adopt towards foreign commercial and shipping interests, and towards Hong Kong as a foreign enclave on the one hand and as a well-run and well-organised entrepôt on the other hand. If one assumes a period of Communist opportunist policy, foreign trade and business with and in the Communist-dominated area will probably not vary greatly in quantity but should at least be less precarious—unless and until the threat of expropriation begins to be felt. Undoubtedly the maintenance or creation of a balance of visible trade using existing facilities (Hong Kong entrepôt, foreign shipping, foreign-owned insurance and commercial houses) would be a vital prop to a new Government, at least until it felt in a position to provide the facilities itself. And any Chinese Government would have to maintain facilities to provide for essential imports (rice, raw materials etc.) which in 1936, a good year, amounted to 17 per cent. of her imports. As against this, however, it must be assumed that a general tightening up of controls would occur with resultant restrictions on remittances and on the possibility of the general range of British goods gaining an established position in the potentially vast Chinese market.

26. The final stage of expropriation or expulsion of foreign commercial and shipping interests and investments, and the undermining of Hong Kong's economic prosperity, may not materialise for some time in view of the extent and essential nature of these interests compared for instance with those in Eastern European countries. But the combination of Chinese Nationalist and Communist feelings may well precipitate this event which, if Shanghai and South China were overrun, would involve a considerable loss to British commercial interests in Shanghai, to British shipping firms operating on coastal trade in South China, and, above all, to the present prosperous economy of Hong Kong.

27. A more detailed consideration of these possible economic effects is given under the several heads below.

(*a*) *British commercial property and investments*

28. The whole situation is laden with 'ifs', but under the present régime British interests are in a bad way and little return is being received from existing investments. Up to date there has always been a hope of improved conditions, which is not likely to materialise under a Communist régime.

29. The total value of British commercial property and investments in China was assessed in 1941 at £300 million of which about one-third is situated in Shanghai. The true figure for the present time cannot be accurately estimated.

(*b*) *China-United Kingdom trade*[5]

---

[5] Negotiations to conclude a new commercial treaty between the UK and China had been stalled for some time. Both parties produced drafts in 1946 but then delays occurred, mainly on the UK side owing to Board of Trade experts being preoccupied with work at Geneva and

30. United Kingdom trade with China is at a comparatively low level at present due to the innumerable difficulties mentioned above. Our main interest lies in increasing exports from China, and in the long run to get a foothold in the potentially great Chinese market.

(i) *Chinese visible exports from Sterling Area*

31. United Kingdom exports to China, which amounted in 1947 to nearly £13 million, will probably be slightly less in 1948. About 50 per cent. consists of banknotes, textile machinery, other machinery, electrical goods and iron and steel manufactures; the remaining 50 per cent. consists of wool tops and miscellaneous goods. Most of this trade passes through Shanghai, and imports of machinery and similar goods from the United Kingdom remain in Shanghai or in other industrial centres, which are mostly north of the Yangtze. Domination of China down to the Yangtze by a Communist Government would therefore be little different in effect from domination of all China by such a Government.

32. Conditions in China have lately been very unfavourable and current trade is neither healthy nor stable. On a long-term view we should certainly want to maintain a foothold in what is potentially one of the greatest markets in the world. A Communist administration would, however, probably restrict imports even more closely than is being done at present by the Central Government to strictly essential goods, especially machinery and capital goods. We should be reluctant to give the Chinese market high priority for the scarcer capital goods or to quote early delivery dates (both of which would probably be demanded) since we do not control our export trade in this way and the volume and importance of Chinese exports to us would not justify it.

33. It is worth noting that even in bad years rice and other foodstuffs and raw materials form a high proportion of China's essential imports and much of this comes from the Sterling Area.

(ii) *United Kingdom visible imports from China*

34. United Kingdom imports from China, which amounted in 1947 to about £7 million, will probably be more in 1948. They consist chiefly of

Havana concerning the International Trade Organisation. At an inter-departmental meeting on 21 October 1947 it was decided to ask the Chinese to negotiate on the basis of the original UK draft, with certain modifications. Sir R. Stevenson, however, advised that it would be better to have no treaty at all than an unsatisfactory one, which was all that could be expected in the existing situation. This was also the view of the British commercial community in China. Their advice was to go slow and hold out for certain essential safeguards on a national and reciprocal basis. 'The upshot', according to Mr. A.L. Scott, 'is that until things settle down one way or another in China, or some pressure is brought to bear on us, we propose like Brer Rabbit to lie fairly low and say nuffin' (letter to Mr R.L. Speaight, 29 April 1948, F 5946/710/10). In the event a commercial treaty was never concluded. A Sino-American treaty was signed at Nanking on 4 November 1946. It was ratified by China at the same time and by the US Senate in June 1948. It came into force in November 1948.

bristles (an important raw material, and China is the main source of supply), vegetable seeds etc., dairy produce (mainly eggs), tung oil and tea. Given financial and political stability and improved transport China could contribute far more than this insignificant amount to our requirements of agricultural produce and raw materials, but she could scarcely become a major source of supply for basic commodities. Most of this trade passes through Shanghai, and many of the areas from which the imports are drawn lie to the North of the Yangtze (the two chief exceptions being the southern province of Kwangtung and the island of Formosa). The effect of domination of China down to the Yangtze by a Communist government would therefore differ only in degree from that of domination of all China by such a government.

35. Unless it is prepared to face widespread suffering and discontent, any Chinese Government must foster at least enough foreign trade to pay for essential imports, of which rice, foodstuffs and raw materials form a high percentage. This need for essential imports would mean that a Communist administration would be under stronger pressure tha[n] the Nationalist Government to take active steps to increase the volume of exports, since it would probably be without any credits from foreign countries, and unable to draw upon such resources as the sterling credits acquired in this country by Chinese industrialists and financiers during the war, which have paid for a proportion of the capital goods sent to China in the last three years. We might therefore be in a better bargaining position than in present circumstances to obtain the sort of commodities we want from China, but, as stated above, the Chinese would undoubtedly want scarce and high priority goods in return.

36. The *general conclusion*, therefore, is that (after a temporary dislocation of perhaps several months) trade between the sterling area and China would not cease under Communist domination. Its maintenance would, however, present new difficulties. If these could be overcome a stable Communist administration should be able to do more than the present régime to provide commodities valuable to us in payment for United Kingdom exports.

(c) Shipping

37. There is as yet no indication of what Communist policy towards foreign shipping will be. Independence of foreign vessels and the closing of the Yangtze to foreign shipping have long been objectives of Chinese nationalist feeling, but the Communists will certainly need shipping for coastal and river traffic, and their policy may well be determined by the amount of the present Chinese merchant tonnage which falls into their hands. British shipowners in the China trade are prepared to trade wherever trade offers.

(i) Coastal shipping between China, Hong Kong and South-East Asia

38. If the Communists allow British vessels to trade at Chinese ports under their control Communist domination of China down to the Yangtze would probably benefit British coastal trade by reintegrating the North

China ports with their economic hinterland and Communist domination of all China would probably not affect trading on the South China coast.

39. If the Communists do not allow British coastal vessels to trade at Chinese ports under their control Communist domination of China down to the Yangtze would be little worse than conditions prevailing until recently, as there has for some time been little profit in the North China coastal trade, but Communist domination of all China would mean very serious losses to British shipping firms, whose trade is now largely based on the South China coast. It would also be a grave blow to Hong Kong, whose shipping prosperity is bound up with the China trade.

40. It is impossible to assess how much of the existing Chinese flag coastal tonnage, which now has the monopoly of the coastal trade and amounts to some half million tons gross, will become available to the Communists.

(ii) *Ocean shipping*
41. The ocean companies are concerned chiefly with Shanghai. Ocean shipping would not be affected if the Communists allowed foreign flag vessels to trade there, but would cease if they did not. If the Communists captured Shanghai's hinterland but not Shanghai itself ocean companies would probably continue their present trade in an attenuated form.

42. The extent of Chinese overseas tonnage is negligible. Therefore, if the Communists were obliged by economic necessity to use overseas vessels, British tonnage should obtain a share.

(iii) *River shipping*
43. The Yangtze, which is navigable by ocean going vessels and is China's main waterway, is at present closed to foreign shipping. If it and Shanghai were opened by the Communists British coastal and ocean companies would be better off than at present.

(iv) *Assets of British shipping firms in China*
44. The shipping firms trading in China and those trading with China, as well as the oil companies, all have extensive shore properties in every port and in addition they own harbour craft such as the tugs and lighters in Tientsin, practically the whole of the dock and repair facilities in Shanghai and a considerable proportion of the harbour craft there as well. The value of these properties was valued in 1941 at £18 million.

(d) *The economy of Hong Kong*
45. Subject to what has been said in paragraphs 24, 25, 26 and 39 above, Communist domination of China down to the Yangtze would probably not affect Hong Kong's economic position if a strong resistance line could be formed at the Yangtze; it might even be benefited, more especially if the use of Shanghai as a port became more difficult and increased imports of essential food, petrol, oil, etc., for China were to be diverted, in whole or in part, through Hong Kong.

46. If the Communists dominated all China, they might provisionally wish for their own purposes to keep Hong Kong as a going concern in British hands. They might, however, take ruthless steps to acquire all Hong

Kong dollar notes held in South China; this could only be partly successful unless the Chinese economy were prosperous and the Hong Kong dollar definitely on the decline—there would be no inducement to surrender Hong Kong dollars voluntarily except for a stronger currency. Hong Kong notes requisitioned by the Communist Government might be used indirectly to obtain sterling credits for purchases for the Chinese Communists or for the USSR. Shares of Hong Kong public utility and dockyard companies would probably fall substantially, but it is considered unlikely that there would be any actual flight of British capital. If the Communists chose to carry on a cold war against Hong Kong on the economic front, they might be able, temporarily at any rate, to paralyse the economic life of the Colony by fomenting strikes. Rumours spread by them in Hong Kong that there was no backing for the Hong Kong dollar might also cause great difficulties; but Chinese exports would no doubt be smuggled into Hong Kong in substantial quantities despite Communist efforts to route them elsewhere.

(*e*) *Economy of South-East Asia*

47. The most serious economic effects of a Communist-controlled China are likely to be:

(i) the probable increase in Communist-inspired labour disturbances in South-East Asia;

(ii) a serious refugee problem, particularly in Hong Kong, whose food resources will consequently be strained to the utmost;

(iii) further disturbances in the rice-producing countries (Burma, Siam, Indo-China) leading to a decrease in the production of rice, on which we, India, and Ceylon rely to feed the increasing populations of our respective territories. Already rice production is lagging well behind pre-war and any decreases in the present inadequate production will have the greatest repercussions on our colonial territories and on the Asian Commonwealth countries. A decrease in rice consumption will provide fertile ground for Communist agitation. This—together with general disturbances in other South-East Asia industries—would cause further disruption of the economy of the area with consequent adverse effects on the production of such vital commodities as rubber, tin, edible oils, etc., which are of such importance to world economic recovery.

(*f*) *Overseas Chinese remittances*

48. It is not expected that after perhaps a temporary interlude Chinese living abroad will wish to discontinue family remittances to a Communist China. Patriotic funds to help the nationalist cause would of course cease, but by far the greater proportion of foreign remittances are family remittances largely to South China. It may be estimated that at present about half these pass through Hong Kong, where they are converted into Hong Kong dollars or Chinese currency for use in China. Hong Kong's

valuable foreign exchange earnings from this traffic will possibly be increased rather than reduced while conditions remain unsettled in China. The risk of attempts at diversion by a strong Chinese Government remain the same, Communist or Kuomintang.

V Possibilities of Counter-Action

49. Certain measures for the emergency evacuation of British residents in China have already been taken. The Commanders-in-Chief, Far East, have for some time been considering the military aspects of the problem in relation to Hong Kong and South-East Asia. Action on the civil side is being taken to put Hong Kong into as great a state of preparedness as possible. The Chiefs of Staff have been invited to consider the strategic implications of the China situation in so far as it threatens the colony of Hong Kong. It is, however, desirable to consider what further measures are open to us to safeguard British interests in the Far East.

China

50. The only Power which could contribute financial, material or military resources for counter-action against the Chinese Communists in China is the United States. For reasons already stated, it seems unlikely that such counter-action will be taken, or if it were taken that it would be effective. As far as the United Kingdom is concerned, our best hope probably lies in keeping a foot in the door. That is to say that, provided there is not actual danger to life we should endeavour to stay where we are, to have *de facto* relations with the Chinese Communists in so far as these are unavoidable, and to investigate possibilities of continued trade in China. It may be that, in consultation with our friends, we shall have a bargaining counter by virtue of our being able to withhold certain essential imports which China must have if the Chinese Communists do not behave. We might be able to insist as a *quid pro quo* that the Communists should respect our trading position and our properties in China. This will require further examination, but seems to offer the only possibility of counter-action in the immediate future. If the Chinese Communist administration fails to obtain effective control of the country, it may be possible to take advantage of internal strains as they manifest themselves to maintain and even improve our position. In order to do this it is essential that we should not abandon our position in China, and we must aim to keep, at any rate, a foot in the door.

South-East Asia

51. The Americans are apparently not prepared to accept any responsibility for South-East Asia, or to take any action at present to maintain the position of friendly Powers there. It therefore seems that it will fall to the Powers geographically situated in the region to take their own measures to meet the Communist menace. It is more than ever essential that the most strenuous efforts should be made to clear up the situation in Malaya as soon as possible. Though it is very desirable that the measures taken by the Governments in the area should be co-ordinated, it

is very doubtful whether in the present political situation in the region it would be possible to align the various territories publicly together. Burma, for example, would find difficulty in associating with French Indo-China and Indonesia, while the French and the Dutch might be equally reluctant to have such an association. Moreover, the Commonwealth countries primarily concerned, i.e., Australia, New Zealand, India and Pakistan, which all have a vital interest in the peace and prosperity of South-East Asia, would on present showing be unwilling to join in any activities involving support of the French and Dutch Governments in this area. It may, therefore, be that the United Kingdom is in the best position to act as the co-ordinating factor though it would be necessary to consider the political consequences very carefully at each stage.

52. In these circumstances there might be advantage in our addressing ourselves to all the interested Powers, setting forth our view of the problems likely to arise as a result of Communist successes in China, and consulting with the Powers concerned as to the best method of dealing with the situation. Such communications might be addressed to the Commonwealth countries, to France, the Netherlands, Burma and Siam. The United States should be kept informed and their support sought. It is desirable, so far as political considerations permit, to ensure that each territory was possessed of police and intelligence services, as well as the requisite legal powers, to deal adequately with any growth of Communist activity, and with these measures in view to arrange for an exchange of information (always provided that this is without risk to our own security) and for frequent consultation. The possibilities of doing this would be considered on receiving the answers to our communications to the various Governments. We might also invite a study of the economic consequences of Communist domination of China for the whole area.

53. In addition to the studies of the military aspects of the problem mentioned in paragraph 49 above, the Chiefs of Staff have been asked to consider the military implications of the situation and the possibility of co-ordinating military measures within the Afghanistan to the Pacific region to meet with any possible strategic threat.

No. 52

Extract from Conclusions of a Meeting of the Cabinet held at 10 Downing St. on 13 December 1948 at 11 a.m.[1]

CM(48)80 [CAB 128/13]

Secret

China: recent developments in the civil war

(Previous Reference: CM(46)1st Conclusions, Minute 1)[2]

3. The Cabinet considered a memorandum by the Foreign Secretary (CP(48)299)[3] covering an appreciation of the military, political and economic consequences of recent developments in the Chinese civil war.

THE FOREIGN SECRETARY said that, as the result of recent military operations, the Government of the Republic of China under President Chiang Kai-shek had virtually lost control of the whole area north of the River Yangtze and it was reasonable to assume that in course of time the Communists would secure control over the rest of China. It was unlikely that the United States Government would be willing to contribute further financial and material resources for the defence of the Kuomintang. The consequences of this situation were examined in detail in the paper annexed to CP(48)299; and he sought authority to discuss with the other Governments immediately concerned the best means of containing the Communist threat in the Far East. The interested Powers should co-ordinate their policies in face of the increasing threat of Communist aggression; but this task was seriously complicated by the hostility provoked throughout Asia by the recent activities of the French in Indo-China and the Dutch in Indonesia. In these circumstances, there would be no point in suggesting at this stage a general conference of all the Powers concerned. He therefore proposed that separate discussions should be initiated with the

---

[1] Present for discussion of this item (F 17714/33/10) were: Mr. Attlee, Mr. Bevin, Mr. Alexander (Minister of Defence), Mr. H. Morrison (Lord President of the Council), Sir S. Cripps (Chancellor of the Exchequer), Mr. H. Dalton (Chancellor of the Duchy of Lancaster), Viscount Addison (Lord Privy Seal), Viscount Jowitt (Lord Chancellor), Mr. J. Chuter Ede (Home Secretary), Mr. G. Isaacs (Minister of Labour and National Service), Mr. A. Bevan (Minister of Health), Mr. G. Tomlinson (Minister for Education), Mr. T. Williams (Minister of Agriculture and Fisheries), Mr. H. Wilson (President of the Board of Trade), Mr. A. Woodburn (Secretary of State for Scotland).

[2] CM 1(46)1, 1 January 1946. At this meeting Mr. Bevin gave a brief account of the discussions concerning the withdrawal of foreign troops from China and Communist representation in the central government that had taken place at the Moscow Conference of Foreign Ministers in December 1945 (see No. 6). He told Cabinet that he had found it embarrassing to be discussing China in the absence of a representative from the Chinese Government (CAB 128/5).

[3] No. 51.

interested Powers, and with the United States Government. He would continue his efforts to promote settlements in Indonesia and Indo-China.[4]

In discussion, the following points were made:

(*a*) No firm conclusions could be reached at this stage on the ultimate nature of Chinese Communism or of the relationship between the Chinese Communist Government and the Soviet Union. The pronouncements of Communist leaders in China were Marxist in philosophy; and the possibility of a close relationship could not be discounted. On the other hand, Far Eastern Communism might develop on Chinese rather than Slav lines. At present, Chinese Communism was an agrarian movement; and it might be forced by economic necessity to modify its principles in order to secure the support of the industrial and mercantile interests. The liberal elements in China, which had been alienated by the Kuomintang, would probably be ready to collaborate with a Communist regime on reasonable terms. In these circumstances, there was some prospect that, at least in the initial stage, a Communist Government might be prepared to adopt a liberal policy towards foreign commercial interests. It would be unwise to pursue a policy which might have the effect of gratuitously driving a Chinese Communist Government into the arms of the Soviet Union, and it was therefore important that the interested Powers should reach agreement as soon as possible on their attitude towards a Chinese Communist Government.

(*b*) Whatever the ultimate character of Chinese Communism, the latest developments in the civil war represented a grave threat to the position of the non-Communist Governments throughout Asia. Was it not time to extend to the Far East the same sort of concerted arrangements for economic and military defence measures as were being built up against Soviet aggression in Western Europe through the European Recovery Programme and the policy of Western Union?

(*c*) THE MINISTER OF DEFENCE said that some concern had been caused over the week-end by a Reuter message from London to the effect that the Government did not intend to send troops to protect British interests in Shanghai. There was no truth in this: on the contrary, the necessary dispositions were now being made.

(*d*) The recent developments in China emphasised the need for an early settlement of Japan's future.

(*e*) While nothing should be said to discourage British interests from remaining in China, it would be inadvisable to offer any positive encouragement which might give rise to claims for compensation.

(*f*) There was no way of preventing an influx of Kuomintang refugees into Hong Kong, but it was essential that the British authorities, in their

[4] On French Indo-China, see No. 59, note 8; on Indonesia, see Nos. 56, note 7 and 57, note 3.

dealings with them, should not give any impression of departing from a strict neutrality between the two sides in the civil war.

(g) The developments in China would throw an increasing strain on the Colonial Governments in Hong Kong and Malaya, and all necessary steps should be taken to strengthen and support the local administrations.

The Cabinet

(1) Expressed general approval of the policy outlined in CP(48)299.

(2) Invited the Foreign Secretary to consult in the first instance with the United States Government on means of containing the Communist threat to Anglo-American interests in Asia.[5]

(3) Took note that, in the light of the results of the approach to be made under Conclusion (2) above, the Foreign Secretary would discuss with the Secretary of State for Commonwealth Relations means of holding similar consultations with Commonwealth Governments.

(4) Invited the Foreign Secretary to consider, in consultation with the Secretary of State for the Colonies and the Minister of Defence, what further steps could be taken to strengthen our position in Colonial territories in Asia.

CABINET OFFICE, *13 December 1948*

[5] Writing to Mr. H.A. Graves, Counsellor in HM Embassy at Washington, on 29 December, Mr. Dening referred to the Cabinet paper and observed: 'It is our hope, though perhaps it is a vain one—that by presenting the Americans with our own considered analysis of the position, we may dispose them to confide to us how their own policy is developing.' He also argued that 'the advantages to the Communists of a coalition seem to me to be such that I should expect them to take this course. But they may nevertheless decide to set up a wholly communist régime.'

Mr. Dening continued that 'unless there is a *concerted* Far Eastern policy soon, the future can only develop to our common detriment . . . American policy failed in China because they failed to appreciate Chinese intransigence; it has virtually failed in Korea because they failed to appreciate Korean intransigence; and it is my personal view that it will eventually fail in Japan because they fail to appreciate Japanese intransigence. Where we shall all be then I shudder to think. Mr. Royall [US Army Secretary] in conversation with the CIGS [Lord Montgomery], expressed the view the other day that the best defence in the Far East would be to abandon Japan and defend a line much further south. I wonder how long it will be before this defeatist outlook finds more general expression. I have an uneasy feeling that, having burnt their fingers, the Americans are adducing reasons to themselves why they should abandon the Far East. This, of course, is what Australia and New Zealand in particular have always feared.' He concluded that his remarks were 'just letting off steam' and could not be divulged to the Americans. But in the New Year a fresh attempt would have to be made to 'bring home' to the Americans 'the realities of the situation and to try to get a Far Eastern policy developed' (F 18545/33/10).

No. 53

Letter from Viscount Elibank[1] to Mr. Bevin

[*F 18018/33/10*]

86, Arlington House, SW1, 14 December 1948

Dear Mr. Bevin,

I had intended to take part in Lord Salisbury's debate on Foreign Affairs in the House of Lords on Wednesday 15th December in order to speak on Chinese affairs and more especially to draw attention to the question of Shanghai. The Debate having been cancelled and owing to the fact that no further opportunity will be available until after the recess by which time it may be too late, I have decided to set out in this letter to you the main points I had wished to make in the Debate in the hope that His Majesty's Government will give them close consideration and see their way to take action.

It will be several weeks probably before the Communist Forces can occupy Nanking as the Yangtse River, as you no doubt know, where the crossings are likely to be made, is about a mile and half wide and about 30 to 40 feet in depth. There is therefore ample time before the occupation to make arrangements for any defensive measures on the spot within our capacity.

It is generally believed amongst those who are well acquainted with the country that the greatest danger to Shanghai after occupation of Nanking, may come from the thousands of Nationalist soldiers retreating after defeat and that the Communist troops are much less likely to cause trouble. The experience hitherto has been that where the Communists have occupied towns in the North, they have not molested foreigners but have themselves tried to restore law and order as soon as possible.

The Americans apparently realize this as their Commander-in-Chief Admiral Badger USN has intimated to a Press Conference that they intend to use their Marines from the two or three Warships stationed at Shanghai, as a Police Force to help to maintain law and order and possibly for the protection from mob action of power plants, rice stocks, unloading of ships etc., but that they were not there to take part in the civil war.

No doubt in this contemplated action the American marines will be protecting not only American nationals and their trade interests but also other Europeans and their trade interests.

In Shanghai there are over three thousand British nationals and apart from British lives, British property in Shanghai has been estimated to be worth anything from £100 million to £150 million.

---

[1] Lt.-Col. Arthur Cecil Murray, 3rd Viscount Elibank (cr. 1911); author and former Liberal MP who served in China in 1900 and as Parliamentary Private Secretary to Sir E. Grey, Foreign Secretary, 1910-14.

Our stake in lives and property and trade is therefore a very large one and I and many others cannot understand why we should not co-operate with the Americans and land British Marines and sailors to take their share in protecting our own nationals and property. The Americans do not hesitate to do so why should we behave in this feeble way. Surely, as the Chinese Government will have run away we would be like the Americans fully justified in landing Marines and sailors for temporary policing. On the other hand what is apparently proposed for our share is that the Marines of HMS Sussex will only be allowed, if the worst comes to the worst, to assist such British as have managed to reach the waterfront.

Do you realize what this means. Let me give you some idea, although you may already know it, of the geography of Shanghai. The Shanghai waterfront is about seven miles long. Very few foreigners live anywhere near it. The vast majority live in the residential roads which radiate out into the country, anything from two to seven miles from the Yangtse River. Between the water front and these foreign residences is a dense rabbit warren of streets almost entirely Chinese. Even the foreigners in Yangtzepoo and Honkow who are nearest to the river would have to make their way through some of the lowest Chinese quarters of Shanghai. How therefore are these unfortunate Britishers to get to the waterfront under the conditions that will exist in the city. It is an impossible position to place them in.

You yourself in your Foreign Affairs speech last Thursday were good enough to pay compliments to the sturdiness of the Shanghai Britons.[2] They would I am sure like to see your words backed up sturdy deeds—at any rate to the extent of our capacity. If the Americans can do it then we can also, and in any event together we should be a stronger force.

I am very glad to observe that His Majesty's Government have stated their determination to defend Hongkong [sic].[3] But may I venture to

---

[2] Speaking during a debate on foreign affairs in the House of Commons on 9 December, Mr. Bevin paid tribute 'to the steadfast manner in which the British communities in China, together with our diplomatic and consular staffs, are facing the difficult situation which is now confronting them' (*Parl. Debs.*, 5th ser., H. of C., vol. 459, col. 567).

[3] Opinion in the FO had been moving steadily in favour of issuing a statement that the British Government intended to remain in Hong Kong. Sir O. Sargent minuted on 8 June: 'If we once begin to hedge and qualify we shall not only demoralise our friends in Hong Kong—not to mention the British officials there—but we shall also encourage the Chinese hotheads to start an agitation in the hope of pushing us still further down the slope of appeasement' (F 8166/154/10). When the transfer of British Naval Headquarters in the Far East from Hong Kong to Singapore in the summer of 1948 prompted a Parliamentary Question asking for an assurance that Hong Kong would remain a Crown Colony, Sir O. Sargent suggested the answer: 'Hong Kong is a British colony and I know of no proposal to alter that situation' (F 9531/154/10). Mr. Rees-Williams's written reply on 7 July was rather more succinct: 'Yes.' (*Parl. Debs.*, 5th ser., H. of C., vol. 453, col. 33). During the Foreign Affairs debate on 10 December (see note 2 above) the Parliamentary Under Secretary of State for Foreign Affairs, Mr. C.P. Mayhew, stated that it was HMG's intention 'to maintain their position in Hong

suggest that in the case of Singapore, we do not forget that Air Defence should be the most important feature in defence of Hongkong. What will Shanghai Britons think of our brave words about Hongkong whilst leaving them practically in the lurch though we have potential help on their doorstep.[4]

Yours sincerely,

ELIBANK

Kong. Indeed, we feel that in this particularly troubled situation the value and importance of Hong Kong as a centre of stability will be greater than ever' (*ibid.*, vol. 459, col. 787).

[4] Mr. Bevin wrote on this letter: 'What is latest plan for China of Chiefs of Staff'. The COS had confirmed to Far Eastern Commanders that the only help expected of them at Shanghai would be to land such troops as might be needed in an emergency to protect the gasworks and waterworks (both British-run) from looting, and to cover a last-minute evacuation of British subjects from selected points on the waterfront (minute by Mr. Scarlett, 16 December). Confirmation had already been received from Washington that the State Department contemplated the use of US Marines at Shanghai not for general protective duties but for the limited protection of American lives. According to Mr. Butterworth, any widening of the Marines' role would be 'like offering American ration tickets to the Chinese population. The prompt result would be an inrush of refugees' (Washington telegram No. 5584 of 8 December, F 17363/33/10).

Replying to Lord Elibank on 20 December, Mr. Bevin described as 'exaggerated' Admiral Badger's remarks at his press conference. He then explained that the British community intended to remain in Shanghai as long as possible, 'in the usual British manner'. If the situation later became so out of hand and threatened lives an emergency plan would be implemented. This plan, drawn up by the Consulate-General in consultation with service representatives, provided for the concentration of British nationals along the waterfront and their embarkation behind a screen of British troops landed for that purpose. Mr. Bevin's information was that the British community in Shanghai had been greatly heartened by the knowledge that this plan existed, and were facing whatever the future might bring 'in a resolute and determined spirit' (F 18018/33/10).

No. 54

Minute by Mr. Scarlett on China: HM Ambassador's movements

[F 17679/33/10]

FOREIGN OFFICE, *30 December 1948*

In his telegram No. 1072 of 30th November (Flag A) Sir R. Stevenson discussed the possibility that Chiang Kai-shek would decide to shift the seat of Government from Nanking to some point in South China and recommended strongly that in this event he and his staff should remain in Nanking merely detaching the Chinese Counsellor to follow Chiang's flag if this seemed desirable.[1] Sir R. Stevenson added that his Commonwealth,

[1] In this telegram (not printed) Sir R. Stevenson expressed the view for the first time that, in view of the certain refusal of the US to become further involved in China, 'the days of the

United States, French, Belgian and Dutch colleagues were making similar recommendations to their Governments.

The Department's inclination was to agree, but before doing so Sir Orme Sargent suggested that we should consult the State Department. This was done, but State Department refuse to take a decision until they can do so in the light of developments and have instructed US Ambassador, Nanking to report any Chinese approach and to await instructions. Subsequent enquiries in Washington have got us no further and it is clear that the Americans will take no decision until the last moment.

Meanwhile, we have returned no direct answer to Sir R. Stevenson.

I suggest that we now take some decision on our own for his guidance and that, on present evidence, we should agree with his recommendations. Since the US Ambassador has got to await instructions from Washington there will be time for Sir R. Stevenson to report the exact circumstances and for the instructions we give him now to be revised if necessary in the light of these.

I submit a draft telegram in this sense.[2]

R.W. SCARLETT

present Chinese Government are numbered'. He argued that it would be unwise to move the British Embassy from Nanking, since Chiang Kai-shek, by moving his capital (Canton thought to be a likely destination), would be attempting 'to bolster up his own vanishing authority' and to involve as many powers as possible in a continual civil war. The moment had passed for this to be in the UK's interests. Moreover, 'were we to leave the capital the eventual return would be more difficult and possibly undignified and certainly would involve our having to take a definite decision about formal recognition of rival Government' (F 16821/33/10).

[2] Mr. Scarlett had earlier minuted (16 December): 'The Americans are clearly incapable of making up their minds on this issue until the last moment.' He agreed with the Ambassador that he would 'lose face' by following 'a beaten Generalissimo into some temporary redoubt'. Sir R. Stevenson was informed that he should remain in Nanking but that the Chinese Counsellor at the Embassy might transfer if the seat of the Chinese Government were moved. As in the case of his American counterpart, the Ambassador was also asked to report the exact circumstances if and when the Chinese Government moved (telegram No. 9 of 3 January 1949, F 17679/33/10).

Chapter V

1949

No. 55

Letter from Mr. C.F.A. Warner[1] to Sir W. Strang[2]

[*PR 197/9*]

Top Secret   FOREIGN OFFICE, *13 January 1949*

My dear William,

I did not know you were going to the Far East until I read it in the newspapers. I was at the time engaged in a clearance of views with Dening about our broad anti-Communist propaganda effort in the Far East and I could not gather the threads together in time to give you a paper or to ask for a short discussion before you left.

2. I am therefore writing to catch you, I hope, in Singapore with a short account of the initiative we have taken and the stage we have reached in exchanges between the Foreign Office on the one hand, and Malcolm MacDonald[3] and Ralph Stevenson on the other, as I think that propaganda will crop up in your discussions with Malcolm MacDonald and Jim Bowker[4] and I hope you will be able to talk to Ralph about it on the basis of this letter.

3. In the first place you may know that Malcolm MacDonald, on his recent visit to London, brought with him a proposal for the creation of a Regional Information Office in Singapore to prepare for the use of both Colonial Governments and our foreign missions in the Far East material—and particularly anti-Communist material—specially adapted for Asiatic consumption. We have agreed to this office being set up: it is not to be a sort of MOI[5] with powers of co-ordination over other Missions or Colonial Governments, but to be a serving unit with a translating and editorial staff, and its mandate is to be limited to S.E. Asia, though it may

---

[1] Assistant Under-Secretary of State and Head of Information Policy Department.

[2] Sir W. Strang was in Singapore at the beginning of a familiarisation tour of the Far East before taking over as Permanent Under-Secretary of State.

[3] Mr. Malcolm MacDonald, UK Commissioner-General for South-East Asia, 1948-55.

[4] HM Ambassador in Rangoon.

[5] Ministry of Information.

offer its material to the rest of the Far East where appropriate and will also supply the Foreign Office and the High Commissioners in India and Pakistan with matter which might be of value to them. Measures are going ahead to set the office up.

4. This, however, we saw as but one step in the face of the very serious situation created by the Communist advances in China. It seemed to us that, envisaging the gradual or, indeed, the almost immediate emergence of the Communists as the paramount power in China, we must consider what, if anything, might be done to render more difficult the consolidation of their power there or to increase their internal security problem as a deterrent to further adventures in the direction of S.E. Asia.[6] Sargent accordingly telegraphed Nanking on 17th, repeating his telegram to catch Ralph Stevenson in Singapore, where he was attending the Conference of heads of Mission and Governors under Malcolm MacDonald (Foreign Office telegram No. 854, repeated to Singapore as No. 1277).[7] He put the question what, if anything, we should do by covert activity, propaganda or even operations to increase this internal security problem of the Chinese Communist administration; and on the other hand what, if anything, we could do to influence fellow-travelling or opportunist Chinese elements (of whom the new administration will presumably need to attract and recruit great numbers) against the almost inevitable Communist policy—at least in foreign affairs—of subservience to Moscow. He also raised with MacDonald as one of the matters which the Conference then being held might consider, whether any development or modification of existing Information organisations in S.E. Asia, including possibly the introduction of covert activities, should be entertained as part of the measures against the Communist threat to the area as a whole. The question of the collection of adequate intelligence was also raised by Sargent.

5. In reply to this initiative, Ralph Stevenson in his telegram No. 1074[8] from Nanking surveyed various considerations which might affect our policy and in particular the importance of whether we, i.e. our Foreign Service posts and the British communities generally, stayed put in China and attempted to enter relations with the new administration and to maintain trade connections with Chinese commercial interests. He declared himself opposed to 'sabotage and similar activities' but, on the other hand, stated that he considered a good deal of unobtrusive counter-propaganda against Communist doctrines could be done by our Information Services so long as the Communists allowed them to operate. He remarked that covert

[6] Earlier, at a meeting of the Russia Committee on 11 November 1948, it was suggested that in view of the deteriorating situation in China, an organisation should be set up in that country with the aim of indoctrinating students or other groups against communism 'by clandestine propaganda or other means'. Mr. C.H. Bateman of the Northern Department explained that a committee to study all implications of a communist victory in China had already been set up and had begun sessions (N 12279/765/38). No records of such a committee have been located.
[7] PR 1064/841/913.
[8] PR 16913/33.

activities by us can only be really successful with the help of a native resistance movement; and he doubted if we could get any enthusiastic help from a people tired of war and discontented with their Government: moreover, the results were not likely to outweigh the danger of retaliation to large British communities and interests remaining, as potential hostages under the Communist administration. He added that as regards the problem of influencing fellow-travelling or opportunist Chinese elements, none of them were likely to respond to any influence which we might try to exert in an effort to dissuade them from joining the Communists; these factions were at present so obsessed with the idea of overthrowing the KMT or Chiang Kai-shek that they were not capable of listening to reason, though they were eventually bound to be disillusioned.

6. We have discussed this reply in the office and we rather feel that there may be some degree of misunderstanding between ourselves and Ralph Stevenson on two counts, namely

(*i*) In proposing covert action we are not envisaging anything violent or acknowledgable. We fully realised (for in the meantime the policy of staying put in China had been decided on) that our first interest was the physical survival of our Foreign Service posts and British communities who are now faced with the prospect of being overrun by the Communists. But we suggested covert action for two reasons; first, because we hold strongly, and Dening agrees, that any information activities to be effective in Asiatic countries should be done through key Asiatic individuals and that open ideological publicity on the European model is to a large extent water off a duck's back in China; secondly, our experience in Europe shows us that it is a vain hope to believe that our Information Offices in Communist-occupied territories will be allowed any significant freedom of action and we have no reason to believe that China will be an exception.

(*ii*) Our reference in Sargent's telegram to the influence we might bring to bear on fellow-traveller or opportunist Chinese seems to have been taken by Ralph to refer to immediate action to deter the Chinese from associating themselves in any way with the Communists. This was not at all in our minds. What we envisaged far more was long-term work, again conducted through as many Asiatic contacts as possible, to promote and exploit the disillusionment which Ralph Stevenson envisaged as coming at a later stage. We wonder whether we should in fact be right in following an entirely inactive policy in regard to these people when we can, after all, deduce the general pattern of Communist policy from the doctrines upon which it is to be founded. It is clear that a large number of Chinese who could be important to us, are not in possession of any of the essential information about Communism which, to a certain extent, by diligent organisation we might be able to put into their hands. Further, it is extremely important to remember that any organisation or covert contacts requires a considerably [*sic*] time to build up. It cannot be laid on to meet a sudden situation without preparation months or even years beforehand. Thus if we do nothing but wait and see which way the cat jumps, when it does jump eventually in the direction of further expansion of Communist influence or at least an attempt at it, we shall be unprepared to meet it and shall have done nothing to put the brakes on such expansion. We are not quite clear whether Ralph Stevenson has taken these factors into account.

7. We are under no illusions as to the value of covert activities: in general, they are inclined to be expensive and only worth entering into as auxiliary measures in times of great crisis. But the ordinary overt media in the Far East suffer severe limitations: broadcasting is not much of a factor;[9] the issue of information bulletins by our offices has a very limited effect, and, in China, may soon be restricted to such an extent that they can have practically no affect at all; cultural activities are necessarily on a small scale; and in general our major themes with which we make some play in the West, such as our social policies and democratic ways of life, are not of much importance or influence upon Asiatics. On the other hand, the role of the key intellectuals in the Far East is, I understand, extremely important: you have an instance in the creation by a handful of intellectuals of a Trotskyist movement in Ceylon, embracing almost a quarter of the population. Under circumstances where overt media is likely to be able to operate but feebly if at all, it seems that we should give further consideration to what a covert organisation directed at such intellectuals might be able to do. It is too early to go into detailed ideas, but I should envisage a small British-controlled covert central organisation disseminating material through Chinese. The main point is that unless we are certain that such a scheme will not be required, we should start planning it at once as it would take anything up to a year to work out, find personnel etc., and it is in the comparatively early stage before the Communists could establish efficient control that it might do good work. Of course, the scheme could be scrapped at any time if circumstances made it desirable.

8. We shall be telegraphing to Ralph Stevenson in reply to the views which I have summarised above and putting some of these points. If you agree that the situation warrants our at least exploring the scheme, could you, if opportunity presents itself, discuss the matter further with Ralph, whose co-operation in working it out would of course be essential.

9. Meanwhile, a second related issue has cropped up of which you will also want to know. We issued an Intel (No. 476)[10] emphasising our view

[9] A scheme to increase the power of Hong Kong radio transmitters from 2.5 kw to 7.5 kw was first considered in February 1949. The purpose was to increase the range of anti-communist broadcasts to southern China. With capital expenditure of £87,000 and recurrent expenditure of £60,000, the scheme was expensive (PR 1728/9). It was abandoned in September 1949 because of the discovery that broadcasts could be jammed in southern China (PR 2824/9).

[10] W 68/7. An Intel was an information telegram.

that we must expect the Chinese Communist leaders to follow the pattern set up by the Communist forces in Europe of setting up broad-based coalitions, and then turn cuckoo and push the other birds out of the nest. In an immediately following guidance Intel (No. 477),[11] we instructed posts outside China that, while avoiding open statements against the Chinese Communists which if repeated might be taken as provocative and prejudicial to relations with them they should not fail to make the following points:

(*a*) The Communist leadership in China must, of course, be regarded as Communist first and Chinese second, and therefore as an instrument of Kremlin imperialism;

(*b*) Point to evidence of a 'divide and rule' policy by the Kremlin, illustrated by their encouragement of a separatist policy in Manchuria, their support of an independent Mongolian Republic, and their diplomatic and military support of Turki separatists in Sinkiang; and

(*c*) That Chinese adherence to the cuckoo-in-the-nest strategy would be a demonstration of the Chinese Communist movement being directed from the Kremlin as are all other Communist parties.

10. In reply to this Ralph Stevenson expressed grave misgivings on the score of the talking points being, in spite of our reservations, too provocative and somewhat speculative in view of our insufficient knowledge at present. He advocated that our publicity line outside China should be modelled on the statement on the Parliamentary debate on foreign affairs of December 9th.[12] This statement goes no further than saying that the Communist armies have obtained control over a vast area of Northern China, that we are watching the situation carefully, and that our Embassy at Nanking, our Consulates and British subjects with business interests in China were remaining at their posts. It is indeed no line at all.

11. We had also, about the same time, telegraphed the substance of an article by Mao Tse-tung in the Cominform Journal which illustrated his subservience to Moscow.

12. A lot of us, not only on the Information side, were rather perturbed by Nanking's attitude. We fully appreciate the first importance of doing nothing that would prejudice the chance of survival of our interests in China in the face of the Communists. On the other hand, it is surely important that the outer world, and particularly the countries of S.E. Asia who may shortly be menaced by Communism and thus bring the menace nearer to our own interests, should know the simple truths which we have enunciated. Moreover, from the information available to us, we do not consider that there is anything speculative in our assessment of the Chinese Communists as Communists first and Chinese second. We think that Ralph probably does not realise that our people do not work on such matters by

[11] *Ibid.*
[12] Cf. No. 53, note 2.

means of official hand-outs, but by off the record methods, mainly by off the record conversations with important local contacts.

13. We are replying to Ralph Stevenson falling in with his wishes as far as we possibly can in recognition of the extremely difficult hand he has to play and the necessity for playing it in the way he wants. Nevertheless, we feel that we cannot indefinitely do nothing outside China about Chinese Communist pretensions. A mainstay of our destructive propaganda aimed at Communism is the demonstration of alien control of national Communist parties and consequent destruction of national sovereignty which is implicit in the whole thing. I may add that our work on these lines is by no means unsuccessful in many countries.

14. If the matters arises, can you also discuss this aspect of it further with Ralph Stevenson, and since he is intimately concerned with that extension of Chinese Communism represented by the overseas Chinese Communists, with Malcolm MacDonald as well.[13]

Yours ever,

CHRISTOPHER WARNER

[13] In response to further FO prompting on the matters raised in this letter in February 1949, Sir R. Stevenson argued: 'Our primary objective in planning should be to enlarge possibilities of the difference between the future Government of China and the Kremlin, but an attempt to discredit Mao Tse-tung before there is any disillusionment in China would be a tactical mistake' (Nanking telegram No. 178 of 11 February, PR 302/16). Mr. Dening thought this approach too cautious. He was concerned that the complete absence of UK activity in the propaganda field was allowing the CCP and Moscow 'to get away with the implantation of their principal thesis in the eyes of the world and of the Chinese, namely that the Chinese Communist Party is in no way related to the Kremlin'. He described the Ambassador's views about discrediting Mao Tse-tung as 'controversial' and argued: '... if we stress the subservence of Mao to the Kremlin we might either hasten the disillusionment of other Communists, or else help to bring about the adoption by Mao of a deliberate policy of deviation. Either of these developments could then profitably be exploited' (minute of 10 March 1949, PR 638/16). Ultimately Sir R. Stevenson accepted a propaganda campaign designed to emphasise (a) Soviet encroachment into Sinkiang, Inner Mongolia and Manchuria, (b) Communist opposition to Islam as a creed and the fate of Islamic communities in Central Asia, and (c) CCP subservience to the Kremlin. To meet the Ambassador's concerns, the propaganda was not to be aimed at China itself. The main purpose would be to convince other Far Eastern governments that Chinese communism was subservient to Moscow and therefore dangerous to their national interests (telegram No. 314 to Nanking of 25 March 1949).

No. 56

Sir A. Nye[1] (New Delhi) to Mr. P. Noel-Baker[2]
(Received 15 January, 1.25 p.m.)

No. X95 Telegraphic [F 943/1015/10]

Immediate. Top Secret   NEW DELHI, *15 January 1949, 2 p.m.*

Your telegram No. Y141 of the 20th December. China[3]

Following is text of reply received from K.P.S. Menon[4] to the message to the Prime Minister contained in your telegram under reference. Begins:

We are in general agreement with Mr. Attlee's analysis of the present situation in China and her immediate prospects. It is clear that Nanking cannot hold out much longer and that Chiang Kai-shek will have to step aside. It is also probable that a coalition Government rather than an out and out Communist Government is likely to emerge. While the Communist party in China appears to have considerable military and political leadership at the top it is lacking in administrative talent and experience and would doubtless like to make use of such elements as are willing to cooperate with it. The present Government is so discredited that many liberal elements will probably associate themselves with the new regime. In order to placate them and to win foreign support in the tremendous task of political and economic reconstruction the new Government will probably adopt a moderate policy at any rate to start with in internal affairs as well as external relations.

3. Compromise is likely to be the key note of the Government's policy and the Chinese have a special genius for it. The Government will probably compromise not only with the Liberals but with the Warlords and Generals and leave them in control of certain parts of the country. It is significant that General Lung Yun,[5] Master of Yunnan Province for over a quarter of a century, is reported to be negotiating with the Communists. So it is said is General Fu Tso-yi[6] who was expected to save Peking and Tientsin from the Communists. The (?Muslim) Governors of North East China are also taking stock of the situation and will probably adapt themselves to it. Regionalism, that ancient curse of China, will probably raise its head again but in Communist hands it may be turned into regional autonomy of the Soviet pattern.

[1] UK High Commissioner in India.

[2] Secretary of State for Commonwealth Relations, 1947-50.

[3] This telegram set out UK policy on China (see Nos. 51 and 52) and requested the views of Pandit Nehru on the situation (F 18186/33/10).

[4] Indian Foreign Secretary.

[5] Former Chairman of Yunnan Province and Chairman in 1949 of the Nationalist Government's Strategy Advisory Committee.

[6] See No. 49, note 2.

4. Heterogeneous Government based on compromise and formed of different elements though dominated by the Communists will not necessarily be dominated by Russia. It seems doubtful whether Russia will be able to stroll in and 'take over' China as she has done in the countries in Eastern Europe. China is too vast, too different ethnically and culturally from the (?Slav group) and too tenacious of her own traditions to be absorbed by Russia even in an ideological sense. Indeed it may be that Communist China may be the first to provide a national counterweight to the USSR. In Europe Russian Communism has achieved political successes primarily in countries which racially differ little from the USSR. In any case they are too small to offer effective resistance. It is different with China. Russia's vast spaces have been her best defence against foreign invaders. China in that respect is almost equally fortunate and her communications are even less developed than those of the USSR.

5. While China will thus retain her independence in a large measure at home she will probably adapt her foreign policy to that of the Soviet Union. Korea which is already half Communist will be the first to feel its impact. Japan would feel it too but for the determination of the United States to erect it as a bastion against Communism. In South East Asia Communism will derive additional strength from the march of events in China and the activities of Communist agents will need more careful watching than ever before. It is, however, doubtful whether Communism will be in a position to subvert existing Governments provided those Governments move with the times. (?Even if) Communist China be in a position to help Communists outside its old borders in a military sense for some time to come, political consolidation and economic rehabilitation will take all its time. India need not therefore fear any serious danger from China directly in the near future. If the Communist victory in China were to lean [*sic*] to (?the) establishment of Communism in Siam or in Colonies under European control the fault would be mainly that of the existing indigenous or Colonial regimes. There is little doubt that the Dutch police action in Indonesia[7] will help the growth of Communism even more than the Communist victories in China. If the Governments of South East Asia recognise in deeds as well as in words the necessity for national independence and the inevitability of social change Communism will be robbed of much of its magic. If on the contrary the major western powers who are so fearful of the spread of Communism in Asia do nothing more

[7] 'Police action' was a euphemism for two large-scale military operations mounted by the Dutch in Indonesia (the East Indies) in July 1947 and December 1948. Both were undertaken in an attempt to eliminate the Indonesian Republic that had been proclaimed during the nationalist revolution in August 1945. By the time of the 1948 offensive there were four army personnel to every police official in Indonesia. Republican political leaders were taken prisoner and strategic positions occupied during the second offensive. In consequence the Dutch faced criticism from the UN and the US. The Truman Administration threatened to exclude the Netherlands from the European Recovery Programme (Marshall Aid) and from the defence negotiations that led to the North Atlantic Treaty. See also No. 57, note 3 below.

to check it than go on calling it a bogey and helping weaklings and puppets to fight nationalism there will be chaos in South East Asia and Communism, which always thrives on chaos, will flourish. A dynamic policy designed to set the genuinely Nationalist Governments of South East Asia on their feet politically and economically is the best and in fact the only antidote to Communism.

6. (*a*) The success of the Communists in China which seems inevitable will thus probably lead to (?the) establishment of a Communist dominated Coalition Government which will follow a moderate policy and will try to avoid conflict with other countries. All its policy, time and energy will be taken up in consolidating its position and in dealing with the devastation caused by the prolonged civil war.

(*b*) The leaders of Communist China are in every sense Marxists but they appear to be able realists and, with a full appreciation of the Chinese background, they will not allow their country to become a mere satellite of Soviet Russia and will follow their own internal policy.

(*c*) Communist China's foreign policy will tend to line up with Soviet Russia more particularly in regard to Korea and Japan especially if other countries show active hostility towards it at the start.

(*d*) The success of Communist China will tend to encourage Communist parties and elements in South East Asia but China will not otherwise directly help Communist parties in those.

(*e*) The effect in South East Asia will depend on the policies of other powers there. If these powers try to crush Nationalist movements then there will be a progressive swing over towards Communism. Communism can only be effectively checked in these countries by Nationalism and Nationalist movements should therefore be helped and encouraged. Any attempt to crush Nationalism and revive any kind of Colonial control will lead to a strengthening of Communism as in the case of Indonesia.

(*f*) Any hostility towards a Communist-controlled China by other countries will tend to throw it more in the Soviet orbit. A realist policy should therefore lead to contracts [*sic*: ?contacts] being maintained with the new Government without any commitments. Future action would depend on developments. Ends.[8]

[8] Copies of this telegram were sent to the Prime Minister and members of the Cabinet.

No. 57

Minute by Mr. Scarlett on the French response to the prospect of Communist successes in China

[F 2277/1015/10]

FOREIGN OFFICE, *15 February 1949*

This useful reaction from Paris to our China paper is the more welcome for being the first of its kind.[1]

Paragraphs 1-10 express agreement with our general analysis of the political and economic factors of the situation. The French Government entertain no illusion about the orthodoxy of the Chinese Communists and, while agreeing that they may for the time being tolerate certain foreign activities, stress the point that such toleration will be dictated simply by necessity. In the international field the French expect the representatives of Communist China to align themselves solidly with Soviet diplomacy. All this is good straight thinking.

In paragraphs 11-15 the French consider what line of policy could best be adopted in China itself. Their first conclusion, which is ours, is that we must accept the fact that any position abandoned now will be lost for good but that if we stick to our guns our presence may be tolerated for a long time in a country 'where logic is not the absolute rule in administrative behaviour'. They intend, like us, to fly the flag to the last. They, too, anticipate some revival of economic life for an interim period and in order to exploit the new Government's weaknesses in this field to the full would see the advantage of taking jointly any chance of economic pressure which may come to light. They will also favour local exchanges of information and collaboration between private enterprises.

They suggest that some political advantage might be drawn from exploiting regional particularism in the southern provinces and fostering it in our business dealing. This point is worth expert examination. Apart from the language barrier in the southern provinces I am not sure how real particularism may be, but it is clearly of great importance to the French to lose no chance of dulling the impact of Communism on the frontiers of Indo-China.

In considering possible means of containing Communism outside China—paragraphs 16-23—the French Government would welcome frequent personal contacts between members of the Foreign Office and the Quai d'Orsay in addition to day-to-day liaison maintained by the Embassies in London and Paris: a regular exchange of specialised security

---

[1] Mr. Scarlett was commenting on a letter from Viscount Hood, Counsellor at HM Embassy in Paris, to Mr. Dening, forwarding comments from the French Government on the memorandum on British views of the situation in China (No. 51) which had been passed to them on 3 January.

information in Saigon and Singapore: the development of economic technical cooperation through the Regional Bureau for South East Asia and Government consultation in advance of meetings in South East Asia of the ECA and FAO.[2] They also favour political consultation with all friendly Powers directly interested in South East Asia and go on to suggest that it would encourage the small Asiatic countries to take positive action against Communism if the United States Government could be induced to show an interest in these consultations. Unluckily, there are signs that the State Department are already shying at just this thought.

I should welcome the observations of South East Asia Department on these concluding paragraphs of the French *Aide-Mémoire*.[3]

P.W. SCARLETT

[2] Economic Cooperation Administration and Food and Agricultural Organisation.

[3] Mr. J.O. Lloyd of South East Asia Department commented on 16 February that while the French paper contained 'several sound ideas' on exchanging intelligence and economic and technical cooperation, political consultation on a wide regional basis would be possible only when there was a settlement of the Indonesian and Indo-China problems. 'It is useless to expect the Burmese or the Indians, not to mention the Pakistanis, Ceylonese, and Australians, to sit at the same table as the French and Dutch to discuss political problems in S.E. Asia as long as the French and Dutch have not reached a settlement in their respective territories satisfactory to the Asian states.' Mr. R.H. Scott agreed: 'The first task for the French is, I think, clearly to put their Indo-China house in order. They cannot do it by force, or by collaboration with us (or the Americans): it can be done only by concessions to the non-communists. It is not for us to say what should be their policy in Indo-China, but we have an interest in seeing that French domestic political differences do not result in prolonging stalemate in Indo-China at a time when communists there can look forward to increased support from China. Incidentally, the Chinese province bordering on Indo-China—Kwangsi—will be one of the last to come under communist influence. But I expect that Hainan will, as ever, be a focus of trouble' (minute of 16 February).

A conference was held in New Delhi between 20 and 23 January 1949, attended by 19 Asian and Pacific countries in addition to India, to discuss the Indonesian situation (see No. 56, note 7). It ended with a resolution urging the UN Security Council to secure the release of Republican leaders, the withdrawal of Dutch troops, the establishment of an interim government, and the transfer of sovereignty to a United States of Indonesia by 1 January 1950. Indonesia became independent on 27 December 1949.

No. 58

Minute by Mr. Scarlett on the recognition question

[F 3305/1023/10]

FOREIGN OFFICE, *17 February 1949*

The problem

The Chinese Communists, who now effectively control a large area of China, are refusing to permit foreign Consulates in territory under their control to communicate either with their respective Governments or with their Embassies in Nanking, and are preventing them from exercising their consular functions. The Communist attitude towards foreign Consulates appears to be a form of pressure designed to force the Governments concerned, including His Majesty's Government, to accord recognition to the Communist régime. The clearest indication of this is contained in a recent report from Nanking to the effect that junior Communist officials in Tientsin are justifying the refusal to recognise foreign Consuls officially on the grounds that diplomatic relations have not yet been established. [1]

Recommendations

1. That as an immediate step, and without prejudice to later recognition when the position in China becomes clearer, we should ask Sir R. Stevenson to brief those of our Consuls with whom he is still in communication, but who are in territory which may shortly be seized by the Communists, to approach the Communists on the following lines:

They should say that the civil war is no concern of ours, and that the question of recognition is one which cannot be decided while the uncertainties of civil war persist. They should point out the functions of our Consulates in looking after the interests of British nationals and in facilitating trade with China, and represent that these functions should be allowed to continue irrespective of the local authority in control. They should ask the Communists, pending settlement of civil strife in China and without prejudice to the question of recognition, to allow our Consulates the full exercise of their functions as hitherto, including free communication with their Governments. They should further assure the Communists that they for their part are quite willing to deal with them on a *de facto* basis while the present situation continues and until the position is clarified.

2. That a similar communication should be made to the Chinese Communist representatives in Hong Kong. This should also contain a specific request to restore communications to HM Consuls-General in Mukden and Tientsin. Mukden has been cut off since the end of November and Tientsin since the end of January. Sir R. Stevenson has recently pointed out that Mr. Harmon, now Public Relations Officer in Hong Kong, who established friendly relations with the Chinese Communist delegation at Chungking during the last stage of the war, and

---

[1] It had earlier been suggested that the Communist authorities in China might be approached through the Communists in Hong Kong. The Governor of Hong Kong advised against this on the grounds that it might ultimately be necessary to take action against the Hong Kong Communists, and that the Chinese Communists had already snubbed a protest by the US Consul-General in Hong Kong about the treatment of the US Consul-General in Mukden (who was said to be virtually under house arrest with no means of communication with the outside world). It was then considered within the FO whether the same purpose would be served if Sir R. Stevenson sent letters through the open post to UK Consular officers in Tientsin and Peking, assuming that the Communists would open them before they were delivered. Messages were delivered, not by letter but in person, to the Mayor of Peking and the Alien Affairs Bureau of the Peking Military Control Commission. They were returned on the grounds that diplomatic relations did not exist, and this approach was therefore abandoned (F 4351, 5971/1023/10).

has been able to maintain some contacts with them since then, might prove an effective channel for such communication.

3. That we should inform the Atlantic Powers and the Commonwealth of the action we are taking under 1 and 2 above, and that we should also inform them of our general views on the recognition question as set out below.

Argument
Views of the Legal Adviser

The Legal Adviser has expressed the emphatic view that it is both legally wrong, and in practice leads to every conceivable difficulty, to refuse to accord any sort of recognition to a Government which in fact effectively controls a large portion of territory. In his submission, the Communist Government in China is already in a position where it must be recognised as *something*; and he suggests that it is both legally right and practically necessary to recognise the Communist Government as at any rate being the *de facto* Government of that part of China which it controls. (We could, of course, at the same time, continue to recognise the Central Government as being the *de jure* Government of the whole of China.) By so doing we should be adopting a similar attitude to that which we adopted towards General Franco during the Spanish Civil War;[2] and we should then have a basis on which to talk to the Communist Government. We have no strong legal grounds for complaint if the Communists treat our Consuls as private persons when we do not recognise their Government, which in fact has effective control over half China, as being anything at all. By accepting the strong element of law in the recognition question, we should be able to justify a politically unpopular step which would really serve our interests by saying that we have recognised in this case not because we like the Chinese Communists, but because the facts of the situation are such that it is legally the proper course to follow. In legal circles the Manchukuo precedent is one that it is not considered desirable to follow again.[3] In any case, it

[2] In October 1936, a provisional government (the Council of National Defence) was set up in Spain under the leadership of General Francisco Franco. The UK did not recognise the new government but acknowledged that General Franco's rebel movement controlled large parts of the country. Once the insurgent army occupied Madrid, the British Government decided to enter into such *de facto* relations with the provisional government as were necessary for the protection of British interests in the areas it controlled (*DBFP*, Second Series, Volume XVII, Nos. 344, 359 and 371).

[3] Japan established the puppet state of Manchukuo in the Chinese province of Manchuria in 1932. The League of Nations passed a resolution against recognition, and set up a commission of enquiry (the Lytton Commission) which recommended that League members should continue to withhold recognition from Manchukuo, 'either *de jure* or *de facto*'. The British Government adhered to this position though Sir John Simon, then Secretary of State for Foreign Affairs, insisted that 'we cannot bind ourselves in perpetuity or limit the freedom of future British Governments if circumstances hereafter change, e.g. by other Powers recognising or by its becoming clear that complete independence from China was the real wish of the people of Manchuria'. British Consular officials were instructed to avoid actions or statements that could be interpreted as an indication that they regarded the new Manchurian government as the

appears to be very doubtful whether the Chinese Communists would be prepared to tolerate the existence of Consuls of non-recognising Governments, as the Japanese did in Manchukuo.

Political considerations

The recommendations above are perhaps less divergent from the views of the Legal Adviser than would appear at first sight. The difference is rather one of emphasis and timing. Far Eastern Department are certainly not proposing any long-term policy of non-recognition in the case of Communist China. They are already face to face with the practical difficulties which arise from non-recognition. But they feel that, for reasons which are set out below, some time must still elapse before HMG accord any form of recognition to the Communists, and in the meantime, they do not wish to neglect any chance of alleviating the position of HM Consuls in Communist-controlled territory.

Our reasons for proposing delaying recognition for the time being are as follows:

(i) The North China People's Government must be regarded as an interim régime which is now in process of converting itself into something else. It is not yet known whether it will prove possible to arrange some form of coalition between the present Central Government and the Communists, nor have the Communists yet decided on their capital. The frontiers of Communist-administered territory are still fluid, and it is impossible to foresee whether there will be a period of stalemate, as in the Spanish Civil War, when the two opposing factions will each be in control of a relatively clearly-defined area.

(ii) On general grounds, we do not wish to appear unduly precipitate in recognising the Communist régime, thereby tending to give the impression that when British interests are at stake we are perfectly prepared to swallow our principles.

(iii) We are anxious to proceed to recognition only on the basis of full consultation with the other Powers concerned.[4]

P.W. Scarlett

---

proper government of the country, while individual technical issues were to be considered on their merits (see *DBFP*, Second Series, Volume XI, Nos. 53, 144, 285, 342).

[4] Mr. Dening noted on 17 February that the US and France, and other powers including members of the Commonwealth, would be 'outraged if we were to make up our minds about recognition without consulting them'. Sir O. Sargent in a minute of 18 February attached particular importance to the establishment of communication with the Consuls-General at Mukden and Tientsin. 'If we fail in this we should have to consider getting them out altogether. We should be severely criticised if anything happened to them because we had failed to look after them adequately.' Mr. Bevin commented: 'I must go into this with great care. I will discuss it.' He discussed the issue with Mr. Dening on 23 February and approved the recommendations made by Mr. Scarlett.

No. 59

Memorandum by Mr. Bevin on the Situation in China

CP(49)39 [CAB 129/32]

Secret   FOREIGN OFFICE, 4 *March 1949*

I circulate herewith, with reference to CP(48)299 of 9th December 1948,[1] a further review of developments in China and South East Asia. An attempt has also been made to assess the economic position of the Government of a Communist-dominated China.

2. As foreshadowed in my previous paper, I have consulted the Chiefs of Staff on the military implications of the situation and the possibility of co-ordinating military measures within the region to meet any possible strategic threat. They have reached the following general conclusions:[2] The spread of Communism into Southern China will cause increased unrest and consequently an increased security commitment throughout South East Asia. It will also increase the threat to our sea communications in war, which would be particularly serious if Formosa were to come under Soviet domination, and increase the difficulties of delivering the air offensive from the Japanese islands. In consequence, the forces required in the area in both peace and war would be increased. Should the Russians establish bases in Southern China, the threat to South East Asia and to our sea communications might become serious. If Communism successfully spreads into the Indian sub-continent, our whole position in South East Asia would become untenable. They go on to suggest that until all countries interested in the area have agreed on a policy for the Far East, the only military consultative and information organisation which is likely to be effective is the exchange of intelligence information on Communist activities and the exchange of police information.

3. In the light of these conclusions and of the political developments outlined in paragraphs 1 to 15 of the attached memorandum, I now recommend

(*a*) that we should pursue our study with those friendly powers to whom we have already communicated the substance of our initial study (CP(48)299);

(*b*) that we should examine further with these same powers possible economic measures in defence of our interests on the basis of paragraphs 16 *et. seq.*

[1] No. 51.
[2] 'General Strategic Implications of the Situation in China as Foreshadowed in the Foreign Office Appreciation', COS(49)29 of 20 January 1949 (DEFE 5/13).

(*c*) that the necessary authority be given to establish liaison between police and intelligence organisations in the area as a whole. I regard this as one of the most useful practical steps to take immediately.

E.B.

ANNEX TO No. 59

The Situation in China

The situation in China was last reviewed in CP(48)299 of 9th December. Since then the Communists have moved down to the North bank of the Yangtse and their hold on North China is now complete. Though President Chiang Kai-shek has retired from the scene to leave the way clear for a settlement by negotiation, there is recent evidence that he is still exerting influence through the Kuomintang 'Old Guard'. A delegation has been sent to Peking on behalf of the Nationalist Government to make preliminary enquiries as to Communist peace terms and the Acting President Li Tsung-jen is reported to be reasonably optimistic that peace negotiations will eventually ensue, but Chiang Kai-shek's continued interference makes it doubtful whether a settlement acceptable to both parties will result. Meanwhile, fighting is at a standstill and the Communists, who clearly feel that time is on their side, appear in no hurry to make any further move. They are reported to be building up their strength on the North bank of the river. They have a well-equipped force of some two million men to their credit while it is doubtful if the Nationalists can now muster more than a million poor troops.

2. Politically, the Nationalist hand has been further weakened by the rival policies within the Government. Most recent reports, however, indicate that the Acting President, who on the transfer of the seat of government to Canton[3] had been virtually alone in Nanking, is regaining control of his scattered ministers. All but the Prime Minister have been brought back to Nanking for a conference. If it is true that his initial peace mission has now returned from the North having been received by Mao Tse-tung, the Acting President's prestige should be greatly restored. The economic situation is deteriorating steadily. The gold Yuan established in August at 12 to the pound was quoted in mid-February at over 5,000. These developments all go to reinforce the tentative view expressed in the previous paper that Communist domination of China must be regarded as inevitable.

[3] Cf. No. 54. The Chinese Government moved from Nanking to Canton at the end of January 1949. Foreign diplomatic personnel transferring at the same time included the Soviet Ambassador. The UK Chinese Counsellor, First Secretary and Military Attaché also moved, as did the US Minister-Counsellor. From Canton, over the course of 1949, the seat of the Nationalist government was moved successively to Chungking, Chengtu and eventually, on 7 December, to Taipeh in Formosa (Taiwan).

3. The present Communist administration in North China is provisional, and at the moment even *de facto* recognition would be premature. In any case His Majesty's Government will have to consult Commonwealth and other friendly Governments before considering recognition. So far it has proved impossible for officials to establish any form of contact with the Communist authorities. There are British and other foreign consulates in the Communist-held towns of Mukden, Peking and Tientsin, but the Communist policy is apparently to cut official consular communications with the outside world and to refuse to recognise the status of consuls until the Governments concerned recognise the Communist régime.

4. The British communities in Mukden, Peking and Tientsin retain their liberty of movement within these cities and seem to be unmolested, but the important British commercial community at Tientsin is gravely disturbed by business conditions since the city fell. Trade is at a standstill, the city is still under a purely military administration, the Communists seem to have no plans for foreign trade, and some firms are short of money, since a new currency has been introduced by the Communists who are unwilling to accept any other, even US dollars, in exchange. HM Ambassador considers, however, that a revival of Tientsin's trade is likely to follow quickly on a political settlement, and many difficulties may be due to Communist suspicions and administrative inexperience. It would be unwise to form any conclusions at this stage.

5. The consultations with friendly Powers as to the best means of containing the Communist threat to all our interests authorised by the Cabinet on 13th December, 1948, have not as yet proved very productive. With the exception of India, Commonwealth countries have offered no comments of substance. India takes the view that a Communist-controlled régime in China would be absorbed by internal problems, which they would handle according to Chinese methods and without accepting Russian dictation, that their foreign policy would be in line with Russia's, that Communists in South East Asia would be encouraged by events in China, but would receive no direct help from there, and that the correct course for other countries would be to help national movements in South East Asia and maintain contacts with the new Government in China without any commitments.[4] The United States Government are actively studying the paper but have not as yet vouchsafed any authoritative views. The French Government have expressed general agreement with our analysis and offered to co-operate generally in the intelligence field,[5] while the initial reaction of the Siamese has been to enquire tentatively what help may be expected from His Majesty's Government and the United States Government to meet the eventualities which we have postulated. We have delayed any approach as yet to the Netherlands and Burma in view of their more immediate pre-occupations.

[4] See No. 56.
[5] Cf. No. 57.

6. The present situation in South East Asia is reviewed briefly in the following paragraphs. A separate paper reviewing the situation as regards defence in Hong Kong and Malaya is being submitted by the Secretary of State for the Colonies.

Burma

7. The position of the Burmese Government in the communal conflict has deteriorated in the last few days. The Karens now appear to have gained control of most of North Burma, while to the South the hold of the Burmese Government on any area except Rangoon and its immediate vicinity is at best tenuous. The Government have promised autonomy within the Burmese Union to the Karens, but this gesture may have been made too late and the Karens may be prepared to continue the fight, fortified by their victories in the North. On the other hand there are indications that they are anxious to negotiate a settlement with the Burmese Government.

8. There have been a number of reports from Burmese sources of Karen co-operation with the Communists. These reports, none of which were reliable or first-hand, may well have been a Burmese exaggeration of the fact that the Karens may have employed dacoits who had been previously been employed by the Communists. The Karens are strongly pro-British and they and the Communists are ideologically at opposite ends of the political spectrum.

9. The question of financial and other assistance to Burma is being discussed by Commonwealth representatives, with the agreement of the Burmese Government, in New Delhi.[6]

India and Pakistan

10. India and Pakistan are well aware of the present chaos in Burma and of the threat to themselves of continued instability there. In both countries the public is following the Government in a growing appreciation of the internal dangers of Communism but, in India at least, the dangers to South East Asia as a whole, arising out of the Communist victories in China, are not yet fully appreciated. In India some 500 Communists have been arrested on the ground that they were planning active sabotage of industrial production and railways. The cease fire which came into effect in Kashmir where the growth of Communist influence gives some cause for concern on 1st January has been well observed and has induced a noticeable improvement in relations between the two Powers. The appointment of a Plebiscite Administrator acceptable to both sides is awaited. He will probably be an American.

---

[6] The meeting was not a success and ended with the Burmese Government protesting about outside interference in domestic politics. On this and subsequent Commonwealth effforts to assist Burma, see S.R. Ashton, 'Britain, Burma and the Commonwealth, 1946-1956', *Journal of Imperial and Commonwealth History*, vol. 29, No. 1, January 2001, pp. 65-91.

Indonesia[7]

11. The Netherlands Government announced their plan on February 26th for the transfer of power to Indonesia. Briefly the intention is to convene a round table conference at The Hague on the 12th March, to be attended by Republicans, non-Republican Indonesians, and the United Nations Commission for Indonesia. This conference will work out plans for the formation of an interim government and the transfer of power much earlier than envisaged in the Security Council resolution. To this extent their plans are in advance of the Security Council resolution, but there is a major obstacle to its acceptance as a satisfactory basis for settlement in accordance with the Security Council resolution in that there is no intention of allowing Republican leaders to go back to Jogjakarta. Unless the Dutch can agree to the Republicans returning to Jogjakarta their plan may miscarry. Meanwhile, the guer[r]illa activities of the Republicans continue, and it is improbable that the Dutch can ever inspire a purely military solution. An early political solution is thus a necessity.

Indo-China

12. Slow progress has been made in the negotiations between ex-Emperor Bao Dai and the French Government on independence for Annam.[8] The main bone of contention is the status of Cochin-China (one of the 3 envisaged provinces of the future Viet Nam) which still remains a French colony as distinct from an 'associated State' of the French Union. It is understood that agreement has been reached on defence, diplomatic representation and economic matters. Bao Dai is not likely to return to Indo-China to head the proposed new Central Government until he has obtained satisfaction on the status of Cochin-China. This depends on a vote of the French Assembly, who do not yet seem to realise the

[7] Cf. Nos. 56, note 7 and 57, note 3.

[8] It had been agreed at Potsdam in 1945 that Indo-China should be divided at the 16th parallel following the Japanese surrender. The UK became responsible for Cochin China (the southern part of Vietnam) and Cambodia; China for Annam, Tongking (the central and northern parts of Vietnam) and Laos. In September 1945 the Communist Viet Minh persuaded Bao Dai, the Vietnamese Emperor, to abdicate in favour of a Democratic Republic of Vietnam (DRV) which was established in the north at Hanoi under the presidency of Ho Chi Minh. In the south of Vietnam, in the absence of any alternative (British instructions went no further than securing Japan's surrender and withdrawal), the French resumed control. In March 1946 France and the DRV reached an agreement that enabled French troops to occupy the north. The DRV was recognised as a free state with its own government and army, belonging to the Indo-Chinese Federation and French Union. British and Chinese troops withdrew from Indo-China in September 1946. Relations between France and the DRV worsened as the former sought to maintain their influence by establishing a separate state of Cochin China in the south. Fighting broke out in November 1946, and over the next three years France attempted to find workable alternatives to the Ho Chi Minh government, mostly centred on a reluctant Bao Dai now living in Paris. On 14 June 1949 qualified independence was conceded to a new state of Vietnam. It included Cochin China, hitherto a bone of contention in the negotiations, its capital was at Saigon and Bao Dai was installed as Chief of State. The Viet Minh immediately denounced the new government and condemned Bao Dai as a French puppet and a traitor.

implications of developments in China and the consequent urgency of reaching a settlement.

Siam

13. The National Declaration of Emergency Decree which Marshal Pibul[9] wished to enforce as soon as possible in order to provide the Siamese Government with powers to deal with the Communist external and internal threat, was promulgated on 23rd February. Critics of Pibul's declaration of Emergency see in it an attempt by the Marshal to further his own ends. Fighting has broken out in Bangkok between units of the Siamese Army and Navy but the Government appears to be in control of the situation and any political opposition appears to have been overcome. The situation is however still rather obscure.

14. On the Siam/Malaya border co-operation between Siamese and Malayan security forces is reported to be improving, but the Siamese forces are handicapped in operations against the bandits by their indifferent equipment. The United Kingdom are providing some military equipment for the Siamese as a matter of urgency: arrangements have also been made for certain training facilities to be given to the Siamese, and for the exchange of intelligence on bandit activities.

Chinese Communists

15. A police raid on the house of a leading Chinese communist in Hong Kong has produced a diary and a series of notes which make it clear that the Chinese Communist Party is just as orthodox in its ideology and just as highly organised as any of its European counterparts.[10] A summary of these

---

[9] Prime Minister of Siam.

[10] The raid took place at an address in Hong Kong on 11 December 1948. According to the Governor, the documents suggested that the address was a Communist headquarters for the Hong Kong area and possibly even for south China. The documents included a diary which, in translation, revealed connections with French Indo-China and the Philippines and a list of addresses for Malaya. It also contained material on Communist policy towards the taking over of Shanghai and the treatment of foreign interests. Here it was suggested that foreign concerns would be allowed to continue only as a matter of expediency; they would function on orders from the 'People's Government' and would be 'dealt with separately' later on. Another document was headed 'Questions Referring to the Present Political Situation and the Party's Policy'. It stated that Communist strength had increased tenfold over the past year and was now 30,000-40,000 in Kwangtung, 10,000 in Kwangsi and 10,000 in Hunan. Other documents included notes on the formation and growth of the CCP, biographies of aspirant members of the Party, household and other accounts and notes on the infiltration of secret societies (F 1559, 4780/1016/10).

In the FO Mr. G. Burgess minuted on 29 January: 'These documents clearly emanate from a party that is orthodox, confident, mature and at the highest level (with which we are in fact in touch here) very well organised. The degree of the CCP's achievements in these respects is I think at least as high as many Western parties. It is certainly on an altogether different level than anyone who speaks of special "Chinese" factors as moderating the CCP or of the individual character of Chinese as working to weaken or alter it, can imagine.' In a later minute of 22 March he disagreed with the view that Mao Tse-tung should be regarded as a 'potential Tito': 'there is plenty of evidence that Mao thinks he is an orthodox Marxist, but that is not the same as being subservient to the Kremlin . . . People who claim to be orthodox Marxists

documents is attached. It has been particularly requested by the Security authorities that the place of origin of these documents i.e. Hong Kong, should be revealed only to Ministers. References in this context to a Chinese Communist interest in the Philippines suggest that it might be useful to inform the Philippine Government of our views on the China situation. This has not been done hitherto since it was felt that the islands were a predominantly American sphere of influence.

Economic considerations

16. The following is an assessment of the major economic problems of a Communist-dominated China, and of possible ways of exploiting to our advantage any economic weaknesses that may emerge. The economic long-term policy of the Communists will be on normal Communist lines and will be directed towards land reform, state industrialisation and the expropriation or expulsion of foreign interests, but it is assumed that in the initial period economic difficulties will be so great that the Communists will perforce move slowly towards these goals, and accordingly that they may be disposed to tolerate foreign interests for a time.

17. Communist economic weaknesses can be summarised under the following heads:

(i) *Finance*

The Communists will have great difficulty in balancing the budget, increasing taxation, diminishing expenditure and maintaining confidence in their currency. They will face the same threat of runaway inflation as the present government but may be expected to take more drastic steps to deal with it.

(ii) *Food and agriculture*

Before the war China normally imported about one million tons of rice a year. This figure will be decreased if the Communists control Formosa, but rice supplies will be insufficient. Internal distribution is another problem (see under *Transport* below). Foreign agricultural machinery, of which the Soviet Union and the satellites cannot supply much, will probably be desired but not immediately essential, nor, owing to the nature of rice agriculture in China, necessarily indispensable.

(iii) *Industry*

Industrialization will require foreign capital, foreign capital goods and foreign technical assistance. It is doubtful whether the Soviet Union and the satellites can provide much of this.

(iv) *Transport*

Adequate distribution of food supplies and economic prosperity depend on the improvement of internal communications and the maintenance of shipping facilities. The Communists will depend on foreign vessels for their overseas trade in any case, and for coastal trade if the present Chinese

without obeying the Kremlin get attacked by the Soviet Press and by the Kremlin's agents. Unless and until that happens to Mao it would surely be safer not to regard him as any sort of Tito, potential or otherwise.'

mercantile marine is denied them. Sufficient river transport will, however, be available. But vast quantities of supplies will be necessary to restore the war damaged railway system, and transport may well prove to be one of the Communists' most serious weaknesses.

(v) *Minerals and raw materials*

China will be almost entirely dependent on non-Communist sources for supplies of rubber, oil, and fertilisers. She will be deficient in raw cotton. The most serious mineral deficiencies will be the ferro-alloy metals.

(vi) *Trade*

Foreign trade has in the past been relatively unimportant in China's economic life, and the Communists will no doubt continue the present Chinese policy of restricting imports to capital goods and basic essentials (oil, rubber, food, etc.). They may very probably wish to increase exports in order to be able to import more.

18. Although United Kingdom trade with China has lately been very small, British merchant and industrial interests are established in China in such strength that they conduct a very large proportion of China's trade with the rest of the world and operate a large number of industrial enterprises in China. Apart from the invisible earnings from these activities the total value of British commercial property and investments in China was assessed in 1941 at £300,000,000. This figure excludes subsequent war damage but the present total value is still very considerable. If British and other non-Chinese interests were to cut their losses promptly and remove whatever property they could it would undoubtedly greatly increase the Communists' difficulties, but from the point of view of the interests concerned the financial loss, as most of the property could not be got out, would be not much less than if the Communists took over all these interests in the first place without compensation.[11] In any case it has been decided on political grounds that British interests should be supported in their desire to keep their foot in the door in China as long as possible, and on economic grounds it would be regrettable to cut ourselves off from a potentially vast market for British goods and a potentially important soft-currency source of supply of essential imports (including eggs, tea, broad beans, bristles, soya beans and flour, and tung oil). With the great internal need in China and our own need for soft currency supplies, potential trade if conditions were at all normal might be at least double pre-war.

19. The best hope for British interests to maintain themselves for some time longer in China seems to lie in the presumed Communist need for the continuing functioning of British public utilities, insurance, banking, commercial and shipping agencies and industrial enterprises until the

[11] An estimate made by the Economic and Industrial Planning Staff in a January 1947 paper put the value of British investments in Shanghai at £107 million. £97,775,000 constituted immovable property (land and buildings). Moveable property (personal belongings, business stocks and equipment, factory machinery and installations) was put at £9,225,000 (F 16267/360/10).

Communists are ready to take them over or have organized alternatives. Whatever economic weapons may be at our disposal for the purpose of protecting British economic interests in China it is considered that they should be held in reserve for as long as the Communists are prepared to tolerate the functioning of British concerns. The probable result of any attempt to bring economic pressure to bear during the first phase would be to expedite the coming of the second phase in which the Communists are likely to attempt some form of expropriation.

20. On the assumption that the existence of foreign economic interests will only be tolerated for as long as their continued functioning is considered by the Communists to be in their own interests, and that a stage will come when some form of expropriation will be attempted, it is clearly of the first importance that we and the other Powers concerned shall endeavour to agree on a common line in the face of this threat. Our objectives in any consultations which may take place should be:

(*a*) to persuade other Powers, and particularly the Americans, who have smaller commercial interests in China than the UK, and who may be tempted to cut their losses at an early stage and to proceed at once to a policy of economic warfare against the Communists, to take no action for as long as foreign interests remain reasonably unmolested;

(*b*) to reach agreement in principle with the other powers concerned on the joint application of possible future measures of economic pressure against the Communists should these later prove necessary and expedient, on the understanding that they are in any case to be held in reserve until such time as the Communists begin to take definitely aggressive action against foreign economic interests. Action on these lines would not of course preclude the denial to China, by agreement with other Powers, of goods of strategic importance, where such denial would be effective.

Ex hypothesi it is clear that any threats by British concerns to shut down their operations (even if concerted through the British Chambers of Commerce) would have little effect on the Communists. Any action would, therefore, have to be taken from outside China; and the summary of Communist economic weaknesses in paragraph 17 above does not reveal any particularly strong card in our hand at the present time. The following possibilities present themselves:

(i) *The licensing of exports from the UK to China*

It is considered that such a system should be introduced only as a last resort, and in any case should apply only to certain materials which we know the Communists have particular need of. It would in any case be no use to introduce a licensing system except on the basis of agreement between the UK and other important potential suppliers, and it would obviously also be necessary to license exports to a number of Far Eastern ports outside China.

(ii) *Oil sanctions*

It is possible that the denial to the Chinese Communists of oil supplies alone might prove to be a weapon of considerable value. Such a sanction could be applied effectively by agreement between the United Kingdom, the United States and the Netherlands.

(iii) *The withdrawal of British shipping*

This might prove to be an effective sanction but would be extremely difficult to operate since the licensing procedure for British vessels is totally unsuitable for such a purpose.

21. While Communist action against British interests in China may perhaps be delayed by suitable tactics, in the long run HMG are likely to be faced with a similar state of affairs as regards expropriated British interests to that in Eastern Europe today, only on a larger scale. By this time we may be better placed in regard to the supply of goods which the Communists most desire, and may therefore be able to minimise our losses, perhaps through a trade and compensation agreement, or if necessary, by threats to impose sanctions on the line of paragraph 20(b) above, or possibly by a combination of the two.

APPENDIX TO No. 59

Chinese Communists

1. The Security authorities in Hong Kong have recently obtained possession of certain documents obviously belonging to one or more influential members of the Chinese Communist Party. These documents paint a revealing picture of the ruthless fervour, efficiency and cynicism of the Chinese Communists and provide abundant evidence that, far from the Chinese Communist Party being moderated by any special 'Chinese' factors, it is strictly orthodox, confident, mature and at the highest level very well organized. There is no trace of Titoism. There are references to a high ranking member of the Chinese Communist Party referred to only as 'F', who appears to enjoy considerable authority and to expound the purest Party line, correcting any deviations. A statement by this authority is, therefore, of considerable importance as showing that the Chinese Communist Party is fundamentally orthodox and is not prepared to accept other parties, however democratic, unless they too are Communists. The statement reads:

The Chinese Communist Party will persist in pursuing the Democratic Revolution to the end, and will consolidate the Proletariat leadership in the Revolution. Under the correct and mature leadership of Chairman Mao, the Chinese Communist Party has become a powerful, unified and genuine Proletariat political Party. The Chinese Revolution has but one course, there being no alternative one . . . Secondly, the 'Common Political Programme' passed by the Coalition Government [Note: the Chinese Communists intend to set up a 'Coalition' government in the near future][12] has to be followed by every and each political party and clique . . .

2. The documents contain numerous references to Communist intentions to use certain politics and parties for their own purposes for so long as it suits them; also to employ intelligent elements as a bridge with the masses, following the step by step process until the complete dictatorship of the proletariat is achieved. Emphasis is laid on the necessity to build generally on the masses. Agrarian reform is discussed as a means to consolidate the support of the peasants, who are 'the Reserve of the Communist Army' and on whom reliance must be placed. But the need to proceed cautiously is stressed, particularly in regard to the selection of new Party members. The whole process of screening candidates for admission and testing their doctrinal purity is described. Considerable space is devoted to the organisation of the Communist Party on orthodox lines. Under 'the problem of Cells', quality and not quantity is preached. There are detailed instructions on how to set about the organisation of Workers in a new field:

'Study and understand the conditions. In the first place make friends with them; reformation to follow later. Mix with them but do not be contaminated by them. Do not relax, but make no haste'. It is suggested that the first Communist propagandist in an untouched village might go in the guise of a hawker, a small shop-keeper or a schoolmaster.

Detailed instructions are also recorded on 'how to consolidate' which means the strengthening of the organisation through a better understanding of the Party line; on self-criticism and other features of Communist conscience-searching and on the 'Purge Problem'. In regard to the last it is interesting to note that a typical purge is cited of 30% of the Party members in Central Hopei Province.

3. Touching on the history of the Chinese Communist Party in South China, the documents reveal that the Southern Committee of the Party dates from 1936. South China is credited with having some loyal and trusted old Party members, but is considered to be weakened at present by the infiltration of opportunist elements and by too much concentration on the intelligentsia. The mistake of ignoring peasants and workers is claimed to have been made. In 1941 the Party was adjusted and in 1942 a further change appears to have taken place which placed the South under the leadership of one referred to as 'Mo'.[13] A lengthy analysis is made of the strong and weak points of South China from a Communist point of view and a plan of campaign mapped out on orthodox lines. The documents assert that the two southern provinces of Kwangtung and Kwangsi are the focal point for Communism in South China. There is mention of the

[12] Brackets as in the original.
[13] This was believed to be Mao Tse-tung himself, 'Mo' being the rendering of the Chinese character 'Mao'.

possible return to South China of a Communist guerrilla unit transferred to North China in 1946, but it seems to have been decided not to rely on the return of this force but to take 'bold action' and 'do our best on our own initiative'.

4. In notes discussing the possible formation of a 'United Front' through coalition with other Democratic Parties it is made clear that any co-operation with other groups is merely a short term policy.

Marshal Li Chai-sum,[14] to whom there are many references, and General Tsai Ting-kai (Marshal Li's associate head of the Kuomintang Revolutionary Committee in Hong Kong) are referred to on a contemptuous note and quite clearly regarded merely as tools; while the Communists' attitude towards the China Democratic League,[15] and the Kuomintang Revolutionary Committee is one of cynicism. They will be used, but if they are given any place in a so-called Coalition Government they will have to enter on the Communist Party's terms and they will be allowed no policy of their own. There is clearly no intention to allow an opposition Party outside the Government. Indeed, the Communist Party show concern lest too many 'Rightists' and 'Opportunists' join the other Democratic Parties so as to be on the winning side and to share in the 'spoils'.

5. There is a lot of material on future Communist policy and the treatment of foreign interests. Pains will be taken to show that the Communist Party rely in no way on foreigners. They will regard foreign industrial concerns—the American-owned power and telephone utilities in Shanghai are specifically cited— as having established themselves through their special privileged position in the past. These concerns will be allowed to continue to function just so long as it is expedient, and it will be made clear that they do so only on orders from the 'People's Government' and that they will be 'dealt with separately later on'. It is stated that foreign shipping should be handled on the lines followed in North Korea. Foreign shipping companies will not be allowed to continue as if nothing has happened. They will have to apply individually for entry permits and it will be impressed upon them that they have no special privileges.

6. The documents record in the purest Communist phraseology important discussions on the method of taking over Shanghai. References are made to a 'vacuum period' with the possibility during that period of

---

[14] *Note in the original:* 'Marshal Li Chai-sum: a native of Kwangsi Province, where he has always enjoyed considerable influence. A military leader of importance who has held many high posts in the Nanking Government. In 1947 he was expelled from the Kuomintang and retired to Hong Kong. In January 1948 he assumed the Chairmanship of an organisation known as "The Kuomintang Revolutionary Committee" which consists of former members of the Kuomintang who have turned against it; most of them have been in political exile in Hong Kong. Li Chai-sum and other leaders have recently gone to North China to join the Communists.'

[15] *Note in the original:* 'Democratic League: a minor left-wing political party outlawed by the Nanking Government in December, 1947, for its relationship with the Chinese Communist Party. During 1948 it established a Headquarters in Hong Kong.'

the 'existence of a chaotic state', and the desire of the 'Democratic Rightists' to prevent this by 'preserving the *status quo* pending handing over to us'. 'F' appears to have rejected these suggestions and decided that there shall be no 'vacuum period'. It seems clear that the Communists do not wish to take over Shanghai as a gift from other 'Democratic Parties' and that they would even prefer to delay action until they can assume control of the city on their own terms.

7. There are many references to Kuomintang officials who are either putting out feelers with a view to enlisting in the Communist ranks, or who are actively working for the Communists while inside the Kuomintang Government. These included a number of personalities connected with the Kwangsi clique, members of the Kuomintang Branches, the Nanking Commissioner of Police, recorded in the documents as having gone to Hainan, and a number of Government Secret Service and Military Officials.

8. On the whole evidence suggests that Hong Kong is more a regional than a purely local centre and this lends support to the view that Hong Kong may be the centre of a 'South China Bureau' and a centre for transmitting directives to neighbouring countries e.g. the Philippines and French Indo China.

No. 60

Sir R. Stevenson (Nanking) to Mr. Bevin

No. 141 [F 3790/1015/10]

Confidential   NANKING, *4 March 1949*

Sir,

The recent Communist successes in China and the prospect of a Communist-dominated Government controlling this country are obviously in process of creating a new situation throughout South-east Asia. The effect of this Communist advance on future developments in that area would in any event be considerable but the presence of many millions of Chinese in Indo-China, Siam, Malaya and Indonesia will undoubtedly make its impact even more serious.

2. My United States, Indian and Australian colleagues and I, myself, have been recently discussing the situation and have gone so far as to formulate our ideas on how it should be dealt with. We fully realise that the matter is outside our respective spheres of competence. But, in view of the fact that it is the position in China, combined with the presence of Chinese populations in South-east Asia, that makes the problem presented so urgent and compelling, we have ventured to produce a joint memorandum setting forth certain proposals. A copy of this memorandum is enclosed herein.

3. You will observe that we postulate an essentially revolutionary condition in South-east Asia which, if not brought under control, will speedily be exploited by the Communists with their easy solution of 'Land to the Tiller' and 'Power to the Worker' with its immense appeal to backward populations. Mere force is of no avail in such circumstances and the only hope is to produce a non-Communist solution of the major issues which the revolution is seeking to solve. A Confederation of South-east Asia is, we consider, the ultimate aim, but in present circumstances it is politically impracticable. But what might, we think, be attainable in the not too distant future would be a permanent Consultative Council composed of the States and territories of this area which could elaborate and apply common policies and provide for an integrated economy capable of resisting Communist economic doctrines. A necessary pre-condition for the creation of such a body would be the attainment of political freedom by Indonesia and Indo-China and the constitutional ability of Malaya to participate at least in common economic policies. It would also be necessary that the Consultative Council should have before it an economic and social programme which would deal realistically with the special problems of the backward societies concerned. Such a programme should, we think, be worked out now by a small committee of political and economic experts, men of the calibre of Lord Hailey,[1] who did the African Survey, appointed by the United Kingdom, the United States, India and Australia, and we suggest this as a first step. It might be convenient in this connexion to employ the services of such bodies as Chatham House, the Foreign Policy Association of the United States of America, the Indian Institute of World Affairs and some such body in Australia.

4. We further suggest that in order to enable the proposed Consultative Council of South-east Asia to give effect to the programme it might be found desirable to create an Advisory Committee consisting of representatives of the Powers from which would have to come the necessary material help and technical advice, viz, United Kingdom, United States of America, India, Australia, France and the Netherlands. We realise that such a Committee even though its functions were purely advisory and exercised only at the invitation of the Consultative Council might be regarded as a kind of 'Imperialist Syndicate'. Were this to prove a valid objection the alternative might be to entrust the advisory functions to the United States of America on the understanding that the other interested Powers would make available the required experts or other assistance within their capacity.

5. The United States, Indian and Australian Ambassadors are addressing similar despatches to their respective Governments. (My Australian

---

[1] William Malcolm Hailey (1st Baron cr. 1936), Indian Civil Service from 1895; Governor of the Punjab 1924-28 and of the United Provinces 1928-30 and 1930-31; Director, Africa Research Survey, 1935-38 and author of *An African Survey* (1938).

colleague is sending his despatch direct to Dr. Evatt in the United Kingdom.)

6. In view of the considerations mentioned in paragraph 2 above, I am sending a copy of this despatch to the Commissioner-General for South-east Asia only.

I have, etc.,

RALPH SKRINE STEVENSON

ENCLOSURE IN NO. 60

Memorandum on the impact of Communist successes in China on South-east Asia

The possibility of a Communist-dominated Government in China has created a new situation in South-east Asia. The immediate effect of the Communist victories in China has been to change the *pace* of events in the adjacent regions, reducing to the minimum the margin of time available for a peaceful transformation of the economy of these countries. The problem arising from the juxtaposition of a Communist controlled China with the semi-colonial economy of the South-east Asian countries may be stated as follows.

2. Till now the dominant issue in all the countries of South-east Asia was the recovery of freedom. This was essentially a political issue and with the independence of India and Burma, the principle may well be said to have been established, though the last chapter in this phase of history still remains to be written in Indo-China and Indonesia. But it is accepted even by the Dutch and the French that their colonies will soon have to gain independence.

3. The achievement of independence does not however solve the problem which these countries have to face, which is one of transforming the typically 'oriental' civilisations of these areas held together by anachronistic social bonds and based on a starvation economy into modern communities, organised on principles of social justice and economic freedom. In short, these countries have to *compress into a short period of time,* the whole process of a century of European evolution, adopt the technology of mid-twentieth century to societies which are still living in the pre-industrial revolution era but with new and destructive ideas sweeping their minds. The resulting condition is essentially revolutionary, both in its process and in its consequences, for it is seeking to force developments and not allowing the slow process of evolution to work.

4. If it is accepted that the situation is revolutionary in its content, then the question immediately follows as to how it can be brought under control and guided into proper channels, for if we do not bring it under control, the Communists with their easy solution of 'Land to the Tiller' and 'Power to the Worker' will step in and take charge.

5. In the circumstances of South-east Asia, the Communist solution has an immense appeal. The situation has been foreseen by the Communist

thinkers who recognise that the transition from feudalism to communism is in a way easier, as the resistance offered will be by classes which have ceased to be socially useful and represent no productive principles in society—the landlords and those who depend on them. In other words the anti-communist element furnished elsewhere in the world by the middle class is completely lacking. That is one of the reasons why Communism is more aggressive in Asia and seems to be less actively resisted by the masses.

6. Any idea that the South-east Asian countries could be persuaded to resist the inroads of Communism by arming its opponents and encouraging the reactionary elements to band together in defence of 'the four freedoms' or the new slogan of free competition is foredoomed to failure for the simple reason that an economic and social revolution is already in being throughout the whole area.

7. How then are we to act? Clearly by accepting the revolutionary content of the situation and providing a solution to the major issues which the revolution is seeking to solve. If the same objectives can be gained with greater safety in a reasonably short time, through a non-Communist solution, then there is every reason to think that Communism can be resisted in this area.

8. It might of course be argued that the alternative to the Communist revolution is really what is being done in India—the attainment of the same objectives by parliamentary methods—that is a revolution controlled by parliament and effectuated through legislation. But the circumstances of South-east Asia do not seem to warrant any hope of successful action along these lines, primarily because there is no established principle of obedience in these countries and secondly because leadership requires an effectuating machinery—a highly trained efficient and loyal service—which notoriously does not exist in these countries.

9. What then is the alternative? The ultimate solution seems clear: a confederation of South-east Asia with a planned and integrated economy, creating out of the small units in this region a viable State following a progressive economic and social policy. In the immediate future such a solution would perhaps be impracticable, if only for the reason that the States which are struggling to acquire their independence like Indo-China, and the States which have only recently acquired independence like Burma, will not even consider anything which may limit their political independence. But the situation created by the existence of a Communist colossus in the North may possibly prove sufficiently dynamic to bring about a change in their attitude, very much in the same manner as the Western European States which are so intensely nationalist have come together in similar circumstances.

10. While this should be the objective, towards which our activities should be directed, it is obvious that since this solution is not capable of immediate realisation, we should have a short-term policy which could be put into effect with the least possible delay. A permanent Consultative Council of the States of this area which will work out common policies and

provide for an integrated economy capable of resisting the pressure of Communist economic doctrines would seem to be the answer. But in order to bring into existence such a Consultative Council, it is necessary as a first step that Indo-China and Indonesia should acquire their political freedom and Malaya should have a constitutional set-up which will enable her at least to participate in economic policies.

11. Such a Consultative Council when brought into being should have before it an economic and social programme which realistically deals with the special problems of their backward societies. Such a programme will have to provide (*a*) for the liquidation of unproductive systems of landowning and for a reorganisation of agriculture with aid of the most modern technology for the purpose of increasing production (*b*) for the absorption into industries of large masses of people now living on land without contributing to the increase of national *production* (*c*) for the integration of the economy of the region so as to avoid wasteful inter-regional *competition* (*d*) for large-scale medical and sanitary facilities which will eliminate the enervating effects of the climatic conditions of the 'monsoon belt', and (*e*) for a common system of education which will provide a background for democratic development: in short a programme of planned economy.

12. The first step, which should be taken *now*, is to utilise to the best advantage the time available before a settlement is arrived at in Indonesia and Indo-China and work out a programme for this region. This can only be done after a careful analysis of the prevailing social and economic conditions. Such a survey should cover not merely the present morphology of these societies, but should be primarily directed towards the shape they should assume in the future: that is, *it must formulate the principles on which the New Society in South-east Asia should be fashioned.*

13. An enquiry of this nature conducted by a group of what are called in America 'social engineers' would provide us with an alternative programme which may blunt the appeal of Communism and tame and regulate the revolutionary process in South-east Asia.

14. The powers most immediately and directly interested in doing so are USA, UK, Australia and India and if the enquiry is entrusted to a small Committee of four or five high level political and economic thinkers from these countries, who have some experience of practical problems, men of the calibre of Lord Hailey who did the African Survey, then a workable and forward looking programme would be available for approval by the Governments concerned.

15. It seems likely, however, that the Governments of South-east Asia, even when working through their own permanent consultative Council would not be able to take full advantage of the programme without material assistance and technical advice. It might therefore be advisable to form some kind of advisory committee parallel to the permanent consultative Council and working in close collaboration with it, composed not only of the four Powers mentioned above but also of France and the

Netherlands whose continuing economic interest in South-east Asia must be considerable. This Committee would be responsible for determining, when invited to do so by the permanent consultative Council and in concert with that body, the amount and the kind of assistance required and its procurement.

No. 61

Memorandum by Mr. Creech Jones on the situation in Malaya and Hong Kong[1]

CP(49)52 [*CAB 129/33*]

Top Secret   COLONIAL OFFICE, 5 *March 1949*

With reference to CM(48)80th Conclusions, Minute 3,[2] it will be of interest to my colleagues to know what steps have been taken to strengthen our position in Hong Kong and Malaya.

Hong Kong

2. After consultation between the Commanders-in-Chief, Far East, the Governor of Hong Kong and the Chiefs of Staff Committee, the Commanders-in-Chief, Far East, have now prepared a revised assessment of the probable threats and of the forces required to meet them. They share the view of the Governor of Hong Kong that the possible short-term threats to Hong Kong are:

(*a*) internal unrest likely to be inspired by the Communist-dominated Trades Unions;

(*b*) large-scale influx of refugees by land and/or by sea;

(*c*) external aggression by guerrilla bands, probably Communist-inspired.

They regard the likelihood of an organised Communist attack on Hong Kong with a view to its rendition, or a full-scale attack supported by Russian specialists, as remote possibilities that need not be considered at present.

---

[1] Only that section of the memorandum dealing with Hong Kong is printed here. The section on Malaya explained the strength of security forces—in addition to the police there were 14,600 British, Gurkha and Malay fighting troops (expected to rise to 15,000 by June 1949) and 26,800 administrative troops. It described the operations in progress and casualties sustained against a few hundred 'hard-core Communists' aided by up to 5,000 armed auxiliaries. Squatters suspected of aiding the Communists were being resettled in areas under close police supervision and those refusing to co-operate were being deported. The European community in Malaya was under strain and making constant demands for more troops. Financial assistance was being provided to maintain the police force in Malaya and to expand the Malay Regiment and other local defence forces.

[2] See No. 52.

3. Threat (*a*) above might occur at any time with little warning if the Communists thought that it would be to their advantage, and we must therefore be prepared to meet it. The Governor thinks that threats (*b*) and (*c*) are less likely to occur than when this question was considered in December. Nevertheless, the threats do exist and, for planning purposes, the Commanders-in-Chief considered that they should be regarded as possible at any time after March, 1949, with probably a month's warning.

4. *Availability of forces*
(i) *Royal Navy*
Existing Naval forces in the Far East are sufficient to meet the threats under all heads if occurring separately or simultaneously, but, if a crisis arose simultaneously in Hong Kong and Shanghai, assistance to Hong Kong should be given priority, and the forces available for the evacuation of Shanghai would be substantially reduced. Moreover, Hong Kong would not be available as a transit base for Shanghai evacuees. A number of harbour craft in Hong Kong are being refitted at once for coastal patrol work when the need for this arises.

(ii) *Army*
If the threats under (*a*), (*b*) and (*c*) occur simultaneously before the end of 1949, two Brigade Groups at least would be required at Hong Kong. One is already available there, and the second would have to be found from outside the Far East area, unless operations in Malaya are to be seriously interfered with. One battalion and one AOP[3] Flight from security forces in Malaya are, however, being earmarked to reinforce Hong Kong, should it be necessary, as a temporary advance guard of the second Brigade reinforcement referred to above (see paragraph 5 below). Shanghai and Burma commitments are likely at any time to put a heavy load on already over-strained resources in this theatre.

(iii) *Royal Air Force*
An Air Force reinforcement would be required to meet the simultaneous occurrence of the threats under (*a*), (*b*) and (*c*), and can be provided from forces available in the Far East provided that the recruitment of the Hong Kong Defence Air Unit is proceeded with. But if any one of the threats arose simultaneously with evacuation from Shanghai and/or Burma, it would be difficult to give full assistance to Hong Kong.

5. The Chiefs of Staff Committee generally agree with the foregoing appreciation. They further agree that no land force reinforcements ought to be sent at the present time to Hong Kong from the United Kingdom, despite the desirability of forestalling an emergency in Hong Kong, but that one Brigade Group should be held in readiness from April till the end of 1949. Two months, however, might have to elapse before reinforcements could arrive in Hong Kong.

[3] Air Observation Post.

6. The following matters have been urgently examined by the Governor in consultation, where necessary, with the local Military Authorities and the British Defence Co-ordination Committee, Far East:

(*a*) *Closing of land frontier*

In the event of a threatened influx of refugees, the frontier could be completely wired in 14 days, the essential minimum being completed in 4 days. The Governor considers that no wiring should be done until the threat appears imminent, as once it is done police and troops will have to guard it, and its erection would cause uneasiness on the frontier and might lead to incidents (there is a tacit understanding at present whereby both Communist guerrillas and Chinese government troops respect the frontier). The Chiefs of Staff Committee have accepted the Governor's recommendations.

(*b*) *Closing of sea frontier*

This question presents considerable difficulties owing to shortage of suitable vessels for patrol work. Immediate steps are being taken by the Naval Commander-in-Chief, Far East, to remedy this situation, and Naval personnel will be made available when required to man additional patrol vessels.

(*c*) *Evacuation of Europeans*

There can be no question of the compulsory evacuation of Europeans from Hong Kong. Plans have been made for the temporary reception of British-sponsored evacuees from China, on their journey to final destinations.

(*d*) *Rationing*

A rationing system is already in existence, and is capable of rapid expansion. Expansion would not, however, have any effect upon immigration into the Colony. Supplies of certain essential foodstuffs are being built up.

(*e*) *Registration*

The Governor has decided to introduce a system of registration in two stages:

(i) voluntary registration of persons at present on the ration strength and of others desirous of being registered (estimated time—four months);

(ii) compulsory registration (not until necessary).

(*f*) *Police*

The Police Force will be expanded to approximately 80 per cent greater strength than 1941 by 31st March. There should also be a certain number of European civilians available as a trained reserve to reinforce senior Police Officers. The present training capacity of the depot is being used to the limit and could not accommodate any further large increase.

(*g*) *Strikes*

There is a possibility that a genuine industrial dispute may be used by the Communists to stir up trouble. Whether they would deliberately initiate industrial and internal strife in the Colony would depend largely on their overall policy towards the Colony and the British Empire generally. Their present action towards foreign interests in China in recent months appears to indicate that they are unlikely to do so, but the danger may arise with little warning. A scheme has been prepared for running the public utility services with volunteer labour, since it is those services whose labour belongs to Communist-controlled Unions. The Naval Commander-in-Chief, Far East, has agreed to provide further man-power, when necessary, to assist in maintaining essential services.

7. The above matters have all been reviewed here, where necessary, with the Chiefs of Staff Committee. The following steps are also being taken:

(a) *Police*

Urgent selection of a small additional number of European Police Officers, required to bring the commissioned personnel of the Hong Kong Police Force up to the necessary strength.

(b) *Supplies*

Special efforts to ensure that, as far as possible, the necessary materials required by local industries in Hong Kong are made available without delay, to minimise possible discontent in industry.[4]

[4] The Cabinet considered this memorandum, together with No. 59, on 8 March (CM(49) 18th Conclusions, Minute 2, CAB 128/15). There was general agreement that every endeavour should be made to maintain trade with China, provided the impression was not created that HMG would compensate UK merchants for serious losses.

On Hong Kong, Mr. Creech Jones explained that he had been advised that any attempt to 'root out' Communism in Hong Kong 'would lead to trouble with the labour unions and might cause internal disorder'. It seemed wiser 'to hold the balance between the different parties so long as no attack was made on the Government'. Some Ministers doubted whether it was advisable to turn a blind eye to Communist activities in Hong Kong, in case a short period of tranquillity was being purchased at the price of eventual serious disturbances when 'a Hong Kong riddled with Communism' would fall easy prey to unrest fomented internally and encouraged from outside. It was accepted that the available defence forces made it difficult to prevent infiltration from China, and that the Communist threat to Hong Kong could not be met by force. Measures of 'political warfare' were needed to strengthen anti-Communist elements. Doubts were expressed as to whether the Communists should be allowed to conduct propaganda work in South-East Asia from headquarters in Hong Kong, but against this it was argued that nothing should be done at this stage to preclude the possibility of the UK's entering into friendly relations with a Communist regime which had established a stable government throughout China. Other factors, such as possible repercussions on isolated groups of UK subjects scattered throughout Communist China, would have to be considered before suppressive action were taken against the Communists in Hong Kong.

At the same meeting it was noted that Mr. Attlee proposed to consider whether formal arrangements should be made for regular consideration by Ministers of the problems of China and South-East Asia. A Cabinet China and South-East Asia Committee was set up on 24 March 1949 with the Prime Minister in the Chair, and the Chancellor of the Exchequer, the Secretaries of State for Foreign Affairs, the Colonies, and Commonwealth Relations, and the Minister of Defence as other members.

No. 62

Sir O. Franks (Washington) to Mr. Bevin

No. 114 Saving: Telegraphic [F 4220/1015/10]

Important. Secret   WASHINGTON, *18 March 1949, 8.30 a.m.*

My telegram No. 79 (5th January): Communist domination of China.[1]
State Department's comments are as follows:
Begins:
Memorandum.

1. The Department of State has studied with care the memorandum regarding China and the influence of present developments in that country upon southern Asia which was handed to the Acting Secretary of State January 5, 1949 by His Excellency the British Ambassador and the subsequent memoranda on this subject handed to officers of the Department by Mr. Graves.[2] A memorandum containing the Department's comments on these documents is enclosed.

2. The Department of State welcomes the opportunity for an exchange of views regarding this important subject and hopes that the discussions which have already been initiated in connexion with the memoranda may be continued.

3. The British memorandum presents a thoughtful and detailed analysis of the effect which present and possible future Communist successes in China may be expected to have upon subsequent developments in China and in other areas of South Asia. This phase of the study is, of course, conjectural in nature, but it appears to be well reasoned. It is helpful to have a wholly independent analysis based upon information obtained through independent channels and reassuring to note that the general estimate of the situation and the conclusions are substantially the same as our own.

4. It is believed that somewhat more emphasis might have been placed upon the growing strength of nationalism in South Asia and the probable incompatibility of this growing force with communism, in the long run. The memorandum points out that it is just conceivable 'that if the Russians sought complete domination of Sinkiang, this might cause a rift with the Chinese Communists, whose nationalism would not take kindly to Russian acquisitiveness'. To Sinkiang might be added Manchuria as a possible source of friction. And whether Soviet acquisitiveness leads to a rift with

---

[1] Sir O. Franks had been instructed on 20 December 1948 to consult the State Department about the UK memorandum on China that had been approved by the Cabinet (see No. 51). Washington telegram No. 79 of 5 January (F 276/1015/10) reported that State Department officials were considering the matter with Mr. Graves (see No. 52, note 5).

[2] Mr. Graves prepared three separate papers for the Americans on (1) the political effects on the adjacent areas of a Communist China, (2) the economic effects, and (3) the possibilities of counter-action (letter to Mr. Scarlett, 18 January 1949 (F 17714/33/10, F 1397/1015/10).

the Chinese Communists or not, it would offend large segments of the Chinese public. Evidence of Moscow domination of a Chinese Communist regime might be expected similarly to offend the nationalist sentiments of large numbers of Chinese. While communists have endeavoured, through persistent propaganda and other methods in other areas of southern Asia, to infiltrate and control nationalist movements with at least temporary advantage to themselves, it appears likely that this marriage of convenience will come to an end as communism shows itself more evidently a tool of either Soviet or Chinese Imperialism. The memorandum mentions the effect of Chinese Communist penetration in Malaya upon the Malayans and suggests that the Chinese Communists might seek a delineation of the Sino-Burmese border unfavourable to Burma. The opportunity which these or similar developments would offer for showing communism not as the protector but rather the destroyer of nationalist aspirations is apparent. If the foregoing is sound, it suggests that measures tending to destroy the false identification of communism with nationalism might be a fruitful means of weakening communism in China and neutralizing the influence of Communist China in other areas of South Asia. It is clear that measures of this nature would be most productive if taken while Communist forces are still attempting to seize control rather than after they have established their characteristic machinery of a police state.

5. The memorandum states that it is desirable 'so far as political considerations permit, to ensure that each territory was possessed of police and intelligence services, as well as the requisite legal powers, to deal adequately with any growth of Communist activity . . .'. It seems desirable, without lessening the importance of such measures, to call attention to their essentially repressive nature and to the equal importance of pursuing a progressive programme which would, in a more positive way, win the loyalty and support of native populations.

6. Finally, a word of caution is desirable regarding dependence upon American material aid in approaching the problems of South Asia. It would be most unfortunate to encourage leaders of South Asia to expect or ask for large amounts of material aid from the United States Government in solving their problems. Although external aid may appear an easy and politically painless solution, it can in no way take the place of soundly conceived measures of self-help. Quite apart from the heavy burden which would be placed upon the American people, experience in China has shown that the extension of external assistance under certain conditions is not an effective means for encouraging a country to face squarely its problems with the determination to help itself. This point is of such importance that a brief review of the experience of the United States in China is desirable by way of emphasis.

7. From 1937 until V-J Day the United States Government authorized grants and credits to the Chinese Government totalling approximately $1.5 billion, of which 55 per cent may be classified as military and 45 per cent as economic assistance. Following V-J Day, the Chinese Government

controlled the major portion of China, of its people and of its resources. In terms of men under arms and quality and quantity of weapons, it was vastly superior to the Chinese Communists. In short, its position in terms of the physical requisites of power was, beyond possible doubt, far better than that of its opponents. To this initial advantage must be added post V-J Day assistance from the United States amounting to approximately $2 billion, which has been almost equally divided between economic and military help. The foregoing sum does not include the very substantial assistance which the Chinese Government received through the transfer to it of surplus property at a fraction of its procurement cost of more than one billion dollars nor does it include assistance which the Chinese Government has received through the assignment of American advisory personnel in the cultural, economic and military fields and through international agencies such as UNRRA. It appears unnecessary to expand further the list of external aid which the Chinese Government has received to establish clearly that the weakness of that government and the cause of its recent reverses may not be found in its lack of material resources, for in this respect it enjoyed unquestionable superiority over the Chinese Communists. This conclusion is further supported by the considered opinion of ranking American military representatives in China that none of the defeats suffered by the Chinese Government armies during the campaigns of 1948 was caused by lack of ammunition or equipment but rather that they may all be attributed to extremely bad leadership and to other morale destroying factors which led to a complete loss of the will-to-fight. Primarily as a result of these conditions, which led to large-scale defections of Nationalist troops and the surrender of military stores intact, the major portion of the military equipment and supplies, exclusive of ammunition, transferred to the Chinese Government by the United States has fallen into the hands of the Chinese Communists.

8. As a matter of fact, it has long been recognized that unless the Chinese Government improved the quality of its leadership and espoused a progressive programme in consonance with the awakening aspirations of the Chinese people it might well succumb to the aggressive and dynamic Communists. American efforts were consequently directed unremittingly towards bringing the Chinese Government to a realization of the essentiality of these measures of self-help and to the understanding of them. Public statements by the President and the Secretary of State and private conversations with Chinese leaders were directed to that end. American aid was used at once to provide an inducement and an opportunity for effective measures of self-help. These efforts were generally unsuccessful and present conditions in China stand as evidence of the essentiality of vigorous self-help to meet the threat of Communism, of the impossibility of substituting external aid for self-help and of the weakness of external aid as inducement to evoke measures of self-help.

Ends.

My observations on this will follow by despatch.[3]

[3] In a letter to Mr Bevin of 22 March, Sir O. Franks commented that there was an 'unfortunate weakness' in the State Department's reply in that it contained 'several isolated comments which have not been developed into any general conclusion and which, without further explanation, are not easy to reconcile with each other'. In the words of Mr. Dean Acheson, US Secretary of State, American policy towards China was one of 'waiting until the dust had settled'. This, according to Sir O. Franks, made it difficult to report US views with any degree of precision. The Ambassador questioned the comments in the State Department's reply about the 'essentially repressive nature' of police and intelligence services: 'In view of the extensive control of such activities in the United States itself it seems rather strange that normal precautionary measures should be thought inappropriate in countries which, in their present state, are naturally more susceptible to communist propaganda.' Sir O. Franks described the remainder of the reply as a 'lament on the failure of United States post-war activities in China' (F 4595/1015/10).

In the FO, Mr. R.H. Scott described the US response as a 'mixture of defeatism and pious advice'. But to the extent that the State Department had been induced to consider these problems, he was 'all for steadily pegging away at the Americans, on the principle of the steady drip wearing away the stone' (minute of 29 April). Mr. Scarlett agreed on 30 April: 'The only hope is to keep on arguing back.'

No. 63

Submission by Mr. Scarlett on a New Airfield at Hong Kong[1]

[F 4273/1381/10]

FOREIGN OFFICE, *21 March 1949*

The Problem

It has been decided to construct a new airport at Deep Bay, in the Leased Territory of Hong Kong. The Colonial Secretary wishes to make this decision public in reply to an inspired Parliamentary Question to be put to him shortly. Before doing so he asks for an assurance that the Secretary of State concurs in the project generally.

Recommendation

I recommend that the Secretary of State should concur.

Argument

The construction of a modern airport of international standards is necessary for the maintenance of Hong Kong's position as a focal point in Far Eastern communications, and on the 26th April, 1948 it was announced in the House of Commons that His Majesty's Government were prepared to make an interest-free loan of £3,000,000 to the Colony

[1] This submission was prepared in response to a letter from the Colonial Office of 23 February, requesting FO views on the text of a proposed statement in the House of Commons about a new airfield at Hong Kong (F 2913/1381/10).

for such construction.[2] The site of the new airport had not then been decided.

It is now considered impracticable to construct the airport on the island of Hong Kong itself, and it is therefore proposed to construct it on the mainland, in part of the territory leased from the Chinese Government in 1898 on a 99 year lease.[3]

Judging from past experience the Chinese Government will not welcome this decision, but they are perhaps less likely to instigate or condone agitation against the project in present circumstances than they would be normally. His Majesty's Ambassador at Nanking is aware of the intention to announce the decision shortly[4] and proposes to inform the Chinese Government simultaneously.[5]

P.W. SCARLETT

[2] *Parl. Debs., 5th ser., H. of C.*, vol. 450, cols. 18-20.

[3] Sir W. Strang, who had been appointed PUS on 1 February 1949, commented on 21 March: 'The existing airfield at Hong Kong is already one of the busiest in the world. It is quite unsuitable as a modern airfield being closely surrounded by hills. It also lies on the edge of the so-called walled city of Kowloon, and is therefore vulnerable in case of disorders. It is impossible to build an airfield on the island of Hong Kong, or on that small area of the mainland which forms part of the colony itself. The only available sites are on the level ground on the western side of the Leased Territory . . . I think I am right in saying that the present airfield is itself situated just inside the Leased Territory, so that we shall not in this respect be making a departure.'

[4] On 21 March Mr. Dening commented on Mr. Scarlett's submission: 'It would be better to make the announcement now, before the Communists get control of the Central Government.'

[5] Sir W. Strang agreed that the proposal should be approved, and the submission was put to Mr. Bevin, who wrote: 'I agree.' He and Mr. Creech Jones met on 23 March and approved the proposal, provided there was no publicity; it was especially important to avoid any reference to the decision in the House of Commons, as Mr. Bevin believed it would lead to trouble from Communist unions in Hong Kong and elsewhere. A local announcement, however, was made in Hong Kong in May to the effect that a survey would be undertaken and that new and better villages would be built to house the people displaced, said to be no more than 1000. The Nationalist government requested details of the boundaries of the proposed airfield, a request Mr. N.C.C. Trench of Far Eastern Department described as 'impudent' (minute of 12 August, F 10876/1381/10).

No. 64

Minutes of a meeting held by the Working Party to consider possible economic sanctions against a Chinese Communist Administration

[*F 5766/1153*]

FOREIGN OFFICE, *13 April 1949*

The Chairman[1] reminded the meeting that the Far Eastern (Official) Committee on Friday, 18th March, invited the Foreign Office to convene a Working Party of representatives of the Treasury, Board of Trade, Ministry of Fuel and Power, Commonwealth Relations Office, Colonial Office and Ministry of Transport, to consider what economic sanctions we could apply if the Chinese Communist Government attempted to suppress our trading interests there, and what measures could be applied by other interested Governments. The Working Party's task was to clarify our own ideas regarding possible sanctions first, as an essential preliminary to an approach to other friendly Governments. The economic section of the latest Cabinet Paper on China (CP(49)39)[2] contained two recommendations: firstly to dissuade other friendly powers, particularly the United States, from taking premature action in the way of sanctions, and secondly to agree in principle with them on what economic sanctions would be practicable and expedient when the time came. The first of these two recommendations was clearly of the greater immediate importance.

Mr. Hugh-Jones enquired whether the Working Party should exclude from their suggestions action such as we have taken in respect of Eastern European countries, i.e. preventing goods of strategic importance from reaching them. The Chairman considered that this could be regarded as excluded from the terms of reference of the Working Party in view of the last sentence of paragraph 20(*b*) of CP(49)39.

Finance

With the approval of the Departments concerned, two British banks have agreed to act for the Communist administration as agents for foreign exchange. The withholding of banking facilities did not, however, appear to offer a useful lever, since foreign banks were likely to be among the first foreign interests to face the threat of expropriation. The possibility of cutting-off overseas Chinese remittances also needed investigating. In reply to a question regarding the possibility of erecting an exchange control wall

---

[1] The meeting was chaired by Mr. F.S. Tomlinson (FO) and attended by Mr. D. Kelvin-Stark (Colonial Office), Mr. W.N. Hugh-Jones and Mr. N.C.C. Trench (FO), Mr. M. Rudd and Miss M.E. Ashe (Treasury), Miss T.W.M. Brunsdon and Mr. W. Gilbert (Board of Trade), Mr. R.C. Mitchell (Ministry of Fuel and Power), Mr. L.J.D. Wakely (Commonwealth Relations Office) and Major-General R.C. Money (Ministry of Transport).

[2] See No. 59.

round Hong Kong, *Mr. Kelvin-Stark* said that to all intents and purposes this was impossible owing to the prevalence of smuggling and to the large number of small banks who were probably willing to undertake illicit transactions. As far as Hong Kong was concerned it would only be possible to stop very large financial deals, or bulk shipments of, for example, petroleum products and machinery, which could not be concealed. Furthermore, if the Hong Kong hinterland were not Communist-controlled, when the time came for imposing sanctions it would be impossible to distinguish between money or materials destined for the hinterland or those which had the hinterland only as their ostensible destination.

The Treasury was invited to prepare a paragraph, in consultation with the Colonial Office, on the subject of finance for inclusion in a general paper embodying the Working Party's findings.

Food and Agriculture

Mr. Tomlinson said that presumably the supply of rice would be the main item under this head. It would be necessary to consult the South East Asia Department of the Foreign Office concerning the possible co-operation of Siam, Burma and South Indo-China.

Industry

Mr. Gilbert pointed out that to deny capital goods which take two or three years to produce would not constitute an effective sanction. *Mr. Tomlinson* quoted passages from Chinese Communist broadcasts, in which it was stated *inter alia* that 'private capital useful to the people's economy will exist and flourish for very much longer than one or two years'. 'The development of light industry as a whole is to be handed over to private enterprise.' Similarly, in finance and trade, 'Under conditions today, private trade is essential . . . it is suicidal to resort to drastic measures. Banks are permitted to continue their business.' *Mr. Hugh-Jones* considered that it was important to determine at what point it was expected that sanctions would be taken. Conditions might differ from area to area and action against foreign interests might be purely unofficial e.g. by organised strikes, boycotts etc. Was there a definite point at which one can say that the interested powers should intervene? It was felt that the solution of this problem, which was recognised to be a real one, was outside the terms of reference of the Working Party. *Mr. Hugh-Jones* considered that sanctions were in any case unlikely to result in British interests being allowed to continue in being, but suggested that they might facilitate the negotiation of a compensation agreement tied to a bilateral trade agreement, as in the case of Eastern European countries.[3] *Mr. Tomlinson* pointed out that in view

---

[3] Mr. Hugh-Jones later claimed that the second half of this sentence did not accord with what he had said, and it was subsequently amended to read 'continue in being. He felt that we should more likely find ourselves in the position of wishing to negotiate a compensation

of its terms of reference, the Working Party would not exclude from its consideration the possibility of sanctions having as their objective the continued existence of threatened British concerns.

Transport

General Money said that so far as British shipping is concerned there is still a Transfer Restriction Act in force and a system of licences to trade. However, these arrangements may be cancelled at any moment. Consideration should, therefore, be given to the possibility of retaining the necessary powers, though the industry would not like this. It was in any case impossible to intervene in order to stop trans-shipment.

The Ministry of Transport was invited to draw up a paragraph on this subject.

Minerals and Raw Materials

It was considered that rubber was an important item under this heading. At the moment, China was importing little raw rubber, and probably obtained its supplies of tyres and tubes from the United Kingdom or United States. *Mr. Gilbert* suggested that it would be worth finding out how great the Chinese production of tyres is, and how far it falls short of requirements. Presumably the United States would shut off the Japanese source of supply in case of need.

As regards raw materials in general, it would be difficult, if not impossible, to arrange for a system of general licencing, but it should be possible to deal with a single item or a small group of specified items.

The Chairman undertook to invite the Economic Intelligence Department to prepare a note on the possibility of withholding a small group of specific items. In particular it would be desirable to consider rubber, ferro-alloy metals and tin. (The question of what the United Kingdom would lose by ceasing to trade with China is referred to in paragraph 18 of CP(49)39, but it would be advisable to include a reference to this point in the Working Party's report.

Oil

Mr. Mitchell described the present situation. China produces only about 50,000 tons of crude oil per annum. She is dependent on British and United States sources for refined products, and for crude oil for the refinery on Formosa, which is run by the Chinese Petroleum Corporation. The value of the installations belonging to foreign countries is approximately £20 millions, of which 40 per cent is British-owned. Trade is not very large: Shell supply some 330,000 tons per annum, U.S. about

agreement. In Eastern Europe we had linked trade and/or payments negotiations with negotiations over compensation questions in order to secure compensation agreements; but in China, when the time came, we might not be able to adopt this procedure, and this would presumably be the occasion for using the threat of sanctions.'

500,000 tons per annum and the Chinese Petroleum Company supply about 450,000 tons per annum, which includes production from the Chinese field and imports from Anglo-Iranian and American companies. The total annual value of refined products is in the neighbourhood of £10 millions. The imposition of sanctions would leave Russia as the only real source of supply, although possibly Mexico might try to send a certain amount. It would be both difficult and expensive for Russia to provide adequate quantities. As regards the types of petroleum products required, those supplied by Shell may provide some guidance. These are as follows:

Aviation spirit	-	30,000 tons p.a.
Motor spirit	-	25,000 " "
Kerosene	-	50,000 " "
Gas Diesel	-	135,000 " "
Fuel Oil	-	84,000 " "

In addition, Anglo-Iranian supply some 195,000 tons of crude oil. 70 per cent of the imported product is shipped in the first instance to Shanghai, presumably because of the facilities for storage and distribution provided there. An alternative distributing point would be difficult to find. *Mr. Gilbert* pointed out that Netherlands co-operation would be required in respect of oil imports.

The Ministry of Fuel and Power were invited to draft a section on the oil position for inclusion in the general report. It would be useful to know the amount which Russia could supply, the general levels of stocks, and the volume of internal transport requiring petroleum fuel. (In reply to a question, *the Chairman* said that in any necessary consultation with oil companies the objective of the present study should *not* be disclosed.) It would be advisable to consult the Economic Intelligence Department regarding the effects of including in the lists of goods to be denied to the Communists materials for internal transport.

The Chairman called attention to the inclusion in the Working Party's terms of reference of the phrase 'to consider . . . what measures could be applied by other interested Governments'. It was agreed that this point would be adequately covered if the Working Party's final report were to include, in its consideration of specific sanctions, appropriate references to the need for the co-operation of other Governments where necessary.

Mr. Tomlinson concluded by saying that when paragraphs on the various subjects had been collected, they would be embodied in a report which will be circulated to members of the meeting for comment, and will then be submitted to the Far Eastern (Official) Committee.

In telegram No. 465 of 22 April Sir R. Stevenson informed the FO that overnight the Communists had effected a crossing of the River Yangtse at Chinkiang between Nanking and Shanghai. The Acting President of the National Government would be leaving shortly for Canton and the Ambassador had been urged by the Acting Chinese Foreign Minister to move to Shanghai at least. Sir R. Stevenson replied that he intended to remain in Nanking (F 5623/1015/10). In telegram No. 496 of 25 April the Ambassasor reported that on the previous evening a small party of Communist soldiers had entered the UK Embassy compound by the main gate. They did not advance more than ten or fifteen yards. Asked to explain their business they replied that they wanted information regarding numbers of people, vehicles, arms and other property in the Embassy and that they proposed to make a search. On Sir R. Stevenson's instructions they were told that a search was not possible and that they needed permission from higher authority. They left 'without further ado'. In the same telegram the Ambassador explained that early in the morning of 25 April an armed party of twelve Communist soldiers had entered the residence of Dr. Stuart, the US Ambassador. They went upstairs to his bedroom, used 'somewhat abusive language' but did not threaten Dr. Stuart or touch anything in the house. They left telling one of Dr. Stuart's servants that the Ambassador was not to leave the compound during the day. Dr. Stuart intended to ignore this order (F 5754/1015/10).

The crossing of the Yangtse had been preceded by nearly two and half months of virtual ceasefire in the civil war as the opposing armies faced each other each other across the river and both sides exchanged mutually unacceptable demands to end the conflict. On 17 April the Communists announced that if their terms were not accepted by 20 April, hostilities would be resumed. On 19 April the frigate HMS Amethyst set sail from Shanghai for Nanking to relieve the destroyer, HMS Consort, and to land supplies for the local British community. On 20 April, upon the expiry of the Communists' ultimatum, Amethyst came under fire from Communist shore batteries and suffered extensive damage and casualties. The Communists claimed that Amethyst opened fire first; also that they were not even sure it was a British ship. Ordered down from Nanking to assist Amethyst, Consort likewise came under fire with the same consequences. Two more British ships, the frigate Black Swan and the cruiser London, arrived that evening. They too were fired upon the following day. Amethyst could not be rescued. The incident that has since borne the ship's name lasted until the end of July and was eventually ended in equally dramatic circumstances (see pp. XVII-XVIII and No. 86).

No. 65

Memorandum by Mr. Bevin and Viscount Hall[1] on the situation in China

CP(49)93 [CAB 129/34]

Secret   CABINET OFFICE, *25 April 1949*

HMS Amethyst

We circulate for the consideration of the Cabinet the text of the statement which it is proposed should be made to Parliament on the *Amethyst* incident (Annex A).[2]

2. Also attached (Annex B)[3] are some details of the incident, not intended to be included in the statement to Parliament, though certain points may have to be brought out in answer to questions which may be raised there.

Shanghai

3. The rapid advance of the Communist armies and the political situation aroused by the *Amethyst* incident also raise certain questions of urgency in connection with our policy in Shanghai. Three telegrams which have been received from HM Ambassador, Nanking, the Consul General, Shanghai and the Flag Officer, 2nd in command, Far East, are attached at Annexes C, D and E respectively.

4. In view of the urgency, the issues raised in these telegrams were considered at a meeting of the Chiefs of Staff this morning and in the afternoon at a meeting between the Foreign Secretary, the Minister of Defence and the First Lord of the Admiralty. As a result, the Prime Minister approved a telegram in reply (Annex F), which has been sent by the Admiralty to the Flag Officer. A similar telegram has been sent by the Foreign Office to the Consul General.

5. The Prime Minister also approved the text of the Admiralty statement (Annex G) which has been issued in London and communicated by the Foreign Office to Nanking and Shanghai.[4]

E.B.   H.

---

[1] First Lord of the Admiralty.

[2] Annex I to this document.

[3] Annex II to this document.

[4] Annexes C-G are not printed. They dealt with the question of the evacuation of UK nationals in Shanghai. Current policy not to evacuate them remained unchanged (see No. 53, note 4). The statement in Annex G announced that HM ships were present at Shanghai solely as refuge for UK nationals and that they would be withdrawn when the need for their presence had passed. It was felt that this statement might lessen the chance that the Communists would object to the presence of the ships.

ANNEX I TO No. 65

Draft Statement on the Amethyst incident[5]

1. The House will wish to have a full account of the circumstances in which His Majesty's Ships were fired upon in the Yangtze[6] river with grievous casualties and damage.

2. I will first explain what our position is with regard to the civil war in China. It has been repeatedly stated in this House that our policy has been governed by the Moscow Declaration of December 1945 in which the United Kingdom, the United States and the Soviet Union declared a policy of non-intervention in China's internal affairs.[7] In view of the considerable British interests in China and of the presence of large British communities, His Majesty's Government decided some months ago that His Majesty's Ambassador and His Majesty's Consular Officers in China should remain at their posts and this was announced to the House by my Rt. Hon. Friend in December. In the disturbed conditions which have prevailed in recent months, warships were stationed at Shanghai and Nanking in the event that a breakdown of law and order as the result of hostilities should require them to assist in the evacuation of British subjects.

3. I should make it clear that the stationing of these ships and their movements from one port to another in China were undertaken with the full knowledge and consent of the National Government of China. I want to make the point therefore that when the incident took place to which I am about to refer HMS *Amethyst* was proceeding on her lawful occasions and that there was no other properly constituted authority to whom His Majesty's Government were under an obligation to notify her movements even had they been in a position to do so.

4. Early on Tuesday, 19th April the frigate HMS *Amethyst* (Lieutenant-Commander Skinner) sailed from Shanghai for Nanking. The objects of her passage were to relieve HMS *Consort* at Nanking, to provide communications for His Majesty's Ambassador, to bring supplies for the British community and to be prepared to carry out their evacuation if need arose. A warship has in fact been maintained at Nanking for a considerable time and passages have been fairly frequent.

5. The opposing Chinese forces have been massed along the banks of the Yangtse for a considerable time and there have been repeated rumours during recent weeks that the Communists were about to cross the river. The passage of the *Amethyst* was accordingly adjusted to meet the military situation. Arrangements were made at the time to avoid the expiration of a Communist ultimatum to the effect that in circumstances they would cross on 12th April. Nevertheless, the necessity for relieving HMS *Consort* as early as possible remained; she was running short of supplies after a long stay at Nanking and a frigate was considered more suitable for this task than a

---

[5] See No. 66, note 6.
[6] After this first mention, all subsequent references in this document appear as Yangtse.
[7] See No. 6.

destroyer. The second Communist ultimatum was due to expire on 21st April. The Flag Officer therefore decided, with the agreement of His Majesty's Ambassador, that the passage should be timed to allow the *Amethyst* to reach Nanking a clear 24 hours before the expiry of this ultimatum. *Amethyst* should therefore have reached Nanking on 20th April. For the same reason the *Consort* was due to leave before *Amethyst*'s arrival. An intelligence report was received on the 19th which confirmed 21st April as the date for the Communist crossing; by the time *Amethyst* received this she was already half-way up the river. In the light of these facts the decision for *Amethyst* to sail was made and this decision was in my opinion correct.

6. What could not have been foreseen before the incidents was the repeated and deliberate attacks by massed artillery on the four warships, and on the Sunderland Flying Boat, whose neutral character and peaceful intentions were all fully known to the Communist forces. For example, both *London* and *Black Swan* were prominently displaying white flags. Perhaps the high light of humanity [*sic*] was the machine-gunning of the men being disembarked from the *Amethyst* under the white flag, many of them seriously wounded, or while still swimming in the water. The same policy appears to be reflected in the refusal of the Communist authorities in Peking even to receive a letter from His Majesty's Consul asking them to order their forces to stop firing and allow our ships to give medical relief and evacuate the wounded.

7. To turn to the narrative of events when *Amethyst* had reached a point on the Yangtse River some 60 miles from Nanking, at about nine o'clock in the morning on the 20th, Chinese time, she came under heavy fire from batteries on the North bank, suffered considerable damage and casualties and eventually grounded on Rose Island. After this, the Captain decided to land about sixty of her crew, including her wounded, who got ashore by swimming or in sampans, being shelled and machine gunned as they did so; we know that a large proportion have, with Chinese help, arrived at Shanghai.

8. Vice Admiral Madden, the Flag Officer 2nd i/c Far Eastern Station ordered the destroyer HMS *Consort* (Commander Robertson) from Nanking to go to *Amethyst*'s assistance, and the frigate HMS *Black Swan* (Captain Jay) from Shanghai to Kiang Yin, 40 miles down river from the *Amethyst*.

9. *Consort* reached *Amethyst* at about three in the afternoon and was immediately heavily engaged. She found the fire too hot to approach *Amethyst* and therefore passed her at speed down river. She turned two miles below and again closed *Amethyst* to take her in tow. But she again came under such heavy fire that she was obliged to abandon the attempt, although she answered the shore batteries with her full armament and signalled that she had silenced most of the opposition. Half an hour later her signals ceased, though in fact she was making a second attempt to take *Amethyst* in tow, having turned down-stream again. This attempt also failed and she sustained further damage and casualties during which her steering

was affected. She therefore had to continue downstream out of the firing area.

10. Meanwhile, the Cruiser HMS *London* (Captain Cazalet), wearing the flag of Flag Officer 2nd i/c, was also proceeding up the Yangtse at best speed.

11. The three ships *London, Black Swan* and *Consort* met at Kiang Yin at about eight that evening. It was found that *Consort* was extensively damaged; she was ordered to proceed to Shanghai to land her dead and wounded and effect repairs.

12. At about two o'clock in the morning of the 21st the *Amethyst* succeeded in refloating herself by her own efforts and anchored two miles above Rose Island. She could go no further as her chart was destroyed. Her hull was holed in several places, her Captain severely wounded, her First Lieutenant wounded, and her Doctor killed. There were only four unwounded officers left, and one telegraphist to carry out all wireless communications.

13. Later the same morning the *London* and the *Black Swan* endeavoured to close the *Amethyst*, but met with heavy fire causing some casualties. The fire was of course returned, but the Flag Officer then decided that it would not be possible to bring the damaged *Amethyst* down river without further serious loss of life in all ships; he therefore ordered the *London* and *Black Swan* to return to Kian[g] Yin.

14. At Kiang Yin they were fired upon by batteries, and suffered considerable casualties and damage. Both ships afterwards proceeded to Shanghai to land their dead and wounded and to effect repairs.

15. That afternoon a Naval and a RAF Doctor, with medical supplies and charts, were flown by a Sunderland aircraft of the Royal Air Force to the *Amethyst*. Both the aircraft and the *Amethyst* were fired upon. The ship was hit, but the Sunderland managed to transfer the RAF Doctor and some medical supplies before being forced to take off. The *Amethyst* then took shelter in a creek.

16. During the night of the 21st-22nd *Amethyst* succeeded in evacuating a further batch of her wounded to a nearby town. After doing so, she moved 10 miles up river under cover of darkness, though under rifle fire from the banks, and again anchored; she then completed the landing of all her more seriously wounded, including her Captain. I am sorry to say that this very gallant officer, who had insisted on remaining with his ship up to this time, died of his wounds soon after. There remained on board three RN officers, 1 RAF Doctor, 52 ratings and 8 Chinese. At about this time Lt. Cdr. Kerans, the Assistant Naval Attaché at Nanking, reached the ship and assumed command.

17. Another courageous effort to reach *Amethyst* was made by the RAF in a Sunderland on the afternoon of the 22nd, but the aircraft was driven off by artillery fire without succeeding in making contact. The *Amethyst* then moved a further four miles up river. She was in close touch with the Flag

Officer, and after a number of courses had been considered it was decided that she should remain where she was.

18. Perhaps I may at this point anticipate two questions which may possibly be asked. First, how was it that HM Ships suffered such extensive damage and casualties, and second, why they were not able to silence the opposing batteries and fight their way through. In answer to the first, I would only say that Warships are not designed to operate in rivers against massed artillery and infantry sheltered by reeds and mudbanks. The Communist forces appear to have been concentrated in considerable strength and are reported as being lavishly equipped with Howitzers, medium artillery and field guns. The above facts also provide much of the answer to the second question only I would add this. The Flag Officer's policy throughout was designed only to rescue HMS *Amethyst* and to avoid unnecessary casualties. There was no question of a punitive expedition and HM ships fired only to silence the forces firing against them.

19. I will at this point briefly summarise the losses and damage which resulted.

The casualties were:

HMS *London*	13 killed	15 wounded
HMS *Consor;*	10 killed	4 seriously wounded
HMS *Amethyst*	19 killed	13 wounded
HMS *Black Swan*	7 wounded	

In addition, an unknown number of the crew of HMS *Amethyst* may have been killed or wounded while they were swimming ashore; some 10 ratings are still missing. Of the damage to the ships, the *London* suffered the most severely, having been holed repeatedly in her hull and upper works. The damage to the *Consort* and the *Black Swan* was less serious. *London* and *Black Swan* have already completed their emergency repairs. The *Amethyst* suffered severe damage but was repaired by the efforts of her own crew to be capable of 17 knots.

20. The House will wish to know whether any steps were taken by our authorities in China to make contact with the Communist authorities. Some time has lapsed since Communist forces overran Mukden, Peking and Tientsin where we have Consular posts. His Majesty's Consular Officers at these posts have been endeavouring for some time past to reach day-to-day working arrangements with the local authorities. Their approaches have, however, been rejected on every occasion without any reason being given for such rejection.

21. When HMS *Amethyst* was fired upon by Communist forces HM Ambassador instructed HM Consular Officer in charge at Peking to communicate to the highest competent Chinese communist authority by whatever means possible a message informing them of this and seeking the issue of immediate instructions by them to their Military Commanders along the Yangtse to desist from such firing. A subsequent message emphasised the urgent need of medical attention of the casualties and reiterated the request for instructions to prevent further firing upon these

ships of the Royal Navy engaged in peaceful and humanitarian tasks. The local Communist authorities, however, refused to accept the Consul's letters.

22. At this time Mr. Edward Youde, a Third Secretary in HM Foreign Service who has a good knowledge of Chinese, volunteered to try and contact the Communist forces north of Pukou in the hope of reaching some Commanding Officer with sufficient authority to stop the firing. HM Ambassador agreed to this attempt and Mr. Youde passed through the Nationalist lines on the night of 21st April. Thanks to his courage and determination Mr. Youde succeeded in reaching the forward headquarters of the People's Liberation Army in Pukou area on 23rd April. He described the situation as he knew it when he left Nanking on 21st April and pointed out to them the peaceful and humanitarian nature of the mission of HMS *Amethyst* and requested that she be allowed to proceed to Nanking or Shanghai without further molestation. Their headquarters took the line that clearance had not been obtained from the People's Liberation Army and that she had entered the war area. They also complained of heavy casualties incurred by their troops as a result of fire from HM Ships. They refused to admit justification or self-defence. After consulting higher authority the headquarters stated that in the circumstances they would be prepared to allow the ship to proceed to Nanking but only on condition that she should assist the People's Liberation Army to cross the Yangtse. Such a condition was obviously unacceptable.

23. My attention has been drawn to a communiqué broadcast by the Communists which said that on the date in question warships on the Yangtse opened fire to prevent its crossing by Communist forces. It was not until the following day that they learned that these ships were not all Chinese but that four British ships were among them. The Communists state that their forces suffered 252 casualties as a result of this firing and claim that His Majesty's Government have directly participated in the Chinese Civil War by firing on Communist positions. These claims are, of course, so far as they relate to His Majesty's Government or the Royal Navy, as fantastic as they are unfounded.

24. If there was any initial misunderstanding as to the nationality of HMS *Amethyst* this would have been speedily resolved had the authorities in Peking acted on HM Ambassador's message. Moreover, had the Communist authorities objected in the past to the movement of British ships on the Yangtse it was always open to them to raise these through our Consular authorities in North China. It is the fact that for reasons best known to themselves the Communists have failed to notify any foreign authority present in areas which they have occupied of the channels through which contact can be maintained and that they have rejected all communications made to them. In these circumstances His Majesty's Government can only reserve their position.

25. The House will wish to join me in expressing sympathy with the relatives of all those who have been killed or wounded in this action and in

expressing admiration of the courage of all those who took part in it. Four names deserve special tribute. Lt. Commander Skinner, RN, the Captain of the *Amethyst*, and Lt. J.C. Weston, RN, his First Lieutenant (who for a short time succeeded his Captain in command of the ship) lost their lives through their devotion to duty. Both were severely wounded but remained at their posts, fighting and manoeuvring the ship and removing the wounded to safety. Both left the ship too late to receive effective surgical aid for themselves.

26. Telegraphist J.L. French showed superlative devotion to duty. He was the only telegraphist left in the *Amethyst* after the early hours of 21st April; and from then onwards his efforts kept the ship in almost continuous communication with Shanghai.

27. The fourth name is that of Mr. Youde, whose one man mission through the Communist Armies I have already described.

28. Without a doubt many other cases of bravery and devotion will be revealed when all the facts are known. But we already have ample evidence that the conduct of the whole ship's company of HMS *Amethyst* was beyond all praise, though a considerable proportion were young sailors under fire for the first time. We have had reports of seamen and marines remaining at their task for up to 24 hours though badly wounded, and of men declining to have their wounds treated until cases they considered more urgent had been dealt with. I have heard too that in HMS *London* and *Black Swan*, when there was a possibility of volunteers being flown to *Amethyst*, there was almost acrimonious rivalry for selection—as they put it 'to go back for more'.

29. In conclusion, I should mention that the United States naval authorities at Shanghai placed their resources unstintingly at our disposal, and the kindness and help of the British communities at Shanghai have been beyond all praise. Finally, the Chinese Nationalist forces in Chinkiang area were most helpful in providing medical aid and stores which they could ill afford. The House will join with me in expressing our gratitude to all of these.

ANNEX II TO No. 65

Supplementary Notes

1. When did *Amethyst* receive intelligence of Communist plans for crossing the river?

Amethyst was already well on her way up river on 19th April when she received a report that the Communists intended to cross on the 21st.

2. Was any attempt ever made to approach the Communists in Peking on any subject before 20th April?

HM Consuls tried to establish relations with Communist authorities, not only at Peking but in other towns, as soon as they entered into occupation. But the Consuls' approaches were consistently rejected and their position as Consuls not recognized.

3. *Amethyst's* position on 22nd April and after.

To return to the *Amethyst's* narrative. By the afternoon of the 22nd she had reached a fairly safe position. Four possible courses of action were considered:

(*a*) to attempt to get down river to Shanghai

(*b*) to attempt to get up river to Nanking

(*c*) to abandon the ship

(*d*) to stay where she was.

Her Commanding Officer held himself ready to follow any of these courses. Reports which began to come in of the crossing of Communist troops above and below her position meant that attempts to reach Shanghai or Nanking at this time would almost certainly end in disaster. Further damage might sink the ship; the crew though in good heart were physically exhausted and of course depleted in numbers; navigation of the Yangtse is always difficult and virtually impossible at night; the radar and gyro compass were out of action and the magnetic compass doubtful. The courageous Captain was unwilling to abandon his ship until the result of the approach of a mission sent to the Communists should be known; there was also a possibility that the Ambassador himself might negotiate a safe passage with the Communist authorities at a later stage or even that the ship might slip down later, after the crew had been rested and the armies had completed their crossing. She was now in a comparatively safe position and in fact was only fired on twice in the next 48 hours. So she remained where she was, shifting berth slightly on two occasions.

4. <u>Risks attendant on passage of the Yangtse.</u>

The passage has always been regarded as one of some risk in case irresponsible elements on either bank opened fire. Nevertheless, the Naval Commander-in-Chief decided that, since there had been no opposition or protests on either side and since our aim was peaceful, the passages should be continued until it became apparent they would be opposed; I fully endorse his decision.[8] The House will of course appreciate that if during these months passages had been stopped because of the uneasy situation, or because of individual scares (of which there were many), the requirements of the Embassy and the British community in Nanking would not have been met. The Navy has always been prepared, and I hope will always be prepared, to take justifiable risks in carrying out its tasks.

5. <u>Have the Americans or French recently had warships at Nanking?</u>

[It is not known whether a US warship has been at Nanking in recent weeks. Information is being urgently obtained through the US Naval Attaché.][9]

---

[8] A marginal note here read: 'Moreover, communists' own propaganda was to encourage people to stop and continue their affairs.'

[9] Brackets in original.

There are no indications that a French warship has been at Nanking in the last 6 weeks.

Both the Americans and French have ships at Shanghai (Woosung).

6. <u>Why was air cover not provided?</u>

Air cover would have been inconsistent with the peaceful intent of HMS *Amethyst*.

In fact, air cover would not have been available. Beaufighters from Singapore could not have arrived before Tuesday, 26th April.

7. <u>Why is Admiral Brind[10] still in London?</u>

The Commander-in-Chief was paying a special visit by air to England to attend exercise Trident with other Commanders-in-Chief. This visit was arranged last January. His presence in London has been most helpful in the handling of the situation. Arrangements have been made for his return by air on Thursday, several days earlier than originally intended.

If he had returned at once he would have been of no service either in the Admiralty or on his station while on passage at this critical time. The Admiralty has complete confidence in Vice-Admiral Madden his Second-in-Command.

8. <u>Did the Nationalist forces fire on HM Ships?</u>

We are advised that they did not.

9. It is undesirable for security reasons to give a detailed explanation of the *Amethyst's* present condition and possible courses of action, unless the *Amethyst's* position has substantially altered by the time this statement is made.

[10] Admiral Sir P. Brind, Commander-in-Chief, Far East Station, 1949-51.

No. 66

Conclusions of a Meeting of the Cabinet held at 10 Downing St. on 26 April 1949 at 10 a.m.

CM(49)28 [CAB 128/16]

Secret

China

(Previous Reference: CM (49)18th Conclusions, Minute 2)[1]

The Cabinet[2] had before them a memorandum by the Foreign Secretary and the First Lord of the Admiralty (CP(49)93) to which were appended

[1] See No. 61, note 4.

[2] Present at this meeting were: Mr. Attlee, Mr. Bevin, Mr. Alexander, Mr. H. Morrison (Lord President of the Council), Sir S. Cripps (Chancellor of the Exchequer), Mr. H. Dalton (Chancellor of the Duchy of Lancaster), Viscount Jowitt, Mr. Noel-Baker, Mr. J. Chuter Ede (Home Secretary), Mr. G. Isaacs (Minister of Labour and National Service), Mr. A. Bevan (Minister of Health), Mr. G. Tomlinson (Minister for Education), Mr. T. Williams (Minister of Agriculture and Fisheries), Mr. H. Wilson (President of the Board of Trade), Mr. A. Woodburn

the draft of a statement to be made in Parliament on the circumstances in which HMS *Amethyst* and other British warships were fired upon in the Yangtse River, and copies of telegrams which had been exchanged with the British authorities in China about the position arising in Shanghai through the rapid advance of the Communist forces on that city.[3]

THE FOREIGN SECRETARY recalled that it had been decided that the British Embassy should remain in Nanking and should not follow the Nationalist Government if it retired to Formosa or some other part of China. Other countries, except the Soviet Government and the Governments associated with it, had decided to pursue a similar policy. Similarly, the Cabinet had agreed on 13th December, 1948,[4] that the British communities in China should not be urged to leave, and these communities were, in fact, maintaining their position with great skill and determination. British warships had been employed in providing communications for the British Embassy at Nanking, bringing supplies to the British community there and preparing, if necessary, to carry out their evacuation. Until recently it had been contemplated that British warships would be used, if necessary, for the evacuation of British civilians from Shanghai.

The Cabinet then discussed in detail the draft statement appended to CP(49)93, about the damage and loss of life in HMS *Amethyst* and other warships, which was to be made by the Prime Minister that afternoon in the House of Commons. A similar statement would be made by the First Lord of the Admiralty in the House of Lords. The main points discussed were as follows:

(a) Paragraph 2 of the statement should refer to the general decision to maintain Embassies and legations at Nanking, and to the fact that several Governments had stationed warships at Shanghai and Nanking to assist in any necessary evacuation of their nationals. The relief of one British warship at Nanking by another warship had been carried out as a routine matter every two or three weeks.

(b) There was some discussion of the question whether reference should be made to the fact that the stationing of British warships and their movements from one port to another in China had been undertaken with the full knowledge and consent of the National Government. Since it was obvious that the authority of the National Government had greatly weakened, it might be said that this was a formal rather than a practical step; and attention was drawn to a statement issued by the Chinese Embassy in London on the previous day that the National Government

(Secretary of State for Scotland), Viscount Hall, Lord Tedder (Marshal of the Royal Air Force and Chief of the Air Staff), Field Marshal Sir W. Slim (Chief of the Imperial General Staff), Lord Fraser of North Cape (First Sea Lord and Chief of the Naval Staff), the Earl of Listowel (Minister of State at the Colonial Office), and Mr. Dening.

[3] See No. 65.
[4] See No. 52.

had advised foreign Powers in February last to withdraw warships from the Yangtse in view of the risk of incidents. The general feeling was, however, that it was necessary to refer to the information which had been given to the National Government, as the authority in control of these areas, though the extent to which that Government had consented to the movement of warships would have to further examined.

(*c*) If precise information was available, the statement should endeavour to meet the criticism that the passage of H.M.S. *Amethyst* had been delayed until too near the time when incidents might occur in consequence of the expiry of the Communist ultimatum on 21st April. It was believed that after the expiry of an earlier Communist ultimatum on 12st April there had been some days when no reliable information was available to the British authorities in China, and it would probably be found that the departure of HMS *Amethyst* from Shanghai for Nanking on the morning of 19th April was the earliest time at which the ship could have sailed, and there was every reason to believe that it would reach Nanking before the expiry of the ultimatum on 21st April. In any event, previous experience suggested that a neutral warship could make its way between the opposing forces, particularly since fighting was not in progress on the banks of the Yangtse on 19th or 20th April.

(*d*) Paragraph 5 of the statement would need some amendment to make it clear that HMS *Consort* had not left Nanking simultaneously with the departure of HMS *Amethyst* from Shanghai, and that, as pointed out in paragraph 8, HMS *Consort* did not leave Nanking until information had been received about the damage done to HMS *Amethyst*.

(*e*) HMS *Amethyst* had displayed the White Ensign and Union Jack; and, if necessary, the point could be made in debate that the first battery that shelled her had ceased fire when further Union Jacks were displayed. Thereafter, another battery opened fire on her and the fire became sustained after the ship had been put temporarily out of control through damage to the wheel house.

(*f*) The reference to the inhumanity of the Communists' conduct in paragraph 6 should be deleted from the narrative of events, and it was for consideration whether, with HMS *Amethyst* still in the Yangtse and the British communities at the mercy of the Communists in the areas under their control, the Government statement should do more by way of censure of the Communists than was required in a statement of facts.

(*g*) The statements about casualties in paragraphs 12 and 19 should be amended in the light of the latest information.[5]

(*h*) Reference might be made to the courage which was being shown by the British communities in Shanghai, Nanking and elsewhere; and to the skilful work done by the British authorities in China in handling a difficult and delicate situation.

---

[5] The final casualty toll on the four ships was 45 dead (20 on Amethyst) and 68 wounded.

The Cabinet were informed that the Speaker was apprehensive about the time which might be taken up by questions and answers consequent upon the Prime Minister's statement, and had suggested that it might be preferable for the Government to move the adjournment of the House and allocate a fixed period for discussion. There was general agreement that, since full information was not yet available, it would be preferable that the Prime Minister, in making the statement, should indicate that, if it was the wish of the House that the subject should be debated when full information was available, facilities for this purpose would be afforded.

The Cabinet

Approved the draft statement on the shelling of HMS *Amethyst* and other warships in the Yangtse to be made by the Prime Minister that afternoon in the House of Commons, subject to amendment on the points raised in discussion.[6]

CABINET OFFICE, *26 April 1949*

[6] The statement was made as intended on the afternoon of 26 April, *Parl. Debs, 5th ser., H. of C.,* vol. 464, cols. 25-46.

No. 67

Extract from Conclusions of a Meeting of the Cabinet held at 10 Downing St. on 28 April 1949 at 10 a.m.[1]

CM(49)30 [CAB 128/15]

Secret

China: Despatch of Reinforcements to Hong Kong
(Previous Reference: CM(49)28th Conclusions)[2]

4. THE SECRETARY OF STATE FOR WAR informed the Cabinet that at their meeting on the previous day (DO(49)12th Meeting) the Defence Committee had considered whether the garrison at Hong Kong should be reinforced. They had decided, subject to the approval of the Cabinet, that one infantry battalion and brigade headquarters should be sent to Hong Kong at once and that the remainder of the brigade group should be sent as soon as practicable thereafter. In addition, certain naval and air reinforcements

[1] Present for this item were: Mr. Morrison (in the chair), Mr. Bevin, Sir S. Cripps, Mr. Dalton, Viscount Jowitt, Mr. Chuter Ede, Mr. Noel-Baker, Mr. Woodburn, Mr. Isaacs, Mr. A. Bevan, Mr. Williams, Mr. Tomlinson, Mr. Wilson, Mr. E. Shinwell (Secretary of State for War), the Earl of Listowel, Sir H. Shawcross (Attorney-General), and Mr W. Whiteley (Parliamentary Secretary, Treasury).

[2] See No. 66.

would also be sent.[3] The Chiefs of Staff considered that, so far as could be foreseen at present, the immediate danger to the security of the Colony was likely to arise from internal unrest, from a large-scale influx of refugees and from external aggression by guerilla [*sic*] bands; and they considered that the reinforcements proposed would suffice to enable the garrison to deal with these threats. The Defence Committee had expressed the hope that it would not be necessary to send young and untrained National Servicemen to Hong Kong, and the War Office would keep this consideration in mind in determining the composition of the brigade group. The despatch of reinforcements to Hong Kong would reduce the strength of the strategic reserve in the United Kingdom to one infantry brigade.

In discussion, the following points were made:

(*a*) Was it not likely that reinforcements on the scale proposed would be inadequate against a serious attack? And, in that event, were we not endangering these men to no purpose? Against this, it was pointed out that it was not suggested that the proposed reinforcements would be sufficient to enable the garrison to resist a major attack. The Chiefs of Staff considered, however, that they would be adequate to meet any threat that could at present be foreseen.

In the light of past experience there was no reason to think that the Communist forces would attack Hong Kong: Communist policy in China had so far been to preserve the existing connections with the non-Communist world. The Cabinet agreed, however, that the Chiefs of Staff should keep the developments in the Far East under close and regular review so that, if there should be any significant change, Ministers would be able to consider urgently what should be their future policy in regard to Hong Kong.

(*b*) It should not be assumed that the Chinese Communists would not be able to launch a full-scale attack on Hong Kong from the mainland. While the Communist forces might not possess the military equipment of a first-class Power, they could exert pressure on Hong Kong by other means, such as a mass movement of refugees, which would be as effective against the Colony as a major direct attack.

(*c*) There was general agreement that the announcement of the decision to reinforce the Hong Kong garrison should be made in the course of the debate on the situation in China in the following week, unless circumstances made it necessary to announce it earlier. Ministers thought it would be inadvisable to refer in this announcement to Communism or to the threat of 'external aggression', but mention might be made of the risks arising from any great influx of refugees into the Colony. Care should be

[3] The principal recommendation was for the despatch of a Fighter Squadron from Malaya and the despatch of a cruiser from the West Indies (sailing time thirty-five days) that had already been ordered.

taken to avoid the use of words which might endanger the position of British communities in China.

The Cabinet

(1) Endorsed the Defence Committee's decision that one infantry battalion and brigade headquarters should be sent to Hong Kong at once, and that preparations should made for the despatch of the remainder of the brigade group as soon as practicable.

(2) Agreed that the decision to reinforce the garrison at Hong Kong should be announced during the forthcoming debate in the House of Commons on the situation in China, unless circumstances made it necessary to announce this earlier.

(3) Invited the Foreign Secretary to settle, in consultation with the Secretary of State for War and the Minister of State for Colonial affairs, the precise terms of the announcement of the decision to reinforce the garrison at Hong Kong.[4]

[4] A draft prepared after inter-departmental discussion read: 'His Majesty's Government have decided that developments in China have made it necessary to take further measures to protect the British Colony of Hong Kong. Arrangements are accordingly being made to reinforce the garrison. It should be clearly understood, however, that it is not the desire or intention of His Majesty's Government to interfere in the internal affairs of China, but solely to prevent the present unsettled conditions from endangering the welfare and safety of the people of Hong Kong or hampering the peaceful pursuit of legitimate trade through Hong Kong with China.'

In submitting the draft to Mr. Attlee on 2 May, Mr. Bevin explained that he would have preferred the omission of the words 'the British Colony of' because of US susceptibilities; they had been specially inserted at the request of the Colonial Office. Mr. Attlee agreed (2 May) and in otherwise approving the draft, he asked why the Colonial Office wanted the words included (FO 800/462, FE/48/8 and 9). Lord Listowel explained that the Governor of Hong Kong wanted to use these words to make it clear that Hong Kong was being protected because it was a British possession. The Governor felt that the words would have a better effect on the morale of Hong Kong's Chinese population, which had been lowered by the Amethyst incident (see No. 65). The Minister of State had no strong views of his own, accepted Mr. Bevin's point about US opinion, and indicated that he would accept Mr. Attlee's judgement (minute to Mr. Attlee, 3 May 1949, F 6678/1192/10).

No. 68

Note by Mr. Attlee on the Defence of Hong Kong

CP(49)100 [CAB 129/34]

Top Secret   10 DOWNING STREET, *3 May 1949*

At their meeting on 28th April (CM(49)30th Conclusions, Minute 4)[1] the Cabinet agreed that their decision to send reinforcements to Hong Kong

[1] See No. 67.

should be announced in the debate on China which is to take place in the House of Commons on Thursday next.

I circulate, for consideration by the Cabinet at their meeting on Thursday, the attached report by the Chiefs of Staff on the defence of Hong Kong.

C.R.A.

ENCLOSURE IN NO. 68
Report by the Chiefs of Staff

The Defence Committee, at their meeting on 27th April, 1949 (DO(49)12th Meeting), when discussing our recommendation on the reinforcements that should now be sent to Hong Kong, invited us to prepare a fresh appreciation of the extent of the threat that was likely to develop against Hong Kong.

2. Our report is attached and is divided into two parts—Annex I, the threat to Hong Kong and Annex II, the defence of Hong Kong. A War Office note on the anti-aircraft defence of the Colony is attached as Annex III.[2]

3. Our conclusions are as follows:

(*a*) If we show our determination to hold the Colony there is little likelihood of a direct Communist attack on Hong Kong.

(*b*) The garrison, reinforced to the strength shown below, would be strong enough to hold local or guerilla attacks; moreover, its presence would show our determination to hold the Colony and should thus deter the Communists from open hostilities:

Navy: Far Eastern squadron augmented by local patrol craft to be manned from the cruisers on station.

Army: Two infantry brigades

One armoured squadron

Two field regiments

One composite AA[3] regiment

Ancillary administrative units.

Air Force: One fighter/ground attack squadron of 16 aircraft

Fighter control and early warning radar

Five Sunderland flying boats.

(*c*) In order to bring the garrison of Hong Kong up to the strength given above, the following military action is now required (in addition to the despatch of the fighter squadron, the battalion and the brigade headquarters ordered to Hong Kong last week):

[2] Only Annex I is printed here.
[3] Anti-Aircraft.

(i) To send to Hong Kong as early as possible the remainder of the brigade group, namely:

Two infantry battalions

One armoured squadron

One field regiment

One composite AA regiment.

(ii) To augment the fighter squadron now being sent to Hong Kong from 8 to 16 equipment aircraft.

(iii) To bring forward and arm additional local patrol craft.

(*d*) Should, however, a large-scale Communist threat develop, further reinforcements of the following order would be required:

Navy: One aircraft carrier

One division of frigates

Army: One division

Air Force: One fighter squadron

One fighter bomber squadron.

The implications of providing reinforcements of this magnitude will clearly require very careful examination. For example, the mobilisation of the units of the division would require the call up of part of Section B of the Army Reserve in addition to Section A, and the provision of the necessary shipping would have wide repercussions.[4]

4. It is particularly important that an early decision be taken to despatch the composite AA regiment mentioned in paragraph 3(*c*)(i) above. There are at present no AA defences in Hong Kong, but, in spite of the poor quality of any possible threat, it is considered that some such defence should be provided for the following reasons:

(*a*) to maintain the morale of the population of the Colony, particularly the Chinese element

(*b*) as a deterrent to an attack;

(*c*) to ensure that, if an attack is made, it meets with opposition, thus tending to increase any lack of determination to press the attack home, and to prevent further attacks.

---

[4] The 'A' and 'B' reserves were categories of the Regular Army Reserve to which soldiers who had completed their service with the Active Army transferred on return to civilian life. Both had a liability to recall for service within the Active Army in certain circumstances. The 'A' Reserve was made up of soldiers who were voluntarily liable to recall in an emergency without recourse to a Royal Proclamation. After a period they transferred to the 'B' Reserve, the larger of the two categories, comprising former regular soldiers who were liable to recall by Royal Proclamation.

Economic blockade

5. Our report does not deal with the threat of an economic land blockade and the effect that this would have on the food supplies of the population of Hong Kong. We understand that there are at present considerable stocks of rice in the Colony and that the bulk of the food supplies for Hong Kong normally comes in by sea. A commitment to supply the population entirely by sea under the conditions that would exist if an economic blockade was declared would, however, have serious implications on the shipping problem.

Recommendation

6. We recommend that:

(*a*) Authority now be given for the despatch of the reinforcements and other action mentioned in paragraph 3(*c*) above.

(*b*) We should be instructed to report from time to time on the military developments in Southern China, with particular reference to the scale of the threat to Hong Kong.

(*c*) We should be instructed to consider how the additional reinforcements indicated in paragraph 3(*d*) above could be provided should a large scale Communist threat to Hong Kong develop.

TEDDER
FRASER
W.J. SLIM

ANNEX I TO ENCLOSURE IN No. 68

The Threat to Hong Kong
Present situation

A Communist Army group has crossed the Yangtze and i[s] now operating against Shanghai. Two further Communist Army groups, totalling some 700,000 men, are in a position to advance into South China.

2. The Chinese Nationalist Army facing this force numbers some 150,000 men but its morale is virtually non-existent and it does not constitute an effective fighting force.

3. The Chinese Nationalist Government has withdrawn from Nanking and is established at Canton but has largely ceased to exercise control over its territory or its forces.

Future developments

4. It now seems more than ever certain that a Communist regime will be established throughout the Chinese mainland and it may not even be necessary for the Chinese Communist Army to continue military operations to achieve this end. In the event, however, of the Nationalist Government re-establishing resistance to the Communists in the South, or if the

Communists decide that it is necessary to eliminate the British Colony of Hong Kong, we consider that the military possibilities are as follows:

(*a*) Owing to the poor state of the roads and the Communist Army's lack of motor transport, the Communists would rely for their advance mainly upon the Hankow-Canton Railway.

(*b*) Allowing time for the collection of rolling stock, and assuming that the amount of rolling stock on the line is the same as in March 1948 and that the Nationalist Forces have not carried out demolitions, we consider that the maximum rate of movement from the Hankow area to Canton and the vicinity of Hong Kong would be as follows:

50,000 men with stores and guns	10 days
100,000 men with stores and guns	15 days
200,000 men with stores and guns	25 days

Further forces could be added to the above if they were thought to be necessary. Over and above any forces advancing from the Yangtze area, there are in South China some 80,000 Communist Forces, formerly guerrillas, but who are now organised on the same lines as the main Communist Armies.

Likelihood of an attack on Hong Kong

5. Any strong Chinese Central Government is likely, in the long run, to desire to terminate the British occupation of Hong Kong. In the early future, however, a stable British regime in Hong Kong may well be considered to be useful to a new Communist Government, as an economic link with the outside world. For some time, moreover, the Communist Government, coming into power after a prolonged civil war, is likely to be occupied with internal affairs. Unless the Communist Government, therefore, were to be tempted by nationalistic ambitions, or alternatively by the possibility of an early conquest, to risk hostilities against the United Kingdom, it seems unlikely that they will undertake an attack upon Hong Kong for some time. Evidence of the British intention to resist any attack on Hong Kong would considerably reduce the likelihood of the Communists deciding to attack the Colony. In any case, they will probably at least make an attempt to obtain its renditions by negotiation before resorting to force.

6. Since, however, the possibility of an early attack on Hong Kong cannot be ruled out entirely, we have estimated below its possible scale and nature.

Possible scale and nature of attack

Internal threat

7. The threat of internal unrest in Hong Kong always exists and could be implemented by the Communists in co-ordination with an armed attack from outside. The Hong Kong Trade Unions are likely under these circumstances to take orders from the Communist authorities in China; the

police force may become unreliable; and the Chinese element in the Volunteer Forces may be disaffected. Should, therefore, the Communists decide to attack the Colony, labour unrest, strikes, demonstrations and mutiny are to be expected. It appears possible that the Communists in Hong Kong may not wait for the armed assistance of the Chinese Communist Army from the North, but may be instructed to cause a revolutionary situation in the Colony by the means mentioned above and this may well be assisted by the 80,000 Communists [*sic*] irregulars in the area.

8. Should it be possible for the Communists to make any sea or air attacks on the Colony, their effect on the morale of the Hong Kong Chinese might be temporarily, at any rate, very serious. Such attacks would further greatly encourage internal strikes by Communist controlled Unions.

9. As a result of the Communist advance to the South the garrison of the Colony would have to contend with the internal security problem created by an attempted large scale influx of refugees.

Land threat

10. Although the Communists will have available a land force of the size described in paragraph 4 above, they would not be able to deploy all these forces against Hong Kong. The landward threat would be limited by the narrowness and difficulties of the approaches to the frontier defences. We are unable to assess accurately the size of force that could be employed without local knowledge of the ground, but we consider that it might amount to the equivalent of 2-3 divisions. In addition, there would undoubtedly be an attempt to land forces in various parts of the Colony by sea. Large numbers of sampans will be available in the Canton River and Mirs Bay and may well be employed in trying to land troops on the Island of Hong Kong and behind the defence line in the New Territories. Recent evidence shows that the Communist Army have managed successfully to collect and man large numbers of local craft for river crossings elsewhere.

11. The present Chinese Communist Armies bear no resemblance to any previous Chinese Army. Their morale, discipline and standard of training is [*sic*] of a high order. The Communist commanders have also shown that they possess sound tactical principles and are able to execute complex plans. Their armament includes a high proportion of automatic weapons and artillery up to 105mm. Their equipment in general is mainly of Japanese and American origin. The amount they possess has undoubtedly increased as a result of recent fighting, since it is reported that a large percentage of the Nationalist Forces have either defected or abandoned their arms, most of which are probably American pattern. Their tanks are few, old and small. They have virtually no motor transport.

Air threat

12. Although it has been known for some time that the Communists have been training on old Japanese aircraft, up to the present they have not made any use of aircraft in operations. It is known that they have obtained some aircraft by defection from Nationalist Forces and 21 aircraft

comprising 3 Liberators, 5 Mustangs, 2 Mitchells and 11 Dakotas have been identified. There may be other aircraft not at present identified. There will also undoubtedly be many others left behind by the Nationalists in an unserviceable condition. Some of these might be made serviceable provided sufficient maintenance personnel could be made available from captured Nationalist troops or civil air companies.

13. The Communists have at present no operational air experience and the morale of those Nationalist aircrews who have defected is low and they are most unlikely to be prepared to press home any attack in the face of any opposition. In view of this, any air threat to the Colony is likely to be short lived, badly conceived and lacking in determination.

14. We do not believe that there is likely to be any further appreciable defection from the Nationalist Air Force but should a peace be arranged, the transfer of the Nationalist Air Forces at present in Formosa would undoubtedly be one of the conditions imposed by the Communists. This might bring some further 450 modern aircraft under Communist control. But unless the Communists are reinforced by Russian personnel, which we consider to be most unlikely at present, the standard of operational technique would remain low and determination to press home the attack would be lacking.

Naval threat

15. At the time of the crossing of the Yangtze, the Nationalist Navy consisted of the following ships:

6 Destroyers
4 Destroyer Escorts
12 Escort Vessels
11 Minesweepers
3 Patrol Boats
12 Submarine Chasers
Some 37 Landing Craft

Some of these are ex-Japanese and were turned over disarmed. A few have been re-armed by the Nationalists and there is nothing to stop the Communists continuing this process.

16. It is known that one ex-Japanese destroyer and probably also six more vessels have surrendered to the Communists. A further four destroyer escorts manned by Chinese are on passage from the United States to China, but it is not known what action they are likely to take.

17. Some of the vessels listed above will have been sunk or damaged in the recent fighting but for any attack on Hong Kong a proportion must be expected to take part, having either surrendered or been captured. The Communists will, however, be incapable of operating these vessels together efficiently or of organising any amphibious operation in Western lines.

No. 69

Extract from Conclusions of a Meeting of the Cabinet held at 10 Downing St. on 5 May 1949 at 10 a.m.[1]

CM(49)32 [*CAB 128/15*]

Secret

China: Despatch of Reinforcements to Hong Kong
(Previous Reference: CM(49)30th Conclusions), Minute 4)[2]

2. The Cabinet had before them a note by the Prime Minister (CP(49)100[3] covering an appreciation by the Chiefs of Staff of the extent of the threat which was likely to develop against Hong Kong and of the forces which would be required to meet that threat.

In discussion, the following points were made:

(*a*) The Chiefs of Staff had set out the reinforcements which would be required to deal with any internal unrest or sporadic guerrilla attacks, and they had indicated further reinforcements would be required if a large-scale Communist threat developed. In making these appreciations they had in mind that, although the Communist armies in China were greatly superior to former Chinese armies, they were not likely to constitute a threat of the kind which would develop if a major power, such as Russia, attacked the Colony.

(*b*) The British community in Hong Kong felt great uncertainty about the Government's ultimate intentions in regard to the Colony and the morale of the Chinese in Hong Kong was low. In these circumstances the Governor of Hong Kong and the Commissioner General for South-East Asia had both urged that the Government should go as far as practicable in the direction of declaring Hong Kong as a British Colony. Any suggestion that the United Kingdom Government might abandon Hong Kong would have profound repercussions in Malaya, Siam and Burma.

(*c*) Ministers felt, however, that they could not ignore the advice they had received that Hong Kong could not be held against attack by a major power operating from the mainland. The Government must be careful to avoid drifting into a position in which, after pouring valuable resources into Hong Kong, they had at the end to withdraw with great material loss and loss of prestige. The aim should be to reinforce the defences of the Colony for the purpose of protecting it against present dangers but to avoid giving

[1] Present for this item were: Mr. Attlee, Mr. Bevin, Mr. Morrison, Mr. Alexander, Mr. Dalton, Viscount Addison (Lord Privy Seal), Viscount Jowitt, Mr. Chuter Ede, Mr. Noel-Baker, Mr. Woodburn, Mr. Isaacs, Mr. Bevan, Mr. Williams, Viscount Hall, Mr. Shinwell, Mr. A. Henderson (Secretary of State for Air), the Earl of Listowel, Mr. Whiteley, Mr. J. Callaghan (Parliamentary Secretary, Ministry of Transport), Lord Fraser of North Cape, Lord Tedder, Sir Gerald Templer (Vice Chief of the Imperial General Staff), and Sir E. Bridges (Treasury).
[2] See No. 67.
[3] See No. 68.

explicit long-term commitments which the Government might be unable to fulfil. From this point of view it was important that Ministers should keep under close and continuous review any developments of the situation in Southern China and Hong Kong.

(*d*) Other Commonwealth countries had been kept in touch with the development of United Kingdom policy in the Far East and would be informed of the decision to reinforce the garrison of Hong Kong. There would, however, be no advantage in attempting at this stage to induce Australia or New Zealand to assist in the defence of Hong Kong. Nor would it be wise to stress in any public statement our consultations with other Commonwealth Governments, since this might be open to the misinterpretation that we were preparing for serious consequences. The United States Government were being kept generally in touch with developments in Hong Kong but could not be associated with specific decisions relating to troop movements.

(*e*) In the public statement about the reinforcement of Hong Kong garrison, the balance of advantage was in favour of giving fairly specific information about the nature of the reinforcements which were being despatched. This information would reassure those who might be inclined to underestimate the force which was being sent, and would at the same time indicate that there was no question of sending forces on the scale required for operations against the Chinese Communists.

(*f*) The decision that newly-recruited National Service men should not normally be included in drafts sent to the Far East would mean that some of the reinforcements sent to Hong Kong might be slightly below strength.

The Cabinet

(1) Agreed to send to Hong Kong as early as possible the remainder of the brigade group whose despatch had been approved in principle by the Cabinet on 28th April, 1949.[4]

(2) Agreed to augment the fighter squadron being sent to Hong Kong from 8 to 16 aircraft, and to collect and arm additional local patrol craft.

(3) Instructed the Chiefs of Staff to report from time to time on military developments in South-East Asia, with particular reference to the scale of the threat to Hong Kong, and to consider how additional reinforcements could be provided if a large-scale Communist threat to Hong Kong developed.

(4) Agreed that the Minister of Defence should announce that day in the House of Commons that the garrison was being reinforced and should give an indication of the nature of the reinforcements that were being sent.[5]

[4] See No. 67.

[5] Briefing Mr. Attlee on 4 May for this item at the Cabinet meeting, Sir N. Brook explained that in a statement welcoming a Hong Kong Trade Mission to the British Industries Fair on 26 April, the Colonial Office had used the words, 'We intend to do our very utmost to maintain Hong Kong as a peaceful haven of refuge from oppression, as a great centre of trade and as a

cultural and educational beacon—in short, as the clearing house of commerce and the shop-window of democracy in the Far East.' The Cabinet Secretary argued that the phrase 'haven of refuge from oppression' implied continued hostility to the Communists in China. He added that the words 'cultural and educational beacon' and 'shop-window of democracy' might suggest that the UK intended to make Hong Kong a centre for anti-Communist activities in the Far East. 'It is one thing', he added, 'to say that we shall defend a British possession against aggression: it is a different matter to imply that we shall use it as a base for conducting "cold war" activities against the mainland' (CAB 21/2428).

Mr. Alexander's statement in the House of Commons on 5 May read as follows:

'His Majesty's Government have decided that developments in China have made it necessary to take further measures for the protection of Hong Kong.

'It should be clearly understood that in reaching this decision, HM Government have been moved solely by the desire and determination to prevent the present unsettled conditions from endangering the welfare and safety of the people of Hong Kong or hampering the peaceful pursuit of legitimate trade through Hong Kong with China.

'Towards this end substantial reinforcements to the garrison are accordingly being sent and will include elements of all arms—land, sea and air. These reinforcements will bring our land forces in Hong Kong up to the strength of two Brigade Groups, each of three battalions, together with ancillary troops, and will include tanks, field guns, anti-aircraft guns and anti-tank guns. The existing air forces will be reinforced with fighters, and the fighter defences will be correspondingly strengthened. Our Far East Squadron will be augmented by an additional cruiser and, should the need arise, by an aircraft carrier' *(Parl. Debs, 5ᵗʰ ser., H. of C.*, vol. 464, cols. 1224-1349).

No. 70

Extract from Conclusions of a Meeting of the Cabinet held at 10 Downing St. on 9 May 1949 at 11 a.m.[1]

CM(49)33 [CAB 128/15]

Secret

China: Defence of Hong Kong
(Previous Reference: CM(49)32nd Conclusions), Minute 4)[2]
2. *The Minister of Defence* drew the attention of the Cabinet to a telegram[3] from the British Defence Co-ordination Committee in the Far East suggesting that, as the Commissioner-General for South-East Asia[4] and the

---

[1] Present for this item were: Mr. Attlee, Mr. Bevin, Mr. Morrison, Mr. Alexander, Mr. Dalton, Viscount Addison, Viscount Jowitt, Mr. Chuter Ede, Mr. Noel-Baker, Mr. Woodburn, Mr. Isaacs, Mr. Bevan, Mr. Williams, Viscount Hall, Mr. Shinwell, Mr. A. Henderson, the Earl of Listowel, Mr. Whiteley, Mr. J. Callaghan, Lord Fraser, Lord Tedder, Sir Gerald Templer, and Sir E. Bridges.

[2] See No. 69.

[3] SEACOS (South-East Asia Chiefs of Staff) 900, 5 May 1949 (F 6911/1015/10), not printed.

[4] See No. 55, note 3.

Commanders-in-Chief of the Land and Air Forces in the Far East would shortly be in London, the Chiefs of Staff should take this opportunity of discussing with them the effects which recent developments in China were likely to have in India and South-East Asia. The Committee suggested that there was urgent need for diplomatic, economic and military action to form a containing ring against further Communist penetration; and that this ring should be formed by the co-ordinated action of many countries, including India, Burma, Siam, French Indo-China and the Dutch East Indies. The Minister added that the Communist forces seemed to be making rapid progress south of the Yangtse, and the need for a co-ordinated policy in respect of Hong Kong might be more urgent than had been assumed in the Cabinet's earlier discussions.

The Cabinet were also informed that Mr. L.D. Gammans, MP,[5] had put down a question for answer by the Prime Minister, asking what approaches had been made to the Governments of other Commonwealth countries regarding the possibility of their contributing towards the defence of Hong Kong. The Australian Minister of Defence was reported to have stated, in reply to questions at a recent Press Conference, that the United Kingdom Government had not yet suggested that Australia might assist in the defence of Hong Kong.

In discussion the following points were made:

(*a*) Other Commonwealth Governments had been kept informed of developments in China and of our decision to reinforce the garrison at Hong Kong. The time had probably come to send them a fuller appreciation of possible future developments and to mention to some of them the possibility of their making some contribution towards the defence of Hong Kong. The Commonwealth Relations Office had been inclined to advise that in the first instance this question should be raised with the older Commonwealth Governments only; and it was agreed that material support in the defence of Hong Kong was more likely to be forthcoming from Australia and New Zealand than from any of the other Commonwealth countries. On the other hand, it was pointed out in the discussion that the first aim of our policy should be to deter the Communist forces in China from making an attack upon Hong Kong and to convince world opinion that it was expedient that the British position there should be maintained. From this point of view it was perhaps even more important that the Commonwealth countries in Asia should express at least moral support of our policy in Hong Kong. India's support, in particular, would have a powerful effect on public opinion throughout Asia.

(*b*) It would be preferable if Mr. Gammans could be persuaded to withdraw his Question, on the ground that it would not be possible at the moment to make any public statement about the attitude of other Commonwealth Governments on this question.

[5] Unionist MP for Hornsey, Middlesex, from 1941.

(*c*) The Cabinet were informed that the proposal made in the telegram from the British Defence Co-ordination Committee in the Far East was consistent with the Foreign Secretary's general desire for closer political co-operation between the various countries of South-East Asia. In discussion, however, doubts were expressed about the expediency of attempting to make common cause with French Indo-China and the Dutch East Indies. The Colonial policies of the French and the Dutch were regarded with great suspicion by the Asiatic peoples; and there would be little prospect of persuading the Government of India to join in discussions on China in which the French and the Dutch were to be represented.

If, therefore, any approach were to be made to the Governments listed in this telegram, it should be related to the situation in South-East Asia generally and should not give prominence to our anxieties about the future of Hong Kong.

(*d*) Ministers should also treat with reserve any suggestion that Hong Kong could be used by the Western Powers as a rallying point for anti-Communist forces in Asia. The Government of India were convinced that in Asia Communism was most dangerous when it could ally itself with nationalism; and they would regard it as playing into the hands of the Communists to represent Hong Kong as an outpost of western democracy in the Far East.

(*e*) The suggestion was made that in the long run it would prove impossible to preserve Hong Kong as a British Colony, and that serious consideration ought now to be given to the possibility of giving it the status of an international port on the analogy of Trieste. It was, however, the general view of the Cabinet that this was not an opportune time to consider so radical a change of policy.

The Cabinet

(1) Agreed that the United Kingdom Government must make every effort to carry other Commonwealth Governments with them in their policy in respect of Hong Kong; and took note that the Secretary of State for Commonwealth Relations would at once formulate, in the light of the discussion, and submit to the Prime Minister, specific proposals about the timing and method of the approach and the basis on which other Commonwealth Governments should be asked whether they would be prepared to assist in the defence of Hong Kong.

(2) Took note that the Prime Minister would arrange for Mr. Gammans, MP, to be asked to withdraw his Question from the Order Paper.

(3) Invited the Minster of Defence to consult with the Foreign Secretary, on his return to London, regarding the scope of the discussions to be held during the forthcoming visit to London of the Commissioner-General for South-East Asia and the Commanders-in-Chief of the Land and Air Forces in the Far East.

(4) Invited the Secretary of State for the Colonies to enquire into the suggestion that Chinese Communists deported from Malaya were finding their way into Hong Kong.

(5) Asked the Secretary of State for the Colonies to circulate, for the information of the Cabinet, a factual appreciation of the present situation in Hong Kong, covering such points as the composition of the population by nationalities, the value of British commercial interests and the importance of the Colony from the point of view of British interests in China generally.

No. 71

Letter from Sir N. Brook (Cabinet Office) to Mr. Dening

[*F 6909/1192/10*]

Secret and Personal   CABINET OFFICE, *12 May 1949*

I[1] have been looking at your paper (FE(O)(49)25)[2] which your Committee is to discuss this morning. I hope you won't mind if I make two suggestions.

(1) I hope that this paper can be expanded so as to comply with the request made in Conclusion (5) of the Cabinet minute of 9 May, viz.

'Asked the Secretary of State for the Colonies to circulate, for the information of the Cabinet, a factual appreciation of the present situation in Hong Kong, covering such points as the composition of the population by nationalities, the value of British commercial interests and the importance of the Colony from the point of view of British interests in China generally.'[3]

What the Cabinet seemed to want was a sort of child's guide to Hong Kong. The particular point raised in discussion was the composition of the population—in particular the proportion of Europeans, and, within that, the proportion of British to other Europeans. This sort of information could be added after paragraph 1 of the draft paper. The Colonial Office might also be able to insert something at that point on the value of British commercial interests in Hong Kong and the importance of the Colony from the point of view of British trade in China generally. The paper would then dispose of that particular remit.

---

[1] Opening and concluding salutations were omitted in the filed copy of this letter.

[2] FE(O)(49)25(Revise), 16 May 1949 (CAB 134/287), was the draft of a Colonial Office memorandum on Hong Kong, prepared for the Far East (Official) Committee, and intended for submission to the China and South-East Asia Committee and then to the Cabinet (see Nos. 74-76).

[3] See No. 70.

(2) I am somewhat concerned about paragraph 5. [4] The Colonial Office seem to be continuing here to press for some further declaration of our intention to hold on to Hong Kong 'at all costs'—presumably for the purpose of putting heart into the British community and friendly elements in South-East Asia. As I think you know, Ministers are quite definitely of the opinion that any such nailing of our colours to the mast would be inexpedient. Their view is that it would be neither militarily nor politically possible for us to remain in Hong Kong if there were a settled Government of China which was one hundred per cent hostile to our staying there. It would be unwise, therefore, for us to make provocative statements, or to take provocative action, which would do anything to stiffen any disposition on the part of the Chinese to get us out of Hong Kong. In fact, it is not perhaps putting it much too high to say that our only hope of hanging on to Hong Kong is to keep quiet about it. In general, the prevalent feeling in the Cabinet is that we should continue to 'stay on the fence' until we see more clearly how strong a Communist Government of China is likely to be and what attitude it will develop towards our remaining in Hong Kong. Meanwhile, we should lie low and, so far as possible, say nothing. Any statement which we may have to make should be framed with the idea in

---

[4] The Colonial Office memorandum for the Far East (Official) Committee reported the governor's view that while Mr. Alexander's 5 May statement (see No. 69, note 5) about reinforcements had been widely welcomed, local opinion still maintained that they were insufficient as they would only bring the garrison up to the strength it had been in December 1941 when the Japanese attacked. The Commanders-in Chief, Far East, were of a similar view. They reported that while reaction to the statement had been good, it had not removed a doubt among a certain section of the Chinese civilian population about whether the UK would be able and willing to defend Hong Kong. The memorandum then continued, in paragraph 5: 'In another despatch which I [Mr. Creech Jones] have just received, the Governor has reported that, for reasons of this kind, of a total population of nearly 2 millions, probably not more than 10,000 persons, including the Police Force and the Permanent Government service, would prove willing to commit themselves by giving the Government their active and wholehearted support in the preservation of internal order and the operation of the minimum essential services, upon which all else depends.'

In the same despatch (No. 15 of 3 May 1949, FE(O)(49)27, CAB 134/287), Sir A. Grantham asked for advice on the extent to which the 'historic role' of Hong Kong as an imperial trading base should now be subordinated to defence needs in a climate of cold war. Hong Kong, he suggested, could either be a thriving commercial entrepôt vulnerable to attack both internally and externally, or it could be an 'unthriving regulation-bound entrepôt' prepared to give 'a reasonable account of itself in war or other emergency'. It could not be both and the Governor argued that 'the very process of preparing Hong Kong to act as a fortress in war drains away its life blood in peace'. If strategic considerations were to take priority, the colony's trade would wither, its revenues would decline, and the UK Government would have to make a substantial contribution. Sir A. Grantham therefore sought confirmation for his assumption that, except in time of war, the primary importance of Hong Kong should be 'economic and not strategic—thus differing from Gibraltar where the roles are reversed'. With the proviso that he should keep in constant touch about security matters with the local military authorities, the Colonial Office believed that there was no alternative but to endorse the Governor's recommendation.

our minds that at some date in the not too distant future we may have to withdraw from Hong Kong—and we ought therefore to avoid saying anything now which would make a subsequent withdrawal even more humiliating.

These views may not be shared by officials on your Committee. At the same time I think the Committee should be aware that Ministers are pretty strongly of this opinion. If the sort of case which is suggested in paragraph 5 of the draft is to be put up by the Colonial Secretary at all, it will need to be supported by a much greater weight of argument if it is to have any chance of getting a hearing at Cabinet.

No. 72

Minutes of a Meeting of the China and South-East Asia Committee of the Cabinet, held at 10 Downing St. on 13 May 1949 at 5 p.m.[1]

SAC(49)4th Meeting [CAB 134/669]

Secret

1. *Shanghai*

The Committee considered a memorandum by the Foreign Secretary (SAC(49)4) on the Shanghai situation.[2]

This explained that, at the end of 1948, a plan had been made for the protection, and if necessary evacuation, of British subjects in Shanghai in the event of a breakdown of law and order.[3] The recent withdrawal of HM ships from Shanghai would, however, mean that, if the Communists seized the Woosung forts at the mouth of the Whangpoo River, they would be cut off from Shanghai, and to that extent the evacuation plan, which had been based on the assumption that HM ships could reach Shanghai, had broken down. In the meantime conditions in the city were serious; Communist forces had sealed it off from its hinterland and shortage of food might lead to widespread rioting. HM Ambassador had taken the view that no action by the interested Powers would be effective in inducing the Chinese not to make a battleground of Shanghai, but their Consuls-General at Shanghai had been instructed to concert a joint appeal to the Chinese Generals in command of the Nationalist forces at Shanghai to spare the city from the consequences which would follow from its continued defence. Sir Ralph Stevenson had left it to the Consul-General to decide whether or not any further statement was needed in order to

[1] Present at this meeting were: Mr. Attlee (in the chair), Mr. Bevin, Mr. Alexander, Mr. Noel-Baker, the Earl of Listowel, Mr. W. Hall (Financial Secretary, Treasury), and Mr. Dening.

[2] Not printed.

[3] See No. 53, note 4.

induce a further reduction in the numbers of the British community, and the Committee were asked to endorse these instructions. The memorandum further recommended that, at the appropriate time, urgent consultation should take place with other Commonwealth Governments and with Atlantic Pact Powers on the question of the possible recognition of the Chinese Communist Government.

The PRIME MINISTER said that he understood that there were some 4,000 British nationals in Shanghai and that very few had left the city in response to the earlier suggestion that those whose continued presence was not essential would be well advised to go. While he recognised the danger that further efforts to reduce the numbers of the British community might result in a general movement to evacuate, he thought that the possibility of securing a further reduction in their numbers ought to be examined urgently. Apart from the risks inherent in the immediate situation, there were grave dangers in leaving so large a number of British nationals as hostages in Communist hands. He understood that merchant vessels could reach Shanghai at 96 hours notice and that, if necessary, they could evacuate the whole British community in about fourteen days.

There was general agreement that it would be advisable to ask HM Consul-General to report urgently whether it would be practicable to take immediate steps to reduce the numbers of the British community.

In further discussion, the following points were made:

(a) The Committee were informed that the Chiefs of Staff did not consider that evacuation by means of merchant ships would be practicable if there should be a further deterioration in the local situation. If, therefore, a decision was delayed, this method might cease to be a practicable solution for the problem of evacuating British nationals from Shanghai.

(b) The MINISTER OF DEFENCE pointed out that, if the Committee took the view that it was not sufficient to plan for the evacuation of British nationals from Shanghai by merchant ships, possibly under armed guard, the only alternative would be to consider the practicability of evacuation under naval and air protection. The Chiefs of Staff had not so far examined this problem, but it was very doubtful whether such an operation would be possible; it would certainly be extremely provocative.

The general view of the Committee was, however, that there were no grounds at present for contemplating drastic action of this nature. Communist treatment of the British communities in other cities which they had taken over, e.g. Peking, Tientsin and Nanking, had been reasonably good; it might be worse in Shanghai if the Nationalists decided to defend the city, but more recently there had been indications that there might after all be a peaceful hand-over. If we took any steps which might be interpreted as a threat of military action, we might precipitate the very situation which we were anxious to avoid.

The Committee:

(1) Invited the Foreign Secretary to ask HM Consul-General in Shanghai to report by 16th May on the possibility of securing a further reduction in the numbers of the British community in Shanghai.

(2) Endorsed the recommendations in SAC(49)4 regarding consultations with Commonwealth and Atlantic Pact Governments on the question of the possible recognition of the Chinese Communist Government.

2. *Hong Kong*

THE PRIME MINISTER said that he was anxious to have an early discussion about long-term policy in respect of Hong Kong. He understood that the Commissioner-General for South-East Asia would be available for consultation very shortly, and he thought that a meeting of the Committee should be arranged as soon as possible after their arrival.

The Committee:

Took note of the Prime Minister's statement.[4]

CABINET OFFICE, *14 May 1949*

---

[4] In a minute to Mr. Bevin (13 May), Mr. Dening commented: 'Sooner or later, however, Ministers will probably have to decide whether Hong Kong is to be held at all costs or whether, in certain circumstances, they are prepared to abandon it with the loss of prestige and the weakening of the general position in South East Asia which must inevitably follow' (F 7103/1015/10).

No. 73

Memorandum by Mr. Noel-Baker on Hong Kong

SAC(49)6 [CAB 134/669]

Secret   COMMONWEALTH RELATIONS OFFICE, *18 May 1949*

At the Cabinet meeting on the 9th May (Conclusions 33(49)2(1))[1] I was invited to submit to the Prime Minister specific proposals about the timing and method of the approach and the basis on which other Commonwealth Governments should be asked whether they would be prepared to assist in the defence of Hong Kong.

I submitted a minute to the Prime Minister accordingly on 12th May and with his approval now circulate it for consideration at the meeting of the China and South-East Asia Committee on the 19th May.

P.J.N-B.

---

[1] See No. 70.

ENCLOSURE IN No. 73

Secret   COMMONWEALTH RELATIONS OFFICE, *12 May 1949*
NO. 50/49

Prime Minister

At the Cabinet meeting on the 9th May I was asked to formulate in the light of the discussion and to submit to you, specific proposals about the timing and method of an approach to other Commonwealth Governments regarding our Hong Kong policy and about the basis on which they should be asked whether they would be prepared to assist in the defence of Hong Kong.

2. As we see it, it is a question not just of defending an isolated Colony, but of identifying Hong Kong as the first point in the East where, if things go wrong, our ultimate determination to repel Communist aggression will have to be successfully demonstrated. If that be so, other like-minded Governments in the Commonwealth association should, in principle, be prepared to support our stand and to assist it. I consider that an approach to Commonwealth Governments at the proper time would be right and I should expect that some Commonwealth Prime Ministers at least would be willing to support our policy. At the same time there are difficulties, both general and particular, in the way of obtaining anything more than moral support for our policy, to which I feel bound to draw attention.

3. There is the general difficulty of the well-known reluctance of even the most co-operative amongst the other Members of the Commonwealth to commit themselves in advance, and in peacetime, to the despatch of military assistance against a hypothetical contingency.

4. In addition there are special considerations in each of the other Commonwealth countries which are examined below.

Canada regards herself as far removed from the dangers in China; internal political difficulties have prevented her from sending crews to help in the Berlin airlift, and she has not forgotten the fate of Canadian troops in Hong Kong in the last war.[2] Indeed this is still at intervals a subject of controversy by the Opposition in the Canadian Parliament, and the Canadian Government are very unlikely to be willing to give any hostage to their opponents before the forthcoming General Election. Canada has taken a strong lead in the formation of the Atlantic Pact, but has never shewn the same interest in the Pacific and, unless the United States were to

---

[2] Two Canadian battalions—The Royal Rifles of Canada and the Winnipeg Grenadiers—were sent to Hong Kong in 1941. Up until this point and unlike the Canadian Air Force and Navy, the Canadian Army had not seen active service in the war. From a Canadian viewpoint the troops were sent to Hong Kong to meet domestic criticism about military inactivity. They left Vancouver on 27 October, arrived on 16 November, and came under attack from Japanese forces three weeks later. They surrendered on Christmas Day. Of the 2,000 Canadian troops, 290 were killed in action, 128 died in prison camps in Hong Kong, 136 died in captivity in Japan, and 4 were killed attempting to escape.

intervene actively, it is unlikely that Canada would feel able to send any military assistance.

Australia and *New Zealand* are the obvious countries, from the point of view of proximity and self-interest, from which to seek material help, but the Australian Prime Minister made it clear last year, when we were wondering whether to approach the Australian Government for military help in Malaya, that it was quite out of the question that the Australian Government should commit themselves to the despatch of troops, and it is very likely that he would take the same stand in the case of Hong Kong. This belief is strengthened by the recent refusal of Australia to be associated in the joint scheme for assistance to Burma. There is also the history of the arrival of Australian troops in Singapore in the last war in time to become prisoners of the Japanese, which is parallel to the memories of Hong Kong in the Canadian mind. New Zealand would no doubt in principle be willing to give any help she could, but her resources are limited and she would find it difficult to be more forthcoming than her partner in the Anzac Pact,[3] which pledges both parties to prior consultation.

While *South Africa* has under the present Nationalist Government come a very long way in defence co-operation with us, it must be recognised that all Governments in the Union think in terms of the African Continent only; our objective is to stimulate their interest in the defence of the Middle East, while relying on Southern Africa as a support area, and we should not wish to prejudice that prospect. Any prospect of her helping us in the Far East should be dismissed.

Very special problems arise in the case of *India* and I deal with these more fully in paragraph 5 below, but it seems most unlikely that in present circumstances Pandit Nehru would agree to despatch troops or other material military assistance to defend Hong Kong.

Pakistan might perhaps be more disposed to consider a request sympathetically, but she has no suitable forces to send and in any case there would be no prospect of her agreeing to send any forces out of Pakistan while the Kashmir question is not settled, and she fears the possibility of an attack from India.

Ceylon has as yet no armed forces that could be used in Hong Kong.

5. I realise that the most valuable moral support that can be obtained would be some statement from Pandit Nehru. It was recognised at the Cabinet meeting that the Government of India would regard it as playing into the hands of the Communists to represent Hong Kong as an outpost of Western democracy in the Far East. I must confess that the prospects of obtaining any favourable response from Pandit Nehru seem to me to be very slender in view of his persistent attacks on 'Colonialism', of his

[3] The Governments of Australia and New Zealand concluded an agreement at Canberra on 21 January 1944 with respect to security arrangements in the South-West and South Pacific regions. ANZAC was the Australia and New Zealand Army Corps.

frequently repeated announcements of neutrality and of his refusal to join up with either the Eastern or Western bloc. It may also be recalled that he gave an appreciation of the Communist threat to China in February last in which he tended to write down the menace from this direction (see his message quoted in telegram Z. No. 13 of 12th February, a copy of which I attach as an appendix).[4]

6. I have thought it right to set out at length the difficulties in handling this question. This does not mean that these cannot be overcome. Paragraph 2 above indicates the common interest of all like-minded Governments in meeting the threat which faces all of us and we should be letting down the principle of Commonwealth consultation if we did not take other Commonwealth Governments as fully as possible into our confidence and invite their support. (We have, of course, already kept them informed of the steps we have taken and shall continue to do this.) We have also forwarded to our High Commissioners for communication to the Governments of Canada, Australia, New Zealand and South Africa, the appreciation by the Chiefs of Staff contained in the Annex to CP(49)100 of 3rd May:[5] the appreciation has been sent to the High Commissioners in India, Pakistan and Ceylon to enable them to take action if it should be decided to make an approach to these Governments.

7. It does not seem that we can fairly approach Commonwealth Governments either for moral or material assistance until we can let them know clearly and definitely what our intentions are in the event of a major Communist threat to Hong Kong developing. If Commonwealth Governments are asked to despatch forces to Hong Kong they will wish to know whether we intend to hold it at all costs or whether there is any thought in our minds of pulling out in the face of a major land threat with consequent loss of prestige: equally if they are to support our policy by public statements, they must know exactly what the full implications of that policy are. Moreover it is important that, in making any request to Commonwealth Governments, we should give a precise indication of the timetable involved and make it clear whether we are asking for immediate assistance to meet the existing emergency, or will require their help at a later stage or will only call for aid if it should be necessary to maintain Hong Kong against a major land threat.

8. There are really two aspects of the problem, involving asking for (a) moral and (b) material, support.

9. As regards seeking moral support, I would, as suggested above, expect that we might obtain strong support from a number of other Commonwealth Governments, though not perhaps in the case of India. Much depends on developments in the campaign, but if any public declarations from Commonwealth Governments are to be sought, the

[4] See No. 56.
[5] Cf. No. 68.

timing should be arranged to coincide with any further statement of policy to Parliament here.

The case of India is very special, but is also crucial. Before we decide on making any approach to Pandit Nehru, I think it would be most helpful to have the advice of Sir Archibald Nye.[6] Mr. Malcolm MacDonald[7] is coming home for consultation on the 18th May and I think it would be invaluable if Sir Archibald Nye could be available at the same time. If you approve, I would therefore propose to instruct him to fly home at once so as to be available for this purpose.

10. As regards material support I should not wish to rule out the prospects of obtaining help from other Commonwealth countries, though in practice I think that any assistance is likely to be limited to Australia and New Zealand. It must be remembered that few Commonwealth countries have mobile forces that can readily be despatched overseas: naval vessels and aircraft could perhaps be made available, but there is not likely to be in the Commonwealth any substantial body of troops that could be moved rapidly to the scene of the action; moreover it should be borne in mind that generally Commonwealth troops are under no liability to serve overseas. If our approach is to have any prospect of success our request must be specific in terms, must be related to forces that are likely to be available and must indicate whether the forces are required for immediate emergency or will only be called for at a later stage. I recommend that the Chiefs of Staff should be asked to examine urgently what requirements they would wish to be sought from other Commonwealth sources, whether these are likely to be available in Australia and New Zealand and, if so, to give a precise indication of the timing involved. For the reasons given in paragraph 7 above, it would be important that in making any approach to other Commonwealth Governments we should be able to give a frank explanation of our intentions in Hong Kong in all the contingencies that are likely to arise.

11. To sum up, I suggest that decisions are required on the following points:

(i) whether it is moral support only or material support that we desire from other Commonwealth countries;

(ii) if we ask for material support we must make it clear whether help is required at once as an immediate measure or only at a later stage as a long-term step. In the former case, Commonwealth Governments are likely to assume that any support given now would imply a determination to hold Hong Kong in which they would be involved. In the latter, we must make it clear at what stage and in what form their help is required. In any event the Chiefs of Staff should be asked to examine these points in detail, bearing in mind that no Commonwealth

---

[6] See No. 56.

[7] See No. 55, note 3.

countries have mobile forces readily available (except India and Pakistan);

(iii) on the question of moral support, it is equally important that in making any approach we should be able to give Commonwealth Governments a clear indication of our own long-term policy;

(iv) in the meantime the Chiefs of Staff appreciation in CP(49)100 of 3rd May has been forwarded to our High Commissioners in Canada, Australia, New Zealand and South Africa for communication to these Governments. The documents have also been sent to the United Kingdom High Commissioners in India, Pakistan and Ceylon, but will not be passed on to those Governments pending a decision here as to an approach to them;

(v) as an immediate step, Sir Archibald Nye should be recalled for consultation.

12. I am sending a copy of this minute to the Foreign Secretary, the Minister of Defence, and the Secretary of State for the Colonies.

P.J.N-B.

No. 74

Memorandum by Mr. Bevin on Hong Kong

SAC(49)7 [CAB 134/669]

Secret   FOREIGN OFFICE, *18 May 1949*

There are certain aspects of the situation which Ministers will wish to consider which are not covered in the memorandum by the Secretary of State for the Colonies (SAC(49)5).[1] These aspects are discussed in the following paragraphs.

Attitude of Communist China

2. Information as to Communist intentions is still scanty, but it seems that some months may elapse before a properly constituted Central Government is established by the Communists. Before that happens it may be expected that Communist domination will have extended to the province of Kwantung with the result that Chinese territory contiguous to the Leased Territories and Hong Kong will be under Communist control.

3. It can be regarded as certain that sooner or later Communist China will seek to recover the Leased Territories and Hong Kong, either by negotiation, or by subversive methods. While an attempt to take Hong

[1] This was a factual appreciation on Hong Kong by Mr. Creech Jones that had been requested by the Cabinet (see No. 70). It was considered with other Hong Kong papers by the China and South-East Asia Committee on 19 May (see No. 75) and then submitted as a Cabinet memorandum on 23 May (see No. 76).

Kong by force cannot be ruled out, it is considered to be the least likely of the courses the Communists will adopt.

4. The first steps which the Communists may be expected to take in order to recover Hong Kong will be to embark on a propaganda campaign designed on the one hand to inflame Chinese opinion against British control and on the other to isolate the United Kingdom in world opinion and more particularly in the opinion of Asiatic countries. There will be references to unequal treaties and to the injustice of the continued retention of what is really part of China by a European imperialist power. The Communists will hope by these tactics to ensure that they can deal with the United Kingdom alone, unsupported by the rest of Asia or by anyone able or likely to offer us support in resisting Communist encroachment.

5. This propaganda campaign is likely to be followed at short notice by attempts to undermine the colony from within through the Chinese population by subversive methods, including infiltration. In this way the Communists will hope so to weaken the position of the Hong Kong Government as to render our position virtually untenable. They may hope thus to force our withdrawal or to be in a position to dictate terms which the situation they have created will compel us to accept.

Political counter-measures

6. Apart from the measures which have already been taken or are contemplated to safeguard our position in Hong Kong and the Leased Territories, it is necessary to consider what political action is possible to counter the Communist tactics outlined above. If it is accepted that the Communist object is to isolate us, then it must be our aim to try to secure in advance the maximum degree of moral support from our friends, and to examine whether any physical support is likely to be forthcoming. We should seek such support from Commonwealth countries, amongst whom the support of India, Pakistan and Ceylon as Asiatic countries is particularly important. We should also seek the support of the United States and, in order to build up a united front, that of Burma and Siam. If we are to obtain this support, it is necessary to consider what our line should be in approaching these countries, whose attitude towards our retention of Hong Kong will vary according to the outlook of the particular countries concerned.

7. On the short term, there is a very good reason for our remaining in possession of Hong Kong and for resisting the Communist advance. The advantages of Hong Kong as a haven and as a well regulated entrepôt for the trade of all powers can be stated with conviction. It can also be stated that to permit the Communists to overrun Hong Kong would be to weaken the position of the whole anti-Communist front in South East Asia and to encourage the growth in strength of Communism through Chinese communities and Communist parties throughout the area. For these reasons it will be possible to justify our determination to hold Hong Kong

at all costs against Communist attempts, whether by propaganda and subversive methods or by force, to wrest it from us.

8. On the long term, it may be more difficult to convince our friends, and more particularly the Asiatic members of the Commonwealth, of our justification for retaining Hong Kong indefinitely as a British colony. From our own point of view it is unthinkable that we should be prepared to discuss the future of Hong Kong except with a stable, unified, democratic and friendly China. Equally we should not be willing to discuss its future with any Chinese Government under duress. Thus we should make it clear that in our view conditions in the foreseeable future render it most unlikely that we shall be prepared to reconsider our continued retention of the colony of Hong Kong and of the Leased Territories.

Approach to other countries for moral support

9. Assuming that an approach to other countries for moral support is agreed upon, it is necessary to study the special considerations in respect of each of the countries concerned. The Secretary of State for Commonwealth Relations has commented separately on the considerations affecting the Commonwealth.[2] The following paragraphs deal with the foreign countries principally concerned.

10. *United States.* It is not possible to estimate accurately what United States reactions would be to a request for moral support in our retention of Hong Kong. In the past American opinion, swayed to a large extent by sentiment and the large missionary element in American contacts with China, tended to be sympathetic to the Chinese view that Hong Kong should be returned to China. The growing menace of Soviet Russia and the Communist advance in China have, it is believed, modified American opinion to some extent, and it is conceivable that the United States Government might be prepared to afford moral support to our retention of Hong Kong on the short term view that this represents part of the general resistance to the advance of Communism. Without putting the matter to the test, there is no certainty, but the line suggested may meet with some response from the United States.

11. *Burma and Siam.* It is doubtful whether, under present conditions, either Burma or Siam would come out openly in support of our retention of Hong Kong, but if approached they might be willing to give their tacit consent to the situation and agree at any rate to resist Communist attempts to stir up public opinion in their countries against us.

12. *France, the Netherlands and Portugal.* It can safely be assumed that France, the Netherlands and Portugal would give us moral support in our retention of Hong Kong. But they are in no position to give us any material support, and owing to Asiatic reactions towards these countries, it would probably be inadvisable to seek their support.

---

[2] See No. 73.

Approach to other countries for material support

13. The problem of obtaining physical support for our retention of Hong Kong in the event of Communist attempts to seize it is a more difficult one. The Secretary of State for Commonwealth Relations has commented separately on the Commonwealth aspect. The reactions of foreign countries may be as follows.

14. *United States.* Though, as indicated above, it is conceivable that the United States might be prepared to come out openly in support of our retention of Hong Kong, they might find difficulty in going so far as to provide military resources in defence of the territory. Here again, without putting the matter to the test, it is not possible to give a definite answer.

15. *Burma, Siam and the Western Union countries.* The Asiatic countries would be unwilling to give us material support even were they in a position to do so, while the European countries are in no position to help us, even if it were desirable that they should do so.

No. 75

Minutes of a Meeting of the China and South-East Asia Committee of the Cabinet, held at 10 Downing St. on 19 May 1949 at 5.30 p.m.[1]

SAC(49) 5th Meeting [CAB 134/669]

Secret

1. *Shanghai*

(Previous Reference: SAC(49)4th Meeting, Minute 1.)[2]

THE FOREIGN SECRETARY made a report to the Committee on the situation in Shanghai. From the latest telegrams from HM Ambassador and HM Consul-General it seemed likely that the Nationalists were not proposing to defend Shanghai and that they would not damage the public utilities. It now seemed probable that the Communists might enter the city very soon, and that the gap between the departure of the Nationalist forces and their arrival would be short. The prospects of a peaceful handover and the avoidance of disorders now seemed better than they had a week ago.[3]

This assessment of the situation was endorsed by the Chiefs of Staff and the Commander-in-Chief, Far East Land Forces.

[1] Present at this meeting were: Mr. Attlee (in the Chair), Mr. Bevin, Mr. Alexander, Mr. Creech Jones, Mr. Noel-Baker, Viscount Hall, Mr. Shinwell, Mr. Henderson, Mr. D. Jay (Economic Secretary, Treasury), Mr. MacDonald, Marshal of the Royal Air Force Lord Tedder, F.-M. Sir W. Slim (CIGS from October 1948), Admiral Sir J. Eccleston (Vice-Chief of the Naval Staff), General Sir N. Ritchie (Commander-in-Chief, Far East Land Forces), Air Marshal Sir H. Lloyd (Air Commander-in-Chief, Far East), Sir N. Brook, Admiral Sir W. Elliot (Chief Staff Officer to the Minister of Defence), Mr. Dening and Mr. J. Paskin (Colonial Office).

[2] See No. 72.

[3] Communist forces entered Shanghai on 23 May.

It was noted that, since the Committee's last meeting, further parties of British subjects had left Shanghai by air; the number of British subjects and others for whom we were responsible now remaining in the city was about three thousand.[4]

The Committee were informed that the position regarding HMS *Amethyst* was unchanged, but that her Captain had been approached by the Communists in an attempt to obtain damaging admissions from him. It was appreciated that the position of *Amethyst* was very unsatisfactory; the continued confinement on board was affecting the morale of her crew, and, if her movement were too long delayed, it might become physically impossible for her to make the passage down the river. It might be possible to negotiate more effectively with the Communist authorities on the subject when they had occupied Shanghai.

The Committee:

(1) Took note of the situation in Shanghai.

(2) Invited the Foreign Secretary to instruct HM Ambassador in Nanking to continue his efforts to reach agreement with the Communist authorities on the subject of HMS *Amethyst*.

2. *Hong Kong*
(Previous Reference: SAC(49)4th Meeting, Minute 5.)
The Committee had before them (i) a memorandum by the Secretary of State for the Colonies (SAC(49)5)[5] giving a factual appreciation of the present situation in Hong Kong; (ii) a memorandum by the Secretary of State for Commonwealth Relations (SAC(49)6)[6] regarding the timing and method of a possible approach to other Commonwealth Governments for assistance in the defence of Hong Kong: and (iii) a note by the Foreign Secretary (SAC(49)7)[7] on some of the external aspects of the Hong Kong situation.

At the request of the Prime Minister, THE COMMISSIONER-GENERAL FOR SOUTH-EAST ASIA gave the Committee an appreciation of the importance of Hong Kong in relation to the situation in South-East Asia generally. In his view, it was imperative that we should both defend Hong Kong against the Communists and make it publicly known that we intended to do so. If we failed to do this, the blow to our prestige would be very serious, especially in countries such as Malaya and Borneo. People in those parts still had nervous memories of the last war; and, if it appeared that we were not going to hold Hong Kong, they would assume that they also would not be defended. The will to resist the Communists in South-East Asia would be undermined, and the whole common front in that area, especially in Siam

[4] Cf. No. 105, note 2 below.   [5] See Nos. 74, note 1 and 76 below.
[6] No. 73.   [7] No. 74.

and Burma, would crumble. It would, in fact, be a major victory for the Communists if they were able to thrust us out of any part of Hong Kong territory. The Chiefs of Staff had shown that we could defend Hong Kong against a Communist attack with our own resources, and we should therefore do so. By making clear our intention to defend the Colony, we might deter the Communists from making a direct attack. We should, therefore, first decide to defend Hong Kong and declare our intention of so doing, and then consult with the other Commonwealth countries and the United States.

THE FOREIGN SECRETARY said that he agreed that Hong Kong must be defended; but he would be opposed to any suggestion that we should strike a provocative attitude by declaring, as had been suggested by the Governor, that we should never leave Hong Kong in any circumstances. In his opinion, the emphasis should be on resistance to aggression. If we once made it clear that we intended to resist aggression, and that we had sufficient forces in Hong Kong to do so, he personally did not think that the Communists would risk an attack. If they did so, however, we should then, while putting up the best resistance possible, bring the matter before the United Nations as an act of aggression. By laying stress on this aspect of the situation, we should have the best chance of obtaining the support of Pandit Nehru, whose whole policy was based on resistance to aggression, and also of mobilising United States opinion, which at the moment was considerably bewildered by the Chinese situation.

THE SECRETARY OF STATE FOR COMMONWEALTH RELATIONS said that he thought it should be possible to enlist the moral support of other Commonwealth Governments, and material support from some of them, if our policy was established on the basis suggested by the Foreign Secretary. The Prime Minister of New Zealand had already made it clear that his Government would support a policy of resistance to a Communist attack on Hong Kong; and, although no official statement had been made on the subject by the Australian Government there were indications that public opinion in Australia would support a vigorous defence of the Colony. There were special reasons why it was unlikely that the Canadian Government would agree to give military aid; in any event it could take no decision on this question until the General Election had taken place. The attitude of the Prime Minister of India was a matter of major importance. His own inclination was to discount the dangers of the Communist advance in China and to regard it as no more than a local movement in fulfilment of the 1911 Revolution; and our first concern must, therefore, be to make sure that there was no danger of his adopting an attitude of open opposition to our policy. There seemed good hope, however, of obtaining his moral support on the basis suggested by the Foreign Secretary, and other Commonwealth Governments would no doubt be willing to use their influence with him at the same time.

There was general support for the Foreign Secretary's suggestion that our policy in Hong Kong should be based on the principle of resistance to aggression; Ministers considered that it should be possible, on this basis, to enlist the maximum degree of support in the event of a Communist attack. But it was emphasised that our moral position would be seriously weakened if we sought the cooperation and help of the French and Dutch Governments in support of our policy, since this would inevitably have adverse reactions on public opinion in South-East Asia and elsewhere.

Discussion turned next on the internal situation in Hong Kong. In discussion, the following points were made:

(*a*) GENERAL SIR NEIL RITCHIE said that, in his opinion, an announcement of policy on the lines suggested by the Foreign Secretary, supported by vigorous action to reinforce the local garrison, would result in a substantial improvement in the internal security position in the Colony.

(*b*) The Committee were informed that the Chiefs of Staff were seriously concerned at the extent to which the defence of Hong Kong might be hampered by the system of divided local command. In their view, the time had come when the Colony ought to be regarded primarily as a fortress and the Civil Governor replaced by a Military Governor, who would also be Commander-in-Chief of the garrison. This change would also emphasise our determination to resist a Communist attack.

On the other hand, it was argued that there were serious risks in regarding Hong Kong as predominantly a fortress. Moreover, the local Government was at present faced with many intricate political and administrative problems, and the withdrawal of the Civil Governor might cause some administrative confusion. Might it not be possible, as an alternative, to give the Governor and the Commander-in-Chief equal powers within the civil and military fields respectively?

THE PRIME MINISTER said that he wished to have a further time to consider this question.

(*c*) Attention was drawn to the practical difficulties arising from the conflicting issues involved in the timing of security measures, to which attention had been drawn in paragraph 10 of SAC(49)5.[8] Some anxiety was expressed lest, as the Communist armies moved southwards, increasing numbers of refugees should seek to enter Hong Kong; experience had shown how movements of refugees could be turned to advantage by an unscrupulous belligerent, and there was in any event a risk that the Communists would use this means of building up a powerful Fifth Column inside the Colony. Should not the Hong Kong Government take urgent steps to prevent a further influx of refugees? Against this, it was pointed out that progress on preventive measures had been hampered by the consideration that certain defence preparations were likely to have a disastrous effect on the economic life of the Colony.

The Committee next discussed the military problems of defending Hong Kong against a large scale attack by Chinese Communist forces from the mainland. An *aide-mémoire* summarising the views of the Chiefs of Staff on

[8] Cf. No. 76, para. 6(iv) below.

this question had been made available to Ministers before the meeting and is annexed to these minutes.[9]

THE CHIEF OF THE AIR STAFF said that the Chiefs of Staff considered that the loss of Hong Kong to a Communist attack would have such serious effects on our whole position in Asia and elsewhere that we ought to take all necessary steps now to prevent this from happening. If we demonstrated our intention to resist attack, the internal situation in Hong Kong would improve: if not, it might prove a fatal source of weakness. The *aide-mémoire* contained a summary of the reinforcements needed to meet the estimated threat of attack and a brief statement of the implications of sending reinforcements to Hong Kong on this scale at the present time.

In discussion of these proposals the following points were made:

(*a*) The proposals for air reinforcement would involve a temporary interference with the Berlin air-lift. It might be possible to arrange for United States aircraft to fill the gap.

(*b*) THE SECRETARY OF STATE FOR AIR said that he was not happy about the proposal to send one long-range fighter squadron from the United Kingdom. If this was done, Fighter Command would be seriously weakened.

In this connection attention was drawn to the fact that an Australian fighter squadron of twenty-four Mustangs was at present stationed in Japan; and the general view was that every effort ought to be made to secure the agreement of the Australian and United States Governments to the transfer of this squadron to Hong Kong.

(*c*) THE CHIEF OF THE IMPERIAL GENERAL STAFF said that the military reinforcements proposed in the *aide-mémoire* represented the minimum required to ensure the successful defence of Hong Kong against a strong attack by Chinese Communist forces. Nevertheless, the implications of sending reinforcements on this scale to Hong Kong was serious, particularly as regards the strength of the Army in the United Kingdom. Moreover, these movements would involve the calling up of 2,000 Army Class A reservists.[10]

THE SECRETARY OF STATE FOR WAR pointed out that there had not been time for full examination of the implication of the proposals contained in the *aide-mémoire*, and that further time would be needed before a final decision could be taken. In particular he was concerned at the proposal for the call-up of Class A reservists: he was very doubtful whether their total strength was as much as 2,000 and he thought the proposal might in any event raise political difficulties. There was also the question whether it might not be necessary to relax the existing rules regarding the posting of semi-trained men overseas.

[9] Not printed: cf. No. 77 below.
[10] See No. 68, note 4.

The Committee:

(1) Took note that the Prime Minister would circulate a paper to the Cabinet on the question how the policy of defending Hong Kong against Communist attack might best be presented to world opinion, and indicating the basis on which other Commonwealth Governments and the United States Government might be asked to support that policy.

(2) Invited the Minister of Defence to circulate a paper to the Cabinet on the military problems involved in the defence of Hong Kong against a large-scale attack by Chinese Communist forces.

(3) Invited the Secretary of State for the Colonies to circulate to the Cabinet a factual appreciation of the present situation in Hong Kong.

CABINET OFFICE, *20 May 1949*

No. 76

Memorandum by Mr. Creech Jones on Hong Kong

CP(49)120 [CAB 129/35]

Top Secret   COLONIAL OFFICE, *23 May 1949*

On 9th May (CM(49)33rd Conclusions, Minute 2(5))[1] the Cabinet asked me to circulate a factual appreciation of the present situation in Hong Kong for the information of my colleagues.

2. *Facts about Hong Kong*
    (i) The Colony consists of (*a*) the island of Hong Kong (approximately 32 square miles), and (*b*) part of the Kowloon Peninsula (approximately 3 square miles) and (*c*) the New Territories (approximately 359 square miles). A map is annexed. (*a*) and (*b*) were ceded outright to Great Britain by China in 1842[2] and 1860[3] respectively; (*c*) was leased to Great Britain by China for 99 years in 1898[4] to meet the Colony's defence needs.
    The length of the land frontier is 12 miles; that of the sea frontier is approximately 200 miles.
    (ii) *Population*
    The estimated total population of Hong Kong is 1,800,000. The non-Chinese elements are as follows:

---

[1] See No. 70.   [2] Treaty of Nanking, 1842.   [3] Peking Convention, 1860
[4] Peking Convention, 1898.

British subjects (United Kingdom and other Commonwealth countries)	6,500
British subjects of Portuguese race	3,000
United States nationals	250
Dutch and Scandinavian	200
French	100
Other non-Asiatics	500
Indians	2,000
Filippinos	200
Stateless	200
Total	12,950

(iii) When ceded to us Hong Kong was a barren rock. British enterprise has turned it into one of the most important and thriving ports and markets of the world. Even when conditions in China were at their best, it was a comparative haven of settled law and order where traders (not least among them Chinese) could conduct their business and thrive as nowhere else in China, except in the treaty ports (especially, of course, Shanghai). This trade has been of great benefit not only to Europe and America, but also to China and to other countries of the Far East. The only stable basis for international trade in the Far East has always been sterling. The Hong Kong dollar circulates not only in the Colony but also over great areas in South China, to the great advantage not only of traders but of the general population in that area. Even before the Communist advance, inept administration in Shanghai had led to the beginning of a flight of industry to Hong Kong, and to a serious decline in shipping business.

(iv) *Hong Kong Trade*

Every month Hong Kong handles about £20,000,000 worth of goods, of which it consumes or produces less than three per cent. In other words, Hong Kong's business is bringing in other people's goods and sending them out again. It provides storage, insurance, banking and shipping facilities for this transit trade, and the Colony has no other major economic role.

The total value of capital invested in Hong Kong is probably of the order of £250,000,000. Perhaps one quarter of this was invested by persons resident, and companies registered, in the United Kingdom. The remaining three-quarters represents local investments. Of this a half is probably non-Chinese (mainly British capital), and the remainder Chinese. The total amount of British capital invested in Hong Kong may therefore be of the order of £156,000,000.

For the purposes of comparison it may perhaps be said that British investment in Shanghai is of the order of £250,000,000.

(v) *British Interests in China in relation to Hong Kong*

British interests in China fall into two classes:

(a) Import-export firms, distributing firms, banking, insurance, agency and shipping firms. As far as it is possible to generalise it may be said that up to 90% of the total business of these firms is directly or indirectly dependent upon Hong Kong;

(b) Industrial, utility and social enterprises in China (e.g. cotton, mining, public utilities, hotels, hospitals, schools) to which Hong Kong is of negligible importance except as indicated in the succeeding paragraph. This second category probably represents the greater part of British property in China.

A number of companies operating entirely in China are registered in Hong Kong under Hong Kong law as 'China companies'. This enables them to maintain their capital in Hong Kong dollars. Communist action to compel registration in China in a currency with little or no practical value would presumably wipe out a large part of the value of the shares of those companies, which at present is probably some millions of pounds. Even companies with little interest in Hong Kong under (b) of the previous paragraph have a considerable interest in Hong Kong from this aspect.

(vi) *Shipping and Industries*

Hong Kong lies roughly midway on the 2,500 mile run from Singapore to Japan. It is one of the finest natural harbours in the world and has been developed as a free port and little else. Its industries are ship-repair and ship-building (up to 10,000 gross registered tons) and its services include registry, insurance, agency, bunkering, banking etc. About 200,000 g.r.t[5] of British shipping is based on Hong Kong.

In 1921, at the peak of its prosperity, entrances and clearances were 43½ million g.r.t., and by 1948 these had recovered to 22 million g.r.t.

In addition there have been important recent developments in light manufacturing industries, the products of which are being exported in considerable quantities to the United Kingdom.

(vii) *Water Supplies*

The Colony's water supply is derived 60% from reservoirs on the island and 40% from the New Territories by pipeline under the harbour. Kowloon is wholly supplied from the New Territories. The present supply is insufficient for the increased population, and hours of supply have to be limited during the dry months. The possibility of increasing reservoir capacity on the island has been examined, but any new scheme would be expensive and inadequate. A project in the New Territories to provide approximately 30,000,000 gallons per day at a cost of approximately £4,000,000, which is considered the only practicable scheme, is now under consideration. (See also paragraph 3(b) below.)

[5] Gross registered tonnage.

3. *Development projects*

We have on hand certain major development projects, for which the continued retention of the New Territories is of particular importance. These include:

(*a*) The projected modern airport near Deep Bay in the New Territories, for which His Majesty's Government has promised an interest-free loan up to £3,000,000;

(*b*) The proposed extension of the water supply catchment areas in the New Territories to supplement existing supplies, already inadequate, for Hong Kong island and Kowloon;

(*c*) Projects for the development of agriculture and fishing at an approximate cost of £500,000 from the Colonial Development and Welfare Vote;

(*d*) The future replanning of the cities of Victoria on Hong Kong island and of Kowloon on the basis of a report prepared by Sir Patrick Abercrombie[6] with assistance from the Colonial Development and Welfare Vote;

(*e*) The rehabilitation of the Hong Kong University is in progress. The Hong Kong Government are making a grant of £250,000 towards this and His Majesty's Government has promised a similar amount. The precise use to which these grants are to be put is still under discussion.

4. *Attitude of Chinese Government towards Hong Kong*

The population of China generally knows little of Hong Kong, but there is a strong irredentist sentiment among the educated and semi-educated with a handy rallying cry for rendition which has an obvious mob-appeal. No Chinese Government, therefore, can afford to be other than basically anti-British over Hong Kong, and there is no reason to suppose that a Communist Government of China will be less so than any other, and good reason to think that its particular ideology and international affiliations may make it more so. We must expect sooner or later increased rather than decreased Chinese pressure for the rendition of Hong Kong.

5. *Position of Communists in Hong Kong*

Hong Kong, being geographically and racially a part of China, has no politics of its own but reflects the politics of China. Immigrants from China far outnumber the Hong Kong Chinese, who themselves have an eye over their shoulder on China. Hong Kong provides a home of refuge for any party in China out of power, and, in accordance with Hong Kong's tradition of neutrality and non-interference in the political affairs of China, supporters of the Kuomintang regime and of the Communists have alike been allowed to reside in Hong Kong provided they obey the law and do not behave so as to damage relations between His Majesty's Government and the Government of China. With the retirement of Chiang Kai-shek

[6] Architect and Professor Emeritus of Town Planning in the University of London.

and the defeat of the National Forces in North China, Kuomintang influence in Hong Kong has greatly declined. More important, Communists inside Hong Kong have left for China, and Communists in Hong Kong have so far shown little signs of attacking the administration.

It has, however, now been reported that an attempt is being made to unify the command of the Communist irregular forces in South China and to establish a liaison office in Hong Kong. Hong Kong Communists have received a Chinese Communist Party Directive to mobilise peasants, intellectuals, overseas-Chinese businessmen, etc., for the purpose of supporting the southward drive by the main Communist forces.

6. *Action in Hong Kong in anticipation of the emergency*
(i) *Food Supplies*
These are at present adequate. A stock of rice, estimated at six months' supply, is held, and the Colony has been stock-piling certain commodities which might run short in an emergency.
(ii) *Police Force*
The Police Force in Hong Kong has recently been greatly expanded, and its strength is now double that of 1941.
(iii) *Possible refugee influx*
Measures have already been concerted to close the land frontier of Hong Kong with military assistance to prevent a serious influx of refugees. The necessary material (barbed wire, pickets, etc.) is available locally. Measures are also in hand to establish, with the assistance of the naval authorities, coastal patrols by sea and land to prevent, as far as possible, any influx across the sea.
(iv) *Measures against subversive activities*
The Government has also taken power to enable it to control more effectively subversive activities. It has not only enacted the Illegal Strikes Ordinance, but has taken powers which have enabled it to close Communist controlled schools such as the Tak Tak College. In connection with outspoken attacks on British and American policy in Communist-controlled newspapers in Hong Kong, the Governor has recently sought guidance on the question of closing these organs down in the last resort, though he appreciates that this could not be done if it were to conflict with His Majesty's Government's general policy or embarrass His Majesty's Ambassador in any negotiations. This matter is still under consideration.

With the concurrence of the Foreign Office the Governor has been authorised to enact legislation to provide for the compulsory registration of all local societies, under which all Triad Societies and all local branches of foreign political parties would become unlawful. The Governor regards this as an essential measure, not only to forestall a demand for the establishment by the Chinese Communist Party of an office in Hong Kong, but also to control the infiltration, under respectable disguises, of Communists. There is no intention of suppressing political activity for the benefit of the Colony, but only political activity which has no relation to the Colony and merely projects external troubles and quarrels into the life of Hong Kong. The proposed legislation would be non-discriminatory. Parties immediately affected would be the Kuomintang, the China Democratic League and the KMT Revolutionary Committee, together with a number of smaller Chinese political parties. (The Communist Party has no branch in Hong Kong, though the majority of the public utility and waterfront labour unions are under Communist influence.) Similar legislation is already in operation in Singapore and will shortly be enacted in the Federation of Malaya.

7. *Attitude of the local population*

My colleagues are aware of the representations which were made to me by the Governor of Hong Kong and the Commissioner-General, South East Asia, supported by a Signal from the Commanders-in-Chief, Singapore, before the debate on 5th May[7] as to the serious effect on the morale of the population of Hong Kong, both British and Chinese (and especially the latter, on whose attitude to us we are so vitally dependent), if we did not make it abundantly clear that we are determined to maintain our position in Hong Kong. In a despatch which reached me after that debate, the Governor informed me that speculation on the part of the highly intelligent and critical public opinion in the Colony has centred not so much on what has been said in the various statements which have been made in the course of the past few months, as on the significance of what appears to have been left unsaid. The plain fact is that, so long as there is any doubt in the minds of the Chinese population of our determination to maintain our position in the Colony, or, in other words, so long as there is a fear that Britain may ultimately abandon Hong Kong, they will not commit themselves to wholehearted co-operation with us in the defence of the Colony. The future risks to themselves would be too great to permit them to do so.

The Governor has also reported that, for reasons of this kind, of a total population of nearly 2 millions, probably not more than 10,000 persons, including the Police force and the permanent Government service, would prove willing to commit themselves by giving wholehearted support in the preservation of internal order and the operation of the minimum essential services, upon which all else depends.[8]

[7] A reference to the debate in the House of Commons on 5 May during which Mr. Alexander made a statement about reinforcing Hong Kong (see No. 69, note 5).

[8] See No. 71, note 4,

No. 77

Memorandum by Mr. Alexander on the defence of Hong Kong
CP(49)118 [CAB 129/35]

Top Secret   MINISTRY OF DEFENCE, *24 May 1949*

1. The Prime Minister has circulated to the Cabinet a memorandum (CP(49)119)[1] on the political considerations involved in meeting the threat to the security of Hong Kong and on the possibility of seeking moral and material support in its defence from other countries of the Commonwealth and the United States. The present paper deals with the military implications of the defence of Hong Kong against a large-scale attack by Chinese Communist forces.

2. Hong Kong may well become the stage for a trial of strength between Communism and the Western Powers. If the Chinese Communist Government are able to force our withdrawal from the Colony, not only would the blow to our prestige throughout the world be irreparable, but the immediate repercussions in South-East Asia would add immeasurably to our defence burdens in that area.

3. On 5th May (CM(49)32nd Conclusions, Minute 2)[2] the Cabinet approved the proposals in CP(49)100[3] for the despatch to Hong Kong of reinforcements which are calculated to enable the garrison to secure the Colony against all threats other than an organised attack by Chinese Communist forces. These threats include:

(*a*) internal unrest, probably sponsored by Communist-inspired trade unions;
(*b*) a large-scale influx of refugees in numbers beyond the capacity of the Colony to absorb;
(*c*) sporadic attacks by Chinese guerrillas.

4. When these reinforcements have arrived—the last battalion is due on 19th July—Hong Kong will have a numerical strength of:

Army: 2 Infantry brigades (4 British, 2 Gurkha battalions)
            24 Anti-tank guns (6-pounders)
            36 Field guns (25-pounders)
            16 Heavy AA guns (3.7 inch)
            12 Light AA guns (Bofors)

---

[1] See No. 78 below.   [2] See No. 69.   [3] See No. 68.

16 tanks

together with ancillary units.

Before they can be considered fully operational, recent reinforcements will require a period of training.

Air Force: 1 Spitfire Squadron (16 aircraft)
1 Flying Boat Squadron (5 Sunderlands)
Fighter control and early warning radar.

Navy: 3 Cruisers
(for whole 6 Destroyers
Far East 5 Frigates
Station) Local control craft.

5. It was made clear in the report by the Chiefs of Staff which the Cabinet considered at their meeting on 5th May that the above forces would not be enough to meet a large-scale Chinese Communist attack should this materialise. Since the nature of the terrain is not an obstacle to infantry, and infiltration by junk and sampan is likely, it is not possible from the information available to give any realistic numerical estimate of the strength that the Chinese Communists may concentrate against Hong Kong. It is, however, estimated that not more than 40,000 Chinese Communist troops could be deployed at any one time in a land offensive. They might be supported by an initial air effort of some 50-60 aircraft (fighters and bombers). The Chiefs of Staff consider that we must be ready by early September if we are to deal with a threat on this scale, should it develop.

6. The Chiefs of Staff are of the opinion that if we make it abundantly clear, by the despatch of certain additional reinforcements and by a suitable public announcement, that we intend to defend Hong Kong against aggression, our defences may never be put to the test; and that if they were, they would be capable of holding the Colony provided adequate measures are taken by the Civil Government to deal with the threat to internal security. The Chiefs of Staff propose therefore that authority should now be given to send to Hong Kong the following further reinforcements:

Army: 28th Infantry Brigade (ex United Kingdom)
Royal Marine Commando Brigade (ex Malta—to be placed under Army command by the Admiralty)
together with supporting units.

Air Force: 1 Fighter Squadron (16 spitfires)
1 Long range Fighter Squadron (16 Hornets).

Navy: 1 Light fleet carrier
4 Destroyers or frigates.

1 Replenishment aircraft-carrier
1 Hospital ship.

In addition it is proposed that a further infantry brigade should be earmarked for despatch if the threat to Hong Kong seriously develops. For this purpose, the Guards Brigade in Malaya is conveniently placed and by September could probably be spared, if necessary, without undue effect on the bandit campaign.

7. If a decision is taken this week, the above reinforcements could all arrive in Hong Kong by early September, with the exception of the Aircraft Replenishment Carrier, which could not be there until a month later. The two fighter Squadrons could, in fact, arrive within 6 weeks of the decision being taken, provided their base maintenance and headquarters personnel could be flown out in aircraft diverted from the Berlin airlift.

8. The arrival of reinforcements on the above scale would bring the garrison of Hong Kong up to the following strength:

Army: 4 Brigades (9 battalions, 3 commandos)
48 Anti-tank guns (12 17-pounders, 36 6-pounders)
54 Field guns (25-pounders)
16 gun Medium Artillery (5.5 inch)
24 Heavy AA guns (3.7 inch)
36 Light AA guns (Bofors)
58 Tanks (52 Comets, 6 Light Tanks)

together with ancillary units.

From September the 2nd Guards Brigade to be earmarked to move from Malaya to reinforce Hong Kong in emergency.

Air Force: 2 Fighter Squadrons (32 spitfires)
1 Long range Fighter Squadron (16 Hornets).
1 Flying Boat Squadron (5 Sunderlands)
Fighter control and early warning radar.

Navy: 3 Cruisers
(for whole 15 Destroyers (or frigates)
Far East   1 Light fleet carrier
Station)   1 Replenishment carrier (in October)
1 Hospital ship
24 Local patrol craft for Hong Kong.

9. The despatch of these further reinforcements will, however, have serious implications elsewhere, of which the principal are as follows:

(*a*) The effect on Western Union of the despatch of further relatively large British forces to the Far East may be considerable.

(*b*) It will be necessary to call up Section 'A' of the Army Reserve (2,200 strong). (This was done for the Shanghai crisis in 1926.)[4]

(*c*) There will be no effective strategic reserve in the United Kingdom until another infantry brigade can be fully armed and equipped.

It will take some three months to do this, during which there will be nothing more than an odd battalion to meet emergency calls for land forces.

(*d*) It will be necessary to relieve the battalion of the Commando Brigade now at Aqaba by an infantry battalion from the Middle East.

The Commando Brigade itself forms part of the forces available to come to the assistance of Transjordan if our treaty is invoked.

(*e*) The present army medical resources can provide the minimum peacetime medical cover for the strength of troops that will be in Hong Kong. If it has to provide even a 'scaled down' medical cover to deal with operations it will entail the withdrawal of specialised personnel now employed in hospitals in the United Kingdom; this will involve closing down some 2,000 out of 5,000 hospital beds, thereby throwing an additional burden on the National Health Service. Otherwise the medical resources necessary will have to come from Section 'B' of the Army Reserve or from outside those at present available to the army. The possibility of approaching other Commonwealth countries for assistance in this should be examined.

(*f*) Our air forces in Germany will be reduced by 1 Fighter Squadron unless replacement is made by a Squadron from the United Kingdom, or, possibly, by an American Squadron.

(*g*) The despatch of 16 Hornet aircraft to Hong Kong will reduce the effective long range fighter force in the United Kingdom by 50 per cent.

An alternative, if the Australians were agreeable would be to move to Hong Kong 16 of the 24 first-line RAAF[5] Mustangs now in South Japan. There is certain to be some delay in getting an Australian reaction to this proposal and it would therefore seem prudent to make preparations to send reinforcements.

(*h*) The airlift required to move essential personnel and equipment for the Spitfire Squadrons from Germany and the Hornet Squadron from this country would entail the withdrawal from the Berlin airlift of two Dakota Squadrons.

(*j*) [*sic*] There will be no operational British aircraft-carrier in the Mediterranean during August and September.

---

[4] The reference is to the events initially sparked in May 1925 when Japanese guards fired on a group of striking Chinese textile workers at a plant in Shanghai, killing a Communist organiser. This led to demonstrations during which a British police inspector ordered his Chinese and Sikh constables to open fire. Four demonstrators were killed and more than fifty wounded, of whom eight died later. More protests and riots followed, with ten more deaths. A general strike was declared and anti-British and anti-Japanese demonstrations broke out all over China.

[5] Royal Australian Air Force.

(*k*) The provision of the necessary shipping presents a most difficult problem. Ways and means of solving it are under urgent consideration.

10. Until the Cabinet have given their approval to the despatch of further reinforcements to Hong Kong on the scale now proposed, an approach cannot be made to the shipping lines or to other Commonwealth countries with a view to their lending us further emigrant ships; nor can other essential preparations be begun for the despatch of troops, aircraft and naval forces.

11. The above proposals represent the maximum effort which the United Kingdom can reasonably make to secure the defence of Hong Kong. Other members of the Commonwealth are also vitally concerned in arresting the spread of Communism south-eastwards in Asia. Australia, New Zealand, India and Pakistan may be prepared to lend us assistance—moral and material—in making Hong Kong secure. The way in which these countries could be of assistance in providing armed forces both now and if the emergency develops is under consideration by the Chiefs of Staff.

Recommendations

12. The Cabinet are asked:
(*a*) to authorise the early despatch to Hong Kong of the reinforcements outlined in paragraph 6 above;
(*b*) to take note of the implications of sending these reinforcements as indicated in paragraph 9 above, in particular

(*i*) the possible effect on Western Union of the despatch of relatively large forces to the Far East;
(*ii*) the need to call up Section 'A' of the Army Reserve, and
(*iii*) the absence for a period of three months of any effective strategic reserve in the United Kingdom.

(*c*) to ensure that immediate steps are taken to gain the moral support of the other countries of the Commonwealth so that at the appropriate moment we can ask them to give us such material aid as they, on the one hand, may be able to provide, and we, on the other hand, require.

No. 78

Memorandum by Mr. Attlee on Hong Kong

CP(49)119 [CAB 129/35]

Top Secret   10 DOWNING STREET, *24 May 1949*

On 5th May the Cabinet authorised the despatch to Hong Kong of reinforcements sufficient to secure the Colony against internal unrest or sporadic attacks by guerrillas. They were, however, unwilling that this decision should be announced in terms implying a long-term policy of maintaining Hong Kong as a British Colony. This unwillingness was based partly on military advice that Hong Kong could not be successfully defended against a full-scale attack by a first class Power, and partly on the knowledge that public opinion in other countries (including some Commonwealth countries) would be unfavourably impressed by any declaration of our intention to hold Hong Kong indefinitely as a Colonial possession (CM(49)32nd Conclusions, Minute 2).[1]

The decision to send these reinforcements was announced by the Minister of Defence, in debate in the House of Commons on 5th May, in the following terms:

'While, as I have made clear, we have scrupulously endeavoured to avoid being involved in the war on the Chinese mainland, we are no less resolute in our attitude as regards territory for which we hold a direct responsibility. Hong Kong has long had a tradition of neutrality and non-interference in the politics of China, and supporters of the Kuomintang and the Communists alike have enjoyed the benefits which have thus been provided, subject to their obeying the law and doing nothing to damage relations between His Majesty's Government and the Government of China. His Majesty's Government have consistently maintained a policy of strict non-interference in the civil war in China, and, in pursuance of this policy, a very vigilant watch is being kept in Hong Kong, and steps have been, and are being, taken to deal with any breach of the conditions under which Chinese nationals, whether Kuomintang or Communist, are allowed to reside there and with disturbance of the peace, however caused. It would not be in the public interest to give details at this stage...'[2]

2. Since then the Communist forces in Southern China have made substantial progress, and the risk of an armed attack against Hong Kong has increased. The Chiefs of Staff have advised that the threat of such an attack may develop at any time after the end of September next and that, if it is to be resisted, we should be ready to meet it from the beginning of September. The Chiefs of Staff have also advised that it should be possible successfully to repel such an attack if it is decided now to send to Hong Kong the further reinforcements described in the memorandum by the Minister of Defence (CP(49)118).[3]

3. Together with the Ministers most directly concerned I have discussed this situation with the Chiefs of Staff, the Commissioner-General for South East Asia and the Commanders-in-Chief of the Land and Air Forces in the Far East.[4] The military implications are discussed in the paper submitted by the Minister of Defence (CP(49)118). My paper is concerned with the

[1] See No. 69.
[2] For that part of Mr. Alexander's statement concerning the reinforcement of Hong Kong, see No. 69, note 5.
[3] No. 77.
[4] See No. 75.

political considerations; and the proposals in the following paragraphs are put forward after consultation with the Foreign Secretary and the Secretary of State for Commonwealth Relations.

4. All the advice that we have received from the authorities on the spot is that any failure on our part to meet this threat to the security of Hong Kong will damage very seriously British prestige throughout the Far East and South East Asia. The peoples of this area remember clearly how Hong Kong was overrun by the Japanese in the last war; and, unless they are convinced of our determination and ability to resist this new threat to Hong Kong, the whole of the common front against Communism in South East Asia, and especially in Siam and Burma, is likely to crumble. On the other hand, a clear indication of our determination to resist such an attack might well succeed in deterring the Communist from making the attempt.

5. In the light of the views expressed in the Cabinet's earlier discussions, I have considered with the Foreign Secretary and the Secretary of State for Commonwealth Relations how best we can present to world opinion a decision to defend Hong Kong against such an attack. We are agreed in recommending that this should be presented as *a decision to resist aggression.* The right to resist aggression, wherever it may occur, is clearly recognised in the United Nations Charter and I therefore propose that we should base on this right our determination to resist aggression against Hong Kong. If the Communists decide to stage an attack on Hong Kong, we should then be in a position to appeal to the Security Council of the United Nations, and would be entitled to the support of the nations who are signatories of the Charter. I do not look to the United Nations for any material support—the Soviet Union would certainly veto any resolution for remedial action—but I base my proposal on the fact that the United Nations Organisation offers the best opportunity of mobilising world opinion and in particular our friends in support of our resistance to aggression.

Approach to other Commonwealth countries and the United States

6. Immediately the decision has been taken to send the necessary reinforcements to Hong Kong and to resist Communist aggression by armed force should it take place, we should notify the other members of the Commonwealth and the United States of our decision and of the basis upon which it rests. The fact that this decision is in accordance with the terms of the United Nations Charter should, we hope, commend itself to those powers who attach importance to the United Nations Organisation and all it stands for.

7. We should be able to obtain strong statements of support from at least the majority of the other Commonwealth Prime Ministers. It would be important, particularly in relation to the older Commonwealth countries, that we should make clear our intentions of defending Hong Kong and our ability to do so. If they are to be asked to support our policy by public statements, they must know exactly what the full implications of that policy

are. The attitude of the different members of the Commonwealth varies and it may be convenient to deal with the countries individually.

8. *Australia and New Zealand.* Australia and New Zealand are the Commonwealth countries most directly affected and incidentally are the only ones who are likely to be able and willing to send material help at an early stage. They would feel that their own security was directly threatened by the loss of Hong Kong and both are likely to support a robust policy on our part. The Prime Minister of New Zealand[5] has already sent a message saying that the possible fate of Hong Kong is a matter of immediate moment. He has said that a second expulsion from this area at this particular time could not fail to have the most damaging consequences and he has asked to be informed of the present position and of the plans which have been drawn up for the effective defence of Hong Kong. Our High Commissioner at Canberra has also reported that the general comment in Australia has been that Australia is vitally concerned in the retention of Hong Kong and must support a firm United Kingdom policy there. At the same time there is in Australia the background of Malaya in the last war with the arrival of Australian troops in time to become Japanese prisoners of war. Our High Commissioners in Canberra and Wellington have already been asked to communicate the appreciation in CP(49)100[6] to the Australian and New Zealand Governments. It is recommended that this should now be followed up by an early approach to the Prime Ministers of Australia and New Zealand, letting them know fully the considerations of policy set out above and informing them of the action we ourselves propose to take by way of further military reinforcements. In this approach we should seek support for our general policy, with a view to making, at the appropriate moment, any requests for material assistance which are recommended in the separate paper by the Minister of Defence.

9. *Canada and South Africa.* The general attitude of Canada and South Africa to a policy on the lines proposed is likely to be similar to that of Australia and New Zealand, though both Canada and South Africa are less directly affected and, for different reasons, would not be likely to send material help. Both are, however, likely to support a policy of resistance to aggression and both would be powerfully impressed by the need to resist the Communist threat. It may be hoped therefore that both Canada and South Africa would give strong moral support to our policy.

10. There is a particular consideration, however, in the case of Canada. The fate of Canadian troops in Hong Kong in the last war[7] has still not been forgotten and this remains a subject of controversy in the Canadian Parliament, where Mr. Drew, the Leader of the Opposition, has been at pains to keep the issue alive. The Canadian General Election is due on 27th June and the Canadian Government may be reluctant to make any

[5] Mr. P. Fraser, Prime Minister of New Zealand, 1940-49.
[6] No. 68.
[7] See No. 73, note 2.

public statement while electioneering is still on. On the other hand, if the United States were to agree to support our policy, Canada would find it much easier to do so.

11. *India.* The attitude of India is crucial in this matter. If we could be assured of India's moral support openly expressed by Pandit Nehru, the effect must be important. On the other hand, refusal on his part to endorse our policy, with, or indeed without, any overt statement, would be highly dangerous in relation to Hong Kong and the situation in South East Asia generally. It may be difficult to obtain any public declaration of support from Pandit Nehru in view of his persistent attacks on 'Colonialism', of his frequently repeated announcements of neutrality and of his refusal to join with either an Eastern or a Western bloc, but we should clearly make every effort. Sir Archibald Nye has been asked to come to London for consultation as to the best way of making an approach to the Government of India and it is hoped that he will be able to handle the matter personally with Pandit Nehru on his return.

12. *Pakistan and Ceylon.* Similar considerations to those affecting India also apply to Pakistan and Ceylon and the action to be taken in relation to them would follow on that taken in the case of India.

13. *United States.* It is not possible to estimate accurately what United States reactions will be to a request for moral support of a policy of defending Hong Kong against aggression. In the past American opinion, swayed to a large extent by sentiment and by the large missionary element in American contacts with China, tended to be sympathetic to the view that Hong Kong should be returned to China. The growing menace of Soviet Russia and the Communist advance in China have, it is believed, modified American opinion, and the United States Government may be prepared to offer moral support to a short-term policy of resisting aggression against Hong Kong as part of the general resistance to the advance of Communism which they favour. A message should be sent to the United States stressing this aspect of the situation as well as the fact that our decision is in accordance with the Charter of the United Nations. It is doubtful whether the United States would be prepared to furnish material support for Hong Kong, but the message might include a request to the United States to consider whether they would be willing to fill the gaps which will be created in Germany (and possibly also in Japan) by a decision to send to Hong Kong some Commonwealth elements from the forces of occupation in those countries.

Summary of Recommendations

14. My recommendations to the Cabinet may be summarised as follows:

(*a*) We should now decide to defend Hong Kong against armed attack by Chinese Communist forces.

(*b*) This decision should be presented as resistance to aggression in accordance with the United States Charter.

(*c*) We should seek moral support for this policy from all the other Commonwealth countries and from the United States.

(*d*) We should also ask, at the appropriate moment, for material assistance from Australia and New Zealand on the lines recommended by the Minister of Defence in CP(49)118.

(*e*) We should ask the United States Government to consider whether they would be willing to fill the gaps created in Germany (and possibly Japan) by the withdrawal of Commonwealth troops for the defence of Hong Kong.

No. 79

Note by Mr. Dening on Mr. Attlee's memorandum on Hong Kong

[*F 7788/1192/10*]

FOREIGN OFFICE, *25 May 1949*

This memorandum by the Prime Minister[1] was drafted in the first instance by the Foreign Office and the Commonwealth Relations Office in consultation together, as a result of a meeting of the China and South East Asia Committee last week at which the Secretary of State was present. The views expressed therein are in accordance with what was said by the Secretary of State at the China and South East Asia Committee. There are therefore no comments on the paper as such.

We feel in the Foreign Office that, of the courses open to the Communists, a direct attack on Hong Kong is the least likely. On the other hand, it would not be safe to ignore the possibility, and the best advice available is that the necessary steps should be taken to put Hong Kong in a state of defence against the possibility of an attack.

Assuming that Ministers decide to take these steps, and to approach the Commonwealth and United States, we think it desirable not to be too provocative in public. As regards India, Sir Archibald Nye advises us that the best we can hope for is that India will not attack our decision to defend Hong Kong. Even this negative support, however, may not be forthcoming if we rattle the sword in the scabbard too loudly. The China policy of the Cabinet is that we should try to keep a foot in the door, which means that our nationals in considerable numbers are remaining in China. We do not want to become involved in open conflict with Communist China over Hong Kong, because that would eliminate all possibility of trying to influence the situation in China proper.

While therefore we should be ready to meet all eventualities in Hong Kong, we must try at the same time to avoid prejudicing our position in China proper. It is possible that we shall eventually reach the point where

[1] No. 78.

it may be in our interests to recognise a Communist government of China, and when that time comes we should wish our bargaining position to be as good as possible.

There is no indication that the Cabinet intend to discuss a suggestion by the Chiefs of Staff that the present Governor of Hong Kong should be replaced by a military Governor.[2] The Governor himself has raised the question whether he should now turn Hong Kong into a fortress,[3] which will inevitably restrict trading facilities there. I have pointed out to the Colonial Office at the official level that the Chinese do not love Hong Kong because it is governed by the British, but because it offers safe and profitable trading facilities. If as a result of military security measures these trading facilities are restricted or cut off, then the Chinese interest in our retention of the colony will dwindle or disappear. It is true that military security measures cannot safely be left till the last moment, but the situation should be weighed very carefully before it is decided to do anything which will interrupt the flow of trade through Hong Kong.

[2] Cf. No. 81.
[3] See No. 71, note 4.

No. 80

Extract from Conclusions of a meeting of the Cabinet held at 10 Downing St. on 26 May 1949 at 9.45 a.m.[1]

CM(49)38 [CAB 128/15]

China
(Previous Reference: CM(49)33rd Conclusions, Minute 2).[2]

3. The Cabinet considered memoranda by the Prime Minister (CP(49)119),[3] the Minister of Defence (CP(49)118)[4] and the Secretary of State for the Colonies (CP(49)120)[5] on the defence of Hong Kong.

THE PRIME MINISTER recalled that on 5th May the Cabinet had authorised the despatch to Hong Kong of reinforcements sufficient to secure the Colony against internal unrest or sporadic attacks by guerrillas.[6]

[1] Present: Mr. Attlee, Mr. Morrison, Sir S. Cripps, Mr. Alexander, Mr. Dalton, Viscount Addison, Viscount Jowitt, Mr. Chuter Ede, Mr. Creech Jones, Mr. Noel-Baker, Mr. Woodburn, Mr. Isaacs, Mr. Bevan, Mr. Williams, Mr. Tomlinson, Viscount Hall, Mr. Henderson, Mr. C.P. Mayhew (Parliamentary Under-Secretary of State for Foreign Affairs), Mr. MacDonald, Sir A. Nye, Lord Tedder, Lord Fraser of North Cape, F-M Sir W. Slim and General Sir N. Ritchie.
[2] See No. 70.   [3] No. 78.   [4] No. 77.   [5] No. 76.   [6] See No. 69

Since then the Communist forces in Southern China had made substantial progress, and the question now arose of sending further reinforcements in order to secure Hong Kong against the risk of direct attack by these forces from the mainland. The Chiefs of Staff had advised that such an attack might be delivered at any time after the end of September; and that, if it was to be resisted with success, an immediate decision should be taken to despatch to Hong Kong the further reinforcements set out in the memorandum by the Minister of Defence (CP(49)118).

The Prime Minister said that, from consultations which he had held with the Commissioner-General for South East Asia and the Commanders-in-Chief of the Land and Air Forces in the Far East, he was satisfied that failure to meet this threat to the security of Hong Kong would damage very seriously British prestige throughout the Far East and South East Asia. Moreover, the whole common front against Communism in Siam, Burma and Malaya was likely to crumble unless the peoples of those countries were convinced of our determination and ability to resist this threat to Hong Kong.

In their earlier discussions the Cabinet had been reluctant to commit themselves to any long-term policy in respect of Hong Kong; and the Prime Minister had therefore considered, in consultation with the Foreign Secretary and other Ministers directly concerned, how a decision to defend the colony could be presented in such a way as to command the support of public opinion in the democratic countries of the world. He had come to the conclusion that it should be presented as a decision to resist aggression; and he recommended that support for such a policy should be enlisted from the Governments of other Commonwealth countries and of the United States.

The following points were made in discussion of the political considerations involved:

(*a*) Policy must take account of the fact that Hong Kong was valuable to us mainly as a centre of trade. In the short term, trade would be seriously interrupted, if not entirely brought to an end, if preparations for the military defence of the Colony were countered by measures of blockade from the mainland. In the long term, if a strong Communist Government established itself in control over the whole of China, it would be impossible for us to maintain Hong Kong as a trading centre unless that Government acquiesced in our continuance there. These considerations seemed to suggest that the aim of our policy should be to find a basis on which a Communist Government of China could acquiesce in our remaining in Hong Kong. If we made it a point of prestige that we should retain Hong Kong as a British possession, it might become a matter of prestige for the Communists to force us to withdraw from it.

As against this, attention was drawn to the importance of our being able to argue from a position of strength in any negotiations with a Chinese Government about our future position in Hong Kong. If we showed no determination to defend the Colony, the risk of its being attacked would be increased; and, if we were forced to withdraw from it, we should have little prospect of persuading a Chinese Government to allow us to return. In the short term, if we showed ourselves determined to remain there, the Communists were unlikely to maintain an economic blockade for any length of time; for the continued interruption of the normal flow of trade between Hong Kong and the mainland was likely to be as embarrassing for the Communists as it would be for the Colony. The temporary interruption of that trade, during a period of tension or actual hostilities, would not do it any lasting injury: it could soon be revived thereafter, as it had been revived since the end of the war.

(*b*) Practical evidence of our determination to defend Hong Kong would have important consequences. First, it might well deter the Communist forces from making a direct attack on the Colony. Secondly, it would rally to our side the wavering elements among the local population and would substantially reduce the threat to internal security. Thirdly, it would strengthen the anti-Communist front throughout South East Asia. The maintenance of our trading position in Hong Kong was doubtless important; but even more important at the present time was the political question whether we must not somewhere make a stand against Communist encroachment in the Far East. If we failed to make this stand in Hong Kong, should we not find it much harder to make it elsewhere in South East Asia?

(*c*) There were, however, dangers in making at this stage any forthright declaration of our determination to defend Hong Kong. Apart from the risk that such a declaration might be regarded as provocative by the Chinese Communists, there was also the danger that a unilateral declaration by the United Kingdom Government would be interpreted, however, it was phrased, as relic of 'Colonialism'. We should find ourselves in an awkward position if, having made the declaration, we failed to enlist a sufficient number of our friends in its support. Although it was fairly clear that we should gain the support of Australia and New Zealand, the attitude of some other Commonwealth Governments was uncertain and it would be unwise to count on the support of public opinion in the United States. Should it not rather be our aim to mobilise as many Governments as possible in support of a policy of resisting aggression against Hong Kong, so that we might appear to be acting as the instrument of an international policy rather than pursuing a selfish policy of our own? There was general support for the view that no declaration of policy should be made until consultations had been held with the Governments of the other Commonwealth countries and of the United States.

(*d*) THE HIGH COMMISSIONER FOR THE UNITED KINGDOM IN INDIA said that there seemed little prospect of persuading Pandit Nehru to make any public declaration of India's support of a policy of defending Hong Kong against aggression by Chinese Communist forces. First, he might think this inconsistent with his general opposition to 'Colonialism'. Secondly, he would be mindful of the French and Portuguese possessions in Pondicherry and Goa; and he would not wish to say anything which might preclude him from objecting, at some later date, to any proposals for strengthening the French or Portuguese garrisons in those places. Thirdly, he had stated that India would not associate herself with power *blocs*, and the declaration made at the end of the April Meeting of Commonwealth Prime Ministers[7] had already been criticised by his political opponents and by some of his political supporters on the ground that it might limit India's freedom of action in international affairs. These critics would be greatly strengthened if, within so short a time after that declaration, Pandit Nehru voiced his public support of a United Kingdom policy for the military defence of Hong Kong. In these circumstances our best hope was to persuade Pandit Nehru to refrain from making any public statement which was critical of our proposed policy in Hong Kong. So long as our action was limited to suppressing internal disorders, he might well be willing to refrain from any such comment. If, however, we were compelled to resist an armed attack by forces operating under the auspices of a Chinese Government, he would find it more difficult to remain silent. From the point of view of avoiding public criticism in India, it would be preferable that we should avoid making any formal declaration of policy.

THE COMMISSIONER-GENERAL FOR SOUTH EAST ASIA said that, from his point of view, he would welcome a public declaration of our determination to defend Hong Kong against aggression. He recognised, however, that the question whether any such declaration should be made must be decided by reference, not so much to local needs, but rather to the wider considerations which had been mentioned in the Cabinet's discussion. From the point of view of strengthening morale in Hong Kong and in South East Asia it would perhaps be sufficient that we should despatch to Hong Kong reinforcements sufficient for its defence.

The following points were raised in discussion of the military implications of defending Hong Kong:

(*e*) To what extent would the successful defence of the Colony be frustrated by failure to control an influx of refugees from the mainland? This had proved a serious difficulty in 1941. The Cabinet were informed that, although the movement of refugees could not be satisfactorily controlled while trade continued between the Colony and the mainland, no insuperable difficulty should arise in a state of siege. Full preparations had been made for dealing with this situation, and the Governor was satisfied that any large-scale influx of refugees could be prevented.

(*f*) Was it clear that adequate water supplies would be available under conditions of siege? The Cabinet were informed that, as the leased territories would be included within the defence area, the water supply

---

[7] Meeting in London in April 1949, the Commonwealth Prime Ministers agreed that India should become a sovereign independent Republic and remain a member of the Commonwealth on the basis that she continued to accept the King as the symbol of the free association of its independent members, and that as such he was the Head of the Commonwealth.

should be sufficient to meet the requirements of the population and of the increased garrison, provided that control was maintained over consumption. It would not be difficult to take precautions against damage by sabotage.

(g) It was hoped that by September the situation in Malaya would have improved sufficiently to allow the Guards Brigade to be moved to Hong Kong without undue risk.

(h) THE SECRETARY OF STATE FOR AIR said that he was not in agreement with the proposal (paragraph 6 of CP(49)118) to include, in the reinforcements to be sent to Hong Kong, a long-range fighter squadron from the United Kingdom. He was reluctant to accept this reduction in the strength of Fighter Command; and he suggested that on this point no final decision should be taken until it was known whether the squadron of Australian Mustangs could be transferred to Hong Kong from Japan.

(i) Some Ministers took the view that it would be undesirable, for political reasons, to proceed with the proposal (Paragraph 9(b) of CP(49)118) to call up Section 'A' of the Army Reserve.

(j) THE MINISTER OF DEFENCE said that a working party of officials had prepared detailed proposals for finding the shipping required for the additional reinforcements set out in CP(49)118.

(k) THE CHANCELLOR OF THE EXCHEQUER said that he proposed to arrange for a representative of the Bank of England to proceed at once to Hong Kong to advise the Governor on currency problems.

The Cabinet:

(1) Approved the proposal to send to Hong Kong the further reinforcements described in CP(49)118, subject to further consideration by the Defence Committee of the proposals (i) to send a squadron of long-range fighters from the United Kingdom and (ii) to call up Section 'A' of the Army Reserve;[8] and authorised the Service Departments to proceed at once with preliminary arrangements for all these movements save those affected by (i) and (ii).

(2) Agreed that for the time being no public announcement should be made that any fresh decision of policy had been taken in respect of Hong Kong or that any further reinforcements were to be sent there.[9]

(3) Invited the Secretary of State for Commonwealth Relations and the Foreign Secretary, respectively, to inform the Governments of the other Commonwealth countries and of the United States of the development

[8] At a meeting of the Defence Committee on 1 June Sir W. Slim argued that 'in view of the political difficulty involved and after a closer study of the detailed implications', the proposed reinforcements should be sent out without calling up Section 'A' of the Army Reserve. The reinforcement would 'suffer in certain respects' but the risk could be accepted. The Defence Committee accepted this judgement (DO 15(49)2, CAB 21/2429).

[9] For the context in which a brief statement was made about the further reinforcements, see No. 81, note 3 below.

of the situation in Hong Kong and of the decision to reinforce the garrison still further; and to ascertain whether those Governments would be prepared to support a policy of defending Hong Kong against aggression by Communist forces from the mainland and, if need be, to make at the appropriate stage public declarations in support of that policy.

(4) Agreed that final decisions regarding the basis of United Kingdom policy in respect of Hong Kong, and the form and timing of any announcement regarding it, should be taken by the Cabinet in the light of the views expressed by the Governments of the other Commonwealth countries and of the United States.

CABINET OFFICE, *26 May 1949*

No. 81

Minutes of a Meeting of Ministers on Hong Kong: Command and Government, held at 10 Downing St. on 1 June 1949 at 6 p.m.[1]

GEN 294/1st Meeting [CAB 130/47]

Top Secret

The Committee had before them the *aide-mémoire* at Annex, reporting the results of a Staff Conference which had taken place earlier in the day on the question of the Command and Government in Hong Kong.

THE MINISTER OF DEFENCE said that the Chiefs of Staff felt that if they were ever put to the test the success or failure of our preparations for the defence of Hong Kong would depend on what was done now; and for this reason they were particularly anxious that a Military Governor should be appointed without delay. He had much sympathy with the logic of this view but believed it would be a mistake to make any such change at a time when we were at pains to secure the moral support of the Commonwealth and the United States to [*sic*] our policy in Hong Kong. He had accordingly discussed with the Chiefs of Staff, the Commissioner General and representatives of the Foreign Office and Colonial Office possible alternative arrangements. The first was that a Supreme Commander might be appointed and given a status equal to that of the present Governor, but it had been generally agreed that this solution would almost inevitably lead to a clash of personalities and could not, therefore, be accepted as

---

[1] Present at this meeting were: Mr. Attlee (in the Chair), Mr. Alexander, Mr. Creech Jones, Mr. H. McNeil (Minister of State, FO), and Mr. P. Gordon-Walker (Parliamentary Under-Secretary of State for Commonwealth Relations).

satisfactory. The second alternative, described in paragraphs 12 and 14 of the Annex, was that there should at once be appointed a Supreme Commander of all the Land, Air and local Naval defence forces in Hong Kong, of high standing and with a good knowledge of the Colony, who would be in a position to influence the Governor; the Governor himself being given confidential instructions to the effect that in the event of a difference of opinion about any major security measures, the military view should prevail. On the whole he was inclined to think that this solution was the right one to adopt and if the Committee agreed he supported the view of the Chiefs of Staff that General Festing would be the right man to appoint as Supreme Commander.[2]

In discussion it was generally agreed that the solution propounded in paragraphs 12 and 14 of the *aide-mémoire* at Annex should be accepted and the Committee then considered the steps that would have to be taken to put this decision into effect.

THE Prime MINISTER said that the first essential would be to secure the co-operation of the Governor. The new arrangement would have to be explained to him and he would have to be given a clear and careful directive which would cover the question of the action he was to take in the event of a difference of opinion about any security measures. While on the one hand he would have to be left in no doubt that if these new arrangements did not work other changes would have to be made, on the other it would be very important to secure his continued co-operation if the situation were to deteriorate and a Military Governor had subsequently to be appointed. The Secretary of State for the Colonies should arrange at once for the drafting of a directive which would then be despatched to the Minister of Defence who would put the whole matter personally to the Governor on his arrival in Hong Kong.[3] There would, of course, be no question of announcing the terms of the directive; nor would it be necessary for the Governor to communicate its terms to his Executive Council.

The Committee:

(1) Agreed to adopt the solution set forth in paragraphs 12 and 13 of the *aide-mémoire* at Annex.

[2] General Sir F. Festing had been GOC Land Forces, Hong Kong, 1945-1946.

[3] Mr. Alexander visited Hong Kong between 6 and 9 June to review security arrangements. He secured Sir A. Grantham's agreement to Sir F. Festing's appointment in 1949 as Commander of British Forces in Hong Kong with the temporary rank of Lieutenant-General (memorandum by Mr. Alexander of 17 June 1949, CP(49)134, CAB 129/35). Mr. Alexander made a brief statement about his visit to Hong Kong in the House of Commons on 22 June. He announced General Festing's appointment and reported that further reinforcements were being sent to the colony but gave no details (*Parl. Debs., 5th ser., H. of C.*, vol. 406, cols. 208-10).

(2) Invited the Secretary of State for the Colonies, in consultation with the Chiefs of Staff and General Festing, to prepare and submit to the Prime Minister the draft of a directive to the Governor of Hong Kong. When approved by the Prime Minister the directive should be telegraphed to the Minister of Defence.[4]

(3) Invited the Minister of Defence on receipt of the directive in (2) above and in the light of the points made by the Prime Minister, to put the matter personally to the Governor of Hong Kong and seek his co-operation in the new arrangements.

(4) Took note with approval that the Chiefs of Staff proposed to nominate General Festing as Commander of all Land, Air and local Naval forces in Hong Kong; but agreed that final confirmation of his appointment should await receipt of a report from the Minister of Defence on his discussions with the Governor.

CABINET OFFICE, *1 June 1949*

ANNEX TO No. 81

Aide-Mémoire
Hong Kong: Command and Government

The Governor of Hong Kong has recently suggested that there is likely to be a clash between trading and defence interests in Hong Kong. This was fully discussed at a Staff Conference this morning at which the Minister of Defence, Mr Malcolm MacDonald, the Chiefs of Staff, General Ritchie and representatives from the Foreign Office and Colonial Office were present.

2. There was general agreement that the real importance of Hong Kong at present is not so much as a trading post or as a potential fortress but because of the effects of what is done there upon the Cold War. This must govern all decisions.

3. It was also generally agreed that the present Governor, for all his deep knowledge of Hong Kong and his many admirable qualities, lacks the one quality—vital at the present time—of leadership.

4. Leadership, not only in military affairs but in economic affairs and government generally, is essential now to Hong Kong both for putting the Colony into a state of defence against external aggression and for

---

[4] The directive confirmed that in the event of a difference of opinion, the views of the Military Commander would prevail. The Governor retained the right to refer any matter considered to be of great importance to the welfare of Hong Kong to the Secretary of State for the Colonies. In the event of an appeal, the Governor was required immediately to inform the British Defence Co-ordination Committee.

preventing the more likely threat to its safety from within, resulting from poor morale.

5. There is no other person available with the necessary qualities who could be found to replace the present Governor.

6. The apparently obvious solution that he should be replaced by a Military Governor is open to the serious objection that, owing to a recent unavoidable change in appointments, no high quality civilian adviser with a long or intimate knowledge of the Colony would be available (as was the case when Admiral Harcourt was Military Governor).[5]

7. Furthermore, the appointment of a Military Governor at this stage might seriously prejudice our attempts to carry the Commonwealth and United States with us in our stand against Communism in Hong Kong. The Foreign Office view is that it would offer more scope for the Chinese Communists to whip up anti-Colonial feeling in Asia against us than would be the case if civil government were preserved.

8. The alternative was therefore suggested that there might be both a civilian Governor and a Military Governor—the latter having overriding powers. This device was successful in Ceylon during the war. Mr. Malcolm MacDonald thought that the Governor might loyally accept such an arrangement and make it work.

9. The Chiefs of Staff, on the other hand, were convinced that this arrangement was bound to lead to a clash of personalities. Almost all decisions of government have some bearing on defence in an outpost like Hong Kong and the very clash which it is desired to avoid would be intensified. The present Governor's position would be undermined and two Heads of Government would mean not greater leadership, but more confused leadership. Moreover, the successful experiment in Ceylon, when prolonged into the peace, was harmful to commerce and industry.

10. The logic of the view of the Chiefs of Staff is difficult to refute. They are, however, equally insistent that adjustments to the machinery of government in Hong Kong ought to be made *now* for the purpose of resisting internal dangers and preparations against external attack.

11. There is clearly no ideal solution. The best arrangement seems to be as follows.

12. A Commander should be appointed to command all the land, air and local naval defence forces in Hong Kong. He would be responsible to the British Defence Co-ordination Committee through the Commanders-in-Chief, Far East. He should be a man of such stature that he would be able to influence the Governor, who tends to be somewhat remote from his usual advisers. Furthermore, he should already have a good knowledge of the Colony so that he would be able to take over as Military Governor in the event of the threat to Hong Kong developing.

[5] See No. 1, note 18. Admiral Harcourt was Commander-in-Chief and Head of Military Administration, Hong Kong, 1945-1946.

13. Two such men are available—Admiral Harcourt and General Festing, who also served in Hong Kong immediately after its liberation. As Admiral Harcourt has already been Governor, however, he could hardly accept a subordinate position.

14. Finally, the Governor should be given private instructions, as has already been suggested by the Colonial Office, that in the event of a difference of opinion about any major security measures, the military view should prevail.

1 June 1949

No. 82

Memorandum by Mr. Noel-Baker on Hong Kong: Attitude of other Commonwealth Countries

CP(49)136 [CAB 129/35]

Top Secret   COMMONWEALTH RELATIONS OFFICE, *17 June 1949*

On 26th May (CM(49)38th Conclusions, Minute 3)[1] the Cabinet invited me to inform the Governments of the other Commonwealth countries of the development of the situation in Hong Kong, and of the decision to reinforce the garrison still further; and to ascertain whether those Governments would be prepared to support a policy of defending Hong Kong against aggression by Communist forces from the mainland, and if need be, to make at the appropriate stage public declarations in support of that policy. Instructions to approach other Commonwealth Governments in this sense were despatched to United Kingdom High Commissioners on 27th May.

2. The purpose of this paper is to indicate the response of other Commonwealth Governments to this approach. The present position may be summarised as follows.

(a) *Canada.* The preliminary view of the Canadian Prime Minister[2] was strongly critical of our intention to retain Hong Kong on the ground that it would be regarded in North America as wrong in principle to endeavour to maintain British rule by force in a Colony which was geographically part of China. It should be emphasised that this was Mr. St. Laurent's first reaction only: he promised to study the question and let us have a more considered view later.[3] In the meantime, the Acting High Commissioner has been asked to put certain further considerations to the Canadian authorities, but it seems improbable that any final indication of the

[1] See No. 80.
[2] Mr. L.S. St. Laurent, Prime Minister of Canada, 1948-57.
[3] For which see No. 103 below.

Canadian Government's attitude will be forthcoming before the Canadian General Election on 27th June.

(*b*) *Australia.* In the first approach made to Mr. Chifley,[4] he agreed that Hong Kong must be defended against any threat in the near future and supported the United Kingdom's decision to reinforce the Hong Kong garrison. (He has agreed to the use of the *Georgic* for carrying reinforcements and it is possible that an Australian troopship may be provided.) But he was unwilling to commit Australia further, even on this short-term policy, because of fears that if it is persisted in over a longer term it may lead to a major clash with a fully organised Communist China, with which (in Mr. Chifley's view) we shall have, at any rate in the long run, to come to terms. Mr. Chifley thought that we should attempt as soon as possible to reach agreement with the Chinese Communists by means of direct negotiations, and that until such negotiations are shown to be impossible, nothing should be done which might discourage the Chinese Communists from preserving and cultivating China's contacts with the West. Our preliminary comments on Mr. Chifley's message, dealing particularly with his suggestion for approaching the Chinese Communists, have already been telegraphed to the High Commissioner at Canberra and a further reply will be sent as soon as Ministers have considered the policy issues involved.

As regards material assistance, Mr. Chifley in his reply of 1st June said that that he felt the Australian Cabinet 'would not be prepared to send material support to meet a full-scale attack on Hong Kong, for this would most likely involve full-scale war with the Chinese Government'. Nevertheless, in an interview with the High Commissioner on 11th June, Mr. Chifley hinted at the possibility of ships and aircraft being sent from Australia, and said that if the United Kingdom made enquiries these would be looked into very carefully. The advice of the High Commissioner was that we should be unwise in these circumstances to make a formal request at the moment. In accordance with his own suggestion he was therefore instructed to ascertain from Mr. Chifley whether the Australian Government would be prepared to entertain favourably a request for certain specified types of assistance, if the United Kingdom were to make it, or alternatively whether Australia was likely to volunteer an offer.

The High Commissioner has now been informed by Mr. Chifley that at its meeting on 14th June there was strong feeling in the Australian Cabinet *against* offering anything in the nature of real military assistance to the United Kingdom at Hong Kong, since this would involve the risk of Australian forces becoming involved in a 'shooting war'; and the view was expressed (with even greater force than in Mr. Chifley's first message) that the right course is to come to early terms with the Chinese Communists. Mr. Chifley has told our High Commissioner that in the light of the Australian Cabinet's views, he would prefer *not* to receive a request from us

[4] See No. 43, note 4.

for land forces, aircraft or warships, since the reply would clearly be in the negative. On the particular question of releasing the Mustangs at present in Japan, Mr. Chifley said that he certainly did not want to join in an approach to General MacArthur for the release of these aircraft, when Australia was now virtually alone in providing these Commonwealth forces in Japan.

The Australian authorities would, however, if desired, readily look into the question of making available *material* such as ammunition and medical supplies, as distinct from personnel. Mr. Chifley also asked for a full statement of the United Kingdom's requirements of medical personnel. This the High Commissioner is supplying. Mr. Chifley has, however, emphasised that any medical personnel would have to be volunteers.

Mr. Fraser[5] has sent a personal message to Mr. Chifley stressing that Hong Kong is vital to Australia and New Zealand and must not be allowed to fall, and informing him of New Zealand's intention (see (c) below) to give material assistance to the United Kingdom.

Mr. Chifley's reply to this makes the Australian attitude a good sharper on a number of points. It reveals Mr. Chifley's embarrassment at the effects that an announcement of New Zealand help would have, and shows that he has asked Mr. Fraser to 'consider most carefully our viewpoint before you reach a final decision'. While the message recognises that 'the British' are entitled and bound to endeavour to retain Hong Kong, and that, for this purpose, some shew of force may be desirable, it somewhat inconsistently argues that there is a danger of over-simplification if the question is regarded as one of making Hong Kong the point to hold back Communist aggression in the Far East. Finally, the message makes it clear for the first time that the Australian Government have it in mind to take 'positive action' to bring the Chinese question, so far as it involves any threat of aggression against Hong Kong, before the Security Council, so that 'conciliation may replace force'.

(c) *New Zealand.* The High Commissioner reports that Mr. Fraser is realistically alive to the vital importance of defending Hong Kong and wholeheartedly accords his moral support to this policy. As regards material assistance, the New Zealand Cabinet have agreed that if the United Kingdom Government require them, three frigates should be placed at our disposal, and Mr. Fraser has indicated that a fourth may be available. A study is being made, at Mr. Fraser's insistence, of the possibility of a New Zealand air contribution also, and the possibility of obtaining medical assistance is also being taken up.

(d) *South Africa.* Dr. Malan[6] has told the High Commissioner that United Kingdom policy in regard to Hong Kong has the moral support of the Union Government. Sir Evelyn Baring[7] has commented that 'as in the days

[5] See No. 78, note 5.
[6] Dr. D.F. Malan was Prime Minister of South Africa.
[7] UK High Commissioner in South Africa.

of General Smuts,[8] the Union Government will be prepared to support generally any line we may wish to take on the advance of Communism in the Far East, but will not offer material help'.

(*e*) *India.* Pandit Nehru's reaction is on the whole more favourable than we expected. He appreciates the necessity for precautionary measures against an armed attack, though he thinks one unlikely. Should this occur, however, he promises that he and his colleagues will examine the situation sympathetically. Meanwhile he strongly endorses the policy of 'giving no offence to the new Chinese Government'. Moreover, the upsurge of nationalism throughout South-East Asia cannot be ignored, and Pandit Nehru trusts that the future of Hong Kong will be viewed by the United Kingdom Government in the same spirit of imaginative statesmanship that they have shown in dealing with problems elsewhere in Asia. From a conversation which the High Commissioner has had with the Secretary of the Indian Department of External Affairs,[9] it is clear that (in view of the position of the French and Portuguese territories in India) the Indian Government would have to reserve liberty of action if the Chinese Communists, instead of taking offensive action, decided to place a demand for the cession of Hong Kong before the Security Council. Sir Archibald Nye reports, moreover, that in view of the probable attitude of the Indian press and public, the less publicity which can be given to the matter the better, since Pandit Nehru and Sir Girja Bajpai would find it difficult in public to maintain as friendly an attitude towards the problem as they are able to do in private.

(*f*) *Pakistan.* Mr. Liaquat Ali Khan[10] has assured the High Commissioner that the United Kingdom Government's policy in regard to Hong Kong has his complete personal sympathy, and that he can see no reason to fear that the Pakistan Government would do anything embarrassing to the United Kingdom. He emphasised the strength of the United Kingdom's position under the Charter.

(*g*) *Ceylon.* Mr. Senanayake[11] welcomes the determination of the United Kingdom Government to make Hong Kong a bastion against Communist aggression. He hopes, however, that we shall exercise great restraint in dealing with internal unrest in Hong Kong, since it would be embarrassing for his Government to support what might seem repressive measures carried out by a Colonial Power. Subject to this, however, he has undertaken to make such public expression of support 'as is possible at the appropriate moment in the light of future developments'.

3. The results of our approach to the other Commonwealth countries about Hong Kong are, thus, broadly as follows:

[8] Prime Minister of South Africa, 1919-24, 1939-48.
[9] Sir Girja Bajpai.
[10] Prime Minister of Pakistan.
[11] Prime Minister of Ceylon.

(i) We have secured a large measure of support for our policy of taking the precautionary measures required to strengthen Hong Kong against internal disturbances or possible armed attack, while on the other hand carefully refraining from striking a provocative attitude. Some doubt has been expressed whether the Chinese Communists will wish to launch a major attack on Hong Kong at all.

(ii) Provided that our present policy is maintained, we have good grounds for hoping that no statements will be made by spokesmen for other Commonwealth countries which might embarrass the United Kingdom Government in their handling of the Hong Kong situation. The New Zealand and South African Governments would be willing to express their moral support for us in public if it becomes expedient to ask them to do so and, in favourable circumstances, other Governments might also be willing to do so.

(iii) The New Zealand Cabinet have already agreed to make three (or possibly four) frigates available, if the need should arise; and other ways in which New Zealand might assist are being explored. After consulting the Australian Cabinet, Mr. Chifley has made it clear that Australia is not prepared to offer land forces, warships or aircraft, though it is possible that some assistance may be forthcoming in respect of volunteer medical personnel.

(iv) But while there is general support among Commonwealth countries for our policy of taking the precautionary measures required to resist aggression, it is clear that there is a wide measure of concern at some of the longer term aspects of the problem. These may be considered under the two heads of:

(*a*) future policy towards China;
(*b*) the 'Colonial' aspect.

(*a*) *Future policy towards China.* In the discussions which took place with Mr. St. Laurent, the Canadian Under-Secretary of State for External Affairs made the point that the Chinese Communists had so far been behaving well; that we should be establishing relations with them; and that evidence was lacking that Communism in China was the same as the Russian brand. Mr. St. Laurent himself also emphasised that the Canadian Cabinet would wish to form an opinion especially from the angle of how things would shape in the Security Council in the event of a clash. The attitude of the Prime Minister of Australia has been described above. In effect, he considers that the main endeavour to secure the future of Hong Kong should be 'by positive means, based on relations between the seemingly new Government and the Western countries'; and that we should enter at once into direct negotiation with the Chinese Communist authorities, with a view to reaching a clear understanding with them about Hong Kong's future. Pandit Nehru, while admitting that aggression must, of course, be resisted, suggests that 'policies may be so framed as to avoid the possibility of such a situation arising'. He personally doubts whether the Chinese

Communists would wish to take action that would mean war with a great power, and foresees many developments in the next two or three months which will progressively change the internal and external situation in China.

(*b*) *The 'Colonial' aspect.* But more important is the reaction of Commonwealth countries to what may be termed the 'Colonial' aspect of the problem. As will be seen from the first reactions of Mr. St. Laurent, this clearly weighs heavily with the Canadian Prime Minister, though we should hope to be able to shake him out of some of his misconceptions. It was only to be expected that, in view of their repeated pronouncements against 'Colonialism', the three 'new' Members of the Commonwealth[12] should feel some hesitation on this score in giving full support for our policy; on the whole, however, their replies are realistic, and are quite as satisfactory as we could have expected. Nevertheless, any announcements about our long term policy for Hong Kong will need careful handling from this point of view. Pandit Nehru has himself raised the point, and has made it clear that he expects the United Kingdom Government to follow a no less enlightened policy in relation to Hong Kong than that already adopted in regard to India, Burma and Ceylon. Moreover, as regards immediate action, the Prime Minister of Ceylon has warned us that his present attitude of warm support for our policy might prove difficult to sustain if there were to be any mishandling of what might appear to be internal unrest, 'since the relationship of a Colony to any metropolitan power is repugnant to the sentiments of Asiatic peoples'. I suggest that this point needs careful watching, and the Secretary of State for the Colonies may wish to bear it in mind in any instructions sent to the Governor on measures to deal with internal unrest.

[12] India, Pakistan and Ceylon.

No. 83

Memorandum by Mr. Creech Jones on Hong Kong: points raised by the United States Government

CP(49)135 [*CAB 129/35*]

Secret   COLONIAL OFFICE, *18 June 1949*

1. In accordance with the conclusions of the meeting of the Cabinet on Thursday, 26th May (CM49)38th Conclusions, Minute 3,)[1] an approach was made to the United States Government to inform them of the development of the situation in Hong Kong and of the decision to reinforce the Garrison still further, and to ascertain whether they 'would be

[1] See No. 80.

prepared to support a policy of defending Hong Kong against aggression by Communist forces from the mainland, and, if need be, to make, at the appropriate stage, public declarations in support of that policy'.

2. Mr. Acheson has now put forward to His Majesty's Government a number of points about Hong Kong. He asks how we would propose to act if the Communists used all measures short of armed attack to secure the retrocession of Hong Kong; what would be the extent and possible duration of the protective measures which might be necessary on our part; and how far British economic interests in Hong Kong would be willing to play their part. The State Department also wish to know what we hope might come from an appeal to the United Nations, particularly in view of the fact that the Chinese Communists are not represented there and are not even an established Government. (See Annex I—telegram from Foreign Secretary).[2]

3. It will be recalled that, in the course of the negotiations preceding the conclusion in 1943 of a treaty abolishing extra-territoriality in China, the Chinese government made a request for the rendition of the New Territories. His Majesty's Government, while refusing to consider this request in connection with extra-territoriality, intimated that, if the Chinese government desired that the question of the lease of these Territories should be reconsidered, that was a matter which, in the opinion of His Majesty's Government, should be discussed when victory was won. The Chinese Government thereupon reserved their right to raise the question later.

4. In the summer of 1946 Generalissimo Chiang Kai Shek referred informally to the desirability of finding an early solution of 'the Hong Kong problem'[3] and, in succeeding months, consideration was given at the official level to the lines on which negotiations with the Chinese might be pursued should the matter go to that length. One of the plans which was considered contemplated the possible rendition of the greater part of the New Territories, but with conditions as to the control of public utilities there (e.g. water supplies and air fields), which would preserve the viability of the Island and Kowloon, which would remain British.[4] In the event,

---

[2] Annexes not printed. Independently, the US Government had decided, both on logistical and strategic grounds, that it would not assist in the defence of Hong Kong. The US Joint Chiefs of Staff advised the National Security Council in June 1949 that a successful defence of the territory would require 'a movement of large-scale forces into China'. This would run the risk of a major military conflict with China and possibly also global war. Strategically, the US defence perimeter in the Pacific under the Truman Administration ran along a line of the Philippines, the Rykus and Japan. It did not include Formosa, Korea, Indo-China or Hong Kong. The US adhered to this position until the outbreak of the Korean War. For a recent discussion see Chi-Kwan Mark, 'A Reward for Good Behaviour: Bargaining over the Defence of Hong Kong, 1949-1957', *The International History Review*, vol. XXII, No. 4, December 2000, pp. 837-61.

[3] See No. 11.

[4] See No. 18.

however, the Chinese Government did not revert to the matter, and no further consideration was given to it.

5. Since then important changes have occurred. At the time when negotiations were contemplated it was hoped that there would be a stable and friendly Government in China, which would play an effective part in the deliberations of the United Nations. Now, insofar as a stable Government of China may emerge, it seems certain that it will be Communist, or Communist-controlled, and sympathetic to Soviet Russia rather than to ourselves. In such circumstances, I feel that it is no longer practicable to consider the New Territories apart from the rest of the Colony. To conclude any arrangement with a Communist Government on any such basis as that mentioned above would inevitably place the Colony in an increasingly precarious position, shorn of defence in depth and without any real assurance that conditions which would be essential to such an arrangement would be faithfully observed.

6. The new situation, therefore calls for re-examination:

(*a*) It is desirable that any line taken should be acceptable to India, Australia, New Zealand and other members of the Commonwealth.

(*b*) The United States Government are not likely to view with favour any uncompromising statement regarding our future possession of Hong Kong. They may stand with us against aggression, but their public is unlikely to discard the view that Britain should remain in China only with the agreement of the Chinese Government.

(*c*) We may well be faced with a request from a Communist Government of China to enter into negotiations about Hong Kong. This is a matter which will require most careful consideration, and my colleagues will no doubt agree that we should embark upon it without further delay.

(*d*) Since in any event the lease of the New Territories expires in 49 years and the life of Hong Kong, e.g. its water supplies, airport facilities, etc., depends in no small part on those Territories, it is the more necessary that we should review our policy for the future of the Colony.

(*e*) Any public reference now to the possibility of future negotiations, or any hint which might leak out that such a possibility is being considered, would have the most damaging effect on morale in Hong Kong at a time when we are endeavouring, by the despatch of reinforcements and in other ways, to strengthen and maintain morale in support of our policy of resistance to Communist aggression.

7. I have consulted the Governor of Hong Kong about the points raised in paragraph 3 of the Foreign Secretary's telegram (Annex I)[5], and I annex a copy of his reply (Annex II). He points out that civil disturbances in Hong Kong would have a prejudicial effect even on that part of its trade (now 80%) which is conducted with countries other than China. Nevertheless, the Governor considers that, in the circumstances envisaged by Mr. Acheson, it will be possible to hold the position in Hong Kong

[5] i.e. those covered in para. 2 of the present memorandum.

indefinitely; and that upon the lifting of the blockade and boycott, and the cessation of internal unrest, the economic recovery of the Colony would probably be rapid.

8. Having regard to the necessity of sending an early reply to Mr. Acheson's enquiries, and to the risk of leakage from the State Department, or from one of the other Commonwealth Governments, who, no doubt, will have to be made aware of our correspondence with the Americans, I suggest that the reply to Mr. Acheson should take the following line:

(*a*) No positive 'assurance' was given to the Chinese Government in 1942.[6] But in 1943 they were informed that, if they desired that the lease of the New Territories should be reconsidered, 'that was a matter which, in the opinion of His Majesty's Government, should be discussed when victory was won'. The Chinese Government thereupon reserved their right to raise the question later. This indication of the willingness of His Majesty's Government to discuss these matters after the war presupposed the existence in China of a stable, unified, democratic and friendly Government. These conditions do not now exist, and it is impossible to forecast when they are likely to arise. But it is assumed that it will be some time before a Government of China emerges with which we could contemplate discussing the future of Hong Kong, or even of the New Territories. Above all, we should certainly not be prepared to discuss these matters under a threat of duress.

(*b*) Nevertheless, we recognise that we are likely to be faced with a request from a Communist Government of China to enter into negotiations about Hong Kong before these conditions are established. We are now considering what our attitude should be to such a request.

(*c*) If the Chinese Communists should try to force our hands by fomenting internal unrest and/or by applying an economic boycott or blockade, it is our intention to maintain order, the essential public services and the economic life of the Colony. In this connection, it is to be noted that over 80% of the trade of Hong Kong is now with countries other than China.

(*d*) Even allowing for the fact that, in the conditions envisaged, it would be necessary to rely on seaborne imports to feed the population of Hong Kong, we see no reason to doubt our capacity to maintain these conditions for as long as may be necessary.

(*e*) (The reply to the State Department's question as to what we hope might come from an appeal to the United Nations is a matter which, I understand, is under consideration by the Foreign Secretary.)

---

[6] As reported in Annex I, the US State Department was under the impression that an assurance had been given to the Chinese Government in 1942 that the UK would be ready after the war to discuss the terms of the leases of the New Territories.

It will be observed that this does not include a reply to Mr. Acheson's enquiry as to the attitude of the British economic interests in the circumstances which he envisages.

9. In view of the terms of paragraph 5 of the Governor's telegram,[7] my colleagues will, no doubt, agree that it will be better to avoid giving an explicit answer in any written communication to the State Department.

A.C.J.

[7] This dealt with the question of a counter blockade against China in the event of action against Hong Kong and read: 'I anticipate that British firms would be willing to play their part at first but if the Communists link boycott of Hong Kong with action against British firms in China it is likely that some of the firms would press for a compromise settlement with the Communists.'

No. 84

Extract from Conclusions of a Meeting of the Cabinet held at 10 Downing Street on 23 June, 1949 at 10 a.m.

CM(49)42 [CAB 128/15]

Secret
China: Defence of Hong Kong[1]
(Previous Reference: CM(49)38th Conclusions, Minute 3)[2]
5. The Cabinet had before them the following memoranda on Hong Kong:

CP(49)134: by the Minister of Defence, reporting on the visit which he had paid to Hong Kong from 6th to 9th June;[3]

CP(49)135: by the Secretary of State for the Colonies, commenting on certain questions which had been raised by the United States Secretary of State when he was asked whether his Government would support a policy of defending Hong Kong against aggression;[4]

CP(49)136: by the Secretary of State for Commonwealth Relations, summarising the response of other Commonwealth Governments to the enquiry whether they would support such a policy.[5]

[1] Present for this item were: Mr. Attlee, Mr. Morrison, Sir S. Cripps, Mr. Alexander, Mr. Dalton, Viscount Addison, Viscount Jowitt, Mr. Chuter Ede, Mr. Creech Jones, Mr. Noel-Baker, Mr. Woodburn, Mr. Isaacs, Mr. Bevan, Mr. Williams, Mr. Tomlinson, Viscount Hall, Mr. Henderson, Mr. Shinwell, Mr. Wilson, Mr. Mayhew, Mt. W.G. Hall (Financial Secretary to the Treasury), Mr. MacDonald, Sir A. Nye, Lord Tedder, Lord Fraser, F-M Sir W. Slim, General Sir N. Ritchie, Sir G. Templer (Vice-Chief of the Imperial General Staff) and Sir J. Eddleston (Vice-Chief of Naval Staff).
[2] See No. 80.
[3] Not printed, but see No. 81, note 3.
[4] No. 83.
[5] No. 82.

THE MINISTER OF DEFENCE and THE SECRETARY OF STATE FOR THE COLONIES informed the Cabinet that action was already being taken to give effect to the specific recommendations made in paragraph 25 of CP(49)134.[6]

Discussion then turned on the attitude of the other Commonwealth Governments. Whole-hearted support, moral as well as material, would be forthcoming from New Zealand; and South Africa had given a firm promise of moral support. The other Commonwealth Governments were, however, reluctant to commit themselves in advance, and evidently entertained misgivings about the long-term prospects of our position in Hong Kong. It was specially disappointing that the Australian Government should have been unwilling to assume any share of responsibility for withstanding Communist encroachment in a part of the world which they professed to regard as being of special concern to them. The Cabinet were, however, informed that, since CP(49)135 was circulated, the Prime Minister of Australia had given a categorical assurance that his Government would not raise the question of Hong Kong at the Security Council without first consulting the United Kingdom Government; and he had also indicated in confidence, that if an attack were actually made upon Hong Kong his Government might well adopt a different attitude on the question of giving material assistance in its defence. The Prime Minister of New Zealand had made it clear that, despite representations from the Australian Government, he was not prepared to withdraw his offer to send three or four frigates to help in the defence of Hong Kong; and, indeed, he was now considering whether he could not also make available some aircraft with crews and ground staff. THE SECRETARY OF STATE FOR COMMONWEALTH RELATIONS said that it might be helpful if he now sent to the Australian Government a fresh appreciation of the position in Hong Kong, which would take account of the impression which the Minister of Defence had formed during his visit.

Discussion then turned on the questions raised by the United States Secretary of State, which were considered in CP(49)135. THE SECRETARY OF STATE FOR THE COLONIES said that, although he had put forward in his paper some tentative suggestions about the reply which might be returned to these questions, he felt that they raised the whole problem of long-term policy in respect of Hong Kong and he thought the time had now come when Ministers must review that problem afresh in the light of the changed conditions in China. THE FOREIGN SECRETARY said that he would propose to avoid sending even an interim reply to Mr. Acheson's questions. He would prefer to undertake at once a thorough review of long-term policy in

[6] This was the concluding paragraph of Mr. Alexander's report on his visit to Hong Kong, and dealt in the main with a series of security matters requiring attention. These involved a speeding up of the registration process for all inhabitants of Hong Kong; an expansion of the Police force (by bringing the number of British officers up to establishment quickly) and of the Hong Kong Volunteer Defence Force (by a campaign of vigorous recruitment); and the appointment of an experienced adviser in Special Branch work.

respect of Hong Kong. From the response to the approaches which had been made to the other Commonwealth Governments and to the Government of the United States, it now appeared that the United Kingdom Government would have to bear the main responsibility for devising effective means of safeguarding British interests in Hong Kong; and he considered that Ministers should lose no time in formulating a positive policy for dealing with the situation. There was general agreement with this view.

The Cabinet

(1) Invited the Secretary of State for Commonwealth Relations to arrange for his Department to prepare, in consultation with the Foreign Office and the Ministry of Defence, a fresh appreciation of the situation in Hong Kong for the information of the Australian Government.

(2) Took note that no reply would be sent for the time being to the questions raised by the United States Secretary of State, as reported in the telegram annexed to CP(49)135.

(3) Invited the Foreign Secretary and the Secretary of State for the Colonies to submit to the China and South-East Asia Committee proposals on long-term policy in respect of Hong Kong.

No. 85

Minute by Mr. Burgess on Communist documents captured in Hong Kong

[F 9267/1016/10]

FOREIGN OFFICE, *25 June 1949*

These documents reached us today.[1] They are being circulated rapidly, because of one rather startling conclusion that it could at least be argued emerges from the programme outlined here.

We know from other captured documents how strictly the CCP stick to their programmes and how long they plan them in advance. These particular examples deal with the economic policy to be followed in South China after it is taken over. They include detailed arrangements for setting up a people's bank, printing JMP notes[2] (with pictures of Mao and a concrete bridge on them), setting up a Communist trading organisation,

[1] A second raid by the colonial police on Communist premises in Hong Kong on 21 April (for the first raid see No. 59, note 10) uncovered a further batch of documents, including the proceedings of the second plenary session of the CCP Central Committee, held between 25 February and 8 March.

[2] Jen Min Piao (Chinese dollar currency introduced by the Communists).

etc. in Kwantung province planned by the CCP well ahead of its liberation (in our calculation still a month or so away).

As such we have some kind of (and certainly the best available) economic blue print for CP economic policy covering Canton and SC.[3] It parallels what has been done in provinces already taken over, Shanghai etc.

A deduction of even greater importance that appears to emerge is a CCP decision *not* to molest Hong Kong following the capture of Kwangtung. Hong Kong is not only *not* included in the plans for Kwangtung but is deliberately excluded. Its problems are analysed separately from those of its hinterland.

Document 6 is the key to this. Here we are dealing with the problem of driving out foreign currencies including the Hong Kong dollar, the chief means of exchange in the future 'liberated' areas. These large-scale plans are not applied to Hong Kong. Further it is categorically assumed that the present *authorities*, as well as the present coinage, will continue to rule in Hong Kong for a period no termination to which is given but which, it emerges, is no short one (document 6, paragraph J, pages 3 and 4).[4]

I have not analysed or even examined carefully the other points in these pps. of vital interest though they may be to Canton. It seemed important to bring the conclusion that the threat to Hong Kong is rather distant to attention at once. SIFE[5] have had these documents for months. They say in their covering note that the papers have not been thought worth analysing as being only of economic importance. But it is precisely from the economic policy of the Communists that one can deduce their political policy. We have found this true over Shanghai. It would seem of particular importance when plans described cover the overall long-term financial and trading policy for the vital Hong Kong area. And long-term political considerations *are* taken into account in this economic analysis e.g. the US slump is catered for as well as the maintenance of the existing régime in Hong Kong.

The details of the economic analysis in fact support the view that Hong Kong, which is referred to as the Colony throughout these documents, will remain an unchallenged one for at least some time. The problems dealt

[3] South China.

[4] None of the documents to which these minutes refer is reproduced here. Document 6, not dated, was entitled: 'Problems on the Issuance of the HK currency, its Circulation, Deflation and Relative Dispositions'. It dealt with the long-term economic organisation of Kwangtung province after its liberation and indicated that in Kwangtung as elsewhere steps would be taken to substitute the Jen Min Piao dollar for other currencies circulating, principally the Hong Kong dollar. Plans to exclude the Hong Kong dollar would not be announced until some three to six months after Kwangtung had been occupied. Significantly, the document envisaged the continuation of colonial administration in Hong Kong after this announcement. Economic plans for the hinterland were developed in detail but no plans were apparently contemplated for Hong Kong itself, nor even for the organisation of economic sabotage.

[5] Security Intelligence Far East.

with flow, as has been said, from Hong Kong's separation from its hinterland in Kwangtung and from the use of different currencies in the Colony and in Kwangtung arising from this political and economic separation. It is significant in calculating the time envisaged by the CCP that even the use of different currencies will not come into operation for a considerable period. Kwangtung has first to be liberated and the trading and financial organisations described set up. It is only 3-6 months after liberation that the banning of the Hong Kong dollar in the liberated provinces is even contemplated for *announcement* and this announcement will only be of the date when the ban will come into force (Document 6, page 5, supplement). The analysis of Hong Kong's economic problems given here only starts from the date on which the ban in the provinces is actually in force or imminent and thus again it assumes that no *early* challenge is intended, or change in Hong Kong's colonial position assumed.

It is further significant that doubt over the status of Hong Kong is introduced but purely as an economic weapon affecting the problems over currency that will face the Colonial administration (Document 6, J1(c)). It is perhaps even more significant that disorders within Hong Kong, whether strikes or incited political disorders, are not so analysed and, query, therefore are not intended, again *immediately* after the Communist troops reach Hong Kong's frontier.

JIC(FE)[6] and the British Defence Co-ordination Committee (FE) in their final revise of JIC(FE)(49)21 on the threat to Hong Kong state as their first conclusion 'the return of Hong Kong to China is an important part of the Chinese Communist programme . . .' (We are asked to comment on this paper and it is suggested that we do so in the light of the conclusions from the documents within.) We had previously reached the conclusion, basing ourselves on speculative evidence, that so far the Chinese Communists have not reached a policy decision as regards Hong Kong (note attached).[7] It is also suggested that we now have positive evidence to show that they may

[6] Joint Intelligence Committee (Far East).

[7] Not printed. This note of 24 June by Mr. Burgess, prepared for Mr. Scarlett's meeting with General Festing (see No. 81), argued that the Chinese Communists themselves had probably not decided on a policy and that they had 'almost certainly not decided on a policy of direct frontal attack'. The captured documents supported these conclusions, as did the indirect evidence of Communist propaganda. Foreign 'imperialism' was constantly attacked but the claim to Hong Kong had never been used. This was in marked contrast to the Communist claim that Formosa should be reunited with the mainland. British administration of Hong Kong was assailed in Communist propaganda, but not British possession of it. The grounds for complaint were the ordinances introduced on 25 May requiring Chinese societies to register with the Government.

The JIC reached the same conclusion. Apart from document No. 6 (see note 4 above), there was no 'hard information' about Communist plans for Hong Kong. However this document could be read as reflecting a decision 'not to molest Hong Kong either internally or externally for a considerable time to come'. It suggested that the trading value of Hong Kong in British hands was of such value to the Communists that they were willing to allow the status quo to continue (JIC(49)44/3 (Final), 23 June 1949, CAB 158/7/1).

have reached a decision *not* to challenge the position for some considerable time though we still have no evidence as to their ultimate intentions. It is also for consideration whether the calculations for the defence plan of the Colony are affected by the deductions we can draw. One can only hope that the defence plans of the Empire have not been disorganised to deal with a speculative threat while ignoring hard evidence tending in the other direction that we have had since 21.4.49.[8]

Whatever may be thought of the wider issue, this Document will be invaluable to Canton and shld. be sent as soon as possible.[9]

G. BURGESS

[8] Mr. Hayter commented here: 'Have we? This seems to be the date of the document, not the date when we got it.'

[9] Mr. Scarlett commented on 27 June: 'It seems to me a perfectly fair political deduction from Document 6 (Flag B) that the Communists are relying on the Govt. of Hong Kong to soak up the HK Dollars on which Kwangtung Province at present lives and that therefore the threat to Hong Kong will not coincide with the arrival of the Communists at the neighbouring coast. This in turn backs up our theory that so long as Hong Kong is useful to the economic life of the Chinese they are the less likely to trouble its peace, by pointing to one way in which the Colony's usefulness has entered Communist calculations.

Even so it seems the greatest pity & a serious reflection on SIFE's powers of evaluation that they did not tumble to this aspect of the matter & that this failure to do so led to the suppression of this paper till now.'

No. 86

Mr. Bevin to Sir R. Stevenson (Nanking)

No. 767 Telegraphic [*F 10022/1219/10*]

Immediate. Secret   FOREIGN OFFICE, *6 July 1949, 6.10 a.m.*

Repeated for information to Hong Kong (for Flag Officer, Second in Command), Shanghai (for Assistant Naval Attaché), and Commander in Chief, Far East Station, Ashore and Afloat.

Amethyst signal 051017 [5th July].[1]

[1] Since the original *Amethyst* incident (see No. 65), negotiations had been in progress in an attempt to secure the ship's release (see No. 75, item 1). These had so far foundered on what the UK considered to be unacceptable Communist terms. *Amethyst* signal 051017 of 5 July indicated that the Communists wanted to include the following clause in a statement about the incident: 'I recognise that HMS AMETHYST and the other three British warships involved in the incident, infringed into China's national river and the CPLA [Chinese People's Liberation Army] frontier zone, without permission of the CPLA being basic fault repetition fault on the part of the British side, regarding this matter.' The clause had been received in Chinese and the translation was that of *Amethyst's* interpreter (F 10023/1219/10). *Amethyst* was at this point under

1. I cannot accept any phraseology which involves our conceding that we were in the wrong. On whatever level it may be conducted the fact remains that this is the first important negotiation we are having with the Communists. If we show willingness to make concessions which jeopardise our whole position in the matter even before actual negotiations begin, the Communists will score such a triumph (which will no doubt be widely publicised) that we may never recover from this initial step.

2. I think it should be made clear to the Communists orally that Amethyst was in the Yangtze with the authorisation of that Government which occupies a seat in the Security Council of the United Nations. I want this to be made clear because it may be that, in the last resort, we shall have to appeal to the United Nations if Amethyst is not released. My guess is that neither the Russians (who still recognise the National Government) nor the Chinese Communists would like the Amethyst case to be brought to the United Nations, and while I do not wish to threaten such action at this stage, I do wish the Communists to know that we are acting within our rights. I am perfectly prepared to negotiate, and if no settlement is reached by direct negotiation, to put the matter if necessary to arbitration. But I cannot accept a position whereby Amethyst continues to be unlawfully detained while I am asked to admit in advance that we were in the wrong, thus jeopardising our whole case.

3. In order to secure the early release of Amethyst I am prepared to agree that the Commander in Chief should admit that the entry of Amethyst into the frontier zone without the concurrence of the CPLA caused a misunderstanding, but you will recall that our reason for not notifying the Communists was that all communications addressed by our officials to Communist authorities up to that time had been ignored. While I do not insist that the reason for non-notification should be included in the statement, I think it should be made clear to the Communists that here too we have good grounds for our attitude.[2]

the command of Lt. Commander J. S. Kerans, Assistant Naval Attaché at Nanking, who had made his way down to the ship after the death of Commander Skinner.

[2] In Nanking telegram No. 1125 of 28 July Sir R Stevenson reported that the prospects of a reasonable settlement did not seem favourable: 'If so time may be soon approaching when in order to break the stalemate we will have to consider alternatives of accepting unquestionably ignominious terms or of resorting to drastic expedients such as scuttling the ship or making a dash for it under cover of darkness with a view to terminating intolerable discourtesy and physical hardship to which the crew are being exposed under intense summer heat of Yangtse Valley' (F 11234/129/10). With the approval of the Commander-in-Chief, Far East Station (see No. 65, note 10), *Amethyst* broke out during the night of 30 July. This was contrary to the wishes of the FO and the Admiralty. Both had requested prior consultation about an escape attempt. The FO was especially concerned that a break-out might have repercussions on British interests, and possibly even British lives, in China. The ship came under fire during the escape. The Communists claimed that *Amethyst* in turn fired on a river steamer causing the deaths of hundreds of passengers. The UK version suggested that Communist batteries had inflicted the damage. A Chinese junk was run down and cut in half by *Amethyst* during the escape (F 11420/1219/10, F 11480/1219/10, F 11508/1219/10).

No. 87

Sir R. Stevenson (Nanking) to Mr. Bevin
(Received 15 July, 4.00 p.m.)

No. 1036 Telegraphic [*F 10513/1015/10*]

Immediate. Secret   NANKING, *15 July 1949, 1.54 p.m.*

Repeated to Washington, Singapore, Ottawa, New Delhi, Canberra.

My immediately preceding telegram (departure of United States Ambassador).[1]

My United States colleague told me and my Commonwealth colleagues today that Communists were seeking to make applicable to him and his staff new regulations governing grant of exit permits to foreign nationals. These regulations stipulate that foreign nationals must obtain 'shop guarantees' before permits can be issued. These are guarantees by an acceptable Chinese business concern that it will be responsible for debts incurred by persons leaving China or for any civil or criminal liabilities. United States Ambassador had gone into the matter as regards the members of his staff who are accompanying him and found that all Chinese firms approached were too frightened to give the required guarantee. Communists had then been asked whether guarantees by foreign firms would be acceptable. No reply has yet been received. As regards himself he had suggested that Communist head of Nanking Foreign National Bureau (an ex-pupil of his) and Mr. Fugh (his Chinese adviser who is in fact accompanying him) should be guarantors. No reply has been received to this suggestion.

2. My Commonwealth colleagues and I were unanimous in regarding Communist attitude as indefensible. Right of unhindered exit of Ambassadors and Diplomatic Staffs with necessary diplomatic privileges and immunities has never been questioned even by states at war. Acceptance of Communist demand for guarantees would thus create a most undesirable precedent. At our suggestion the whole matter has been referred by the United States Ambassador to the State Department for a ruling. It is much to be hoped that United States Government will not (repeat not) give way on this matter of principle even if it means that the heads of Missions will be held here as hostages.

---

[1] Nanking telegram No. 1035 of 15 July explained that the US Ambassador was making preparations 'to leave some time next week'. The date was being kept secret because safe conduct was not being sought from the Nationalists. After his departure the US Chargé d'Affaires would be Mr. Lewis Clarke in Canton.

3. In the case of my Afghan colleague who, I understand, received an exit permit before the issue of the new regulations, the guarantee was furnished by the official whom he has left in charge of Afghan Legation. I have passed this information on to my United States colleague.

4. My Commonwealth colleagues would be grateful if the contents of this telegram and of my immediately preceding telegram could be communicated to their respective Governments.[2]

---

[2] A compromise was reached on 27 July whereby the State Department agreed that the US Embassy at Nanking would act as the necessary guarantor for the Communist authorities. By such means Dr. Stuart and his staff obtained exit permits and left China on 2 August. The State Department was anxious that the Ambassador should leave before the publication of its White Paper on China (*FRUS, 1949*, vol. viii, pp. 799-809.) This was eventually published on 5 August (see No. 91, note 2).

No. 88

Mr. Bevin to Sir F. Hoyer-Millar (Washington)[1]

No. 1067 [*F 11001/1023/10*]

Secret   FOREIGN OFFICE, *21 July 1949*

Sir,

The United States Ambassador[2] called on me today at his request to talk about China.

2. Mr. Douglas said that Mr. Dean Acheson was anxious to continue the exchanges which I had had with him during the Council of Foreign Ministers in Paris with particular reference to China.[3] We were confronted with a number of problems of concern to both our countries, such as the question of recognition of a Communist régime; the effect of such

---

[1] HM Minister in Washington.

[2] Mr. Lewis Douglas.

[3] Mr. Bevin discussed China with Mr. Acheson at a meeting of the Council of Foreign Ministers at Paris in May 1949. Referring to this, and another private conversation about China with Mr. Acheson in Washington when, on both occasions, Mr. Bevin had spoken of the UK and the US taking 'a trip round the world' to see if they could develop common policies, Mr. Douglas commented: 'Mr. Acheson hopes that we can have a thorough and frank exchange of views regarding the Far East in a "matey sort of way" as you expressed it in Paris when the question of Hong Kong was discussed. You will recall that the United Kingdom has strongly urged the need of a firm position in case the Communists attack Hong Kong and has asked for our support. Would this not imply the need for a firm position all along the line?' Mr. Douglas enclosed with his letter a short memorandum on 'Far Eastern Problems Requiring an Urgent Solution' that dealt with the issues mentioned in paragraph 2 of Mr. Bevin's letter to Sir F. Hoyer-Millar. The memorandum concluded by suggesting that other interested governments should be consulted: 'We think first steps along such lines should be taken by the Asiatic states, preferably under Nehru's leadership' (letter to Mr. Bevin of 22 July 1949, F 10976/1023/10).

recognition in the United Nations Organisation; the question of trading with China and whether such trade would not strengthen the hands of the Communists. Mr. Acheson would like all these problems to be discussed between us. The State Department had not yet formed a view as to whether the scope of such discussions should be extended to include other interested countries, notably the Members of the British Commonwealth, and they would welcome our opinion on this.

3. I told Mr Douglas that I would think the matter over, and let him have a reply. Quite frankly, I had not expected to be confronted with the China problem so soon. At present I was concerning myself with the Middle East, and with the Kashmir problem between India and Pakistan. I agreed that the China problem must be considered too, and I hoped I should be in a position to discuss it with Mr. Acheson when I went with the Chancellor to Washington.

4. I have since sent a letter to Mr. Douglas, saying that I am very willing that our officials should consult together on the problems which he outlined to me, and I have said that I will look into the question further when I return from the Continent.[4]

I am, &c.,
ERNEST BEVIN

[4] Mr. Dening minuted on 22 July: 'For the past 3 years we have been trying to get the Americans to be frank with us over China and Japan and all our efforts have failed. The Americans have gone their own way, with unhappy results for everyone. Now they are asking us to discuss China and Japan ... I think we should welcome this as the best way in which to try to keep American policy on the right lines. It will not involve us in any wider commitments; it will merely mean a more active diplomacy by us in FE affairs which we are well equipped by past experience to conduct.' Mr. Scarlett added (22 July): 'The S of S commented that we must stop the Americans from talking about "under Nehru's leadership". This would not be acceptable to some of the other powers concerned.'

No. 89

Record by Mr. Scarlett of a Meeting with the China Association on 28 July[1]

[*F 11603/1153/10*]

FOREIGN OFFICE, *29 July 1949*

MR. KESWICK, who is Chairman of the China Association, explained that he had asked Mr. McNeil to receive them only after the most exhaustive discussion with the members of the Association about the position and future of British interests in Communist China. Individual firms were now persuaded that they were facing a situation in which they could no longer help themselves. They had therefore turned to the China Association for advice and before giving that advice he had felt bound to ask whether His Majesty's Government could see any hope for the future or had any advice or help to offer the British firms concerned with the China trade. The financial position of all firms was serious: for many it was already desperate. This arose from two factors: on the one hand the sterling exchange rate was unrealistic and on the other, the Communist authorities had tied wages to the price of rice which was soaring in terms of local currency. At the same time, the Nationalist blockade[2] which HMG regarded as illegal was effective so far as the port of Shanghai was concerned and imports had consequently ceased. A few British firms still had stocks to market and were therefore able to meet their wages bill by local sales but this could not last long. Already the majority were living on remittances from London at the rate of £350,000 monthly and this, besides being bad finance, represented a burden which could not be carried for long. Reuters Agency had already decided to close down. Sir Victor

---

[1] The China Association was represented at this meeting by Mr. Keswick (see No. 1, note 11), Sir John Masson (Butterfield and Swire), Mr. Cockburn (Chartered Bank), Mr. Vignoles (Shell Company), and Mr. Mitchell (see No. 39, note 3). The FO was represented by Mr. McNeil, Mr. Dening, and Mr. Scarlett.

[2] In an attempt to isolate Communist-held ports in China the Nationalist government used its air and naval predominance to announce, on 20 June 1949, that the coastal region within Chinese territorial waters from the mouth of the Liao Ho River in North China (East longitude 122 degrees 20 minutes and North latitude 40 degrees 30 minutes) to the estuary of the Mia-Chiang River (East longitude 119 degrees 40 minutes and North latitude 26 degrees 15 minutes) would be temporarily closed and all foreign ships were strictly prohibited from sailing into this region. It was then announced that from midnight on 26 June any alien ship violating this rule would be restrained, and that any foreign ship endangering itself through violation of this rule would have to bear all responsibility. At the same time the line of closure was extended from the estuary of the Minkiang River (East longitude 119 degrees 40 minutes and North latitude 26 degrees 15 minutes) to the western tip of the Tienpai Hsien (East longitude 111 degrees 20 minutes and North latitude 21 degrees 30 minutes).

Sassoon[3] who owned vast interests had decided to cut his losses. Lesser firms had already reached a similar decision individually but were seeking guidance from the Association before actually implementing these. If the outcome of this meeting was that HMG could offer no hope of taking action to mitigate the situation, Mr. Keswick felt that the Association could only advise members to cut their losses as soon as they felt they must.

Against this background he had two questions to ask: (1) would HMG consider taking active steps to break the Nationalist blockade of Shanghai, with or without the co-operation of the United States? (2) if not, would HMG examine the possibility of blocking remittances of sterling to China as a gambit to bring the Communist authorities to their senses? He realised that such a course was fraught with difficulties and would entail considerable hardship to individuals and possibly even physical danger. His only excuse for recommending it was that the Association felt that some drastic remedy was needed to meet a growingly desperate situation.

The MINISTER OF STATE assured the Association of the very real concern and anxiety with which both the Foreign Office and HMG were following the fortunes of British firms in China at the present time. He felt, however, that he could do British business no greater disservice than to use any words which might engender optimism. His impression of all he had heard and read about Communist policies in China was that, whether from blank ignorance or deliberate policy, the Communists were deliberately avoiding contacts with foreign traders unless forced to make them by immediate and compelling circumstances.

As to Mr. Keswick's first point, he could assure the Association that the possibility of dealing with the Nationalist blockade had been recently considered by Ministers who had reached the conclusion that in this matter HMG should not act without the co-operation of the United States. We had sought this co-operation to effect a limited objective, namely the convoying of essential relief supplies into Shanghai but the State Department had refused initially to go along with us. We had now gone back to them again and were awaiting their reply.[4] Though he could hold out little hope that this would be more favourable, we had not necessarily said our last word to Washington and our views might yet prevail. He expressed this qualified optimism in the belief that the US Government

---

[3] Governing Director, E.D. Sassoon Banking Company Ltd.

[4] Briefing Mr. Attlee on 12 August about the blockade of Shanghai, Mr. McNeil observed: 'The present position is that, as a result of our representations, the Americans have agreed to make a parallel approach to the Chinese National Government asking them to permit ships to enter Shanghai without interference. The Americans, of course, want the ships through primarily for evacuation purposes. We on the other hand want them through for supply purposes... Our policy is beginning to diverge from that of the Americans, who are advocating the withdrawal of American firms from China. Our policy is that so long as our trading concerns are prepared to stay, we should encourage them to do so. Our interests in China are far greater than those of the United States, and to uproot them entirely would be grave at any time, and particularly so just now' (FO 800/462, FE/49/17).

were not actuated in their refusal by deliberate policy since, to the best of our belief, they had in fact little or no policy towards China at the present time. In the field of diplomacy the Chinese Ambassador had been sternly spoken to and we had also made strong representations against the blockade to the Chinese authorities in Canton and in Formosa. He could only assure the Association that HMG would do everything they could to influence the situation and that the Association would be kept confidentially informed of our progress.

As to the question of blocking sterling remittances, Mr. McNeil said that this was a new thought to him. It was clearly one which would need the fullest and most careful consideration and it would be explored in conjunction with other interested Departments forthwith.[5]

P.W. SCARLETT

[5] At the end of the meeting Mr. Keswick explained to Mr. McNeil his own view that whatever the political complexion of its government, China would have to raise loans on the international market. There was nothing left in mainland China to serve as security and so far as Mr. Keswick was aware the only potential security for a loan lay in Formosa. He understood that Formosa was not yet legally Chinese territory because of the delay in concluding a Japanese peace treaty and he wondered whether this might provide an opportunity to ventilate the possibility of Formosa being placed under international control. According to the record, Mr. McNeil 'could not begin to think how such a change in status could be negotiated within the United Nations but he agreed that it was worth examining further among ourselves'.

No. 90

Sir A. Grantham (Hong Kong) to Mr. Creech Jones
(Received 10 August, 8.40 p.m.)

No. 824 Telegraphic [*FO 800/462*]

Secret   HONG KONG, *10 August 1949*[1]

Repeated to Nanking, No. 125. Savingram to Commissioner General Singapore.

Chinese Communist Party Dissensions and Intentions.

Fitzgerald,[2] former British Council Representative in Peking, arrived here three days ago from Peking. He was the bearer of an important message from Chou En Lai for HMG. This message was passed to him by Michael Keon, Australian journalist, who represented United Press in Peking and stayed on there after foreign correspondent facilities were withdrawn. Keon was in Nanking early in 1947 during time of Communist-

[1] Time of despatch is not recorded on the filed copy.
[2] British Council records indicate that a Mr. C.P. Fitzgerald served in China but his dates are not clear.

Nationalist negotiations. At that time he was Press Head to Australian Embassy, [and] was rather a troublesome character. In Nanking he came into contact with Chou En Lai and number of other communist officials; subsequently he visited 'liberated' Shantung for several months having by this time left the Australian Embassy. Keon, although he has been personally abused in Peking communist press as a foreign correspondent, has privately maintained his previous contacts and seen them from time to time.

2. About two months ago Fitzgerald was asked by Wen Ching, Chou En Lai's Secretary, if he was prepared to meet Chou. He was asked on no account to reveal that he had seen Chou and he was to refer to him as a 'very high communist official'. For various reasons Chou did not wish to use consular channels for transmitting a message to HM Government and in giving Keon message he emphasized repeatedly that greatest care should be taken to keep his name out. Fitzgerald's departure from Peking provided that suitable opportunity of getting message safely out.

Chou's message is as follows:

3. There are two parties or groups within Chinese Communist Party. (*a*) One group is wholly convinced that third world war is inevitable and will come soon. China must in this war line up (with) Soviet Union and it would be mere waste of time to establish any relations with the Western Powers. Leaders of this group are Liu Shao Chi (leading theorist and organiser of the party who is violently pro-Russian) and Peng Teh Huai.[3] (Li Li San,[4] it should be noted, is not considered so important inside Communist China as he is outside.)

(*b*) Second group comprises those who took part in Nanking peace talks and is headed by Chou himself. Other principal figures are Yeh Chien Ying (present Mayor of Peking) and (corrupt groups) Lin Piao.[5] This group wish to normalise relations with West. They do not think third world war is necessarily imminent. They wish to bring China back to normal and create peaceful conditions under which social reforms and (corrupt group) can be completed.

4. Mao Tse Tung himself has succeeded in remaining generally above these party dissensions. In the meantime these two groups are contending and ultimately party line will be that of party which prevails. Present position is:

(*a*) Chou considers his group is in ascent. Time and events are playing for them. Economic difficulties which New China is now experiencing show the need for peace and normal relations with the West. He says that

---

[3] Military commander and member of CCP Politburo from 1945.

[4] *De facto* party leader from 1928, dismissed on Stalin's orders in 1930, spending the next fifteen years as an involuntary exile in Russia.

[5] Commanding general of Communist armies, acknowledged as an exceptional military strategist.

other group generally understands nothing about the outside world and modern economic conditions and are apt to over simplify the problem.

(*b*) Chou stresses that it must be realised that Chinese Communist Party have won greatest victory in Chinese history. They have come to stay. They are hundred per cent convinced communist and they consider communism is the only answer to China's problems. They realise it will be slow and lengthy and it may take lifetime of all of them.

(*c*) Chou's line (corrupt group) he hopes for normal diplomatic relations with Western powers on a basis equal and reciprocity (whatever that may mean). He says that if he is in charge of foreign policy it would not necessarily follow that China's veto in Security Council would always follow Soviet vote. He would follow China's interest and would use China's vote to reconcile rather than to aggravate existing conflict between the West and Soviet bloc.

(*d*) Chou group do not (repeat do not) control propaganda bureau and organs of CCP. He therefore asks that party be judged by their acts not by their words. Propaganda line may be extravagant and lip service will be paid to solidarity with Russia. Chou asks HMG to see further than this.

5. When originally giving this message to Keon, Chou En Lai stressed that it was not urgent and that it did not call for any action yet. The party line had not yet been cleared and struggle was still continuing. In any event nothing much could be done before a central Government for communist China had been established.

6. On 15th July Keon saw Chou En Lai at (latter's?) request. He said that message still stood. He went on to say that an open disagreement had now arisen between two groups over the question of Russia's demands for concessions in Manchuria. Uranium has been discovered north of Chiamussu in Manchuria and Russians have asked for concessions. They have also asked for concessions for uranium deposits in Sinkiang. In Central Committee of CCP Lin Piao had taken an exceedingly strong line on this question. He expressed his strong hatred of all foreigners. He recalled how his wife had been tortured by the KMT whom he regarded as instrument of foreign imperialists. He said Russians were foreigners as much as anyone else and that one imperialist was as bad as any other. He would therefore resist Russian imperialism as he would any other. It appears that Lin Piao's forces in the People's Liberation Army are as numerous as all other units combined, and he still effectively controls all forces in Manchuria, as well as units at Shanhaikuan and along the two main trunk railways.

7. The rift over Russian demands for concessions has aggravated the tension between the two groups and Lin Piao's forthrightness has strengthened the position of Chou En Lai's group. Chou En Lai is apparently much distressed at these dissensions occurring at moment when victory is in sight but he believes that they will be overcome. The victory of one group over the other will be signalled by purges and possible

liquidation of all opposition elements and unity of CCP will thus be maintained.[6]

8. Chou's message has already been passed on to Americans through David Barratt Assistant US Military Attaché in Peking. Thorn[7] passed it on to War Department who in turn passed it to State Department and it seems that it got back to Doctor Stuart. Chou is understood to have been apprehensive that message should reach Stuart as he feared it would get to the ear of latter's Chinese private secretary Philip Fu whom he did not trust. Barrett is reported to have had one interview with Chou but it is not satisfactory. Barrett asked whether in the event of war with Russia the communists would welcome landing US forces in China. Chou gave emphatic 'no'.

9. Finally Fitzgerald told me that he understands that preparatory committee of consultative conference has already taken all decisions and that when conference meets probably in September or early October it will merely rubber-stamp these decisions. Only decision that he knows to be final is that Peking will be the Capital.[8]

[6] The same message had been conveyed to the US Government in June. The State Department sent a response with instructions that, as a safeguard against possible distortion, it should be communicated 'on plain paper without signature or designation source'. Prior to his departure from China an invitation was extended to Dr. Stuart to meet Mao Tse-tung and Chou En-lai in Peking. It was declined. For details, see *FRUS 1949*, vol. viii, pp. 357-410 (pp. 384-85 for the reply) and 766-69.

[7] No reference to an official of this name has been found in State Department records. Possibly this is a reference to Mr. W.L. Thorp, Assistant Secretary for Economic Affairs, who worked on US aid to China in 1948.

[8] While conceding that China might ultimately become another Soviet satellite, the Far Eastern Department had not ruled out the possibility of its becoming another Yugoslavia. Mr. Dening saw no reason for a change in the UK policy of 'keeping a foot in the door and of waiting to see how things work out'. He assumed that as they were moving towards evacuation and the severance of contacts with the Chinese Communists, the Americans would regard the message as a plant and urge that it should be ignored. Mr. Dening did not think the message called for a reply from the UK 'at present' but concluded: 'The Department's view remains, however, that we should not be openly hostile to Communist China, and that our only hope of exercising any influence on the future of a Communist-dominated China will be through our interests which are already there' (minute of 16 August, F 12075/1015/10).

Mr. E.E. Tomkins, an Assistant Private Secretary to Mr. Bevin, minuted on 17 August: 'The S/S says that this move of Chou En-lai's reminds him very much of the attitude adopted at one time or another by various less extremist politicians in Soviet satellite states. He points out that whether we respond to approaches from so called moderates or not, the extremists always won. All in all, the S/S tends to the view that this move is in accordance with standard Soviet tactics.'

Asked to comment, Sir R. Stevenson suggested that the round-about method by which the message had been communicated, and the time elapsed since its delivery, militated against its accuracy. He regarded neither Mr. Keon nor Mr. Fitzgerald as reliable messengers. But whether the message was a 'serious and honest approach or a rhetorical gesture', the Ambassador thought that it provided an 'authoritative insight into the inner Councils of the Chinese Communists' and that it was important for this reason. He put forward two possible interpretations. First, that it was designed to lull UK and US apprehensions that the increasing virulence of Communist propaganda would result in the abandonment of trade. Secondly, that it was an attempt by Chou En-lai to ingratiate himself with foreign powers in anticipation that he might have to seek asylum in Hong Kong or Japan to escape a purge (Nanking telegram No. 1370 of 30 August, F 12952/1015/10).

No. 91

Record of a conversation between Mr. McNeil and Mr. Kennan[1]

[FO 800/462]

Top Secret   FOREIGN OFFICE, *11 August 1949*

Conversations with Mr. Kennan on the Far East were interrupted by his visit to France. In the interval before their resumption the U.S. Embassy presented a note officially suggesting Anglo-U.S conversations on this subject.

A. *China*

Mr. Kennan said that the State Department were expecting shortly to publish a White Paper[2] on past events in China which they hoped would confound their critics. It was likely to contain material (including General Wedemeyer's Report)[3] which would come as a surprise to the American public.

2. As to the future, the Americans are studying whether there remain in China any elements capable of offering effective resistance to the Chinese Communists and worthy of support. If such elements are found to exist the United States would support them but the prevailing view is that no elements exist which can really be relied upon not to come to terms with the Communists, or to maintain effective resistance.

[1] Mr. G.F. Kennan, Director of the Policy Planning Staff in the US State Department, who visited London for discussions in July-August 1949. Only that part of the record dealing with China is reproduced here.

[2] Department of State Publication 3573, *United States Relations with China, With Special Reference to the Period 1944-1949* (Washington, Government Printing Office, 1949). The White Paper was in fact published on 5 August (see No. 87, note 2). For documentation about whether and when it should be published, see *FRUS 1949*, vol. ix, pp. 1365ff. The White Paper was intended to counter domestic criticism of US policy in China but it had the opposite effect. In large part this was because it seemed contradictory. In a Letter of Transmittal to the President dated 30 July, Mr. Acheson argued that the outcome of the civil war in China was 'beyond the control of the government of the United States'. But while the Letter then suggested that the civil war was 'the product of internal Chinese forces, forces which this country has tried to influence but could not', it also maintained that China was being exploited by a party in the interests of a 'foreign imperialism' (State Department Publication 3608, *A Summary of American-Chinese Relations*).

[3] See No. 28.

3.   As regards the Communists themselves, Mr. Kennan said there was some evidence—though he would not wish to exaggerate it—that they were becoming somewhat restive over Russian activities at Dairen and Port Arthur. This was perhaps natural since Russia was the only remaining power with extra-territorial rights in Chinese Territory. He seemed to think that this might have some propaganda value but it was pointed out to him that we were more vulnerable than the Americans in this regard since the Chinese Communists would tend to look upon the Hong Kong leased territories as being also extra-territorial.

4.   The Americans are studying what to do about the Chinese Communists, and want to consult with us. Their preliminary view is that, on a governmental level, we should make no concessions to the Chinese Communists unless they recognise and adhere to the principle of reciprocity. The State Department have not much sympathy with the American community in Shanghai whom they regard as hostages. The community were given the opportunity to go and did not do so because they hoped to make money. That being so the Administration appear to regard them as an embarrassment not meriting much consideration.

5.   The Americans want to go into the whole question of trade policy with us. Reference was made to the recent talks in London on the question of the control of strategic raw materials.[4] Mr. Kennan was told that this question is being referred to the Ministers here. As part of this submission we are considering whether we, together with the Americans and the Dutch, cannot so control supplies of oil to the Chinese Communists as to ensure that they are not able to build up stocks for military purposes. Reference was made to the difficulty of getting our respective merchant interests to exercise restraint in trading with the Communists. Mr. Kennan said he recognised that we could not prevent our merchants from trading. What we must try to ensure is that governments make no concessions to the Communists unless and until they recognise that they must treat us properly.

6.   On Hong Kong, Mr. Kennan said that the Americans regard this as a problem for the United Kingdom, but they would be very interested to know how we propose to handle the situation, and to what extent we expect American support.

7.   On the subject of Formosa, Mr. Kennan said the State Department had been considering a number of courses and were not quite certain which to follow. He appeared to have no confidence that the Nationalist forces in Formosa, numbering some 300,000, would offer effective resistance to Communist penetration since they brought Communist infiltration with them from the mainland. He thought it by no means impossible that a Communist regime would establish itself in Formosa as a result of defections from the Nationalist side. A development towards which

---

[4] Cf. No. 94, Annexes D and E.

the Americans would not be unsympathetic would be if the Formosans themselves were to revolt against Chinese misrule. In that event the whole issue might be aired before the United Nations. Since we and the Americans were suspect, Mr. Kennan thought it might be useful if some Asiatic country like the Philippines or India would take up the Formosa issue. It was pointed out to him that neither India nor the Philippines had any representation in Formosa, so that they did not know what was going on there. At present India is tending to take a rather unrealistic view about Chinese communism.

8. When the conversations were resumed on July 23rd Mr. Kennan was told, with reference to the approach made by Mr. Douglas to the Secretary of State about talks on China,[5] of the Secretary of State's suggestion to Mr. Douglas that, after discussions at the official level, he should discuss the whole question with Mr. Acheson during his forthcoming visit to Washington. Reference was also made to the Secretary of State's suggestion that Mr. Dening might accompany him for these talks. Mr. Kennan was asked whether he thought these suggestions would be welcome.

9. Mr. Kennan said that Mr. Acheson had become fully conscious of the fact that the Far East had tended to be bypassed in view of the urgency of the European and Middle East problems. He had now given directions that a full study was to be made of the whole situation. Mr. Kennan therefore thought that we should find the Americans both willing and ready to cover the whole field during the Secretary of State's forthcoming visit to Washington. It was agreed that it would be desirable to have discussions at the official level in order to prepare the way for these talks. As regards the press, Mr. Kennan said the American attitude would be that when Foreign Ministers met together it was natural that they should cover the whole field of subjects of mutual interest. It would therefore be unnatural if the Secretary of State and Mr. Acheson were not to discuss Far Eastern questions when they met in Washington.[6]

[5] See No. 88.

[6] The record continued with a discussion of Japan and South-East Asia. On the question of resistance to Communism in South-East Asia, Mr. Kennan 'made it clear that the Americans consider the main task to fall to members of the British Commonwealth. The United States could not contemplate joining any pact like the North Atlantic Pact with South-East Asia. The most they might be prepared to do would be to join in a pact which covered the fringe of the Asiatic continent, to include countries such as the Philippines, Australia and New Zealand.' The impression was left that the US expected the UK to take the lead in South-East Asia. The Americans would not consider military commitments and it would probably be difficult to persuade them to give economic help. Mr. Kennan argued that the military threat to South-East Asia from Russia was negligible and that the countries concerned had to learn that in the event of war 'they must be capable of defending themselves'. Cf. Nos. 108, note 2, and 116.

No. 92

Memorandum by Mr. Bevin and Mr. Creech Jones on Hong Kong[1]
CP(49)177 [CAB 129/36]

Secret   *19 August 1949*

On 23rd June (C.M.(49)42nd Conclusions, Minute 5) the Cabinet invited us to submit proposals on long-term policy in respect of Hong Kong.[2] As our colleagues are aware, the United States authorities have asked us for information about our policy towards Hong Kong (telegram No. 113 of 8th June from the United Kingdom Delegation to the Council of Foreign Ministers, Paris, at Annex A).[3] There is also outstanding a considered reply to the telegram No. 365 of 1st June (at Annex B)[4] from the United Kingdom High Commissioner in Australia outlining the attitude of the Australian Prime Minister towards the situation in Hong Kong.

2. At Annex C we give some factual information about Hong Kong, some notes on the value to ourselves, to the local inhabitants, and indeed to China itself, of the maintenance of the British connexion, and on our ability to maintain our position there in the face of Chinese hostility. Annex D is a summary of assurances given by His Majesty's Government since 1942 about the future of Hong Kong; and a map of the Colony is also annexed.

3. Our consideration of the problem of Hong Kong has led us to the conclusion that, since it is not possible to predict with any certainty how the situation will develop in China, it is not possible or desirable to attempt to determine a long-term policy for the future of Hong Kong. In some respects the situation we are faced with in Hong Kong is similar to that which faced us—and to some extent still faces us—in Berlin. Just as we cannot foresee with certainty how the future of Berlin will develop but are convinced of the necessity of remaining there, so we are impelled to remain in Hong Kong without any clear indication of the extent or duration of the military commitment involved. In both cases the threat of Russian and Communist expansionism necessitates holding what we have and not withdrawing.

4. In the case of Hong Kong there are (over and above our unassailable legal right to be there) other cogent reasons for our remaining. These reasons are summarised in paragraph 3 of Annex C.[5]

---

[1] The Annexes to this memorandum are not printed.

[2] See No. 84.

[3] Cf. No. 83.

[4] Cf. No. 82.

[5] The reasons had remained unchanged since the 1946 analysis (see No. 18). They were: the interests and wishes of the inhabitants of Hong Kong; the value of Hong Kong as a port and place of exchange for international trade in the Far East; the strategic value of Hong Kong; and

334

5. The weakness of our future position in Hong Kong arises from the fact, which we must accept, that both Nationalism and Communism in China are likely to have as their aim the eventual recovery by one means or another not only of the Leased Territories but also of the ceded areas of the Colony. Such recovery could be attempted by the threat or actual use of force; by pressure, or by peaceful negotiation.

Threat or Actual Use of Force

6. We have already taken steps to meet the threat or actual use of force, and, the position being thus safeguarded, it may well be found that no threat will develop. We have indicated clearly that we are not prepared to allow interference by the Chinese Communists in our own territories, and this indication of policy has strengthened local morale. Were we, however, to withdraw our forces, and thus allow it to be implied that we are not prepared to stand our ground, the results throughout South-East Asia would be disastrous. There is no doubt that the successes of the Chinese Communists have already had a profound effect in this region, where there are very large Chinese populations. It is a characteristic of Chinese, wherever they may be, to come to terms with the Government in being in China proper. There are already signs, for example in Siam, that this process has begun. Unless it is made unmistakably clear that the Governments of South-East Asia territories are firmly determined to fulfil their obligations and to suppress Chinese Communist interference in their affairs, there is a very real danger that Chinese communities in these areas will support the Communist cause, not so much from conviction as from a traditional tendency to give way to the inevitable.

7. We cannot afford to allow South-East Asia to become dominated by Communism. Apart from our historical obligations towards Malaya and the fact that it is our most important dollar earner, South-East Asia is a provider of foodstuffs and raw materials which are essential to the economy of the West as a whole. From the economic point of view alone, the loss of this region would be a disaster. Politically and strategically the consequences would be equally grave.

8. The fact that Asian peoples tend as a rule to swing in the direction of greater power makes it essential that we should not weaken at Hong Kong. For weakness there would be interpreted without any doubt as the beginning of a general retreat, and the Asian peoples would immediately begin to turn their thoughts towards making terms with the new power of Communism as the only visible alternative.

9. It can be argued that in our straitened circumstances we cannot afford to remain so extended so far from the centre of our own activities and commitments in Europe and the Middle East. But the preceding paragraphs provide evidence that we cannot afford to abandon our position

the expressed or implied undertakings given by HMG that no alteration in the status of Hong Kong was contemplated.

in South-East Asia. Nor shall we be entirely alone and without support if we decide to stay. The United States Secretary of State is reported as having said at a recent press conference that, if any action were taken against Hong Kong which the United States considered a violation of the Charter of the United Nations, then the United States would fully meet its obligations under the Charter. If support of our position in Hong Kong is to be maintained, it is important to explain it fully to our friends and in particular to the other members of the British Commonwealth and the United States.

The Use of Pressure

10. The same considerations as those mentioned above apply to attempts by the Chinese Communists to render our position in Hong Kong untenable by stirring up internal unrest, strikes, &c. Only the evidence that we are prepared to deal with these attempts will convince the Chinese population of Hong Kong that stable government under British aegis will continue. Given that conviction, they will prefer British law and order to Chinese chaos and disorder, even though they will not admit this in public; if they lack that conviction they will come to terms with the Communists even though they may fear and dislike them.

Peaceful Negotiations

11. There remains to be considered an attempt by a Chinese Government to recover Hong Kong through peaceful negotiation. The Chinese Government of the day raised the question of the termination of the lease of the New Territories at the time of the surrender of our extra-territorial rights in China in January 1943. They were told that in the view of His Majesty's Government it was a matter for consideration 'after victory was won.' The 'Hong Kong problem' was raised again by Chiang Kai-shek in 1946 and also by Dr. Wellington Koo, then Chinese Ambassador in London, but it was not pressed.[6] It is hardly a live issue any longer with the National Government of China.

12. If and when a Communist Central Government of China is set up, it is conceivable that they may seek to initiate discussions with the United Kingdom about the future of Hong Kong. This presupposes that we, together with other Powers, have entered into diplomatic relations with the new Government. For our part, however, we must postulate that in addition we should not be prepared to discuss the future of Hong Kong with the new Government unless it were friendly, democratic, stable and in control of a united China.

13. We cannot agree to negotiate about Hong Kong with a Government which is unfriendly, since we should be negotiating under duress. We should equally refuse to discuss the future of Hong Kong with a Government which is undemocratic, since we should not be prepared to hand the people of Hong Kong over to a Communist regime. Finally, we should be unwilling to discuss Hong Kong with a China which is not

[6] See No. 11.

336

united, because its future would be likely to become a pawn in the contest between conflicting factions. Unless there were a stable Government we could not rely on it to preserve Hong Kong as a secure free port and place of exchange between China and the rest of the world.

14. On the basis of present information a Communist Government of China, when it is set up, is unlikely to fulfil any of the conditions enumerated in the preceding paragraph. The question of discussing the future of Hong Kong is therefore likely to be academic for some time to come, and no useful purpose would be served at this stage by trying to estimate how we should meet a hypothetical situation.

15. The lease of the New Territories is due to expire in 1997. It does not seem likely that when that time comes any Chinese Government will be prepared to renew the lease. Without these territories Hong Kong would be untenable, and it is therefore probable that before 1997 the United Kingdom Government of the day will have to consider the status of Hong Kong. But we are surely not justified some two generations in advance of the event in attempting to lay down the principles which should govern any arrangement which it may be possible to reach with China at that time. In the intervening years there will be developments of one kind or another in China, and it is upon these developments that the willingness or otherwise of the United Kingdom Government of the day to reach an accommodation will probably depend.

Conclusion

16. The conclusion which we reach is therefore that, while we should be prepared to discuss the future of Hong Kong with a friendly and democratic and stable Government of a unified China, the conditions under which such discussions could be undertaken do not exist at present and are unlikely to exist in the foreseeable future. Until conditions change, we intend to remain in Hong Kong, and should so inform other Commonwealth Governments and the United States, while refraining in public from pronouncements which exacerbate our relations with China.

Recommendations

17. We recommend—

(i) that the Foreign Secretary be authorised to communicate to the United States Secretary of State for his confidential information the conclusion of this paper and the reasons which have led to it, and that he should seek the support of the United States Government;
(ii) that the Lord Privy Seal[7] should similarly inform other Commonwealth Governments.

The people of Hong Kong are very sensitive to the slightest suggestion that His Majesty's Government might be contemplating negotiations with China about Hong Kong and the merest hint at present that this possibility was being even considered, let alone discussed with other Governments,

[7] Viscount Addison.

would destroy the confidence which it has taken considerable military reinforcements to build up. Every precaution should therefore be taken to guard against any leakage and the importance of this should be stressed in the approaches to other Governments.[8]

E.B.
A.C.J.

[8] In discussion of this memorandum in Cabinet on 29 August some Ministers suggested that the only chance of maintaining a UK presence in Hong Kong was to enlist US support in placing the colony under an international régime. If such a proposal were to be put forward at all, it should be put forward quickly, before conditions in China deteriorated further. Against this it was argued that any move over Hong Kong would be interpreted as a sign of British weakness in the Far East, and that this would undermine all the efforts being made to stem Communist encroachment throughout South-East Asia. In further discussion attention was drawn to the use of the word 'democratic' in paragraphs 12 and 16 of the memorandum. If accepted, this would have the effect of precluding the UK from discussing Hong Kong at any time with a Communist government of China. The Cabinet endorsed, as an interim policy, the conclusion set out in paragraph 16, subject to the omission of the words 'and democratic'. Mr. Bevin was invited to give further consideration to the suggestion that Hong Kong might be placed under international control and, if he thought it practicable, to ascertain whether the US Government was likely to support such a policy (CM 54(49)2, CAB 128/16).

No. 93

Letter from Mr. MacDonald (Singapore) to Sir W. Strang

[F 13405/1023/10]

SINGAPORE, 19 August 1949

My dear William,

I feel that I should send you this note to put on record an aspect of our relations with Communist China which affects us here in Malaya. I have not set this down in writing before, because I assumed—no doubt with complete justification—that the point made in it is fully in the minds of those in the Foreign Office, as well as in the Colonial Office, who have to give advice to Ministers on the question of recognising a Communist or Communist-dominated Government in China. But it strikes me that I should now make the point in writing so that you are specifically aware of a difficulty which may be created for us in Malaya and British Borneo.

The diplomatic recognition of a Communist Government in China would land us in some difficult consequences in Malaya and British Borneo, which, I think, would not arise on anything like the same scale in any part of the British Empire in relation to the recognition of a Communist Government of any other foreign country. It is as follows. In the Federation of Malaya, Singapore and the three territories in British Borneo there are large local Chinese populations. In Singapore and the

Federation in particular they have a powerful influence in local politics and other affairs. Diplomatic recognition of the Communist authorities in China would naturally give those authorities the right to appoint Consuls-General and Consuls in these five countries as well as elsewhere in the world. The existence of Chinese Communist Consular Representatives amidst the local Chinese populations would be dangerous. No doubt a part of their instructions from their Government would be to do everything possible to stimulate anti-British Chinese Nationalism amongst these Chinese. The local Chinese character being what it is, many in the population would be sensitive to pressure from the Consular Representatives.

This, therefore, is a consideration on the side of postponing as long as possible diplomatic recognition of a Communist Government in China. I do not, of course, suggest that this consideration should outweigh wider and more important considerations, but only that it should be given due weight. From our local point of view here it looms very large, and is capable of causing very serious trouble for us. The same of course applies in several other countries in South-East Asia, but that is a matter for decision by the Governments of those countries.

I am sending a copy of this letter to Sir Thomas Lloyd[1] in the Colonial Office.[2]

Yours ever,
MALCOLM MACDONALD

[1] Permanent Under-Secretary at the Colonial Office.

[2] Mr. MacDonald returned to this theme in a further letter to Sir W. Strang on 22 August. He enclosed a copy of a letter (15 August) he had received from Sir F. Gimson, the Governor of Singapore, that made the same point about the possible repercussions in Singapore if the UK recognised a Communist government in China. Sir W. Strang replied to both letters on 2 September, pointing out that nothing was likely to happen over recognition until a central Communist government had been established in China. He explained the position of the FO to the effect that, if the UK refused to recognise a Communist government, this would serve only to increase Communist hostility and make the danger to South-East Asia still more acute. There was also the question of Chinese Communist representation in the United Nations to consider. The FO believed that if the Communists were recognised this would not in itself signify approval of Communist actions. Suitable propaganda could make this clear. The UK had relations with the Soviet Union but no one was in any doubt about the UK attitude towards the actions of the Soviet Government. If Communist consuls were appointed in Malaya and Singapore, the local authorities would no doubt consider in advance what measures might be taken to restrict their capacity to do harm. The FO requested prior consultation before such measures were taken.

No. 94

Memorandum by Mr. Bevin on China

CP(49)180 [CAB 129/36]

Secret   FOREIGN OFFICE, 23 August 1949

I invite my colleagues to consider certain developments which have taken place in China since this question was last considered by the Cabinet,[1] and to concur in the recommendations made in this paper.

2. The United States Ambassador called on me on 21st July and stated that the United States Secretary of State had expressed a desire to consult with me about China.[2] I told him that I would be prepared to do this when I visited Washington in September and that meanwhile I was quite willing that conversations should take place at the official level. Certain departmental views on the China situation, which will be found at Annex A, have been communicated to the American Embassy in London for transmission to the State Department in fulfilment of this undertaking, and on the understanding that they were without commitment to Ministers. I concur in these views and consider they should now be endorsed.

3. The position is thus that I am under an obligation to discuss our policy towards China during my forthcoming visit to Washington. It is complicated by the fact that, as will be shown below, United States policy has tended in recent weeks to diverge from the policy outlined in C.P.(48) 299 of 9th December, 1948,[3] and approved by the Cabinet on 13th December (C.M.(48)80th Conclusions, Minute 3).[4]

Present Situation in China

4. The Communist advance in China continues. The port of Foochow, in the province of Fukien opposite Formosa, has fallen and it is suspected that Canton will be overrun by the Communists in September. There is evidence that the authorities of the province of Kwangtung in which Canton is situated are making arrangements to come to terms with the Communists. In addition to the southward drive, there is a drive westward towards Chungking, which may also be expected to fall before very long. In the province of Yunnan, which adjoins Burma and Indo-China, the position is confused, but there is a distinct prospect that this province too will go over to the Communists in the comparatively near future. To all intents and purposes, therefore, the Communists will shortly be in control of the greater part of China and will have extended to the borders of the New Territories of Hong Kong.

[1] See No. 59.   [2] See No. 88.   [3] See No. 51.   [4] See No. 52.

5. The political future is still obscure. In broadcasts and public pronouncements the Chinese Communists reiterate the orthodoxy of their Marxist-Leninist ideology, their support of the Soviet Union and the Cominform and their opposition to British and American 'imperialism'. In the field of practical politics, little has been done to remedy the ills of China to which the Communists have become heirs, and there is as yet no evidence of a co-ordinated economic policy. It appears probable that a Central Government will be set up in the autumn. A message from a high Communist authority to His Majesty's Government, received at third hand after some delay, suggests that there is a conflict between those Communists who are fanatical supporters of the Soviet Union, and, believing in the imminence of a third world war, consider it not worth while to seek an arrangement with the Western Powers; and those who, while 100 per cent. Communist, consider that the consolidation of their position must be a slow process and that it is necessary to enter into relations and to trade with the West.[5] The extreme faction is said to control the propaganda machine, and this is said to explain why Communist publicity is wholly hostile to the Western Powers. That there is a conflict within the Chinese Communist Party is believed to be a fact; for the rest it remains to be seen how a Communist Central Government, when it is set up, will behave towards the Western Powers.

Position of British Trading Interests in Communist China

6. The position of our trading communities in Communist China gives cause for serious concern. There has been no physical molestation on the part of the Communists, though their attitude has on the whole been unco-operative and aloof. The threat of crippling taxation is already causing British trading interests to wonder whether they will be able to continue in such circumstances. The Communists continue to have no dealings with our Embassy at Nanking or with our Consulates in Communist China.

Nationalist Blockade

7. The chief cause for the present serious situation has, however, been the Nationalist blockade of Shanghai and Tientsin. The latter may now become ineffective as a result of the occupation by Communist forces of some of the Miao Islands at the entrance of the Gulf of Pechili. But the blockade of Shanghai has been effective in preventing the entry or exit of merchant vessels (with the exception of one small ship, which managed to run the blockade). The Blue Funnel Steamship *Anchises* was bombed and machine-gunned by Nationalist aircraft and became a casualty for which compensation is be claimed.[6]

---

[5] See No. 90.

[6] *Anchises*, a UK merchant ship, was bombed and machine-gunned by Chinese Nationalist aircraft as part of the blockade of Communist-held ports on the morning of 21 June 1949. The incident took place at the mouth of the Whangpoo River, a tributary of the Yangtse, on which Shanghai is situated. *Anchises* ran aground and suffered casualties and was strafed again on 22

8. The result of this blockade now is that British firms in Shanghai are in a parlous condition. The exchange [rate] is entirely fictitious and is tied to the price of rice. Firms are without funds to pay wages and in order to avoid labour troubles it is proving necessary, according to the China Association (which represents the London offices of British firms in China), to remit sterling from London to the extent of some £350,000 or more a month.[7] It has been represented to me that this drain cannot continue and that many firms will be forced to close down before long. Some of them who have stocks can carry on until these are exhausted, but even of these some have decided to close down if the situation does not improve.

9. This very serious situation could be at any rate alleviated if it were found possible to send ships to Shanghai which could bring in relief supplies (e.g., International Refugee Organisations stores, household and medical supplies). As one means of doing this an approach was made to the United States Government suggesting that parallel representations be made to the Nationalist Government to permit the passage of ships for relief purposes. The United States Government at first returned a negative reply to this suggestion, but eventually agreed to make a parallel approach on the understanding that their emphasis would be upon that evacuation of their nationals rather than upon relief. Since ships bringing in supplies could be used for evacuation, we saw no reason to argue this point, and representations were accordingly made by the United Kingdom and United States representatives at Canton on 15th August.

10. The United States Government have now received a reply to the effect that the National Government agree in principle to a repatriation vessel calling at Shanghai. They would not permit carriage of cargo which might be of direct value to the Communists, but would allow other inward cargo provided it is 'limited to the minimum amount regarded as essential to secure Communist permission for the ship's entry'. They will not permit the carriage of any cargo from Shanghai. No reply has yet been made to the United Kingdom Government.

The National Government's reply to the United States Government does not appear to meet the requirements of British merchants in Shanghai, since a single ship will not be sufficient for the purposes of relief. It may, on the other hand, meet United States requirements for evacuation. If

---

June. HMS *Black Swan* on patrol at the Far East station was unable to assist her because UK warships were not at liberty to help British shipping in internal Chinese waters. The Commander-in-Chief, Far East, issued orders that HM ships on the Yangtse patrol should (*a*) fire at aircraft for their own self-defence, and (*b*) fire at aircraft that had attacked UK or other neutral merchants vessels whether inside or outside territorial waters. Cabinet considered the matter on 22 June. Ministers were inclined to approve these orders but the Chief of the Air Staff, Lord Tedder, explained that it would not be easy to identify aircraft with accuracy. There was a risk of action being taken against civilian or other inoffensive aircraft. Cabinet therefore recommended further consideration of the matter by officials ('Bombing of British Shipping in the Yangtse', memorandum by Viscount Hall of 22 June 1949, CP(49)133, CAB 129/35).

[7] See No. 89.

United States needs are satisfied, it is not improbable that the National Government will decline to lift the blockade any further in order to meet United Kingdom needs.

11. In the meantime the Shanghai situation continues to deteriorate, and the attitude of the British community there is indicated in Shanghai telegram No. 694 of 18th August (Annex B).[8] I consider that the time has come when we must make up our minds to follow one of two courses. The first would be to reverse the policy we have so far adopted and indicate to the British communities in Communist China that they can count on no support or relief and should make up their own minds whether in the circumstances they will remain. The second would be, if the Nationalists fail to meet our request to give safe-conduct to our ships to proceed to Shanghai with relief supplies, to decide to escort ships through the blockade. As a first step we should inform the United States Government of our intention and express the hope that even if they felt unable to subscribe to this policy, they would not publicly oppose it. Having already represented formally to the Nationalist Government our view that the blockade which they are conducting is illegal, we should then proceed to carry out our intention to escort ships. Before doing so, it would of course be necessary to secure an undertaking of safe-conduct and speedy turn-round from the Communist authorities at Shanghai, which should not prove impossible. The views of His Majesty's Ambassador in China on the blockade will be found at Annex C.[9]

Divergence between the United Kingdom and United States Policies in China

12. It is desirable to consider here the extent to which United Kingdom policy is tending to diverge from that of the United States. The United States Government were informed in December last year of the general sense of the view which the Cabinet then took of the situation in China (C.P.(48)299 of the 9th December, 1948) and were invited to consult with

---

[8] Not printed. This telegram explained that the local British business community was willing to remain and to continue in its efforts to reach an understanding with the Communist régime, but needed at the same time reassurance that the UK Government wanted them to stay and considered it safe for them to do so. A number of managers of trading and industrial concerns wanted to 'hang on' but having regard for the safety of their staffs, they had reached a point where they would have to close down unless they could be assured of support from HMG. The telegram also explained that it was 'vitally urgent' to establish communications with Hong Kong, even if Kuomintang approval were not forthcoming. It ended by expressing the hope that the UK Government would be able to formulate a policy allowing the British business community to remain without causing offence to the Americans who were now committed to evacuation.

[9] Not printed. Annex C is Nanking telegram No. 1234 of 13 August in which Sir R. Stevenson argued that 'having rightly taken the decision to "keep a foot in the door" in China we should now do all we can to help our people to hold on'. With or without US support, he suggested that Commonwealth governments should tell the Nationalist Government that they were 'compelled to relieve the discomfitures of our communities so far as we can by sending supplies to them by sea and removing those of our nationals who wish to go'.

us. Since then, consultation has taken place between His Majesty's Embassy in Washington and the State Department, but beyond indicating their anxiety about the control of the flow of strategic raw materials to Communist China the United States Government have never given any clear indication of their policy, though on the whole they have seemed disposed to concur in our view that our nationals should remain in China and that we should jointly follow a policy of keeping 'a foot in the door'.

13. Recently, however, without any prior warning, United States policy seems to have taken a sharp turn in the direction of retreat. While on the one hand the State Department issued a White Paper[10] of some 1,100 pages which sought to justify the past policy of the United States in China and liberally castigated the Nationalist Government of China, on the other they appear to have decided that it is no longer desirable that they should keep a foot in the door, and to be desirous of evacuating their nationals from China as soon as possible (it is for this purpose that they want ships to pass through the blockade). The State Department have decided to close their Consulates at Canton, Kunming, Chungking and Tihwa, and drastically to reduce their staffs at Nanking and Shanghai. They have asked His Majesty's Government to take charge, not only of their consular properties, but also of American interests. To this I have agreed, since, in spite of the embarrassment which it may cause, the resentment which would be aroused in the United States were we to refuse would be likely to affect our relations adversely at this critical time.

14. The fact that the United States have asked our Consuls to take charge of their interests suggest that they do not intend to quarrel with our intention to remain in China. It is difficult to understand what the present trend of American policy denotes, but there is understood to be a school of thought which considers that Communist China should be allowed to relapse into complete chaos, which will encourage the Chinese people to overthrow the Communist régime. This is diametrically opposite to our own view as outlined in Annex A to this memorandum, namely, that if we are not to drive Communist China into the arms of Moscow we must do our utmost to maintain Western contacts.

15. It is easier for the United States to cut their losses in China than for the United Kingdom to do so. Their trading interests are fewer and not so deep-rooted and their communities are smaller. Moreover, the total loss of their trading interest means less to the United States than a similar loss means to the United Kingdom in our present economic and financial condition.

16. We are faced with the dilemma that unless we can persuade the United States authorities to agree with us we must either agree to differ and pursue our own policy of keeping a foot in the door, or abandon the whole of our interests in China in order to follow in the American wake. The fact that the United States have asked us to take charge of their

---

[10] See No. 91, note 2.

interests in China suggest that they are not unwilling that we should adopt a different course from their own, and in the circumstances I recommend that we should adhere to the policy of remaining in China as long as we can.

The Extent of our Commitments

17. It is necessary to examine whether, by adopting a different policy from that of the United States, we are entering into commitments, which are in excess of our capabilities in our present straitened circumstances. The answer, I think, is that we should, in fact, be entering into no major commitments. The only step which His Majesty's Government are being asked to take at present is to ensure that merchant vessels are able to enter the port of Shanghai in order to bring relief to our merchant communities. If, in the event, there is no relief and British firms decide to close down, we shall be asked to provide facilities for evacuation, and this we should be prepared to do. Apart from the fact that the escorting of British merchant ships might entail a clash with the rapidly disintegrating Nationalist Government of China, we are not likely to be called upon to accept any major risks or to incur any vast expenditure. If in the event our policy of keeping a foot in the door proves to be a failure and we have to withdraw from China altogether, we shall be no worse off than if we withdraw now.

Position of His Majesty's Ambassador in China

18. I pass now to the position of our Ambassador in China. The United States Government, who at one time advocated that like-minded Powers should take concerted action, withdrew their Ambassador from Nanking for consultation without waiting for other Powers. The French Ambassador, who is ill in Shanghai, has received instructions to return as soon as he is fit to travel. The Netherlands Ambassador, who has reached retiring age, has been recalled. The Indian Ambassador at Nanking has recommended that he should be recalled to New Delhi for consultation before the formation of a coalition Government. The lack of shipping and air transport renders it unlikely that any head of foreign missions at Nanking will be able to leave for the time being.

19. Sir Ralph Stevenson remains at Nanking. But when it appears likely that a Communist Central Government is about to be set up, I consider it will be desirable to withdraw him for consultation. For if he then remains at Nanking the Communist Government may demand either immediate recognition or his immediate withdrawal, which might place us in an embarrassing position and force us to make a decision before we are ready to do so. As indicated in Annex A, the question of recognition of a Communist Government is closely connected with the question of Chinese representation in the United Nations Organisation, and it will clearly be necessary to consult with other Commonwealth Governments and with the United States and France before deciding upon an act of recognition.

20. In the above circumstances I propose to authorise Sir Ralph Stevenson to withdraw when it appears likely that Communist Central

Government is about to be set up.[11] On present information this may be in September or October of this year. We should notify other Commonwealth Governments and the United States of our intention.

Control of Strategic Materials

21. At their meeting on 22nd July (SAC(49) 6th Meeting, Minute 1)[12] the China and South-East Asia Committee decided the terms of the reply to be made to the United States Government's representations on the subject of the control of the flow of strategic materials to China. This reply did not satisfy the United States Government and a memorandum on the subject, which will be found at Annex D, was handed to the Minister of State on 3rd August.

22. Though it is not clear that the United States have any grounds for their apparent anxiety on this question, it is clear that they attach great importance to it, and I have been warned that the matter will be raised during my forthcoming visit to Washington. I recommend that I should be authorised to reply in the terms of the draft which will be found at Annex E.

Summary of Recommendations

I recommend that:

(1) If a satisfactory reply is received from the Nationalist Government about the passage of relief ships, immediate steps should be taken to arrange for their passage to Shanghai with the necessary relief stores.

(2) If, as appears probable, the Nationalists only agree to the passage of single vessels for repatriation purposes, the decision be taken in principle to escort British merchant vessels past the blockade to Shanghai; and that the United States Government be informed of this decision, which should not be put into effect until their reaction is known.

(3) I be authorised to discuss our policy towards China with Mr. Acheson on the basis of this paper and in particular of Annex A; that I should seek to persuade him that this policy is the right one; but that if the United States do not feel able to follow it themselves, they should not criticise us for so doing.

(4) His Majesty's Ambassador at Nanking be instructed to withdraw for consultation when it becomes apparent that a Central Communist Government of China is about to be set up; and that the other members of the Commonwealth, the United States, France and other friendly powers be informed of our intention.

(5) I be authorised to reply to the State Department on the lines of Annex E on the control of the flow of strategic materials to China.

[11] See No. 100, note 1. Having received an assurance of safe passage from the Nationalist authorities that were blockading Shanghai, Sir R. Stevenson left Nanking by ship and arrived in Shanghai on 17 October. Two days later he sailed for Hong Kong and arrived on 21 October.

[12] CAB 134/669.

(6) Other Commonwealth Governments also be informed of our intentions as regards recommendations (1), (2), (3) and (5).[13]

E.B.

Annex A

China: Report by Officials

FOREIGN OFFICE,*15 August 1949*

General

There do not seem to be any further grounds for hope that the Communists will fail in their bid for complete power in China. Effective or prolonged resistance cannot be expected from the discredited Nationalist Government, which can no longer hope for large-scale outside assistance, nor, *a fortiori,* from any splinter factions into which the Nationalist Government may disintegrate. Planning must therefore be on the assumption of Communist domination of the *whole* of China in the near future.

2. There is no doubt that the present leaders of the Chinese Communist Party are orthodox Marxist-Leninists and that their present strongly pro-Soviet policy constitutes a serious threat to Western political and economic interests not only in China but also in South-East Asia.

3. As regards South-East Asia, it would appear of cardinal importance to encourage the establishment of an effective anti-Communist front to prevent Communist encroachment beyond the borders of China. As regards China itself, it is considered that at the present stage any outside attempt to prevent the Communists from attaining complete power would not only be bound to fail but would rally the traditionally xenophobe

---

[13] Before this memorandum was considered in Cabinet on 28 August, a reply was received from the Nationalist Government on the question of relief ships. It stipulated that there should be one ship only and that any evacuation should be carried out in one operation. Chinese naval officers would board the ship and Chinese warships would escort it. These conditions were regarded in the FO as unacceptable ('China', note by Mr. Bevin, 25 August, CP(49)184, CAB 21/1947). Before the Cabinet met, the FO Legal Adviser questioned the legality of any attempt on the part of the UK to escort ships past the blockade (minute by Mr. Scarlett, 26 August, F 12748/1023/10).

In Cabinet Mr. Bevin announced his intention to consult the Law Officers on the issue of the blockade. Ministers were informed of the opinion of the Chiefs of Staff that an operation to run the blockade would be feasible, although assurances would be needed in advance that the ships would not be fired upon from the river banks by Communist forces. Ministers were also informed that any attack on a UK escort convoy in the open seas would have to be treated as an act of war; in response the UK would launch air strikes on Nationalist bases in the Chusan peninsula and in Formosa. Cabinet approved the other recommendations in the memorandum (CM 54(49)1, CAB 21/1947).

Chinese behind their new rulers, and that to display a general and avowed hostility to the new régime is calculated to drive it further into the arms of Moscow.

4. It is therefore considered that the only hope of encouraging the emergence in China of a less anti-Western tendency is to give the new régime time to realise both the necessity of Western help in overcoming its economic difficulties, and the natural incompatibility of Soviet imperialism with Chinese national interests (e.g., in Manchuria).

Every opening for emphasising that Moscow's designs are incompatible with a strong and independent China should be seized. In general, we wish to avoid as far as possible head-on conflict with the Communists at present, though we have no intention of pursuing a policy of appeasement on major issues.

Economic

5. For the following reasons it is considered that Western commercial and financial interests should endeavour to maintain themselves in China for as long as possible:

(*a*) If and when the Communists begin to realise the necessity for trade with the West in overcoming their economic difficulties, it is to be presumed that their first advances will be made not to Governments but to private concerns, and it is therefore important that there should be Western concerns in China which can be approached. If at a later stage the Communists wish to make an approach to Governments, it is considered that their proposals should be considered on their own merits. His Majesty's Government have of course, no intention of making official advances to the Communists, but they equally do not wish to show open hostility by dissuading British commercial interests from entering into normal commercial relations with them.

(*b*) Although there can be no doubt about the fundamental hostility of Chinese Communism to foreign mercantile committees [*sic*: communities], it nevertheless remains possible that experience may induce a more realistic attitude in the Communist authorities, who are at present themselves to some extent prisoners of their own propaganda. There may be few grounds for optimism as to the future; but we should be unwise to abandon what remains of our position in China until it becomes abundantly clear that is it untenable. It is of course practically certain that long-established and deep-rooted commercial establishments and connections, once abandoned, could never be restored.

(*c*) In view of its position in Hong Kong and South-East Asia, the United Kingdom has, of course, every reason for being anxious to avoid mercantile transactions of a kind which might result in increasing the military strength of Communist China. It is not considered, however, that the continuance of normal trade in civilian requirements need result in any perceptible accreditation to the war potential of a Communist administration in China, while any hardships resulting from the cessation of trade would fall, in the major industrial towns at any rate, on the population as a whole. These would, of course, be represented by the Chinese Communists as entirely due to the hostility of the 'Imperialist Powers'.

(*d*) It is recognised that foreign economic interests in China are likely sooner or later to be faced with the threat of expropriation. Provided that the normal channels of commerce are still open the Communist desire for trade with the West may conceivably be strong enough for some sort of trade and compensation agreements to be secured eventually.

(*e*) But perhaps more important than the foregoing considerations is the fact that foreign trading communities constitute a major element in Western influence in China. We consider that it is of the first importance to maintain for as long as possible the maximum Western contact and influence behind the Asian Iron Curtain, particularly bearing in mind that it may conceivably prove that one of the tasks most beyond the powers of the Communist régime may be that of regimenting and controlling the deep-rooted trading propensities of the individual Chinese. So long as hope remains of exploiting the Chinese instinct to trade to the detriment of the Communist cause complete abandonment of our position in China would appear to be premature, to say the least.

(*f*) Finally, in the long term, the potentialities of China under a strong and efficient Government as a source of raw material and foodstuffs and as an export market should not be forgotten. It would be a misfortune should at some future time these potentialities be realised if the Western world were then cut off from what might become available. It must still be our hope that opportunities will eventually arise for co-operation by the Western world with an effective Chinese Government for the economic development of the country for the benefit of the Far East and the world as a whole. The severance of existing commercial links with China would run entirely counter to such an objective, however remote it may seem for the present.

6. For the above reasons although our merchants in China may eventually have to cut their losses and leave, it is considered that it is neither in our political nor in our economic interests that they should do this if it can be avoided; and we do not share the view, which we gather to be that of the United States authorities, that foreign merchants who have stayed behind have put themselves in the position of hostages in their search for private gain and are therefore deserving of little sympathy. Moreover, it must be remembered that the British firms in China are private traders. The decision whether it is worth while for them to continue to try to keep alive their activities must still primary be theirs. His Majesty's Government would not in existing circumstances feel justified in seeking to prevent those who are willing and able to go on trading and

would certainly not wish to be responsible by such prevention for any ensuing losses.

7. This does not, of course, mean that British mercantile communities in China would be advised to continue indefinitely to do business on humiliating and unequal terms. It is intended that British concerns in China should be encouraged to co-operate fully with each other, and with the commercial communities of other friendly Powers, so that as trade opportunities offer they will be in a position to take advantage of Communist needs to secure improvements in the conditions under which they are permitted to operate.

Evacuation

8. As indicated above, His Majesty's Government are not in favour of a premature abandonment of British interest in China, and they consider that the longer British merchants and British missionaries (the two main elements of the British communities in China) are able to maintain a footing in China the more hope there is of maintaining British political and economic interests.

9. Broadly speaking the British communities in China are still determined to maintain themselves if they can, though of recent weeks there has been feeling in favour of evacuation. If British nationals want to leave His Majesty's Government will certainly furnish such assistance as they can to enable them to do so, but it is not proposed, at present at least, to advise them to do so wholesale.

Recognition

10. The charter of the United Nations (Articles 23 and 27 (3)) appears to be so framed that unless there is a Chinese representative the Security Council can take decisions only on procedural matters. It therefore seems essential that *de jure* recognition should not be withdrawn from one Chinese Government until *de jure* recognition can be accorded to its successor. The question of continuing to recognise the Nationalist Government and of according recognition to the Communists thus appear to be two facets of the same problem.

11. No question of according *de jure* or *de facto* recognition to the Communists can arise until the Communists form a Government claiming to be of national character. However, there are various indication that the Communists hope by their present offensive southwards to acquire so much territory as to be clearly the effective rulers of China. They will then probably set up a Government, to which Soviet recognition will doubtless promptly be accorded. The Communists apparently hope that this stage will be reached by mid-autumn 1949.

12. It is thus likely that the recognition question will become acute in the next few months. There are, however still too many undetermined factors for detailed consideration of the action to be taken in all possible contingencies to be profitable at this stage. The issues therefore can be usefully discussed only in general terms.

13. At the worst, the relations of the British Commonwealth and North Atlantic Powers with a Communist Chinese Government after recognition may follow the pattern of their relations with Soviet satellite States in Eastern Europe. There is, however, the possibility that the pattern will eventually develop along the lines of our present relationship with Yugoslavia, and it is therefore considered that the Western Powers should be careful not to prejudice future possibilities by developing an openly hostile attitude towards a Communist regime from the outset.

14. The political objections to precipitate recognition of a Communist régime are obvious. On the other hand, to withhold recognition from a Government in effective control of a large part of China is legally objectionable and leads to grave practical difficulties regarding the protection of Western interests in China.[14] It is most unlikely that the fulfilment of any special conditions can be exacted in return for recognition of the Communist régime, and it is therefore probable that after a certain stage delay in proceeding with recognition might seriously prejudice Western interests in China without any compensating advantages being obtained. The Chinese Communists themselves are unlikely to be seriously inconvenienced by the withholding of recognition. For their part they will probably decline to enter into diplomatic relations with any power which continues to recognise the Nationalist Government.

15. Since the Nationalist Government is not considered to be any longer capable of maintaining effective resistance, the question of its continued recognition by the Powers should be considered on a basis of practical convenience rather than of sentiment. If there is Nationalist control in Formosa and/or in Western China, it may be considered sufficient to regard the authority there as the *de facto* authority in control. The most important factor governing continued recognition of the Nationalist Government will, however, be the question of United Nations representation.

16. As regards Chinese representation in the United Nations Organisation, it seems probable that, according to the Communist timetable as far as it can be estimated, the National Government will continue to represent China during the forthcoming session of the Assembly. But the possibility cannot be excluded that a change of China's representation will become a live and controversial issue even while the Assembly is in session. It is impossible to determine in advance what the attitude of the Commonwealth and North Atlantic Powers should be in such an event, but clearly it will be desirable that there should be close and continuing consultation between them.

---

[14] Of the two main economic departments in the UK, the Treasury, while less convinced than the FO that the Communists would not resort to threats against UK interests, shared the FO view that the UK should maintain a commercial foothold in China (T 236/1814). The Board of Trade was not convinced that recognition would improve the survival chances of British interests; it favoured recognition but was not inclined to press for it (F 18316/1023/10).

ANNEX D

CONTROL OF TRADE WITH CHINA

Aide-Mémoire from American Embassy

3 August 1949

1. Although it is recognised that the final form of the United Kingdom's reply to the United States proposals regarding the control of trade with China is still subject to confirmation of other interested British Departments, the Department of State has read with disappointment the tentative British response, which the Foreign Office recently communicated to the Embassy.

2. During the meeting held in the Foreign Office beginning 21st July, 1949, the United States representatives stressed on several occasions their belief that it was highly important that the Western Powers demonstrate their bargaining strength *vis-à-vis* the Chinese Communist régime for protection, if necessary, of western interests in China, and that those Powers be in a position possibly to influence the orientation of that régime through the concerted control of selected exports of key importance to the Chinese economy. The Department of State, consequently, is seriously concerned that the proposed United Kingdom response represents far less than the absolute minimum requirements for joint protective measures in view of the present Chinese situation.

3. Any failure to demonstrate effective western control over selected key imports would represent the abandonment of the most important single instrument available for the defence of mutual vital western interests in China and the Far East generally. Yet the proposed United Kingdom response would appear to imply the desirability of a completely passive role by the Western nations in their economic relations with China. Such a rôle would extend not only to all strategic aspects of the China problem, but would cast serious doubt on the possibility of arriving at an effective joint approach towards the mutually agreed objective of combating the spread of communism throughout Asia.

4. In regard to the specific implementation of a positive approach, the Department of State has the following comments:

5. The Department understands that the United Kingdom is prepared to keep the flow of 1A strategic goods and materials[15] to Communist China and Northern Korea under control, since it is, of course, necessary to prevent possible transhipments via China to the Soviet orbit. It also appreciates the importance which the United Kingdom attaches to securing, before the United Kingdom can extend its export controls over 1A items to cover transhipment in Hong Kong and Singapore, prior

---

[15] 1A items were strategic materials, the export of which to China was prohibited. 1B items constituted all other materials and their export to China would have to be closely watched.

assurance from the Belgian, French and Dutch Governments that these Governments are prepared to take similar action covering both their metropolitan and Far East colonial territories. The Department is pleased, in this connection, to assure the United Kingdom Government that SCAP[16] is now controlling strategic exports to China in accordance with the proposed United States-United Kingdom policy, and that, furthermore, the United States Government is prepared to obtain Philippine co-operation.

6. The Department agrees that joint control of petroleum shipments is important, but regards it as only one aspect of a common general control pattern.

7. Although the Department of State and the Foreign Office thus appear to be largely in accord regarding the above two types of controls, and although the Department hopes that the United Kingdom Government may be able to extend control over the transhipment of 1A items through its Far Eastern colonies, 1A and petroleum export controls alone would not be adequate to permit the Western Powers to demonstrate their bargaining strength *vis-à-vis* the Chinese Communist régime, to influence the orientation of that régime, and therefore to combat the spread of communism throughout Asia. The reasons for this are that (*a*) China depends relatively little upon imports of 1A items, and (*b*) petroleum controls not only would be effected largely through informal arrangements with private companies rather than through governmental export licensing, but in addition China's petroleum purchases over the foreseeable future are likely to be far below normal civilian requirements.

8. The Department therefore believes that it is principally through the inclusion of selected 1B items in the present pattern of the United Kingdom's 1A licensing system that the Western Powers can secure leverage in dealing with the Chinese Communists. More exchange of information would not be sufficient for this purpose.

9. The selective character of the 1B items which might be included under 1A controls was evident in the discussions between United Kingdom and United States representatives acting as a subcommittee of the United Kingdom-United States group. It will be recalled that this subcommittee selected five categories of goods in the 1B category which might be suitable for control in respect of China:

> All essential types of mining equipment.
> Essential power generating equipment.
> Really essential transport equipment.
> Steel mill equipment.
> Petroleum products.

[16] Supreme Command(er) Allied Powers.

In addition there were a number of miscellaneous items in these categories which were regarded as of key importance to the Chinese economy.

10. The Department wishes therefore to reopen with the Foreign Office the matter of controlling these items, and suggests that the following factors be taken into account:

The Foreign Office has already indicated its desire to control the export of petroleum products. The same reasoning would appear to require control of the other categories studied by the subcommittee.

The difficulties of including 1B items in the present pattern of the United Kingdom's 1A licensing system are recognised. It is not understood, however, why the control of selected 1B exports to China could not be effected through the creation of a new list under which licences would be required in effect only for exports to China and adjacent areas. This would limit procedural deterrents on Britain's general export trade to a marginal scope.

The question of discrimination seems hardly relevant. Not only does the present pattern of United Kingdom export licensing involve open discrimination as between broad areas of the world, but, as maintained successfully in GATT and ECE[17] conferences, the present world situation obviously justifies discrimination on security.

In connection with Asia restricting the spread of communism is clearly a security matter for the Western Powers. Control over the export of selected 1B items *vis-à-vis* Communist China is as important for the mutual security interests of the western world as is the control of 1A items to Eastern Europe. Certainly as far as Asia is concerned the mutual security interests of the western world must be considered at least as much in terms of political and economic strategy as in terms of direct military factors.

11. In conclusion, it is difficult for the Department of State to understand what 'political and administrative difficulties' might be so great as to outweigh the importance of solidarity in the adoption of a strategy for the maximum protection of United States-United Kingdom mutual, vital long-range interests.

Annex E

Control of Trade with China

Draft Reply to American Embassy Aide-Mémoire of 3 August

Upon receipt of the American Embassy's Aide-mémoire of 3rd August, the United States proposals regarding the control of trade with China were

---

[17] General Agreement on Tariffs and Trade; Economic Commission for Europe.

once again made the subject of careful study by the interested Departments of His Majesty's Government.

2. The objectives of the United States proposals appear to be:

(*a*) to ensure that Western trade with China does not have as a direct consequence an increase in the military strength of the Chinese Communist administration; and

(*b*) in the words of the American Embassy's Aide-mémoire, 'to influence the orientation of that (the Chinese Communist) régime, and therefore to combat the spread of Communism throughout Asia.' It appears to be the United States view that this end might be achieved by demonstrating to the Chinese Communists the economic bargaining strength of the West through the concerted control of selected exports of key importance to the Chinese economy.

3. It is perhaps unnecessary to emphasise that there is no difference between His Majesty's Government and the United States Government as to the importance of these aims. Indeed, His Majesty's Government, because of their position in Hong Kong and South-East Asia, have immediate and compelling reasons for being anxious to secure the achievement of both objectives.

His Majesty's Government consider that, as far as the first of these two objectives is concerned, they have already taken steps which safeguard the position. They have, for example, not only effectively prohibited the export from the United Kingdom of weapons of war of any kind destined for the Chinese National Government, but have refused to permit the transshipment in Hong Kong of military equipment so destined irrespective of its country of origin. They have done this because experience has shown that such shipments usually eventually result in an accretion to the military strength of the Chinese Communists. In any case, the fact that the American Embassy's Aide-Mémoire under reference lays almost exclusive stress on the importance of controls, not from the narrower and more direct security point of view, but in the light of broader political considerations, suggests that it is to this latter aspect of the question that the United States Government now wish to draw especial attention.

5. It has already been stated that His Majesty's Government fully share the United States Government's anxiety to take such steps as may be effective and practicable to influence the Communist régime in China in the direction of more moderate and co-operative courses. Indeed, His Majesty's Government noted with gratification that the United States Aide-Mémoire implies the practicability of the exertion of Western influence on the Chinese Communists, since it is because they share this view that His Majesty's Government do not favour a general policy of evacuation but on the contrary believe it important that the maximum Western influence should continue to be exerted in China. The basic difference between the two Governments on this issue appears to be that His Majesty's

Government see no grounds for believing that the imposition of export controls of the kind proposed is likely to produce this desirable result.

6. It is understood that the United States proposals do not contemplate any immediate interference in the export to China of the list 1B items which have been suggested for control, and that the powers which it would be necessary to assume would, in fact, be held in reserve; the argument being that the mere assumption of these powers would provide an effective demonstration of Western bargaining strength and might also have the desirable political consequences mentioned above.

7. His Majesty's Government find it difficult to see the force of this argument. The Chinese Communists are presumably aware that a sovereign State has the power to control its own exports. The assumption of controls for this purpose would be regarded as a threat to impose economic sanctions and it is hard to see why such a step should be any more effective than an announcement designed to remind the Chinese Communists of the economic bargaining position of the West.

8. In any case, experience has shown that Communist Governments regard commercial relations as being entirely dissociated from political relations: they have consistently shown themselves to be unwilling to modify their political principles for the sake of commercial advantages, but they have at the same time demonstrated their willingness to trade freely, in so far as it is advantageous to them, with capitalist countries with whom they are in acute political divergence.

9. The American Embassy's Aide-mémoire refers to the subject of petroleum products in the following terms:

'The Foreign Office has already indicated its desire to control the export of petroleum products. The same reasoning would appear to require control of the other categories studied by the sub-committee.'

There is, however, an important difference between the United Kingdom objective in regard to petroleum products and the United States objective in regard to the other categories proposed for control. The United States proposal is that this latter group of items should be controlled, not because of its immediate security importance but because of the general political bargaining strength which it is asserted that such controls would bestow. As has already been stated, His Majesty's Government are sceptical of the efficacy of export controls aimed at a modification of the political alignment of the Chinese Communist régime, and are not disposed to institute controls for such a purpose. In the case of petroleum products, however, there is an obvious security interest. It is clearly of direct security importance to prevent the Chinese Communists from acquiring substantial reserves of petroleum products. Although the military operations of the Communists within China have not involved any substantial consumption of petroleum products, plans must be made on the assumption that sooner or later they will endeavour to expand beyond the frontiers of China. For such a purpose substantial quantities of petroleum products might well be indispensable. His Majesty's Government have to give particular consideration to the case of Hong Kong. It is considered that any overt attack on Hong Kong from the Chinese mainland could be successfully resisted unless the aggressor were able to acquire, at any rate temporarily, command of the air and sea. It was because of considerations of this order that the communication recently made by the Foreign Office to the American Embassy laid particular stress on the importance of petroleum products.

10. His Majesty's Government have indicated to the United States Government in another context that they see important advantages in the continued maintenance in China for as long as possible of Western commercial and financial interests. It is precisely because they are anxious to secure the second of the two objectives referred to in paragraph 2 above that they do not wish to show open hostility to the Chinese Communists by dissuading British commercial interests from entering into normal commercial relations with them. This does not mean that their policy in this regard can be considered as purely passive as is suggested in the United States Aide-Mémoire. On the contrary, they consider it to be of importance to maintain their general position in China for as long as possible in order to permit the carrying out of a flexible policy of exerting influence and pressure whenever opportunity offers. They do not, however, consider that the means proposed by the United States Government are likely to lead to the desired result.

No. 95

Memorandum on International Control of Hong Kong

[*F 13280/1061/10*]

Secret   FOREIGN OFFICE, *5 September 1949*

At the Cabinet Meeting on the 29th August it was asked in connexion with the Cabinet Paper on Hong Kong (C.P.(49)177), whether the possibility of establishing an international regime for Hong Kong had been considered.[1]

2. This possibility was reviewed departmentally after the end of the war, when future policy in Hong Kong was under active consideration.[2] The sole argument adduced in favour was that short of total rendition to China the only solution of the Hong Kong problem likely to commend itself to United States anti-colonial feeling would be an international regime in which the United States Government would participate.

[1] See No. 92, note 8.
[2] See note before No. 18.

3. The suggestion then made was that Hong Kong might be placed under international control, with the Chinese Government and His Majesty's Government having a predominant share in the administration and control, and made a free port open to every nation on equal terms; and that such a scheme might be brought into appropriate relationship with the United Nations.

4. It was thought doubtful whether the Chinese would welcome such arrangements, but the overriding disadvantage was felt to be that extremely dangerous opportunities would be offered to mischief making by the Soviets, who could not be excluded from the international control. It was also felt that the Soviets would thereby acquire an admirable foothold in South East Asia, with consequences pleasing neither to the United Kingdom, China nor the USA. The proposal was therefore ruled out at that time.

5. In present circumstances no proposal for international control of Hong Kong would be welcome to the United States Government unless both the USSR and Communist China were excluded. It would probably be impossible to prevent this were United Nations endorsement for transference of Hong Kong to international control sought, and it is doubtful whether it would be consonant with the spirit of the United Nations Charter to make a transfer without seeking such endorsement. If a transfer excluding the Communist Powers were made without reference to the United Nations, those Powers would have an opportunity for damaging attacks in the United Nations on colonial imperialism and disregard for the wishes of colonial peoples.

6. It is equally doubtful whether many friendly Powers would be willing to participate in international control. The United States Government itself might well be reluctant to put itself in a position where it might become involved in a head-on collision with Communist China for the sake of what its opponents would doubtless call a disguised British colony, and few if any of the Western Powers would at present undertake new and potentially extensive commitments in the Far East. As for the Commonwealth, India, Pakistan and Ceylon would almost certainly refuse to participate, in view of their general public position that Asiatic peoples should be self-governing.

7. International control would be even more offensive to Chinese nationalistic susceptibilities than the present British control, as it would appear to defer *sine die* the return of Hong Kong to China. The Chinese Communist authorities would regard such action as a challenge and would probably be forced by Chinese public opinion into immediate counter-action.

8. Finally, it is already sufficiently difficult for the present integrated and well-established British administration to maintain itself against Chinese hostility, and the difficulties would be far greater for a newly established, inexperienced and less closely integrated international regime.

9. While therefore international control of Hong Kong may perhaps at some date in the future be a suitable subject for further consideration, the practical objections in present circumstances are overwhelming.

10. It should be added that there are equally conclusive arguments against trusteeship, i.e., normal national administration supervised by the United Nations through the Trusteeship Council. In the first place the United Nations would be most unlikely to agree to a trusteeship over Hong Kong without convincing evidence that its inhabitants do not want to return to Chinese sovereignty, and would doubtless wish to set up a Commission to ascertain the wishes of the inhabitants by a plebiscite. Secondly, even if a plebiscite were to record a majority for remaining under British sovereignty and Hong Kong were placed under United Kingdom trusteeship, the goal to which the Trusteeship Council would work would have to be the attainment of self-government or independence. Soviet and Chinese influence in the Council, together with the lukewarm attitude of other Powers, would ensure that the administration of Hong Kong became impossible.

No. 96

Record of a meeting on China held at the State Department in Washington on 13 September 1949[1]

[F 14070/1023/10]

Top Secret   WASHINGTON, *13 September 1949*

Mr. Acheson recalled that a special Advisory Committee under Dr. Jessup had been looking into the question of United States policy in China and he had now seen their recommendations, with which he was in general agreement. He was anxious to get the question of China removed from the field of internal party politics.

The general conclusions reached by the Advisory Committee were as follows:

The United States Government should avoid giving any appearance of running after the Communists, and should on the contrary leave it to the Communists to come to them.

---

[1] Present at this meeting were, for the US: Mr. Acheson. Mr. Douglas, Dr. P. Jessup (Ambassador at Large), Mr. G.C. McGhee (Assistant Secretary of State for Near Eastern and Asian Affairs), Mr. Butterworth, and Mr. J.C. Satterthwaite (Director of the Office of Near Assistant and African Affairs). The UK was represented by Mr. Bevin, Sir O. Franks, Mr. Dening, and Mr. R.E. Barclay, formerly Acting First Secretary, Washington, now head of FO Personnel Department.

For the US record of Mr. Dening's separate meeting with State Department officials on 13 September, see *FRUS 1949*, vol. ix, pp. 76-78.

They should keep on the look-out for the emergence of any genuine resistance groups in China, but should not be in too much of a hurry to give such groups their support. At the moment there was no national leader of sufficient stature in sight. They should, however, be constantly on the look-out for the development of a Chinese version of Titoism. This was not the moment for conciliatory gestures to the Communists, which would only be represented as a sign of weakness, and in any case would be unacceptable to the American public. The aim should be to let the Chinese Communists learn by bitter experience that the position of a satellite of Russia had little to recommend it. Every effort should be made to show up any Soviet actions which were contrary to China's interests. At the moment the United States Government had few weapons with which they could do any harm to the Communists, though the position in this respect would gradually change. They should, however, certainly avoid doing anything to help them.

The policy recommended for the United States Government might be summarised as follows:

(*a*) No premature recognition and no recognition until the Communist regime had obtained firm control over the greater part of China;

(*b*) Insistence on recognition by the new regime of China's international obligations;

(*c*) The policy to be followed should, as far as possible, be concerted between the Atlantic Powers;

(*d*) There should be no economic warfare against the new regime, but it should be made to pay its way. For example, there should be no haste to offer loans. The United States Government should try to secure agreement on the general prohibition of the import into China of the items specified on the I.A. list.[2] As regards items on the I.B. list, the necessary machinery of control, export licences, &c., should be instituted, but no attempt should be made at present to prevent these goods from reaching China.

Mr. Acheson also referred to the complication presented by the present state of affairs in Formosa, but said that there seemed no possibility of any useful initiative there at present.

Mr. Bevin said that His Majesty's Government were in no hurry to recognise the Communist regime. On the other hand, the British were in a rather different position from the Americans in China, since their commercial interests were very much greater. The British community had been advised to stay where they were, and the British consular officers were remaining at their posts. It would scarcely be possible at this stage to advise the British community to clear out. To do so would have a very demoralising effect in Hong Kong and in the rest of the area. The grant of recognition would have to depend on how the Communist Government

[2] See No. 94, note 14.

behaved. It would certainly not be given if they tried to use threats, and it would be necessary to ensure that they accepted their international obligations. At the same time he thought there was a risk, if the Western Powers remained too obdurate, that the Chinese would be driven further into the arms of Moscow. It was important to avoid doing anything which would discourage them from being Chinese first and foremost.

Mr. Acheson said he agreed that the objective must be to encourage a split with Moscow. He thought, however, that there was a danger that premature recognition would serve to discourage the anti-Communist forces in China.

It was agreed that the maximum publicity, by means of pamphlets or otherwise, should be given to the action of the Russians in removing all the available machinery and equipment from Manchuria.

Mr. Acheson said that the United States Government quite understood that because of the much more extensive British interests in China the behaviour of His Majesty's Government was bound to be somewhat different from that of the United States Government. It was a difference in situation rather than a difference in policy, and as long as the objective of the two Governments remained the same he did not think it mattered greatly if there was some divergence on tactics.

After some further discussion of the question of exports to Communist China, *Mr. Bevin* confirmed that he agreed that every effort should be made to prevent the entry into Communist China of any goods on the 1.A. list. He undertook to look again into the possibility of setting up machinery for the control of goods on the 1.B. list.[3]

---

[3] Hong Kong was also discussed at this meeting. Mr. Bevin read out the amended version of paragraph 16 of CP(49)177 (see No. 92, note 8) and said that if there were aggression against Hong Kong, this would be resisted with all available forces. All necessary precautionary steps had been taken and the UK authorities were confident of their ability to face armed aggression, economic blockade or subversive activities from within. Mr. Acheson thought the policy described by Mr. Bevin 'sound and reasonable' and deserving of US support (F 14110/1192/10).

No. 97

Record of a meeting on developments in China held at the State Department in Washington on 17 September 1949[1]

[*F 14440/1023/10*]

Secret   FOREIGN OFFICE, *17 September 1949*

Mr. Bevin said that the policy of His Majesty's Government had been to try to keep a foot in the door in China. We were accordingly not withdrawing any of our Consults [*sic*] or advising our communities to leave. On the question of recognition, His Majesty's Government were determined to proceed with great caution and to remain in close consultation with the United States, French and other Governments concerned. There was, of course, the awkward problem of Chinese representation on the Security Council, which made it important not to proceed in too much of a hurry. There was, he thought, a slight difference in tactics in China between the British and the Americans, since the Americans were more inclined to withdraw their Consuls and to advise their communities to leave.

Mr. Bevin then said he had heard that there was a new development in that two American ships were trying to run the blockade. *Mr. Butterworth* confirmed that the State Department had had a report to this effect. The owners had been told that they could not have the assistance of the United States Navy in running the blockade. On the other hand, the United States Government was not in a position to forbid them making the attempt if they wished to take the risk. Mr. Butterworth added that provided satisfactory assurances were received from both sides the SS *General Gordon* would go to Shanghai on about 23rd September, primarily for the purpose of removing American citizens and others who wished to be evacuated.

Mr. Bevin asked whether the United States and French Governments considered the blockade to be legal. *Mr. Butterworth* replied that the United States Government had told the Nationalist Government that they could not regard their announcement as constituting a legal blockade.

M. Bonnet said that the French Government had taken a similar line. The question was, however, largely academic, since they had no ships on the spot. In reply to an enquiry from Mr. Bevin, *M. Schuman* said that he did

[1] Present at this meeting were, for the US: Mr. Acheson, Mr. Butterworth, Mr. Satterthwaite, Mr. L.T. Merchant (Counsellor of US embassy on special detail to Formosa), and Mr. D MacArthur 2nd (Chief of Division of West European Affairs). France was represented by M. R. Schuman (Foreign Minister), M. H. Bonnet (Ambassador in Washington) and M. B. Clappier (Directeur du Cabinet, Quai d'Orsay). Mr. Bevin, Sir O. Franks, Mr. Dening, and Mr. Barclay represented the UK.

not think the relief ship which the French had at one time contemplated sending would materialise. In reply to a further enquiry from Mr. Bevin, *M. Bonnet* said that the French had considerable interests in China and quite a large community of merchants and missionaries. For the time being the community were staying where they were. The French Ambassador, however, would come away for consultation at the beginning of October.

Mr. Bevin said he did not want to give the appearance that His Majesty's Ambassador was running away, and he therefore hoped to arrange that his withdrawal should ostensibly be for consultation with Mr. MacDonald in Singapore. Once out, however, he would not, of course, go back. All the British Consuls would remain at their posts. In reply to an enquiry from M. Schuman, *Mr. Butterworth* said that the United States Government were withdrawing all their Consuls with the exception of those at Shanghai, Tsingtse (though he might come away later) and of course Hong Kong. They would naturally also retain an establishment in Nanking. He thought that there would probably be about 800 holders of American passports who would stay on in Shanghai.

Mr. Bevin said that the Chinese Ambassador in Washington had told him that the Nationalists were holding the Communist forces outside Canton, and had tried to argue that the Communists were now behind their time-table. *Mr. Butterworth* said that Marshal Li's[2] representative had complained that Chiang Kai-shek was not providing enough gold and silver, and he thought that there would be serious difficulties by October.

The three Ministers agreed that all they could do was to keep in close consultation on the whole situation. They also agreed that it was likely that a Communist Government would be set up on 10th October.

Mr. Acheson then spoke about the problem of recognition and explained the attitude of the United States Government in similar terms to those he had used at his meeting with Mr. Bevin on 13th September.[3] He added that though he hoped it would be possible for the three Governments to keep in close step, there would be no recriminations if they felt obliged to move separately. *M. Schuman* mentioned that a special consideration with the French Government was that until the Communists controlled the territory along the Indo-China frontier, there could be no question of recognition.

Mr. Bevin said that he had already made clear the attitude of His Majesty's Government with regard to Hong Kong, which they would certainly defend against aggression. The Portuguese Minister for Foreign Affairs had called to see him and had raised the question of Macao. The Portuguese Government had sent troops there, but were doubtful of their

[2] Li Tsung-jen (see 37, note 9), now Acting President of the Nationalist Government.

[3] See No. 96.

ability to hold out against an attack. It was, of course, possible that there would be Communist aggression against Hong Kong, Macao or Indo-China. His Majesty's Government had made it clear that if attacked they would fight, but the French and Portuguese Governments had not yet taken a public stand.

Mr. Acheson said the Portuguese Minister for Foreign Affairs had also told him that reinforcements had been sent, but that the Portuguese would not be able to resist a determined attack. M. da Mata[4] had asked about the United States military liaison officers in Hong Kong, and had been told that they were merely the service attachés from Canton under a different guise. He had also enquired what the United States Government would do if Hong Kong were attacked. Mr. Acheson said he had replied that they had not been asked to help, but any aggression would be a violation of the United Nations Charter and the United States Government would fulfil its obligations under the Charter.

Mr. Butterworth commented that the Governor of Macao did not appear to take the situation too seriously. He had not wanted troop reinforcements, the sending of which he regarded as provocative. He claimed that he had no internal problems, and was confident that he could hold the situation.

M. Schuman asked what his colleagues thought would happen about Chinese representation in the Security Council if the Nationalist Government collapsed. Would it be possible for the Security Council to function. *Mr. Acheson* said he thought the United States Government would take the line that the absence of one of the permanent members of the Council need not prevent it from functioning. However, this was a very technical point which he thought could best be left to the lawyers.[5]

[4] Portuguese Foreign Minister.
[5] For the US record of this meeting, see *FRUS 1949*, vol. ix, pp. 88-91.

No. 98

Minute from Sir W. Strang to Mr. Attlee on the Shanghai Blockade

[FO 800/462]

FOREIGN OFFICE, *29 September 1949*

PRIME MINISTER

You will recall that Ministers decided after considering C.P. (49) 180 on 29th August[1] that there could be no question of breaking the Shanghai blockade by naval action unless the Law Officers took the view that such action was legally justifiable. The Law Officers were unable to take this view and in consequence no action was taken.

2. In the weeks which have elapsed since this question was put to the Cabinet, we have been under continuing pressure from the China Association (which represents British merchant interests in China) to do something about the blockade. This pressure has increased as a result of the fact that two American merchant ships have succeeded in reaching Shanghai (it is not yet known whether they have succeeded in getting out). These vessels ran the blockade, unlike the *General Gordon* which entered and left Shanghai for evacuation purposes by arrangement between the Nationalist and United States governments. In the past few weeks five merchant ships have succeeded in entering Shanghai, while three have been intercepted by the Nationalist Navy.

3. Two British shipping firms: Messrs. Matheson and Co. and Messrs. John Swire, now wish to sail ships to Shanghai on 4th October. Both firms are loading ships in Hong Kong and are eager to sail them to Shanghai without passengers after due advertisement (the Americans publicly advertised their sailings in advance). The firms have stated their willingness to take the commercial risk if they can be assured that an incident with the Nationalist Navy will not be embarrassing to HMG. They argue that they would have done so long since but for two practical considerations:

(1) The terms of an advice to shipping issued by the Deputy Commander-in-Chief, Far East which made it impossible for them to obtain insurance cover from their normal [sources].[2]

(2) The consideration that they did not wish to run counter to the policy of HMG as expressed by the Admiralty.

4. The following political factors are involved:

---

[1] This should read 28 August, see No. 94, note 13.

[2] In the filed copy of the document a word or words are missing at this point in the text.

(1) Although the economic situation of Shanghai has deteriorated less rapidly than was at first expected thanks to effective *ad hoc* measures taken by the Communist administration to feed the population and maintain essential services, the situation of the trading community is nearly desperate and worsening every day that seaborne supplies are cut off. As an indication of the degree of difficulty, one firm with a stake in China estimated at £5 million decided last week to cut its losses and close down. This is the first major collapse on the British front; and when the decision becomes public knowledge, the will of others to resist is likely to weaken. The China Association have stated that sterling is being remitted to Shanghai at the rate of £360,000 monthly for maintenance.

(2) The Nationalist Government's situation is steadily deteriorating. The recent defection of a Nationalist destroyer must have weakened their blockade of Shanghai.

(3) The US Government can hardly raise an objection to British merchantmen taking the same risks that two of their own merchant fleet have taken. The State Department enquired recently whether we had it in mind to force the blockade; this was before the two American vessels succeeded in reaching Shanghai. They were told that no decision had been taken.

5. I attach at Annex A a draft statement which we think will meet the desire of British merchants for an indication of the views of HM Government while making it clear that vessels will enter territorial waters at their own risk. I think we should do what we can to encourage British ships to sail to Shanghai if they are prepared to do so, and though it is possible that the Nationalists may turn them back, I hardly think that the Nationalists would risk an actual attack on British merchant ships (except when they lie alongside the wharves in Communist-controlled Shanghai).

6. At Annex B[3] you will find the existing instructions of the Commander-in-Chief, Far East Station, for the protection of British merchant vessels. I am advised by the Legal Advisor of the Foreign Office that the action contemplated in (*b*) runs contrary to the opinion of the Law Officers, which states that 'we do not know of any reason in principle or on authority which would make it lawful to escort ships into the territorial and national waters of a foreign and sovereign power carrying relief supplies for the British community to Shanghai when it was unlawful to

---

[3] The instructions in Annex B explained that merchant ships would be entitled to Royal Navy protection in full on the high seas up to the three-mile limit of territorial waters. Shipowners would be required to arrange a clear communication system with HM ships and also to make their courses and rendezvous as arranged. Once in territorial waters merchant ships would not be escorted and HM ships would only enter to protect them if they had been attacked or bombed. If arrested in territorial waters and turned back they would have to comply.

escort ships with their cargoes'. While provision (*b*) does not suggest that ships will be escorted when they enter territorial waters, it does suggest that HM ships would enter to protect them if they were actually attacked or bombed. You may consider that, in spite of the legal opinion, the declining authority of the Nationalist Government renders it unnecessary to modify this provision. If, however, you consider that the risk is not an acceptable one, it will be necessary for the Commander-in-Chief to make it clear to British merchant ships that he will in no circumstances be prepared to enter territorial waters, even if ships are attacked. In either event the text of the statement in Annex A would remain as it is.

7. In brief, the recommendations are that the text at Annex A (which has the concurrence of the Admiralty and Ministry of Transport) should be communicated to British merchant concerns here; and that the provisions for protection contained in Annex B should be communicated by the Commander-in-Chief, Far East Station to British merchant ships, either as they stand, or amended as necessary.[4]

ENCLOSURE IN NO. 98

Annex A: Note for Draft Statement to China Association

SHANGHAI BLOCKADE

It has never been the intention of His Majesty's Government to prevent British merchantmen from pursuing their normal trade with China. On the contrary it is their wish that normal trade be resumed as soon as possible. But when advice was sought by shipping interests on the effect of the proclamation by the Nationalist Government closing certain ports, the Commander-in-Chief assessed the possibility of interference by Chinese warships and gave it as his view (which in the circumstances at the time was accepted by HM Government) that the control of the Yangtse entrance by the Nationalists was complete.

2. In the intervening months experience has shown that of the attempted voyages to and from Shanghai, five have been successful and three have failed. This experience indicates that the closure of the port of Shanghai is not complete.

3. It is for shipowners to decide whether voyages to Shanghai are to be attempted. If they decide to resume their services to Shanghai, they should ascertain from the Commander-in-Chief, Far East Station the scale of protection that can be given to them and the requirements they must comply with. It must be made clear, however, that HM ships will not escort British merchant vessels into Chinese territorial waters, which they will therefore enter at their own risk.

---

[4] Mr. Attlee noted: 'Approved. C.R.A. 29.9.49.'

No. 99

Report by the Joint Intelligence Committee for the Chiefs of Staff

JIC(49)48(Final) [*CAB 158/7/1*]

Top Secret   MINISTRY OF DEFENCE, *30 September 1949*

THE IMPLICATIONS OF A COMMUNIST SUCCESS IN CHINA

We examine the likely effects of the civil war in China on our strategic position in South East Asia and Japan.

2. For the purpose of this examination we have assumed that:

(*a*) no major war has broken out between Russia and the Western Powers;

(*b*) the Chinese Communists have set up a Government over the whole of China except Formosa;

(*c*) Hong Kong and Macao will remain in British and Portuguese hands respectively.

Conclusions

3. (*a*) In spite of economic and political difficulties, we expect at least in the near future, that there will be no important divergence between the policy of the Chinese leaders, and we consider that the resources of China Proper must be counted within the Russian orbit. We consider nevertheless that China may be discounted as a major industrial asset to the Soviet bloc for a number of years to come.

(*b*) The policy of the Chinese Communist Government will be aimed at the immediate recovery of Formosa, and eventually of Hong Kong and Macao. Chinese membership of the United Nations and the Security Council will be utilised, once *de jure* recognition of the Chinese Communist Government has been secured, to support Soviet policy particularly over Asiatic questions. Economically and militarily, China will be of little value to the Soviet Union in the short term. In the event of war, bases on the China coast would probably be available to the Soviet Navy and, providing it were possible to arrange for the transportation of adequate supplies, Chinese airfields would be of value to the Russian Air Forces.

(*c*) With the establishment of a Communist Government in China, the Communists will be in a favourable position to further the spread of Communism step by step into South East Asia. Therefore, unless preventive action is taken and substantial material support given by the Western Powers to indigenous Governments, the countries of SE Asia, in their turn, may fall under Communist control. Should Siam fall, a land threat to Singapore will develop. Should Burma fall it is likely that India would be so preoccupied with the security of her Eastern frontier and the internal situation in frontier areas that, even if she were prepared to do so, she would be unable to contribute to Commonwealth defence commitments.

(*d*) Although the Chinese Communist Army has not been tested in modern battle, and although it lacks heavy equipment and support weapons on a European scale it is considered their best troops are the equal of the average Russian soldiers, and that they are capable of aggressive action in other countries of SE Asia, should this be the policy of the Chinese Communist Government. There is no Communist Air Force at present but there is no doubt that a force capable of supporting the Army could be formed with Russian assistance. Chinese Communist Naval Forces can be expected to establish control of the approaches to ports a short time after the final Communist victory in China. In the much longer term it can be expected to extend its influence into the China Sea.

(*e*) In all countries of SE Asia there is a Chinese Community, whose majority (with the possible exception of Burma where the Chinese are predominantly of the shop-keeping class) would probably support the policy of a Communist Chinese Government in China. These Chinese, therefore, constitute a potentially dangerous fifth column but they are disliked by the indigenous peoples and the more closely they align themselves with the Communist regime in China, the greater will be the hostility of the indigenous peoples towards Communism.

(*f*) The success of the Chinese Communists will encourage the Japanese Communist Party and strengthen the bargaining position of the Japanese Government *vis-à-vis* the Allied Administration. The Chinese Communist success will weaken the authority of the South Korean republican government and increase the Communist threat in the Philippines.

Recommendations

4. We recommend that the Chiefs of Staff approve this report and forward copies to the Minister of Defence and, subject to his approval, to the Foreign Office and the British Defence Co-ordination Committee, Far East.[1]

ANNEX TO No. 99

We have previously appreciated that the ultimate object of the Soviet Union is the establishment of Communism, directed from Moscow, throughout the world. It thus seems probable that the Russian long-term

---

[1] On the question of China's industrial potential and the aims of Communist China beyond its own borders, this JIC assessment reached broadly the same conclusions as those that appeared in an FO regional survey (3 October 1949) of Soviet policy in the Far East. Where perhaps the emphasis differed slightly was in the FO expectation that on balance, Communist China was likely to become 'an effective instrument of Soviet policy, to which it will be indirectly geared through Communist Party control'. On Korea, the FO anticipated that so long as the Americans remained in Japan, it was unlikely that the Russians would either instigate, or offer support to, an invasion of the South from the North (N 9575/1023/38).

intention in the Far East and South East Asia, including the Indian sub-continent, is to achieve the establishment there of Communist Governments, obedient to Moscow, and thereby to eliminate from Asia the political and economic influence of the Western Powers and the military threat from the east.

Sino-Russian Relations

2. In order to estimate the degree of control likely to be exercised by the Soviet Leaders over Chinese Communist parties and the Chinese authorities, both in China proper and in the outlying provinces, we have examined below the relations of the Soviet Government and the leaders of Communist China.

Russian Relations with the Outer Provinces of China

3. *Mongolian People's Republic,* was formerly a province of China, called Outer Mongolia. It was occupied after the Russian Revolution by the Red Army, which was not withdrawn until 1924 when an autonomous government had been established. After a plebiscite in 1945 the Central Chinese Government agreed to the 'independence' of this Republic. The Mongolian People's Republic has become a Russian satellite state closely controlled from Moscow. The Mongolian Army is equipped and supplied with advisory personnel from the Soviet Union.

4. *Inner Mongolia,* on the other hand, remains technically a part of China. A Communist regime under Yun Tse, a Sinicised Mongol trained in Moscow and president of the Inner Mongolian Communist Party, was established in 1947 in the presence of Russian and Outer Mongolian forces, covering the Mongol areas in Jehol, Chahar, Suiyuan and North West Manchuria. Yun Tse himself, however, has announced that Inner Mongolia is a constituent part of the Chinese Republic and that the people, although not of Han stock, are Chinese.

5. *Sinkiang* likewise remains a Chinese province. By skilful exploitation, however, of the tribes on the Russian border, the Russians and their agents have arranged the establishment of a regime favourable to themselves in the north.

6. *Manchuria* was occupied by Russian forces in 1945. When they withdrew, taking with them £200 million worth of industrial assets, they left behind a situation in which a government under Li Li-San, a communist trained in Moscow, was subsequently able to take over. By virtue of the Yalta agreement and the Sino-Soviet Treaty of August 1945, the Russians enjoy substantial control of the Chinese Eastern railway and the South Manchurian railway. They have refortified Port Arthur as a naval base and retained special privileges in Dairen.

Russian Relations with China Proper

7. The Chinese Communist leaders are orthodox Communists and have repeatedly denounced the nationalistic deviation of Yugoslavia. The particular interests of China Proper, however, both internal and external,

may require special tactics; and if not skilfully guided by Russian policy may become a deviation. The basis of those particular interests is economic and they are discussed below.

8. Whereas the industrial proletariat is the usual instrument of Marx-Leninism, the economy of China Proper is almost wholly agricultural, and the 'Peasant question', or the difficulty of preserving the alliance between the 'Proletarian Vanguard' and the 'mass of labouring peasants' has always been a problem for communist planners. The Soviet Union is unlikely to be willing to divert to China the necessary technicians and material from projects to which she is already committed in her own Far Eastern territories. The commercial co-operation of the Western Powers will therefore be necessary for any reasonably rapid industrial development or improvement of the standard of living in China Proper.

9. The Communist Party in China Proper will therefore be confronted with special economic difficulties in bringing Chinese Communism into line with communism as it is understood in Moscow, and will at least be compelled to go slow. These special difficulties are in turn likely to limit the degree of Russian control of the Central Chinese Communist Government.

Future Relations

10. The political shape to be imposed upon the whole of China including the outer Provinces will remain to be seen when China Proper has been overrun by Communist armies. The leaders of the Chinese Communists in all areas have either been trained in Moscow, or have learned their Communism from those who have been trained there. It might therefore be expected that a gigantic new Far Eastern communist state will arise, or a new far eastern union of Soviet Republics. Mao Tse-tung has himself forecast a 'federation' of Chinese Democratic Republics but whether the focus of power in such a federation would be wholly Russian, even if ostensibly Chinese, or genuinely Chinese, it is at present impossible to forecast.

11. Since China became a Republic, no Chinese Government has ever succeeded in controlling the whole of China including the outlying provinces, and it is hardly likely that an alien government in Moscow will be more successful. Moreover, Russian imperialism in the Far East has not in the past been notably successful, and it is open to doubt whether the Soviet leaders have sufficient technical man power, specialist knowledge and political skill to exploit the opportunity offered by the success of the Communist cause in China. Direct Russian control of the whole of China is therefore improbable.

12. Present indications suggest that in China Proper the provincial organisation will be replaced by a small number of regional administrations controlled, to an extent still unknown, by a Communist Central Government. All of these will no doubt be co-ordinated and controlled by the Chinese Communist Party pursuing the Moscow line. Outer Mongolia, a direct neighbour of the Soviet Union, will remain firmly controlled

economically, politically, and militarily, to all intents and purposes an integral part of the Soviet Union. The Soviet leaders are likely to make special efforts to retain control of Manchuria, another neighbour, which is of particular economic importance by reason of its industrial potential and sea ports, and of strategic importance by virtue of its naval base and communications. The degree of Russian control of Inner Mongolia and of Sinkiang will depend on the relations between the Soviet Union and China Proper.

Summary

13. The new driving force of communism in the Far East and the skill and energy of its Chinese leaders, of which the success of the communist armies is ample evidence, should not be under-estimated. In spite of the economic and political difficulties mentioned above it is reasonable to expect, at least in the near future, that there will be no important divergence between the policy of the Chinese leaders and the policy of the Soviet Leaders, and that the resources of China must be counted within the Russian orbit.

Potentialities of China as an ally of the Soviet Union

14. We review below the significance of the incorporation of China within the Russian orbit.

Political Potentialities

15. An efficient and resolute Government of China could exercise a powerful influence throughout the Far East and South East Asia by virtue of the Asiatic aspirations formerly exploited by the Japanese and of the considerable population established abroad from the borders of Australia to the borders of India. Although in the past many Chinese abroad have been prosperous and contented, they have usually supported the Chinese Central Government and returned to China in their old age. The new Communist Government is likely to aim at gaining the support of the overseas Chinese, and by exploiting this loyalty, they would have (except possibly in Burma where the Chinese are predominantly of the shop-keeping class) the makings of a dangerous fifth column which could do much to make untenable the position of the Western Powers in Indo-China and Malaya, to reverse the present inclinations of the Government of Siam, and to reverse the initial inclinations of the Nationalist Government of Indonesia.

16. The relevant political objectives hitherto announced by the Chinese communists are the elimination of feudalism and of Anglo-American imperialism in China, and, in particular, an end to American interference in Chinese affairs and the complete withdrawal of British forces from the vicinity of China. No announcement has been made about Hong Kong but it has been unofficially suggested that they will wish to 'discuss' it. There can be no doubt that the recovery of Hong Kong and Macao is among the ultimate aims of Chinese Communist policy. The Communists will also undoubtedly claim Formosa which is at present administered by the

Chinese Nationalist Government. It would be in the Russian interest for all these questions to be taken up.

17. The Soviet Leaders will no doubt afford the Communist Government of China their diplomatic support in securing *de jure* recognition and its admission as a member of the Security Council of the United Nations. They could thereupon encourage it to play an active part, in the Russian interest and against the Anglo-Americans, in the proceedings of the United Nations, particularly in respect of the Japanese Peace Treaty, the Korean question, and other Asiatic issues such as the problems of Indonesia, Formosa and Kashmir.

Economic Potentialities

Inner Mongolia

18. Inner Mongolia's limited economic resources are as yet little developed.

Sinkiang

19. Sinkiang trades almost exclusively with the Soviet Union. It has deposits of tungsten ore and oil and the Soviet Union is reported to be negotiating for concessions to work these deposits. Great efforts are being made to bind Sinkiang economically to the Soviet Union. There are small widely separated resources of Uranium ore.

Manchuria

20. Manchuria is rich agriculturally and has abundant timber. There are large reserves of coal (mainly bituminous) and of iron ore, in addition to a great variety of other metals. These resources were developed by the Japanese who built up a substantial engineering industry in the province. Towards the end of World War II when the Red Army occupied Manchuria, the province was denuded of most of its industrial equipment, including steel-making plant. Since then Manchurian industry has been barely sufficient for local needs, but food production has been adequate and surpluses have been exported to the Soviet Union and to Communist-dominated Northern China. A trade agreement between Manchurian authorities and the Soviet Union was signed in Moscow on the 30th July. So far as is known this is the first economic agreement signed by the Chinese Communists in pursuit of their announced policy of seeking such trade treaties with the Russians and their Satellites. Under the agreement the Soviet Union promises to furnish industrial equipment, oil, motor vehicles, textiles, and medical goods in return for soya beans, vegetable oil, maize and rice from Manchuria. The agreement is on a barter basis and, unlike most Soviet-Satellite trading agreements, covers one year only. According to unconfirmed reports a three-year plan for the economic rehabilitation of Manchuria has been agreed between the Soviet Union and the administration, and a Russian economic adviser has established his headquarters in Harbin. A number of locomotives and certain industrial machinery and plant are to be lent to the province by the Soviet Union

and some of the looted machinery has even been returned, but Russia's chief concern at the moment seems to be in maintaining Manchuria as a source of foodstuffs and raw materials. The industrial potential power exists and it may be here that the Soviet Union will find it worth while to extend help. If so, developments could be significant, for the basis laid by the Japanese is very extensive.

China Proper

21. China has little or no heavy industry. Communications are either primitive or chaotic, but the communists have already worked hard to improve them. Before any economic advantages can accrue to the Soviet[s] it will be essential, as a first step, to restore and improve communications and secondly to make China self-sufficient in foodstuffs so that a greater proportion of her foreign currency earnings can be spent on much needed capital equipment. Such earnings are earmarked for this purpose by the Communist economic programme.

22. The only economic advantage that is likely to accrue to the Soviet Union in the near future from Communist China is that country's output of tungsten, tin, antimony, and tung oil. To this might be added the vast resources of unskilled labour. There are small resources (which are being worked on a small scale) of Uranium ore in South China, in the area where the boundaries of Kiangsi, Hunan and Kwangtung provinces meet.

23. Domestic assets for future industrial developments include large coal reserves, considerable deposits of iron ore and some non-ferrous metals. At present, however, China lacks capital equipment and the skilled labour required to develop industry on any appreciable scale. The shortage of technical and administrative staff of every kind also increases the extent to which the industrial future of China depends upon foreign assistance. Whereas it may be difficult for the Soviet Union to spare capital, equipment or skilled labour to help China to any significant degree, it is not impossible that some development of industrial exports to the Far East may occur if the political inducement is thought sufficient. We believe nevertheless that China proper may be discounted as a major industrial asset to the Soviet bloc for a number of years to come.

Military Potentialities

Naval

24. The Chinese Communists have acquired some 60 warships from the Nationalists, including 6 Escort Destroyers. Although the efficiency of the personnel must at the moment be very low and the standard of maintenance of the ships is poor, this force does provide a solid basis on which to build. A number of the officers, including two senior officers, who have defected were British trained. The necessary senior staff officers to build up the required administration and organisation, which they are so seriously lacking, are thus available. We have, furthermore, good evidence

for supposing that ex-Nationalist officers and men who have been captured or who have defected are being trained and indoctrinated in Manchuria.

25. Chinese Communist Naval Forces are possibly capable of supporting small scale military operations, and it is to be expected that effective control of the approaches to ports can be established soon after the final Communist victory in China. In the long term, however, the Chinese Communist Government must realise that the surest means of protecting their sea frontier will lie in the exercise of sea-air power in the China Sea—the more so since the US garrisons in Japan and any unfriendly forces remaining in Formosa must represent a threat from that quarter. The creation of a powerful fleet might therefore become an important part of Chinese military policy. Such a fleet would fill the power-vacuum in the West Pacific caused by the elimination of the Japanese Fleet, and might well inspire the Chinese to adopt the Japanese policy of the greater East Asia Co-prosperity Sphere. It would, however, take many years of steady development for Chinese industry to become capable of building a large modern fleet, and the Soviet Union can hardly be expected to assist China to an extent which would give her naval predominance in the Western Pacific.

26. Considerable strategic advantages would be gained by the Soviet Union in the event of war from the use of the following ports by Russian submarines:

> Chusan Archipelago
> Foochow
> Swatow
> Amoy
> Yulin   )   Hainan (Developed by the
> Suma   )   Japanese during World War II)
> Hoihow   )
> Hongkong   ) Should these come under
> Macao   )
> Takao   ) the control of the Chinese
> Tsoying) Formosa)
> Keelung)   ) Communist Government

If the Russian surface forces in the Far East were developed to the extent of being able to dispute the control of the China Sea, some of these ports would also be of value to them in the event of war.

Army

27. The present strength of the Communist Army is believed to be about 2½ million, but this includes Korean, Japanese and Mongolian elements together with a large militia. The Chinese Communist Army is, however, at present in the process of re-organisation. When this is completed the field force is likely to consist of 1,400,000 men organised in 70 armies. With a population of 480 million, however, there is virtually no limit to the size

of the Army which could be raised. Although the Chinese Communist troops have not yet been tested in modern battle we estimate the standard of the best to be equal to that of the average Russian soldier. The Chinese Communist Armies are well equipped with all light weapons, but we consider it will be many years before they possess heavy equipment and supporting arms on a similar scale to a first-class European Army.

Air Forces

28. No operational Communist Air Force has appeared in the field and no operational air units are known to exist. A number of aircraft are, however, held and training is reported to be taking place in N. Manchuria and also in the Soviet Union.

29. Following is an estimate of Communist aircraft holdings in China:

Source of Supply	Aircraft Type	No. of Aircraft	Remarks
Japanese	Bomber) Fighter) Transport) Trainer)	100 to 150	It is considered unlikely that more than 30-50 are now serviceable.
Russian	Types as) above but) likely to) be mainly) Trainers)	40 to 80	These may be ex-lend lease aircraft.
American	Liberator) Mustang) Mitchell) Dakota)	22 to 50	These aircraft have been captured on airfields or flown over by Nationalist deserters.

30. There is little doubt that a Communist Air Force could be formed with Russian Assistance. Should it be possible to arrange for the transportation of adequate supplies, Chinese airfields would be of value to Russian air forces in the event of war.

Implications in South East Asia outside China

31. Once the Chinese Communists have established their rule throughout China the Communist Parties in the neighbouring countries in SE Asia may expect to receive some support more tangible than political directives and small quantities of smuggled weapons. The frontiers of Burma and FIC[2] with China are long and are extremely difficult to close. It is

[2] French Indo-China.

reasonable, therefore, to expect that aid on the lines of that given to the Greek Communists will be given to the Communists in Burma and to Ho Chi Minh. This will probably take the form of arms, and of incursion initially of Chinese guerilla bands. If these tactics are successful Burma and French Indo-China may be used in turn as bases for further Communist aggression against their neighbours. We therefore examine the further implications of such a development on the internal situation of the other countries of South East Asia.

French Indo-China

32. The factors affecting the future of the (Communist) Viet Minh movement in French Indo-China are the degree of co-operation it may expect from the Chinese Communists, the support the Emperor Bao Dai may expect from the Vietnamese, the degree to which Bao Dai's regime is recognised by neighbouring countries, and the success of French military operations.

33. The crucial factor is the degree of co-operation which Viet Minh may expect from the Chinese Communist. Ho Chi Minh is a Moscow trained Communist and it is reasonable to assume that arrangements for collaboration between Viet Minh and the Chinese Communists do exist. Bao Dai is generally suspect as a puppet of the French and although the latter are now doing their best to strengthen his position by assurances that Viet Nam is an independent and sovereign state, he will have a long way to go before he commands the allegiance of a majority of the Vietnamese. Mistrust of Bao Dai's regime as the creation of 'French Imperialism' is fairly widespread throughout South East Asia, and it is unlikely to be recognised until it has proved its ability to stand on its own feet. As to the military operations, so far as the present threat is concerned, the French Chief of Staff has stated that the French forces properly reinforced can, and will, hold their positions in Tonkin, and we agree with this appreciation provided the external threat does not develop before the present French plan is *fulfilled*. The French have also shown that they are conscious of the major external threat. President Auriol[3] has recently emphasised that Viet Nam is an independent State and a candidate for membership of the United Nations; by so doing he has made an international issue of any major Communist interference in Indo-China.

34. Should the Viet Minh with the assistance of the Chinese Communists be able to force the French to withdraw the immediate result would be a threat to Siam. This would cause the Siamese to be reluctant to continue to co-operate in anti-bandit measures on the Malayan border to which they have now agreed, and to seek definite guarantees from the Western Powers in exchange for long term co-operation.

[3] President of the French Republic.

Burma

35. It is not possible to predict the outcome of the present civil war in Burma, or the extent of the aid which might be derived from Communists in Yunnan. Burma is so divided in itself and so lacking in strong leaders that the country would fall an easy prey to a determined fifth column reinforced from outside.

36. In the past Communist Party directives to the Communists in Burma have been transmitted via the Communist Party of India. Since the early part of 1948 the influence of Mao Tse-Tung and the Communist Party of China in Burma has been at least as strong as that of the Communist Party of India.

37. There has recently been a significant increase of Communist influence in the Arakan, the Irrawaddy Valley and the Upper Chindwin area, and with sufficient assistance from the Chinese Communists in China it is possible that the whole of Burma may come under Communist control. The immediate implications of such a situation are:

(*a*) A threat to the Burmese export rice trade, with serious repercussions on the food situation especially in Malaya, Ceylon and India.

(*b*) A threat to India and possibly Pakistan, with a consequent pre-occupation of the governments of those countries with the security of their frontiers in that direction and with internal security in the border areas.

Siam

38. The Communist Party in Siam is relatively weak amongst the Siamese, but disproportionately strong amongst the two to three million Chinese. (The total population of Siam is seventeen and a half million.) The Free Thai movement is alleged to have obtained a promise of full CCP (Siam) backing and support for Pridi's[4] next attempt at a coup d'état. If successful in this, the Communists would attempt to infiltrate and gain control of the Siamese Government by their now well established technique. There is, however, no immediate likelihood of this occurring. Should either French Indo-China (FIC) or Burma be brought under Communist domination a determined Communist effort, based on one of these countries, to establish a favourable regime in Siam can be expected, which the present Government would be unlikely to be able to prevent.

Malaya

39. At present it appears as if the Malayan Chinese bandits may at least succeed in implementing that part of their strategic plan which envisaged concentration in the Betong salient of Siam on the North Malaya border.

---

[4] Nai Pridi Panomyong, war-time resistance leader in Siam who fled the country when Field Marshal Pibul (see No. 59, note 8) came to power after a *coup* in 1947. Nai Pridi's supporters staged an unsuccessful *coup* in his favour in 1948 and there were rumours that a further attempt had been made in February 1949.

In the absence of effective Siamese military and police operations in this area, these bandits will succeed in reorganising. The recent agreement for the mutual co-operation of Siamese and Malayan police in the border area is an important first step towards a concerted Malayan-Siamese approach to this danger. If Siam falls under Communist domination, they will probably receive direct logistical support, and will be able to return to the offensive in Malaya with increasing confidence.

40. The bulk of the Malayan Chinese may become less inclined to resist threats and extortions and to take an active stand against their bandit co-nationalists. Already it is clear that even those Chinese in Malaya who denounce the present terrorist campaigns are not prepared to base their denunciation on the fact that this a Communist movement. Further, the interest shown by certain sections of the Chinese community in the presence of Tan Kah Kee[5] in liberated China, as a member of the Preliminary Constituent Committee, and other evidence of the influence of the Liberation movement, show that events in China are likely to make the Malayan Chinese more inclined to adopt a 'fellow-travelling' line. The Government are attempting to counter this tendency by a policy of weaning the Chinese from their loyalty and affiliation to China and encouraging exclusive loyalty to Malaya.

Indonesia

41. It appears likely that in the near future Dutch sovereignty will have passed to a native nationalist government which will probably initially be opposed to Communism. The Chinese in Indonesia, who conduct much of the trade of the region, will be left without Dutch protection on which they have relied in the past and can expect little sympathy from the Indonesians jealous of their success. Though the Chinese in Indonesia have been lukewarm in their attitude to Nationalist China since the war, their need for support to guard their interests in Indonesia may cause them to renew their ties with a successful regime in China. The Communists possibly aided by the Chinese will make the overthrow of the nationalist government their first task. It is impossible at the moment to forecast the outcome of the possible struggle for power.

North Borneo and Sarawak

42. Communist influence is at present negligible although the small nucleus which already exists among the Chinese communities may become strengthened and expand with encouragement from China. It may be necessary to admit numbers of Chinese from the Federation and Singapore into North Borneo if the development of the Colony is to proceed as planned; but immigrants will be carefully screened and will be liable to

[5] Tan Kah Kee was a leading Chinese industrialist in Singapore who urged the Malayan Chinese to end lawlessness on the ground that disorder would lead to unemployment and therefore reduce remittances to families in China.

repatriation. The immigration laws and administration of all three Borneo territories are meanwhile being tightened up. The Police Forces are being reorganised and expanded and there seems no reason to suppose that when this process is completed the local forces will not be able to deal with any internal security threat which may develop in the foreseeable future.

South-East Asian Nationalism

43. The force of nationalism in South-East Asia is a factor which may now militate against a further development of communism in the area. One of the chief assets of the Communists in these countries has hitherto been their support of nationalism. The Russians have professed to play the role of the champions of the oppressed peoples against the tyranny of the Imperialist plutocrats and the Communists in pursuing the anti-Imperialist path were, until lately, aligned with bourgeois national liberation movements. Nevertheless, the principal nationalistic movement in Malaya, for example, is anti-Communist. In Burma and India, despite the recession of British power, the communists profess that the anti-Imperialist struggle is continuing, and, being determined that the proletarian revolution shall follow the political revolution, they have turned against the bourgeois nationalists in power and denounce them as tools of the Imperialists. Such was the intention of the Communist rebellion against the Indonesian Republic in 1948, but the tactics employed brought only discredit to the Communists.

44. In the past, nationalistic elements have looked to the Soviet Union for moral support, but now, where they have established independent government, they find that the Soviet Union, unlike the Western Powers, offers them no practical assistance. Chinese immigrants in South-East Asia are a perpetual irritant to the indigenous peoples and the fact that the Chinese are presumably now the spearhead of Communism in South-East Asia may further divert support from the Soviet Union. The more closely the immigrant Chinese align themselves with the Communist regime in China, the greater may become the hostility of the indigenous peoples towards communism. Thus a rift, which should be capable of exploitation, has appeared in South-East Asia between communism and moderate nationalism, and the sinophobia of the indigenous peoples will contribute to widen it. Exploitation of this rift between communism and moderate nationalism will largely depend upon the extent to which Communists can be made to appear as enemies rather than friends of existing independent Governments. No such policy is of course applicable in places such as Singapore where the population has a Chinese majority.

45. It would be a mistake, however, to assume that the threat can be readily averted by skilful propaganda or diplomacy only. Material support in the way of military equipment will also be essential if the indigenous governments are to regain or maintain their control over their territories. It will be equally important to prove that the military power of the West is predominant, and that in the ultimate resort the West can and will defend

its interests in the East. If it can be shown that the West is competent to resist Communism in Malaya, in Hong Kong, and in Indo-China, moderate opinion in South-East Asia will be reassured. It is becoming steadily more apparent that the Communists intend to push on in South-East Asia as far as possible until they reach the limits of possible exploitation in present circumstances, and there appears to be little prospect of a pause for consolidation. Open aggression against the states of South-East Asia is unlikely, but aggression by indirect subversive means is to be expected and will be effectively checked only when it meets superior force and recognises that that force is backed by the Western Powers.

Implications in the Far East outside China

Japan

46. The communisation of Japan, which is still the only country in Eastern Asia which has considerable reserves of highly-skilled industrial manpower, and organising and technical ability, would be an indispensable element in the successful communisation of Asia. It must be assumed, therefore, that the eventual incorporation of Japan into the Soviet sphere occupies an important place in Soviet plans. The extremely thorough and successful indoctrination which has obviously been undergone by Japanese prisoners-of-war now being repatriated from Soviet territory lends colour to this view. The success of the Chinese Communists has undoubtedly been an important element in the steady growth of Communist influence in Japan. It is unlikely, however, that the Japanese Communist Party will gain sufficient strength under existing conditions to prove a serious embarrassment to the occupation authorities. It is, of course impossible to forecast how long the military occupation in its present form will continue.

47. The success of the Communists in China has clearly enhanced the importance of Japan to the Western Powers as the one remaining relatively secure non-Communist area in Eastern Asia. There are indications that the Japanese have seized on this aspect of the situation, with the result that the possibility of an improvement in their own bargaining position *vis-à-vis* the Western Powers has somewhat blinded them to the real nature of the threat to Japanese security presented by the spread of Communism on the Asiatic mainland.

48. In the long run it is hard to see how Japan can hope to attain economic viability without a substantial flow of trade with China. The degree of Japan's dependence on trade with China may have important political consequences within Japan. There are already reports of Japanese merchants making contacts with the Japanese Communist Party in the apparent belief that when the time comes they will only be able to get a firm footing in the China market if they appear to be of the right political complexion.

Philippines

49. The Government of the Philippines are at present firmly anti-communist and the President has publicly associated himself, even at the

present late stage, with the Chinese Nationalist Government.[6] The Communist movement of the Philippines, however, which is believed to be in touch with the Chinese Communist Party, is likely to be encouraged and reinforced by the Communist success in China. The agrarian revolutionary movement (Hukbalahap) is led by an avowed Communist, and dock labour is under communist influence.

Korea

50. North Korea is a Satellite State on much the same pattern as the People's Democracies of Eastern Europe. The chances of survival of the government of the Republic of Korea (the democratic administration in the south) will be diminished by the establishment of a Communist Government in China.[7]

[6] Chiang Kai-shek flew from Formosa to Baguio in Luzon to the north of Manila to meet President Quirino of the Philippines in July 1949. His purpose was to discuss the formation of an anti-Communist front in the Pacific region and closer economic co-operation between China and the Philippines (F 1031/1015/10).
[7] The Chiefs of Staff approved this report on 14 October (COS 152(49)13, DEFE 4/25).

No. 100

Mr. Bevin to HM Representatives Overseas

Information No. 371 Telegraphic [F 14878/1023/10]

Confidential   FOREIGN OFFICE, *7 October 1949, 11.45 a.m.*

His Majesty's Consul-General at Peking has made the following official communication to the Chinese Communist Ministry of Foreign Affairs:

[Begins]
'His Majesty's Government in the United Kingdom are carefully studying the situation resulting from the formation of the Central People's Government.[1] Friendly and mutually advantageous relations, both commercial and political, have existed between Britain and China for many generations. It is hoped that these will continue in the future. His Majesty's Government in the United Kingdom therefore suggest that, pending completion of their study of the situation, informal relations should be established between His Majesty's Consular Officers and the appropriate authorities in the territory under the control of the Central People's Government for the greater convenience of both Governments and promotion of trade between the two countries.'
[Ends].

[1] Mao Tse-tung proclaimed the establishment of the People's Republic of China on 21 September 1949; a Communist government was inaugurated in Peking on 1 October.

2. Although from the strictly legal point of view this communication could be interpreted as implying *de facto* recognition, it merely constitutes a further attempt to induce the Communist authorities to enter into working relations with His Majesty's Consular Officers pending a decision on the recognition question. His Majesty's Government's declared policy of consulting other friendly governments on this question remains, of course, unchanged.

3. We do *not* intend to release this communication to the press and it seems unlikely that the Chinese will do so. Above is for your guidance and for use only in the event of this statement becoming publicised.[2]

---

[2] Sir W.E. Beckett, Legal Adviser to the FO, minuted on 10 October on the recognition issue: 'In this connexion we have studied UK record of conversations between Ministers at Washington [see Nos. 96 and 97] and note that the word "recognition" was employed in those conversations without any definition. We consider however that the Ministers were concerned with *de jure* recognition since they were discussing *inter alia* Chinese representation on the Security Council, and do not think they had this kind of *de facto* recognition in mind.'

The State Department in Washington was not consulted about this message in advance and did not receive the text until six days after it had been communicated to Peking. Mr. Acheson complained that it implied *de facto* recognition and requested 'full consultation' over any future action contemplated by the UK. According to the Secretary of State, President Truman 'thought that the British had not played very squarely with us on this matter' (*FRUS 1949*, vol. ix, p. 132). Mr. Bevin found the situation 'embarrassing' and he explained to the US Ambassador that a 'mistake in the Department' had caused the delay in informing Washington (F 15683/1023/10).

No. 101

Minute by B.A. Casey[1] for Chiefs of Staff Committee

COS(49)330 [*CAB 21/2429*]

Top Secret. Guard   MINISTRY OF DEFENCE, *7 October 1949*

HONG KONG—POLICY IN WAR

I have the honour to forward for the information of the Chiefs of Staff a paper by the Commanders-in-Chief, Far East, on Defence Policy for Hong Kong in a war with Russia.

2. The paper has been discussed in the British Defence Co-ordination Committee and the Commissioner General has expressed himself personally as in agreement with it. He does not wish, however, to endorse it formally until he is satisfied that the Governor of Hong Kong is in general agreement. The paper is accordingly being sent to Hong Kong for early concurrence or comment and will, if necessary, be discussed with the Governor in November, which is the first likely opportunity.

---

[1] Secretary, Chiefs of Staff Committee.

3. I am further to state that the Commissioner General has not yet had any correspondence with the Foreign Office on the subject matter of the paper.

B.A. CASEY

ANNEX TO NO. 101

DEFENCE POLICY FOR HONG KONG IN A WAR WITH RUSSIA

Introduction

1. With the southward advance of the Chinese Communist armies the threat to Hong Kong has greatly increased and in consequence substantial reinforcements of all three Services have been sent to the Colony. This fact indicates the importance attached by His Majesty's Government at the present time to resisting further Communist expansion in the Far East and to preserving the integrity of territories for which it is responsible. The defence policy for Hong Kong during the present period of cold war is thereby clearly established. Should war break out, however, it will be necessary to review this policy in the light of many new factors.

2. For the purposes of this paper we regard the island colony of Hong Kong and the area acquired or leased under separate agreements with the Chinese government as a unified whole. We do not consider that our argument need be complicated by an attempt to assess the different degrees of moral right and obligation which the United Kingdom possesses in the different parts of the Territory.

The Aim of the Paper

3. The aim of this paper is to discuss our defence policy in relation to Hong Kong in a war with Russia.

Assumptions

4. We have made the following assumptions:

(*a*) Russia will be the main enemy in war, but within the theatre Communist China is likely to present the primary threat, both by attack from her armed forces and on account of her active encouragement of subversive activity and militant Communism.

(*b*) The Commonwealth and the United States will be allied from the outset.

(*c*) So long as the cold war continues in the Far East the maintenance of our position in Hong Kong will remain a most important part of our cold war strategy.

5. Since we are not conversant with proposed American strategy in the Far East we have assumed that no direct American contribution is likely for the defence of Hong Kong.

Military factors affecting our defence policy in Hong Kong

6. Hong Kong is a base whence naval and air offensive operations could be undertaken against coastal shipping and, in the case of air operations, against road and rail communications. The effectiveness of operations of this type other than at short range will, however, be restricted by lack of airfield facilities, even when Deep Bay airfield is developed. From Hong Kong, therefore, a limited contribution only could be made towards delaying any intended enemy advance into South East Asia.

7. It is difficult at this stage accurately to assess the scale of attack likely to be developed against Hong Kong in a war which takes place in several years time. It is possible that the Chinese Communists would receive some assistance from Russia, especially in the air. On the other hand factors such as economic difficulties, shortage of both military and industrial equipment and fuels, and the innate disinclination of the Chinese to be controlled by others might alienate them from close co-operation with Russia, and might even cause internal division within China herself. Until these factors become clear, however, it would be wise to assume that the Chinese Communists alone could attack the Colony with land forces limited only by the terrain and their technical and logistic weakness. For some time to come, any such attack would almost certainly be assisted by a very serious internal security problem amongst the large and unreliable Chinese population.

8. We consider that the minimum garrison which would have a good chance of holding Hong Kong against a full scale Chinese Communist attack of this nature would be of the order of two divisions and four fighter squadrons, together with adequate naval forces and shipping for their supply.

9. It is most unlikely that as large a force as this could be made available in war to garrison Hong Kong. Even were the threat to diminish, and the forces required consequently to be reduced, the units needed for this task would certainly represent a major part of the total Far East garrison.

10. The availability of reinforcements for Hong Kong from within the theatre would depend upon the strength of the garrison available for the Far East as a whole, the state of affairs in French Indo-China, Thailand, Burma and Indonesia, and the situation in Malaya as affected by events in these neighbouring territories.

11. Were the Communists to extend their sphere of domination south-westwards it might be necessary to devote all our available resources to the security of Malaya since it forms the lynchpin of our position in the Far East. In this case unless reinforcements were available from outside the theatre, they would of necessity have to come from Hong Kong.

12. Although the contribution outlined in paragraph 6 above could hinder an enemy advance in South East Asia it could not indefinitely prevent it. Therefore the garrison required for Hong Kong might well be better employed to oppose the enemy in the more decisive regions of the theatre.

13. Were the Chinese Communists to be given appreciable Russian help, particularly in the air, Hong Kong might be rendered indefensible and it must therefore be regarded as an insecure base.

14. Hong Kong with its present population produces only about one tenth of its own food requirements and few other essential needs. Its maintenance and supply would therefore be a severe liability, placing an added burden on both our rice and shipping resources. The local defence of the harbour could only be provided at the expense of other ports. Furthermore, the possibility of enemy U-boat action would compel protection for such shipping, thus straining our anti-submarine resources. The maintenance and supply of Hong Kong can therefore only be regarded as acceptable in return for powerful advantages.

15. Hong Kong contains facilities which could be of value to the enemy. It could be used as an advanced U-boat base to attack our southern shipping routes. Our intelligence advice is, however, that these routes are unlikely to be the main target for the enemy U-boat offensive. Were the enemy able to continue coastal shipping operations the port facilities, which are better than those in Canton, would assist him to ease the strain on his inland communications. Its air facilities would add nothing to those already available to him. The denial to the enemy of a great port by demolition has been proved to be an enormous undertaking. Therefore continued occupation by us is desirable but not, on this score alone, essential.

The Economic Factor

16. Hong Kong's considerable economic importance in peacetime lies predominantly in its entrepôt trade. This trade depends on access to China, free movement of shipping of all types and the availability for trade of large quantities of manufactured goods and raw materials. Such goods as are manufactured in Hong Kong are, with the exception of ship-building and textiles, of no importance in war. The supply of raw materials for these manufactures would in any case be uncertain. In addition, cessation of the entrepôt trade would cause bankruptcy in the Colony and compel the payment of a subsidy. It is possible that in China there may be opportunities even in war for exerting economic and political pressure from Hong Kong with the object of undermining Chinese co-operation with Russia. Should, however, such co-operation be fully effective, Hong Kong would be not only of negligible economic value in war but also a financial drain on the United Kingdom.

Political Factors

17. Hong Kong is British territory. We therefore have a paramount duty and moral obligation towards the inhabitants.

18. In the East the value of 'face' is highly rated and the maintenance of our position in Hong Kong, particularly if accompanied by offensive action there, might influence the attitude of neighbouring countries in our favour. Nevertheless the military factors outlined above indicate that in war Hong Kong is not vital and will be very expensive in both men and materials.

We must, therefore, consider the implications of withdrawal, in spite of the gravity of such a decision.

19. The effect of a withdrawal from Hong Kong upon the other countries in the theatre would be conditioned by their attitude towards ourselves and the enemy at the time. Were they to be mainly anti-Communist, or were they 'sitting on the fence', our withdrawal from Hong would have a much more serious effect than if they had already definitely declared their hostility towards us. Memories are long in the East, and a withdrawal would be regarded by Asians as likely to be the start of a train of events similar to 1941.

20. In the independent countries, Thailand and Burma, a withdrawal would result in a loss of prestige for the Western Powers and a lack of confidence in the ability of the British to provide support in the face of the Russian threat. Were they favourably disposed to us at the time, a weakening of the anti-Communist front and a strengthening of the Communist faction in those countries would follow. They would consequently be less inclined to help our war effort, which they might indeed seek to hinder. Were they to be avowedly pro-Communist their cause would receive encouragement.

21. In the dependent countries, Indo-China and Malaya, a British withdrawal would greatly encourage the Communist and subversive movements whose cause would be strengthened. Consequently the threat to internal security within the countries concerned would be increased.

22. The repercussions in Indonesia would be as for those in a dependent or independent country according to its position at the time.

23. These ill effects would be mitigated in any particular country were that country to benefit by the diversion of forces from Hong Kong to its own area.

24. It can be seen from the foregoing that in general the effect of a withdrawal upon the anti-Communist countries of the theatre would be serious, though not so serious in the case of those countries already hostile towards us. We see no reason to suppose, however, that it would be disastrous so long as we were to retain our position in Malaya.

25. In particular the effect would be further conditioned by the timing of such a withdrawal. Should withdrawal become necessary its timing would have to take into account our moral obligation to British citizens to permit them time to readjust their lives and business interests, and the desirability of realising our capital assets in the Colony.

26. Withdrawal could take place:

(*a*) *At, or very shortly before, the outbreak of war*
This would have the disadvantage that we would have either to keep the local inhabitants in ignorance of our intention to abandon them or by announcing our projected departure lose all bargaining power *vis-à-vis* the Chinese Government.

(b) After the outbreak of war

This would be open to the same disadvantages as (*a*) above and might have, in addition, the character of a military defeat with great loss of 'face' and the serious political repercussions which that implies.

27. A third alternative would be to give up Hong Kong as a result of direct diplomatic negotiations between the United Kingdom Government and China. Such a course might satisfy the requirements of paragraph 25 above, and would have the additional advantage of mitigating any appearance of a surrender to *force majeure* on our part.

28. There are, however, certain extremely cogent objections to the course suggested in paragraph 27 above. In view of our treaty rights in Hong Kong, its rendition to China would be regarded throughout South East Asia as a sign of weakness. This would be all the more serious if the rendition wore made to a Communist China since all the advantages of possession of Hong Kong would in that case be handed over to an actual enemy in the cold war period and a potential enemy in a hot war. Moreover were such a course to be decided upon we might find that, by taking counsel of our fears of an attack which might never materialise, we had forfeited the great advantages which we obtain from Hong Kong in peace. We would also discard the benefits gained by making a firm stand in the Colony during the cold war.

29. Therefore we are opposed to such a course. But there is another alternative which might avoid both the disadvantages of having to defend, by ourselves, the colony in war and also the objections to negotiating its peaceful rendition to a Communist China. If it is considered that we cannot hold Hong Kong there is a good case for action through the United Nations organisation to put the Colony on such an international footing that we could obtain the peacetime benefits from Hong Kong without bearing the heavy responsibility for its defence unsupported. This raises questions with which it is beyond our competence to deal but we mention it as the only means which appears to us to offer a satisfactory solution to the problem.

The Importance of Hong Kong within the Far East Theatre: Summary of Deductions

30. In war Hong Kong can make a contribution to retarding the enemy's military advance in South East Asia but its influence in this respect could be useful but not decisive.

31. It is difficult at this stage accurately to assess the threat to Hong Kong in a war taking place in several years time. Against Chinese Communists alone Hong Kong could probably be held by a garrison of two divisions and four fighter squadrons, together with adequate naval forces and shipping for their supply. Such a force should be regarded as a minimum requirement until the threat can be assessed more accurately. It is, however, most unlikely that as large a garrison as this could be made available for the Colony in a war against Russia.

32. Even were the threat to decrease the forces required to exert the degree of influence referred to in 30 above would represent a major part of the wartime garrison for the Far East, and might well be better employed in those parts of the theatre where a decisive contribution could be made.

33. If appreciable Russian assistance were available to the enemy, Hong Kong might be indefensible, and must therefore be regarded as an insecure base.

34. The maintenance and supply of Hong Kong in war would place a heavy burden upon our resources. Its reinforcement from within the theatre, at any rate during the early stages, might well be impossible.

35. Hong Kong's economic value in war would be negligible.

36. The factors of prestige and politics which in the Far East play so important a part in strategy are difficult to evaluate. Nevertheless it is evident that were we forced to evacuate Hong Kong under conditions of apparent political duress, or worse still military defeat, it would have a markedly adverse effect upon our prestige in the theatre and would be of encouragement to the enemy. It is quite clear that to adopt the course of evacuating the Colony and handing it to China by diplomatic negotiation well before the outbreak of war would have most serious disadvantages.

Conclusions

37. We conclude that in view of:

(*a*) our obligations to the inhabitants of the Colony;
(*b*) the desirability of obtaining the full benefits from our cold war strategy of reinforcing Hong Kong;
(*c*) the need to retain the advantages conferred upon us in peace by the Colony;
(*d*) the fact that the wartime threat to Hong Kong cannot as yet be accurately assessed;

it would be wrong at this stage to assume that we shall be unable to hold Hong Kong in war and to regard withdrawal as inevitable. We would, however, qualify this statement by emphasising that our ability to hold Malaya and Singapore must not be prejudiced by any policy adopted regarding Hong Kong.

38. We would point out that until the threat becomes clarified, it would be wise to assess the garrison needed to defend Hong Kong in war at two divisions and four fighter squadrons, together with adequate naval forces and shipping for their supply.

39. If the defence of the Colony continues to need large forces which can be ill spared from other more important parts of the theatre, or if it appears certain that the Chinese Communists will receive backing from Russia sufficient to enable them to mount an overwhelming attack upon the Colony, it will be necessary to reconsider our policy regarding Hong Kong. The essence of the problem is to balance, from both the political and military points of view, the disadvantages of withdrawing from Hong

Kong against the advantages of releasing the garrison for operations elsewhere.

40. Finally, we would emphasise that in writing this paper our intention has been to present the problem of Hong Kong in relation to the Far East theatre only. We of course realise that any decision which may be taken upon the strategic policy for the Colony must be related to the world-wide Commonwealth and allied war plans.[2]

[2] When this paper was considered by the British Defence Co-ordination Committee, Far East on 15 November 1949, Mr. Dening explained that the FO and Colonial Office had agreed that the problem of Hong Kong should be treated like that of Berlin; 'the enemy must be defied even though it was not possible to see the eventual outcome'. Mr. Dening suggested that it was not an opportune time to reopen the question of the colony's future. Sir A. Grantham agreed with the paper's conclusions and Mr. MacDonald proposed that the paper should be reviewed again by the committee in six or twelve months' time. Recommending that the Chiefs of Staff should do no more than take note of the paper, the Joint Planning Staff reiterated that it was not UK policy to defend Hong Kong against an attack by a first class power in possession of the mainland. The reinforcements of all three services despatched to Hong Kong earlier in the year would be required in other theatres in the event of war (JP(49)118(Final) of 16 December 1949, CAB 21/2429).

In April 1950 one component in these reinforcements—the Royal Marine Commando Brigade (see No. 76)—was transferred to Malaya. The colonial authorities in Hong Kong opposed the transfer, which was undertaken as part of a renewed drive against Communist insurgents in Malaya (FC 1192/14 and COS 63(50)3, 24 April 1950, DEFE 4/30). In approving the transfer, the Chiefs of Staff wanted to impose a 'firm limit' on further military reinforcements to Malaya. They did not want Malaya to become a 'bottomless pit devouring all our resources', as this would play 'straight into Russia's hands'. Any further reinforcement of the Far East could not be drawn from the UK. If subsequently there were an emergency in Hong Kong, the Commando Brigade would have to be returned from Malaya (FC 1192/17).

The garrison was temporarily reduced still further when two battalions were sent to Korea upon the outbreak of the Korean War in June 1950. Hostilities in Korea prompted a further review of Hong Kong defence policy. This envisaged a limited war against China as a result of a Chinese assault on Hong Kong. The Chiefs of Staff considered that the capture of the colony would have 'grave repercussions on the Allied position in the Far East and South-East Asia, and would be a severe shock to British prestige generally'. Communist forces in China were said to have grown appreciably (200,000 in the Canton area as opposed to the 40,000 estimate of May 1949), and the Korean War had demonstrated that Russian-trained forces were now better equipped and more efficient. To hold Hong Kong it was suggested that three infantry divisions and an armoured regiment would be required, together with other land and air and naval support units. In the short term it was considered unrealistic to rely on US and Commonwealth assistance. Their forces would not arrive in time. UK forces could not now be drawn from Malaya where the risk of defeat 'would be fatal to our whole position in the Far East'. Reinforcements would have to be drawn from other theatres (Germany or the Middle East) or by partial mobilisation. 'By causing us to divert forces to a theatre remote from our vital interests' the Chiefs of Staff argued that both courses 'would play straight into the Communists' hands. The former would greatly weaken our position in Europe and the Middle East, and the latter would throw a severe strain upon our economy.' Recommending a series of military, political, civilian and deception measures (the latter intended to make it appear that the garrison was larger than it was) to safeguard Hong Kong, the Chiefs of Staff concluded: 'If, therefore, Hong Kong is to be retained, it must, as far as possible, be by a policy designed to deter the Chinese from launching an attack' (report to Cabinet Defence Committee, DO(50)74, 15 September 1950, CAB 131/9).

No. 102

Letter from Sir A. Gascoigne[1] (Tokyo) to Mr. Dening

[*F 15700/1015/10*]

Personal & secret   TOKYO, *8 October 1949*

Dear Bill,

The Governor of Hong Kong (who has been staying here for the past week) and I spent an hour with the Supreme Commander in the latter's office this morning. Although a part of what MacArthur said was a repetition of what he said to me in the past, I think that you may like to learn the upshot of the conversation.

2. The interview was arranged for Sir Alexander Grantham, and the situation in China formed, therefore, the main topic of conversation. I opened the ball by remarking that I had heard that the head of the Chinese Nationalist Government Mission here, General Chu Shih-ming, had left Tokyo that morning for a short visit to Formosa. The Supreme Commander explained that, according to Chu, he had been sent for by Chiang Kai-shek; Chu had not, however, explained clearly the exact reason for this. MacArthur suggested that it might be that Chu had decided to see the Generalissimo on questions pertaining to the upkeep of the Chinese Mission here (which had not been paid since last May!), and also with a view to stabilising his own position with the Nationalists, to whom he was definitely committed. At the interview which MacArthur had given to Chu before his departure, the latter had stated that the Nationalist Generals in South China were determined to make an all-out last attempt to stand before Canton, but that he (Chu) had no great illusions regarding the eventual fate of that city. MacArthur had asked him how long he thought that the Canton could hold out, but Chu had not given him any clues.[2]

3. Sir Alexander then asked for MacArthur's opinion upon the Chinese situation in general, whereupon MacArthur aired his well-known views on the effects of totalitarianism upon the countries in which it held sway; *inter alia* he pointed to the deadening effect which this form of government

[1] UK Political Representative in Japan with rank of Ambassador, 1946-1951.
[2] Communist forces occupied Canton on 16 October.

always had upon the external and internal commercial activities of the countries concerned (*vide* article 6 of my despatch No.161).[3]

4. Turning to the question of the recognition of the Chinese Communist Government, MacArthur remarked that no doubt the British Government would recognise Peking before the United States Government did. The British would do this from economic, not political, motives; for they, unlike the United States, had important vested interests in the country. While he appreciated the pressure which was being exerted upon the United Kingdom Government by British commercial concerns in China, he would like to see the problem of recognition dealt with in another way. He suggested that British economic interests (which, if they attempted to carry on in China under the Reds would certainly be 'gipped' in the end) should be compensated, and that they should cut their losses and leave China for the present. There would then be no reason, he felt, for His Majesty's Government to recognise the Chinese Communist Government; indeed there would be every reason for them not to do so.

5. Turning then to the strategic aspect of the China situation, the General explained at some length why, in his opinion, the Chinese communists could, as he put it, be 'choked out of existence' by an Anglo-Saxon economic blockade. China was not in the same position as the Russian satellite states in Eastern Europe. The latter could be reached from the Soviet Union and supplied by Russia with what they needed. China could not be so supplied by Russia owing to the poor communications between the two countries (here followed a longish dissertation upon the defects of the Trans Siberian Railway and the length of time (four months) taken by Russia to marshal her forces for her week's war against Japan in 1945). Russia had not been able to send many supplies from Russia to help the Chinese Communist armies, who had received most of their munitions and equipment from United States sources either in the form of material traded with or captured from the Chinese Nationalist armies, or in the shape of American stores (140 shiploads) dumped at Vladivostock in 1945

---

[3] In this despatch of 12 September, Sir A. Gascoigne reported a conversation between Mr. MacDonald and General MacArthur at Tokyo on 10 September. The General, who was in 'expansive mood' on the subject of how, having been baulked in Europe, the Russians were now seeking to expand their influence throughout Asia, gave three reasons for his view that Russian communism was never successful in raising the living standards of those living under its sway. First, the political treatment of the people was such that 'they could not continue effectively to produce the fruits of the soil'. Secondly, it was difficult to market products because internal transport systems were so poor. Finally, the financial basis for the conduct of foreign trade was 'a stumbling block'. Russia would therefore not succeed in rehabilitating the Chinese economy. By contrast the General argued that if only the US and the British Commonwealth 'meticulously' examined the situation in China, they would find 'a vast field open to them for their industrial and commercial projects'. Mr. MacDonald explained that with the greater part of China dominated by the Communists, it was difficult for UK and US businesses to recover their China trade. Agreeing, the General 'acknowledged that this would be difficult and that he could not at present say precisely how this was to be done' (F 14533/1057/23).

for the supply of the Russian armies then fighting against Japan. Given therefore that China could receive but little material assistance from the West (Russia), she would have to trade with the Anglo-Saxon powers from the East. The Pacific was an 'Anglo-Saxon lake'; we could do what we liked there; we could virtually impose a blockade of China's Eastern seaboard, which would result in Communist China being eventually forced out of existence by reason of the economic chaos which would ensue throughout the land because of the total stoppage of supplies from outside. (You will observe that this suggestion for a blockade appears on the face of it at any rate to conflict with what MacArthur said recently to MacDonald, as reported in paragraph 6 of my despatch No. 161).[4]

6. Sir Alexander then addressed a question to the Supreme Commander regarding the present legal status of the island of Formosa, and MacArthur explained that it had only been placed under the 'trusteeship' of China until such time as it might legally be placed under the sovereignty of China by decisions taken at a Japanese peace conference. Sir Alexander remarked that if we recognized the Communist Government of China as being a *de jure* authority over Chinese territory, complications would seemingly arise over the status of Formosa, which would still be in Nationalist hands. General MacArthur replied that he felt convinced that Formosa would never be given up to the Chinese Communists by the Allies.

7. To sum up, MacArthur feels, as he always has felt, that his Government's handling of the Chinese situation has been wrong from the word 'go', and that the Communists would, if the United States had dealt with China with a firm hand from the start, have been completely defeated. He believes apparently that it would be possible now to make things so difficult for the Peking Government economically (through a Pacific blockade) that they would eventually fall, and that from the resulting chaos a new China might be born. The burden of his argument is, of course, that as the Chinese Communists have 'nothing at the back of them' (because Russia is unable to assist them materially), we should cash in on that happy state of affairs by 'smothering' the Reds at birth in the manner described above. But he fully realizes, I think, that his suggestions are not likely to come to fruition.

Sir Alexander and I came away feeling that while we had been treated to an interesting exposé of the China situation, the General's ideas for dealing with Communist China would be difficult of achievement.

8. I am sending a copy of this letter to the Chancery at Washington.

Yours ever,
JOE GASCOIGNE

---

[4] See note 3 above.

No. 103

Memorandum by Viscount Addison[1]

CP(49)202 [CAB 21/2429]

Secret   COMMONWEALTH RELATIONS OFFICE, *11 October 1949*

In C.P. (49) 136 of 17th June,[2] the Secretary of State for Commonwealth Relations summarised the replies received up to that time from other Commonwealth Governments to our approach about Hong Kong. As my colleagues will recall, the preliminary view of the Canadian Prime Minister was strongly critical of our intention to retain Hong Kong on the ground that it would be regarded in North America as wrong in principle to endeavour to maintain British rule by force in a Colony which was geographically part of China. In his memorandum of 17th June Mr. Noel-Baker emphasised that this was Mr. St. Laurent's first reaction only. Indeed, his views were given during a hurried week-end visit to Ottawa in the middle of an Election campaign, when, in view of the previous history, it might have been very embarrassing for the Government if the issue of Hong Kong had been raised.

2. Mr. St. Laurent promised to study the matter further and to let us have the considered views of the Canadian Government later. These have now been received in the form of an aide-mémoire dated 2nd September, which was handed to our High Commissioner at Ottawa, and which is reproduced as an Annex to this paper.

3. It will be seen that the Canadian Government fully appreciate the reasons why, in present circumstances, the United Kingdom has determined to make of Hong Kong a point where it will demonstrate its intention to resist Communist aggression in the Far East, and hope that 'this decision of the United Kingdom Government to defend Hong Kong will strengthen the will of all the threatened countries of East Asia to resist Communist infiltration or overt aggression.' The Canadian Government also pledge their full support to the United Kingdom Government, should we feel obliged to draw the attention of the Security Council to an attack on Hong Kong by the Chinese Communists.

4. My colleagues will wish to be aware of the much more forthcoming attitude now adopted by the Canadian Government, which is in refreshing contrast to Mr. St. Laurent's first reactions.

A.

[1] Lord Privy Seal.
[2] See No. 82.

ANNEX TO No. 103

DEPARTMENT OF EXTERNAL AFFAIRS, CANADA

OTTAWA, *2 September 1949*

Aide-Mémoire: Hong Kong

The memorandum of 28th May, 1949, and related papers setting forth the considerations which impelled the United Kingdom Government to decide to send reinforcements to Hong Kong, in order to be able to deal with any probable attack by the Chinese Communists, have been studied carefully.

The Canadian Government fully appreciates the reasons why the United Kingdom Government, under present circumstances, has determined to make of Hong Kong a point where it will demonstrate its intention to resist Communist aggression in the Far East. The threat of Communist domination over all South-East Asia carries far-reaching implications for all free countries. It is to be hoped that this decision of the United Kingdom Government to defend Hong Kong will strengthen the will of all the threatened countries of East Asia to resist Communist infiltration or overt aggression.

It is noted from the papers prepared for the consideration of the United Kingdom Government that emphasis is placed, in preparing for the defence of Hong Kong, on not unduly provoking Chinese reaction. The Canadian Government is in sympathy with this point of view. An aspect of this question is the possibility that the Communists might make use of the Hong Kong issue to provoke anti-British and anti-foreign agitation throughout China, which might well jeopardise the safety and welfare of all foreign nationals there.

It is noted further that, should the Chinese Communists attack Hong Kong, the United Kingdom Government would draw this action to the attention of the Security Council of the United Nations. In such circumstances the Canadian Government would lend its full support to the United Kingdom Government in the Security Council.

It is realised, however, that in the United Nations the Soviet *bloc* may endeavour to fit the Hong Kong issue into the framework of a general contention that the Western Powers are denying to the inhabitants of Asiatic territories the right of self-determination and are standing in the way of the progress of Asiatic countries to full freedom and independence. The Canadian Government, mindful of the danger that this type of propaganda may meet with some success, particularly in South-East Asia, would be glad to learn from the United Kingdom Government what line it is considering taking in the United Nations to counter the possible use of the Hong Kong issue by the Soviet *bloc* for propaganda purposes.[3]

[3] When first approached on this issue, Mr. St. Laurent compared the situation to that of the Dutch in Indonesia and expressed concen that difficulties might arise 'on general grounds of race, colour and geography'. Over Indonesia, and despite Canadian friendship with, and sympathy for, the Dutch, the Prime Minister believed there was a 'point beyond which we could not support them'. He asked for a memorandum setting out the British legal and political position in Hong Kong, 'and an estimate of the factors involved in their policy' (Mr. A.D.P. Heeney, Canadian Under-Secretary of State for External Affairs, to Mr. Brooke Claxton, Canadian Minister of National Defence, 23 June 1949, National Archives of Canada, RG 25, vol. 4732, file 50,0634, part 1). Mr. L. Pearson, the Canadian Minister for External Affairs, submitted a memorandum on 22 August. In the meantime Canada had asked for the views of the Governments of India and the United States and these were explained in Mr. Pearson's submission. The memorandum suggested that it would be 'more discreet to make an oral rather a written reply' to the UK approach. It included a statement that Mr. St. Laurent might make to Sir A. Clutterbuck, the UK High Commissioner in Ottawa. The statement closely resembled the *aide-mémoire* reproduced here. Mr. Pearson emphasised that it made no specific reference to 'moral support' for UK policy. Mr. St. Laurent spoke to Sir A. Clutterbuck on 30 August and the UK High Commissioner received a written version on 2 September. Canadian views about Hong Kong were also made known to the Indian and US Governments and to the Government of New Zealand, the latter having requested to be informed about them. The editors are grateful for these references to Dr. G. Donaghy, Historian in the Historical Section of the Canadian Department of Foreign Affairs and International Trade.

No. 104

Letter from Mr. Dening to Air Marshal Sir W. Elliott[1]

[*F 15856/10127/10*]

Top Secret   FOREIGN OFFICE, *18 October 1949*

I have seen SEACOS 978 of 13th October from the British Defence Coordination Committee to the Chiefs of Staff about Formosa.[2]

I quite understand the anxiety of the Far Eastern Commanders-in-Chief, but I am afraid that we have no optimism about the future of Formosa. I discussed this subject with the State Department when I was in Washington, and they told me that the United States Chiefs of Staff had come to the conclusion that they could not intervene to save Formosa from falling into Communist hands (I think the State Department would not wish the United States Chiefs of Staff to know that they had told me this).

[1] Chief Staff Officer, Ministry of Defence, and Deputy Secretary (Military) to Cabinet.

[2] This telegram to the Ministry of Defence stressed the strategic importance of Formosa (Taiwan) and expressed concern that developments in China over the last six months had greatly increased the risk of the island falling into Communist hands. It suggested that the UK and the US might review, militarily as well as politically, whether action to forestall a Communist capture of the island should be considered.

The United States had been doing what they could to aid the island economically, but it had nevertheless fallen into economic chaos owing to the large influx of Nationalist troops and refugees. As a result the population were growing very discontented. There were already elements of communism in the island, and there was every reason to believe that there had been communist infiltration amongst the refugees and the troops evacuated from the mainland.

In short, I found that the Americans took the same gloomy view about Formosa which we have in this Department. My guess is that the United States Joint Chiefs of Staff have concluded that, as long as they retain bases in Japan, Okinawa and the Philippines, they can neutralise Formosa if it becomes hostile. If the Americans are unwilling to intervene to save the situation, it is quite certain that we cannot do so with any success. I would not like to estimate how long Chiang Kai-shek[3] can retain possession of Formosa, but I think we must accept the possibility that sooner or later it will turn communist. If anyone has any intelligent suggestions as to how this can be averted, we should be very glad to receive them.

M. E. DENING

[3] Chiang Kai-shek arrived in Formosa on 10 December 1949. Thereafter the island reverted to its traditional Chinese name of Taiwan.

No. 105

Memorandum by Mr. Bevin on Recognition of the Chinese Communist Government

CP(49)214 [CAB 129/37]

Secret   FOREIGN OFFICE, *24 October 1949*

The Communist Government of the People's Republic of China, which was set up on the 1st October, 1949, has expressed a desire to enter into diplomatic relations with foreign Powers. The Soviet Union and satellite Powers have already accorded *de jure* recognition. We shall have to make up our minds in due course whether or not to recognise the Communist Government as the *de jure* Government of China, but before we do so we are committed to consultation with other Commonwealth countries, with the United States and with other friendly Powers. Since our interests in China are very much greater than those of the other Powers, we should not necessarily feel bound by the views of other Powers, but it is obviously desirable to obtain the largest measure of agreement possible and in particular the agreement of other Commonwealth countries.

2. The question of recognition is to some extent bound up with the complaint to the United Nations Assembly of the Nationalist Government

of China. This item is on the agenda of the Political Committee,[1] and the attitude of the Powers in that Committee will necessarily have some bearing on their attitude towards the Communist Government. I set out in the following paragraphs the considerations which I think should govern our own attitude towards these two related questions.

I. RECOGNITION

Argument

3. The Nationalist Government were our former allies in the war and since the war they have been a useful friend in the United Nations. To-day, however, they are no longer representative of anything but their ruling clique and their control over the remaining metropolitan territories after the fall of Canton is tenuous. British interests can reap no advantage from continued recognition of this shadowy Government, since they lie almost entirely within Communist control. In the United Nations Organisation the continued recognition of the Nationalist Government offers the temporary advantage of a vote which in the past has usually been cast in our favour, whereas a Communist vote is likely to be cast against us. But this is hardly an advantage which can be maintained indefinitely.

4. For the time being the Communist Government of the People's Republic of China is the only alternative. The Communists are now the rulers of most of China. The fall of Canton has brought them to the Hong Kong frontier. It would be a mistake to disregard the fact that they are, on their own statements, orthodox Marxist-Leninists who openly declare their strong partiality for the Soviet Union and its methods. How long they will last, how 'orthodox' their methods will be and how strong their leadership will prove is yet to be seen. They have trade to offer and we have an immovable stake in their territory which can only be maintained by trade. Too long delay in according them recognition cannot fail to make them ill-disposed towards us. We may thereby gratuitously vitiate our future relations. Similarly, delay will increase the existing tendency of the Communist Government to look to the Soviet Union, and may induce the feeling that they can tighten their belts and do without Western economic assistance. A considerable number of Russian technicians have already arrived in North China and it may be expected that the Soviet Union will take full advantage of the fact that they are first in the field. It is possible that in due course friction may develop between the Russians and the Chinese, but we cannot take advantage of this unless we are in relations with the Communist Government.

5. As regards our own trading interests, we have advocated the policy of keeping a foot in the door. If this policy is to bear fruit (and British firms are remitting sterling from London to the tune of £360,000 a month for

---

[1] The Political Committee of the UN General Assembly dealt with political and security issues.

maintenance) it can only be done by according full and early recognition. On political as well as practical grounds we should therefore decide to recognise the new regime.[2]

6. I am advised by the Legal Adviser of the Foreign Office that the recognition of the Chinese Communist Government as the *de jure* Government of China in the present circumstances cannot be said to be contrary to the principles and practice of international law, having regard to the proportion of Chinese territory controlled by the Communist Government, the firmness of its control there on the one hand and the small proportion of Chinese territory held by the Nationalists and the tenuous nature of Nationalist control, where it exists, on the other hand. The best writer on recognition in international law says: 'So long as the revolution has not been fully successful, and so long as the lawful Government, however adversely affected by the fortunes of the civil war, remains within national territory and asserts its authority, it is presumed to represent the State as a whole.... So long as the lawful Government offers resistance which is not ostensibly hopeless or purely nominal, the *de jure* recognition of the Revolutionary Party as a Government constitutes premature recognition which the lawful Government is entitled to regard as an act of intervention contrary to international law.'

7. I consider that it can be asserted that the resistance of the Nationalist Government in China is now ostensibly hopeless, and its control over any portion of Chinese territory on the mainland hardly more than nominal, and on this political appreciation of the facts of the situation my Legal Adviser considers *de jure* recognition of the Communist Government to be legally justifiable.

8. Our present position in regard to recognition is that His Majesty's Consul-General in Peking has made a communication in the following terms to the Chinese Communist Government:

'His Majesty's Government in the United Kingdom are carefully studying the situation resulting from the formation of the Central People's Government. Friendly and mutually advantageous relations, both commercial and political, have existed between Britain and China for many generations. It is hoped that these will continue in the future. His Majesty's Government in the United Kingdom therefore suggest that pending completion of their study of the situation, informal relations should be established between His Majesty's Consular Officers and the appropriate authorities in the territory under the control of the Central

[2] In August 1949 it had been estimated that there were about 4,476 UK nationals in China, of whom the majority (3,721) were in Communist-held areas (F 12398/1611/10). In October the number of British subjects in Shanghai was about 2,250 (Shanghai telegram No. 881, 14 October 1949, F 15942/1611/10).

People's Government for the greater convenience of both Governments and promotion of trade between the two countries.'[3]

I am advised that this message can be interpreted as according recognition to the Communist Government as the *de facto* Government of the territories which they control, but no reply has been received from the Communist Government and our original assumption that the Communists would be satisfied with nothing less than *de jure* recognition appears to be correct. In my speech to the United Nations Assembly on 26th September I stated that China had entered into certain international obligations which we feel must be honoured, and that a wise approach to the handling of these problems will be in the interest of the whole world. There has been no further public indication of our attitude towards the question of recognition.

Attitude of other Powers

9. India and Australia have made communications to the Chinese Communist Government similar in nature to that quoted above, and Portugal and Denmark have instructed their representatives to do the same.

10. It is clear from the talks which I had in Washington with Mr. Acheson and M. Schuman that the United States are not in favour of early *de jure* recognition and that France, because of her position in Indo-China, is afraid of the consequences of such recognition.[4] The attitude of the State Department is influenced by the attacks in Congress upon its China policy. In an effort to meet these attacks the State Department published on 30th July a voluminous White Paper on China which, however, failed to stifle the critics and indeed provided them with further ammunition.[5] In the circumstances it must be recognised that the State Department will be influenced in its attitude more by internal American politics than by the realities of the situation in China. The French are influenced by the views of their High Commissioner in Indo-China, who appears to believe that *de jure* recognition of the Communist Government will endanger the constitutional structure which has recently been set up under the Emperor Bao Dai.[6] This view is not shared by the French Ambassador in China, but it is nevertheless likely to influence the French Government in the direction of deferring *de jure* recognition.

11. Of the other foreign Powers with whom we have been in consultation, the Dutch may conceivably hesitate to recognise the Chinese Communist Government in view of the Indonesian situation, though this is

[3] See No. 100.   [4] See No. 97.
[5] See No. 91, note 2.   [6] See No. 59, note 8.

not certain. The other European Powers may be expected to follow our lead.

12. Of the other Commonwealth Powers, Canada may be reluctant to take a line unpalatable to the United States. Her interests in China are not extensive, and she may feel that in the circumstances she can afford to be out of step with the rest of the Commonwealth. Australia and India are believed to be in favour of early recognition. The other members of the Commonwealth have no direct representation in China, but will probably keep in line with the United Kingdom.

13. It will be necessary to consult both with other Commonwealth countries and other friendly foreign Powers before reaching a decision to recognise the Chinese Communist Government. Other Commonwealth Governments might be invited to instruct their High Commissioners in London to confer with me, thus affording evidence of the principle of Commonwealth consultation.

II. Chinese Nationalist Motion in United Nations Assembly

14. There is the related question of the Nationalist Government's complaint to the United Nations Assembly. They have secured time in the First Committee to invite attention to the infringements by the Soviet Union of the terms and spirit of the Sino-Soviet Treaty of Friendship of 1945. The question may come up for debate about mid-November. It is extremely doubtful if the Chinese can make a case against the USSR, and the move can only have for object a vain and belated attempt to make political capital. We have told the Chinese that we would consider supporting their case if they can make one. The United States Government were initially rather more forthcoming, but have since realised the weakness of their position. Their White Paper on China has unfortunately provided abundant material to show the extent of American intervention in China and the rottenness and corruption which have led to the defeat of the Nationalist Government and to the assumption of power by the Communists. The State Department now realise that the Soviet Union is likely to take full advantage of the opportunity thus provided, and it may be expected that there will be a violent attack upon the status of the Nationalist Government and its claim to represent China in the United Nations Organisation.

15. If we hold the views outlined in Section I of this paper and in consequence propose eventually to recognise the Communist Government, it follows that we should no longer support in any degree this Chinese resolution. Anything we say, however anodyne, can hardly fail to be embarrassing *vis-à-vis* the new regime, while our support of the Nationalist Government could not fail to make us ridiculous in the face of the available evidence. Our best course would therefore seem to be to instruct the United Kingdom representative to take no part whatever in the debate and to abstain from voting. We should explain our intentions and our

reasons to Commonwealth Governments and other friendly Powers in advance.

III. Timing of Recognition

16. It is clear from the preceding paragraphs that we cannot take a decision as to the date when *de jure* recognition should be accorded to the Chinese Communist Government until we have consulted with other Powers. We have also to consider the impact of recognition upon United Kingdom interests in the Far East. There is to be a conference at Singapore from 2nd-4th November under the chairmanship of Mr. Malcolm MacDonald, which will be attended by all His Majesty's Representatives in the Far East, including His Majesty's Ambassador to China, and also by the three Far Eastern Commanders in Chief. This will afford a suitable opportunity to discuss the implications of recognition, and it is desirable therefore to await the outcome of this conference before reaching a decision.

Recommendations

17. I invite my colleagues to agree that:

(1) I should consult with the United States and other friendly Powers on the basis of this paper;

(2) our views be communicated to other Commonwealth Governments and that they be invited to instruct their High Commissioners in London to confer with me on the question of recognition;

(3) no decision as to the date of recognition be taken until the results of these consultations are known and until a report is received on the outcome of the Singapore conference.[7]

---

[7] Briefing Mr. Bevin, officials explained that this paper had not raised the question of whether assurances should be sought from the Chinese Communists that they would respect China's international obligations. That such assurances should be given was the view of the Australian Minister for External Affairs, Dr. Evatt. In a statement Dr. Evatt had gone so far as to say, not only that the UK, the US and Australia were 'in complete accord' on the matter but also that recognition would not be forthcoming unless China gave specific assurances respecting the territorial integrity of neighbouring countries. Mr. Bevin's brief explained that no such assurances had been sought from the 'satellite' governments in Eastern Europe and added that 'in the light of our bitter memories of the fate of non-aggression pacts at the hands of totalitarian states', it was 'inconceivable' that the UK would request guarantees for the territorial integrity of China's neighbours (minute initialled by Mr. F.S. Tomlinson for Mr. Dening, 26 October, F 16459/1023/10). Ministers supported this view when CP(49)214 was discussed in Cabinet. Dr. Evatt's statement 'did not correctly represent the views of the United Kingdom Government' (CM 62(49)7, 27 October, CAB 128/16).

No. 106

Sir O. Harvey[1] (Paris) to Mr. Attlee

No. 285 Saving [F 16978/1023/10]

Secret   PARIS, 11 *November 1949*[2]

Repeated to Washington No. 171, Saigon No. 27, Singapore No. 19 Saving
My telegram No. 284 Saving.
Following from Secretary of State.[3]
We then turned to consideration of our attitude towards the Chinese
Communist Government, M. Schuman spoke first and said that this was a
problem which faced all our three Governments and which in particular
became more acute for him as Communist forces advanced towards Indo-
China. The problem was essentially a political one which must be
considered not only as affecting the three Powers represented at the
meeting but also in its broader context in relation to United Nations
affairs. M. Schuman said that the guiding consideration for France must be
the question of what Government was master of the country bordering on
Indo-China since it would be difficult for France to recognise a
Government if its area of authority did not go this far. M. Schuman
expressed his concern at the possibility of Nationalist armies flooding into
Indo-China.

2. He then turned to the problem of Bao Dai.[4] He said that following
the traitorous acts of Ho Chi Minh in 1946 it might have appeared that
France was acting purely in her own interest.[5] M. Schuman pointed out,
however, that the relationship between Ho Chi Minh and the Communists
in China was well known and that by opposing Ho Chi Minh, France was
erecting a barrier against the advance of Communism. He stressed that
France had dealt with this problem with determination and as a result had
run into great administrative, military and financial difficulties. At the
present time the military situation was relatively good, though he could not
say what would happen if two to three hundred thousand Communist
troops were just across the frontier and if they were co-operating with Ho
Chi Minh in subversive activities.

---

[1] HM Ambassador in Paris.

[2] Times of despatch and receipt not recorded on filed copy.

[3] Mr. Bevin was in Paris for a Conference of Foreign Ministers of Belgium, France, Holland,
Luxembourg, the UK and the US on policy towards Germany. The Petersberg Agreements,
admitting the recently established West German Government to a number of international
organisations and amending the Occupation Statute, were signed in the French capital on 22
November. This telegram reported Mr. Bevin's discussions with Mr. Acheson away from the
Conference about Yugoslavia (R 10709/1102/92).

[4] See No. 59, note 8.

[5] V. *ibid.*

3. M. Schuman then said that, since the Ho Chi Minh agreement was unilaterally violated in March, 1949, the French had sought for another leading figure and had found Bao Dai. He urged the importance of the utmost support for Bao Dai, who had undertaken to act in accordance with French policy and who was prepared to proceed on his own initiative, but at the same time was given to over much reflexion and required a lot of assurances. Bao Dai was also worried about whether French policy with respect to himself was supported and approved by the Governments of Great Britain and the United States. In these circumstances M. Schuman said that he had a concrete proposal to put to us. Would we inform Bao Dai that our Governments approved of him and French policy towards him? M. Schuman stressed that he did not mean that we should recognise Bao Dai at this stage. He knew that until the French Agreement with Bao Dai was ratified recognition could not take place. He did, however, urge once more upon us the importance which he attached to an expression of goodwill from our Governments.

4. Mr. Acheson having referred to our previous conversations on this subject[6] said that his Government felt strongly that, so long as there was any opposition to the Communist regime, it would be a stab in the back for this opposition if we were to accord the Communist Government recognition. He said that his Government attached great importance to obtaining an assurance from the Communist Government that they would accept their international responsibilities. He referred to the ill treatment of the American Consul at Mukden[7] and to the generally impossible attitude of the Communists towards Europeans generally. They were moreover violating treaties and he thought it essential to have an assurance from the Communists that they would accept at any rate some degree of responsibility. He had the draft of a message which he proposed to send through his representative in Peking to Chou En Lai. The object of this approach was to find out how the Communists would in the present and in the future treat foreigners, and he thought that the Communists might consider that a favourable reply to his communication would also result in a more favourable reaction in the future from the Western Powers. He stressed, however, that if any major Western Power were to weaken in its attitude towards the Communists at this stage and afford recognition, then he would clearly get no reply.

5. He then turned to the subject of Bao Dai and said that his Government were anxious to give all possible help. He added that he had recently spoken to Pandit Nehru about Bao Dai and had found that Pandit Nehru did not consider that Bao Dai was a strong enough character to survive. We had previously agreed that it would be as well to obtain Asian support for recognition of Bao Dai before the Western Powers were to grant recognition themselves in order to avoid giving the impression that

[6] See Nos. 96 and 97.
[7] See No. 58, note 1.

the Western Powers were trying to influence opinion towards Bao Dai. Finally he said that his Government would sympathetically consider any proposals put forward by France, but that in the meantime she must straighten out the constitutional position so that others Powers could proceed to recognition.

6. He then referred to a communication which the Nationalist Government had made to the United States Government asking for permission to chase bandits into Indo-China. It seemed obvious to him that all they wanted was a line of retreat, so they had been told that this was a matter which should be taken up through their own representatives in Paris.

7. I said that all these questions had been receiving consideration by the conference of our Far Eastern Representatives at Singapore.[8] There were talks going on in Canberra and I intended to meet the Commonwealth High Commissioners in London next week. We had to consider the effect of recognition of the Chinese Communist Government on Asia as a whole and we must be prepared to recognise it within a reasonable time. It was important that we should try to keep India in step as there had been a danger that she might act prematurely. I said that I thought that Pandit Nehru's trip to the United States had had a useful effect. On my return I would discuss the matter again with my colleagues. Meanwhile I could say that our policy was to keep in step with the Asian members of the Commonwealth on the one hand and with the United States and France on the other.

8. There were several factors that made for delay. It would be unfortunate to act while the United Nations Assembly was still sitting and China was on the agenda, and I knew that M. Stikker[9] was anxious that we should take no step before the transfer of power in Indonesia. The Australians were anxious that recognition should not be granted until after their elections. For all these reasons I could give no definite answer at once. We were holding the position in Hong Kong well, but I was worried about events in Formosa. The Nationalists had a large force of aircraft there and I was afraid that, in accordance with their usual practice, they would allow this important equipment to fall into the hands of the Communists.

9. I then turned to Indo-China. Here I said the immediate obstacle was that France had not yet ratified. We should be ready to take the necessary steps if they did. We should try to get some Asian power, perhaps Siam or Ceylon, to extend recognition, but I doubted whether we could get India to do so. I offered the suggestion that it might make matters easier if the French would transfer the administration of Indo-China from their Colonial Office to the Foreign Office. M. Schuman interposed to say that this could be done by the French Government without reference to

[8] See No. 108.
[9] Dutch Foreign Minister.

Parliament after ratification had taken place. I continued by saying that recognition by us would then have a much greater psychological effect. I undertook to consider the matter further and do what I could to help M. Schuman.

10. I continued by saying that the position of Tibet was one of great concern to India. I understood that Pandit Nehru would welcome unilateral declarations of interest in Tibet by the great Powers. The situation in Burma too was causing grave concern and I was worried at the possible repercussions in Burma when recognition of the Chinese Communist Government was announced. For all these reasons I could not consider the problems of China and Indo-China in isolation.

11. Mr. Acheson confirmed Pandit Nehru's great interest in Tibet though he had not made any suggestion about a unilateral declaration. He added that when Pandit Nehru arrived in the United States he was ready for precipitate action with regard to the recognition of the Chinese Communist Government but in later conversations with the State Department he showed signs of cooling off and had evidently been giving consideration to the effect on Burma.

No. 107

Minute by Mr. A.A.E. Franklin[1]

[F 17349/1261/10]

FOREIGN OFFICE, *23 November 1949*

Some of the more purple bits within provide a good quasi missionary counter-blast to the over-righteous indignation of the Shanghai 'taipans' that somebody else's war is being allowed to interfere with their business.[2] I

---

[1] Far Eastern Department, China (Political) Section (served in China, 1937-42 and 1947-49).

[2] This minute was written in response to appeals by representatives of British companies with trading interests in China that the UK Government should help them break the Nationalist blockade of Shanghai. Mr. Keswick of Jardine Matheson and Mr. Swire of Butterfield and Swire were incensed in November that two of their ships (the *Tsinan* and *Wosung*) had been detained in territorial waters and that a third (the *Louise Moller*) had been shelled by a Chinese Nationalist warship (F 17322/1261/10). FO and Admiralty officials devised a scheme whereby UK warships might place themselves in the line of fire between a merchant ship and a Chinese gunboat in order to jockey the gunboat out of position. However the First Sea Lord, Lord Fraser of North Cape, expressed doubts about the plan on the grounds that it was not reasonable to place upon the Navy responsibility for any trouble that might arise. Sir R. Makins, Deputy Under-Secretary of State at the FO, described this attitude as 'deplorable'. He found it 'almost incredible' that the Navy was allowing itself to be defied by what was in effect a single Chinese gunboat. 'In earlier days the local commanders would have jockeyed the Chinaman out of position without instructions' (minute of 18 November, F 17774/1261/10). So long as the UK continued to recognise the Nationalists as the *de jure* Government of China, no solution to the problem could be found. The UK could only address strong protests to the

should add that I have a little knowledge and a lot of respect for many of the sterling qualities of the Treaty Port communities—but political acumen is not one of them. In the concessions, the Municipal Councils of extra-territorial days, while admittedly an irritant in Chinese patriotic eyes, provided in many ways a remarkably successful experiment in local self-government. On what were mud flats they provided roads, drains, schools, hospitals, wharves for Chinese as well as foreigners. Admittedly the motives were never disinterested. Business first and never mind who kills what and why as long as we can keep out of it, has always been the Treaty Port line. Perhaps they would never have survived had it been any other. Their contacts with the Chinese and their knowledge of China has always been negligible. On the other hand, long before the 'White Ensign' ever appeared on the scene, the Chinese enjoyed a sense of superiority and a wall complex that among other things was useful in shutting out foreigners. Mao Tse-tung, as a patriot, doubtless shares many of the prejudices of the late-lamented Empress Dowager, the grey coolie uniform notwithstanding. In their reactions and psychology the Chinese Communists, where the Soviet indoctrination leaves room for Chinese emotions, skip the era of more liberal, western influences, which on both Nationalist and Communist grounds are in any case taboo, and revert not entirely surprisingly to an 18th Century frame of mind. In this respect they are in the classical Chinese tradition. At best the foreigner is a necessary evil. To show him that he is not allowed to boss anybody about, you concentrate on humiliating him and making him lose face. The charm of the process is that by so doing you yourself gain face and the common man of China will undoubtedly think the more of you for it if you succeed in pulling it off.

Some appreciation of the traditional Chinese conception of international affairs is absolutely essential to an understanding of what is going on now. The recognition problem must among other things be seen in this light. The same holds good for the present position of the Embassies and for that of the foreign trader in China. If you succeed in locking up a foreign official, you very nearly score a bull's eye. If you successfully ignore official communications you also score handsomely. If a second communication follows the first, and is similarly ignored, your score is doubled. To play this game really skilfully, you must of course be able to play one foreign devil off against another, preferably of a different nationality. As they

Chinese Ambassador in London, reserve to itself the right to take action against any Nationalist ship found laying mines, and ask the US Government to put strong pressure on the Nationalist authorities to refrain from air attack and mine-laying. Nor would recognition of the Chinese Communists as the *de jure* Government result in any immediate or material change in the position as far as action by HM ships inside China's territorial waters was concerned. The Communists would first have to approve any such action (F 18725/1261/10, F 18757/1261/10).

usually all think they are cleverer than each other, it is all the easier to deal with them in this kind of way. In the case of the merchants as their sole motive is greed, this process becomes even easier. Their ships must not wear their national flags. Once they have left port, they must not be allowed to return. Prior to the privilege of calling at one of your ports, they must obtain permits. Recently in Tientsin this regulation was interpreted to mean that ships had to have left port (Hong Kong) en route to Tientsin, before a petition was allowed to be submitted for a permit to call at Tientsin. Similarly, in the recent case of the 'Tsinan' and 'Wosang', it was assumed by the owners that in spite of the fact that the blockading Nationalist warship prevented the ship from proceeding, the Communist authorities would nevertheless not permit her to return to Shanghai. As the owners are primarily trading with the Communists, it is not entirely surprising that this point was not over-emphasised in the accounts of the troubles of these two ships. Frustrations and extortions of various kinds, of course, exist for all foreign traders in China to-day. The hope of the foreign communities that recognition will bring this state of affairs to an end is certainly not borne out by historical precedents. Terms of trade are likely to be dictated by the Chinese authorities and this means they will almost certainly be arbitrary. Official representations will almost certainly wherever possible be ignored.

As far as the present treatment of the Embassies and Missions is concerned, Lords MacCartney [*sic*], Napier and Amherst,[3] all 18th Century and early 19th Century Ambassadors, would have found the ground extremely familiar. In 1793 the Ambassador (Lord MacCartney) proceeding to Peking is quoted as being 'well aware of the tenaciousness of the Chinese Court, in enacting ceremonies, on which the humiliation on the one part contributed perhaps to render most Embassies so grateful to the other'. The Ambassador having been made to go through the ceremony of 'prostration' etc. eventually admits that his Embassy had no practical effect whatever, no trade points were settled and no alterations in regulations effected.

---

[3] Lord Macartney led an Embassy to China during 1792-94. He refused to *kowtow* to the Emperor, a salutation performed by kneeling on both knees and touching the floor nine times with the forehead. When pressed he said he would only *kowtow* if a Chinese official of his own rank did likewise before a portrait of King George III. His insistence persuaded the Chinese to waive this part of the ceremony when he was presented to the Emperor. The permission sought by Lord Macartney to have a British Minister resident in China was not conceded. Lord Amherst's Embassy in 1816 had a similar purpose and foundered for the same reason: the Ambassador refused to prostrate himself before the Emperor. Lord Napier was appointed Chief Superintendent of Trade in China in 1833. He failed in his attempts to break the custom whereby trade was conducted through Chinese merchants. Lord Napier wanted to deal direct with the Chinese authorities but was unable to convince the Viceroy at Canton. Ordered by the Viceroy to return to Macao, Lord Napier at first refused and was only persuaded to comply because he became ill. He died at Macao in October 1834.

In 1817 Mr. Ellis[4] in his account of Lord Amherst's Embassy writes: 'It is impossible not to reflect without some mortification upon the result of the two British Embassies to the Court of Peking, both were undertaken for the express purpose of obtaining, if not additional privileges, at least increased security for trade, the failure of both has been complete ... To the mode in which Lord MacCartney's Embassy was conducted, I am inclined to give the most decided approbation. If ever impression is to be produced at Peking, it must be from an intimate knowledge of our political and military strength.'

Of Lord Napier's mission we read: 'On July 25th, 1834, the Mission proceeded to Canton and endeavoured to open direct official communication with the Viceroy, and the Governor of Hong Kong, but reception of letters was refused...' (Letters are now returned to Consulates by double registered mail.)

Of Napier's successors we read: 'they could only maintain themselves by sinking their character as British national envoys and submitting to the indignities which the Chinese more than ever delighted in imposing on them, increasing in virulence in proportion to the extent to which they were accepted.'

While the Chinese have in the meantime learnt a lot from Moscow and over and above this rather old-fashioned Chinese technique will now also add the more modern conceptions of spy-mania and the People's Court, the above sort of background should not be ignored in our dealings with the new rulers of China.

A.E.E. FRANKLIN

[4] Chronicler of the Amherst Embassy (*Journal of the Proceedings of the late Embassy to China*, 1817).

No. 108

Memorandum by Mr. Bevin on South-East Asia and the Far East: Conference of HM Representatives and Colonial Governors[1]

CP(49)244 [*CAB 129/37*]

Secret   FOREIGN OFFICE, *26 November 1949*

My colleagues will recall that on 18th October I circulated to them a memorandum (CP (49) 207) about our general policy in South East Asia and the Far East.[2] That memorandum was designed to serve as guidance

[1] The Conference was held at Bukit Serene in Singapore.

[2] This was a review of the UK in South-East Asia and the Far East, the first study of UK policy since that produced in December 1945 (see No. 1, note 17). It started from the premise that UK influence in the areas in question was an important factor in the preservation of world peace and of direct benefit to the UK itself. As in the case of the 1945 study, it recommended

to the delegates attending a conference of H.M. Representatives and Colonial Governors in the area. In the present memorandum I give, for the information of my colleagues, an account of the proceedings of that conference.

that the UK should concentrate on South-East Asia. Here the aim should be build up 'some sort of regional association ... in partnership with the association of Atlantic powers'. The paper reached the following broad conclusions: (1) The main problem in the Far East lay not with the inhabitants but with the US 'whose policies we must endeavour to influence along lines acceptable to ourselves'. (2) The UK object in China should be 'to keep a foot in the door' in the hope of maintaining China's contacts with the West and being in a position to take advantage of any rift between Communist China and the Soviet Union. (3) A greater measure of regional co-operation in South-East Asia was at present only practicable in the economic field. Though its own resources were insufficient to meet the large demands likely to be made, the UK had the major role play in promoting regional economic co-operation. This role should be played as unobtrusively as possible and Asian countries encouraged to assume the initiative where this could be done safely. (4) In all fields—political, economic and military—the Commonwealth countries of Asia (India, Pakistan and Ceylon), together with the UK and Australia and New Zealand, provided a nucleus on which to build. (5) South-East Asia was not yet ripe for greater political collaboration either internally or with the West. (6) The security of South-East Asia was the most pressing problem, but for the time being the UK could only work with individual countries. (7) Only if the UK showed a willingness and an ability to bring about greater Asian solidarity would the Americans be prepared to assist or come into any regional arrangement. (8) No plans would be 'really successful' without US participation and to secure this would be the main object of UK policy (CAB 129/37).

In that section which dealt with individual countries in   South-East Asia, the paper suggested that it was too early to foresee the outcome of the Bao Dai experiment in French Indo-China (see No. 59, note 8). Mr. Attlee agreed with the overall analysis of the paper but minuted on 22 October: 'I rate the chances of the continuance of French rule and influence in Indo-China very low. I think that France has missed the bus' (F 15857/1055/61).

When the Cabinet discussed this paper on 27 October Sir S. Cripps, Chancellor of the Exchequer, urged that the impression should not be given at the Singapore Conference that the UK would be able to continue the existing scale of its financial and material aid to South-East Asia. Commitments in respect of India and Pakistan and to a lesser extent Ceylon and Burma had been running at a rate of £200 million a year, and the UK's economic position (a new dollar crisis had precipitated the devaluation of sterling on 18 September) made it necessary to make substantial reductions in this expenditure in the future. The general reduction that was required in unrequited exports to various parts of the world involved as a corollary US agreement to an integrated overseas investment policy. In discussion it was suggested that it would be impracticable to maintain UK political influence in South-East Asia while arranging for the US to provide much of the capital investment that was required. The American experience in China, however, might make the US government more receptive to collaborative proposals in Asian affairs on the basis of the UK providing the experience and the US the finance. The Cabinet approved the paper as guidance for the Singapore Conference, subject to any necessary modifications to make clear the limited scope for future UK financial commitments to South-East Asia. Ministers also took note that the Chancellor was reviewing the whole field of overseas investment policy and that he would endeavour to secure early agreement on the subject with the US government (CM 62(49)8, CAB 128/16).

2. The conference was held from 2nd to 4th November under the Chairmanship of Mr. Malcolm MacDonald, Commissioner General in South East Asia. The Ministerial representative of His Majesty's Government was the Parliamentary Under-Secretary of State for the Colonies, Mr. Rees-Williams, and the Foreign Office were represented by Mr. M.E. Dening. The following were also present: His Majesty's Representatives at Nanking, Tokyo, Bangkok, Rangoon, and Manila, the Acting British Consuls General at Saigon and Batavia, the United Kingdom Deputy High Commissioner in New Delhi, the Governors of Singapore and Hong Kong, the High Commissioner for the Federation of Malaya, the Chief Secretaries of North Borneo and Sarawak, and the Commanders-in-Chief, Far East.

3. The conference was similar in form to the conference of His Majesty's Representatives convened by Mr. MacDonald in November, 1948, though wider in scope since, on this occasion, H.M. Ambassadors in China and Japan, H.M. Minister in the Philippines, and the United Kingdom Deputy High Commissioner in New Delhi were present.

4. My colleagues will already have seen the telegrams from Singapore reporting the conclusions reached by the conference on various subjects. These conclusions are now being studied. Where consultation with my colleagues is necessary before action is taken arising out of the conference, I shall circulate papers dealing with specific subjects. In particular, I shall circulate a further paper about recognition of the Communist Government of China.

5. The main purpose of the conference was to exchange views, and I think my colleagues will agree that it served this purpose well and that its conclusions, the substance of which I give below, deserve careful study.

Conclusions of the Conference

6. *Recognition of the Communist Government of China*

The conference agreed that British interests in China and Hong Kong demanded the earliest possible *de jure* recognition of the Communist Government of China. The general situation in South East Asia also made it desirable that recognition should be accorded before the end of this year. It was agreed that recognition should be accompanied by three measures:

(*a*) His Majesty's Government should state unilaterally that they assume that the new Government accept China's existing international obligations.

(*b*) At the same time as recognition is granted, resistance to Communism in South East Asia should be strengthened.

(*c*) British propaganda should explain that there is no inconsistency in a policy which recognises the Communist Government in China and at the same time intensifies resistance to Communism in South East Asia.

7. *Probable effects of recognition of Communist China in South East Asian countries*

It was agreed that, as far as United Kingdom territories were concerned, recognition of Communist China would in no way affect the attitude of the Chinese communities of those territories. These communities have already tacitly accepted the Chinese Communist Government. The appointment of Chinese Communist Consuls in colonial territories would present the Colonial Governments with a difficult problem, but by itself this should not be allowed to delay the granting of recognition. Of the foreign territories in South East Asia only Burma and Indo-China would be sensibly affected by the granting of recognition. In Burma it would encourage the near-Communist tendencies of the powerful Burmese Socialist Party, and in Indo-China it would seriously undermine the confidence of Bao Dai and the confidence of the Indo-Chinese people in Bao Dai (but see paragraph 9 below). In the case of India it would be India's responsibility to safeguard the *status quo* in Tibet as far as this could be done by a unilateral declaration.

8. *South East Asian Regional Problems—General*

(*a*) The conference welcomed a statement by Mr. Rees-Williams of His Majesty's Government's policy in South East Asia based on the memorandum circulated with CP (49) 207. It was agreed that the long-term objective of His Majesty's Government's policy in South East Asia should be the creation of a regional pact through which the Governments of the area could work in partnership with the countries belonging to the North Atlantic Pact and also with Australia and New Zealand. Since, however, the present situation in South East Asia was not favourable for attempts to create such a pact in the near future an initial approach should be made by the stimulation of economic co-operation in the region.

(*b*) The conference considered that the danger from Communism was so great and imminent in South East Asia that energetic short-term action was required irrespective of steps which it might be possible to take to attain the long-term objective. In the opinion of the conference the Chinese Communists were unlikely to attempt military aggression beyond their frontiers; but it was thought that they could be expected to stimulate conspiracy against and subversion of orderly government in South East Asia at the earliest opportunity.

(*c*) It was agreed that Indo-China would probably be the immediate objective of Communist action in this sense and that thereafter attempts would be made to overthrow the existing regimes in Siam and Burma. If these attempts were successful the South East Asian Communist Parties would have gained control over the great rice-growing countries of the world and through them would have a strangle-hold on the whole of Asia. Moreover, the frontiers of Malaya and India would be directly threatened and the long-term policy of His Majesty's Government would have become impracticable.

(*d*) The conference therefore concluded that South East Asia should be regarded as a region in which an emergency exists and that policy towards it should be pursued with a proper consequential note of urgency.

9. *Indo-China*

The conference concluded that if the Bao Dai experiment failed French withdrawal from Indo-China would become inevitable, with disastrous effects on our general strategic position in South East Asia. It was therefore recommended that every possible assistance should be given to the French in their attempt to rally and consolidate the Vietnamese national movement round Bao Dai. Specifically, the conference made four recommendations:

(*a*) that His Majesty's Government should grant *de facto* recognition to Bao Dai immediately after the transfer of power on 1st January, *and de jure* recognition after ratification by both parties of the agreement between the French and Bao Dai;
(*b*) that His Majesty's Government should encourage the French Government to make all possible concessions to Bao Dai, to transfer Indo-Chinese affairs from the Ministry of Overseas France to the Ministry of Foreign Affairs, and to give assurances that they would agree to the extension of Vietnamese diplomatic representation abroad;
(*c*) that His Majesty's Government and the United States Government should publish a declaration about the Tongkinese frontier similar to Mr. Acheson's declaration about the Hong Kong frontier (in which he pointed out at a press conference that if Hong Kong were attacked the United States would be prepared to carry out its obligations as a member of the Security Council);
(*d*) that the present ban on close co-operation with the French authorities in Indo-China with regard to anti-Communist propaganda should be lifted.

10. *Siam*

The conference considered that it was essential, in view of Siam's strategic importance, to do everything possible to strengthen the determination of the present Siamese Government to resist Communist infiltration and pressure. In order to do this and in order to maintain the political stability of Siam under the existing regime it was recommended that every effort should be made to meet Siam's requirements in the purchase of military equipment and in the strengthening of her economic position (for example, by permitting her if possible to float a public loan in London next year, and by allowing for political factors in negotiations in such matters as British war claims against Siam).

11. *Burma*

The conference concluded that, since the chaotic situation in Burma rendered that country acutely vulnerable to infiltration and exploitation by the Chinese Communists, every effort must be made to promote a settlement of the dispute between the Burmese Government and the Karens. It was recommended that this matter should be discussed with the Government of India with a view to devising some solution at an early date.

12. *Machinery for dealing with the emergency in South East Asia*
The conference concluded that measures taken in London to deal with the needs of the South East Asian area needed to be accelerated. It was recommended that early steps should be taken to ensure that inter-departmental consultation reached quick decisions on requests for assistance for South East Asia.

13. *United States Representation in South East Asia*
The conference considered that United States representation in South East Asia was not on the whole of very high calibre and, since it was essential that the United States Government should be able to see the South East Asian picture correctly through the eyes of their own observers, it was hoped that Dr. Jessup's[3] forthcoming tour in South East Asia would lead to a greater realisation by the United States Government of the emergency in South East Asian affairs.

[3] See No. 96, note 1.

No. 109

Minutes by Sir G. Jebb[1] and Mr. Dening on Recognition of the Chinese Communist Government

[*F 18695/1023/10*]

FOREIGN OFFICE, *3 and 6 December 1949*

Mr. Dening
I have read with interest the Cabinet Paper CP (49) 244 of the 26th November regarding the conclusions of the conference at Bukit Serene.[2]
2. I note that the 'conference agreed that British interests in China and Hong Kong demanded the earliest possible *de jure* recognition of the Communist Government of China', and further that 'the general situation in South East Asia also made it desirable that recognition should be accorded before the end of this year.
3. I suppose that as regards China it is thought that if we recognise we shall be able to provide in some way or other for the protection of our interests in Shanghai and the other centres concerned. I suppose also, however, that recognition is not absolutely certain to result in these

[1] Deputy Under-Secretary of State (Political), FO, from February 1949.
[2] See No. 108.

interests being protected, though I take it that the idea is that the Chinese Communists will be dependent on certain assistance and trade, which only the Western Powers can supply, and this fact will therefore necessitate their agreeing to the survival of certain large British interests or at any rate to their not being liquidated beyond a certain period of time.

4. It is however the second conclusion that puzzles me, rather, probably because the reasons behind it are not, I think, stated in the paper. Indeed, reading the paper as a complete ignoramus I would have supposed that, whereas the 'Chinese' reasons for recognising were fairly clear, the 'South East Asia' reasons given point rather against, than for recognition. Thus we are told that

(a) 'The appointment of Chinese Consuls in Colonial territories would present the Colonial Governments with a difficult problem';
(b) 'Burma and Indo-China would be sensibly affected by the granting of recognition';
(c) 'In Indo-China it (recognition) would seriously undermine the confidence of Bao Dai and the confidence of the Indo-Chinese people in Bao Dai';
(d) 'If the Bao Dai experiment failed French withdrawal from Indo-China would become inevitable, with disastrous effects on our general strategic position in South East Asia.'

5. As I have said, all these seem to be reasons *against* recognizing, and though there are no doubt many powerful reasons *for* recognizing, they certainly do not emerge from this particular paper.

6. I expect that all that is necessary in order to silence these doubts is for you to refer me to some other paper! The only real point on which I would like guidance is why exactly 'recognition must be agreed before the end of this year'?

G.J.

3.12.49

Sir G. Jebb

I have asked that a copy of the draft Cabinet paper,[3] which is to be considered by the FE(O)Ctee on 8th December, should be sent to you.

I agree that the Bukit Serene conclusions did not bring out the arguments, and that was the first thing which struck me when I got back. The arguments *for* early recognition were to me quite unexpected as regards Malaya and Singapore, but less unexpected as regards Hong Kong. But clearly the Governors of Singapore and Hong Kong and the High Commissioner of Malaya knew what they were talking about.

---

[3] 'Recognition of the Chinese Communist Government', FE(O)78, 2 December 1949 (CAB 134/288). The draft is not reproduced here; for the final version see No. 110.

The argument was this. The three territories have vast Chinese populations (2 million in Hong Kong, 60% of Singapore and 40% of Malaya). These populations have strong national ties with China and, without appreciating the consequences of assumption of power by a Communist Govt., they have been on the whole elated by recent developments which, they feel, put China on the map once more. Whereas they have so far co-operated with our colonial govts., their loyalties will be divided if we remain hostile to the Chinese Communist Govt. and refuse to recognise it. They fear that we may stop remittances to China, which are very important to them, and that we shall prevent them from maintaining their ties with the Motherland. In time these considerations will tend to make them less co-operative with the colonial govts. *Ergo* there is a need for early recognition.

The Governors thought there was no difficulty in reconciling in the local Chinese mind recognition of a Chinese Communist Govt. *in China* and suppression of Communist terrorists by all the means at our disposal in Malaya. We have always made it quite clear that what the Chinese do in China is their business but that we will not tolerate attempts by Communist minorities to seize power in the territories for which we are responsible. The two things are not incompatible.

It was the two Govs. and the HC[4] [for Malaya] who wanted recognition 'as early as possible' and the rest of us who said 'at any rate by the end of the year'. The arguments for the later are contained in the conclusions of the draft Cabinet paper.

I hope this hastily scribbled minute makes the position clear?

M.E.D.

3.12.49

Yes—thank you very much.

But I shd. have thought that, since the French are apparently strongly opposed to early recognition (for obvious & valid reasons) & the Dutch plead for it to be delayed until at least after Jan. 1st, we might have deferred our recognition date until say Jan. 15th?

What do you think?

G.J.

5.12.49

But we don't think the French reasons are either strong or valid really,[5] and as for the Dutch, their transfer of power is now due to take place on 27th Dec. On the other hand the morale of our communities in China (who have had no proper diplomatic representation since last April) is low

---

[4] High Commissioner.

[5] Sir G. Jebb commented here: 'Then the passage in the CP on the Bukit Serene Conference quoted in para 4 (c) of my minute should be revised.'

and Hong Kong is faced with a number of difficulties owing to non-recognition. Most serious of all, however, are the considerations in the second sentence of para. 27.[6]

India is now in any case likely to recognize before 29th.

M.E.D.

6.12.49

[6] This is a reference to paragraph 27 of the draft Cabinet paper. It appears in the final version (see No. 110) as paragraph 29.

No. 110

Memorandum by Mr. Bevin on Recognition of the Chinese Communist Government

CP(49)248 [CAB 129/37]

Secret   FOREIGN OFFICE, *12 December 1949*

I. Introduction

C.P. (49) 214 of 24th October set out the case for and against recognition of the Chinese Communist Government and drew the conclusion that on political as well as practical grounds, we should recognise the Peking Administration.[1] In the light of this appreciation of the situation the Cabinet on 27th October (CM (49) 62nd Conclusions, Minute 7) authorised consultation with the rest of the Commonwealth, the United States and other friendly Powers on the basis of the views set out in CP (49)214.

2. The results of these consultations are set forth below.

II. Attitude of Foreign Governments

3. *United States.* The United States Government felt strongly that as long as there was any opposition to the Communist régime it would be a stab in the back if recognition were to be accorded. They attached great importance to obtaining an assurance that the Communist Government is prepared to accept China's international obligations. Mr. Acheson, at a press conference on 7th December, reiterated the view that recognition of the Chinese Communist Government in the immediate future would be premature and that even consideration of recognition was premature. Subsequently, Mr. Acheson expressed the hope to Sir Oliver Franks that there will be 'a large-ish time gap between a decision on the date and the act of recognition' in order that public opinion in the United States may be properly prepared. He also expressed the hope that we should not seek concerted action by members of the Commonwealth, since he feared that

[1] See No. 105.

this would tend to give emphasis to the suggestion that the British and Americans were going their separate ways. The United States Government would accordingly favour an arrangement whereby members of the Commonwealth would accord recognition 'at several intervals of time.'

4. *France.* The guiding consideration for France is her difficult situation in Indo-China and the fear that *de jure* recognition of a Chinese Communist Government without any corresponding gesture of approval towards the Bao Dai Administration would jeopardise the prospects for the latter. On the general political issues involved in recognition the French Government's views coincide fairly closely with our own. They would like to see a united front maintained, since recognition by some, in advance of others, might lead to discrimination, but at the same time they would be loath themselves to accord *de jure* recognition to the Communist Government until the control of South-West China has passed into their hands. They have expressed the hope that we shall delay our recognition of the Chinese Communist Government as long as possible, and though they may well expect that we shall accord recognition in the fairly near future, they may reproach us if we do.

5. *Netherlands.* The Netherlands Government are in general sympathy with what they call our 'realistic approach.' They are, however, anxious not to accord recognition before the transfer of sovereignty in Indonesia. This is now due to take place on 27th December, and recognition in the neighbourhood of that date is unlikely to raise any acute problem for the Dutch.

6. While the *Scandinavian* countries are generally prepared to accord recognition as soon at we have done so, the *Italian* and *Portuguese* Governments are somewhat more hesitant and are most certainly influenced in this by the American attitude to recognition. The *Belgian* Government have associated themselves with the French desire that our recognition should be delayed as long as possible.

7. Of the attitudes of the Powers mentioned above, clearly that of the United States is of the utmost importance. Moreover, whatever the attitude of the United States Government, there will certainly be widespread dislike in the United States of the necessity of recognition. There may well be criticism of our action, and unless carefully handled this may become vocal in Congress. Mr. Acheson's views, recorded in paragraph 3, therefore merit serious consideration. As regards France and Belgium, our Brussels Treaty relationship would naturally incline us to meet their wishes as far as is practicable. On the other hand, neither France nor Belgium plays a leading part in Asian affairs, and European reactions to recognition are not, on balance, the most important.

8. In *Asia*, *Burma* has indicated a desire to accord recognition soon after 11th December, and may be unwilling to defer the date. *Siam*, which before 1946 had no relations at all with China, may be reluctant to accord recognition, while the *Philippines* may conceivably follow the lead of the United States.

III. Attitude of other Commonwealth Governments

9. Commonwealth views reveal a wide measure of agreement, and while there is some divergence as to timing or tactics, in no case have the reasons which had led us to decide in principle in favour of recognition been disputed. The most important points of difference are that *Australia* on the one hand is against immediate recognition[2] and would prefer to see the question put on the agenda of the Colombo Conference,[3] while *India* on the other hand is anxious to accord recognition as soon as the present Session of the General Assembly is over. India has indicated that she may in fact accord recognition at some time between 15th and 26th December. The Australian Government, in addition, consider that some prior assurance should be obtained from the Communist Government to the effect that they would assume China's international obligations and respect the territorial integrity of China's neighbours. The views of Australia and New Zealand have been influenced by the general elections in both countries.

The views of the new Government of the New Zealand are as yet unknown.[4]

10. *Ceylon, Pakistan, Canada* and the *Union of South Africa* have expressed views which agree generally with our own, although in the case of Canada there is reluctance to march too far out of step with the United States, and the Canadian Government have recently stated that they would prefer to postpone their recognition until after the Ceylon Conference. The Government of the Union of South Africa have also indicated that they would prefer not to be in 'the first batch' to recognise.

IV. Singapore Conference

11. The Conference of His Majesty's Representatives in the Far East, which was held in Singapore between 2nd and 4th November, considered that the situation in South-East Asia and the Far East demands that *de jure* recognition should be accorded to the Communist Government of China at the earliest possible moment.[5] They recommended that no formal conditions should be attached to such recognition. In their view recognition should be accompanied by a strengthening of our resistance to the spread

[2] See *ibid.*, note 7.

[3] A conference of Commonwealth Foreign Ministers was held in Colombo, the capital of Ceylon, in January 1950 to consider economic aid and development in South and South-East Asia. A Commonwealth Economic Consultative Committee was created, and Colombo became the headquarters of a Commonwealth Technical Assistance Committee. A Colombo Plan was published in May 1950 and began operating in July 1951.

[4] Like Australia, New Zealand was against recognition.

[5] See No. 108.

of Communism in South-East Asia. The Conference, in addition, emphasised the need for:

(*a*) an extensive propaganda campaign to explain that recognition does not imply any inconsistency with our policy of opposition to Communism,

(*b*) every effort to minimise the adverse effects of any disagreement with the United States over recognition.

It was emphasised at the Conference that recognition of a Chinese Communist Government in China and increased resistance to Communism in South-East Asia were not necessarily incompatible. What happens in China is the business of the Chinese and we should merely be recognising an accomplished fact; what happens in South-East Asia is the concern of the Governments there which are opposed to Communism.

12. The Legal Adviser of the Foreign Office has given it as his opinion that our recognition should be without conditions, since no change in the international obligations of a State are brought about by a change of régime, and it is, therefore, unnecessary to insist on explicit acceptance of this principle by a new régime. Indeed, to do so has its disadvantages, since this opens the way to the argument that a new régime is only bound by the previous obligations of the country if it expressly says that it will be. To seek such an assurance would not strengthen our position in law. On the other hand, it would certainly give consolation to bodies such as the Council of Foreign Bondholders, who have large vested interests in China. But since an awkward answer from the Chinese to such an approach, if made, would speedily dispel any hope in the hearts of those interested, it would probably be better tactics to make a quite separate public statement in answer to an inspired Parliamentary Question, which would not invite any comment from the Chinese Communist Government.

V. Timing of Recognition

13. At the meeting in London on 15th November with the Commonwealth High Commissioners the Foreign Secretary made the suggestion that it would probably suit the convenience of Commonwealth and other friendly Governments if the act of recognition was delayed until a date early in the New Year, since by then the Chinese motion in the United Nations Assembly would be out of the way, the Australian and New Zealand elections would be over, the Netherlands Government should have transferred sovereignty to Indonesia and the French Government should have ratified their agreement with Bao Dai.

14. In the light of the Indian Government's views referred to in paragraph 9 above, it seems probable that India will accord recognition in December whether other Commonwealth countries recognise or not. Since United Kingdom interests in China are far greater than those of any other Commonwealth country, and since we have also to consider our position in

Hong Kong and our vital interests in Malaya and Singapore, it seems clear that a firm decision should be taken without delay. With a view to holding India on the one hand and on the other to stimulating the less ready among the other friendly Governments, all have been informed that His Majesty's Government expect to take a decision between 12th and 19th December.

VI. Effects of Recognition

15. It will be appreciated that recognition does not itself make the Communist authorities the rulers of China. They are that already. Recognition is no more than an acceptance of a fact, which its withholding would not alter. Nor, in view of the almost total collapse of the Nationalist Government, can it any longer cogently be argued that recognition would undermine what might otherwise have been effective resistance to Communism. Conversely, to withhold recognition from the Communist Government now that no other effective authority exists in China would imply a deliberate policy of boycotting China. The effects of such a negative policy on our long-term relations with China as well as on our trading interests in China need no elaboration.

16. Politically, recognition implies our willingness to enter into diplomatic relations with the new Government and does not signify approval of its ideology or outlook. It follows logically from recognition that we would accept the Communist Government's claim to represent China in all international organisations. Her vote, by contrast with that of the Nationalist Government, would almost certainly be cast against us on most major issues. The political advantages of recognition are calculated on the assumption that we cannot afford to ignore, however much we may disapprove its political orientation, a government which has effective authority over a vast territory and population. Similarly, it is assumed that without relations with this Government, we shall be in no position to exert any influence on its future development.

17. We have had no diplomatic representation with the Nationalist Government since Canton fell on 14th October, so that the withdrawal of recognition from that Government presents no immediate practical problem in China. His Majesty's Consular Officers would remain in Nationalist areas, including Formosa, and maintain *de facto* relations with the local authorities.

Military Effects

18. The Chiefs of Staff have studied the military aspects of recognition and have reached the conclusion that *de jure* recognition of the Chinese Communist Government is likely, on balance, to have an adverse effect on our military position in the Far East and South-East Asia. The military

disadvantages will not be sufficient, however, to outweigh any strong political or economic advantage which might accrue from recognition.[6]

Treaty Rights

19. While the Chinese Communist Government have on the one hand announced their willingness to 'establish diplomatic relations with any and all foreign Governments willing to observe the principles of equality, *mutual* interest, and mutual respect for territorial sovereignty,' their press on the other hand has announced that *all* Kuomintang agreements are liable to re-examination and revision. We should therefore assume that, irrespective of any unilateral statement we make about the Communist Government's assumption of China's international obligations, in fact it is improbable that these obligations will be regarded as binding. Delay in recognition is, however, unlikely to lead to any satisfactory assurances on this point, and in the absence of relations, the Treaty rights are themselves of no value. Recognition may therefore lead to a laborious and unpromising series of negotiations on the revision of existing treaties with China and in particular of the Sino-British Treaty (1943) on relinquishment of extra-territorial rights, on which our existing rights of property ownership and of travel, and our rights in respect of shipping and consular representation in China are based. Similar considerations apply to the various Financial, Air and other Agreements. We should have no illusions in this respect, but should be prepared to insist on strict reciprocity.

Propaganda

20. In the propaganda field we may expect that, at the worst, the Chinese press and radio will continue their attacks upon 'Western imperialism', and that Chinese Communist propaganda will follow the Moscow pattern. In such circumstances recognition of a Chinese Communist Government should not in any way deter us from taking appropriate counter-measures in the territories for which we ourselves are responsible, or from encouraging our friends in South and South-East Asia to do the same. In this country careful publicity will be required to explain that recognition implies neither approval nor disapproval of the ideology or outlook of the new Government but is merely an acceptance of the fact that they are now rulers of China.

British Trading Interests

21. While recognition is unlikely to provide any immediate panacea for British trading interests in China and to a lesser extent Hong Kong, it may be expected to provide that minimum protection necessary to their continued existence. While the new régime is not at present so corrupt as its predecessor, its authority may well prove even more arbitrary and

[6] COS(49)421, 5 December 1949 (copy in F 18519/1023/10).

vexatious in its regulations. Its realisation of its need for some Western trade is, however, indicated by the very fact that the foreign trading communities have not been uprooted. In individual cases, their position, particularly under the totalitarian juridical system of the 'People's Courts,' may prove precarious.

Hong Kong

22. At the Bukit Serene Conference the Governor of Hong Kong expressed himself in favour of early recognition of the Chinese Communist Government in view of the very large Chinese population in Hong Kong and the New Territories. It is true that with recognition all Chinese Government assets will necessarily be regarded as vested in the new Government. This may create a difficult problem for the Governor of Hong Kong, but it may be less embarrassing than the present position in this respect. The Governor of Hong Kong, who recognises that the appointment of a Communist representative after recognition cannot be avoided, would prefer that such a representative should continue to have the undefined status which the Nationalist representative at present enjoys, though his present title of 'Special Commissioner for Kwangtung and Kwangsi' should if possible be changed to 'Special Commissioner for Hong Kong.' On balance it is thought preferable not to press for the appointment of a Consul-General, who might insist on exercising privileges not at present exercised by the Special Commissioner.

Malaya and Singapore

23. The Governor of Singapore and the High Commissioner for Malaya both favour early recognition of the Chinese Communist Government, since they feel that continued non-recognition will be misunderstood by the large Chinese population in these territories and render them less co-operative. It is recognised that the appointment of Chinese Communist consuls will create difficulties. It is felt that the appointment of Communist consuls cannot be long delayed, though any possible delay should be contrived while the present emergency remains. While Chinese Communist consuls can facilitate communications, their presence is not essential to the conduct of subversive Communist activities in Malaya, which can easily be stepped up by the infiltration of Communist agents who may or may not have affiliations with Chinese consulates.

Chinese Nationalist Representation in London

24. On the day that we choose for according *de jure* recognition to the People's Republic of China it will be necessary to inform the present Chinese Ambassador of this decision and to request him to consider himself henceforward as a private person. Dr. Cheng,[7] who has a life-long

[7] Dr. Cheng T'ien-his, Ambassador of the Nationalist Government in the UK since 1946.

connexion with the United Kingdom and is a Bencher of the Middle Temple, is certain to ask for permission to establish residence in this country. It is recommended that this should be granted and that the same concession be allowed to any members of his staff who can make out a reasonable case. In practice the majority will probably opt for service under the new régime.

25. As regards consulates, having regard to the position in Malaya and Singapore, it may be desirable not to close the Nationalist Consulates forthwith but to allow them to continue until such time as the Chinese Communist Government notify us of their intention to take over. In the interim period, the position of Nationalist consuls will be anomalous, but it is by no means improbable that certain consular staffs will go over to the Communist side and take service under the Communist Government.

British Representation in Nationalist China

26. As stated in paragraph 17 above, we have no diplomatic representatives in Nationalist China. Day-to-day business with the Nationalist authorities on the Chinese mainland will be carried on through His Majesty's Consul at Kunming so long as Kunming remains in Nationalist hands and through His Majesty's Consul in Formosa. These officers should be left at their posts and should maintain local contact with the local authorities as before on a *de facto* basis.

United Nations

27. The Soviet Union and certain satellites have already expressed the view in the United Nations Assembly that the present Chinese delegation no longer represents China. Until, however, the status of the various Chinese representatives in the United Nations is changed by a decision of some organ or organs of the United Nations, they will presumably continue to retain their seats. This question is of particular significance in relation to the Security Council, where, in accordance with the normal procedure, the Chinese representative will be in the chair in January 1950, when the Kashmir dispute may still be under consideration by the Council. While there seems to be no reason why the United Kingdom should take any initiative in the matter (since it would not be convenient for us for the Nationalist representative to retain his seat in the Security Council until such time as he is displaced by some generally accepted decision), we must accept the position that after recognition we shall have to cast our vote for the admission of the Communist representative. Assuming that we have accorded *de jure* recognition to the Chinese Communist Government, our attitude should be, if approached by that Government, that the replacement of the various Nationalist representatives by Chinese Communists is a matter for the United Nations and concerns the United Kingdom only as an individual member of that organisation.

28. We must nevertheless accept the fact that a difficult position is bound to arise sooner or later, and that no precedent exists for the expulsion of

representatives who refuse voluntarily to vacate their seats which are claimed by a successor Government. If, as we may suppose, the United States delay recognition of the Chinese Government, there may be the two extremes that the United States openly support the Nationalist representatives, while the Soviet Union (and presumably Yugoslavia, who has recognised the Chinese Communist Government) will refuse to do business with them. In between these two extremes the situation may be that the United Kingdom and India, for example, who by then will have recognised the Chinese Communist Government, will refuse to take sides in the matter until the question of representation has been thrashed out. It must be admitted that such a situation will not be conducive to the smooth working of the Security Council, or indeed the other organs concerned. But since the Soviet Union and its satellites have already taken their stand in the matter, the situation is likely to arise whether the United Kingdom and India recognise the Chinese Communist Government or not.

CONCLUSION

29. We have now reached the stage when we have consulted with friendly Governments on this question and have to make up our own minds. There is an obvious danger if recognition is delayed too long, and the time may not be very far distant when, if it is withheld any further, the Chinese Communist Government will begin to put pressure upon our interests in China, and even demand the withdrawal of our officials. We shall then be compelled either to accord recognition under duress or to withhold it indefinitely as a gesture against coercion. To adopt the first alternative would be to weaken our whole position and prestige in the Far East. To adopt the second would be to sacrifice our interests in China which we have been at such pains to maintain. Therefore though it is possible that we may not carry all the friendly Governments with us and though it may be difficult for the United States to follow our lead, at any rate for some time to come, everything points to the conclusion that we should now decide to accord *de jure* recognition to the Chinese Communist Government at an early date.

30. If this conclusion is accepted, it is suggested that the Chinese Communist Government should be notified at an early date of our decision to accord *de jure* recognition. An opportunity should be given for friendly Governments, if they feel so disposed, to synchronise their own action with ours.

RECOMMENDATIONS

31. I invite my colleagues to agree that:

(*a*) A decision be taken to accord *de jure* recognition to the Chinese Communist Government at an early date.

(*b*) Other Commonwealth Governments, the United States and other friendly Powers be notified of our decision and the reasons for making it and invited, they feel so disposed, to synchronise their action with that of His Majesty's Government in the United Kingdom.[8]

[8] The Cabinet considered and approved the conclusions to this memorandum on 15 December. Ministers recommended that the governments of other Commonwealth countries and of friendly powers (including the US) should be informed of the UK decision to recognise Communist China and of the date when recognition was to be accorded, in an attempt to ensure that as many as possible of them would extend recognition to the new Chinese government on or about the same date (CM 72(49)3, CAB 128/16).

No. 111

Note on 'Christmas Ship' to be chartered by HMG for round trip to Hong Kong/Shanghai and back

[*F 18402/1261/10*]

FOREIGN OFFICE, *12 December 1949*

On December 5th His Majesty's Consul-General at Shanghai[1] asked us if His Majesty's Government would consider chartering a 'Christmas ship' to make the round trip Hong Kong/Shanghai possibly calling southward bound at Fuchow and Swatow. The ship would carry passengers, mail and possibly foodstuffs and medical supplies (but no commercial cargo). The reason for running the ship was to boost the morale of Shanghai's British community. British merchant vessels owing to the Nationalist blockade have stopped running and the community is said to be 'greatly depressed'.

2. The Treasury, who have been sounded, are prepared to sanction charter of such a ship. The Ministry of Transport have agreed that their Hong Kong representative assist in making necessary arrangements with shipping companies concerned, if we decide to go ahead. Their representative has been asked for his urgent comments. HM Consul-General, Shanghai, has been informed of the above and also that we are anxious to help. He now assures us that no difficulty regarding entry permits for such a ship is anticipated as far as the Communist authorities are concerned.

3. As regards the blockade difficulty, HM Consul-General, Shanghai, originally suggested that since a permit for the ship's journey might not be given by the Nationalists, or at any rate given in time, we content ourselves with letting them know that we are running a ship but make no special request for a permit. He considers that if HM Ships at the mouth of the

[1] Sir R. Urquhart.

Yangtse signalled the Nationalist guardship requesting them not to interfere with this ship, no further action would be necessary. On the other hand, Mr. Hutchison[2] in Nanking points out that it might be undesirable for a ship chartered by HMG to put herself in a position where she might be obliged to comply with orders from a Nationalist gunboat and where she could not rely upon assistance from HM Ships in the vicinity unless she were in extreme distress.

4. It is now for decision:

(1) whether we should go ahead with the proposals to charter a ship and run the possible risk of trouble with the Nationalists and now approach the Admiralty with a view to instructions being sent to the Commander-in-Chief, Far East for his assistance in arrangements to get the ship through;

(2) whether we should inform the Nationalist authorities in Formosa of the proposed journey. This could be done either by applying for a special permit for the ship basing this application on the 'relief' character of the ship or by merely letting them know that we intend to run the ship; or

(3) whether we drop the whole proposal.

5. In reaching our decision we should take into account the fact that the Shanghai British community would be greatly encouraged if we were able to get a ship with passengers and mail in. This would also to some extent counter the criticism that HMG is indifferent to their fate and has done nothing about putting an end to the 'farcical' blockade position. On the other hand, there is the risk of getting involved with the Nationalists and either, if they object to the ship's proceeding to Shanghai turning back (which would put us in an extremely foolish light) or of proceeding despite their orders in which case HM Ship might have to intervene. Any incident prior to recognition would be extremely unfortunate since it might distort the whole picture as far as recognition is concerned. A decision on these points must be taken soon if the ship is to get to Shanghai by Christmas. In any case it seems imperative that the ship should have left Shanghai on its return journey before HMG's final decision on recognition is announced.

Recommendations

(1) That we provisionally go ahead with the proposal to run the ship and approach the Admiralty with a view to the assistance of C-in-C Far East being obtained in making necessary arrangements to get ship through.

(2) That HM Consul at Tamsui be asked immediately to inform Chinese authorities in Formosa that we propose to send a 'relief' ship carrying passengers, mail and certain foodstuffs and medical supplies (but no commercial cargo) and requesting them to issue instructions to Nationalist guardship not to intervene.

---

[2] Formerly Commercial Counsellor at Shanghai (see No. 13, note 2), Mr. Hutchison was promoted to Nanking as a Minister (Commercial) in October 1947. Following the UK's recognition of the Communist Government in January 1950 he was appointed to Peking as British Chargé d'Affaires (see No. 121, note 2).

(3) If reply to HM Consul, Tamsui clearly indicates that Nationalists would prevent passage of 'relief' ship by force, the proposal to send her should be dropped.[3]

[3] The proposal to charter a Christmas relief ship to Shanghai was ultimately abandoned. The Treasury would not authorise the indemnity guarantee sought by the ship's owners against loss or damage, and the ship could not be got in and out of Shanghai before 20 December when the Nationalists planned to start new mine laying. Finally, if the ship could not reach Shanghai until after the new year it would run into clearance difficulties with the Communists and become entangled in the recognition issue (minute by Mr. A.A.E. Franklin of 16 December, F 19089/1261/10).

No. 112

Report by the Joint Intelligence Committee

JIC(49)44/16 Final [CAB 158/7/1]

Top Secret   MINISTRY OF DEFENCE, *14 December 1949*

We have again reviewed developments in South China with particular reference to the threat to Hong Kong. Our seventeenth report is at Annex.

2. Provided there are no important developments in South China over Christmas, we intend to submit our next report on Wednesday, 4th January 1950.

Conclusions

3. There is no evidence that the Chinese Communists intend to attack Hong Kong in the near future. After British recognition of the Chinese Communist regime there is a possibility of isolated Nationalist air attacks on Kaitak airfield.

ANNEX TO NO. 112

A Review of the Threat to Hong Kong on 13th December 1949

Military Situation

1. The situation between Canton and the Leased Territories remains unchanged, with no signs of a build up of Communist forces, nor of any indications of Communist military intentions towards Hong Kong. The Chinese Communist armies have continued to advance in west and south China, and Communist troops are rapidly approaching the Indo-China frontier. Yunnan province is now controlled by provincial troops who, with their Governor, transferred their allegiance to the Communists on the 10th December, 1949.

Political

2. The Peking Conference of the World Federation of Trade Unions, which was attended by delegates from South East Asian countries and from other countries including the Soviet Union and its satellites, appealed for

insurrections against imperialism in Vietnam, Burma, Indonesia, Malaya, the Philippines and Japan. The fact that uprisings were called for in the British Colony of Malaya, and yet Hong Kong was not mentioned in the opening speech by the President of the Chinese Federation of Labour, would seem to bear out the opinion already expressed that the Chinese Communists do not plan any immediate action against the Colony.

Situation in Hong Kong

3. *External.* River steamer services to Canton have still not been resumed nor, with the exception of a number of coal trains, have through rail services. There are indications that an increased effort is being made by the Communist frontier control to prevent smuggling (particularly of rice) into the Colony.

4. *Air Threat.* It is reported by the Air Attaché in Formosa that, after British recognition of the Chinese Communist regime, there is a possibility that aircraft flown by irresponsible aircrew members of the Nationalist Air Force may attack Kaitak airfield. At present there are some 65 China National Corporation aircraft grounded there. The scale of attack in these circumstances would be small and probably limited to single aircraft. In the most unlikely event of Nationalist approval being given for such an attack, up to 40 medium and heavy bombers could be used initially.

5. *Internal.* Public morale remains steady. Food and water stocks are satisfactory. Labour is generally quiet. Despite visa controls which now apply to immigrants from all places except Macao and the Communist areas of China, the influx into the Colony continues. The excess over departures for the week ending 4th December was 3429, bringing the total recorded influx since 30th November, 1948 to 210,423. The Governor has been asked for an estimate of the further numbers which can be accepted and whether he yet proposes any control over arrivals from Canton or regulation or entry across the frontier.

Communist Amphibious Training

6. A further report supporting our previous views[1] that Communist Amphibious Training is taking place has now been received. It indicates that training on the Lower Yangtse has been in progress since the 1st August, 1949. Exercises involve infantry and artillery units and training in night assaults. There has also been mention of the construction of some LC(A)[2] type craft powered by 80 H.P. engines. These reports may indicate Communist intentions to attack the Chusan Group. We still, however, maintain our view[3] that Chinese Communists are not at present in a position to make a successful opposed invasion of Formosa and that the likelihood of an attempted invasion early in 1950 has diminished.

[1] JIC(49)44.14 Final, 16 November 1949, CAB 158/7/1.
[2] Landing Craft (Assault).
[3] JIC(49)103 Final, 2, November 1949, CAB 158/8/2.

Conclusions

7. There is no evidence that the Chinese Communists intend to attack Hong Kong in the near future. After British recognition of the Chinese Communist regime, there is a possibility of isolated Nationalist air attacks on Kaitak airfield.

No. 113

Note on China: Proceedings at Lake Success[1]

[*F 19416/1023/10*]

FOREIGN OFFICE, *14 December 1949*

When the Debate on China in the First Committee of the United Nations Organisation opened on the 25th November, the Soviet delegate stated that the Chinese Delegation could only represent a fictitious government which had no authority in China and thus had no right to initiate the Debate. The Soviet Delegation would not participate in the discussion nor recognise any decision adopted on it.

The Debate gave rise to three resolutions:

1. By China urging the Assembly to determine 'that the USSR has by obstructing the National Government of China and by giving aid to the Chinese Communists, violated the Charter of the United Nations and the Treaty of Friendship and Alliance between China and the USSR of the 14th August, 1945': urging 'all Member States to desist and refrain from giving any military and economic aid to the Chinese communists: recommending all Member States not to accord diplomatic recognition to any régime organised by the Chinese communists and calling upon all Member States to refrain from taking advantage of the present situation in China for any purpose that is incompatible with the political independence and territorial and administrative integrity of China.'

2. By United States of America, Australia, Mexico, Pakistan and the Philippines. The operative paragraphs of this resolution as finally amended read as follows:

'The General Assembly desiring to promote the stability of international relations in the Far East, calls upon all states

To respect the political independence of China and be guided by the principles of the United Nations in their relations with China.

[1] This note about the UN debate on China was one of two attachments to a minute by Mr. Dening briefing Mr. Bevin about the Cabinet paper (No. 110) and the date when the UK should recognise Communist China. The other attachment was a draft telegram to Commonwealth and other friendly governments (France and the US) justifying the UK decision to extend recognition along the lines argued in the Cabinet paper.

(2) To respect the right of the people of China now and in the future to choose freely their political institutions and to maintain a Government independent of foreign control.

(3) To respect existing treaties relations [*sic*] to China and

(4) To refrain from

(*a*) Seeking to acquire spheres of influence or to create foreign controlled régimes within the territory of China

(*b*) Seeking to obtain special rights or privileges within the territory of China.'

3. By Equador, Cuba and Peru. Which, as finally amended, reads:

'Considering that item 68 'Threats to the political independence and territorial integrity of China and to the peace of the Far East resulting from Soviet violation of the Sino-Soviet Treaty of Friendship and alliance of 14th August, 1945 and from Soviet violations of the Charter of the United Nations' is of special importance and involves the fundamental principles of the Charter; considering the resolution on promotion of stability of international relations in the Far East the General Assembly authorises the Interim Committee of the General Assembly if it considers such action would promote the stability of international relations in the Far East to examine any violations of the principles contained in that resolution.'[2]

When it came to the Vote, the three-power resolution was adopted by 23 in favour, 19 against (including UK, US and Soviet block) and 14 abstentions. The five-power resolution was adopted by 47 votes in favour, 5 against (Soviet block) and 5 abstentions. The Chinese resolution was withdrawn but the Chinese delegate indicated that he wished to re-introduce it into the Interim Committee. When the item was considered by the Plenary Session of the Assembly on the 7th and 8th December, the five-power resolution was adopted by 45 votes in favour and 5 against and

[2] An earlier draft of the five-power resolution that had been sponsored by the US caused some anxiety in the FO and was described as 'dangerous'. These concerns were only partially allayed by the amended resolution put forward. The earlier draft had called on all states 'To respect the sovereignty of China and to refrain from the threat or use of force against its territorial integrity or political independence'. To the FO, the call to respect China's sovereignty 'offers a handle to anyone to attack our position in Hong Kong', while the reference to refraining from the use of force against China's territorial integrity might invite attack on the UK for its decision to reinforce the Hong Kong garrison. The substitution of these phrases still left the FO with concerns about the words 'Chinese people' in paragraph 2 of the resolution. This could include 'the overseas Chinese anywhere, e.g. Malaya or Manhatten [*sic*] and given the Chinese view of nationality it is difficult to devise any alternative form of words to exclude them'. Subsections (*a*) and (*b*) of paragraph 4 were open to objection on the grounds that they could lead to attacks on the position of Hong Kong. They might also embarrass the UK and the US in their respective objectives in Cyrenaica and Tripolitania (telegram Y455 to UK High Commissioner in India, repeated to other High Commissioners and UK Delegation in New York, 24 November 1949, F 17812/1023/10). Formerly Italian colonies, Cyrenaica and Tripolitania were united as the independent state of Libya in December 1951. Both the UK and the US wanted to establish military bases in Libya to exclude Soviet influence.

the three power resolution by 32 votes in favour with 5 against and 17 abstentions (including UK, Australia and Canada).

The three-power resolution is bound to be considered by the Interim Committee sometime early in the New Year but if in the meantime the Chinese Delegation have been succeeded by representatives of the new régime it is to be hoped that it may be allowed to die.

No. 114

Mr. Bevin to Sir O. Franks (Washington)

No. 11571 Telegraphic [*F 19057/1023/10*]

Secret   FOREIGN OFFICE, *16 December 1949, 6.30 p.m.*

Recognition of Chinese Communist Government.

Please seek an interview with Mr. Acheson and convey to him the following personal message from me.

Begins.

I want you to know that the Cabinet have now taken a decision in principle to extend *de jure* recognition to the Chinese Communist Government. The actual date of recognition has not yet been fixed, but I am thinking in terms of 2nd January 1950, though I do not wish to be held to that date. I am anxious that no publicity should be given to our decision until we are ready to notify the Chinese Government.

I also wish you to know that we have deferred a decision on this matter as long as we felt able, but having taken into account all the circumstances and all the views expressed by other Governments, we nevertheless feel we must now proceed to recognition. There are some factors which affect us specially, not only our interests in China but the position in Hong Kong and also in Malaya and Singapore, where there are vast Chinese communities. We are advised that continued non-recognition is liable to cause trouble there which we cannot afford to risk, and we have had to bear this in mind.

As you know, we also take the view that to withhold recognition indefinitely is to play straight into the hands of the Soviet Union. We feel that the only counter to Russian influence is that Communist China should have contacts with the West, and that the sooner these contacts are established the better.

Our recognition will merely acknowledge the inescapable fact that the Chinese Communist Government is in effective control in China. This does not in the least lessen our determination to resist communism in South East Asia and elsewhere. What happens in the territories for which we are responsible is very much our business, and we intend to stimulate resistance to communism with all the means at our disposal, and hope like-minded countries will do the same.

While for obvious reasons, we cannot accompany the act of recognition with a statement in public that it does not denote approval of the Chinese Communist Government, this is as you know the fact. All of us after all recognise the Soviet Union and satellites. We acknowledge the existence of these governments, though we certainly do not approve of them, and by recognising the Chinese Communist Government we shall be doing no more than acknowledging a fact, as we have done with the Soviet Union and the satellites.

Such then is the position which I want to put to you frankly. I had hoped that we might be able to take action together in this matter, but if the United States feel unable to accord recognition I shall quite understand the position. As you know, we want to keep in close association with you, but we have to be careful not to lose our grip of the situation in Asia and to take account into account the views of our Asian friends.

I am grateful for the views which you expressed to Sir Oliver Franks about this question of recognition on 8th December (Washington telegram No. 5726 of 8th December) which I have taken into account in discussion with my colleagues.[1] I am consulting with Commonwealth and other Governments with whom we have been in touch on this question, but it is of course for them to make up their own minds. Ends.

You will no doubt ask Mr. Acheson if he has any comments on this communication and indicate that I shall be grateful to receive a reply.[2]

[1] This telegram explained the points made by Mr. Acheson to Sir O. Franks that were put before the Cabinet in No. 110, paragraph 3 (F 18481/1023/10).

[2] Mr. Acheson replied on 23 December regretting the UK decision as he had hoped for a common course of action on the question of recognition. The US Government had yet to decide whether to issue a statement explaining its own position that recognition was unwise, and it trusted that on all other matters of mutual concern in the Far East, the UK and the US would feel able to pursue a common policy. This would be especially important in stimulating local resistance against the spread of Communism. Mr. Acheson also stressed that consideration should be given to the effect the timing of the UK's decision might have on the Vietnam problem (*FRUS 1949*, vol ix, pp. 241-42).

No. 115

Mr. Bevin to Sir O. Harvey (Paris)

No. 3391 Telegraphic [FO 800/462]

Immediate. Secret   FOREIGN OFFICE, *16 December 1949, 6 p.m.*

Recognition of Chinese Communist Government.
Please seek an interview with M. Schuman and deliver to him the following personal message from me.
Begins.

We have decided to recognise the Chinese Communist Government and I want to give you the earliest notice of our decision as I know how important it is to your Government.

2. The date on which we shall announce the decision to the Chinese is not yet fixed, but I am thinking in terms of 2nd January 1950, though I do not wish to determine the exact date until I have the views of other Governments.

3. I do not think it necessary to go over the reasons for this decision. They are all fairly obvious. We cannot indefinitely go on ignoring the effective government of a vast territory like China. I shall be happy if the French Government take a similar decision, but if you cannot I shall understand the special difficulties of your position arising out of the Indo-China situation. You will remember our conversation in Paris in November.[1] I share your anxiety about Indo-China. South East Asia is a region of great importance to both our Governments. I earnestly trust that our recognition of China will not add to your difficulties in Indo-China—my considered view is that worse dangers would flow from non-recognition than from recognition of China—and I hope that neither your own authorities on the spot, nor Bao Dai and his administration, will misinterpret our action.

4. I therefore suggest that a message should be passed to Bao Dai through your channels to warn him of our impending recognition of the Chinese Government. I would prefer you not to do this yet, but to wait till just before the event. By that time I hope that we shall have seen our way clear to *de facto* recognition of Viet Nam as an Associated State of the French Union. We shall not make public our decision about Viet Nam until after the Colombo Conference (when I shall try to carry other Commonwealth Governments with me in taking similar action), but I do know that you feel that an advance intimation to Bao Dai, in confidence, would help him and you. I cannot however yet give you the necessary assurance. Much depends on the actions of your Government in the next fortnight. It will help me greatly in putting the case to other Commonwealth Governments if I can point to the fact that substantial authority has been transferred to Bao Dai, and above all if I can point to a public declaration by the French Government of a programme and time-table for the transfer of full effective powers to Bao Dai.

5. I beg you to let me have urgently an account of the measures you have in mind in this connexion. I shall study it carefully and sympathetically and hope that as a result I shall be able before recognition of China takes effect to tell you of our decision about Viet Nam.[2]

[1] See No. 106.

[2] Vietnam (with Bao Dai as Head of State), Cambodia and Laos became 'Associated States within the French Union' as a result of agreements signed in Paris on 2 February 1950. The UK and US recognised the three Associated States on 7 February. Ho Chi Minh's Democratic

Republic of Vietnam had been recognised by Communist China on 18 January and by the Soviet Union on 30 January.

No. 116

Sir O. Franks (Washington) to Mr. Bevin (Received 18 December, 1.17 a.m.)

No. 5855 Telegraphic [*FO 800/462*]

Immediate. Secret   WASHINGTON, *17 December 1949, 6.54 p.m.*

For Secretary of State from Oliver Franks.

At dinner with Hume Wrong[1] and myself Acheson made several remarks about the Far East and the Indian Ocean. He was talking at large so that to my mind importance attaches to the drift of his thoughts rather than their detailed expression.

2. He started off by saying that he thought the world across the Pacific Ocean would be the principal preoccupation of the State Department in 1950. He and his advisers had changed their views on what were likely to be the immediate consequences of the successful conquest and occupation of China by the Communists. They now thought there was likely to be early expansion south and east beyond the borders of China. This expansion would be especially dangerous, if it took place, where there were considerable Chinese settlements.

3. He had been scratching together what dollars he could and believed he could lay hands on about 75 millions. He expected to use this in Indonesia and Indo-China with possibly a little bit of help to spare for Siam. With the aid these dollars represented, quite a job could be done in building up the régimes in these countries. At this point Acheson interpolated a paean of praise about French achievements in Indo-China. They had done far more than they had ever let on. Bao Dai had a good chance and the thing to do was to press early recognition on the French. The American Government in distinction from its earlier views would be ready to recognise and help Indo-China as soon as the French had acted.

4. He then said that all this made the Colombo Conference[2] a most important event. His mind was moving in terms of some rough geographical division of responsibilities. The Americans would look after Indonesia, Philippines, Indo-China with a little to spare for Siam. The Commonwealth would see to the help of the countries in the Indian Ocean. He had in mind especially Burma: then there was our own position

[1] Canadian Ambassador in Washington.

[2] See No. 110, note 3.

in Malaya and our interest overlapping theirs in Siam. Acheson clearly was hoping that in some way India and the United Kingdom would be able to tidy up the mess in Burma so as to prevent the Chinese appearing over the hump.[3]

5. He said that he would like to talk with Mike Pearson[4] about these ideas before the Colombo Conference and this was tentatively arranged with Hume Wrong.

6. I did not take part very much in this expression of views. I did ask what evidence there was to account for the American change of view about the misbehaviour of the Chinese. The only reply I got was that the Communists would, by aggrandisement in the south, direct the gaze of the Chinese people from Manchuria. I also said that I personally had doubts about spheres of influence rather than joint policies and operations. To start with Hong Kong did not fit in and I did not want Acheson to feel that now the Americans have at last got interested in South East Asia they need not think at all about the Indian Ocean. We may want them to think a good deal about some of the countries round that Ocean, for example in connexion with the tripartite talks. I therefore discouraged any sharp divisions of interest or function.

[3] Cf. Nos. 91, note 6, and 108, note 2.

[4] This is a reference to Mr. Lester Pearson, the Canadian Minister for External Affairs.

No. 117

Mr. Bevin to Mr. Hutchison (Nanking)[1]

No. 196 [*F 19055/1023/10*]

Confidential   FOREIGN OFFICE, *19 December 1949*

Policy of His Majesty's Government regarding recognition of the Chinese Communist Government

Sir,

The Chinese Ambassador called on me to-day and brought with him a report from the political correspondent of *Reynolds News* of 18th December, to the effect that His Majesty's Government had decided to proceed to the recognition of the Communist Government in China without waiting for France or America and that an announcement would be made before the end of the year.

2. Dr. Cheng Tien Hsi asked me whether in fact any foundation existed for such an article. I told him that the actual date of recognition had not

[1] See No. 111, note 2.

been fixed. I said I must be frank with him. Great Britain had tried to maintain a steadying influence on the whole position, but it was quite clear that the Nationalist armies were offering no resistance, and the Communists were marching through China and taking it over. In this situation it was impossible for us to refuse to recognise this new Government which had been thrown up by a revolutionary and civil war and which was now in possession of nearly the whole country. It was not a question of opinion, but of fact; and, though I felt extremely sorry for him and his colleagues, we could not go on blindly as if nothing had occurred. I told the Ambassador that we had decided on recognition in principle, but had not fixed a date. We were in communication with other Governments who would be affected by our action.

3. Dr. Cheng Tien Hsi then asked me whether we would cease to recognise the Nationalist Government. I said that no such decision had been taken. The matter was being considered with regard to those territories which the Nationalist Government still controlled, but circumstances were changing very fast. I would see him before the actual act of recognition took place and communicate to him what our position was in this matter.

4. The Ambassador said that the inference that Great Britain and the British Commonwealth were willing to recognise Communist China had demoralised the Nationalist forces. I told him that I could not accept that. The Nationalist forces had been demoralised for a long time. In fact, during the whole of the difficult period for those Governments who wanted to be friendly with China, we had not had one word regarding policy from Chiang Kai-shek or his Government, and this could not be attributed to any act of ours. We had tried to act in the most friendly manner, and I felt that his assertions were unjustified.

5. Dr. Cheng then said that he was left in a very difficult position. He did not know whether he had been sentenced to political death or whether he was wanted to carry on. I said this was usually the outcome of revolutionary conditions and although I felt sorry for him I could not help him very much. We had enjoyed the most friendly relations, and I wanted to do everything I could, but the interests of His Majesty's Government demanded that a decision must now be taken.

I am, &c.,
ERNEST BEVIN

No. 118

Sir D. Kelly[1] *(Moscow) to Mr. Bevin (Received 20 December, 1.27 p.m.)*

No. 1088 Telegraphic [F 19061/10338/10]

Secret   MOSCOW, *20 December 1949, 12.16 p.m.*

My telegram No. 1078.[2]

I have been considering what significance should be attached to Mao Tse-tung's visit to Moscow.

2. It seems unlikely that he should have made the journey simply to be present at Stalin's seventieth birthday celebrations. Even if this were the original motive, I should expect some tangible political result to emerge. The most likely conjecture is that the opportunity will be taken to sign a treaty of friendship and mutual aid similar to those linking the Soviet Union with the satellites. This treaty would presumably be proclaimed with a burst of publicity which, besides announcing eternal friendship between the two peoples, would emphasise the disinterested help which the Soviet Union was prepared to give to war-ravaged China. Within the framework of this treaty the basis would be laid for the further development of their political, economic, technical, cultural and possibly military relations.

3. It is perhaps worth noting that in the short speech which he made on his arrival here Mao showed no excessive deference to the Soviet Union, but on the contrary gave an indication of his feeling of equality by referring repeatedly to their two 'great peoples' and 'the two great States'. It is a fair assumption that he will do his best to avoid any specific re-affirmation of the more onerous provisions of the Sino-Soviet Treaty of 1945, and it is likely that the more contentious problems arising out of that Treaty (e.g. Dairen) will be left over for future settlement. Indeed, it is quite possible that the new agreement (if there is one) will be in the general terms which are now standard practice and that its relationship to the 1945 Treaty and the precise status of the latter will be ignored altogether or left deliberately vague.

Foreign Office please pass to Washington as my telegram No. 81.[3]

[1] HM Ambassador at Moscow, 1949-51.

[2] This telegram reported Mao Tse-tung's arrival in Moscow the previous day and his reception at the railway station by a Soviet delegation led by Mr. Molotov (F 18923/10338/10).

[3] Mao Tse-tung remained in the Soviet Union for nine weeks. His visit ended with the signing of a Sino-Soviet Treaty of Friendship, Alliance and Mutual Assistance on 14 February 1950. The treaty provided for mutual assistance should Japan, or any country in alliance with Japan, engage directly or indirectly in acts of aggression. It also stipulated that Soviet rights over the Manchurian railways and over the ports of Dairen and Port Arthur would terminate with the conclusion of a Japanese peace treaty or, failing that, by 1952 at the latest. The Soviet Union thus agreed to surrender the gains made in the 1945 treaty with Nationalist China (see No. 3) but in fact the ports were not handed over until after the death of Marshal Stalin in

March 1953. Finally the treaty made provision for the establishment of joint-stock Sino-Soviet companies in China and for a Soviet loan worth 300 million dollars at a one per cent rate of interest. This was a negligible sum when compared with the low cost finance made available to the Soviet satellite countries in Eastern Europe.

No. 119

Minute from Mr. Bevin to Mr. Attlee

[*FO 800/462*]

FOREIGN OFFICE, *23 December 1949*

PRIME MINISTER

You will recall that when the Cabinet considered recognition of the Chinese Communist Government it was left to me to decide on the date when recognition should take place.[1] After carefully considering all the replies we have received from various governments, in particular the fact that India has decided to recognise on the 30th and that the French have asked me, because of the situation in Indo-China, to defer recognition as long as possible, I have come to the conclusion that we should notify the Chinese Communist Government of our intention to accord *de jure* recognition on 6th January 1950. Messages are being drafted to all the various governments (in consultation with the Commonwealth Relations Office as far as Commonwealth countries are concerned).

2. I will not bother you with these messages, but would like your approval of the action proposed in the attached timetable.[2]

ERNEST BEVIN

[1] See No. 110, note 8.

[2] Mr. Attlee approved this action on 24 December. Mr Acheson was informed of the decision on the same day. From 6 January 1950 *de jure* recognition of the Nationalist Government would be withdrawn and the Chinese Ambassador in London would no longer be recognised. Together with his staff he would be offered asylum in the UK if he so desired. The UK Consul in Formosa would continue to maintain *de facto* relations with the local authorities (telegram No. 11751 to Washington of 24 December, F 19274/1023/10).

Chapter VI

1950

The plight of British commercial interests in China worsened during the early months of 1950. This was partly the result of the continuing Nationalist blockade that now intensified as KMT aircraft bombed Shanghai. But the problems of the blockade were compounded by the attitude of the Communist authorities towards foreign firms. Arbitrary and potentially crippling taxation levies were imposed and firms were not allowed to lay off labour that was no longer needed. State controls were speedily established over both the supply and marketing of raw materials. With their reserves virtually exhausted a number of UK concerns reached the conclusion for themselves that it was impossible to continue. In January 1950 the manager of the Kailin Mining Administration, the largest British concern in China, informed the Chinese Government that the company intended to withdraw.

The prospect of losing the whole of British investment in China began to worry Ministers and officials, not because, over the long-term, this was not expected but because it was happening so quickly and lending encouragement to the Communists to hasten the process. In April 1950 Mr. Bevin expressed his concern to Cabinet about the loss of prestige that would be involved in a total withdrawal from China (FE(O)(50)16, 13 April 1950, CAB 134/290, and CP(50)73, 20 April 1950, CAB 129/29). Although full diplomatic relations had yet to be established, the FO continued to justify the decision to extend de jure recognition in January. As well as the commercial argument about protecting UK trading interests, there was the 'fundamental political reason' that to withhold recognition would imply a deliberate policy of boycotting China. This in turn would cement still further the ties between China and the Soviet Union and neither the UK nor the US had the power to create a 'sanitary cordon' around China. Further justification for recognition was provided in the position of Hong Kong and in the presence of large Chinese populations in Malaya and elsewhere in South-East Asia.[1] *If*

---

[1] After the extension of *de jure* recognition to the Communists, the British colonial authorities in South-East Asia urged again that Chinese Consuls should not be appointed in their territories (see No. 93). The FO argued that this would mean Communist retaliation with a demand for the withdrawal of HM Consuls in China. At the very least this would make continued trade with China almost impossible and if the rupture extended to a total break in relations, this would have the political consequences the UK was most anxious to avoid (FO memorandum, 'The Political and Economic Implications of Break in Relations with China', FE(O)(50)30 Revise, 16 May 1950, CAB 134/290). Although it was agreed that Chinese Consuls would not be accepted in Malaya during the Emergency, China made no request to send representatives.

in time there had to be a break in relations with China it was important from the standpoint of world opinion that responsibility should rest with the Chinese Government.

The FO envisaged four possible ways in which the situation in China might develop: (a) Russian influence would continue to grow with the result that China would become a Soviet satellite; (b) Russian attempts to dominate would foster Titoism; (c) the Government of the People's Republic would fail to maintain effective control over the whole country and dissident opposition would emerge; (d) the Communists would achieve unqualified success and China would become a great power capable of standing on its own feet. The ultimate outcome could not as yet be foreseen but the odds against China becoming a great power unaided were said at the time to be considerable.

Against the background of this analysis Mr. Hutchison, the Chargé d'Affaires who transferred from Nanking to Peking in February 1950, was instructed to approach the Chinese authorities with proposals designed to alleviate the condition of British business in China. The mutual advantage of continued trade to both countries was stressed. Local loans at reasonable rates were suggested for firms whose reserves were exhausted but who wished to continue. Direct financial assistance to the firms was considered but ruled out on the grounds that it would in effect mean the UK financing a number of public utilities in China with no guarantee that ultimately they would not be nationalised. Permission was requested to discharge uneconomic labour and in cases where firms had no current orders, it was suggested that they should be allowed to close down and be placed on a care and maintenance basis in a manner that would enable them to resume production when conditions improved. Greater freedom of movement for British subjects was also requested, together with exit permits for those wishing to leave (telegram No. 518 to Peking, 2 May 1950, FC 1106/69, and memorandum to the Chinese Government of 24 May 1950, FC 1106/178).

Simultaneously the FO favoured action to break the blockade but recognised that it would not be wise to act independently without either US support or at least tacit approval. Neither was forthcoming when the matter was raised in Washington in March. The State Department insisted that the blockade should not be seen in isolation and suggested instead that American and British officials should examine the whole of the China situation, including the vexed issue of China's representation at the UN (FC 1022/263). In effect US and UK tactics over China continued to diverge. While recognising what they described as the 'distorted propaganda value of the blockade', the Americans maintained that its economic and administrative effects on the Communists were not to be discounted. The British doubted that the blockade was having any material effect on the Communists who were portrayed as having little regard for popular hardship or suffering. The UK argued that the blockade was serving only to increase Soviet influence in China (FRUS, 1950, vol. iii, pp. 992-94).

By April 1950 the American view of developments in China had been placed in an entirely different context. In that month the Administration approved NSC-68, a major analysis of US defence objectives and programmes prepared by the National Security Council (ibid., vol. i, pp. 234-92). Basing their outlook upon a polarisation of world power in which 'slave society' was said to confront the free, the authors of NSC-68 asserted that the Soviet Union was 'animated by a new fanatic faith' and that the aim of Soviet leaders was total domination of the Eurasian land mass. To resist this hegemonic drive, NSC-68 argued that the US needed sufficient military power to deter aggression against itself and to fight limited wars abroad. The result was to be an unprecedented increase in US defence spending.

The new US outlook dictated by NSC-68 explains why Mr. Attlee and Mr. Bevin were unable to persuade Mr. Acheson to consider any compromise over China when the Secretary of State visited London in May 1950. Mr. Bevin found the discussions 'a little disappointing', although it had been agreed in advance that the Foreign Secretary would not press UK policy on China to such an extent as to risk alienating the sympathy and support of the US government (Series II, Volume I, No 3, and Series II, Volume II, Nos. 28, 56, 80). After this Mr. Bevin was more inclined towards an independent line. In June he considered whether the UK should move its position from abstention to one of support for Communist China on the question of China's representation at the UN.² He also contemplated replacing Mr. Hutchison by an experienced official of higher rank. Mr. Dening was regarded as Britain's Ambassador-designate and, as a means of expediting negotiations on the position of UK firms, Mr. Bevin toyed with the idea of sending a special mission to China (FC 1051/4).³

It was at this point, in late June 1950, that the Korean War started.⁴ Communist North Korea's attack on its southern neighbour was viewed in Washington as immediate vindication of the analysis put forward in NSC-68. President Truman ordered the US Seventh Fleet to neutralise the Formosa Straits, a move that finally ended the Nationalist blockade of Shanghai. But it was China's entry into the war in October 1950 that put

---

[2] Two weeks before the outbreak of the Korean War, Mr. Attlee approved an FO proposal that the UK should modify its policy of waiting for a majority UN decision and vote in favour of Communist China's representation. Temporarily put on hold when the war started, the new policy was supported by Mr. Bevin in August—he argued that China was essentially an Asian problem on which the UK could not afford to ignore the views of such countries as India, Pakistan and Ceylon—and confirmed by the Cabinet in September. See Series II, Volume IV, pp. xi, xiv-xv, and Nos. 7, 35 and 42.

[3] Under cover of a wider tour of Asian and Pacific countries between October 1950 and April 1951, secret arrangements were made for Mr. Dening to visit China at the beginning of the tour. The aim was not to achieve practical results but to persuade the Chinese authorities that their suspicions of the non-Communist world were without foundation. He failed to obtain an entry visa and the visit was abandoned at the end of October when China entered the Korean War and sent troops into Tibet (FC 1022/515 and FZ 1026/12).

[4] China's entry into the war revived the former debates about the nature of Chinese communism and its relationship with Moscow. In contrast to its earlier assessments (see e.g. No. 55 and 99, note 1), FO analysis maintained that Communist China was not a satellite of Moscow but that it was a menace to peace and stability in Asia. Thus while agreeing with the US on the second point, the FO parted company with America on the first. US tactics in relation to China were said to be counter-productive in that they had strengthened the extremists and the pro-Russian elements in China, and frightened the small countries in South-East Asia. The policy advocated for the UK was one of recognition and negotiation, the latter from positions of strength, firmness and patience. Series II, Volume, IV, No. 123.

paid to any prospect of negotiations with the Communists to protect British firms. The firms' assets and properties, however, were never expropriated or confiscated. They were forced into such debt by taxes and regulations that they had to close, leave China voluntarily and hand over what remained of their assets to the Chinese Government. Their withdrawal was announced in May 1952 and subsequent UK losses were estimated at between £200 million and £250 million. In 1937, when British influence in China had been at its height, the number of British subjects in China was 20,000. By the middle of 1951 it was no more than about 1,700.[5] Concluding a review of how British interests in China had been treated by the Communist government, Mr. Herbert Morrison, Mr. Bevin's successor at the FO from March 1951, observed: 'All this suggests a deliberate and consistent policy of squeezing out by degrees those British—and indeed Western—interests which are not of practical use and assistance to the Chinese. This policy, including the gradual exclusion of foreign Consuls, is in many ways similar to that which was applied in Soviet Russia after 1927.' It was 'an unhappy story as a whole' and not one to which the UK Government wished, 'at this stage, to give official publicity' (FO Intel No. 109 of 21 May 1951, B 11/25).

[5] Non-essential British subjects and US nationals were advised to leave China in October 1950. This advice was repeated in May 1951 and business leaders already thinking of liquidating and leaving were informed that it would be unwise to postpone their plans in anticipation that the situation might improve. By the end of 1951 the number of British subjects in China was put at under a thousand. Shipping was available to evacuate them but because of the war in Korea it was unclear whether ships would be allowed to call at Chinese ports or even for British subjects to leave China at all (FC 1582/27). On the firms, see Aron Shai, *The fate of British and French firms in China, 1949-1954: imperialism imprisoned* (Basingstoke, Macmillan, 1996).

No. 120

Mr. Bevin to HM Representatives Overseas on the establishment of Diplomatic relations with China

Information No. 129 Telegraphic [GC 11/64]

Secret   FOREIGN OFFICE, *26 June 1950*

I give below a review of the discussions in Peking on the establishment of diplomatic relations between China and the United Kingdom. My two immediately following Intels contain respectively the texts of communications on this question exchanged between the two Governments[1] and a list[2] showing the countries which have recognised the Central People's Government and the dates on which they did so.

2. The Central People's Government was formally established in Peking on 1st October 1949. On 6th January His Majesty's Government accorded *de jure* recognition to the Central People's Government, and expressed their

[1] See No. 121.
[2] Not printed.

willingness to enter diplomatic relations. On 9th January the Central people's Government acknowledged receipt of this note and similarly expressed their willingness to enter into diplomatic relations, and invited His Majesty's Government to send a representative to Peking 'to carry on negotiations on preliminary and procedural questions on the establishment of diplomatic relations.'[3] On 13th February His Majesty's Chargé d'Affaires[4] arrived in Peking. On 2nd March he had an initial interview with the Vice-minister for Foreign Affairs, and the Chinese Government then requested clarification on two main questions:

(1) His Majesty's Government's attitude on Chinese representation in the United Nations; and
(2) His Majesty's Government's attitude on Chinese State property in Hong Kong.

On 17th March His Majesty's Government's replies to these questions were communicated to the Chinese Government. After a considerable interval, on 8th May the Chinese Government, having made it clear that they did not regard His Majesty's Government's earlier replies as satisfactory, requested further clarification. His Majesty's Government's reply to the Chinese Government's communication of 8th May was delivered by His Majesty's Chargé d'Affaires at Peking on 17th June.

3. The attitude of the Chinese authorities to His Majesty's Chargé d'Affaires may be of interest. For the purpose of conducting the discussions on the establishment of diplomatic relations, Mr. Hutchison has been accepted in his capacity as His Majesty's Chargé d'Affaires. The Chinese Government undertook to extend all facilities both to Mr. Hutchison and his staff. The transport arrangements for his move from Nanking to Peking, together with his staff and archives, were entirely satisfactory. His Majesty's Chargé d'Affaires is accorded what amounts to diplomatic privileges and these seem to be extended to his staff. In Peking Mr. Hutchison lives in the old Embassy compound. He has diplomatic wireless facilities and can communicate with London, Nanking, Shanghai, Canton and Kunming in code and cypher. These posts have wireless transmitting facilities. It has proved possible to arrange for the King's Messenger to travel from Hong Kong to Peking. The Chinese authorities agreed to the issue of an entry and exit permit for this courier, and it is considered that there would be no difficulty in establishing a regular courier service to Peking.

4. Mr. Hutchison and his staff have been treated with courtesy in Peking. At the interviews with the Vice-Minister for Foreign Affairs he has also invariably been treated with consideration. It should, however, be noted that in the course of these interviews it has not in fact so far proved

---

[3] See No. 121, note 2.
[4] Only an accredited Head of a Diplomatic Mission abroad is entitled to use the appellation 'His/Her Majesty's'. The correct usage for a Chargé d'Affaires is 'The British Chargé d'Affaires'.

possible to exchange views frankly and freely. The interviews in fact have been formal in character. The exchanges are communicated orally and some supplementary comment is occasionally made by one side or the other. Texts of the oral communications are made available.

5. In these discussions the Chinese in theory claim they are doing no more than making a stand on two main principles:

(1) The complete severance of relations with the 'Kuomintang reactionary clique',
(2) The demonstration of a friendly attitude to the Central People's Government by the Government wishing to establish relations.

Governments who have recognised the Peking Government must, it seems, pass these tests if they are to qualify for diplomatic relations. The answers to the tests appear to be found in the attitude of the recognising Government to (1) Chinese representation in the United nations; (2) Chinese State property in their territory.

6. These tests have not been put to the Government of the USSR or to those of the Eastern European satellites. It is, however, worth noting that so far no Chinese missions have been opened in any of the East European capitals, although the various East European satellites have for some time already had their representatives in Peking. The appointment of a Chinese Ambassador to Warsaw has now, however, been announced and missions may therefore shortly be opened in East European capitals. The Chinese Ambassadors to India and Sweden have so far not proceeded to take up their appointments, although a Chargé d'Affaires is expected to leave for New Delhi shortly. At present the Central People's Government is represented only in Moscow. We have only in the last few days for the first time heard of the existence of a Chinese diplomatic passport, and although Peking was 'liberated' more than a year and a half ago, we have not so far heard of any ordinary passports having been issued; nor with very rare exceptions have any requests for the issue of visas to or via British territory been received through Chinese Government channels, or for that matter by individual application. (Visas are of course not required for travel from China to Hong Kong.) Travel, it will be seen, is not encouraged.

7. As far as news is concerned, our mission, apart from telegraphic correspondence and copies belatedly received of Hong Kong papers and the *North China Daily News* published in Shanghai, which carries some Reuters' reports (though Reuters are not mentioned), is largely dependent on the BBC and other broadcasting stations and on the Chinese press. The foreign news contained in the Chinese press has an exclusively Tass[5] background. Letters from the United Kingdom to Peking, however, get through by ordinary mail regularly and fairly quickly (about one month) but are liable to unofficial censorship.

[5] Soviet news agency.

8. While Mr. Hutchison is regarded as 'the British Government's representative for the purpose of conducting negotiations on the establishment of diplomatic relations', he has, nevertheless, communicated in writing with the Chinese Ministry for Foreign Affairs on quite a number of questions not connected with the discussions on the establishment of diplomatic relations, including questions such as the seizure of the former military barracks; the repatriation of Chinese refugee soldiers from Hong Kong; British commercial interests in China; assaults on British subjects; issue of permits for the Shanghai repatriation ship; exit and entry facilities for individual British subjects in cases of special difficulty; Hong Kong immigration control measures; the alleged sabotage of CNAC/CATC planes in Hong Kong.[6] While these communications have not invariably been formally acknowledged, they have in certain cases proved effective in obtaining the desired result. The Chinese for their part have similarly on occasion transmitted communications to Mr. Hutchison, including copies of messages to the Secretary-General of the United Nations, protests regarding Hong Kong immigration regulations, alleged sabotage of several CNAC/CATC aircraft, and detention of these aircraft, also matters arising out of the upkeep of the Chinese Embassy premises in London. While far from satisfactory, it nevertheless provides at any rate some channel of communication.

9. Mr. Hutchison and his staff can move freely inside Peking and for some distance in the neighbouring countryside. Contacts with Chinese exist, although as a result of caution on the Chinese side they are somewhat limited by 'pre-liberation' standards. No contacts, other than the outwardly friendly but nevertheless formal contacts of the staff of the

[6] Seventy-one aircraft in Hong Kong were the property of two Chinese air transport companies: the Chinese National Aviation Corporation and the Central Air Transportation Corporation. The former was incorporated under Chinese law and owned 80 per cent by the Chinese Nationalist Government and 20 per cent by Pan-American Airways. The latter was never incorporated and was a department of the Chinese Nationalist Government. As early as June 1949 the Governor of Hong Kong had asked for the removal of the aircraft on the grounds that their maintenance had become an inconvenience and that there was a risk of the rapidly advancing Communists laying claim to them. Ownership of the aircraft became a disputed issue in November 1949 when the managing directors of the two companies defected to the Communists taking eleven aircraft with them. The Communists maintained that the remaining seventy-one planes were their property but in December 1949 two US citizens signed a contract with the Nationalist government purchasing the assets of both companies. They later sold their interest to Civil Air Transport Incorporated, a company incorporated in the US. The US Government supported the claims of the US company. The aircraft then became the subject of protracted legal proceedings during which the Americans expressed frequent concern that Communist sympathisers among the workforce were sabotaging them at the maintenance base and workshops where they were being held. Later, when China became involved in the Korean war, Washington was concerned that China's military potential should not be increased by the acquisition of the aircraft (B 11/15).

Ministry of Foreign Affairs, exist with any other Chinese Government officials or Communist Party members. No opportunity for conversation or exchange of views with Chinese Government officials on any general questions has proved possible since the departure from the scene of the Nationalists. It is, however, worth recording that on the occasion of The King's Birthday some 250 guests attended a garden party given by Mr. Hutchison. The guests included the Chef de Protocole and two secretaries, and a 'sprinkling of Chinese' in addition to Soviet and East European representatives as well as those of friendly Governments.

10. His Majesty's Consular Officers in the meantime remain unrecognised and have no official contacts with the Chinese authorities. They are treated as 'private' residents and as such have on the whole been reasonably treated. Consular offices have not been closed and consuls continue to advise and assist British subjects and perform notarial functions. Their position is, however, for obvious reasons far from easy. In their personal capacity they have on occasion been able to maintain unofficial and strictly limited contacts with the personnel of the Chinese Foreign Affairs Department. No courier facilities exist.

11. In conclusion, on the more general question of the establishment of diplomatic relations, it should be noted that the Chinese Communist press has recently played up in its propaganda the question of His Majesty's Government's insincerity and duplicity as revealed in the course of exchanges which have taken place in Peking, and in their attitude in the United Nations voting on Chinese representation. The boot is, of course, to a very large extent on the other foot, and the sincerity of the Chinese Government is highly questionable. As realists, they are perfectly aware that the question at issue is whether diplomatic relations are established irrespective of the fact that there are a large number of conflicting interests and outstanding issues. The Chinese press has on occasion indulged in considerable abuse at our expense, while comment in the press in this country and on the BBC has on the whole been moderate. Similarly, the Chinese are quite well aware that their attitude to Communist subversive activities in Malaya scarcely reveals any reciprocity as far as demonstrating a friendly attitude is concerned. They must also be perfectly well aware that their admission into the United Nations (about which they are possibly not in any great hurry) would have been considerably expedited had they displayed any really genuine desire to establish diplomatic relations in a normal and reasonable manner with us. This they have not so far done. Attention is drawn to these points, since there is on occasion a tendency to assume that we, rather than the Chinese, have been 'sticky' or 'holding out' or perhaps even 'insincere' in our overtures to the Central people's Government.

12. To sum up, the future of the discussions on the establishment of diplomatic relations is uncertain, and the 'Peking talks' have so far been characterised by a reluctance on the part of the Chinese to make it possible to reach talking terms with them.

13. As pointed out in my No. 112 Intel, of 7th June,[7] it has perhaps been insufficiently appreciated that there are in fact no negotiations in the normal sense between the United Kingdom and the Chinese Government, and the latter have so far not sought to impose conditions for the establishment of relations. While it is clear that the two issues which are holding up progress are Chinese representation in the United Nations and the case of the aircraft in Hong Kong, the Chinese Government have so far not done more than to ask for a clarification of our attitude on these two questions. There has been no bargaining, and no demands have been made.

14. No attempt is made here to assess the extent to which the Chinese Government may be influenced in the policy they are adopting in this matter by the Soviet Union.

15. The above is for your confidential information only.

[7] GC 11/63.

No. 121

Mr. Bevin to HM Representatives Overseas

Information No. 130 Telegraphic [*GC 11/64*]

Secret   FOREIGN OFFICE, *26 June 1950*

My immediately preceding Intel.[1]

Following are texts of communications exchanged between His Majesty's Government and the Central People's Government on recognition and the establishment of diplomatic relations:

Text of Note on Recognition communicated to the Chinese Minister for Foreign Affairs by His Majesty's Consul-General at Peking on 6 January, 1950

'Sir,

I have the honour to inform your Excellency that His Majesty's Government in the United Kingdom of Great Britain and Northern Ireland, having completed their study of the situation resulting from the formation of the Central People's Government of the People's Republic of China, and observing that it is now in effective control of by far the greater part of the territory of China, have this day recognised that Government as the *de jure* Government of China. In these circumstances. His Majesty's

[1] See No. 120.

Government, in response to Chairman Mao Tse-tung's proclamation of 1st October, 1949, are ready to establish diplomatic relations on the basis of equality, mutual benefit and mutual respect for territory and sovereignty and are prepared to exchange diplomatic representatives with the Central People's Government.

2. Pending the appointment of an Ambassador, Mr. J.C. Hutchinson has been nominated as His Majesty's Chargé d'Affaires *ad interim*. Accordingly I have the honour to request that you will receive him and transact official business with him in that capacity, and further that he may be granted all necessary facilities for the transfer of himself, his staff and the archives of His Majesty's Embassy from Nanking to Peking.

ERNEST BEVIN,
His Britannic Majesty's Principal
Secretary of State for Foreign Affairs

Text of the Reply to our Note on Recognition signed by the Chinese Minister for Foreign Affairs and delivered to His Majesty's Consul-General at Peking on 9 January, 1950

On behalf of the Central People's Government of the People's Republic of China, I hereby acknowledge the receipt of your telegram of 6th January, 1950, transmitting the information that the Government of the United Kingdom of Great Britain and Northern Ireland is ready to establish diplomatic relations with the Central People's Government of the People's Republic of China on the basis of equality, mutual benefit and mutual respect for the territory and sovereignty.

I hereby inform you that the Central People's Government of the People's Republic of China is willing to establish diplomatic relations with your Government on the basis of equality, mutual benefit and mutual respect for the territory and accept Mr. J.C. Hutchison whom you have appointed as Chargé d'Affaires *ad interim* as the representative of the Government of the United Kingdom of Great Britain and Northern Ireland sent to Peking to carry on negotiations on the question of establishment of diplomatic relations between our two countries.[2] The

[2] The wording here in this Chinese interpretation of Mr. Hutchison's status is significant. In effect the Communist Government agreed to treat Mr. Hutchison as a Chargé d'Affaires but they did not officially recognise him as such. In subsequent communications Mr. Hutchsion and his successors were referred to as 'Negotiating Officer'. They were not accorded diplomatic status. The position changed in 1954 as a result of contacts established between the UK and China during the Geneva Conference. The British Chargé d'Affaires in Peking, Mr. (later Lord) Trevelyan, was given diplomatic status and in September 1954 a Chinese officer of similar rank (Huan Hsiang) was appointed to London.

Central People's Government of the People's Republic of China will give all necessary facilities for the transfer, of Mr. Hutchison, his staff and archives from Nanking to Peking.

CHOU EN-LAI

Oral Communication made by Chinese Vice-Minister for Foreign Affairs to His Majesty's Chargé d'Affaires on 2 March, 1950

Of questions concerning establishment of diplomatic relations between China and the United Kingdom, the most important, which must be settled first, is question of severance of relations between His Majesty's Government and Kuomintang remnant of reactionaries. The Chinese Government consider, as His Majesty's Government has announced the establishment of diplomatic relations with the Chinese People's Republic, it should not continue to maintain any diplomatic intercourse with Kuomintang. The British delegate to Security Council, however, on 10th January concurred with the American delegate's opinion that a decision to take action as proposed by Soviet delegate would be premature and when Soviet delegate's proposal was put to a vote on 13th January the British delegate abstained. This action in effect means that His Majesty's Government continues to recognise the legality of so-called 'delegate' of Kuomintang remnant of reactionary clique and refuses to accept delegate of legal Government of Chinese people. Similar action was subsequently taken by British delegates in other organisations of United Nations, e.g., the Economic and Social Council The Chinese therefore consider His Majesty's Government should clarify their attitude to this question and demonstrate by actual deeds their complete severance of diplomatic intercourse with Kuomintang remnant reactionaries and their sincerity in desiring to establish diplomatic relations with Chinese People's Republic. The Central People's Government consider that this question is one the practical settlement of which is essential for the establishment of diplomatic relations between China and United Kingdom. Furthermore, the Chinese Government hope that His Majesty's Government will inform them clearly of their attitude to various organisations of Kuomintang remnant clique at present in Hong Kong and to all Chinese nationals['] property there.

At this interview the Vice-Minister for Foreign Affairs said they hoped that His Majesty's Chargé d'Affaires would be able to make an early statement of the attitude of His Majesty's Government in both these questions and further added the hope that he would see him again soon. His Majesty's Chargé d'Affaires described the tone of the meeting as courteous and friendly.

Oral Communication made by His Majesty's Charge d'Affaires on 17 March in reply to Questions raised by the Central People's Government at his interview on 3 March with the Chinese Vice-Minister for Foreign Affairs

As already indicated to the People's Government, His Majesty's Government in the United Kingdom withdrew recognition from the former Nationalist Government of China on 6th January, 1950, on which day they notified *de jure* recognition of the People's Government. No diplomatic relations have existed with the former Nationalist Government since that date. The Chinese Embassy in London is closed and the former Ambassador enjoys no diplomatic status.

The present position in the United Nations has, in the view of His Majesty's Government in the United Kingdom, no connexion with the facts of the position as already stated. A decision as to whether the former Nationalist representatives should be expelled from their seats in the various organs of the United Nations can only be reached collectively and the effect of the action that has been prematurely taken to seek a decision by vote has furnished concrete evidence that this course does not produce the desired result. Our experience since the setting up of the United Nations has proved to us that collective decisions in the desired direction are brought about by consultation, and not by publicly registering a vote in opposition to the majority. When His Majesty's Government in the United Kingdom abstained from voting in the Security Council on the issue of the expulsion of the former Nationalist representative, this did not constitute an expression of view in favour of the former Nationalist representative or against the People's Government representative. The decision to abstain was taken because there was at that time no likelihood of a majority decision and it was consequently premature for the question to be raised. The considerations which applied in the Security Council apply equally in other organs of the United Nations. In general, His Majesty's Government would of course welcome the appearance of representatives of the People's Government in all organs of the United Nations as soon as the majority of members of those organs are disposed to vote in favour of that Government's admission. They will themselves vote in favour of such admission as soon as they are assured that the taking of a vote will not simply result in the rejection of the People's Government's candidates.

The stay in Hong Kong of individual Chinese who may have held positions of responsibility in organisations connected with the former Kuomintang Government or been members of the Kuomintang does not mean that His Majesty's Government recognise them as representatives of the Kuomintang or as having any political status at all. They are given asylum in Hong Kong subject to good behaviour; this being ordinarily accorded in international practice.

Furthermore, the Hong Kong Societies Ordinance of 1949 makes registration of all societies compulsory and expressly prevents the registration of all societies and organisations which are affiliated with political parties abroad. Thus the true operation in Hong Kong of these societies and organisations which cannot be registered is rendered illegal. While individual membership of foreign political parties is still permitted, group activities are thus banned.

As regards Chinese national property, the recognition by His Majesty's Government of the Central People's Government produces in British law (using this term as a comprehensive expression to cover both the United Kingdom and Hong Kong and other colonies) the effect that the right to exercise control over Chinese State property now falls to the Central People's Government. If, however, the Central People's Government cannot obtain actual possession and control of any such property because other persons are holding it and refuse to give it up on demand, the executive cannot settle such disputes, and it will be necessary for the Central People's Government to have recourse to the Courts.

Oral Communication made by Chinese Vice-Minister for Foreign Affairs to His Majesty's Charge d'Affaires at Peking on 8 May, 1950

The Central People's Government of the People's Republic of China, having made a factual survey of and studied the British Government's oral reply of 17th March, 1950, to questions raised by the Central People's Government in negotiations on preliminary and procedural matters pertaining to the establishment of diplomatic relations between China and Britain, hereby make the following notification:

1. *On the question of China's right of representation in the United Nations*

On the question of China's right of representation in the United Nations what the Central People's Government of the People's Republic of China stress is not the number of favourable votes but rather to see in the process of voting whether the countries which have formally severed relations with remnant cliques of Kuomintang reactionaries and are willing to establish diplomatic relations have in fact really severed diplomatic relations with remnants of Kuomintang reactionaries and are really taking a friendly attitude towards the Central People's Government, thus the Central People's Government consider as unsatisfactory the British Government's explanation of its decision to abstain from voting in organs of the United Nations on the question of China's right of representation and consider as especially unsatisfactory the fact that British delegates continue to abstain from voting in all affiliated organs of the United Nations. The Central People's Government deem it necessary that the British Government should show with actual deeds that it has definitely severed diplomatic relations with the remnant of the cliques of Kuomintang reactionaries and that it is truly sincere in its wish to establish diplomatic relations with the Central People's Government of the People's Republic of China.

2. *On the attitude of the British Government towards the various organs of remnant cliques of the Kuomintang reactionaries in Hong Kong and towards Chinese State property in Hong Kong*

Through oral communication made by Mr. Hutchison, the Central People's Government of the People's Republic of China are aware of the attitude of the British Government towards the various organs of the remnant cliques of Kuomintang reactionaries and towards the Chinese State property in United Kingdom, Hong Kong and other British Colonies, which in effect is that the British Government definitely recognise the full right of the Central People's Government to exercise control over Chinese State property in the aforementioned territories.

On the third section of oral communication made by Mr. Hutchison, the Central People's Government of the People's Republic of China wish to make the following statement: only the Central People's Government and persons appointed by it for the purpose have the right to administer Chinese State property now in the United Kingdom, Hong Kong and other British Colonies, the property rights in which belong to the People's Republic of China: no infringement, damage, detention, transfer or interference by anyone using any means can be tolerated. These property rights and rights of administration of the Central People's Government should receive the full respect of the British Government. Because of the fact that British authorities in Hong Kong have impeded aircraft, which are in direct possession of China's National Aviation Corporation and the Central Air Transport Corporation (both under Civil Bureau of Central People's Government) from taking off and returning to China, and because of the fact that British authorities in Hong Kong have not really in a fully responsible manner protected those aircraft, seven of which were sabotaged as a result, the Central People's Government consider that the British Government have not yet in actual action showed full respect for the State property rights and the right to administer these properties of the Central People's Government. The Central People's Government of the People's Republic of China therefore hope that the British Government will give further clarification in regard to the above-mentioned two questions, namely, the question of China's right of representation in the United Nations and the question of China's property rights in Hong Kong.

Oral Communication made by His Majesty's Charge d'Affaires at Peking on 17 June, 1950, in reply to the Chinese Government's Communication of 8 May, 1950, on the Establishment of Diplomatic Relations

His Majesty's Government in the United Kingdom having taken note of the oral communication made on behalf of the Central People's Government on 8th May, 1950, by Mr. Chang Han-fu to His Majesty's Charge d'Affaires at Peking, in response to His Majesty's Government's earlier oral communication of 17th March, 1950, have the following observations to make.

2. His Majesty's Government accorded *de jure* recognition to the Central People's Government on 6th January, 1950, and at the same time they expresssed their willingness to enter into diplomatic relations with the Central People's Government. They subsequently instructed His Majesty's Chargé d'Affaires to proceed to Peking, where he arrived on 13th February, 1950, to discuss preliminary and procedural questions on the establishment of diplomatic relations. They note, however, that since that date five months have elapsed without any clear or final intimation having been received from the Central People's Government as to whether they for their part are in fact sincerely desirous of the early establishment of diplomatic relations. They further note that the Central People's Government have in advance of the establishment of diplomatic relations raised certain general issues, including questions of substance. These issues His Majesty's Government are perfectly prepared to discuss, but they would point out that they are issues which would be susceptible of more satisfactory discussion once effective diplomatic relations had been established. His Majesty's Government would indeed invite the attention of the Central People's Government to the fact that the very purpose and meaning of diplomatic relations between two Governments is amongst other things to facilitate the discussion of matters of mutual interest and also of disagreement.

3. With a view to avoiding any further delays or misunderstandings His Majesty's Government therefore consider it both desirable and necessary to take this opportunity of reiterating their readiness to establish diplomatic relations with the Central People's Government on a basis of equality, mutual benefit and mutual respect for territory and sovereignty and also of expressing their willingness to an exchange of Ambassadors. They also wish to state that they would now welcome an early reaffirmation by the Central People's Government of their readiness, as stated in their communication of 9th January, 1950, to establish diplomatic relations with His Majesty's Government on a similar basis. They would further welcome an early intimation of whether the Central People's Government in fact wish to proceed with an exchange of Ambassadors.

4. On the further clarification of the replies communicated by His Majesty's Charge d'Affaires on 17th March, requested by the Central People's Government in their oral communication of 8th May, 1950, His Majesty's Government have the following observations to make:

(i) *On the question of Chinese Representation in the United Nations*

(a) As already indicated in their earlier reply of 17th March His Majesty's Government severed relations with the former Nationalist Government on 6th January on which day they notified *de jure* recognition of the Central People's Government. His Majesty's Government therefore consider that their position in this respect was both clear and definite.

(b) In regard to Chinese representation in the organs of the United Nations, His Majesty's Government wish to make it clear that they would welcome the representatives of the Central People's Government in these organs. They will vote for these representatives at the appropriate moment, but they consider that it is for them to determine the appropriate moment in the light of the prevailing circumstances. His Majesty's Government's attitude on this matter is generally known to all member States of the United Nations and has been based on the accepted democratic principle that, in an international organisation such as the United Nations, a collective majority decision is the only method of settling such issues and can best be reached by a process of consultation. In the meanwhile the fact that His Majesty's Government have abstained from voting on this issue when it has been raised in the various organs of the United Nations in no way indicates approval of the Nationalist representation or opposition to the representation of the Central People's Government, nor has the abstention of His Majesty's Government in any way prejudiced the solution of the question. Although this question will no doubt be settled in due course in each principal organ of the United Nations in turn, it would in the view of His Majesty's Government be most appropriate and effective if a lead could be given by the Security Council. In this connexion His Majesty's Government desire to draw the attention of the Central People's Government to the steps which they have taken to persuade other members of the Council to cast their votes in favour of the admission of the Central People's Government's representatives and thus secure an early decision in that body

(*c*) His Majesty's Government consider that their attitude as outlined above is clear and explicit and will contribute to the earliest possible admission of the representatives of the Central People's Government to the United Nations. They accordingly invite the Central People's Government to reconsider their comments on this question in the light of the above observations.

(*ii*) On the question of Chinese State Property

(*a*) As already indicated in their earlier reply of 17th March, the recognition by His Majesty's Government produces the effect in British Law that the right to exercise control of Chinese State property now falls to the Central People's Government. It is observed that the Central People's Government although they take note of the acceptance of this principle by His Majesty's Government, nevertheless seek to show that, in relation to certain aircraft in Hong Kong, His Majesty's Government are in fact repudiating the very principle which they have enunciated. His Majesty's Government therefore consider it necessary to restate their view that where the question at issue is whether a property is Chinese State property or the property of a third party who claims it, that question is one which in British territory can only be established by the Courts. This clearly applies in the case of the CNAC–CATC Aircraft since the ownership of these aircraft is in dispute. Once the ownership of the aircraft has been finally established by the Courts, the property rights of the owner will of course be fully respected. The Central People's Government will be aware that it is precisely to safeguard the position regarding the ownership of these aircraft that an Order in Council was made on 10th May. There can, however, be no question of His Majesty's Government entering into discussions on the ownership of these aircraft at a time when the matter is *sub judice*. It is for the Courts and not for His Majesty's Government to decide on their ownership.

(*b*) His Majesty's Government are replying separately to the communication of the Central People's Government on the subject of the sabotage to seven of the aircraft in Hong Kong. It is sufficient therefore to state for the purpose of this communication that His Majesty's Government are unable to accept the Central People's Government's contention that the Government of Hong Kong afforded inadequate protection of these aircraft.

(*c*) His Majesty's Government invite the Central People's Government to reconsider their comments on the question of Chinese State property, particularly in Hong Kong, in the light of the above observations. In this connexion they would also add that the fact that the recognition of the Central People's Government produces the effect in British law that the right to exercise control of Chinese State property now falls to the Central People's Government is only one example of a broader principle of international law, namely that the Central People's Government now being the Chinese Government succeeds to all the rights and correspondingly to all obligations of the Chinese State.

Index of Main Subjects and Persons

This index is designed to be used in conjunction with the Chapter Summaries. References in this index are to page, rather than document numbers.